New Perspectives on

MICROSOFT®
WINDOWS® 2000
PROFESSIONAL

Introductory

JUNE PARSONS & DAN OJA
MediaTechnics

JOAN & PATRICK CAREY
Carey Associates

COURSE
TECHNOLOGY

Thomson Learning™

ONE MAIN STREET, CAMBRIDGE, MA 02142

Australia • Canada • Denmark • Japan • Mexico • New Zealand • Philippines
Puerto Rico • Singapore • South Africa • Spain • United Kingdom • United States

New Perspectives on Microsoft Windows 2000 Professional—Introductory is published by Course Technology.

Senior Editor	Donna Gridley	Associate Product Manager	Melissa Dezotell
Senior Product Manager	Rachel A. Crapser	Editorial Assistant	Jill Kirn
Product Manager	Catherine V. Donaldson	Text Designer	Meral Dabcovich
Senior Production Editor	Catherine G. DiMassa	Cover Art Designer	Douglas Goodman
Developmental Editor	Mary Kemper		

© 2000 by Course Technology, a division of Thomson Learning

For more information contact:

Course Technology
1 Main Street
Cambridge, MA 02142
Or find us on the World Wide Web at: http://www.course.com.

For permission to use material from this text or product, contact us by
Web: www.thomsonrights.com
Phone: 1-800-730-2214
Fax: 1-800-730-2215

Trademarks

Course Technology and the Open Book logo are registered trademarks and CourseKits is a trademark of Course Technology. Custom Edition is a registered trademark of Thomson Learning.

The Thomson Learning Logo is a registered trademark used herein under license.

Some of the product names and company names used in this book have been used for identification purposes only and may be trademarks or registered trademarks of their respective manufacturers and sellers.

Disclaimer

This textbook was published based on the release candidate version of Microsoft Windows 2000, and was not tested against final software. It is to be distributed for review purposes only.

Course Technology reserves the right to revise this publication and make changes from time to time in its content without notice.

ISBN 0-7600-7093-8

Printed in the United States of America

1 2 3 4 5 6 7 8 9 10 BM 04 03 02 01 00

PREFACE

The New Perspectives Series

About New Perspectives

Course Technology's **New Perspectives Series** is an integrated system of instruction that combines text and technology products to teach computer concepts, the Internet, and microcomputer applications. Users consistently praise this series for innovative pedagogy, use of interactive technology, creativity, accuracy, and supportive and engaging style.

How is the New Perspectives Series different from other series?

The **New Perspectives Series** distinguishes itself by **innovative technology**, from the renowned Course Labs to the state-of-the-art multimedia that is integrated with our Concepts texts. Other distinguishing features include **sound instructional design, proven pedagogy**, and **consistent quality**. Each tutorial has students learn features in the context of solving a realistic case problem rather than simply learning a laundry list of features. With the **New Perspectives Series**, instructors report that students have a complete, integrative learning experience that stays with them. They credit this high retention and competency to the fact that this series incorporates critical thinking and problem-solving with computer skills mastery. In addition, we work hard to ensure accuracy by using a multi-step quality assurance process during all stages of development. Instructors focus on teaching and students spend more time learning.

Choose the coverage that's right for you

New Perspectives applications books are available in the following categories:

Brief: approximately 150 pages long, two to four "Level I" tutorials, teaches basic application skills.

Introductory: approximately 300 pages long, four to seven tutorials, goes beyond the basic skills. These books often build out of the Brief book, adding two or three additional "Level II" tutorials. The book you are holding is an Introductory book.

Comprehensive: approximately 600 pages long, eight to twelve tutorials, all tutorials included in the Introductory text plus higher-level "Level III" topics. Also includes two Windows tutorials and three or four fully developed Additional Cases.

Advanced: approximately 600 pages long, cover topics similar to those in the Comprehensive books, but offer the highest-level coverage in the series. Advanced books assume students already know the basics, and therefore go into more depth at a more accelerated rate than the Comprehensive titles. Advanced books are ideal for a second, more technical course.

Office: approximately 800 pages long, covers all components of the Office suite as well as integrating the individual software packages with one another and the Internet.

Brief
2-4 tutorials

Introductory
6 or 7 tutorials, or Brief + 2 or 3 more

Comprehensive
Introductory + 4 or 5 more tutorials. Includes Brief Windows tutorials and Additional Cases

Advanced
Quick Review of basics + in-depth, high-level coverage

Office
Office suite components + integration + Internet

Custom Editions

Choose from any of the above to build your own Custom Editions or CourseKits

Custom Books The New Perspectives Series offers you two ways to customize a New Perspectives text to fit your course exactly: *CourseKits*™ are two or more texts shrink-wrapped together, and offer significant price discounts. *Custom Editions*© offer you flexibility in designing your concepts, Internet, and applications courses. You can build your own book by ordering a combination of topics bound together to cover only the subjects you want. There is no minimum order, and books are spiral bound. Contact your Course Technology sales representative for more information.

What course is this book appropriate for?

New Perspectives on Microsoft Windows 2000 Professional—Introductory can be used in any course in which you want students to learn some of the most important topics of Windows 2000 Professional, including organizing files with Windows Explorer, personalizing your Windows environment, bringing the World Wide Web to the desktop, searching for information, and connecting computers over a phone line. This book assumes students have had little or no prior computer experience.

Proven Pedagogy

CASE

Tutorial Case Each tutorial begins with a problem presented in a case that is meaningful to students. The case turns the task of learning how to use an application into a problem-solving process.

The problems increase in complexity with each tutorial. These cases touch on issues important to today's business curriculum.

45-minute Sessions Each tutorial is divided into sessions that can be is designed to be completed in about 45 minutes to an hour (depending upon student needs and the speed of your lab equipment). Sessions allow instructors to more accurately allocate time in their syllabus, and students to better manage their own study time.

Each numbered session begins with a "session box," which quickly describes the skills students will learn in the session.

1.

2.

3.

Step-by-Step Methodology We make sure students can differentiate between what they are to do and what they are to read. Through numbered steps – clearly identified by a gray shaded background – students are constantly guided in solving the case problem. In addition, the numerous screen shots with callouts direct students' attention to what they should look at on the screen.

TROUBLE?

TROUBLE? Paragraphs These paragraphs anticipate the mistakes or problems that students may have and help them continue with the tutorial.

Tutorial **Tips** ⊢

Tutorial Tips Page This page, following the Table of Contents, offer students suggestions on how to effectively plan their study and lab time, what to do when they make a mistake, how to use the Reference Windows, MOUS grids, Quick Checks, and other features of the New Perspectives Series.

"Read This Before You Begin" Page Located opposite the first tutorial's opening page for each section of the text, the Read This Before You Begin Page helps introduce technology into the classroom. Technical considerations and assumptions about software are listed to save time and eliminate unnecessary aggravation. Notes about the Data Disks help instructors and students get their files in the right places, so students get started on the right foot.

Quick Check

Quick Check Questions Each session concludes with meaningful, conceptual Quick Check questions that test students' understanding of what they learned in the session. Answers to the Quick Check questions are provided at the end of each tutorial.

Reference Windows   Reference Windows are succinct summaries of the most important tasks covered in a tutorial and they preview actions students will perform in the steps to follow.

Task Reference   Located as a table at the end of the book, the Task Reference contains a summary of how to perform common tasks using the most efficient method, as well as references to pages where the task is discussed in more detail.

End-of-Tutorial Review Assignments, Case Problems, Internet Assignments and Lab Assignments Review Assignments provide students with additional hands-on practice of the skills they learned in the tutorial using the same case presented in the tutorial. These assignments are followed by four to five Case Problems that have approximately the same scope as the tutorial case but use a different scenario. In addition, some of the Review Assignments or Case Problems may include Exploration Exercises that challenge students, encourage them to explore the capabilities of the program they are using, and/or further extend their knowledge. Each tutorial also includes instructions on getting to the text's Student Online Companion page, which contains the Internet Assignments and other related links for the text. Internet Assignments are additional exercises that integrate the skills the students learned in the tutorial with the World Wide Web. Finally, if a Course Lab accompanies a tutorial, Lab Assignments are included after the Case Problems.

File Finder Chart   This chart, located at the back of the book, visually explains how students should set up their Data Disks, what files should go in what folders, and what they'll be saving the files as in the course of their work.

The Instructor's Resource Kit for this book contains:

- Electronic Instructor's Manual
- Make Data Disk program for Level I and Level II tutorials (Tutorials 1–2, and 3–6)
- Course Test Manager Testbank
- Course Test Manager Engine
- Figure Files
- WebCT
- Course Labs
- Sample Syllabus

These teaching tools come on CD-ROM. If you don't have access to a CD-ROM drive, contact your Course Technology customer service representative for more information.

The New Perspectives Teaching Tools Package

Electronic Instructor's Manual   Our Instructor's Manuals include tutorial overviews and outlines, technical notes, lecture notes, solutions, and Extra Case Problems. Many instructors use the Extra Case Problems for performance-based exams or extra credit projects. The Instructor's Manual is available as an electronic file, which you can get from the Instructor Resource Kit (IRK) CD-ROM or download it from **www.course.com**.

Data Files   Data Files contain all of the data that students will use to complete the tutorials, Review Assignments, and Case Problems. A Readme file includes instructions for using the files. See the "Read This Before You Begin" page/pages for more information on Student Files.

Course Labs: Concepts Come to Life These highly interactive computer-based learning activities bring concepts to life with illustrations, animations, digital images, and simulations. The Labs guide students step-by-step, present them with Quick Check questions, let them explore on their own, test their comprehension, and provide printed feedback. Lab icons at the beginning of the tutorial and in the tutorial margins indicate when a topic has a corresponding Lab. Lab Assignments are included at the end of each relevant tutorial. The Labs available with this book and the tutorials in which they appear are:

Using a Keyboard	Using a Mouse	Using Files	The Internet: World Wide Web	Web Pages & HTML
Tutorial 1	Tutorial 1	Tutorial 2	Tutorial 5	Tutorial 5

Figure Files Many figures in the text are provided on the IRK CD-ROM to help illustrate key topics or concepts. Instructors can create traditional overhead transparencies by printing the figure files. Or they can create electronic slide shows by using the figures in a presentation program such as PowerPoint.

Course Test Manager: Testing and Practice at the Computer or on Paper Course Test Manager is cutting-edge, Windows-based testing software that helps instructors design and administer practice tests and actual examinations. Course Test Manager can automatically grade the tests students take at the computer and can generate statistical information on individual as well as group performance.

Online Companions: Dedicated to Keeping You and Your Students Up-To-Date Visit our faculty sites and student sites on the World Wide Web at **www.course.com**. Here instructors can browse this text's password-protected Faculty Online Companion to obtain an online Instructor's Manual, Solution Files, Student Files, and more. Students can also access this text's Student Online Companion, which contains Student files and all the links that the students will need to complete their tutorial assignments.

More Innovative Technology

Course CBT Enhance your students' Office 2000 classroom learning experience with self-paced computer-based training on CD-ROM. Course CBT engages students with interactive multimedia and hands-on simulations that reinforce and complement the concepts and skills covered in the textbook. All the content is aligned with the MOUS (Microsoft Office User Specialist) program, making it a great preparation tool for the certification exams. Course CBT also includes extensive pre- and post-assessments that test students' mastery of skills. These pre- and post-assessments automatically generate a "custom learning path" through the course that highlights only the topics students need help with.

SAM How well do your students *really* know Microsoft Office? SAM is a performance-based testing program that measures students' proficiency in Microsoft Office 2000. SAM is available for Office 2000 in either a live or simulated environment. You can use Course Assessment to place students into or out of courses, monitor their performance throughout a course, and help prepare them for the MOUS certification exams.

WebCT WebCT is a tool used to create Web-based educational environments and also uses WWW browsers as the interface for the course-building environment. The site is hosted on your school campus, allowing complete control over the information. WebCT has its own internal communication system, offering internal e-mail, a Bulletin Board, and a Chat room.

Course Technology offers pre-existing supplemental information to help in your WebCT class creation, such as a suggested Syllabus, Lecture Notes, Figures in the Book/ Course Presenter, Student Downloads, and Test Banks in which you can schedule an exam, create reports, and more.

Acknowledgments

We want to thank all of the New Perspectives Team members for their support, guidance, and advice. Their insights and team spirit were invaluable. Thanks to our reviewers: Jody Baty, Ralph Brasure, Liberty University; and Sally Tiffany, Milwaukee Area Technical College. Our appreciation goes to Catherine DiMassa, Senior Production Editor. Thanks also to Greg Bigelow, John Bosco, Li-Juian Jang, and all the QA testers. We are grateful to Donna Gridley, Christine Guivernau, Catherine Donaldson, Karen Shortill, and Melissa Dezotell for their editorial support, and to Karen Seitz for her marketing efforts.

June Parsons, Dan Oja, Joan & Patrick Carey

We would also like to acknowledge and thank our five little sons, Stephen, Michael, Peter, Thomas, and John Paul, for their unfailing love, cheer, and faith in us.

Joan & Patrick Carey

TABLE OF CONTENTS

Tutorial 3   WIN 2000 3.03

*Organizing Files with
Windows Explorer*

**Structuring Information on a Disk at Kolbe
Climbing School**

Tutorial 4   **WIN 2000 4.01**

*Personalizing Your Windows
Environment*

Changing Desktop Settings at Companions, Inc.

Tutorial 5   WIN 2000 5.01

*Bringing the World Wide Web
to the Desktop*

Using Active Desktop at Highland Travel

Tutorial 6   **WIN 2000 6.01**

Searching for Information

**Using the Search Feature to Locate Files for a
Speechwriter**

Appendix A WIN 2000 A.01

Connecting Computers Over a Phone Line

Reference **Window List**

Tutorial **Tips**

These tutorials will help you learn about Microsoft Windows 2000 Professional. This book is about Windows 2000 Professional. For those who have Windows 2000 Millennium, you might notice some differences. The tutorials are designed to be worked through at a computer. Each tutorial is divided into sessions. Watch for the session headings, such as Session 1.1 and Session 1.2. Each session is designed to be completed in about 45 minutes, but take as much time as you need. It's also a good idea to take a break between sessions.

Before you begin, read the following questions and answers. They will help you plan your time and use the tutorials effectively.

Where do I start?

Each tutorial begins with a case, which sets the scene for the tutorial and gives you background information to help you understand what you will be doing. Read the case before you go to the lab. In the lab, begin with the first session of a tutorial.

How do I know what to do on the computer?

Each session contains steps that you will perform on the computer to learn how to use Microsoft Windows 2000 Professional. Read the text that introduces each series of steps. The steps you need to do at a computer are numbered and are set against a shaded background. Read each step carefully and completely before you try it.

Some steps may ask you to print. Check with your instructor to see if he or she wants you to provide printed documents.

How do I know if I did the step correctly?

As you work, compare your computer screen with the corresponding figure in the tutorial. Don't worry if your screen display is somewhat different from the figure. The important parts of the screen display are labeled in each figure. Check to make sure these parts are on your screen.

What if I make a mistake?

Don't worry about making mistakes—they are part of the learning process. Paragraphs labeled "TROUBLE?" identify common problems and explain how to get back on track. Follow the steps in a TROUBLE? paragraph only if you are having the problem described. If you run into other problems:

- Carefully consider the current state of your system, the position of the pointer, and any messages on the screen.

- Complete the sentence, "Now I want to…" Be specific, because identifying your goal will help you rethink the steps you need to take to reach that goal.

- If you are working on a particular piece of software, consult the Help system.

- If the suggestions above don't solve your problem, consult your technical support person for assistance.

How do I use the Reference Windows?

Reference Windows summarize the procedures you will learn in the tutorial steps. Do not complete the actions in the Reference Windows when you are working through the tutorial. Instead, refer to the Reference Windows while you are working on the assignments at the end of the tutorial.

How can I test my understanding of the material I learned in the tutorial?

At the end of each session, you can answer the Quick Check questions. The answers for the Quick Checks are at the end of that tutorial.

After you have completed the entire tutorial, you should complete the Review Assignments and Projects. They are carefully structured so that you will review what you have learned and then apply your knowledge to new situations.

What if I can't remember how to do something?

You should refer to the Task Reference at the end of the book; it summarizes how to accomplish tasks using the most efficient method.

Now that you've read the Tutorial Tips, you are ready to begin.

New Perspectives on

MICROSOFT®

WINDOWS® 2000

PROFESSIONAL

Read This Before You Begin

To the Student

Make Data Disk Program

To complete the Level I tutorials, Review Assignments, and Projects, you need three Data Disks. Your instructor will either provide you with Data Disks or ask you to make your own.

If you are making your own Data Disks you will need three blank, formatted high-density disks and access to the Make Data Disk program. If you want to install the Make Data Disk program to your home computer, you can obtain it from your instructor or from the Web. To download the Make Data Disk program from the Web, go to www.course.com, click Data Disks, and follow the instructions on the screen.

To install the Make Data Disk program, select and click the file you just downloaded from www.course.com, 6548-9.exe. Follow the onscreen instructions to complete the installation. If you have any trouble obtaining or installing the Make Data Disk program, ask your instructor or technical support person for assistance.

Once you have obtained and installed the Make Data Disk program, you can use it to create your Data Disks according to the steps in the tutorials.

Course Labs

The Level I tutorials in this book feature three interactive Course Labs to help you understand Using a Keyboard, Using a Mouse, and Using Files concepts. There are Lab Assignments at the end of Tutorials 1 and 2 that relate to these Labs. To start a Lab, click the **Start** button on the Windows 2000 taskbar, point to **Programs**, point to

Course Labs, point to **New Perspectives Course Labs**, and click the name of the Lab you want to use.

Using Your Own Computer

If you are going to work through this book using your own computer, you need:

- ■ **Computer System** Microsoft Windows 2000 Professional must be installed on a local hard drive or on a network drive. This book is about Windows 2000 Professional—for those who have Windows 2000 Millennium, you might notice some differences.

- ■ **Data Disks** You will not be able to complete the tutorials or exercises in this book using your own computer until you have your Data Disks. See "Make Data Disk Program" above for details on obtaining your Data Disks.

- ■ **Course Labs** See your instructor or technical support person to obtain the Course Lab software for use on your own computer.

Visit Our World Wide Web Site

Additional materials designed especially for you are available on the World Wide Web. Go to http://www.course.com.

To the Instructor

The Make Data Disk Program and Course Labs for this title are available in the Instructor's Resource Kit for this title. Follow the instructions in the Help file on the CD-ROM to install the programs to your network or standalone computer. For information on using the Make Data Disk Program or the Course Labs, see the "To the Student" section above. Students will be switching the default installation settings to Web style in Tutorial 2. You are granted a license to copy the Data Files and Course Labs to any computer or computer network used by students who have purchased this book.

OBJECTIVES

In this tutorial you will:

- Start and shut down Windows 2000

- Identify the objects on the Windows 2000 desktop

- Practice mouse functions

- Run software programs, switch between them, and close them

- Identify and use the controls in a window

- Use Windows 2000 controls such as menus, toolbars, list boxes, scroll bars, option buttons, tabs, and check boxes

- Explore the Windows 2000 Help system

LABS

Using a Keyboard

Using a Mouse

EXPLORING THE BASICS

Investigating the Windows 2000 Operating System

CASE

Your First Day on the Computer

You walk into the computer lab and sit down at a desk. There's a computer in front of you, and you find yourself staring dubiously at the screen. Where to start? As if in answer to your question, your friend Steve Laslow appears.

"You start with the operating system," says Steve. Noticing your puzzled look, Steve explains that the **operating system** is software that helps the computer carry out operating tasks such as displaying information on the computer screen and saving data on your disks. (Software refers to the **programs**, or **applications**, that a computer uses to perform tasks.) Your computer uses the **Microsoft Windows 2000 Professional** operating system—Windows 2000, for short.

Steve explains that much of the software available for Windows 2000 has a standard graphical user interface. This means that once you have learned how to use one Windows program, such as Microsoft Word word-processing software, you are well on your way to under-standing how to use other Windows software. Windows 2000 lets you use more than one program at a time, so you can easily switch between them—between your word-processing software and your appointment book software, for example. Finally, Windows 2000 makes it very easy to access the **Internet**, the worldwide collection of com-puters connected to one another to enable communication. All in all, Windows 2000 makes your computer effective and easy to use.

Steve recommends that you get started right away by starting Microsoft Windows 2000 and practicing some basic skills.

SESSION 1.1

In this session, in addition to learning basic Windows terminology, you will learn how to use a pointing device, how to start and close a program, and how to use more than one program at a time.

Starting Windows 2000

Using a Keyboard

Windows 2000 automatically starts when you turn on the computer. Depending on the way your computer is set up, you might be asked to enter your username and password.

To start Windows 2000:

1. Turn on your computer.

TROUBLE? If you are asked to select an operating system, do not take action. Windows 2000 will start automatically after a designated number of seconds. If it does not, ask your technical support person for help.

TROUBLE? If prompted to do so, type your assigned username and press the Tab key. Then type your password and press the Enter key to continue.

TROUBLE? If this is the first time you have started your computer with Windows 2000, messages might appear on your screen informing you that Windows is setting up components of your computer. If the Getting Started with Windows 2000 box appears, press and hold down the Alt key on your keyboard and then, while you hold down the Alt key, press the F4 key. The box closes.

After a moment, Windows 2000 starts. Windows 2000 has a **graphical user interface** (**GUI,** pronounced "gooey"), which uses **icons,** or pictures of familiar objects, such as file folders and documents, to represent items in your computer such as programs or files. Microsoft Windows 2000 gets its name from the rectangular work areas, called "windows," that appear on your screen as you work (although no windows should be open right now).

The Windows 2000 Desktop

In Windows terminology, the area displayed on your screen when Windows 2000 starts represents a **desktop**—a workspace for projects and the tools needed to manipulate those projects. When you first start a computer, it uses **default** settings, those preset by the operating system. The default desktop, for example, has a plain blue background. However, Microsoft designed Windows 2000 so that you can easily change the appearance of the desktop. You can, for example, add color, patterns, images, and text to the desktop background.

Many institutions design customized desktops for their computers. Figure 1-1 shows the default Windows 2000 desktop and two other examples of desktops, one designed for a business, North Pole Novelties, and one designed for a school, the University of Colorado. Although your desktop might not look exactly like any of the examples in Figure 1-1, you should be able to locate objects on your screen similar to those in Figure 1-1. Look at your screen and locate the objects labeled in Figure 1-1. The objects on your screen might appear larger or smaller than those in Figure 1-1, depending on your monitor's settings.

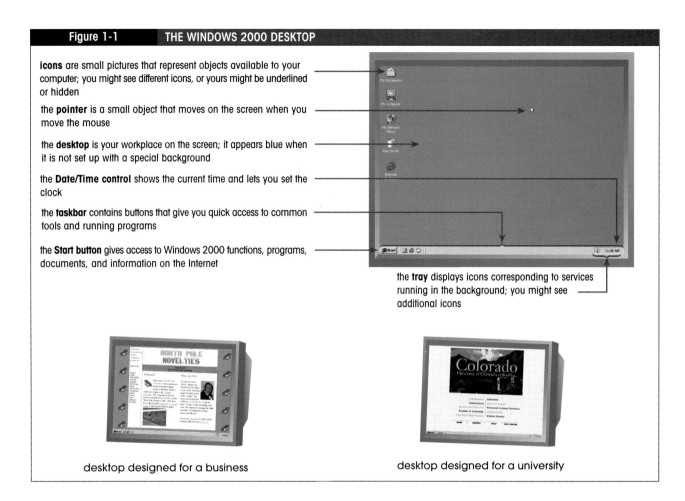

| Figure 1-1 | THE WINDOWS 2000 DESKTOP |

icons are small pictures that represent objects available to your computer; you might see different icons, or yours might be underlined or hidden

the **pointer** is a small object that moves on the screen when you move the mouse

the **desktop** is your workplace on the screen; it appears blue when it is not set up with a special background

the **Date/Time control** shows the current time and lets you set the clock

the **taskbar** contains buttons that give you quick access to common tools and running programs

the **Start button** gives access to Windows 2000 functions, programs, documents, and information on the Internet

the **tray** displays icons corresponding to services running in the background; you might see additional icons

desktop designed for a business

desktop designed for a university

If the screen goes blank or starts to display a moving design, press any key to restore the Windows 2000 desktop.

Using a Pointing Device

Using a Mouse

A **pointing device** helps you interact with objects on the screen. Pointing devices come in many shapes and sizes; some are designed to ensure that your hand won't suffer fatigue while using them. Some are directly attached to your computer via a cable, whereas others function like a TV remote control and allow you to access your computer without being right next to it. Figure 1-2 shows examples of common pointing devices.

The most common pointing device is called a **mouse**, so this book uses that term. If you are using a different pointing device, such as a trackball, substitute that device whenever you see the term "mouse." Because Windows 2000 uses a graphical user interface, you need to know how to use the mouse to manipulate the objects on the screen. In this session you will learn about pointing and clicking. In Session 1.2 you will learn how to use the mouse to drag objects.

You can also interact with objects by using the keyboard; however, the mouse is more convenient for most tasks, so the tutorials in this book assume you are using one.

Figure 1-2	POINTING DEVICES

traditional two-button mouse

traditional three-button mouse

mouse designed especially to prevent hand fatigue

to hold the mouse, place your forefinger over the left mouse button and place your thumb on the left side of the mouse

your ring and small fingers should be on the right side of the mouse

use your arm, not your wrist, to move the mouse

newer mouse includes a "wheel" that you can use to move through documents more easily

touch pad pointing devices have no moving parts; you slide your finger to move the pointer and tap to click

trackball pointing devices feature a ball that you roll with your finger

trackballs and touchpads are often embedded into notebook computers

Pointing

You use a pointing device to move the pointer over objects on the desktop. The pointer is usually shaped like an arrow ⃕ , although it can change shape depending on where it is on the screen and on what tasks you are performing. Most computer users place the mouse on a **mouse pad**, a flat piece of rubber that helps the mouse move smoothly. As you move the mouse on the mouse pad, the pointer on the screen moves in a corresponding direction.

You begin most Windows operations by positioning the pointer over a specific part of the screen. This is called **pointing**.

To move the pointer:

1. Position your right index finger over the left mouse button, as shown in Figure 1-2, but don't click yet. Lightly grasp the sides of the mouse with your thumb and little fingers.

TROUBLE? If you want to use the mouse with your left hand, ask your instructor or technical support person to help you use the Control Panel to swap the functions of the left and right mouse buttons. Be sure to find out how to change back to the right-handed mouse setting, so that you can reset the mouse each time you are finished in the lab.

2. Place the mouse on the mouse pad and then move the mouse. Watch the movement of the pointer.

TROUBLE? If you run out of room to move your mouse, lift the mouse and place it in the middle of the mouse pad. Notice that the pointer does not move when the mouse is not in contact with the mouse pad.

When you position the mouse pointer over certain objects, such as the objects on the taskbar, a "tip" appears. These "tips" are called **ScreenTips**, and they tell you the purpose or function of an object.

To view ScreenTips:

1. Use the mouse to point to the **Start** button 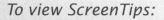, but don't click it. After a few seconds, you see the tip "Click here to begin," as shown in Figure 1-3.

   TROUBLE? If the Start button and taskbar don't appear, point to the bottom of the screen. They will then appear.

Figure 1-3	VIEWING SCREENTIPS

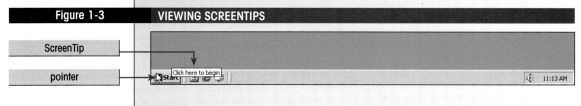

ScreenTip

pointer

2. Point to the time on the right end of the taskbar. Notice that today's date (or the date to which your computer's time clock is set) appears.

Clicking

Clicking is when you press a mouse button and immediately release it. Clicking sends a signal to your computer that you want to perform an action on the object you click. In Windows 2000 most actions are performed using the left mouse button. If you are told to click an object, click it with the left mouse button, unless instructed otherwise.

When you click the Start button, the Start menu appears. A **menu** is a list of options that you use to complete tasks. The **Start menu** provides you with access to programs, documents, and much more. Try clicking the Start button to open the Start menu.

To open the Start menu:

1. Point to the **Start** button ![Start].

2. Click the left mouse button. An arrow ▶ following an option on the Start menu indicates that you can view additional choices by navigating a **submenu**, a menu extending from the main menu. See Figure 1-4.

Figure 1-4	START MENU

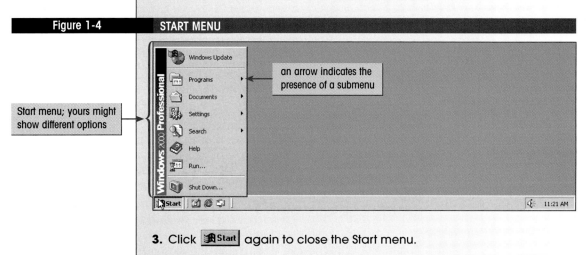

an arrow indicates the presence of a submenu

Start menu; yours might show different options

3. Click ![Start] again to close the Start menu.

Next you'll learn how to select items on a submenu.

Selecting

In Windows 2000, pointing and clicking are often used to **select** an object, in other words, to choose it as the object you want to work with. Windows 2000 shows you which object is selected by highlighting it, usually by changing the object's color, putting a box around it, or making the object appear to be pushed in, as shown in Figure 1-5.

Figure 1-5	SELECTED OBJECTS

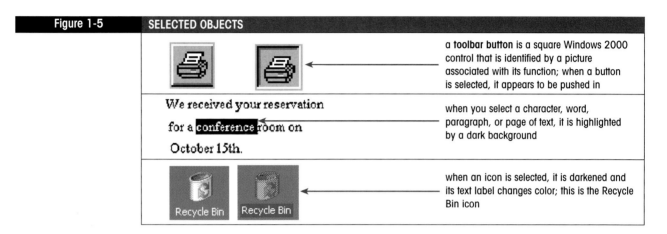

a **toolbar button** is a square Windows 2000 control that is identified by a picture associated with its function; when a button is selected, it appears to be pushed in

when you select a character, word, paragraph, or page of text, it is highlighted by a dark background

when an icon is selected, it is darkened and its text label changes color; this is the Recycle Bin icon

In Windows 2000, depending on your computer's settings, some objects are selected when you simply point to them, others when you click them. Practice selecting the Programs option on the Start menu to open the Programs submenu.

To select an option on a menu:

1. Click the **Start** button ⊞Start and notice how it appears to be pushed in, indicating it is selected.

2. Point to (but don't click) the **Programs** option. After a short pause, the Programs submenu opens, and the Programs option is highlighted to indicate it is selected. See Figure 1-6.

Figure 1-6	PROGRAMS SUBMENU

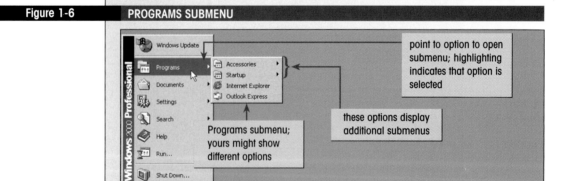

point to option to open submenu; highlighting indicates that option is selected

these options display additional submenus

Programs submenu; yours might show different options

TROUBLE? If a submenu other than the Programs menu opens, you selected the wrong option. Move the mouse so that the pointer points to Programs.

TROUBLE? If the Programs option doesn't appear, your Start menu might have too many options to fit on the screen. If that is the case, a double arrow ⌄ appears at the top or bottom of the Start menu. Click first the top and then the bottom arrow to view additional Start menu options until you locate the Programs menu option, and then point to it.

3. Now close the Start menu by clicking [Start] again.

You return to the desktop.

Right-Clicking

Pointing devices were originally designed with a single button, so the term "clicking" had only one meaning: you pressed that button. Innovations in technology, however, led to the addition of a second and even a third button (and more recently, options such as a wheel) that expanded the pointing device's capability. More recent software—especially that designed for Windows 2000—takes advantage of the additional buttons, especially the right button. However, the term "clicking" continues to refer to the left button; clicking an object with the *right* button is called **right-clicking**.

In Windows 2000, right-clicking both selects an object and opens its **shortcut menu**, a list of options directly related to the object you right-clicked. You can right-click practically any object—the Start button, a desktop icon, the taskbar, and even the desktop itself—to view options associated with that object. For example, the first desktop shown in Figure 1-7 illustrates what happens when you click the Start button with the left mouse button to open the Start menu. Clicking the Start button with the right button, however, opens the Start button's shortcut menu, as shown in the second desktop.

Figure 1-7	CLICKING WITH THE LEFT AND RIGHT MOUSE BUTTONS

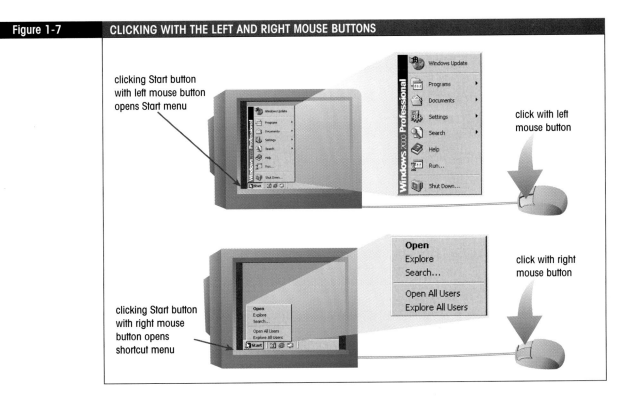

Try using right-clicking to open the shortcut menu for the Start button.

To right-click an object:

1. Position the pointer over the Start button.

2. Right-click the **Start** button [Start]. The shortcut menu that opens offers a list of options available to the Start button.

TROUBLE? If you are using a trackball or a mouse with three buttons or a wheel, make sure you click the button on the far right, not the one in the middle.

TROUBLE? If your menu looks slightly different from the one in Figure 1-8, don't worry. Different systems will have different options.

Figure 1-8	START BUTTON SHORTCUT MENU

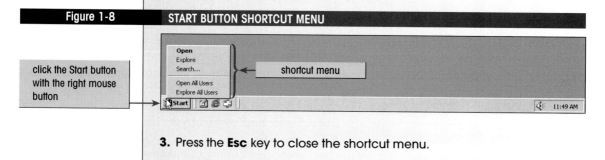

click the Start button with the right mouse button

3. Press the **Esc** key to close the shortcut menu.

You again return to the desktop.

Starting **and Closing a Program**

To use a program, such as a word-processing program, you must first start it. With Windows 2000 you usually start a program by clicking the Start button and then you locate and click the program's name in the submenus.

The Reference Window below explains how to start a program. Don't do the steps in the Reference Windows as you go through the tutorials; they are for your later reference.

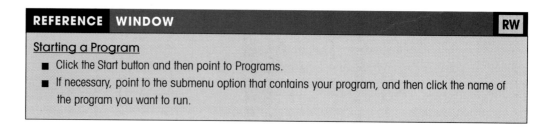

REFERENCE WINDOW   **RW**

Starting a Program
- Click the Start button and then point to Programs.
- If necessary, point to the submenu option that contains your program, and then click the name of the program you want to run.

Windows 2000 includes an easy-to-use word-processing program called WordPad. Suppose you want to start the WordPad program and use it to write a letter or report. You open Windows 2000 programs from the Start menu. Programs are usually located on the Programs submenu or on one of its submenus. To start WordPad, for example, you select the Programs and Accessories submenus.

If you can't locate an item that is supposed to be on a menu, it is most likely temporarily hidden. Windows 2000 menus use a feature called **Personalized Menus** that hides menu options you use infrequently. You can access hidden menu options by pointing to the menu name and then clicking the double arrow ≫ (sometimes called a "chevron") at the bottom of the menu. You can also access the hidden options by holding the pointer over the menu name.

To start the WordPad program from the Start menu:

1. Click the **Start** button 🔳**Start** to open the Start menu.

2. Point to **Programs**. The Programs submenu appears.

3. Point to **Accessories**. The Accessories submenu appears. Figure 1-9 shows the open menus.

   TROUBLE? If a different menu opens, you might have moved the mouse diagonally so that a different submenu opened. Move the pointer to the right across the Programs option, and then move it up or down to point to Accessories. Once you're more comfortable moving the mouse, you'll find that you can eliminate this problem by moving the mouse quickly.

   TROUBLE? If WordPad doesn't appear on the Accessories submenu, continue to point to Accessories until WordPad appears.

Figure 1-9	START MENU

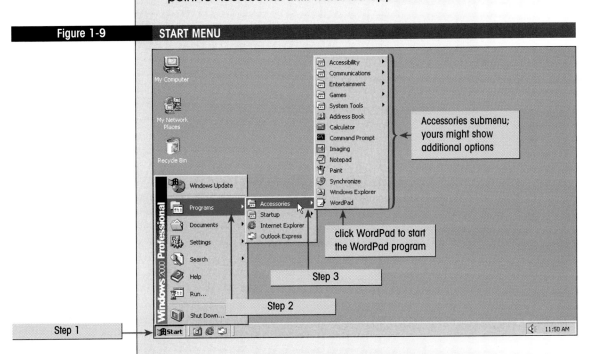

4. Click **WordPad**. The WordPad program opens, as shown in Figure 1-10. If the WordPad window fills the entire screen, don't worry. You will learn how to manipulate windows in Session 1.2.

Figure 1-10	THE WORDPAD PROGRAM

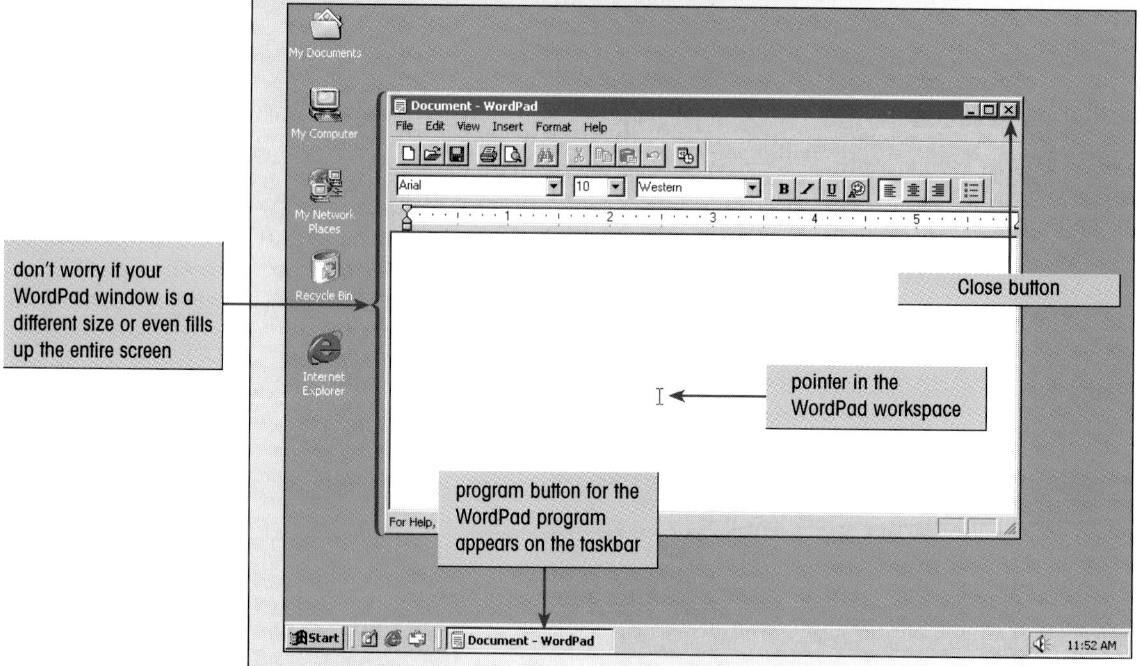

don't worry if your WordPad window is a different size or even fills up the entire screen

Close button

pointer in the WordPad workspace

program button for the WordPad program appears on the taskbar

When a program is started, it is said to be **open** or **running**. A **program button** appears on the taskbar for each open program. You click program buttons to switch between open programs. When you are finished using a program, click the Close button ☒.

To exit the WordPad program:

1. Click the **Close** button ☒. See Figure 1-10. You return to the Windows 2000 desktop.

Running **Multiple Programs**

One of the most useful features of Windows 2000 is its ability to run multiple programs at the same time. This feature, known as **multitasking**, allows you to work on more than one project at a time and to switch quickly between projects. For example, you can start WordPad and leave it running while you then start the Paint program.

To run WordPad and Paint at the same time:

1. Start WordPad again and then click the **Start** button 🏁Start again.

2. Point to **Programs** and then point to **Accessories**.

3. Click **Paint**. The Paint program opens, as shown in Figure 1-11. Now two programs are running at the same time.

TROUBLE? If the Paint program fills the entire screen, don't worry. You will learn how to manipulate windows in Session 1.2.

Figure 1-11	THE PAINT PROGRAM

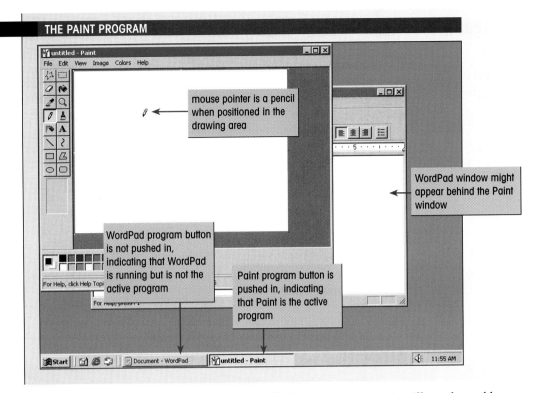

What happened to WordPad? The WordPad program button is still on the taskbar, so even if you can't see it, WordPad is still running. You can imagine that it is stacked behind the Paint program, as shown in Figure 1-12. Paint is the active program because it is the one with which you are currently working.

Figure 1-12	PROJECTS STACKED ON A DESK

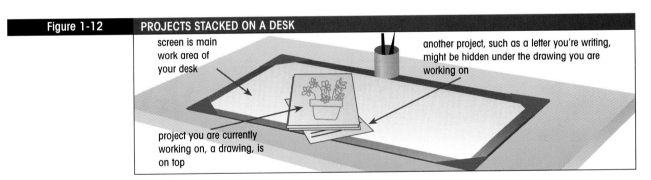

Switching Between Programs

The easiest way to switch between programs is to use the buttons on the taskbar.

To switch between WordPad and Paint:

1. Click the button labeled **Document - WordPad** on the taskbar. The Document - WordPad button now looks as if it has been pushed in, to indicate that it is the active program, and WordPad moves to the front.
2. Next, click the button labeled **untitled - Paint** on the taskbar to switch to the Paint program.

The Paint program is again the active program.

Accessing the Desktop from the Quick Launch Toolbar

The Windows 2000 taskbar, as you've seen, displays buttons for programs currently running. It also can contain **toolbars**, sets of buttons that give single-click access to programs or documents that aren't running or open. In its default state, the Windows 2000 taskbar displays the **Quick Launch toolbar**, which gives quick access to Web programs and to the desktop. Your taskbar might contain additional toolbars, or none at all.

When you are running more than one program but you want to return to the desktop, perhaps to use one of the desktop icons such as My Computer, you can do so by using one of the Quick Launch toolbar buttons. Clicking the Show Desktop button 🗇 returns you to the desktop. The open programs are not closed; they are simply made inactive and reduced to buttons on the taskbar.

To return to the desktop:

1. Click the **Show Desktop** button 🗇 on the Quick Launch toolbar. The desktop appears, and both the Paint and WordPad programs are temporarily inactive. See Figure 1-13.

   TROUBLE? If the Quick Launch toolbar doesn't appear on your taskbar, right-click the taskbar, point to Toolbars, and then click Quick Launch and try Step 1 again.

Figure 1-13	ACCESSING THE DESKTOP

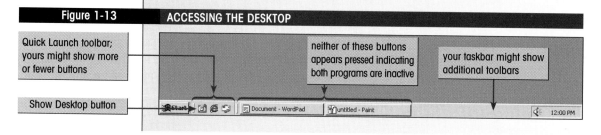

Quick Launch toolbar; yours might show more or fewer buttons

Show Desktop button

neither of these buttons appears pressed indicating both programs are inactive

your taskbar might show additional toolbars

Closing Inactive Programs from the Taskbar

It is good practice to close each program when you are finished using it. Each program uses computer resources, such as memory, so Windows 2000 works more efficiently when only the programs you need are open. You've already seen how to close an open program using the Close button ❌. You can also close a program, whether active or inactive, by using the shortcut menu associated with the program button on the taskbar.

To close WordPad and Paint using the program button shortcut menus:

1. Right-click the **untitled – Paint** button on the taskbar. To right-click something, remember that you click it with the right mouse button. The shortcut menu for that program button opens. See Figure 1-14.

2. Click **Close**. The button labeled "untitled – Paint" disappears from the taskbar, indicating that the Paint program is closed.

3. Right-click the **Document – WordPad** button on the taskbar, and then click **Close**. The WordPad button disappears from the taskbar.

Figure 1-14 **PROGRAM BUTTON SHORTCUT MENU**

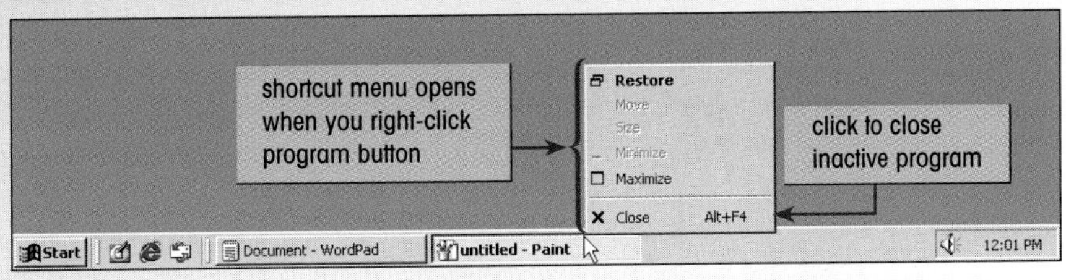
shortcut menu opens when you right-click program button
Restore
Move
Size
Minimize
Maximize
Close Alt+F4
click to close inactive program
Start
Document - WordPad
untitled - Paint
12:01 PM

Shutting **Down Windows 2000**

It is very important to shut down Windows 2000 before you turn off the computer. If you turn off your computer without correctly shutting down, you might lose data and damage your files.

You should typically use the "Shut Down" option when you want to turn off your computer. However, your school might prefer that you select the Log Off option in the Shut Down Windows dialog box. This option logs you out of Windows 2000, leaves the computer turned on, and allows another user to log on without restarting the computer. Check with your instructor or technical support person for the preferred method at your lab.

To shut down Windows 2000:

1. Click the **Start** button Start on the taskbar to display the Start menu.
2. Click the **Shut Down** menu option. A box titled "Shut Down Windows" opens.

   TROUBLE? If you can't see the Shut Down menu option, your Start menu has more options than your screen can display. A double arrow appears at the bottom of the Start menu. Click this button until the Shut Down menu option appears, and then click Shut Down.

   TROUBLE? If you are supposed to log off rather than shut down, click the Log Off option instead and follow your school's logoff procedure.

3. Make sure the **Shut Down** option appears in the box shown in Figure 1-15.

   TROUBLE? If "Shut down" does not appear, click the arrow to the right of the box. A list of options appears. Click Shut Down.

Figure 1-15 **SHUTTING DOWN**

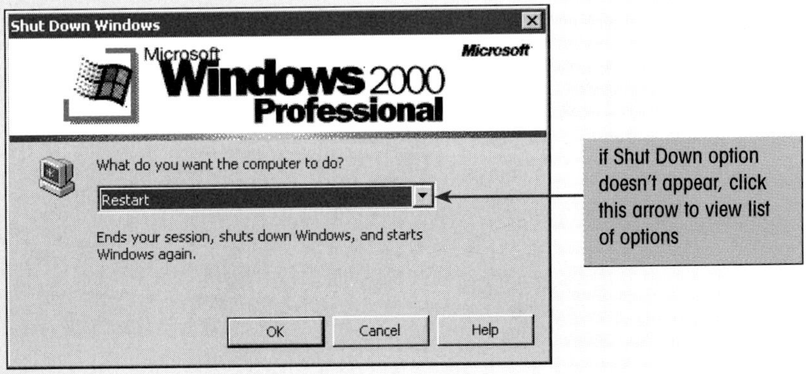
Shut Down Windows
Microsoft
Windows 2000 Professional
Microsoft
What do you want the computer to do?
Restart
Ends your session, shuts down Windows, and starts Windows again.
OK
Cancel
Help
if Shut Down option doesn't appear, click this arrow to view list of options

4. Click the **OK** button.

5. Wait until you see a message indicating it is safe to turn off your computer. If your lab staff has requested you to switch off your computer after shutting down, do so now. Otherwise leave the computer running. Some computers turn themselves off automatically.

Session 1.1 QUICK CHECK

1. What is the purpose of the taskbar?

2. The _____ feature of Windows 2000 allows you to run more than one program at a time.

3. The _____ is a list of options that provides you with access to programs, documents, submenus, and more.

4. What should you do if you are trying to move the pointer to the left edge of your screen, but your mouse bumps into the keyboard?

5. Even if you can't see an open program on your desktop, the program might be running. How can you tell if a program is running?

6. Why is it good practice to close each program when you are finished using it?

7. Why should you shut down Windows 2000 before you turn off your computer?

SESSION 1.2

In this session you will learn how to use many of the Windows 2000 controls to manipulate windows and programs. You will also learn how to change the size and shape of a window; how to move a window; and how to use menus, dialog boxes, tabs, buttons, and lists to specify how you want a program to carry out a task.

Anatomy of a Window

When you run a program in Windows 2000, it appears in a window. A **window** is a rectangular area of the screen that contains a program or data. Windows, spelled with an uppercase "W," is the name of the Microsoft operating system. The word "window" with a lowercase "w" refers to one of the rectangular areas on the screen. A window also contains controls for manipulating the window and for using the program. Figure 1-16 describes the controls you are likely to see in most windows.

Figure 1-16	WINDOW CONTROLS
CONTROL	**DESCRIPTION**
Menu bar	Contains the titles of menus, such as File, Edit, and Help
Sizing buttons	Let you enlarge, shrink, or close a window
Status bar	Provides you with messages relevant to the task you are performing
Title bar	Contains the window title and basic window control buttons
Toolbar	Contains buttons that provide you with shortcuts to common menu commands
Window title	Identifies the program and document contained in the window
Workspace	Part of the window you use to enter your work—to enter text, draw pictures, set up calculations, and so on

WordPad is a good example of a typical window, so try starting WordPad and identifying these controls in the WordPad window.

To look at window controls:

1. Make sure Windows 2000 is running and you are at the Windows 2000 desktop.

2. Start WordPad.

   TROUBLE? To start WordPad, click the Start button, point to Programs, point to Accessories, and then click WordPad.

3. On your screen, identify the controls labeled in Figure 1-17. Don't worry if your window fills the entire screen or is a different size. You'll learn to change window size shortly.

Figure 1-17	WORDPAD WINDOW CONTROLS

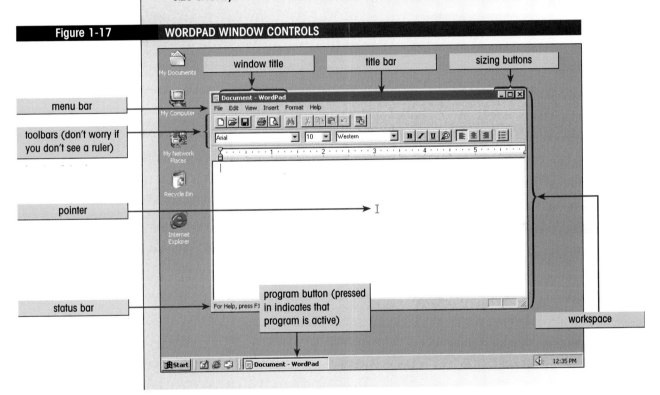

Manipulating a Window

There are three buttons located on the right side of the title bar. You are already familiar with the Close button. The Minimize button ▬ hides the window so that only its program button is visible on the taskbar. The other button changes name and function depending on the status of the window (it either maximizes the window or restores it to a predefined size). Figure 1-18 shows how these buttons work.

Minimizing a Window

The Minimize button hides a window so that only the button on the taskbar remains visible. You can use the Minimize button when you want to temporarily hide a window but keep the program running.

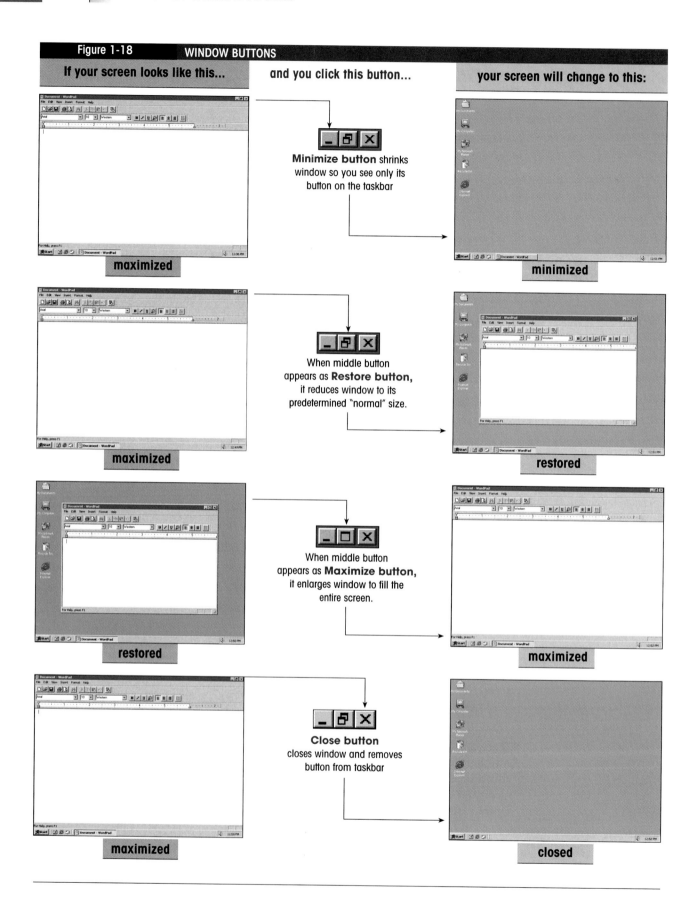

Figure 1-18   **WINDOW BUTTONS**

If your screen looks like this...   and you click this button...   your screen will change to this:

maximized

Minimize button shrinks window so you see only its button on the taskbar

minimized

maximized

When middle button appears as **Restore button,** it reduces window to its predetermined "normal" size.

restored

restored

When middle button appears as **Maximize button,** it enlarges window to fill the entire screen.

maximized

maximized

Close button closes window and removes button from taskbar

closed

> **To minimize the WordPad window:**
>
> 1. Click the **Minimize** button ▭. The WordPad window shrinks so that only the Document - WordPad button on the taskbar is visible.
>
> TROUBLE? If you accidentally clicked the Close button and closed the window, use the Start button to start WordPad again.

Redisplaying a Window

You can redisplay a minimized window by clicking the program's button on the taskbar. When you redisplay a window, it becomes the active window.

> **To redisplay the WordPad window:**
>
> 1. Click the **Document - WordPad** button on the taskbar. The WordPad window is restored to its previous size. The Document - WordPad button looks pushed in as a visual clue that WordPad is now the active window.
>
> 2. The taskbar button provides another means of switching a window between its minimized and active state: Click the **Document - WordPad** button on the taskbar again to minimize the window.
>
> 3. Click the **Document – WordPad** button once more to redisplay the window.

Maximizing a Window

The Maximize button enlarges a window so that it fills the entire screen. You will probably do most of your work using maximized windows because they allow you to see more of your program and data.

> **To maximize the WordPad window:**
>
> 1. Click the **Maximize** button ▢ on the WordPad title bar.
>
> TROUBLE? If the window is already maximized, it will fill the entire screen, and the Maximize button won't appear. Instead, you'll see the Restore button ⧉. Skip Step 1.

Restoring a Window

The Restore button ⧉ reduces the window so it is smaller than the entire screen. This is useful if you want to see more than one window at a time. Also, because of its smaller size, you can drag the window to another location on the screen or change its dimensions.

> **To restore a window:**
>
> 1. Click the **Restore** button ⧉ on the WordPad title bar. Notice that once a window is restored, ⧉ changes to the Maximize button ▢.

Moving a Window

You can use the mouse to move a window to a new position on the screen. When you click an object and hold down the mouse button while moving the mouse, you are said to be **dragging** the object. You can move objects on the screen by dragging them to a new location. If you want to move a window, you drag its title bar. You cannot move a maximized window.

To drag the WordPad window to a new location:

1. Position the mouse pointer on the WordPad window title bar.

2. While you hold down the left mouse button, move the mouse to drag the window. A rectangle representing the window moves as you move the mouse.

3. Position the rectangle anywhere on the screen, then release the left mouse button. The WordPad window appears in the new location.

4. Now drag the WordPad window to the upper-left corner of the screen.

Changing the Size of a Window

You can also use the mouse to change the size of a window. Notice the sizing handle 🔲 at the lower-right corner of the window. The **sizing handle** provides a visible control for changing the size of a window.

To change the size of the WordPad window:

1. Position the pointer over the sizing handle 🔲. The pointer changes to a diagonal arrow ↘ .

2. While holding down the mouse button, drag the sizing handle down and to the right.

3. Release the mouse button. Now the window is larger.

4. Practice using the sizing handle to make the WordPad window larger or smaller, and then maximize the WordPad window.

You can also drag the window borders left, right, up, or down to change a window's size.

Using **Program Menus**

Most Windows programs use menus to organize the program's menu options. The menu bar is typically located at the top of the program window and shows the titles of menus such as File, Edit, and Help.

Windows menus are relatively standardized—most Windows programs include similar menu options. It's easy to learn new programs, because you can make a pretty good guess about which menu contains the option you want.

Selecting Options from a Menu

When you click any menu title, choices for that menu appear below the menu bar. These choices are referred to as **menu options** or **commands**. To select a menu option, you click it. For example, the File menu is a standard feature in most Windows programs and contains the options typically related to working with a file: creating, opening, saving, and printing a file or document.

To select the Print Preview menu option on the File menu:

1. Click **File** on the WordPad menu bar to display the File menu. See Figure 1-19.

TROUBLE? If you open a menu but decide not to select any of the menu options, you can close the menu by clicking its title again.

Figure 1-19	FILE MENU

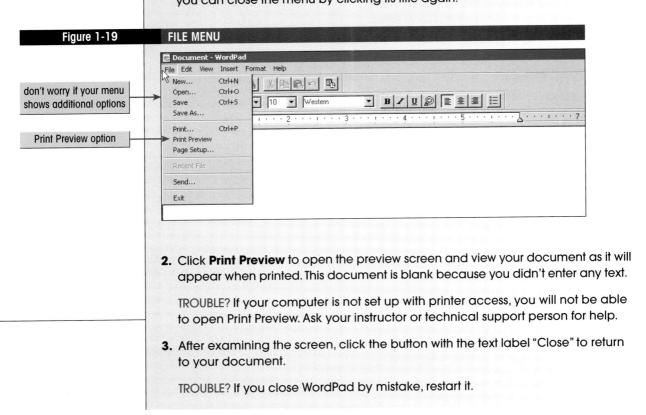

don't worry if your menu shows additional options

Print Preview option

2. Click **Print Preview** to open the preview screen and view your document as it will appear when printed. This document is blank because you didn't enter any text.

TROUBLE? If your computer is not set up with printer access, you will not be able to open Print Preview. Ask your instructor or technical support person for help.

3. After examining the screen, click the button with the text label "Close" to return to your document.

TROUBLE? If you close WordPad by mistake, restart it.

Not all menu options immediately carry out an action—some show submenus or ask you for more information about what you want to do. The menu gives you hints about what to expect when you select an option. These hints are sometimes referred to as **menu conventions**. Figure 1-20 describes the Windows 2000 menu conventions.

Figure 1-20	MENU CONVENTIONS

CONVENTION	DESCRIPTION
Check mark	Indicates a toggle, or "on-off" switch (like a light switch) that is either checked (turned on) or not checked (turned off)
Ellipsis	Three dots that indicate you must make additional selections after you select that option. Options without dots do not require additional choices—they take effect as soon as you click them. If an option is followed by an ellipsis, a dialog box opens that allows you to enter specifications for how you want a task carried out.
Triangular arrow	Indicates the presence of a submenu. When you point at a menu option that has a triangular arrow, a submenu automatically appears.
Grayed-out option	Option that is not available. For example, a graphics program might display the Text Toolbar option in gray if there is no text in the graphic to work with.
Keyboard shortcut	A key or combination of keys that you can press to activate the menu option without actually opening the menu
Double arrow	Indicates that additional menu options are available; click the double arrow to access them

Figure 1-21 shows examples of these menu conventions.

Figure 1-21 — **EXAMPLES OF MENU CONVENTIONS**

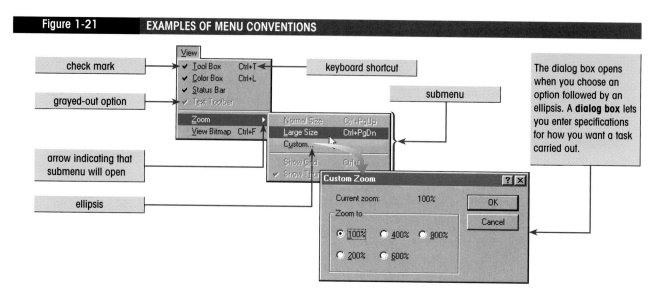

Using **Toolbars**

Although you can usually perform all program commands using menus, toolbar buttons provide convenient one-click access to frequently used commands. For most Windows 2000 functions, there is usually more than one way to accomplish a task. To simplify your introduction to Windows 2000 in this tutorial, we will usually show you only one method for performing a task. As you become more accomplished at using Windows 2000, you can explore alternate methods.

In Session 1.1 you learned that Windows 2000 programs include ScreenTips, which indicate the purpose and function of a tool. Now is a good time to explore the WordPad toolbar buttons by looking at their ScreenTips.

To find out a toolbar button's function:

1. Position the pointer over any button on the toolbar, such as the Print Preview button ☒. After a short pause, the name of the button appears in a box near the button, and a description of the button appears in the status bar just above the Start button. See Figure 1-22.

Figure 1-22 — **TOOLBAR BUTTON AIDS**

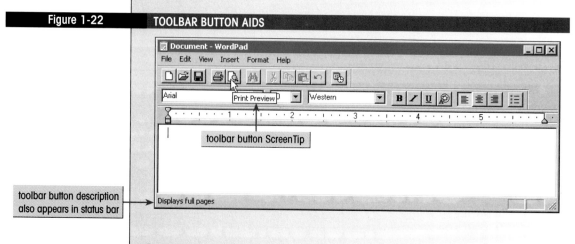

2. Move the pointer over each button on the toolbar to see its name and purpose.

You select a toolbar button by clicking it.

To select the Print Preview toolbar button:

1. Click the **Print Preview** button 🔍. The Print Preview screen appears. This is the same screen that appeared when you selected Print Preview from the File menu.

2. After examining the screen, click the button with the text label "Close" to return to your document.

Using **List Boxes and Scroll Bars**

As you might guess from the name, a **list box** displays a list of choices. In WordPad, date and time formats are shown in the Date/Time list box. List box controls usually include arrow buttons, a scroll bar, and a scroll box, as shown in Figure 1-23.

To use the Date/Time list box:

1. Click the **Date/Time** button 🗓 to display the Date and Time dialog box. See Figure 1-23.

Figure 1-23	LIST BOX

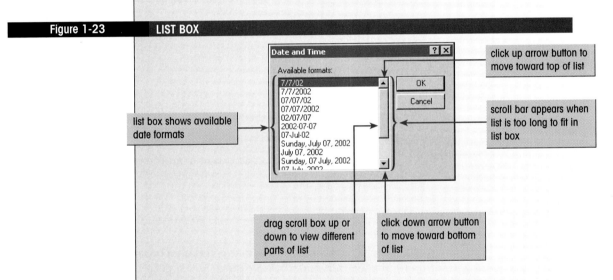

2. To scroll down the list, click the **down arrow** button ▼. See Figure 1-23.

3. Find the scroll box on your screen. See Figure 1-23.

4. Drag the **scroll box** to the top of the scroll bar. Notice how the list scrolls back to the beginning.

    TROUBLE? You learned how to drag when you learned to move a window. To drag the scroll box up, point to the scroll box, press and hold down the mouse button, and then move the mouse up.

5. Find a date in the format "July 07, 2002." Click that date format to select it.

6. Click the **OK** button to close the Date and Time dialog box. This inserts the current date in your document.

You can access some list boxes directly from the toolbar. When a list box is on the toolbar, only the current option appears in the list box. A **list arrow** appears on the right of the box and you can click it to view additional options.

To use the Font Size list box:

1. Click the **Font Size** list arrow, as shown in Figure 1-24.

Figure 1-24	FONT SIZE LIST ARROW

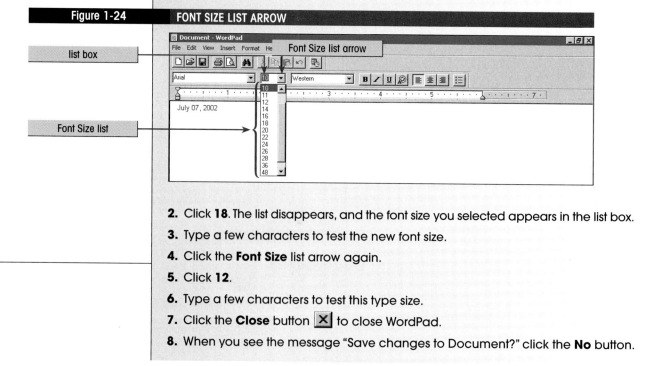

2. Click **18**. The list disappears, and the font size you selected appears in the list box.

3. Type a few characters to test the new font size.

4. Click the **Font Size** list arrow again.

5. Click **12**.

6. Type a few characters to test this type size.

7. Click the **Close** button ☒ to close WordPad.

8. When you see the message "Save changes to Document?" click the **No** button.

Using **Dialog Box Controls**

Recall that when you select a menu option or button followed by an ellipsis, a dialog box opens that allows you to provide more information about how a program should carry out a task. Some dialog boxes group different kinds of information into bordered rectangular areas called **panes**. Within these panes, you will usually find tabs, option buttons, check boxes, and other controls that the program uses to collect information about how you want it to perform a task. Figure 1-25 describes common dialog box controls.

Figure 1-25	DIALOG BOX CONTROLS

CONTROL	DESCRIPTION
Tabs	Modeled after the tabs on file folders, tab controls are often used as containers for other Windows 2000 controls such as list boxes, radio buttons, and check boxes. Click the appropriate tabs to view different pages of information or choices.
Option buttons	Also called **radio buttons**, option buttons allow you to select a single option from among one or more options.
Check boxes	Click a check box to select or deselect it; when it is selected, a check mark appears, indicating that the option is turned on; when deselected, the check box is blank and the option is off. When check boxes appear in groups, you can select or deselect as many as you want; they are not mutually exclusive, as option buttons are.
Spin boxes	Allow you to scroll easily through a set of numbers to choose the setting you want
Text boxes	Boxes into which you type additional information

Figure 1-26 displays examples of these controls.

Figure 1-26	EXAMPLES OF DIALOG BOX CONTROLS

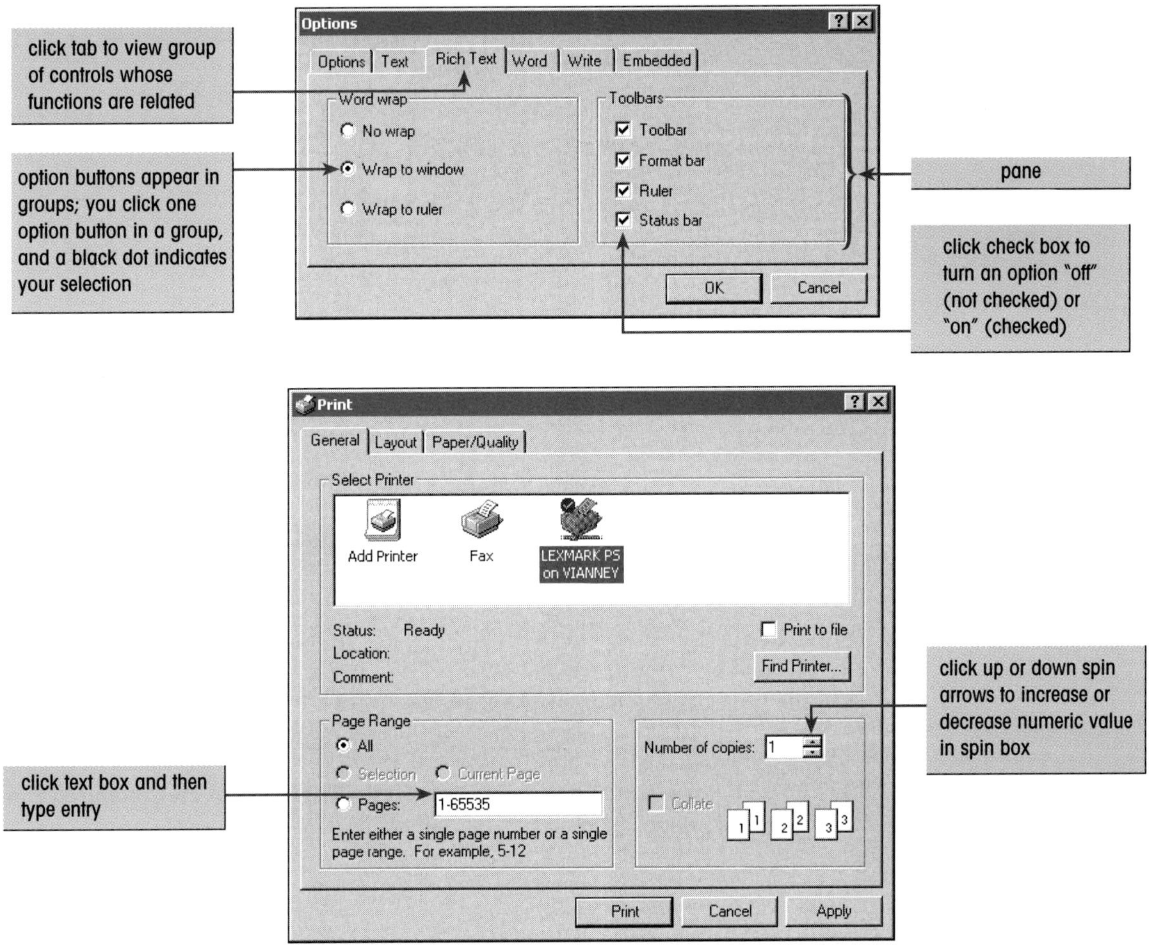

click tab to view group of controls whose functions are related

option buttons appear in groups; you click one option button in a group, and a black dot indicates your selection

Options   ? X

Options | Text | **Rich Text** | Word | Write | Embedded

Word wrap
○ No wrap
◉ Wrap to window
○ Wrap to ruler

Toolbars
☑ Toolbar
☑ Format bar
☑ Ruler
☑ Status bar

OK   Cancel

pane

click check box to turn an option "off" (not checked) or "on" (checked)

Print   ? X

General | Layout | Paper/Quality

Select Printer

Add Printer   Fax   LEXMARK PS on VIANNEY

Status: Ready
Location:
Comment:

☐ Print to file

Find Printer...

click up or down spin arrows to increase or decrease numeric value in spin box

Page Range
◉ All
○ Selection   ○ Current Page
○ Pages: 1-65535
Enter either a single page number or a single page range. For example, 5-12

click text box and then type entry

Number of copies: 1

☐ Collate   1 1   2 2   3 3

Print   Cancel   Apply

Using **Help**

Windows 2000 **Help** provides on-screen information about the program you are using. Help for the Windows 2000 operating system is available by clicking the Start button on the taskbar, then selecting Help from the Start menu. If you want Help for a program, such as WordPad, you must first start the program, then click Help on the menu bar.

When you start Help, a Windows Help window opens, which gives you access to help files stored on your computer as well as help information stored on Microsoft's Web site. If you are not connected to the Web, you have access only to the help files stored on your computer.

To start Windows 2000 Help:

1. Click the **Start** button.

2. Click **Help**. The Windows 2000 window opens to the Contents tab. See Figure 1-27.

TROUBLE? If the Contents tab is not in front, click the Contents tab to view the table of contents.

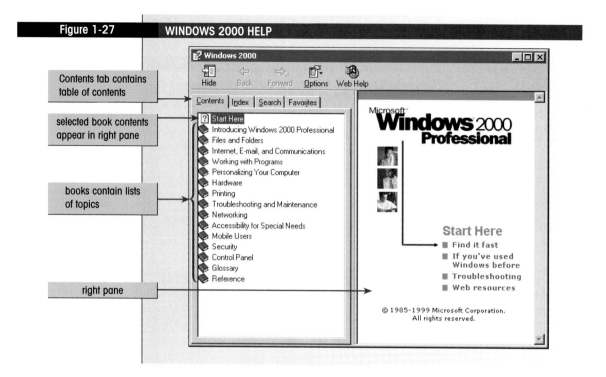

Figure 1-27   WINDOWS 2000 HELP

Help uses tabs for the four sections of Help: Contents, Index, Search, and Favorites. The **Contents tab** groups Help topics into a series of books. You select a book 📖 by clicking it. The book opens, and a list of related topics appears from which you can choose. Individual topics are designated with the ? icon. Overview topics are designated with the 🔖 icon.

The **Index tab** displays an alphabetical list of all the Help topics from which you can choose. The **Search tab** allows you to search the entire set of Help topics for all topics that contain a word or words you specify. The **Favorites tab** allows you to save your favorite Help topics for quick reference.

Viewing Topics from the Contents Tab

You know that Windows 2000 gives you easy access to the Internet. Suppose you're wondering how to connect to the Internet from your computer. You can use the Contents tab to find more information on a specific topic.

To use the Contents tab:

1. Click the **Internet, E-mail, and Communications** book icon 📖. A list of topics and an overview appear below the book title.

2. Click the **Connect to the Internet** topic icon ?. Information about connecting to the Internet appears in the right pane. See Figure 1-28.

| Figure 1-28 | LOCATING INFORMATION ABOUT HOW TO CONNECT TO THE INTERNET |

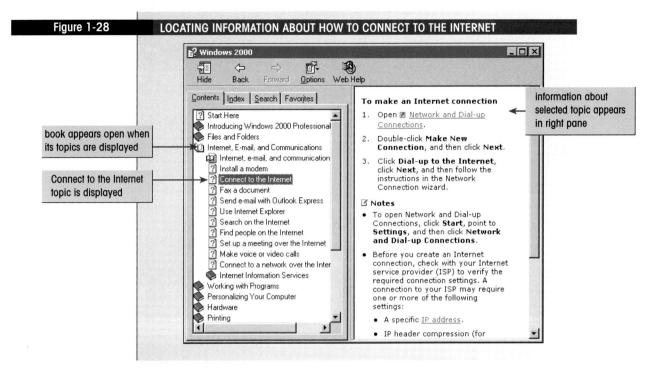

book appears open when its topics are displayed

Connect to the Internet topic is displayed

information about selected topic appears in right pane

Selecting a Topic from the Index

The Index tab allows you to jump to a Help topic by selecting a topic from an indexed list. For example, you can use the Index tab to learn more about the Internet.

To find a Help topic using the Index tab:

1. Click the **Index** tab. A long list of indexed Help topics appears.

   TROUBLE? If this is the first time you've used Help on your computer, Windows 2000 needs to set up the Index. This takes just a few moments. Wait until you see the list of index entries in the left pane, and then proceed to Step 2.

2. Drag the scroll box down to view additional topics.

3. You can quickly jump to any part of the list by typing the first few characters of a word or phrase in the box above the Index list. Click the box and then type **Internet**.

4. Click the topic **searching the Internet** (you might have to scroll to see it) and then click the **Display** button. When there is just one topic, it appears immediately in the right pane; otherwise, the Topics Found window opens, listing all topics indexed under the entry you're interested in. In this case, there are four choices.

5. Click **Using Internet Explorer** and then click the **Display** button. The information you requested appears in the right pane. See Figure 1-29. Notice in this topic that there are a few underlined words. You can click underlined words to view definitions or additional information.

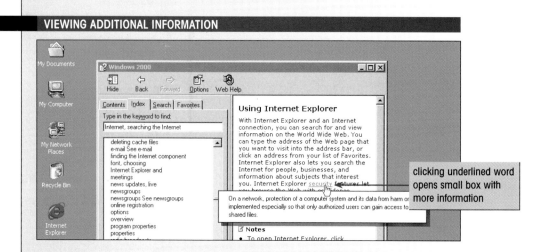

Figure 1-29 **USING THE INDEX TO LOCATE INFORMATION**

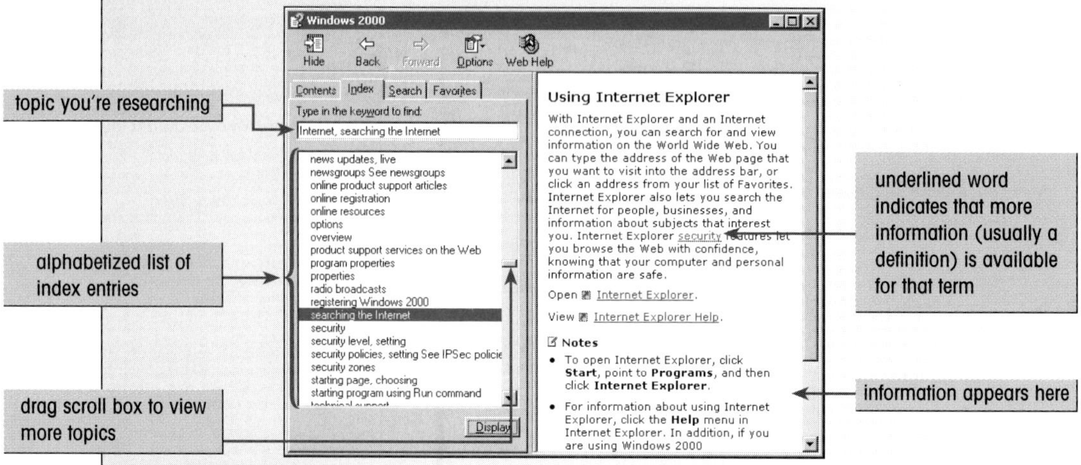

topic you're researching

alphabetized list of index entries

drag scroll box to view more topics

underlined word indicates that more information (usually a definition) is available for that term

information appears here

6. Click **security**. A small box appears that defines the term "security." See Figure 1-30.

Figure 1-30 **VIEWING ADDITIONAL INFORMATION**

clicking underlined word opens small box with more information

7. Click a blank area of the Windows 2000 window to close the box.

The third tab, the Search tab, works similarly to the Index tab, except that you type a word, and then the Help system searches for topics containing that word. You'll get a chance to experiment with the Search and Favorites tabs in the Review Assignments.

Returning to a Previous Help Topic

You've looked at a few topics now. Suppose you want to return to the one you just saw. The Help window includes a toolbar of buttons that help you navigate the Help system. One of these buttons is the **Back** button, which returns you to topics you've already viewed. Try returning to the help topic on connecting to the Internet.

To return to a Help topic:

1. Click the **Back** button. The Internet topic appears.

2. Click the **Close** button ☒ to close the Windows 2000 window.

3. Log off or shut down Windows 2000, depending on your lab's requirements.

Now that you know how Windows 2000 Help works, don't forget to use it! Use Help when you need to perform a new task or when you forget how to complete a procedure.

You've finished the tutorial, and as you shut down Windows 2000, Steve Laslow returns from class. You take a moment to tell him all you've learned: you know how to start and close programs and how to use multiple programs at the same time. You have learned how to work with windows and the controls they employ. Finally, you've learned how to get help when you need it. Steve is pleased that you are well on your way to mastering the fundamentals of using the Windows 2000 operating system.

Session 1.2 QUICK CHECK

1. What is the difference between the title bar and a toolbar?

2. Provide the name and purpose of each button:
   a. [_]   b. [□]   c. [🗗]   d. [✕]

3. Describe what is indicated by each of the following menu conventions:
   a. Ellipsis...   b. Grayed-out   c. ▶   d. ✔

4. A(n) _____ consists of a group of buttons, each of which provides one-click access to important program functions.

5. What is the purpose of the scroll bar? What is the purpose of the scroll box?

6. Option buttons allow you to select _____ option(s) at a time.

7. It is a good idea to use _____ when you need to learn how to perform new tasks.

REVIEW ASSIGNMENTS

1. **Running Two Programs and Switching Between Them** In this tutorial you learned how to run more than one program at a time, using WordPad and Paint. You can run other programs at the same time, too. Complete the following steps and write out your answers to questions b through f:
   a. Start the computer. Enter your username and password if prompted to do so.
   b. Click the Start button. How many menu options are on the Start menu?
   c. Run the Calculator program located on the Accessories menu. How many program buttons are now on the taskbar (don't count toolbar buttons or items in the tray)?
   d. Run the Paint program and maximize the Paint window. How many programs are running now?
   e. Switch to Calculator. What are two visual clues that tell you that Calculator is the active program?
   f. Multiply 576 by 1457 using the Calculator accessory. What is the result?
   g. Close Calculator, then close Paint.

Explore ▶ 2. **WordPad Help** In Tutorial 1 you learned how to use Windows 2000 Help. Almost every Windows 2000 program has a Help feature. Many users can learn to use a program just by using Help. To use Help, start the program, then click the Help menu at the top of the screen. Try using WordPad Help:
   a. Start WordPad.
   b. Click Help on the WordPad menu bar, and then click Help Topics.
   c. Using WordPad Help, write out your answers to questions 1 through 4.
      1. How do you create a bulleted list?
      2. How do you set the margins in a document?
      3. How do you undo a mistake?
      4. How do you change the font style of a block of text?
   d. Close WordPad.

Explore

3. **The Search Tab** In addition to the Contents and Index tabs you worked with in this tutorial, Windows 2000 Help also includes a Search tab. Windows 2000 makes it possible to use a microphone to record sound on your computer. You could browse through the Contents tab, although you might not know where to find information about microphones. You could also use the Index tab to search through the indexed entry. Or you could use the Search tab to find all Help topics that mention microphones.

   a. Start Windows 2000 Help and use the Index tab to find information about microphones. How many topics are listed?
   b. Now use the Search tab to find information about microphones. Type "microphone" in the box on the Search tab, and then click the List Topics button.
   c. Write a paragraph comparing the two lists of topics. You don't have to view them all, but indicate which tab seems to yield more information, and why. Close Help.

4. **Getting Started** Windows 2000 includes Getting Started, an online "book" that helps you discover more about your computer and the Windows 2000 operating system. You can use this book to review what you learned in this tutorial and pick up some tips for using Windows 2000. Complete the following steps and write out your answers to questions d–j.

   a. Start Help, click the Contents tab, click Introducing Windows 2000 Professional, and then click Getting Started online book. Read the information and then click Windows 2000 Professional Getting Started.
   b. In the right pane, click New to Windows? Notice the book icons in the upper-right and upper-left corners of the right pane.
   c. Read each screen, and then click the right book icon to proceed through the Help topics. Alternately, you can view specific Getting Started Help topics by clicking them on the Contents tab. To answer the following questions, locate the information on the relevant Help topic. All the information for these questions is located in Chapter 4—"Windows Basics." When you are done, close Help.
   d. If your computer's desktop style uses the single-click option, how do you select a file? How do you open a file?
   e. What features are almost always available on your desktop, regardless of how many windows you have open?
   f. How can you get information about a dialog box or an area of the dialog box?
   g. How does the Getting Started online book define the word "disk"?
   h. If your computer is connected to a network, what Windows 2000 feature can you use to browse network resources?
   i. Why shouldn't you turn off your computer without shutting it down properly?

5. **Favorite Help Topics** You learned in this tutorial that you can save a list of your favorite Help topics on the Favorites tab. Try adding a topic to your list of favorites.

   a. Open a Help topic in the Help system. For this assignment, click the Contents tab, click Personalizing Your Computer, and then click Personalizing your workspace overview.
   b. Click the Favorites tab. The topic you selected appears on the right, and the topic name appears in the lower-left corner.
   c. Click the Add button. The topic appears in the box on the Favorites tab. This provides you an easy way to return to this topic.
   d. Click the Remove button to remove the topic from the Favorites list.

PROJECTS

1. There are many types of pointing devices on the market today. Go to the library and research the types of devices available. Consider what devices are appropriate for these situations: desktop or laptop computers, connected or remote devices, and ergonomic or standard designs (look up the word "ergonomic").

Use up-to-date computer books, trade computer magazines such as *PC Computing* and *PC Magazine*, or the Internet (if you know how) to locate information. Your instructor might suggest specific resources you can use. Write a one-page report describing the types of devices available, the differing needs of users, special features that make pointing devices more useful, price comparisons, and what you would choose if you needed to buy a pointing device.

2. Using the resources available to you, either through your library or the Internet (if you know how), locate information about the release of Windows 2000. Computing trade magazines are an excellent source of information about software. Read several articles about Windows 2000 and then write a one-page essay that discusses the features that are most important to the people who evaluated the software. If you find reviews of the software, mention the features that reviewers had the strongest reaction to, pro or con.

3. Upgrading is the process of placing a more recent version of a product onto your computer. When Windows 2000 first came out, people had to decide whether or not they wanted to upgrade to Windows 2000. Interview several people you know who are well-informed Windows computer users. Ask them whether they are using Windows 2000 or an older version of Windows. If they are using an older version, ask why they have chosen not to upgrade. If they are using Windows 2000, ask them why they chose to upgrade. Ask such questions as:
   a. What features convinced you to upgrade or made you decide to wait?
   b. What role did the price of the upgrade play?
   c. Would you have had (or did you have) to purchase new hardware to make the upgrade? How did this affect your decision?
   d. If you did upgrade, are you happy with that decision? If you didn't, do you intend to upgrade in the near future? Why, or why not?

   Write a single-page essay summarizing what you learned from these interviews.

4. Choose a topic to research using the Windows 2000 online Help system. Look for information on your topic using three tabs: the Contents tab, the Index tab, and the Search tab. Once you've found all the information you can, compare the three methods (Contents, Index, Search) of looking for information. Write a paragraph that discusses which tab proved the most useful. Did you reach the same information topics using all three methods? In a second paragraph, summarize what you learned about your topic. Finally, in a third paragraph, indicate under what circumstances you'd use which tab.

LAB ASSIGNMENTS

Using a Keyboard

Using a Keyboard To become an effective computer user, you must be familiar with your primary input device—the keyboard. See the Read This Before You Begin page for information on installing and starting the lab.

1. The Steps for the Using a Keyboard Lab provide you with a structured introduction to the keyboard layout and the function of special computer keys. Click the Steps button and begin the Steps. As you work through the Steps, answer all of the Quick Check questions that appear. When you complete the Steps, you will see a Summary Report that summarizes your performance on the Quick Checks. Follow the directions on the screen to print the Summary Report.

2. In Explore, start the typing tutor. You can develop your typing skills using the typing tutor in Explore. Take the typing test and print out your results.

3. In Explore, try to improve your typing speed by 10 words per minute. For example, if you currently type 20 words per minute, your goal will be 30 words per minute. Practice each typing lesson until you see a message that indicates that you can proceed to the next lesson.

Create a Practice Record, as shown here, to keep track of how much you practice. When you have reached your goal, print out the results of a typing test to verify your results.

Practice Record
Name:
Section:
Start Date: Start Typing Speed: wpm
End Date: End Typing Speed: wpm
Lesson #:   Date Practiced/Time Practiced

Using a Mouse A mouse is a standard input device on most of today's computers. You need to know how to use a mouse to manipulate graphical user interfaces and to use the rest of the Labs. See the Read This Before You Begin page for information on installing and starting the lab.

1. The Steps for the Using a Mouse Lab show you how to click, double-click, and drag objects using the mouse. Click the Steps button and begin the Steps. As you work through the Steps, answer all of the Quick Check questions that appear. When you complete the Steps, you will see a Summary Report that summarizes your performance on the Quick Checks. Follow the directions on the screen to print the Summary Report.

2. In Explore, create a poster to demonstrate your ability to use a mouse and to control a Windows program. To create a poster for an upcoming sports event, select a graphic, type the caption for the poster, then select a font, font styles, and a border. Print your completed poster.

QUICK CHECK ANSWERS

Session 1.1

1. The taskbar contains buttons that give you access to tools and programs.
2. multitasking
3. Start menu
4. Lift the mouse up and move it to the right.
5. Its button appears on the taskbar.
6. To conserve computer resources such as memory.
7. To ensure you don't lose data and damage your files.

Session 1.2

1. The title bar identifies the window and contains window controls; toolbars contain buttons that provide you with shortcuts to common menu commands.
2. a. Minimize button shrinks window so you see button on taskbar
   b. Maximize button enlarges window to fill entire screen
   c. Restore button reduces window to predetermined size
   d. Close button closes window and removes button from taskbar
3. a. ellipsis indicates a dialog box will open
   b. grayed-out indicates option is not currently available
   c. arrow indicates a submenu will open
   d. check mark indicates a toggle option
4. toolbar
5. Scroll bars appear when the contents of a box or window are too long to fit; you drag the scroll box to view different parts of the contents.
6. one
7. online Help

OBJECTIVES

In this tutorial you will:

- Format a disk

- Enter, select, insert, and delete text

- Create and save a file

- Open, edit, and print a file

- Create and make a copy of your Data Disk

- View the list of files on your disk and change view options

- Move, copy, delete, and rename a file

- Navigate a hierarchy of folders

LABS

Using Files

WORKING WITH FILES

Creating, Saving, and Managing Files

CASE

Distance Education

You recently purchased a computer in order to gain new skills so you can stay competitive in the job market. You hope to use the computer to enroll in a few distance education courses. **Distance education** is formalized learning that typically takes place using a computer and the Internet, replacing normal classroom interaction with modern communications technology. Distance education teachers often make their course material available on the **World Wide Web**, a popular service on the Internet that makes information readily accessible.

Your computer came loaded with Windows 2000. Your friend Shannon suggests that before you enroll in any online courses, you should get more comfortable with your computer and with Windows 2000. Knowing how to save, locate, and organize your files will make your time spent at the computer much more productive. A **file**, often referred to as a **document**, is a collection of data that has a name and is stored in a computer. Once you create a file, you can open it, edit its contents, print it, and save it again—usually using the same program you used to create it.

Shannon suggests that you become familiar with how to perform these tasks in Windows 2000 programs. Then she'll show you how to choose different ways of viewing information on your computer. Finally, you'll spend time learning how to organize your files.

SESSION 2.1

In Session 2.1, you will learn how to format a disk so it can store files. You will create, save, open, and print a file. You will find out how the insertion point differs from the mouse pointer, and you will learn the basic skills for Windows 2000 text entry, such as entering, selecting, inserting, and deleting. For the steps of this tutorial you will need two blank 3½-inch disks.

Formatting a Disk

Before you can save files on a floppy disk, the disk must be formatted. When the computer **formats** a disk, the magnetic particles on the disk surface are arranged so that data can be stored on the disk. Today, many disks are sold preformatted and can be used right out of the box. However, if you purchase an unformatted disk, or if you have an old disk you want to completely erase and reuse, you can format the disk using the Windows 2000 Format command. This command is available through the **My Computer window**, a feature of Windows 2000 that you use to view, organize, and access the programs, files, drives and folders on your computer. You open My Computer by using its icon on the desktop. You'll learn more about the My Computer window later in this tutorial.

The following steps tell you how to format a 3½-inch high-density disk, using drive A. Your instructor will tell you how to revise the instructions given in these steps if the procedure is different for your lab.

Make sure you are using a blank disk (or one that contains data you no longer need) before you perform these steps.

To format a disk:

1. Start Windows 2000, if necessary.

2. Write your name on the label of a 3½-inch disk and insert your disk in drive A. See Figure 2-1.

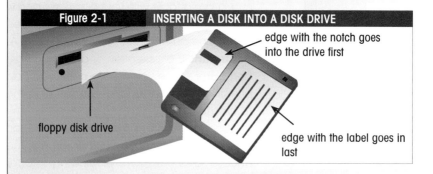

| Figure 2-1 | INSERTING A DISK INTO A DISK DRIVE |

edge with the notch goes into the drive first

floppy disk drive

edge with the label goes in last

   TROUBLE? If your disk does not fit in drive A, put it in drive B and substitute drive B for drive A in all of the steps for the rest of the tutorial.

3. Click the **My Computer** icon on the desktop. The icon is selected. Figure 2-2 shows this icon on your desktop.

   TROUBLE? If the My Computer window opens, skip Step 4. Your computer is using different settings, which you'll learn to change in Session 2.2.

4. Press the **Enter** key to open the My Computer window. See Figure 2-2 (don't worry if your window opens maximized).

TROUBLE? If you see a list of items instead of icons like those in Figure 2-2, click View, and then click Large Icons. Don't worry if your toolbars don't exactly match those in Figure 2-2.

TROUBLE? If you see additional information or a graphic image on the left side of the My Computer window, Web view is enabled on your computer. Don't worry. You will learn how to return to the default Windows 2000 settings in Session 2.2.

| Figure 2-2 | MY COMPUTER WINDOW |

My Computer icon; don't worry if yours looks different

3½ Floppy (A:) icon

your window might contain different icons and have a different look

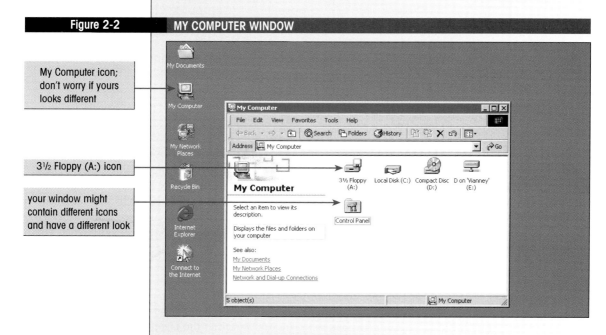

5. Right-click the **3½ Floppy (A:)** icon to open its shortcut menu, and then click **Format**. The Format dialog box opens.

6. Make sure the dialog box settings on your screen match those in Figure 2-3.

| Figure 2-3 | FORMATTING A FLOPPY DISK |

capacity is 1.44 MB

file system is FAT

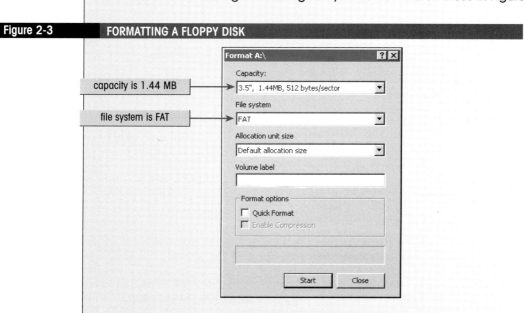

By default, Windows 2000 uses the FAT (File Allocation Table) file system for floppy disks. A **file system** is the way files are organized on the disk. Windows 2000 supports other file systems such as FAT32 and NTFS, but this is a more advanced topic.

7. Click the **Start** button to start formatting the disk.

8. Click the **OK** button to confirm that you want to format the disk (the actual formatting will take a minute to perform). Click the **OK** button again when the formatting is complete.

9. Click the **Close** button.

10. Click the **Close** button ☒ to close the My Computer window.

Now that you have a formatted disk, you can create a document and save it on your disk. First you need to learn how to enter text into a document.

Working **with Text**

To accomplish many computing tasks, you need to enter text in documents and text boxes. This involves learning how to move the pointer so the text will appear where you want it, how to insert new text between existing words or sentences, how to select text, and how to delete text. When you type sentences of text, do not press the Enter key when you reach the right margin of the page. Most software contains a feature called **word wrap**, which automatically continues your text on the next line. Therefore, you should press Enter only when you have completed a paragraph.

If you type the wrong character, press the Backspace key to back up and delete the character. You can also use the Delete key. What's the difference between the Backspace and Delete keys? The **Backspace** key deletes the character to the left, while the **Delete** key deletes the character to the right. If you want to delete text that is not next to where you are currently typing, you need to use the mouse to select the text; then you can use either the Delete key or the Backspace key.

Now you will type some text, using WordPad, to practice text entry. When you first start WordPad, notice the flashing vertical bar, called the **insertion point**, in the upper-left corner of the document window. The insertion point indicates where the characters you type will appear.

To type text in WordPad:

1. Start WordPad and locate the insertion point.

TROUBLE? If the WordPad window does not fill the screen, click the Maximize button ☐ .

TROUBLE? If you can't find the insertion point, click in the WordPad **document window**, the white area below the toolbars and ruler.

2. Type your name, pressing the Shift key at the same time as the appropriate letter to type uppercase letters and using the Spacebar to type spaces, just as on a typewriter.

3. Press the **Enter** key to move the insertion point down to the next line.

4. As you type the following sentences, watch what happens when the insertion point reaches the right edge of the page:

This is a sample typed in WordPad. See what happens when the insertion point reaches the right edge of the page. Note how the text wraps automatically to the next line.

TROUBLE? If you make a mistake, delete the incorrect character(s) by pressing the Backspace key on your keyboard. Then type the correct character(s).

> TROUBLE? If your text doesn't wrap, your screen might be set up to display more information than the screen used for the figures in this tutorial, or your WordPad program might not be set to use Word Wrap. Click View, click Options, make sure the Rich Text tab is selected, click the Wrap to window option button, and then click the OK button.

The Insertion Point Versus the Pointer

The insertion point is not the same as the mouse pointer. When the mouse pointer is in the text-entry area, it is called the **I-beam pointer** and looks like Ⅰ. Figure 2-4 explains the difference between the insertion point and the I-beam pointer.

Figure 2-4	THE INSERTION POINT VS. THE POINTER

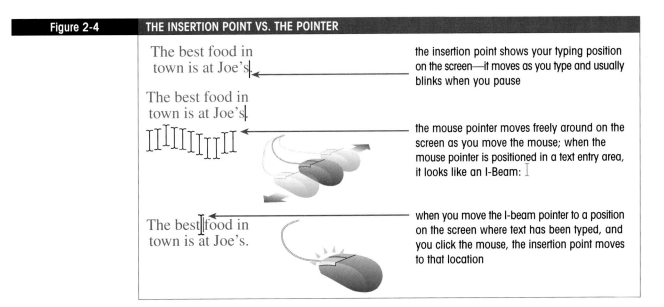

The best food in
town is at Joe's⏐ ◄——— the insertion point shows your typing position on the screen—it moves as you type and usually blinks when you pause

The best food in
town is at Joe's⏐ ◄——— the mouse pointer moves freely around on the screen as you move the mouse; when the mouse pointer is positioned in a text entry area, it looks like an I-Beam: Ⅰ

The best⏐food in
town is at Joe's. ◄——— when you move the I-beam pointer to a position on the screen where text has been typed, and you click the mouse, the insertion point moves to that location

When you enter text, the insertion point moves as you type. If you want to enter text in a location other than where the mouse pointer is currently positioned, you move the I-beam pointer to the location where you want to type, and then click. The insertion point jumps to the location you clicked. In most programs, the insertion point blinks, making it easier for you to locate it on a screen filled with text.

To move the insertion point:

1. Check the locations of the insertion point and the I-beam pointer. The insertion point should be at the end of the sentence you typed in the last set of steps. The easiest way to locate the I-beam pointer is to move your mouse gently until you see the pointer. Remember that it will look like ⌖ until you move the pointer into the document window.

2. Use the mouse to move the I-beam pointer just to the left of the word "sample" and then click the mouse button. The insertion point should be just to the left of the "s."

   TROUBLE? If you have trouble clicking just to the left of the "s," try clicking in the word and then using the arrow keys to move the insertion point one character at a time.

3. Move the I-beam pointer to a blank area near the bottom of the workspace and then click. Notice the insertion point does not jump to the location of the I-beam pointer. Instead the insertion point jumps to the end of the last sentence or to the point in the bottom line directly above where you clicked. The insertion point can move only within existing text. It cannot be moved out of the existing text area.

Selecting Text

Many text operations are performed on a **block** of text, which is one or more consecutive characters, words, sentences, or paragraphs. Once you select a block of text, you can delete it, move it, replace it, underline it, and so on. To deselect a block of text, click anywhere outside the selected block.

If you want to delete the phrase "See what happens" in the text you just typed and replace it with the phrase "You can watch word wrap in action," you do not have to delete the first phrase one character at a time. Instead, you can select the entire phrase and then type the replacement phrase.

To select and replace a block of text:

1. Move the I-beam pointer just to the left of the word "See."

2. While holding down the mouse button, drag the I-beam pointer over the text to the end of the word "happens." The phrase "See what happens" should now be highlighted. See Figure 2-5.

TROUBLE? If the space to the right of the word "happens" is also selected, don't worry. Your computer is set up to select spaces in addition to words. After completing Step 4, simply press the Spacebar to type an extra space if required.

| Figure 2-5 | SELECTING TEXT |

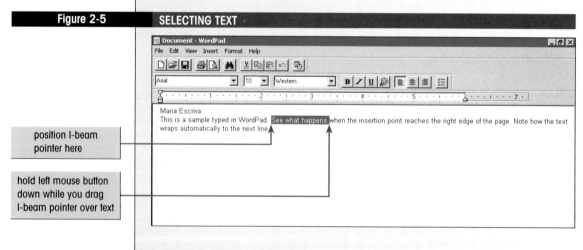

position I-beam pointer here

hold left mouse button down while you drag I-beam pointer over text

3. Release the mouse button.

TROUBLE? If the phrase is not highlighted correctly, repeat Steps 1 through 3.

4. Type **You can watch word wrap in action**

The text you typed replaces the highlighted text. Notice that you did not need to delete the selected text before you typed the replacement text.

Inserting a Character

Windows 2000 programs usually operate in **insert mode**—when you type a new character, all characters to the right of the insertion point are pushed over to make room.

Suppose you want to insert the word "page" before the word "typed" in your practice sentences.

To insert text:

1. Move the I-beam pointer just before the word "typed" and then click to position the insertion point.

2. Type **page**

3. Press the **Spacebar**.

Notice how the letters in the first line are pushed to the right to make room for the new characters. When a word gets pushed past the right margin, the word-wrap feature moves it down to the beginning of the next line.

Saving a File

As you type text, it is held temporarily in the computer's memory, which is erased when you turn off the computer. For permanent storage, you need to save your work on a disk. In the computer lab, you will probably save your work on a floppy disk in drive A.

When you save a file, you must give it a name, called a **filename**. Windows 2000 allows you to use up to 255 characters in a filename—this gives you plenty of room to name your file accurately enough so that you'll know the contents of the file by just looking at the filename. You may use spaces and certain punctuation symbols in your filenames. You cannot use the symbols \ / ? : * " < > | in a filename, because Windows uses those for designating the location and type of the file, but other symbols such as & ; - and $ are allowed.

Another thing to consider is whether you might use your files on a computer running older programs. Programs designed for the Windows 3.1 and DOS operating systems (which were created before 1995) require that files be eight characters or less with no spaces. Thus when you save a file with a long filename in Windows 2000, Windows 2000 also creates an eight-character filename that can be used by older programs. The eight-character filename is created from the first six nonspace characters in the long filename, with the addition of a tilde (~) and a number. For example, the filename Car Sales for 1999 would be converted to Carsal~1.

Most filenames have an extension. An **extension** (a set of no more than three characters at the end of a filename, separated from the filename by a period) is used by the operating system to identify and categorize the file. In the filename Car Sales for 1999.doc, for example, the file extension "doc" identifies the file as one created with Microsoft Word. You might also have a file called Car Sales for 1999.xls—"xls" identifies the file as one created with Microsoft Excel, a spreadsheet program. When pronouncing filenames with extensions, say "dot" for the period, so that the file Resume.doc is pronounced "Resume dot doc."

You usually do not need to add extensions to your filenames because the program you use to create the file does this automatically. Also, Windows 2000 keeps track of file extensions, but not all computers are set to display them. The steps in these tutorials refer to files by using the filename without its extension. So if you see the filename Practice Text in the steps, but "Practice Text.doc" appears on your screen, don't worry—these refer to the same file. Also don't worry if you don't use consistent lowercase and uppercase letters when saving files. Usually the operating system doesn't distinguish between them. Be aware, however, that some programs are "case-sensitive"—they check for case in filenames.

Now you can save the WordPad document you typed.

To start saving a document:

1. Click the **Save** button 🖫 on the toolbar. The Save As dialog box opens, as shown in Figure 2-6.

Figure 2-6	SAVING A FILE

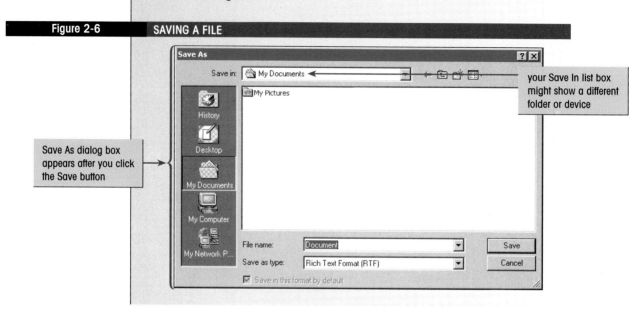

Save As dialog box appears after you click the Save button

your Save In list box might show a different folder or device

You use the Save As dialog box to specify where you want to save your file (on the hard drive or on a floppy disk, in a folder or not, and so on). Before going further with the process of saving a file, let's examine some of the features of the Save As dialog box so that you learn to save your files exactly where you want them.

Specifying the File Location

In the Save As dialog box, Windows 2000 provides the **Places Bar**, a list of important locations on your computer. When you click the different icons in the Places Bar, the contents of those locations will be displayed in the white area of the Save As dialog box. You can then save your document directly to those locations. Figure 2-7 displays the icons in the Places Bar and gives their function.

Figure 2-7	ICONS IN THE PLACES BAR

ICON	DESCRIPTION
History	Displays a list of recently opened files, folders, and objects
Desktop	Displays a list of files, folders, and objects on the Windows 2000 desktop
My Documents	Displays a list of files, folders, and objects in the My Documents folder
My Computer	Displays a list of files, folders, and objects in the My Computer window
My Network P...	Displays a list of computers and folders available on the network

To see this in action, try displaying different locations in the dialog box.

To use the Places Bar:

1. Click the **Desktop** icon in the Places Bar.

2. The Save As dialog box now displays the contents of the Windows 2000 desktop. See Figure 2-8.

| Figure 2-8 | USING THE PLACES BAR |

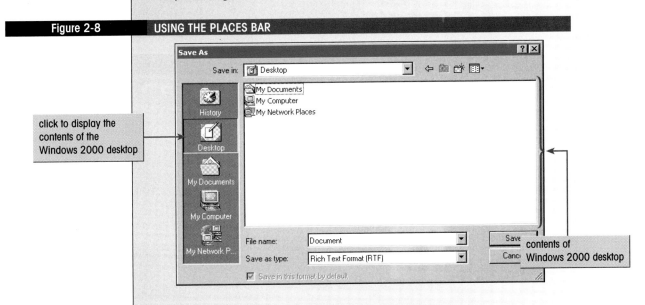

click to display the contents of the Windows 2000 desktop

contents of Windows 2000 desktop

3. Click the **My Documents** icon to display the contents of the My Documents folder.

Once you've clicked an icon in the Places Bar, you can open any file displayed in that location, and you can save a file into that location. The Places Bar doesn't have an icon for every location on your computer, however. The **Save in** list box (located at the top of the dialog box) does. Use the Save in list box now to save your document to your floppy disk.

To use the Save in list box:

1. Click the **Save in** list arrow to display a list of drives.

2. Click **3½ Floppy (A:)**.

   Now that you've specified where you want to save your file, you can specify a name and type for the file.

Specifying the File Name and Type

After choosing the location for your document, you have to specify the name of the file. You should also specify (or at least check) the file's format. A file's **format** determines what type of information you can place in the document, the document's appearance, and what kind of programs can work with the document. There are five file formats available in WordPad: Word for Windows 6.0, Rich Text Format (RTF), Text, Text for MS-DOS, and Unicode Text. The Word and RTF formats allow you to create documents with text that can use bold-faced or italicized fonts as well as documents containing graphic images and scanned photos. However, only word-processing programs like WordPad or Microsoft Word can work with those files. The three text formats allow only simple text with no graphics or special formatting, but such documents are readable by a wider range of programs. The default format for WordPad documents is RTF, but you can change that, as you'll see shortly.

Continue saving the document, using the name "Practice Text" and the file type Word 6.0.

To finish saving your document:

1. Select the text **Document** in the File name text box and then type **Practice Text** in the File name text box. The new text replaces "Document."

2. Click the **Save as type** list arrow and then click **Word for Windows 6.0** in the list. See Figure 2-9.

Figure 2-9	COMPLETED SAVE AS DIALOG BOX

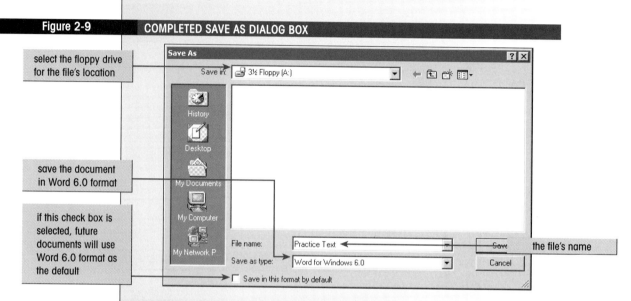

select the floppy drive for the file's location

save the document in Word 6.0 format

if this check box is selected, future documents will use Word 6.0 format as the default

the file's name

Note that if you want all future documents saved by WordPad to use the Word 6.0 format as the default format rather than RTF, you can select the Save in this format by default check box. If you select it, the next time you save a document in WordPad, this format will be the initial choice, so you won't have to specify it.

3. Click the **Save** button in the lower-right corner of the dialog box.

4. If you are asked whether you are sure that you want to save the document in this format, click the **Yes** button.

Your file is saved on your Data Disk, and the document title, "Practice Text," appears on the WordPad title bar.

Note that after you save the file the document appears a little different. What has changed? By saving the document in Word 6.0 format rather than RTF, you've changed the format of the document slightly. One change is that the text is wrapped differently in Word 6.0 format. A Word 6.0 file will use the right margin and, in this case, limit the length of a single line of text to 6 inches.

What if you try to close WordPad before you save your file? Windows 2000 will display a message—"Save changes to Document?" If you answer "Yes," Windows will display the Save As dialog box so you can give the document a name. If you answer "No," Windows 2000 will close WordPad without saving the document. Any changes you made to the document will be lost, so when you are asked if you want to save a file, answer "Yes," unless you are absolutely sure you don't need to keep the work you just did.

After you save a file, you can work on another document or close WordPad. Since you have already saved your Practice Text document, you'll continue this tutorial by closing WordPad.

To close WordPad:

1. Click the **Close** button ☒ to close the WordPad window.

Opening a File

Suppose you save and close the Practice Text file, then later you want to revise it. To revise a file you must first open it. When you open a file, its contents are copied into the computer's memory. If you revise the file, you need to save the changes before you close the program. If you close a revised file without saving your changes, you will lose them.

There are several methods to open a file. You can select the file from the Documents list (available through the Start menu) if you have opened the file recently, since the Documents list contains the 15 most recently opened documents. This list is very handy to use on your own computer, but in a lab, other student's files quickly replace your own. You can also locate the file in the My Computer window (or in **Windows Explorer**, another file management tool) and then open it. And finally, you can start a program and then use the Open button within that program to locate and open the file. Each method has advantages and disadvantages.

The first two methods for opening the Practice Text file simply require you to select the file from the Documents list or locate and select it from My Computer or Windows Explorer. With these methods the document, not the program, is central to the task; hence, this method is sometimes referred to as **document-centric**. You need only to remember the name of your file—you do not need to remember which program you used to create it.

Opening a File from the My Computer Window

If your file is not in the Documents list, you can open the file by selecting it from the My Computer window. Either way, Windows 2000 uses the file extension (whether it is displayed or not) to determine which program to start so you can manipulate the file. It starts the program, and then automatically opens the file. The advantage of both methods is simplicity. The disadvantage is that Windows 2000 might not start the program you expect. For example, when you select Practice Text, you might expect Windows 2000 to start WordPad because you used WordPad to create it. Depending on the programs installed on your computer system, however, Windows 2000 might start Microsoft Word instead. Usually this is not a problem. Although the program might not be the one you expect, you can still use it to revise your file.

To open the Practice Text file by selecting it from My Computer:

1. Open the **My Computer** window, located on the desktop.

2. Click the **3½ Floppy (A:)** icon in the My Computer window.

   TROUBLE? If the 3½ Floppy (A:) window opens, skip Step 3.

3. Press the **Enter** key. The 3½ Floppy (A:) window opens.

4. Click the **Practice Text** file icon.

   TROUBLE? If the Practice Text document opens, skip Step 5.

5. Press the **Enter** key. Windows 2000 starts a program, and then automatically opens the Practice Text file. You could make revisions to the document at this point, but instead, you'll close all the windows on your desktop so you can try the other method for opening files.

   TROUBLE? If Windows 2000 starts Microsoft Word or another word-processing program instead of WordPad, don't worry. You can use Microsoft Word to revise the Practice Text document.

6. Close all open windows on the desktop.

Opening a File from Within a Program

The third method for opening the Practice Text file requires you to open WordPad, and then use the Open button to select the Practice Text file. The advantage of this method is that you can specify the program you want to use—WordPad, in this case. This method, however, involves more steps than the method you tried previously.

You can take advantage of the Places Bar to reduce the number of steps it takes to open a file from within a program. Recall that one of the icons in the Places Bar is the History icon, which displays a list of recently opened files or objects. One of the most recently opened files was the Practice Text file, so it should appear in the list.

To start WordPad and open the Practice Text file:

1. Start **WordPad** and, if necessary, maximize the WordPad window.

2. Click the **Open** button 📂 on the toolbar.

3. Click **History** in the Places Bar.

The Practice Text file doesn't appear in the list. Why not? Look at the Files of Type list box. The selected entry is "Rich Text Format (*.rtf)". What this means is that the Open dialog box will display only RTF files (as well as drives). This frees you from having to deal with the clutter of unwanted or irrelevant files. The downside is that unless you're aware of how the Open dialog box will filter the list of files, you may mistakenly think that the file you're looking for doesn't exist. You can change how the Open dialog box filters this file list. Try this now by changing the filter to show only Word documents.

To change the types of files displayed:

1. Click the **Files of type** list arrow and then click **Word for Windows (*.doc)**

   The Practice Text file now appears in the list.

2. Click **Practice Text** in the list of files. See Figure 2-10.

Figure 2-10	THE OPEN DIALOG BOX

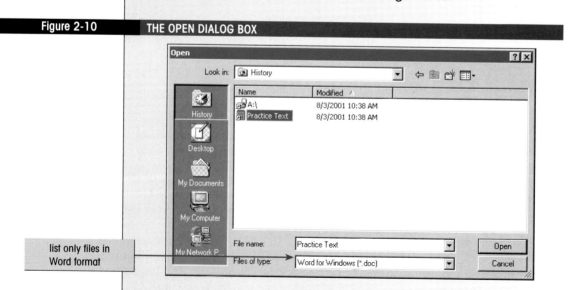

list only files in Word format

3. Click the **Open** button. The document should once again appear in the WordPad window.

Now that the Practice Text file is open, you can print it.

Printing **a File**

Windows 2000 provides easy access to your printer or printers. You can choose which printer to use, you can control how the document is printed, and you can control the order in which documents will be printed.

Previewing your Document Before Printing

It is a good idea to use Print Preview before you send your document to the printer. **Print Preview** shows on the screen exactly how your document will appear on paper. You can check your page layout so that you don't waste time and paper printing a document that is not quite the way you want it. Your instructor might supply you with additional instructions for printing in your school's computer lab.

To preview, then print, the Practice Text file:

1. Click the **Print Preview** button 🔍 on the toolbar.

TROUBLE? If an error message appears, printing capabilities might not be set up on your computer. Ask your instructor or technical support person for help, or skip this set of steps.

2. Look at your document in the Print Preview window. Before you print the document, you should make sure the font, margins, and other document features look the way you want them to.

TROUBLE? If you can't read the document text on screen, click the Zoom In button as many times as needed to view the text.

3. Click the **Close** button to close Print Preview and return to the document.

Now that you've verified that the document looks the way you want, you can print it.

Sending the Document to the Printer

There are three ways to send your document to the printer. The first approach is to print the document directly from the Print Preview window by clicking the Print button. Thus once you are satisfied with the document's appearance, you can quickly move to printing it.

Another way is to click the Print button 🖨 on your program's toolbar. This method will send the document directly to your printer without any further action on your part. It's the quickest and easiest way to print a document, but it does not allow you to change settings such as margins and layout. What if you have access to more than one printer? In that case, Windows 2000 sends the document to the default printer, the printer that has been set up to handle most print jobs.

If you want to select a different printer, or if you want to control how the printer prints your document, you can opt for a third method—selecting the Print command from the File menu. Using this approach, your program will open the Print dialog box, allowing you to choose which printer to use and how that printer will operate. Note that clicking the Print button from within the Print Preview window will also open the Print dialog box so you can verify or change settings.

To open the Print dialog box:

1. Click **File** on the WordPad menu bar and then click **Print**.

2. The Print dialog box opens, as displayed in Figure 2-11. Familiarize yourself with the controls in the Print dialog box.

Figure 2-11 | **THE PRINT DIALOG BOX**

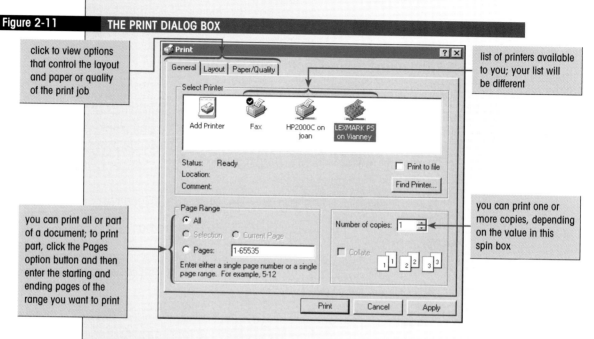

click to view options that control the layout and paper or quality of the print job

list of printers available to you; your list will be different

you can print all or part of a document; to print part, click the Pages option button and then enter the starting and ending pages of the range you want to print

you can print one or more copies, depending on the value in this spin box

3. Make sure your Print dialog box shows the Print range set to "All" and the Number of copies set to "1."

4. Select one of the printers in the list (your instructor may indicate which one you should select) and then click the **Print** button. The document is printed.

5. Close WordPad.

TROUBLE? If you see the message "Save changes to Document?" click the No button.

You've now learned how to create, save, open, and print word-processed files—essential skills for students in distance education courses that rely on word-processed reports transmitted across the Internet. Shannon assures you that the techniques you've just learned apply to most Windows 2000 programs.

Session 2.1 QUICK CHECK

1. A(n) _____file_____ is a collection of data that has a name and is stored on a disk or other storage medium.

2. _____Formatting_____ erases all the data on a disk and arranges the magnetic particles on the disk surface so that the disk can store data.

3. True or False: When you move the mouse pointer over a text entry area, the pointer shape changes to an I-beam.

4. What indicates where each character you type will appear? *insertion bar*

5. What does the History icon in the Places Bar display?

6. A file that you saved does not appear in the Open dialog box. Assuming that the file is still in the same location, what could be the reason that the Open dialog box doesn't display it? *File type list is different*

7. What are the three ways to print from within a Windows 2000 application? If you want to print multiple copies of your document, which method(s) should you use and why?

SESSION 2.2

In this session, you will learn how to change settings in the My Computer window to control its appearance and the appearance of desktop objects. You will then learn how to use My Computer to manage the files on your disk; view information about the files on your disk; organize the files into folders; and move, delete, copy, and rename files. For this session you will use a second blank 3½-inch disk.

Creating Your Data Disk

Starting with this session, you must create a Data Disk that contains some practice files. You can use the disk you formatted in the previous session.

If you are using your own computer, the NP on Microsoft Windows 2000 menu option will not be available. Before you proceed, you must go to your school's computer lab and find a computer that has the NP on Microsoft Windows 2000 program installed. If you cannot get the files from the lab, ask your instructor or technical support person for help. Once you have made your own Data Disk, you can use it to complete this tutorial on any computer running Windows 2000.

To add the practice files to your Data Disk:

1. Write "Disk 1 - Windows 2000 Tutorial 2 Data Disk" on the label of your formatted disk (the same disk you used to save your Practice Text file).

2. Place the disk in drive A.

3. Click the **Start** button **Start**.

4. Point to **Programs**.

5. Point to **NP on Microsoft Windows 2000 – Level I**.

   TROUBLE? If NP on Microsoft Windows 2000 - Level I is not listed, ask your instructor or technical support person for help.

6. Click **Disk 1 (Tutorial 2)**. A message box opens, asking you to place your disk in drive A (which you already did, in Step 2).

7. Click the **OK** button. Wait while the program copies the practice files to your formatted disk. When all the files have been copied, the program closes.

Your Data Disk now contains practice files you'll use throughout the rest of this tutorial.

My Computer

The My Computer icon, as you have seen, represents your computer, with its storage devices, printers, and other objects. The My Computer icon opens into the My Computer window, which contains an icon for each of the storage devices on your computer. My Computer also gives you access to the **Control Panel**, a feature of Windows 2000 that controls the behavior of other devices and programs installed on your computer. Figure 2-12 shows how the My Computer window relates to your computer's hardware.

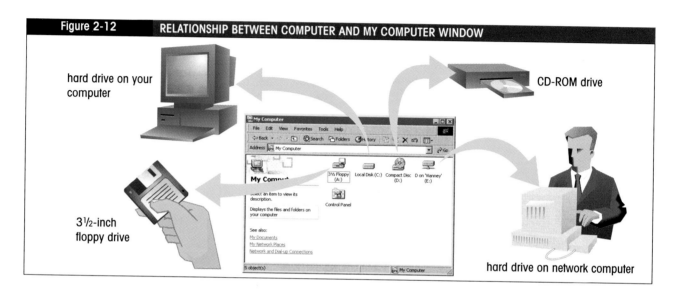

Figure 2-12   RELATIONSHIP BETWEEN COMPUTER AND MY COMPUTER WINDOW

hard drive on your computer

CD-ROM drive

3½-inch floppy drive

hard drive on network computer

Each storage device that you have access to has a letter associated with it. The first floppy drive on a computer is usually designated as drive A (if you add a second floppy drive, it is usually designated as drive B), and the first hard drive is usually designated drive C. Additional hard drives will have letters D, E, F and so forth. If you have a CD-ROM drive, it will usually have the next letter in the alphabetic sequence. If you have access to hard drives located on other computers on a network, those drives will sometimes (though not always) have letters associated with them. In the example shown in Figure 2-12, the network drive has the drive letter E.

You can use the My Computer window to organize your files. In this section of the tutorial, you'll use the My Computer window to move and delete files on your Data Disk, which is assumed to be in drive A. If you use your own computer at home or work, you will probably store your files on drive C instead of drive A. In a school lab environment, you can't always save your files to drive C, so you need to carry your files with you on a floppy disk. Most of what you learn about working on the floppy drive will also work on your home or work computer when you use drive C (or other hard drives).

Now you'll open the My Computer window.

To open the My Computer window and explore the contents of your Data Disk:

1. Open the My Computer window.

2. Click the **3½ Floppy (A:)** icon and then press the **Enter** key. A window appears showing the contents of drive A; maximize this window if necessary. See Figure 2-13.

Figure 2-13 **CONTENTS OF DATA DISK**

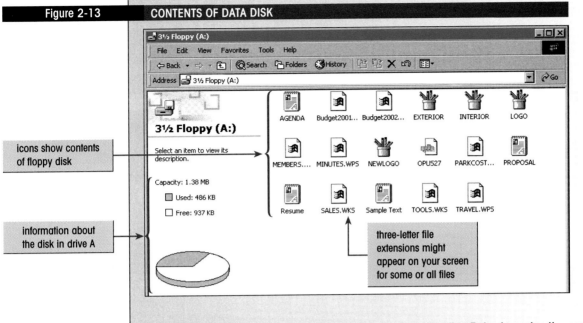

icons show contents
of floppy disk

information about
the disk in drive A

three-letter file
extensions might
appear on your screen
for some or all files

TROUBLE? If the window appears before you press the Enter key, don't worry.
Windows 2000 can be configured to use different keyboard and mouse combinations to open windows. You'll learn about these configuration issues shortly.

TROUBLE? If you see a list of filenames instead of icons, click View on the menu
bar and then click Large Icons on the menu.

Changing the Appearance of the My Computer Window

Windows 2000 offers several different options that control how toolbars, icons, and buttons
appear in the My Computer window. To make the My Computer window look the same as
it does in the figures in this book, you need to ensure three things: that only the Address and
Standard toolbars are visible, that files and other objects are displayed using large icons, and
that the configuration of Windows 2000 uses the default setting. Setting your computer to
match the figures will make it easier for you to follow the steps.

Controlling the Toolbar Display

The My Computer window, in addition to displaying a Standard toolbar, allows you to display
the same toolbars that can appear on the Windows 2000 taskbar, such as the Address toolbar or
the Links toolbar. These toolbars make it easy to access the Web from the My Computer
window. In this tutorial, however, you need to see only the Address and Standard toolbars.

To display only the Address and Standard toolbars:

1. Click **View**, point to **Toolbars**, and then examine the Toolbars submenu. The
   Standard Buttons and Address Bar options should be preceded by a check mark.
   The Links and Radio options should not be checked. Follow the steps below to
   ensure that you have check marks next to the correct options.

2. If the Standard Buttons and Address Bar options *are not checked*, then click
   them to select them (you will have to repeat Step 1 to view the Toolbars
   submenu to do this for each option).

3. If the Links or Radio options *are checked*, then click them to deselect them (you will have to repeat Step 1 to view the Toolbars submenu to do this for each option).

4. Click **View** and then point to **Toolbars** one last time and verify that your Toolbars submenu and the toolbar display look like Figure 2-14.

| Figure 2-14 | CHECKING VIEW OPTIONS |

Standard Buttons toolbar

Address Bar toolbar

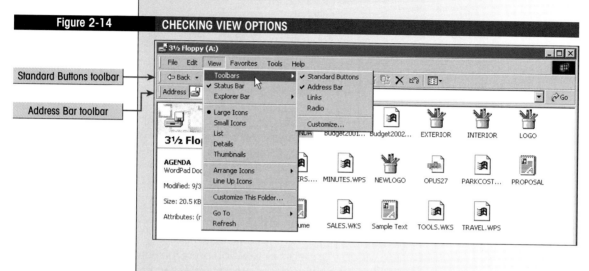

TROUBLE? If the check marks are distributed differently than in Figure 2-14, repeat Steps 1–4 until the correct options are checked.

TROUBLE? If your toolbars are not displayed as shown in Figure 2-14 (for example, both the Standard and Address toolbars might be on the same line, or the Standard toolbar might be above the Address toolbar), you can easily rearrange them. To move a toolbar, drag the vertical bar at the far left of the toolbar. By dragging that vertical bar, you can drag the toolbar left, right, up, or down.

Changing the Icon Display

Windows 2000 provides five ways to view the contents of a disk—Large Icons, Small Icons, List, Details, and Thumbnails. Figure 2-15 shows examples of these five styles.

| Figure 2-15 | VIEWING STYLES |

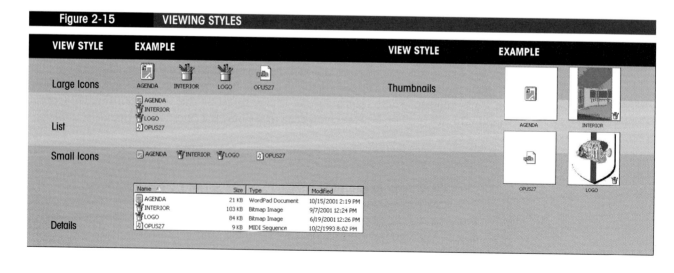

The default view, **Large Icons view**, displays a large icon and title for each file. The icon provides a visual cue to the type of the file, as Figure 2-16 illustrates. You can also get this same information with the smaller icons displayed in the **Small Icons** and **List** views, but in less screen space. In Small Icons and List views, you can see more files and folders at one time, which is helpful when you have many files in one location.

Figure 2-16	TYPICAL ICONS IN WINDOWS 2000

FILE AND FOLDER ICONS

	Text documents that you can open using the Notepad accessory are represented by notepad icons.
	Graphic image documents that you can open using the Paint accessory are represented by drawing instruments.
	Word-processed documents that you can open using the WordPad accessory are represented by a formatted notepad icon, unless your computer designates a different word-processing program to open files created with WordPad.
	Word-processed documents that you can open using a program such as Microsoft Word are represented by formatted document icons.
	Files created by programs that Windows does not recognize are represented by the Windows logo.
	A folder icon represents folders.
	Certain folders created by Windows 2000 have a special icon design related to the folder's purpose.

PROGRAM ICONS

	Icons for programs usually depict an object related to the function of the program. For example, an icon that looks like a calculator represents the Calculator accessory.
	Non-Windows programs are represented by the icon of a blank window.

All of the three icon views (Large Icons, Small Icons, and List) help you quickly identify a file and its type, but what if you want more information about a set of files? **Details view** shows more information than the Large Icon, Small Icon, and List views. Details view shows the file icon, the filename, the file size, the program you used to create the file, and the date and time the file was created or last modified.

Finally, if you have graphic files, you may want to use **Thumbnails view**, which displays a small "preview" image of the graphic, so that you can quickly see not only the filename, but also which picture or drawing the file contains. Thumbnails view is great for browsing a large collection of graphic files, but switching to this view can be time-consuming, since Windows 2000 has to create all of the preview images.

To see how easy it is to switch from one view to another, try displaying the contents of drive A in Details view.

To view a detailed list of files:

1. Click **View** and then click **Details** to display details for the files on your disk, as shown in Figure 2-17. Your files might be listed in a different order.

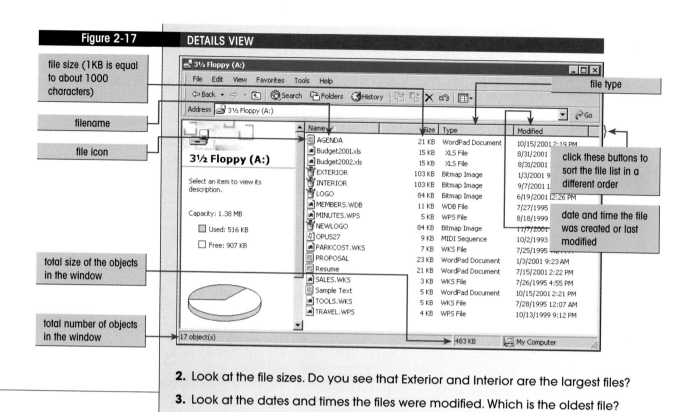

Figure 2-17 DETAILS VIEW

- file size (1KB is equal to about 1000 characters)
- filename
- file icon
- total size of the objects in the window
- total number of objects in the window
- file type
- click these buttons to sort the file list in a different order
- date and time the file was created or last modified

2. Look at the file sizes. Do you see that Exterior and Interior are the largest files?

3. Look at the dates and times the files were modified. Which is the oldest file?

One of the advantages that Details view has over other views is that you can sort the file list by filename, size, type, or the date the file was last modified. This helps if you're working with a large file list and you're trying to locate a specific file.

To sort the file list by type:

1. Click the **Type** button at the top of the list of files.

   The files are now sorted in alphabetical order by type, starting with the "Bitmap Image" files and ending with the "XLS File" files. This would be useful if, for example, you were looking for all the .doc files (those created with Microsoft Word), because they would all be grouped together under "M" for "Microsoft Word."

2. Click the **Type** button again.

   The sort order is reversed with the "XLS File" files now at the top of the list.

3. Click the **Name** button at the top of the file list.

   The files are now sorted in alphabetical order by filename.

Now that you have looked at the file details, switch back to Large Icon view.

To switch to Large Icon view:

1. Click **View** and then click **Large Icons** to return to the large icon display.

Restoring the My Computer Default Settings

Windows 2000 provides other options in working with yc options fall into two general categories: Classic style and Wel of working with windows and files that resembles earlier versi system. **Web style** allows you to work with your windows work with Web pages on the World Wide Web. For example you can double-click the file icon (a **double-click** is clickir quickly) or click the file icon once and press the Enter key. would simply click the file icon once, and the file would open. You could also create y own style, choosing elements of both the Classic and Web styles, and add in a few customized features of your own.

In order to simplify matters, this book will assume that you're working in the Default style, that is the configuration that Windows 2000 uses when it is initially installed. No matter what changes you make to the configuration of Windows 2000, you can always revert back to the Default style. Try switching back to Default style now.

To switch to the Default style:

1. Click **Tools** and then click **Folder Options** on the menu.

2. If it is not already selected, click the **General** tab.

   The General sheet displays general options for working with files and windows. Take some time to look over the list of options available.

3. Click the **Restore Defaults** button.

4. Click the **View** tab.

   The View sheet displays options that control the appearance of files and other objects. You should set these options to their default values as well.

5. Click the **Restore Defaults** button.

6. Click the **OK** button to close the Folder Options dialog box.

Working with Folders and Directories

Up to now, you've done a little work with files and windows, but before going further you should look at some of the terminology used to describe these tasks. Any location where you can store files on a computer is referred to as a **directory**. The main directory of a disk is sometimes called the **root directory**, or the **top-level directory**. All of the files on your Data Disk are currently in the root directory of your floppy disk.

If too many files are stored in a directory, the list of files becomes very long and difficult to manage. You can divide a directory into **subdirectories**, also called **folders**. The number of files for each folder then becomes much fewer and easier to manage. A folder within a folder is called a **subfolder**. The folder that contains another folder is called the **parent folder**.

All of these objects exist in a **hierarchy**, which begins with your desktop and extends down to each subfolder. Figure 2-18 shows part of a typical hierarchy of Windows 2000 objects.

PART OF A TYPICAL HIERARCHY OF WINDOWS 2000 OBJECTS

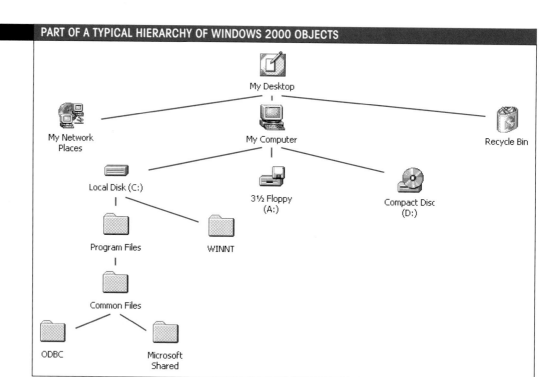

Creating a Folder

You've already seen folder icons in the various windows you've previously opened. Now, you'll create your own folder called Practice to hold your documents.

To create a Practice folder:

1. Click **File** and then point to **New** to display the submenu.

2. Click **Folder**. A folder icon with the label "New Folder" appears.

3. Type **Practice** as the name of the folder.

   TROUBLE? If nothing happens when you type the folder name, it's possible that the folder name is no longer selected. Right-click the Practice folder, click Rename, and then repeat Step 3.

4. Press the **Enter** key.

   The folder is now named "Practice" and is the selected item on your Data Disk.

5. Click a blank area next to the Practice folder to deselect it.

Navigating Through the Windows 2000 Hierarchy

Now that you've created a subfolder, how do you move into it? You've seen that to view the contents of a file, you open it. To move into a subfolder, you open it in the same way.

To view the contents of the Practice folder:

1. Click the **Practice** folder and press the **Enter** key.

2. The Practice folder opens. Because there are no files in the folder, there are no items to display. You'll change that shortly.

You've seen that to navigate through the devices and folders on your computer, you open My Computer and then click the icons representing the objects you want to explore. But what if you want to move back to the root directory? The Standard toolbar, which stays the same regardless of which folder or object is open, includes buttons that help you navigate through the hierarchy of drives, directories, folders, subfolders and other objects in your computer. Figure 2-19 summarizes the navigation buttons on the Standard toolbar.

Figure 2-19		NAVIGATION BUTTONS
BUTTON	**ICON**	**DESCRIPTION**
Back	⬅	Returns you to the folder, drive, directory, or object you were most recently viewing. The button is active only when you have viewed more than one window in the current session.
Forward	⮕	Reverses the effect of the Back button.
Up	⬆	Moves you up one level in the hierarchy of directories, drives, folders, and other objects on your computer.

You can return to your floppy's root directory by using the Back or the Up button. Try both of these techniques now.

To move up to the root directory:

1. Click the **Back** button ⬅.

Windows 2000 moves you back to the previous window, in this case the root directory of your Data Disk.

2. Click the **Forward** button ⮕.

The Forward button reverses the effect of the Back button and takes you to the Practice folder.

3. Click the **Up** button ⬆.

You move up one level in hierarchy of Windows 2000 objects, going to the root directory of the Data Disk.

Another way of moving around in the Windows 2000 hierarchy is through the Address toolbar. By clicking the Address list arrow, you can view a list of the objects in the top part of the Windows 2000 hierarchy (see Figure 2-20). This gives you a quick way of moving to the top without having to navigate through the intermediate levels.

Figure 2-20 A HIERARCHY OF OBJECTS DISPLAYED IN THE ADDRESS LIST BOX

Now that you know how to move among the folders and devices on your computer, you can practice manipulating files. The better you are at working with the hierarchy of files and folders on your computer, the more organized the hierarchy will be, and the easier it will be to find the files you need.

Working with Files

As you've seen, the Practice folder doesn't contain any files. In the next set of steps, you will place a file from the root directory into it.

Moving and Copying a File

If you want to place a file into a folder from another location, you can either move the file or copy it. **Moving** a file takes it out of its current location and places it in the new location. **Copying** places the file in both locations. Windows 2000 provides several different techniques for moving and copying files. One way is to make sure that both the current and the new location are visible on your screen and then hold down the right mouse button and drag the file from the old location to the new location. A menu will then appear, and you can then select whether you want to move the file to the new location or make a copy in the new location. The advantage of this technique is that you are never confused as to whether you copied the file or merely moved it. Try this technique now by placing a copy of the Agenda file in the Practice folder.

To copy the Agenda file:

1. Point to the **Agenda** file in the root directory of your Data Disk and press the *right* mouse button.

2. With the right mouse button still pressed down, drag the **Agenda** file icon to the **Practice** folder icon; when the Practice folder icon turns blue, release the button.

3. A menu appears, as shown in Figure 2-21. Click **Copy Here**.

Figure 2-21 | **COPYING A FILE**

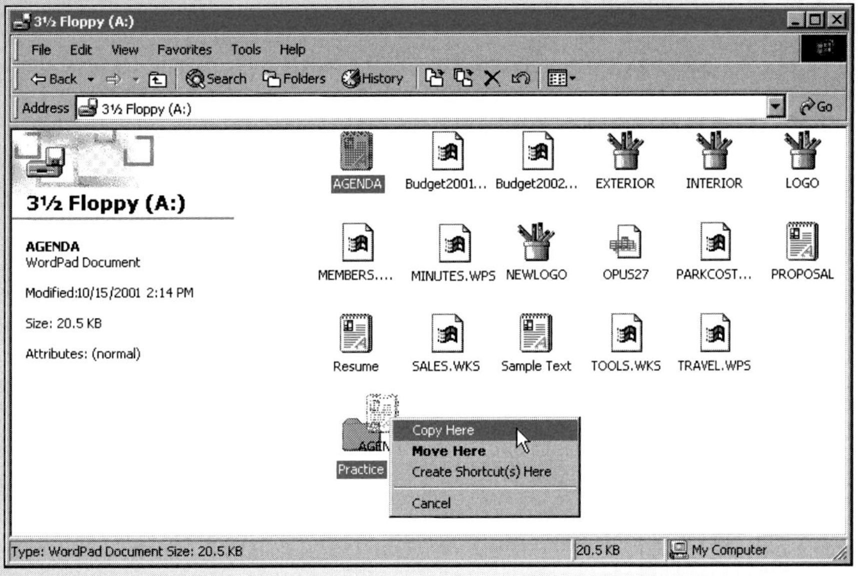

> **TROUBLE?** If you release the mouse button by mistake before dragging the Agenda icon to the Practice folder, the Agenda shortcut menu opens. Press the Esc key and then repeat Steps 1 and 2.

4. Double-click the **Practice** folder.

The Agenda file should now appear in the Practice folder.

Note that the "Move Here" command was also part of the menu. In fact, the command was in boldface, indicating that it is the default command whenever you drag a document from one location to another on the same drive. This means that if you were to drag a file from one location to another on the same drive using the left mouse button (instead of the right), the file would be moved and not copied.

Renaming a File

You will often find that you want to change the name of files as you change their content or as you create other files. You can easily rename a file by using the Rename option on the file's shortcut menu or by using the file's label.

Practice using this feature by renaming the Agenda file "Practice Agenda," since it is now in the Practice folder.

To rename the Agenda file:

1. Right-click the **Agenda** icon.

2. Click **Rename**. After a moment the filename is highlighted and a box appears around it.

3. Type **Practice Agenda** and press the **Enter** key.

TROUBLE? If you make a mistake while typing and you haven't pressed the Enter key yet, you can press the Backspace key until you delete the mistake, then complete Step 3. If you've already pressed the Enter key, repeat Steps 1-3 to rename the file a second time.

The file appears with a new name.

Deleting a File

You should periodically delete files you no longer need so that your folders and disks don't get cluttered. You delete a file or folder by deleting its icon. Be careful when you delete a folder, because you also delete all the files it contains! When you delete a file from a hard drive on your computer, the filename is deleted from the directory but the file contents are held in the Recycle Bin. The Recycle Bin is an area on your hard drive that holds deleted files until you remove them permanently; an icon on the desktop allows you easy access to the Recycle Bin. If you change your mind and want to retrieve a file deleted from your hard drive, you can recover it by using the Recycle Bin. However, once you've emptied the Recycle Bin, you can no longer recover the files that were in it.

When you delete a file from a floppy disk or a disk that exists on another computer on your network, it does not go into the Recycle Bin. Instead, it is deleted as soon as its icon disappears—and you can't recover it.

Try deleting the Practice Agenda file from your Data Disk. Because this file is on a floppy disk and not on the hard disk, it will not go into the Recycle Bin, and if you change your mind you won't be able to get it back.

To delete the Practice Agenda file:

1. Right-click the icon for the Practice Agenda file.

2. Click **Delete** on the menu that appears.

3. Windows 2000 asks if you're sure that you want to delete this file. Click the **Yes** button.

4. Click the **Close** button ⊠ to close the My Computer window.

If you like using your mouse, another way of deleting a file is to drag its icon to the Recycle Bin on the desktop. Be aware that if you're dragging a file from your floppy disk or a network disk, the file will *not* be placed in the Recycle Bin—it will still be permanently deleted.

Other Copying and Moving Techniques

As was noted earlier, there are several ways of moving and copying. As you become more familiar with Windows 2000, you will no doubt settle on the technique you like best. Figure 2-22 describes some of the other ways of moving and copying files.

Figure 2-22	METHODS FOR MOVING AND COPYING FILES	
METHOD	**TO MOVE**	**TO COPY**
Cut, copy, and paste	Select the file icon. Click **Edit** on the menu bar and **Cut** on the menu bar. Move to the new location. Click **Edit** and **Paste**.	Select the file icon. Click **Edit** on the menu bar and **Copy** on the menu bar. Move to the new location. Click **Edit** and **Paste**.
Drag and drop	Click the file icon. Drag and drop the icon in the new location.	Click the file icon. Hold down the Ctrl key and drag and drop the icon in the new location.
Right-click, drag and drop	With the right mouse button pressed down, drag the file icon to the new location. Release the mouse button and click **Move Here** on the menu.	With the right mouse button pressed down, drag the file icon to the new location. Release the mouse button and click **Copy Here** on the menu.
Move to folder and copy to folder	Click the file icon. Click **Edit** on the menu bar and **Move to Folder** on the menu bar. Select the new location in the Browse for Folder dialog box.	Click the file icon. Click **Edit** on the menu bar and **Copy to Folder** on the menu bar. Select the new location in the Browse for Folder dialog box.

The techniques shown in Figure 2-22 are primarily for document files. Because a program might not work correctly if moved into a new location, the techniques for moving program files are slightly different. See the Windows 2000 online Help for more information on moving or copying a program file.

Copying an Entire Floppy Disk

You can have trouble accessing the data on your floppy disk if the disk is damaged, is exposed to magnetic fields, or picks up a computer virus. To avoid losing all your data, it is a good idea to make a copy of your floppy disk.

If you wanted to make a copy of an audiocassette, your cassette player would need two cassette drives. You might wonder, therefore, how your computer can make a copy of your disk if you have only one floppy disk drive. Figure 2-23 illustrates how the computer uses only one disk drive to make a copy of a disk.

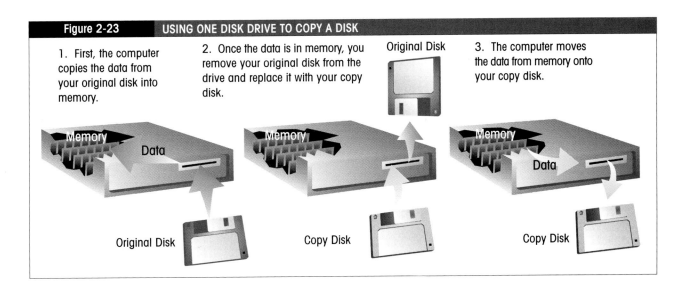

Figure 2-23	USING ONE DISK DRIVE TO COPY A DISK

1. First, the computer copies the data from your original disk into memory.

2. Once the data is in memory, you remove your original disk from the drive and replace it with your copy disk.

3. The computer moves the data from memory onto your copy disk.

Original Disk

Memory

Data

Original Disk

Memory

Copy Disk

Memory

Data

Copy Disk

REFERENCE WINDOW   RW

Copying a Disk

- Insert the disk you want to copy in drive A.
- In My Computer, right-click the 3½ Floppy (A:) icon, and then click Copy Disk.
- Click Start to begin the copy process.
- When prompted, remove the disk you want to copy, place your second disk in drive A, and then click OK.

If you have an extra floppy disk, you can make a copy of your Data Disk now. Make sure you copy the disk regularly so that as you work through the tutorials in this book it will stay updated.

To copy your Data Disk:

1. Write your name and "Windows 2000 Disk 1 Data Disk Copy" on the label of your second disk. Make sure the disk is blank and formatted.

   TROUBLE? If you aren't sure if the disk is blank, place it in the disk drive and open the 3½ Floppy (A:) window to view its contents. If the disk contains files you need, get a different disk. If it contains files you don't need, you could format the disk now, using the steps you learned at the beginning of this tutorial.

2. Make sure your original Data Disk is in drive A and the My Computer window is open.

3. Right-click the **3½ Floppy (A:)** icon, and then click **Copy Disk**. The Copy Disk dialog box opens.

4. Click the **Start** button and then the **OK** button to begin the copy process.

5. When the message "Insert the disk you want to copy to (destination disk)..." appears, remove your Data Disk and insert your Windows 2000 Disk 1 Data Disk Copy in drive A.

6. Click the **OK** button. When the copy is complete, you will see the message "Copy completed successfully." Click the **Close** button.

7. Close the My Computer window.

8. Remove your disk from the drive.

As you finish copying your disk, Shannon emphasizes the importance of making copies of your files frequently, so you won't risk losing important documents for your distance learning course. If your original Data Disk were damaged, you could use the copy you just made to access the files.

Keeping copies of your files is so important that Windows 2000 includes a program called Backup that automates the process of duplicating and storing data. In the Projects at the end of the tutorial you'll have an opportunity to explore the difference between what you just did in copying a disk and the way in which a program such as the Windows 2000 Backup program helps you safeguard data.

Session 2.2 QUICK CHECK

1. If you want to find out about the storage devices and printers connected to your computer, what window could you open?

2. If you have only one floppy disk drive on your computer, it is usually identified by the letter _____.

3. The letter C is typically used for the _____ drive of a computer.

4. What information does Details view supply about a list of folders and files?

5. The main directory of a disk is referred to as the _____ directory.

6. What is the topmost object in the hierarchy of Windows 2000 objects?

7. If you have one floppy disk drive, but you have two disks, can you copy the files on one floppy disk to the other?

REVIEW ASSIGNMENTS

1. **Opening, Editing, and Printing a Document** In this tutorial you learned how to create a document using WordPad. You also learned how to save, open, and print a document. Practice these skills by copying the document called **Resume** into the Practice folder on your Data Disk. Rename the file **Woods Resume**. This document is a resume for Jamie Woods. Make the changes shown in Figure 2-24. Save your revisions in Word for Windows 6.0 format, preview, and then print the document. Close WordPad.

Figure 2-24

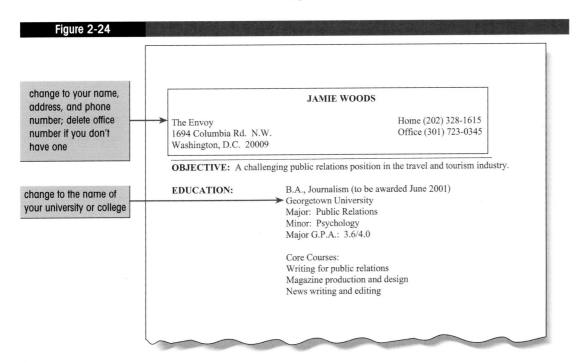

change to your name, address, and phone number; delete office number if you don't have one

JAMIE WOODS

The Envoy
1694 Columbia Rd. N.W.
Washington, D.C. 20009

Home (202) 328-1615
Office (301) 723-0345

OBJECTIVE: A challenging public relations position in the travel and tourism industry.

change to the name of your university or college

EDUCATION:

B.A., Journalism (to be awarded June 2001)
Georgetown University
Major: Public Relations
Minor: Psychology
Major G.P.A.: 3.6/4.0

Core Courses:
Writing for public relations
Magazine production and design
News writing and editing

2. **Creating, Saving, and Printing a Letter** Use WordPad to write a one-page letter to a relative or a friend. Save the document in the Practice folder on your Data Disk with the name **Letter**. Use the Print Preview feature to look at the format of your finished letter, then print it, and be sure to sign it. Close WordPad.

3. **Managing Files and Folders** Using the copy of the disk you made at the end of the tutorial, complete steps a through f below to practice your file-management skills, and then answer the questions below.

   a. Create a folder called Spreadsheets on your Data Disk.
   b. Move the files **Parkcost**, **Budget2001**, **Budget2002**, and **Sales** into the Spreadsheets folder.
   c. Create a folder called Park Project.
   d. Move the files **Proposal**, **Members**, **Tools**, **Logo**, and **Newlogo** into the Park Project folder.
   e. Delete the file called **Travel**.
   f. Switch to the Details view and write out your answers to Questions 1 through 5:
      1. What is the largest file or files in the Park Project folder? _logo files_
      2. What is the newest file or files in the Spreadsheets folder? _newlogo_
      3. How many files (don't include folders) are in the root directory of your Data Disk? _7_
      4. How are the Opus and Exterior icons different? Judging from the appearance of the icons, what would you guess these two files contain? _bitmap / winamp_
      5. Which file in the root directory has the most recent date? _sample text_

4. **More Practice with Files and Folders** For this assignment, you need a third blank disk. Complete steps a through g below to practice your file-management skills.

   a. Write "Windows 2000 Tutorial 2 Assignment 4" on the label of the blank disk, and then format the disk if necessary.
   b. Create another copy of your original Data Disk, using the Assignment 4 disk. Refer to the section "Creating Your Data Disk" in Session 2.2.
   c. Create three folders on the Assignment 4 Data Disk you just created: Documents, Budgets, and Graphics.
   d. Move the files **Interior**, **Exterior**, **Logo**, and **Newlogo** to the Graphics folder.
   e. Move the files **Travel**, **Members**, and **Minutes** to the Documents folder.
   f. Move **Budget2001** and **Budget2002** to the Budgets folder.
   g. Switch to Details view and write out your answers to Questions 1 through 6:
      1. What is the largest file or files in the Graphics folder?
      2. How many word-processed documents are in the root directory? *Hint*: These documents will appear with the WordPad, Microsoft Word, or some other word-processing icon, depending on what software you have installed.
      3. What is the newest file or files in the root directory (don't include folders)?
      4. How many files in all folders are 5 KB in size?
      5. How many files in the root directory are WKS files? *Hint*: Look in the Type column to identify WKS files.
      6. Do all the files in the Graphics folder have the same icon? What type are they?

5. **Searching for a File** Windows 2000 Help includes a topic that discusses how to search for files on a disk without looking through all the folders. Start Windows Help, then locate this topic, and answer Questions a through c:

   a. To display the Search dialog box, you must click the _Start_ button, then point to _help_ on the menu, and finally click _history_ on the submenu.
   b. Do you need to type in the entire filename to find the file? _no_
   c. How do you perform a case-sensitive search?

6. **Help with Files and Folders** In Tutorial 2 you learned how to work with Windows 2000 files and folders. What additional information on this topic does Windows 2000 Help provide? Use the Start button to access Help. Use the Index tab to locate topics related to files and folders. Find at least two tips or procedures for working with files and folders that were not covered in the tutorial. Write out the tip in your own words and include the title of the Help screen that contains the information.

right click on file a folder and select "send to"

7. **Formatting Text** You can use a word processor such as WordPad to format text, that is, to give it a specific look and feel by using bold, italics, and different fonts, and by applying other features. Using WordPad, type the title and words to one of your favorite songs and

then save the document on your Data Disk (make sure you use your original Data Disk) with the filename Song.

   a. Select the title, and then click the Center ▤ , Bold **B** , and Italic *I* buttons on the toolbar.

   b. Click the Font list arrow and select a different font. Repeat this step several times with different fonts until you locate a font that is appropriate for the song.

   c. Experiment with other formatting options until you find a look you like for your document. Save and print the final version.

PROJECTS

1. Formatting a floppy disk removes all the data on a disk. Answer the following questions using full sentences:

   a. What other method did you learn in this tutorial for removing data from a disk?

   b. If you wanted to remove all data from a disk, which method would you use? Why?

   c. What method would you use if you wanted to remove only one file? Why?

2. A friend who is new to computers is trying to learn how to enter text into WordPad. She has just finished typing her first paragraph when she notices a mistake in the first sentence. She can't remember how to fix a mistake, so she asks you for help. Write the set of steps she should try.

3. Computer users usually develop habits about how they access their files and programs. Follow the steps below to practice methods of opening a file, and then evaluate which method you would be likely to use and why.

   a. Using WordPad, create a document containing the words to a favorite poem, and save it on your Data Disk with the name Poem.

   b. Close WordPad and return to the desktop.

   c. Open the document using a document-centric approach.

   d. After a successful completion of step c, close the program and reopen the same document using another approach.

   e. Write the steps you used to complete steps c and d of this assignment. Then write a paragraph discussing which approach is most convenient when you are starting from the desktop, and indicate what habits you would develop if you owned your own computer and used it regularly.

Explore   4. The My Computer window gives you access to the objects on your computer. In this tutorial you used My Computer to access your floppy drive so you could view the contents of your Data Disk. The My Computer window gives you access to other objects too. Open My Computer and write a list of the objects you see, including folders. Then open each icon and write a two-sentence description of the contents of each window that opens.

Explore   5. In this tutorial you learned how to copy a disk to protect yourself in the event of data loss. If you had your own computer with an 80 MB hard drive that was being used to capacity, it would take many 1.44 MB floppy disks to copy the contents of the entire hard drive. Is copying to floppy disks a reasonable method to use for protecting the data on your hard disk? Why, or why not?

   a. As mentioned at the end of the tutorial, Windows 2000 also includes an accessory called Backup that helps you safeguard your data. Backup doesn't just copy the data—it organizes it so that it takes up much less space than if you simply copied it. This program might not be installed on your computer, but if it is, try starting it (click the Start button, point to Programs, point to Accessories, point to System Tools, and then click Backup) and opening the Help files to learn what you can about how it functions. If it is not installed, skip Part a.

   b. Look up the topic of backups in a computer concepts textbook or in computer trade magazines. You could also interview experienced computer owners to find out which method they use to protect their data. When you have finished researching the concept of the backup, write a single-page essay that explains the difference between copying and backing up files, and evaluates which method is preferable for backing up large amounts of data, and why.

Using Files

LAB ASSIGNMENTS

Using Files In this Lab you manipulate a simulated computer to view what happens in memory and on disk when you create, save, open, revise, and delete files. Understanding what goes on "inside the box" will help you quickly grasp how to perform basic file operations with most application software. See the Read This Before You Begin page for instructions on starting the Using Files Course Lab.

1. Click the Steps button to learn how to use the simulated computer to view the contents of memory and disk when you perform basic file operations. As you proceed through the Steps, answer all of the Quick Check questions that appear. After you complete the Steps, you will see a Quick Check Summary Report. Follow the instructions on the screen to print this report.

2. Click the Explore button and use the simulated computer to perform the following tasks:
   a. Create a document containing your name and the city in which you were born. Save this document as NAME.
   b. Create another document containing two of your favorite foods. Save this document as FOODS.
   c. Create another file containing your two favorite classes. Call this file CLASSES.
   d. Open the FOOD file and add another one of your favorite foods. Save this file without changing its name.
   e. Open the NAME file. Change this document so that it contains your name and the name of your school. Save this as a new document called SCHOOL.
   f. Write down how many files are on the simulated disk and the exact contents of each file.
   g. Delete all the files.

3. In Explore, use the simulated computer to perform the following tasks.
   a. Create a file called MUSIC that contains the name of your favorite CD.
   b. Create another document that contains eight numbers and call this file LOTTERY.
   c. You didn't win the lottery this week. Revise the contents of the LOTTERY file, but save the revision as LOTTERY2.
   d. Revise the MUSIC file so that it also contains the name of your favorite musician or composer, and save this file as MUSIC2.
   e. Delete the MUSIC file.
   f. Write down how many files are on the simulated disk and the exact contents of each file.

QUICK CHECK ANSWERS

Session 2.1
1. file
2. Formatting
3. True
4. insertion point
5. a list of recently opened files and objects
6. The Files of Type list box could be set to display files of a different type than the one you're looking for.
7. From the Print Preview window, using the Print button on the toolbar, and using the Print command from the File menu. If you want to print multiple copies of a file, use either the Print button from the Print Preview window or the Print command from the File menu—both of these techniques will display the Print dialog box containing the options you need to set.

Session 2.2
1. My Computer
2. A
3. hard
4. filename, size, type, and date modified
5. root or top-level
6. the Desktop
7. yes

New Perspectives on

MICROSOFT®

WINDOWS® 2000

PROFESSIONAL

Read **This Before You Begin**

To the Student

Make Data Disk Program

To complete the Level II tutorials, Review Assignments, and Projects, you need three Data Disks. Your instructor will either provide you with Data Disks or ask you to make your own.

If you are making your own Data Disks you will need three blank, formatted high-density disks and access to the Make Data Disk program. If you want to install the Make Data Disk program to your home computer, you can obtain it from your instructor or from the Web. To download the Make Data Disk program from the Web, go to www.course.com, click Data Disks, and follow the instructions on the screen.

To install the Make Data Disk program, select and click the file you just downloaded from **www.course.com**, 7093-8.exe. Follow the onscreen instructions to complete the installation. If you have any trouble obtaining or installing the Make Data Disk program, ask your instructor or technical support person for assistance.

Once you have obtained and installed the Make Data Disk program, you can use it to create your Data Disks according to the steps in the tutorials.

Course Labs

The Level II tutorials in this book feature two interactive Course Labs to help you understand Internet: World Wide Web and Web Pages & HTML concepts. There are Lab Assignments at the end of Tutorial 5 that relate to these Labs. To start a Lab, click the **Start** button on the Windows 2000 taskbar, point to **Programs**, point to **Course Labs**, point to **New Perspectives Course Labs**, and click the name of the Lab you want to use.

Using Your Own Computer

If you are going to work through this book using your own computer, you need:

- **Computer System** Microsoft Windows 2000 Professional must be installed on a local hard drive or on a network drive. This book is about Windows 2000 Professional—for those who have Windows 2000 Millennium, you might notice some differences.

- **Data Disks** You will not be able to complete the tutorials or exercises in this book using your own computer until you have your Data Disks. See "Make Data Disk Program" above for details on obtaining your Data Disks.

- **Course Labs** See your instructor or technical support person to obtain the Course Lab software for use on your own computer.

Visit Our World Wide Web Site

Additional materials designed especially for you are available on the World Wide Web. Go to **http://www.course.com**

To the Instructor

The Make Data Disk Program and Course Labs for this title are available in the Instructor's Resource Kit for this title. Follow the instructions in the Help file on the CD-ROM to install the programs to your network or standalone computer. For information on using the Make Data Disk Program or the Course Labs, see the "To the Student" section above. You are granted a license to copy the Data Files and Course Labs to any computer or computer network used by students who have purchased this book.

OBJECTIVES

In this tutorial you will:

- "Quick" format a floppy disk

- View the structure of folders and files in Windows Explorer

- Select, create, and rename folders in Windows Explorer

- Navigate through devices and folders using navigation buttons

- Select a single file, a group of files, all files, or all files but one

- Create a printout showing the structure of folders and files

- Move and copy one or more files from one disk to another

- Display lists of recently opened files

ORGANIZING FILES WITH WINDOWS EXPLORER

Structuring Information on a Disk at Kolbe Climbing School

CASE

Kolbe Climbing School

Bernard Kolbe knew how to climb before he could ride a bike. In college he started what is now one of the most popular guide services in the Front Range, the Kolbe Climbing School, known to locals as "KCS." KCS offers guided climbs in the Front Range area, especially in Rocky Mountain National Park and nearby climbing areas such as Lumpy Ridge. While most clients simply want to learn rock and sport climbing, a few want guides for longer alpine climbs and ice climbing.

Since he started his business, Bernard has handled the paperwork using yellow pads, clipboards, and manila folders. Recent conversations with his insurance agent and accountant, though, convinced him that he needs to keep better records on his employees, clients, and the use and condition of his equipment. The KCS offices adjoin a business services office, so Bernard rented some computer time and began creating the files he needs, storing them on a floppy disk.

Not too long ago, Bernard asked if you could help him out with KCS recordkeeping. You agreed (in exchange for some free climbing lessons) and got to work updating the client files on his floppy disk. When Bernard first gave you the disk he warned you that it could use a little organization, so you began by creating a folder structure on the disk.

This morning, you walked into the office to find that Bernard had spent yesterday evening at the rented computer adding new files to his disk. You realize you need to show him the folder structure you created so he can learn to use it. You point out that an important part of computerized recordkeeping is creating and using a system that makes it easy to find important information. Bernard is willing to learn more (it's too cold to climb anyway), so the two of you head over to the business services office to spend some time looking over Bernard's files.

SESSION 3.1

In this session, you will learn how Windows Explorer displays the devices and folders your computer can access. Understanding how to manipulate this display is the first step in using Windows Explorer to organize files, which will make you a more productive Windows user. In this tutorial you will work with files and folders on a floppy disk. If you have your own computer or are in a business environment, you will more likely work with files and folders on a hard drive. You will discover that file management techniques are practically the same for floppy disks and hard drives. For this tutorial, you will need two blank 3½-inch disks.

Creating Your Data Disk with Quick Format

Before you begin, you need to prepare a new Data Disk that contains the sample files you will work with in Tutorials 3 and 4. You can make your Data Disk using the NP on Microsoft Windows 2000 menu.

If you are using your own computer, the NP on Microsoft Windows 2000 menu will not be available. Before you proceed, bring a blank disk to your school's computer lab and use the NP on Microsoft Windows 2000 menu to make your new Data Disk. Once you have made the disk, you can use it to complete this tutorial on any computer that runs Windows 2000.

When you want to erase the contents of a floppy disk, you can use the Quick format option rather than the Full format that you use on a new disk. A Quick format takes less time than a Full format because, instead of preparing the entire disk surface, a Quick format erases something called the file allocation table. The **file allocation table (FAT)** contains information that your operating system uses to track the locations of all the files on the disk. By erasing the FAT, you erase all the information that tells the computer about the files on the disk, and so the disk appears empty to the computer. Note that to merely delete a few files from a floppy disk, you don't need to format the disk; you can just select the files (as you'll learn in this tutorial) and delete them.

To Quick format your Data Disk:

1. Write "Disk 2—Windows 2000 Tutorials 3 & 4 Data Disk" on the label of your disk.

2. Place your disk in drive A.

   TROUBLE? If your 3½-inch disk drive is B, place your disk in that drive instead, and for the rest of this tutorial substitute drive B wherever you see drive A.

3. Open the My Computer window.

4. Right-click the **3½ Floppy (A:)** icon.

5. Click **Format** to display the Format dialog box.

6. Click the **Quick Format** check box, as shown in Figure 3-1.

Figure 3-1	FORMAT DIALOG BOX

Format A:

Capacity:

3.5", 1.44MB, 512 bytes/sector

File system

FAT

Allocation unit size

Default allocation size

Volume label

Format options

☑ Quick Format

☐ Enable Compression

Start   Close

click to Quick format a disk

7. Click the **Start** button and then click the **OK** button.

TROUBLE? If an error message appears, it is possible your disk capacity is double-density instead of high-density. Make sure you are using a high-density disk.

8. Wait a few moments. When the formatting is complete, click the **OK** button and then click the **Close** button.

9. Close the My Computer window.

Now that you have formatted your disk, you can make a Data Disk for Tutorials 3 and 4.

To create your Data Disk:

1. Click the **Start** button 🏁 **Start**, point to **Programs**, point to **NP on Microsoft Windows 2000-Level II**, and then click **Disk 2 (Tutorials 3 & 4)**.

2. When a message box opens, click the **OK** button. Wait while the program copies the practice files to your formatted disk. When all the files have been copied, the program closes.

Windows **Explorer**

The root directory of Bernard's disk contains three folders—Clients, Gear, and Guides—plus the files he hasn't yet organized.

One tool for file organization tasks, you tell Bernard, is Windows Explorer. **Windows Explorer** is a program included with Windows 2000 that is designed to simplify file management tasks. Through an easy-to-navigate representation of the resources on your computer, Windows Explorer makes it easy to view, move, copy, or delete your files and folders.

Many of the techniques you used in Tutorial 2 with the My Computer window apply to Windows Explorer—and vice-versa. A window like the My Computer window can be modified to appear like Windows Explorer. So as you learn about Windows Explorer, keep in mind that you can apply these tools to almost any Windows 2000 window that displays the contents of a folder or drive.

Starting Windows Explorer

As with other Windows 2000 applications, you start Windows Explorer using the Start menu. It is possible that on your desktop is a Windows Explorer icon, which you can click to start Windows Explorer easily.

To start Windows Explorer:

1. Make sure your Data Disk is in drive A, click the **Start** button ▐Start▌, point to **Programs**, point to **Accessories**, and then click **Windows Explorer**.

   TROUBLE? If you can't see Windows Explorer on the Accessories menu, the menu item has been temporarily hidden. Click the two arrows pointing down to display the complete menu, and then click Windows Explorer.

2. If the Exploring window is not maximized, click the **Maximize** button ▢.

Like the My Computer window, the Exploring window can display the Standard, Address, Links, and Radio toolbars and a status bar. For this tutorial, you need to make sure you can see the Standard toolbar, the Address bar, and the status bar. These are the default settings for Windows 2000. To match the figures in this tutorial, you should also display the files in Large Icons view rather than the other views offered by Windows 2000.

To set up the appearance of Windows Explorer:

1. Click **View** and then point to **Toolbars**. Make the necessary changes so that the Standard Buttons toolbar and the Address Bar are the only toolbars displayed.

2. If necessary, reopen the View menu. Make sure that Status Bar is checked and the Large Icons option is selected. If Status Bar is not checked, click Status Bar. If Large Icons is not selected, open the menu again if necessary and then select Large Icons.

Displaying the Explorer Bar

Windows Explorer is divided into two sections called **panes**. The left pane, also called the **Explorer bar**, shows different ways of locating specific files or folders on your computer. The pane on the right displays lists of these files and folders (similar to the view of files and folders you had in examining the contents of the floppy disk in Tutorial 2).

The Explorer bar can be displayed in one of four ways: as a Search pane, a Favorites pane, a History pane, or a Folders pane. The **Search** pane includes tools to help you search for a particular file or folder on your computer. The **Favorites** pane displays a list of your favorite files and folders on your computer and sites on the World Wide Web. The **History** pane organizes the files and folders on your computer by the date you last worked with them. The **Folders** pane organizes your files and folders based on their location in the hierarchy of objects on your computer. To move between these different panes, you click the appropriate button on the Standard Buttons toolbar or choose the appropriate option from the View menu. Note that the Explorer bar is available in any Windows 2000 window that displays files and folders. You can, for example, use the Explorer bar in the My Computer window.

You'll start working with Windows Explorer by making sure that the Folders pane is displayed.

To view the Folders pane:

1. Click **View** and then point to **Explorer Bar**.

2. Make sure that the Folders option has a check mark next to it. If it does not, click Folders; otherwise click a blank area of the screen to close the View menu. Your Exploring window should now resemble Figure 3-2.

Figure 3-2	WINDOWS EXPLORER OVERVIEW

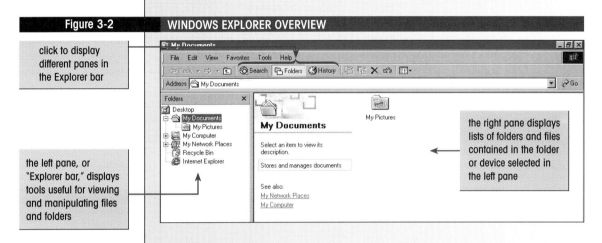

click to display different panes in the Explorer bar

the left pane, or "Explorer bar," displays tools useful for viewing and manipulating files and folders

the right pane displays lists of folders and files contained in the folder or device selected in the left pane

TROUBLE? Depending on the configuration of your computer, your Windows Explorer window may look slightly different from the one displayed in Figure 3-2.

The Folders pane initially displays a list of the objects on your desktop: the My Documents folder, the My Computer window, the My Network Places window, the Recycle Bin, and Internet Explorer. If your desktop contains other folders or objects, those will be displayed as well. The right pane of the Exploring window displays the contents of the object selected in the Folders pane. In this case, the My Documents folder is the selected object, and it contains only one item—the My Pictures folder. An icon for this object is therefore displayed in the right pane.

Working with the Folders Pane

To see the devices and resources available to your computer, you can scroll through the list of objects in the Folders pane. Each object in the list has a small icon next to it. In this session you will use the Folders pane to explore your computer's contents. Explorer uses the icons shown in Figure 3-3, among others, to represent different types of storage objects.

Figure 3-3	STORAGE DEVICE ICONS		

ICON	REPRESENTS	ICON	REPRESENTS
	Floppy disk drive		Network disk drive
	Hard disk drive on your computer		Shared disk drive
	CD-ROM drive		Zip drive

Opening an Object in the Folders Pane

Like a file cabinet, a typical storage device on your computer contains files and folders. These folders can contain additional files and one or more levels of subfolders. If Windows Explorer displayed all the storage devices, folders, and files on your computer at once, it could be a very long list. Instead, Windows Explorer allows you to open devices and folders only when you want to see what they contain. Otherwise, you can keep them closed.

The small icon next to each object in the list, called the **device icon** or **folder icon**, represents the device or folder on your computer. Many of these icons also have a plus box or minus box next to them, which indicates whether the device or folder contains additional folders. Both the device/folder icon and the plus/minus box are controls that you can click to change the display in the Exploring window. You click the plus box to display folders or subfolders, and you click the minus box to hide them. (You can also refer to clicking the plus box as "expanding" the view of the file hierarchy, and clicking the minus box as "collapsing" the view of the file hierarchy.) You click the device/folder icon to control the display of object contents in the right pane.

You begin assisting Bernard by showing him how you've structured the folders on drive A, which is located in the Windows 2000 hierarchy beneath the My Computer icon. You explain to him how the plus/minus boxes can be used to open the My Computer icon and then the drive icon for his floppy disk.

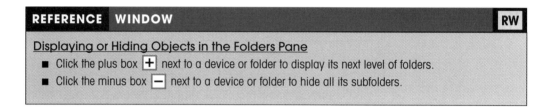

REFERENCE	WINDOW		RW

Displaying or Hiding Objects in the Folders Pane
- Click the plus box ⊞ next to a device or folder to display its next level of folders.
- Click the minus box ⊟ next to a device or folder to hide all its subfolders.

To display or hide the levels of folders on drive A:

1. Click ⊞ to the left of the My Computer icon in the Folders pane.

2. Click the ⊞ to the left of the 3½ Floppy (A:) device icon. The folders in the root directory of drive A appear in the left pane, and the plus box in front of drive A changes to a minus box ⊟. See Figure 3-4.

Figure 3-4	FOLDERS ON DRIVE A, DISPLAYED IN THE FOLDERS PANE

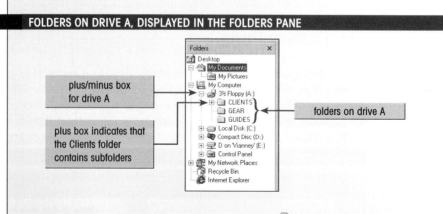

TROUBLE? The 3½ Floppy (A:) device icon 🖫 might appear with a different name on your computer. This is the icon representing the device that contains your Data Disk. In the steps in this tutorial, this icon is called simply drive A.

TROUBLE? If you initially see a minus box in front of the device icon for drive A, your drive A folders are already visible in the left pane. You don't need to click the icon in Step 1.

3. Click ⊟ in front of 3½ Floppy (A:). Now the Folders pane shows only drive A, without the folders it contains.

4. Click ⊞ in front of 3½ Floppy (A:) one more time to redisplay the folders on the drive.

When you click the plus box ⊞ next to drive A, you do not necessarily see all the folders on the drive. You only see the first level of folders. If one of these folders contains subfolders, a plus box appears next to it. The Clients folder on drive A has a plus box next to it, indicating that it contains subfolders. When you originally created the structure for Bernard's disk, you grouped his clients into Advanced and Basic, and then grouped the Advanced clients by their primary interests—Alpine, Ice, and Sport.

To view the subfolders for Clients:

1. Click ⊞ next to the Clients folder. You see that Clients contains two subfolders: Advanced and Basic. Because there is a ⊞ box next to the Advanced folder, you know it contains subfolders as well.

2. Click ⊞ next to the Advanced folder. Now you see three additional subfolders: Alpine, Ice, and Sport. See Figure 3-5.

Figure 3-5	ENTIRE FOLDER AND SUBFOLDER STRUCTURE ON DRIVE A

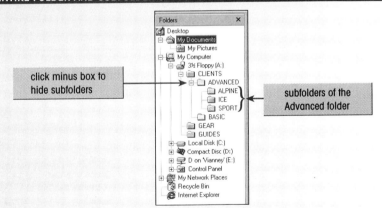

click minus box to hide subfolders

subfolders of the Advanced folder

3. Click ⊟ next to the Clients folder to hide its folders. Notice that you were able to "collapse" the entire Clients folder hierarchy by clicking the Clients minus box; you didn't have to click each level.

4. Click ⊞ next to the Clients folder again. Note that the entire folder structure is displayed again—including the subfolders—because the last time you collapsed the Clients folder, you had all its subfolders displayed.

Selecting an Object in the Folders Pane

To work with a device or folder in the Folders pane, you first click it to select it, and Windows highlights it. It is important to understand that using the plus/minus box does not select a device or folder. Notice that as you were clicking the plus/minus boxes in front of the folders in drive A, the right pane still displayed the contents of the My Documents folder.

To select a device or folder, you must click its icon, not its plus/minus box. When you select a device or folder, it becomes active. The **active** device or folder is the one the computer uses when you take an action. For example, if you want to create a new folder on drive A, you first need to select drive A in the Folders Explorer bar. It then becomes the active drive. If you don't first activate drive A, the new folder you create will be placed in whatever device or folder is currently active—it could be a folder on the hard drive or network drive. How do you know which device or folder is active? You can know in three ways. First, it is selected. Second, its name appears in the Address bar and finally, its contents appear in the right pane.

You can experiment with changing the active device and folder by selecting drive A and then selecting the Clients folder.

To select devices and folders:

1. Click 🖴 **3½ Floppy (A:)** if necessary. To show that drive A is selected, the computer highlights the label and displays it in the Address Bar.

2. Click 📁 **Clients** in the Folders pane. The computer highlights the label "Clients" and displays it in the Address bar. Its contents appear in the right pane. See Figure 3-6.

Figure 3-6	THE ACTIVE DEVICE OR FOLDER IN THE FOLDERS PANE

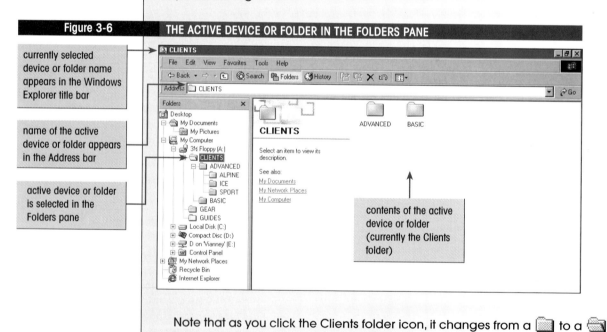

currently selected device or folder name appears in the Windows Explorer title bar

name of the active device or folder appears in the Address bar

active device or folder is selected in the Folders pane

contents of the active device or folder (currently the Clients folder)

Note that as you click the Clients folder icon, it changes from a 📁 to a 📂 indicating that the folder is "open," that is it's become active, and its contents are displayed in the right pane of the Explorer window.

Creating a New Folder

You can create a new folder using the same techniques you used to create new folders in Tutorial 2. You just have to make sure that you've selected the correct object in the Folders pane before inserting the new folder.

Bernard tracks gear usage for ropes and other types of equipment such as carabiners, belay plates, and so on. His disk already contains a folder named "Gear" that contains files for each of the KCS ropes. You decide to create two new subfolders within the Gear folder: one for all files having to do with ropes and the other for files having to do with hardware equipment.

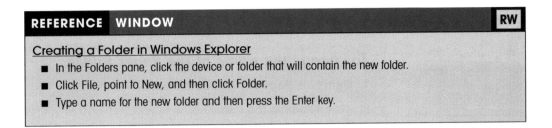

REFERENCE WINDOW   **RW**

Creating a Folder in Windows Explorer
- In the Folders pane, click the device or folder that will contain the new folder.
- Click File, point to New, and then click Folder.
- Type a name for the new folder and then press the Enter key.

The Clients folder is currently active. If you create a new folder now, it will become a subfolder of Clients. Because you want to create the two subfolders in the Gear folder, you must make the Gear folder active.

To create the new subfolders within the Gear folder:

1. Click 📁 **Gear** in the Folders pane to activate the Gear folder.

2. Click **File** on the menu bar, point to **New**, and then click **Folder**. A folder icon labeled "New Folder" appears in the right pane. The folder name is selected, and anything you type will replace the current name.

3. Type **Hardware** as the title of the new folder, and then press the **Enter** key. Now create the second subfolder of the Gear folder for all the rope files.

   TROUBLE? If you pressed Enter twice by mistake, Hardware becomes the active folder. Be sure Gear is still the active folder; click the Gear folder icon in the left pane, if necessary.

4. Click **File**, point to **New**, click **Folder**, type **Ropes** as the name of the second folder, and then press the **Enter** key.

5. Click ⊞ next to the Gear folder in the left pane to see the new folders in the left pane. See Figure 3-7.

| Figure 3-7 | CREATING NEW FOLDERS |

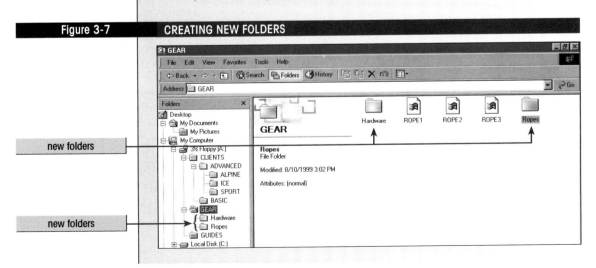

new folders

new folders

As you and Bernard go over the current folder structure, you realize that a complete inventory of the KCS gear also includes the harnesses climbers wear to attach themselves to the rope for protection in case they fall. Because harnesses aren't considered hardware, you decide that the harness inventory files should go in the same folder with the ropes. Thus, you need to rename the Ropes folder "Ropes and Harnesses." You rename a folder by right-clicking the folder icon in either the Folders pane or the right pane and then clicking the Rename command.

To change the name of the Ropes folder:

1. Right-click **Ropes** in the Folders pane.

2. Click **Rename**. The folder name is selected, and anything you type will replace the current name.

3. Type **Ropes and Harnesses** as the new folder name, and then press the **Enter** key.

The new name now appears in both the left and right panes, although it might be truncated if the panes are too narrow to display it.

Adjusting the Width of the Folders Pane

As you create or view more and more levels of folders, the Explorer bar might not be wide enough to display all the levels of folders. As a result, you might not be able to see all the device and folder icons. Whether or not this occurs depends on how long your folder names are and how wide the All Folders Explorer bar was in the first place. You can change the width of the Exploring window panes by dragging the dividing bar that separates the two panes.

REFERENCE WINDOW   **RW**

Adjusting the Width of the Explorer bar
- Move the mouse pointer to the dividing bar between the left and right panes.
- When the arrow-shaped pointer ⬚ changes to a double-ended arrow ⟷, hold down the left mouse button and drag the dividing line right or left, as necessary.
- When the dividing bar is in the desired position, release the mouse button.

To increase the width of the Explorer bar:

1. Move the mouse pointer to the dividing bar between the two panes. The ⬚ pointer changes to a ⟷ pointer.

2. Hold down the left mouse button while you drag the dividing bar about one-half inch to the right, as shown in Figure 3-8.

| Figure 3-8 | ADJUSTING THE WIDTH OF THE EXPLORER BAR |

double-ended arrow appears when you drag the dividing bar

3. Release the mouse button. Use this method as necessary when you work with the Explorer Bar.

4. Click the **Close** button ☒ to close the Exploring window. You return to the Windows 2000 desktop.

Session 3.1 QUICK CHECK

windows

1. _Explorer_ is an alternative to using My Computer for file management tasks.

2. The Exploring window is divided into two panes. Describe each pane, using one sentence for each pane. *left pane -*

3. True or False: If you see folders with the same names in both the right and left panes of the Exploring window, the folders are duplicates and you should erase those in the right pane. *false*

4. True or False: The Folders pane displays all the files in a folder. *false*

5. A folder that is contained in another folder is referred to as a(n) *subfolder*.

6. You click the _+ box_ to expand the display of folders in the Folders pane.

7. If you want to create a new folder on drive A, what should you first click in the Folders pane? *the a: icon*

8. True or False: The Explorer Bar exists *only* in Windows Explorer. You cannot use the Explorer Bar in the My Computer window. *false*

SESSION 3.2

In Session 3.2 you will work with the right pane of the Exploring window, which displays folders and files. You'll learn how to select multiple files from the right pane. You'll work with different methods of moving and copying files from one location to another. You'll also see how to print a copy of the Explorer window to use as a reference later on.

Working with Files in Windows Explorer

Now that you've worked with the Explorer bar, it's time to put the right pane of Windows Explorer to use. You've already created a folder structure for Bernard's files. Now you have to work on putting the right files into the proper folders. To do this you have to learn how to select and work with multiple files in the Explorer window. Before getting started, you should reopen the Data Disk.

To open the Data Disk:

1. Make sure your Data Disk is in drive A, and then start Windows Explorer. Set up Windows Explorer so that the Standard Buttons toolbar, Address Bar, and Folders pane are all visible.

2. Locate and click the 🖫 **3½ Floppy (A)** in the Folders pane to display the contents of the root directory of drive A.

3. Click **View** on the menu bar and then click **Details** to display the file icons in Details view.

Working with files displayed in the right pane is exactly like working with files displayed in the My Computer window or any Windows 2000 window that displays a list of files. You can use the View command, switching from Large Icons view to Details or Thumbnails view. You can click the Back ⬅, Forward ➡ and Up buttons 🔁 buttons to navigate through the hierarchy of objects in your computer. You can open a file by clicking its icon and pressing the Enter key. You can rename a file by right-clicking its icon and choosing the Rename command from the menu. Selecting which files to work with is the same as well.

Selecting Multiple Files

You select files by clicking the file's icon in the right pane of the Explorer window. If you want to select multiple files, Windows 2000 provides several different ways of accomplishing this. The first technique you'll explore is how to select all of the files in a folder. You can do this by using one of the commands in the Windows Explorer menu.

To select all of the files in the root directory:

1. Click **Edit** on the menu bar and then click **Select All**. Explorer highlights the files and folders to show that they are selected. Note that the status bar indicates that 19 objects are selected and that the total size of the selection is 158 kilobytes. See Figure 3-9.

Figure 3-9 | **SELECTING ALL FILES IN A FOLDER**

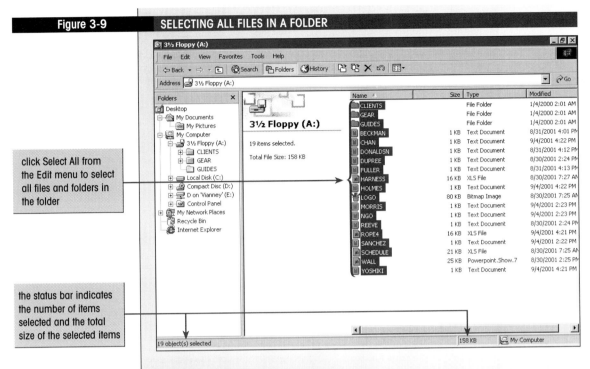

click Select All from the Edit menu to select all files and folders in the folder

the status bar indicates the number of items selected and the total size of the selected items

2. **Deselect the files by clicking any blank area. The highlighting is removed to indicate that no files are currently selected.**

What if you want to work with more than one file, but not with all the files in a folder? For example, suppose Bernard wants to delete three of the files in a folder. In Explorer there are two ways to select a group of files. You can select files listed consecutively using the Shift key, or you can select files scattered throughout the right pane using the Ctrl key. Figure 3-10 shows the two different ways to select a group of files.

Figure 3-10 | **TWO WAYS TO SELECT A GROUP OF FILES**

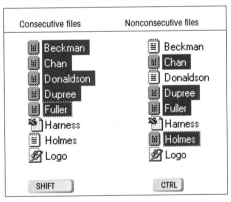

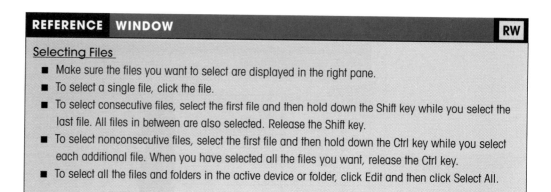

First try selecting a set of consecutive files, and then a set of nonconsecutive files scattered within a folder.

To select groups of files:

1. Make sure the right pane displays the root directory of drive A and then click the **Beckman** file icon.

2. Hold down the **Shift** key while you click the **Fuller** file. Release the **Shift** key. The Beckman and Fuller files and all files in between are selected. See Figure 3-11.

Figure 3-11   SELECTING CONSECUTIVE FILES

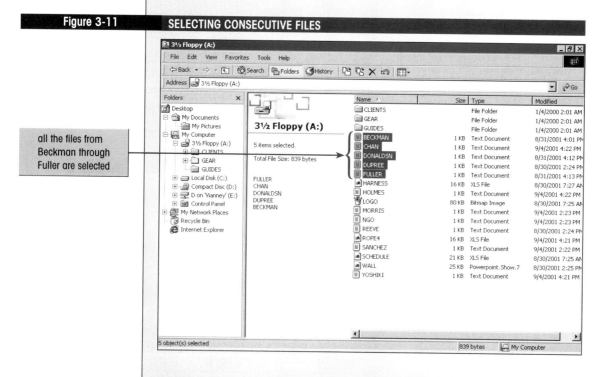

all the files from Beckman through Fuller are selected

3. Now select a set of nonconsecutive files. First click the **Reeve** file. Notice that selecting this file automatically deselects any selected files.

4. Hold down the **Ctrl** key and select the **Morris** file and then the **Sanchez** file. All three files should be selected. Release the **Ctrl** key. See Figure 3-12.

Figure 3-12   SELECTING NONCONSECUTIVE FILES

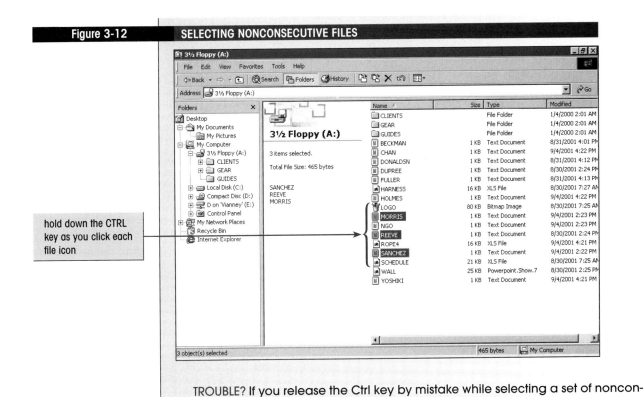

hold down the CTRL key as you click each file icon

TROUBLE? If you release the Ctrl key by mistake while selecting a set of nonconsecutive files, press it again and select the files you want.

While selecting multiple files with the Ctrl key, you can deselect any file by clicking it again while holding down the Ctrl key. You can also select more files by holding down the Ctrl key again, then selecting the additional files. The files do not need to be in consecutive order for you to select them as a group.

To select and deselect additional files:

1. Hold down the **Ctrl** key and click the **Chan** file to select it. Four files are now selected.

2. Keep holding down the **Ctrl** key and click the **Sanchez** file to deselect it. Now three files are selected: Chan, Morris, and Reeve.

Suppose you want to select all the files in a folder except one. You can use the Invert Selection menu option to select all the files that are not selected.

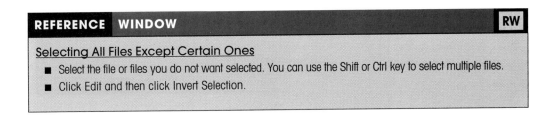

REFERENCE WINDOW   **RW**

Selecting All Files Except Certain Ones
- Select the file or files you do not want selected. You can use the Shift or Ctrl key to select multiple files.
- Click Edit and then click Invert Selection.

To use Invert Selection to select all files except Dupree:

1. Click the **Dupree** file icon.

2. Click **Edit** and then click **Invert Selection**. All the folders and files except Dupree are now selected.

3. Click a blank area to remove the highlighting for all the files on drive A.

Selecting Files in Web Style

Up to now, you've been selecting files using the Windows 2000 default method. You may be more comfortable using a "Web-style" method, in which files are selected and deselected by simply pointing to the file icon with the mouse pointer. To select consecutive files, you point to the first file in the list, hold down the Shift key and then point to the last file in the list. To select a group of individual files, you hold down the Ctrl key as you point to each file in the list. The advantage of this method is that there are fewer mouse-clicks involved for each action, something people with computer-related hand and wrist problems would need.

To turn on the Web-style file selection:

1. Click **Tools** and then click **Folder Options**.

2. Click the **General** dialog sheet tab, if necessary, to display the General dialog sheet.

3. Click the **Single-click to open an item (point to select)** option button. See Figure 3-13.

Figure 3-13   **TURNING ON WEB-STYLE FILE SELECTION**

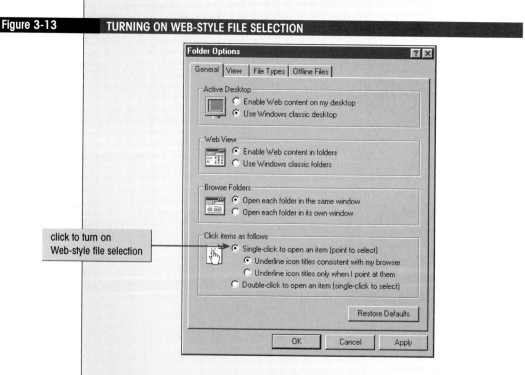

click to turn on
Web-style file selection

At this point, if you click the OK or Apply buttons, you can start selecting files by pointing at them, rather than clicking. However, since this book assumes that you'll use the Default option, you'll close this dialog box *without* enacting any changes.

4. Click the **Cancel** button to close the Folder Options dialog box without making any changes.

You may find that this method of file selection works best for you. Try experimenting on your own later.

Printing **the Exploring Window**

You are almost ready to start moving Bernard's files into the appropriate folders. Bernard would like to identify the files that need to be moved. He wonders if there's a quick way to get a hard copy (that is, a paper copy) of the Exploring window so he can write on it. You tell him you can temporarily store an image of your computer screen in memory using the Print Screen key. Then, you can start the WordPad program and paste the image into a blank WordPad document. Finally, you can print the document, which will contain an image of your screen—in this case, the Exploring window. It can be handy to have a printout of the structures of certain important devices for reference, so this is a good procedure to learn.

To print the Exploring window:

1. Make sure the right pane still displays the contents of drive A; if not, click **3½ Floppy (A:)** in the left pane.

2. Click ☐ next to 3½ Floppy (A:), FlooClients, Advanced, and Gear as necessary so that all the folders and subfolders on Bernard's disk are visible.

3. Press the **Print Screen** key. Although it seems as if nothing happens, an image of the Exploring window is stored in memory.

   TROUBLE? If you cannot locate the Print Screen key, it might be accessible through another key on your keyboard or it might be labeled with an abbreviation such as "PrtScn." Ask your instructor or technical support person for help.

4. Start WordPad.

5. Maximize the WordPad window if necessary, type your name and the date at the top of the WordPad window, and then press the **Enter** key twice.

6. Click the **Paste** button 📋 and then scroll to the top of the document (also scroll left, if necessary). The picture of the Exploring window appears in the WordPad document. See Figure 3-14.

| Figure 3-14 | WINDOWS EXPLORER SCREEN IMAGE IN WORDPAD |

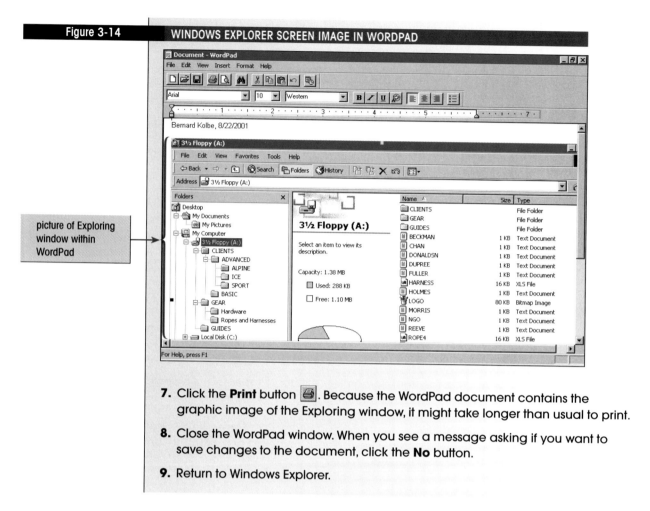

picture of Exploring window within WordPad

7. Click the **Print** button 🖨. Because the WordPad document contains the graphic image of the Exploring window, it might take longer than usual to print.

8. Close the WordPad window. When you see a message asking if you want to save changes to the document, click the **No** button.

9. Return to Windows Explorer.

Bernard annotates the printout as shown in Figure 3-15. His notes show you where to move the files in the root directory.

Figure 3-15	BERNARD'S PRINTOUT

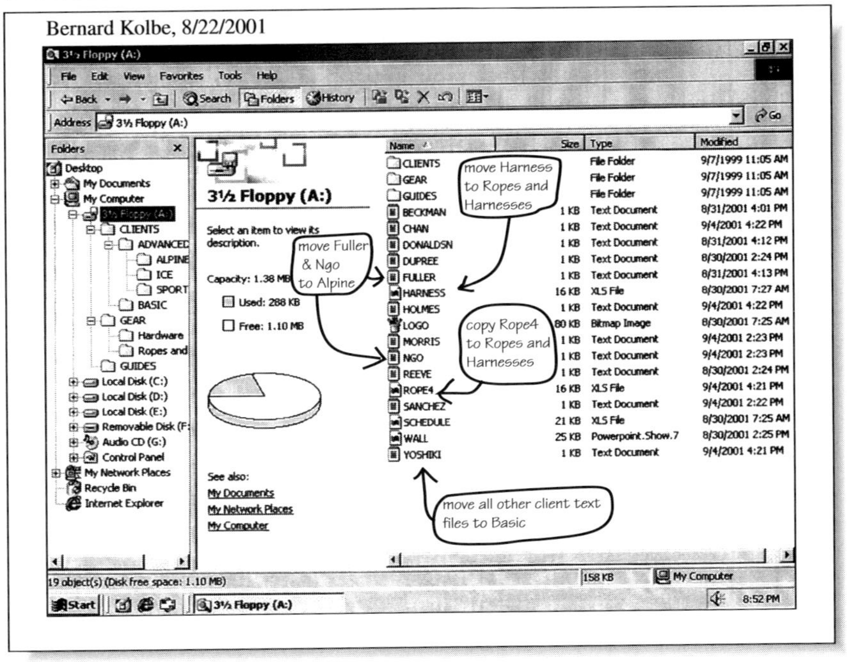

Moving **Files in the Explorer Window**

You've already had some experience in moving files. You saw in Tutorial 2 how you could right-click an object and drag it into a folder on a floppy disk, choosing whether to copy or move the file. Moving files in Windows Explorer is exactly the same, except that you have the added benefit of using the Folders pane to navigate the hierarchy of Windows 2000 objects. Because the Folders pane can display a detailed tree of folders and devices, you can easily move a file to almost any location on your computer.

Bernard has already marked the printout you created to show which files you need to move. You begin by moving the Harness file from the root directory to the Equipment folder.

To move the Harness file:

1. Make sure that the active device in the Folders pane is the 3½ Floppy (A:) drive and that in the Folders pane you can see both the Hardware and the Ropes and Harnesses subfolders of the Gears folder.

2. Hold down the right mouse button while you drag the Harness file icon from the right pane to the Ropes and Harnesses folder, as shown in Figure 3-16.

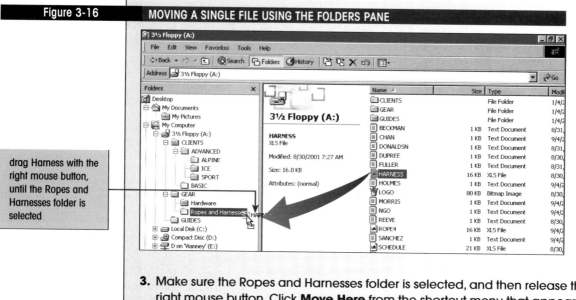

Figure 3-16 **MOVING A SINGLE FILE USING THE FOLDERS PANE**

drag Harness with the right mouse button, until the Ropes and Harnesses folder is selected

3. Make sure the Ropes and Harnesses folder is selected, and then release the right mouse button. Click **Move Here** from the shortcut menu that appears.

TROUBLE? If you selected the wrong folder, click Cancel on the shortcut menu and repeat Steps 1 through 3.

TROUBLE? If you moved the file to a different folder by mistake, click Undo Move from the Edit menu and then repeat Steps 1 through 3.

The Harness file is moved to the new folder, and it disappears from the right pane.

4. Click ▦ **Ropes and Harnesses** in the Folders pane. The Harness file should appear in the right pane.

If you use other Windows programs, you know that in most programs you drag objects with the left mouse button. Although you can drag files in Windows Explorer with the left mouse button, be careful. When you use the left mouse button, Windows Explorer will not open the shortcut menu. Instead, it will simply move or copy the file to the folder you selected, depending on the circumstances. When you drag a file from one folder to another on the same drive, Explorer moves the file. However, when you drag a file from a folder on one drive to a folder on a different drive, Explorer copies the file; it does not move it. Therefore, to prevent mistakes and lost files, most beginners should use the right mouse button to drag files.

Bernard recently purchased a fourth rope, and he is tracking its use in the file Rope4. He wants a copy of the Rope4 file in the Ropes and Harnesses folder.

To copy the Rope4 file into the Ropes folder:

1. Click ▤ **3½ Floppy (A:)** in the Folders pane to view the files in the root directory once again.

2. Hold down the right mouse button while you drag the **Rope4** icon from the root directory to the Ropes and Harnesses folder.

3. Make sure the Ropes and Harnesses folder is selected, and then release the right mouse button.

4. Click **Copy Here** from the shortcut menu. Rope4 is copied from the root directory to the Ropes and Harnesses folder. Notice that Rope4 is still displayed in the right pane for drive A, because you copied the file rather than moved it.

5. Click ▨ **Ropes and Harnesses** in the Folders pane and notice that Rope4 now appears in this folder along with the Harness file.

Moving Files with Cut and Paste

Although dragging works well when you can see the file in the right pane and its destination folder in the Folders pane, this will not always be the case. Instead of dragging, you can use the Cut, Copy, and Paste buttons on the Standard Buttons toolbar to move or copy objects. The Cut, Copy, and Paste commands are also available on the selected objects' shortcut menus.

REFERENCE WINDOW   **RW**

Moving or Copying Files with Cut, Copy, and Paste

- Select the file you want to copy or move. If you want to copy or move a group of files, first use the Shift or Ctrl key to select the files to be moved.
- Click the Cut command on the Edit menu to move the files, or the Copy command on the Edit menu to copy them.
- Select the device or folder into which you want to place the copied or cut files.
- Click Edit, and then click the Paste command.

Bernard wants to move the three rope files from the Gear folder to the Ropes and Harnesses folder. The rope files are listed consecutively, so you should use the Shift key to select these three files and then you move them as a group. Then use the Cut and Paste commands to move the files.

To move the rope files to the Ropes and Harnesses folder:

1. Click the ▨ **Gear** folder in the left pane to activate the Gear folder and view the other rope files, which also need to be moved into the Ropes and Harnesses folder.

2. Select the three rope files, **Rope1**, **Rope2**, and **Rope3** using the usual techniques to select multiple files.

3. Click **Edit** on the menu bar and then click **Cut**.

4. Click the **Ropes and Harnesses** folder in the Folders pane.

5. Click **Edit** and then click **Paste** to move the files to the Ropes and Harnesses folder. The Ropes and Harnesses folder now contains Harness, Rope1, Rope2, Rope3, and Rope4.

If you cut or copy a file or set of files but then neglect to paste them into a destination folder, don't worry. Windows Explorer doesn't actually carry out the cut or copy until you paste. It simply flags the file until it actually performs the action desired. Thus, if you close Windows Explorer without having pasted a file, the file remains in its original position.

Using the Move To Folder and Copy To Folder Commands

You've got Bernard's gear files organized, so now it's time to look at the new client files he added. Mark Fuller and George Ngo are interested exclusively in alpine climbing, so you'll move the Fuller and Ngo client files into the Alpine folder. If you want to move these folders without having to work with the Folders pane, you can do so with the Move To Folder and Copy To Folder commands. These commands display a dialog box from which you can navigate the hierarchy of objects on your computer, explicitly choosing the folder that you want to move or copy the file selection to.

REFERENCE WINDOW | **RW**

Moving or Copying Files with the Move To Folder and Copy To Folder commands
- Select the file you want to copy or move. If you want to copy or move a group of files, first use the Shift or Ctrl key to select the files to be moved.
- Click Edit and Move To Folder to move the file(s).
- Click Edit and Copy To Folder to copy the file(s).
- Locate the folder you want to move or copy the files to in the Browse For Folder dialog box.

Try this technique now by moving the Fuller and Ngo files into the Alpine folder.

To move files using the Move To command:

1. Click 🖳 **3½ Floppy (A:)** in the Folders pane to display the files on the floppy disk's root directory.

2. Select the **Fuller** and **Ngo** files.

3. Click **Edit** on the menu bar and then click **Move To Folder**.

   The Browse For Folder dialog box opens and displays the hierarchy of objects and folders on your computer.

4. Click ➕ in front of the My Computer icon to display the contents of that object.

5. Move through the rest of the hierarchy of objects by clicking ➕ in front of the 3½ Floppy (A:) icon and then clicking the ➕ boxes in front of the Clients and then the Advanced folders.

6. Click the 📁 **Alpine** folder icon to select this folder. The Browse For Folder dialog box should appear as shown in Figure 3-17.

| **Figure 3-17** | **MOVING FILES USING THE MOVE TO FOLDER COMMAND** |

by clicking the New Folder button, you can create a new folder and at the same time move files into that folder

7. Click the **OK** button to move the files into the Alpine folder.

8. Click the **Alpine** folder in the Folders pane to confirm that the Ngo and Fuller files have been moved to that location (there should now be 5 files).

Moving Files of Similar Type

You need to move the remaining client files from the root directory into the Basic folder. You can combine some of the methods you have already learned to complete this task most efficiently. If you are in Details view, you'll see that the client files (the ones with people's names) are all text files. If you arrange these files by type, they'll all be next to each other, so you can select them as a group and move them together to the Basic folder. You'll use the technique of cutting and pasting to accomplish this task.

To move a group of related files to a new folder:

1. Click 💾 **3½ Floppy (A:)** to display the files of the floppy drive's root directory.

2. If necessary, click **View** and then **Details** on the Explorer menu to display the files in the root directory in Details view.

3. Click the **Type** button. The client text files are now grouped together.

   TROUBLE? The Type button is at the top of the third column under the Address Bar in the right pane.

4. Use the Shift key to select the **Beckman** and **Yoshiki** text files and all the files in between.

5. Right-click the selection, click **Cut**, right-click the **Basic** folder icon in the Folders pane, and then click **Paste**. The files move from the root directory into the Basic folder.

Bernard's disk is now reorganized, with the appropriate files in the gear and client folders.

Moving or Copying Files Between Drives

So far all the moving and copying you've done has been within a single drive—the floppy drive. Often you will want to move or copy files between drives, for example between your floppy drive and your hard drive, or between one floppy drive and another. You can do this using the same techniques you've learned so far: dragging and dropping with the right mouse button, using cut and paste, and so forth.

Moving Files from the Floppy to the Hard Drive

In your computer lab you will rarely need to copy a file from your floppy drive to the hard drive of a lab computer. However, if you have a computer at home, you might frequently want to move or copy files from your floppy disk to your hard drive, to take advantage of its speed and large storage capacity. To practice this task, copy the Excel spreadsheet file named Schedule to the hard drive.

To copy a file from a floppy disk to the hard drive:

1. If necessary, scroll through the left pane so you can see the icon for drive C.

2. Click ▭ **(C:)** in the Folders pane. Your drive C icon might appear slightly different if it is a network or shared drive.

3. Click **File**, point to **New**, and then click **Folder** to create a new folder on drive C.

   TROUBLE? If a message warns you that you can't create a folder on drive C, you might be on a computer that restricts hard drive access. Ask your instructor or technical support person about other options for working on a hard drive, and read through the rest of this section to learn how you would work on a hard drive if you had the opportunity.

4. Type **Climbing** as the name of the new folder and then press the **Enter** key.

   TROUBLE? If there is already a Climbing folder on the hard drive, you must specify a different name. Use the name "Climb" with your initials, such as "ClimbJP." Substitute this folder name for the Climbing folder for the rest of this tutorial.

5. Click ▭ **3½ Floppy (A:)** in the Folders pane (you might have to scroll to see it) to display its contents in the right pane.

6. Right-click the **Schedule** file in the right pane of the Explorer window.

7. Click **Copy**. Locate and then right-click the **Climbing** folder on drive C in the Folders pane (you might have to scroll to see it).

8. Click **Paste**. The original Schedule file remains in the root directory of drive A. A copy of the file now appears in the Climbing folder on drive C.

9. Click ▭ **Climbing** on drive C if necessary to ensure that the Schedule file was copied onto the hard drive.

The Schedule file is now in the Climbing folder on your hard drive.

Copying Between Floppy Drives with the Send To Command

You notice that Bernard has a file on his disk called Wall; you ask him about it. He explains that it is a PowerPoint file that contains a slide presentation for the local Parks and Recreation Department, proposing the construction of an indoor climbing wall. You tell Bernard you would love to help him develop the slide show; if he gave you a copy of the file on a new disk, you could work on it on your computer at home. Although you could use the Copy Disk command you used in Tutorial 2 to copy the entire disk, you want only the Wall file on the new disk.

If your computer has only one floppy disk drive, you can't just drag a file from one floppy disk to another, because you can't put both floppy disks in the drive at the same time. So how do you copy the file from one floppy to another? You first copy the file from the first floppy disk—the source disk—to a temporary location on the hard drive, then you insert the second floppy disk—the destination disk—into drive A; finally, you move the file from the hard drive to the second floppy disk. Figure 3-18 shows this procedure.

Figure 3-18 | **COPYING A FILE TO THE HARD DISK AND THEN TO A DIFFERENT FLOPPY DISK**

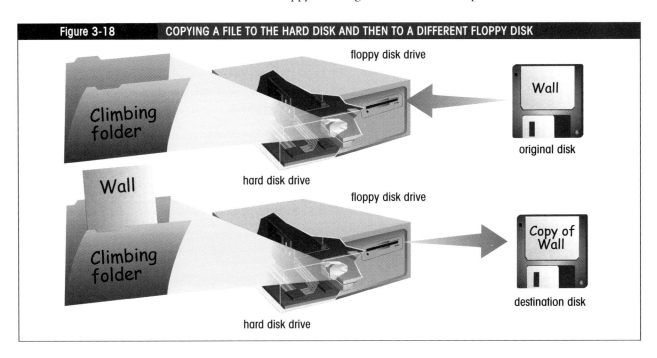

floppy disk drive

Climbing folder

original disk

Wall

hard disk drive

Wall

floppy disk drive

Climbing folder

Copy of Wall

destination disk

hard disk drive

REFERENCE WINDOW | **RW**

__Copying a File from One Floppy Disk to Another__
- Make sure you have a folder on the hard drive to which you can copy a file. If necessary, create a new folder on the hard drive.
- Copy the file to the hard drive.
- Take your Data Disk out of the floppy drive and insert the floppy disk to which you want the file copied.
- Click View and then click Refresh to view the contents of the second disk.
- Move the file from the hard drive to the floppy disk that is now in the floppy disk drive.

To move a file from the hard drive to the destination disk, you use another Windows 2000 feature: the Send To command. The Send To command provides a simple one-click method of sending any file on your computer's hard drive to your floppy drive (you can also use the Send To command to send files to other locations on your computer, such as the Desktop.) Be aware however, that the Send To command can only send files to the root directory of the floppy drive; you can't direct a file to a specific folder within the floppy drive.

To carry out this procedure, you need two disks: your Data Disk and another blank, formatted floppy disk.

To copy a file from one floppy disk to another:

1. Click **3½ Floppy (A:)** in the Folders pane (you might have to scroll to see it) to display its contents in the right pane.

2. Right-click the **Wall** file to select it and then click **Copy**.

3. Right-click the **Climbing** folder on drive C and then click **Paste** to copy the file into the folder.

4. After the copy is complete (the drive A light goes out), remove your Data Disk (the source disk).

5. Write "Wall disk" on the label of your second disk, the destination disk. Insert the Wall disk (the destination disk) into drive A.

6. Open the Climbing folder on drive C.

7. Right-click the **Wall** file, click **Send To**, and then click **3½ Floppy (A)** (see Figure 3-19).

Figure 3-19	COPYING A FILE TO THE FLOPPY DISK WITH THE SEND TO COMMAND

The file should now be copied into the destination disk.

8. Click **3½ Floppy (A:)** and make sure the Wall file is safely on the disk, then remove the destination disk from drive A.

9. Place your Data Disk back in drive A, click **View**, and then click **Refresh** to view the files on the Data Disk.

This example shows how you can quickly copy a file to your floppy disk by using the Send To command. The Send To command saves you the trouble of navigating through the hierarchy of Windows 2000 objects. The Send To command can also be used to send files as faxes or e-mail messages.

Since this exercise was an example to give you experience in copying from the floppy to the hard drive, and since you don't want to clutter up your hard drive with unneeded files, you should delete the Climbing folder before continuing on.

You can do so easily by simply removing the Climbing folder from drive C. If you weren't able to move any files to drive C, you can skip these steps.

To delete the Climbing folder from drive C:

1. Right-click the **Climbing** folder icon in the Folders pane.

2. Click **Delete** to display the Confirm Folder Delete dialog box.

TROUBLE? If a message appears telling you that you can't perform this operation, your system administrator might have restricted the deletion privileges from the hard drive. Continue reading the rest of the instructions to understand the process.

3. Make sure the Confirm Folder Delete message indicates that the Climbing folder will be moved to the Recycle Bin.

TROUBLE? If a different filename appears in the Confirm Folder Delete dialog box, click the No button and go back to Step 1.

4. Click the **Yes** button to delete the folder from drive C.

5. Click the **Close** button ☒ to close the Exploring window. You return to the Windows 2000 desktop.

You look over the structure of folders and files on Bernard's disk and realize that, as his business increases, this structure will become increasingly useful. You've used the power of Windows Explorer to simplify tasks such as locating, moving, copying, and deleting files. You can apply these skills to larger file management challenges when you are using a computer of your own and need to organize and work with the files on your hard drive.

Session 3.2 QUICK CHECK

1. You hold down the _____ key when you select files, to select consecutive files, whereas you hold down the _____ key to select nonconsecutive files.

2. How do you set up Windows 2000 to select files by simply pointing at them (rather than by pointing and clicking)?

3. What view must you be in, and what button do you click, to view files organized by date?

4. How can you make a printout of your computer screen? *prt scrn, paste into word/print*

5. Why is it a good habit to use the right mouse button, rather than the left, to drag files in Windows Explorer? *proper shortcuts*

6. True or False: You can copy a file from one floppy disk to another even if you only have one floppy disk drive in your computer, if you have access to a hard drive. *true*

7. True or False: When you delete files or folders from the floppy disk, they go into the Recycle Bin. *false*

8. If you want to copy a file from your hard drive directly to the root directory of your floppy disk (without having to navigate through the hierarchy of Windows 2000 objects), what command can you use? *send to*

SESSION 3.3

In this session you'll learn how to view a list of recently opened files with the History pane. You'll learn how to search through the History list based on date, number of times accessed, and most recently accessed, and by site. You'll learn how to search in the History pane to locate a specific file you've recently used.

Viewing Your File History

Now that you've finished working with the Folders pane in Windows Explorer to organize your files, Bernard is interested in the other organizational tools that Explorer offers. You decide to introduce him to the History pane, which displays a history of the files and objects that Bernard has opened recently (within the last week). For example, if Bernard remembers opening a particular file last Tuesday, but can't remember the file's location, he might still be able to locate it with the History pane by viewing a list of files opened on that date.

Displaying the History Pane

Like the Folders pane, the History pane is displayed in the Explorer Bar. You open the History pane using the View command on the menu bar.

To open the History pane:

1. Open Windows Explorer.

2. Click **View**, point to **Explorer Bar**, and then click **History**.

Explorer displays the History pane as shown in Figure 3-20.

Figure 3-20	DISPLAYING THE HISTORY PANE

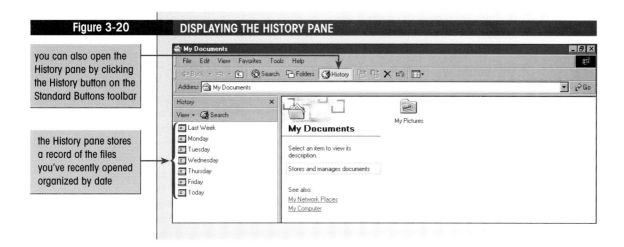

you can also open the History pane by clicking the History button on the Standard Buttons toolbar

the History pane stores a record of the files you've recently opened organized by date

The history pane shows an icon for each of the last few days you've worked with the computer as well as an icon for the entire previous week. Each icon displays a list of the files, folders, Web pages, and other objects, that were opened during those times. Thus, if Bernard needs to locate the file that he worked on last Tuesday, he can do so by opening the Tuesday icon in the History pane. Try this now.

To view objects opened on Tuesday:

1. Click 🔲 **Tuesday** in the History pane.

2. Within the Tuesday icon are the various files and sites Bernard has opened recently (yours will be different). For example, if he's used this computer to access the Web, those Web sites will be listed along with local sites, such as the My Computer window. Bernard is interested only in the files he's accessed on his computer.

3. Click the **My Computer** icon listed under Tuesday in the left pane.

Depending on what files you've opened during that time, you'll see a variety of icons at this point. Figure 3-21 displays the list of files accessed by Bernard on Tuesday. Your list of files will be different.

Figure 3-21	FILES OPENED ON TUESDAY

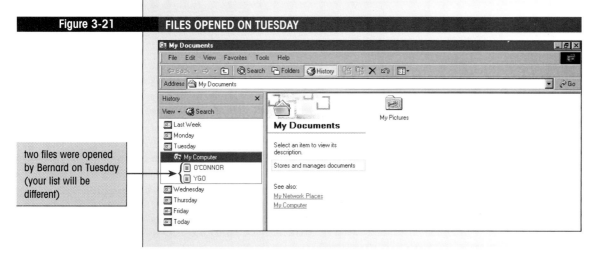

two files were opened by Bernard on Tuesday (your list will be different)

If Bernard wanted to open one of these files (the O'Connor file for instance) he could do so by clicking the file icon, and Windows 2000 would open the file. One important point: if the file has been moved since Tuesday, then Windows 2000 will not be able to open the file because it will be looking for it in its previous location.

Other Views in the History Pane

You have several choices of how to view the list of recently opened files. You can view the recent file list:

- By the date that the files were opened (the default)
- By the site where the files reside
- By the number of times you've opened each file
- By the order in which you've opened the files on the current day

For example, if Bernard knows that he's opened the O'Connor file a lot recently, he may decide that it's quicker to view the History pane organized by the number of times each file has been opened. The O'Connor file would probably be near or at the top of that list. Bernard asks to see how to show such a list.

To view the list of files ordered by most visits:

1. Click **View** in the History pane.

2. Click the **By Most Visited** option.

3. Windows Explorer displays a list of recent files organized by the number of times you've visited or opened the files. The files you've visited most often are displayed at the top of the list. See Figure 3-22.

| Figure 3-22 | THE HISTORY LIST ORDERED BY THE MOST VISITED FILES |

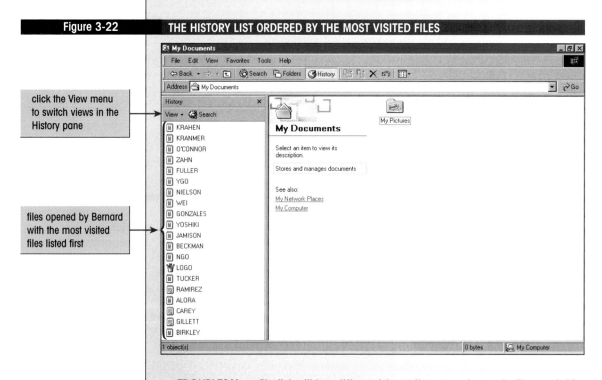

click the View menu to switch views in the History pane

files opened by Bernard with the most visited files listed first

TROUBLE? Your file list will be different from the one shown in Figure 3-22.

Once again, Bernard could click the O'Connor file icon to open that file directly without having to know where the file is located within the Windows 2000 hierarchy of objects. The only limitation is that if the file is located on a CD-ROM or floppy disk, that disk must be in place before the file can be accessed.

In this case, Bernard is doing a lot of work with a floppy disk, so that disk is most likely to be in place. If he wants to quickly move back and forth between the files he's opened recently, he might find it most useful to have the History pane organized in order of the files he's visited in the current day.

To view the list of recently opened files:

1. Click **View** in the History pane and then click **By Order Visited Today**.

Figure 3-23 shows the files that Bernard has opened in the current day, with the most recent files listed first.

| Figure 3-23 | DISPLAYING FILES OPENED IN THE CURRENT DAY |

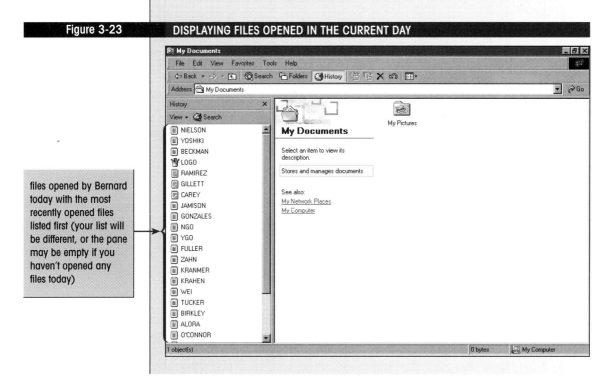

files opened by Bernard today with the most recently opened files listed first (your list will be different, or the pane may be empty if you haven't opened any files today)

The final view option, By Site, becomes useful when you use your computer to tour the World Wide Web. Those Web pages that you visit will then be organized by the different Web sites in the By Site view. Since Bernard is working *only* with files on his own computer—the My Computer site if you will—there's no value in viewing the History list by site.

Searching the History Pane

Bernard finds the History pane a useful tool for locating the files he's recently worked with. But he wonders what he would do if he didn't know where the file was located, wasn't sure when he last accessed the file, and was a bit unclear on the file's name. For example, Bernard knows that he's opened a client's file sometime in the last week, but he's not sure of the file-name. He can't remember if it's spelled "Kranmmer," "Kranmar," "Kranmere," or "Kranmer," he just knows that it starts with a "Kran." Could the History pane still help him locate the file?

He could, by trial and error, work through the various views of the History pane to locate the file, but it would be quicker and more instructive to use the Search command. With the Search command you can specify the name or part of a name of a recently opened file, and Windows Explorer will then locate the file for you (assuming that you've worked with the file within the last week). You show Bernard how to do this with the "Kran" file.

To locate the "Kran" file:

1. Click the **Search** button in the History pane.

2. Type **Kran** in the Search For text box.

3. By typing "Kran" you are limiting your search only to files with the text "kran" in their filenames, such as "<u>Kran</u>mer" or "C<u>krank</u>".

4. Click the **Search Now** button.

The Kranmer file is listed in the History pane, as shown in Figure 3-24. This is the file that Bernard is looking for. However, since you haven't actually opened the Kranmer file recently, it won't show up in your History pane.

Figure 3-24	LOCATING THE KRANMER FILE

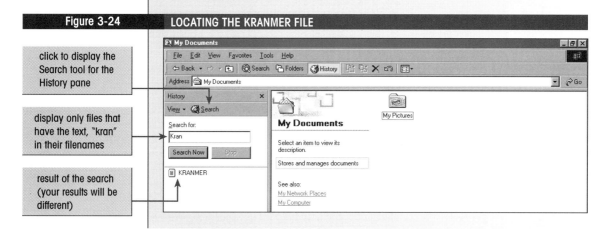

click to display the Search tool for the History pane

display only files that have the text, "kran" in their filenames

result of the search (your results will be different)

The Search tool in the History pane is limited to searching through the list of files you've opened within the last week. If you want to perform a more general search for *any* file located on your computer (whether you've opened it or not), you can do so with the Search pane. The Search pane is a rich tool containing many features for complex and detailed searches. You'll get a chance to explore some of the features in a later tutorial.

You've completed your work with Windows Explorer. You remind Bernard that each of the tools and techniques you've shown him can be used with most of the windows in Windows 2000. For example, if he wants to use the History or Search panes in the My Computer window, he can do so.

To finish your work:

1. Close Windows Explorer.

2. Remove your floppy disk from the floppy drive.

Session 3.3   QUICK | CHECK

1. True or False: This History pane contains a list of all of the files you've ever opened on your computer. _false_

2. True or False: If a file is moved from its original location, the History pane will display the new file location. _false_

3. To display a list of files you've most often visited, click _by most visited_ from the History pane view menu.

4. The By Site view option in the History pane is useful if you are using your computer to access the _www_ .

5. True or False: The Search tool in the History pane can be used to locate any file on your computer. _true_

REVIEW ASSIGNMENTS

1. **Copying Files to the Hard Drive** Bernard wants to place his sport-climbing client files (those in the Sport folder) on the hard drive to work with them on an advertisement campaign. The Sport folder is a subfolder of Advanced, which is itself a subfolder of Clients.

   a. Using the Wall disk you used in Session 3.2, Quick format the disk, then make a new Data Disk, using the Level II Disk 2 option.
   b. Start Windows Explorer and then create a new folder on drive C called Advertise.
   c. Copy the files in the Sport folder on your Data Disk to the Advertise folder on the hard drive.
   d. Open the Advertise folder on the hard drive to display the files it contains.
   e. Print the Exploring screen from WordPad (using the steps in this tutorial), including your name and the date on the printout.
   f. Delete the Advertise folder from the hard drive when your printout is complete.

2. **Creating a New Folder and Copying Files** Bernard now wants a folder that contains all the clients he has, because he'd like to do a general mailing to everyone, advertising an expedition to the Tetons. (*Hint*: The client files are all text files, so consider viewing the files in the root directory by type. Don't forget that there are also client files in the Clients folder and its subfolders.)

   a. Create a folder called All Clients on the drive A root directory, and then copy all the text files from the root directory into the All Clients folder.
   b. Open the Clients folder and then all its subfolders one at a time, and copy the text files from each of those folders into the new All Clients folder.
   c. Print out the Exploring screen from WordPad (using the steps in this tutorial), showing the contents of the All Clients folder arranged by name. Be sure to include your name and the date on your printout.
   d. Delete the All Clients folder from the floppy disk when your printout is complete.

3. **Copying Between Floppy Disks** Suppose someone who doesn't know how to use Windows Explorer (she missed class) wants to copy the Guides folder from her Data Disk to another floppy disk—but she doesn't want the entire contents of the Data Disk. Try this yourself, and as you go through the procedure, write down each step so that this student will be able to follow the steps and make a copy of Guides. Keep in mind that she doesn't know how to use Explorer.

4. **Restructuring a Disk** Use Quick Format to format the second disk you used in Session 3.3 (the "Wall" disk). Now make a new Data Disk, using the Level I Disk 1 menu option rather than the Level II Disk 2 option. (Disk 1 contains the files you used in Tutorial 2.) Rearrange the files on the disk so they correspond to Figure 3-27. Delete any files or folders not shown in

the figure. Print out the Explorer screen from WordPad (using the steps from this tutorial) that shows your new organization and the files in the Yellowstone Park folder arranged by size.

Figure 3-25

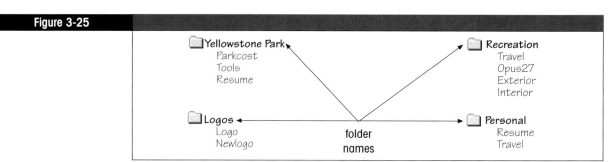

5. **Creating a Folder Structure** When you complete your computer class, you are likely to use a computer for other courses in your major and for general education requirements such as English and Math. Think about how you would organize the floppy disk that would hold the files for your courses, and then prepare a disk to contain your files. If you're not a student, prepare a disk using fictitious data.

   a. Make a sketch of this organization.
   b. Use Quick Format to erase the contents of the second disk you used in Session 3.3 (the Wall disk).
   c. Create the folder structure on your Data Disk (even though you don't have any files to place in the folders right now). Use subfolders to help sort files for class projects (your composition course, for example, might have a midterm and a final paper).
   d. Make sure all folders and subfolders are displayed in the left pane, and then paste an image of the Exploring screen into WordPad (using the steps in this tutorial). Be sure to include your name and the date, but don't print anything yet.
   e. Use WordPad to write one or two paragraphs after your name explaining your plan. Your explanation should include information about your major, the courses you plan to take, and how you might use computers in those courses. Print the document when it is finished.

6. **Exploring Your Computer's Devices, Folders, and Files** Answer each of the following questions about the devices, folders, and files on your lab computers. You can find all the answers using the Exploring window. Note that your answers will vary from those of other students because different computers have different devices, folder hierarchies, and files.

   a. How many folders (not subfolders) are on drive C?
   b. How many of these folders on drive C have subfolders? What is the easiest way to find the answer to this question?
   c. Do you have a Windows folder on drive C? If so, how many objects does it contain? What is the easiest way to answer this question?
   d. Do you have a folder named My Documents on drive C? If so, what is the size of the largest file in this folder?
   e. Does your computer have a CD-ROM drive? If so, what drive letter is assigned to the CD-ROM drive?
   f. Does your computer have access to a network storage device? If so, indicate the letter(s) of the network storage device(s).
   g. How much space do the files in the root directory of drive C occupy? How much free space is left on drive C?
   h. What file has been most recently opened?
   i. Of the files most recently opened, which file has been opened most often?

7. **Separating Program and Data Files** Hard drive management differs from floppy disk management because a hard drive contains programs and data, whereas a floppy disk (unless it is an installation disk that you got from a software company) generally only contains data files. On a hard drive, a good management practice is to keep programs in folders separate from data files. Keeping this in mind, read the following description, draw a sketch of the folder structure described, and then make a sketch of how the current structure could be improved.

The Marquette Chamber of Commerce uses a computer to maintain its membership list and track dues. It also uses the computer for correspondence. All the programs and data used by the Chamber of Commerce are on drive C. The program for the membership database is in a folder called Members. The data file for the membership database is in a subfolder of Members called Member Data. The accounting program used to track income and expenditures is in a folder called Accounting Programs. The data for the current year is in a folder directly under the drive C icon called Accounting Data 2001. The accounting data from 1999 and 2000 is stored in two subfolders of the folder called Accounting Programs. The word-processing program is in a folder called Word. The documents created with Word are stored in the Member Data folder. Finally, Windows 2000 is stored in a folder called Windows, which has 10 subfolders.

8. **Using the Send To Command** The Send To command provides an efficient way to send files to the root directory of the floppy disk. Use the Windows Explorer Help system to learn about the Send To command. Then write the steps you would take to use this command to send a file on your floppy disk to your computer's desktop. How would you add other options to the Send To command (for example, to send files directly to the My Documents folder)?

PROJECTS

1. Shortly after graduation, you start working for your aunt and uncle, who own a thriving antique store. They hope to store data about their inventory and business on the computer they recently purchased. They have hired you to accomplish this task. Your Aunt Susan asks you to organize her client files and to prepare some financial statements. Your Uncle Gabe wants you to create customized forms for invoicing and inventory. Two part-time employees, Julia and Abigail, have asked you to help develop documents for advertising. You realize that a folder structure would be helpful to keep things straight.

   a. Create a folder on your Data Disk named Antiques.
   b. Create the following subfolders: Customers, Finances, Invoices, Inventory, and Advertising.
   c. Create each of the documents listed below in WordPad and save them to the correct folders on your Data Disk:

Customers subfolder:	Inventory subfolder:
Harrington	Furniture
Searls	Art
Finances subfolder:	Advertising subfolder:
Budget	Anniversary Sale
Profit and Loss	Winter Clearance
Balance Sheet	
Invoices subfolder:	
Sales	
Vendors	

   d. In Windows Explorer, display the entire Antiques folder hierarchy in the left pane, and display the contents of the Finances subfolder in the right pane. Press the Print Screen key. Then open a new WordPad document, type your name and the date at the top, and paste an image of the Exploring window into the document. Print the document. Close WordPad, but don't save the changes.

2. Uncle Gabe decided to have his financial statements prepared by an accountant, so you need to copy the files in the Finances subfolder onto a different disk that you can give to the accountant. Use the folders and files you created in Project 1. You will need a blank floppy disk and the ability to access your computer's hard drive to complete this project. Uncle Gabe wants to know how to copy files to a new disk, so as you copy the files, write down in detail what you are doing so he can repeat this procedure by following your directions.

   a. Create a folder on your hard drive called Accountant.
   b. Copy the three files in the Finances folder on your Data Disk to the Accountant folder on your hard drive, using the drag technique.

c. Copy the contents of the Accountant folder to the blank disk, using the cut-and-paste technique.

d. Delete the Accountant folder from your hard drive.

3. Two of the methods you've learned for moving files between folders are the drag-and-drop method and the cut-and-paste method. Answer the following questions:

a. Can you think of any situations in which you could not use drag and drop to move a file in Windows Explorer?

b. In such a situation, what should you do instead?

c. Which method do you prefer? Why?

4. Windows 2000 enables users to extensively customize their working environment. For each item, first write the steps you take to make the change, and then comment on the benefits or disadvantages of using the following options in the Exploring window:

a. Details view or List view

b. Displaying or hiding the status bar

c. Displaying or hiding the Folders pane

d. Switching from the Folders pane to the History pane

e. Displaying or hiding the Standard Buttons option (for this option, also address how you accomplish your work without the Standard buttons visible)

QUICK CHECK ANSWERS

Session 3.1

1. Windows Explorer

2. The left pane, displays tools, such as the Folders pane, History pane, and Search pane, used to organize the files on your computer; the right pane displays the contents of the object selected in the right pane.

3. False

4. False

5. subfolder

6. plus box

7. the drive A device icon

8. False

Session 3.2

1. Shift, Ctrl

2. Click Folder options from the Tools menu and then choose the Single-click to Open option button from the General dialog sheet.

3. Details

4. Press the Print Screen key, paste the image into WordPad, and print the WordPad document.

5. Using the right mouse button opens a shortcut menu that gives you the choice to move or copy.

6. True

7. False

8. the Send To command

Session 3.3

1. False

2. False

3. By Most Visited

4. World Wide Web

5. False

OBJECTIVES

In this tutorial you will:

- Place a document icon on the desktop and use Notepad's time-date stamp

- Create and delete shortcuts to a drive, a document, and a printer

- Change desktop appearance

- Configure your taskbar

- Create and modify taskbar toolbars

- Edit your Start menu

- Use the Control Panel to access system settings

PERSONALIZING
YOUR WINDOWS ENVIRONMENT

Changing Desktop Settings at Companions, Inc.

CASE

Companions, Inc.

Bow Falls, Arizona, is a popular Sun Belt retirement mecca that is also a college town with several distinguished universities. Beth Yuan, a graduate of Bow Falls University, realized that the unusual mix of ages in her town might be perfectly suited to a service business. She formed Companions, Inc. to provide older residents with trained personal care assistants who help with housecleaning, home maintenance, and errands. Many of Beth's employees are students at local colleges who like the flexible hours and enjoy spending time with the elderly residents. In addition to employees who work directly with clients, Beth has hired office staff people who help manage the day-to-day tasks of running a business.

The offices of Companions, Inc. are equipped with computers that are used to maintain client records, schedule employees, manage company finances, develop training materials, and create informational documents about Beth's business. Beth recently upgraded her computers to Windows 2000. She has heard that it's easy to change Windows 2000 settings to reflect the needs of her office staff. She asks you to find a way to make it easier to access documents and computer resources. She would also like you to give the desktop a corporate look and feel.

SESSION 4.1

In this session, you will learn how to place a Notepad document icon on the desktop and how to "stamp" the document with the time and date. You will create shortcuts to the objects you use most often, including your computer's floppy drive, a document, and a printer. You will learn how to use the icons you create and how to restore your desktop to its original state.

Document-centric Desktops

Windows 2000 automatically places several icons on your desktop, such as the My Computer and the Recycle Bin icons. You can place additional icons on the desktop that represent objects such as printers, disk drives, programs, and documents, making it easier for you to access them. For example, you can create an icon on your desktop that represents your resume. To open this document, you would use its icon. You would no longer have to navigate menus or windows or even locate the program you used to create the document. A desktop that gives this kind of immediate access to documents is called **document-centric**.

Creating a Document Icon on the Desktop

Employees in the Companions, Inc. offices keep a log of their telephone calls, using the Notepad accessory. Notepad, like WordPad, allows you to edit simple text documents, but because it does not include the formatting options provided by WordPad, it is used only for text documents with no formatting. Notepad includes a time-date stamp that automatically inserts the time and date whenever you open the document. Figure 4-1 shows you a Notepad document with automatic time-date stamps.

Figure 4-1	NOTEPAD DOCUMENT WITH TIME-DATE STAMP

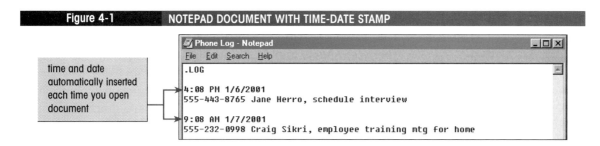

time and date automatically inserted each time you open document

You create a new document on the desktop by right-clicking the desktop and then selecting the type of document you want from a list. A **document icon** appears on the desktop to represent your document. The appearance of the document icon depends on the type of document you create. For example, a Notepad document icon appears as 📄, whereas a WordPad document icon appears as 📄. When you open the document represented by the icon, the operating system checks the file's extension to determine which program it should start.

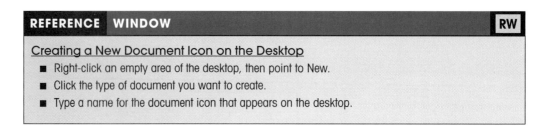

REFERENCE WINDOW **RW**

Creating a New Document Icon on the Desktop
- Right-click an empty area of the desktop, then point to New.
- Click the type of document you want to create.
- Type a name for the document icon that appears on the desktop.

The phone log is a perfect candidate for a document icon because employees use it so frequently. When you use the document icon to open the document, Windows 2000 locates and starts the appropriate program for you (in this case, Notepad).

To create a Notepad document icon on the desktop:

1. Right-click a blank area of the desktop and then point to **New**. The menu shown in Figure 4-2 opens.

> TROUBLE? If no menu appears, you might have clicked with the left mouse button instead of the right. Repeat Step 1.

> TROUBLE? If your list of options on the New menu looks different from the one in Figure 4-2, don't worry. The document types that appear on the New menu depend on the programs installed on your computer.

> TROUBLE? If the objects on your screen take up more or less space than those shown in the figures, don't worry. Your monitor settings are different.

Figure 4-2	CREATING A NEW TEXT DOCUMENT

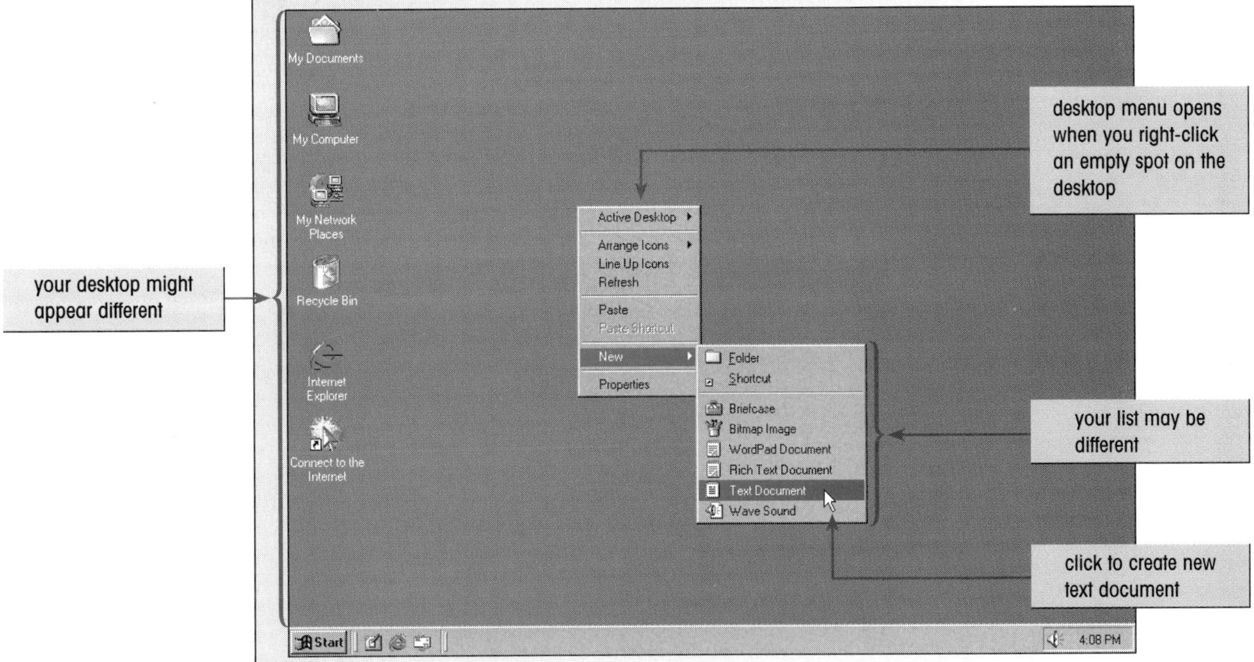

your desktop might appear different

desktop menu opens when you right-click an empty spot on the desktop

your list may be different

click to create new text document

2. Click **Text Document**. A document icon for your new text document appears on the desktop. See Figure 4-3. Its default filename, "New Text Document," is selected so you can assign it an appropriate name.

> TROUBLE? If you receive an error message when you try to create a new document on the desktop, your lab might not allow you to make any changes to the desktop. Ask your instructor which sections of this tutorial your lab allows you to complete.

Figure 4-3 **DOCUMENT ICON**

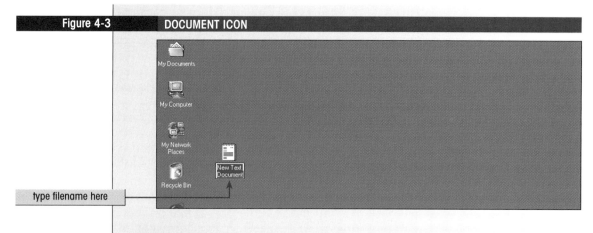

type filename here

3. Type **Phone Log** as the name of your document.

TROUBLE? If nothing happens when you type the document name, you might have inadvertently pressed a key or mouse button that deactivated the document icon. Right-click the New Text Document icon, click Rename, and then type Phone Log.

4. Press the **Enter** key. See Figure 4-4.

TROUBLE? If you see a message about changing the filename extension, click No, type Phone Log.txt, and then press Enter. Your computer is set to display file extensions, and because you didn't supply one with the title, the operating system deletes the extension unless you click No and supply an extension.

Figure 4-4 **PHONE LOG DOCUMENT ICON**

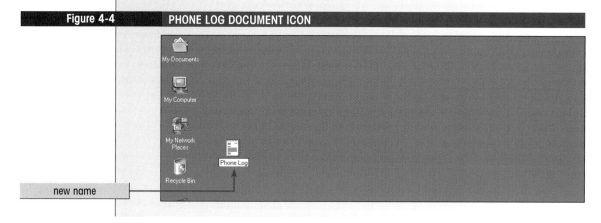

new name

You can often identify an object's type by the appearance of its icon. The Phone Log document icon 🗒 identifies a Notepad text document. Later in this tutorial you'll identify other icons that represent other object types.

Opening a Document on the Desktop

When you use a desktop document icon to open a document, Windows 2000 starts the appropriate program, which in this case is Notepad, so you can edit the document.

To open the Phone Log:

1. Double-click the **Phone Log** icon. Windows 2000 starts Notepad. See Figure 4-5.

| Figure 4-5 | PHONE LOG DOCUMENT OPENS IN NOTEPAD |

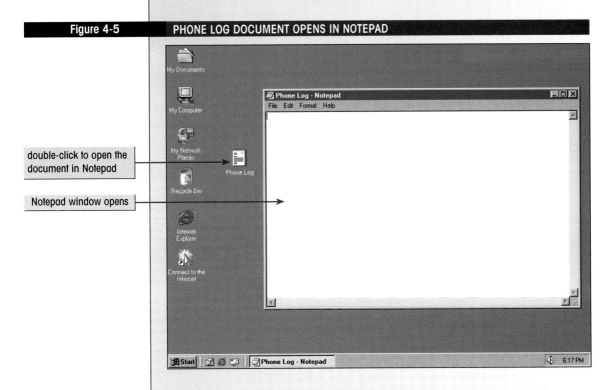

double-click to open the document in Notepad

Notepad window opens

TROUBLE? If the Notepad window hides the Phone Log document icon, drag and resize the window as necessary to view both the icon and the window. If the window is maximized, you'll first need to restore it.

Creating a LOG File

Notepad automatically inserts the date when you open a document only if the document begins with .LOG, in uppercase letters. Your next step is to create a document with .LOG at the beginning and to enter some text. Then you will save the document and close it, so that next time you open it, the time and date will be entered automatically.

To set up the Phone Log document:

1. Type **.LOG**. Be sure to first type the period and to use uppercase letters.

2. Press the **Enter** key to move to the next line.

3. Type **Phone Log for** and then type your name.

4. Press the **Enter** key.

5. Click the **Close** button ⊠ to close Notepad.

6. Click **Yes** to save the changes.

Now you will test the Phone Log document to see if an automatic time-date stamp appears when you open it.

To test the .LOG feature:

1. Open the Phone Log document.

2. Make sure your document contains a time and date stamp. See Figure 4-6.

Figure 4-6	TIME-DATE STAMP

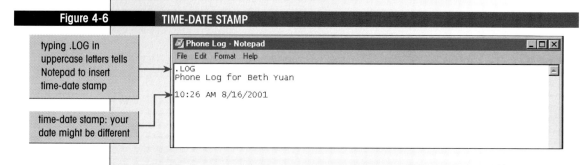

typing .LOG in uppercase letters tells Notepad to insert time-date stamp

time-date stamp: your date might be different

3. Now enter your first phone log entry: type **941-555-0876 Charlene Maples, prospective client needs household help 5 hrs/week.**

4. Press the **Enter** key. See Figure 4-7.

Figure 4-7	FIRST PHONE LOG ENTRY - NOTEPAD

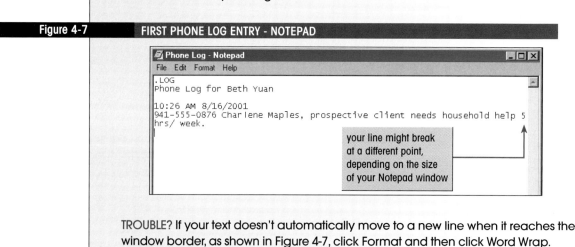

your line might break at a different point, depending on the size of your Notepad window

TROUBLE? If your text doesn't automatically move to a new line when it reaches the window border, as shown in Figure 4-7, click Format and then click Word Wrap.

5. Click the **Close** button ☒ to close Notepad.

6. Click **Yes** to save the changes.

Using **Shortcuts**

Beth uses her floppy drive regularly and would like an easier way to access it. One way is to create a shortcut on the desktop to her floppy drive. A **shortcut** is an icon that "points" to an object on your computer. You can create shortcuts to access drives, documents, files, Web pages, programs, or other computer resources such as a printer.

A shortcut icon is identified by the arrow in the lower-left corner. For example, a document icon might appear as 📄, while the shortcut icon for the same document would appear as 📄. One advantage of shortcuts is that you can store your documents in one location, but place shortcuts to those documents in several different locations (such as on your desktop), making it easier to access those files or objects directly without having to navigate through the Windows 2000 hierarchy.

Creating Shortcuts

Windows 2000 provides several different ways of creating shortcuts. For example, you can right-click an object and choose "Create Shortcut(s) Here." Figure 4-8 summarizes the various techniques you can use to create shortcuts. Which one you choose is a matter of personal preference.

Figure 4-8	METHODS FOR CREATING SHORTCUTS
METHOD	**DESCRIPTION**
Copy and Paste Shortcut	Use Windows Explorer or My Computer to locate and select the file icon. Click **Edit** and **Copy** from the menu bar. Move to the new location. Click **Edit** and **Paste Shortcut**.
Drag and Drop	Use Windows Explorer or My Computer to locate and select the file icon. Click the file icon. Drag and drop the icon in the new location, holding down the **Alt** key.
Right-click Drag and Drop	Use Windows Explorer or My Computer to locate and select the file icon. With the right mouse button pressed down, drag the file icon to the new location. Release the mouse button and click **Create Shortcut(s) Here** in the menu.

Be aware that the technique of dragging and dropping with your left mouse button does not work the same way for all objects. For example, if you drag and drop a document icon from one folder to another on the same drive, the document is moved to the new location. However, if you drag and drop a program or drive icon, a shortcut is created at the new location. This is because a program might not work correctly if moved into a new location (Windows 2000 expects to find it in the folder in which it was installed), and so the default is to create a shortcut rather than move the file. Similarly, Windows 2000 cannot move a drive or disk, so it creates a shortcut instead. Finally, if you drag and drop a document between one drive and another, the document is copied and *not* moved.

If this seems confusing, remember you can always tell which task Windows 2000 is performing by observing the icon as you drag it into the new location. If the icon has a shortcut arrow, a shortcut is being created. If no shortcut arrow is present, the file is being moved to the new location. If a plus box appears, the file is being copied to the new location.

REFERENCE WINDOW	RW

Creating a Shortcut on the Desktop
- Use Windows Explorer or My Computer to locate the icon that represents the program, document, or resource for which you want to create a shortcut.
- Make sure you can see a blank area of the Windows 2000 desktop, and that none of the windows is maximized.
- Hold down the right mouse button and drag the icon for the shortcut to the desktop, and then release the mouse button to display the menu.
- Click Create Shortcut(s) Here.

Creating a Shortcut to a Drive

Now you will create a shortcut to your floppy drive. Once this shortcut is on the desktop, you can open it to view the contents of your Data Disk, or you can move or copy documents to it without having to start Windows Explorer. You'll begin by making a new Data Disk, since the one you used in Tutorial 3 no longer contains the necessary files. You can use your original Data Disk if you don't need it anymore, or you can use a new, blank disk.

To make a new Data Disk and then create a shortcut to your floppy drive:

1. Format your disk so that it contains no files.

   TROUBLE? If you don't remember how to format a disk, refer to Tutorial 3.

2. Click the **Start** button ![Start], point to **Programs**, point to **NP on Microsoft Windows 2000-Level II**, and then click **Disk 2 (Tutorials 3 & 4)**.

   TROUBLE? Don't worry if your menu items appear abbreviated.

3. When a message box opens, click the **OK** button. Wait while the program copies the practice files to your formatted disk. When all the files have been copied, the program closes. If necessary, close any open windows.

4. Start the Windows Explorer program.

   TROUBLE? To start Windows Explorer, click the Start button, point to Programs, point to Accessories, and then click Windows Explorer.

5. Make sure the Exploring window is open, but not maximized.

   TROUBLE? If the Exploring window is maximized, click ![icon]. If necessary, resize the Exploring window further so you can see an empty part of the desktop.

6. Locate the device icon ![icon] for **3½ Floppy (A:)** in the Folders pane of the Exploring window.

   TROUBLE? If the Folders pane does not appear, click View, point to Explorer Bar, and then click Folders.

7. Hold down the right mouse button while you drag the device icon ![icon] for 3½ Floppy (A:) from the Folders pane into an empty area of the desktop.

   TROUBLE? If you dragged with the left mouse button instead of the right, you'll get a message saying you can't move or copy the item and asking if you want to create a shortcut instead. Click the No button and then repeat Step 7 so you learn the correct method.

8. Release the mouse button. Notice the menu that appears, as shown in Figure 4-9.

Figure 4-9	CREATING A SHORTCUT TO DRIVE A

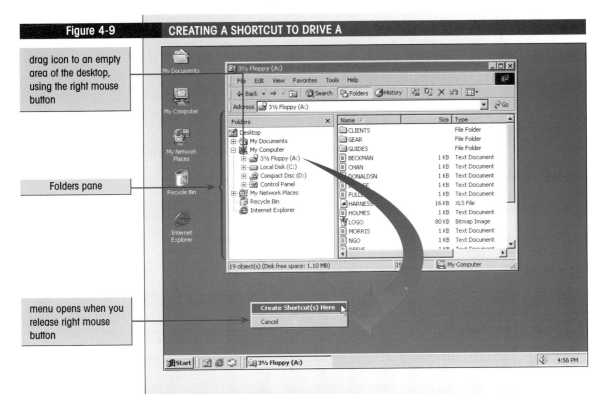

drag icon to an empty area of the desktop, using the right mouse button

Folders pane

menu opens when you release right mouse button

9. Click **Create Shortcut(s) Here**.

10. Click the **Close** button ☒ to close Windows Explorer. A shortcut labeled "Shortcut to 3½ Floppy (A:)" now appears on the desktop (yours may be in a different location). See Figure 4-10.

Figure 4-10	SHORTCUT TO DRIVE A

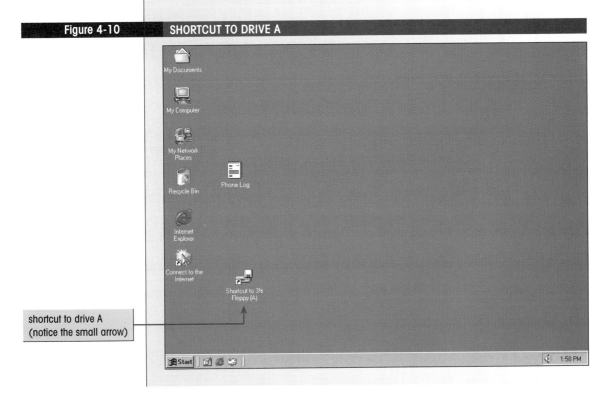

shortcut to drive A (notice the small arrow)

Now you can test the shortcut to see how it gives you immediate access to the contents of the disk in drive A.

To test the 3½ Floppy (A:) shortcut:

1. Double-click the **3½ Floppy (A:)** shortcut icon. A window opens, showing the contents of the disk in your 3½ Floppy (A:) drive.

2. Click the **Close** button X to close the 3½ Floppy (A:) window.

Beth often works at her home office, and she'd like to store the log on a disk that she carries back and forth. To move the log to a floppy disk, all she has to do is drag the Phone Log icon to the 3½ Floppy (A:) shortcut icon. You'll do this using the Cut and Paste method of moving a document.

To move the document from the desktop to a floppy disk:

1. Right-click the **Phone Log** icon on your desktop and then click **Cut** on the menu.

2. Right-click the **3½ Floppy (A:)** icon and then click **Paste** on the menu. The Phone Log icon disappears from the desktop.

When you moved the document icon to the drive A shortcut, the file itself was moved to the disk in drive A and off your desktop. Beth can now take the disk home with her and use a shortcut to drive A on her desktop there to open the file. Practice this now, using the shortcut you just created. (You could also open drive A from My Computer or Windows Explorer, but it is handier to use the drive A shortcut.)

To open the Phone Log document from the new 3½ Floppy (A:) window and add a new entry:

1. Use the 3½ Floppy (A:) shortcut icon to open the drive A window. Scroll through the window, if necessary, to verify that the Phone Log document is on your Data Disk.

   TROUBLE? If you don't see the Phone Log document on your Data Disk, click the Undo button (or click Edit, then click Undo Move), and then repeat the previous set of steps for moving a document to a floppy disk.

2. Open the **Phone Log** document from the 3½ Floppy (A:) window.

   Notice that another time-date stamp is entered.

3. If necessary, click the last line of the phone log so you can type a new entry.

4. Type **941-555-1248 Frank Meyers, next week's home care schedule**.

5. Press the **Enter** key.

6. Click the **Close** button X to close Notepad.

7. Click **Yes** to save the changes.

Creating a Shortcut to a Document

The Phone Log document is now on a floppy disk, as Beth requested; however, it no longer has an icon on the desktop. If you want to access the Phone Log document (now saved on your Data Disk) directly from the desktop, you can create a shortcut that automatically starts Notepad and opens the Phone Log from your Data Disk.

To create a shortcut to the Phone Log document on your Data Disk:

1. Resize the 3½ Floppy (A:) window as necessary to see both the Phone Log icon in the window and a blank area of the desktop.

2. Hold down the right mouse button while you drag the **Phone Log** icon from the 3½ Floppy (A:) window onto the desktop, and then release the mouse button.

3. Click **Create Shortcut(s) Here** on the menu.

   An icon labeled "Shortcut to Phone Log" now appears on the desktop.

4. Click the **Close** button ⊠ to close the 3½ Floppy (A:) window.

5. Hold your mouse pointer over the icon for the new shortcut and note the ScreenTip that appears next to the icon, indicating the location of the source document (in this case, on the root directory of drive A). See Figure 4-11.

| Figure 4-11 | CREATING A SHORTCUT TO THE PHONE LOG DOCUMENT ON DRIVE A |

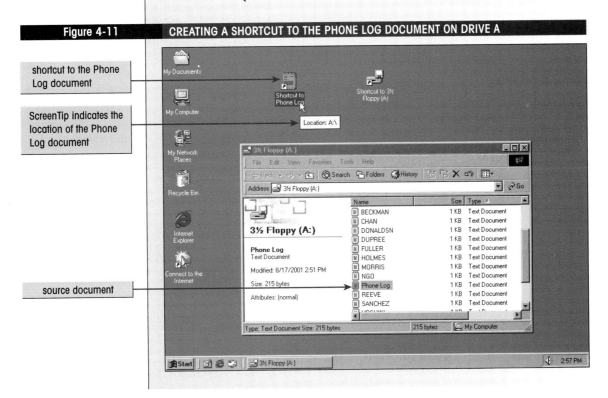

shortcut to the Phone Log document

ScreenTip indicates the location of the Phone Log document

source document

Now you can test the shortcut to see if it automatically opens the Phone Log.

To test the Phone Log shortcut:

1. Click the **Shortcut to Phone Log** icon and press the **Enter** key. Windows 2000 starts the Notepad program and then opens the Phone Log document on your Data Disk.

2. Type: **941-555-7766 Trinity River Accounting** below the new time-date stamp, and then press the **Enter** key.

3. Click the **Close** button ☒ to close Notepad.

4. Click **Yes** to save the changes.

The shortcut icon you just created and tested is different from the Phone Log icon you created at the beginning of this tutorial. That icon was not a shortcut icon. It was a document icon representing a document that was actually located on the desktop. The shortcut icon currently on your desktop represents a document located on your Data Disk.

If you delete a document icon, you also delete the document. If you delete a shortcut icon you don't delete the document itself, because it is stored elsewhere; you are just deleting the shortcut that points to the document. If you were to remove your Data Disk from drive A, the shortcut to the Phone Log would no longer work because the source document would no longer be available.

You might notice that some of the icons on your desktop, such as My Computer and the Recycle Bin, don't have arrows and are therefore not shortcut icons. These icons are installed by the operating system and cannot be removed (although they can be hidden).

Creating a Shortcut to a Printer

You now have an efficient way to open the Phone Log and to access your floppy drive. Now you want to add a printer shortcut to the desktop so that employees can easily print their phone logs and other documents.

You create a printer shortcut in much the same way as you created a shortcut for the floppy drive: by locating the printer icon and then dragging the icon onto your desktop. You can locate your printer's icon by opening the Printers window located on your computer's Start menu.

To create a printer shortcut:

1. Click the **Start** button ⊞Start, point to **Settings**, and then click **Printers**.

2. Position the pointer over the icon of the printer for which you want to create a shortcut.

   TROUBLE? If you are using a computer that is not connected to a network or printer, read through the following steps for later reference.

   TROUBLE? If more than one printer is listed and you do not know which printer you usually use, use the default printer, identified with the ● icon.

3. Hold down the right mouse button while you drag the printer icon to the desktop.

4. Release the right mouse button to drop the printer icon on the desktop.

5. Click **Create Shortcut(s) Here** on the menu. The printer shortcut appears. See Figure 4-12.

Figure 4-12	CREATING A SHORTCUT TO A PRINTER

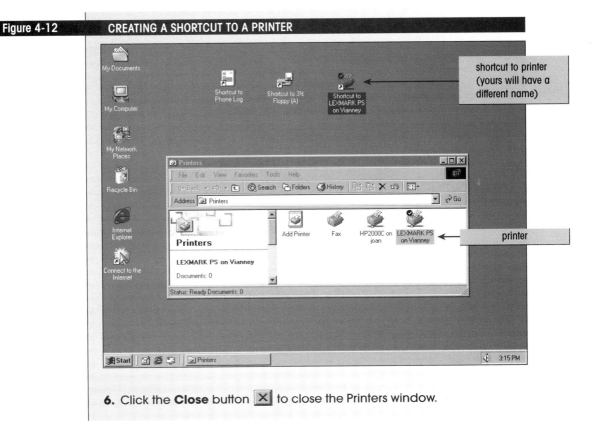

6. Click the **Close** button ❌ to close the Printers window.

Once a printer shortcut icon is on the desktop, you can print a document by dragging its icon to the printer shortcut icon. Think of the steps you save by printing this way: you don't have to open any programs or search through menus to locate and open the document and then locate the Print dialog box. Practice printing using the Phone Log document icon on your Data Disk.

To print the Phone Log document using the printer shortcut icon:

1. Drag the **Shortcut to Phone Log** icon with the left mouse button and drop it on the **Shortcut to Printer** icon that you just created.

2. When you release the mouse button, watch as Windows 2000 starts the Notepad program, opens the Phone Log, and then prints the Phone Log. (Normally Windows 2000 would simply close the program, but because your document has an automatic time-date stamp, the document is changed every time you open it. Thus, Windows 2000 asks if you want to save changes to the document before closing it. You don't need to save it because you don't have any new phone entries to log.)

3. Click **No**. Windows 2000 closes Notepad without saving the new time-date stamp.

Identifying Shortcut Icons on the Desktop

Your desktop now has three new shortcut icons. Although the names of the shortcut icons help you identify what the shortcuts are for, the icons themselves help you identify the shortcut type. Figure 4-13 shows the types of icons you might see on a desktop and the objects they represent.

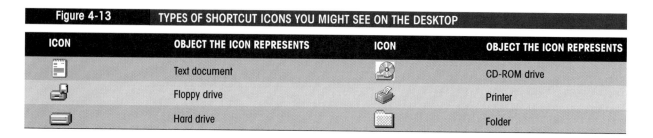

Figure 4-13	TYPES OF SHORTCUT ICONS YOU MIGHT SEE ON THE DESKTOP		
ICON	**OBJECT THE ICON REPRESENTS**	**ICON**	**OBJECT THE ICON REPRESENTS**
	Text document		CD-ROM drive
	Floppy drive		Printer
	Hard drive		Folder

When you are opening a document represented by a desktop icon, you can usually identify which program Windows 2000 will start by looking at the icon representing the document.

Deleting Shortcut Icons

If you are working on your own computer, you can leave the printer and drive icons in place, if you think you'll find them useful. Otherwise, you should delete all the shortcuts you created so that the desktop is restored to its original condition for the next user. You can delete them all at once.

To delete your shortcuts:

1. Click the printer shortcut icon to select it.

2. Press and hold down the **Ctrl** key, then click the floppy drive shortcut icon, the printer shortcut icon, and the Phone Log shortcut icon, so that all three icons are highlighted. Make sure no other icons are highlighted. If they are, deselect them.

3. Press the **Delete** key.

4. Click **Yes** if you are asked if you are sure you want to send these items to the Recycle Bin.

Your desktop is restored to its original appearance.

QUICK CHECK

1. True or False: On a document-centric desktop, the quickest way to open a document is by locating the program that created the document, starting the program, and then using the Open command to locate and open the document.

2. True or False: You can create a document with an automatic time-date stamp in Notepad by typing "log" at the beginning of the document.

3. What happens if you delete a document icon that does not have an arrow on it?

4. What happens if you delete a shortcut icon?

5. What happens if you drag and drop a document icon from one drive to another, using the left mouse button? What happens if you drag and drop the document icon within the same drive?

SESSION 4.2

In this session, you'll change the appearance of your desktop by working with the desktop's property sheets. You'll experiment with your desktop's background and appearance, enable a screen saver, try different colors to see how they look, and modify desktop settings to explore your monitor's capabilities. As you proceed through this session, check with your instructor or technical support person before you change settings on a school lab computer, and make sure you change them back before you leave.

Changing **Desktop Properties**

In Windows 2000, you can think of all the parts of your computer—the operating system, the programs, and the documents—as individual objects. For example, the desktop is an object, the taskbar is an object, a drive is an object, a program is an object, and a document is an object. Each object has **properties**, or characteristics, that you can examine and sometimes change. The desktop itself has many properties, including its color, its size, and the font it uses. Most objects in Windows 2000 have property sheets associated with them. A **property sheet** is a dialog box that you open to see or change an object's properties. To open an object's property sheet, you right-click the object and then click Properties on the shortcut menu that appears.

To view desktop properties:

1. Right-click an empty area of the desktop to open the shortcut menu.

2. Click **Properties** to open the Display Properties dialog box. See Figure 4-14.

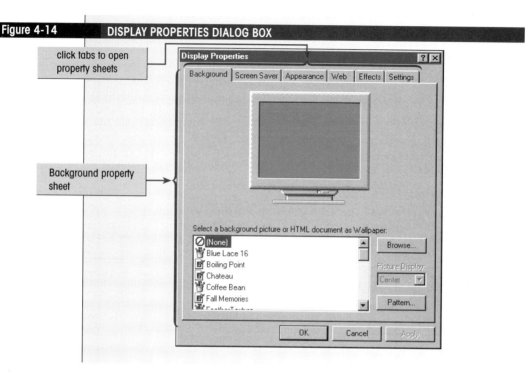

Figure 4-14   **DISPLAY PROPERTIES DIALOG BOX**

click tabs to open property sheets

Background property sheet

The Display Properties dialog box has several tabs along the top. Each tab corresponds to a property sheet. Some objects require only one property sheet, but the desktop has many properties associated with it, so there are more tabs for it. The Background tab appears first. To view a different property sheet, you click its tab.

Changing Your Desktop's Background

Beth wants the staff computers in the Companions, Inc. offices to have a corporate look. You can change the desktop background color, or you can select a **wallpaper**—a graphic or other type of file that you designate to give your desktop a different appearance—using the Wallpaper list on the Background property sheet. The image of a monitor at the top of the Background property sheet lets you preview the wallpaper. You can also choose a **pattern**, a design or shape that uses the current background color and is repeated over the entire desktop. When you change the background, you are not placing a new object on the desktop; you are simply changing its appearance. If you choose a wallpaper that doesn't occupy the entire background, you can choose a pattern that "fills in" the area around the wallpaper. When a pattern is in effect and you choose a wallpaper that occupies the entire background, the wallpaper covers up the pattern, and not the other way around. Either way, you can continue to work with the desktop just as you always have.

You'll first experiment by choosing a pattern, and then by choosing a wallpaper and a graphic.

To select a pattern:

1. Look at the Wallpaper list and check if a wallpaper is already selected. If one is, write the name down, because you will restore this setting later. Then scroll to the top of the Wallpaper list, click **(None)**, and then click the **Apply** button.

2. Click the **Pattern** button. The Pattern dialog box opens.

3. Click the **Boxes** pattern in the Pattern list. The preview changes to show the Boxes pattern. See Figure 4-15.

TROUBLE? If the Boxes pattern isn't available, choose a different one.

TROUBLE? If you have installed desktop themes, a feature that changes the look of your desktop and desktop icons, you need to turn this feature off before you can work with patterns. Click the Start button, point to Settings, and then click Control Panel. Locate and open Desktop Themes, and note the theme your computer is using. To temporarily disable desktop themes, click the Theme list arrow, and then click Windows Default. Click the OK button, close any open windows, and repeat Steps 1–3. When you are finished with this section, restore your themes setting to its original state.

Figure 4-15	SELECTING A DESKTOP PATTERN

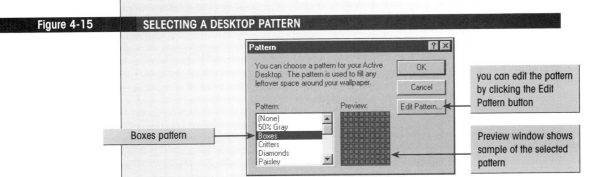

4. Scroll toward the bottom of the Pattern list and then click **Weave**. The preview now shows the Weave pattern.

5. Click the **OK** button to close the Pattern dialog box and then click the **Apply** button in the Display Properties dialog box to see how this pattern appears on the entire desktop. See Figure 4-16.

Figure 4-16	WEAVE PATTERN APPLIED TO THE DESKTOP

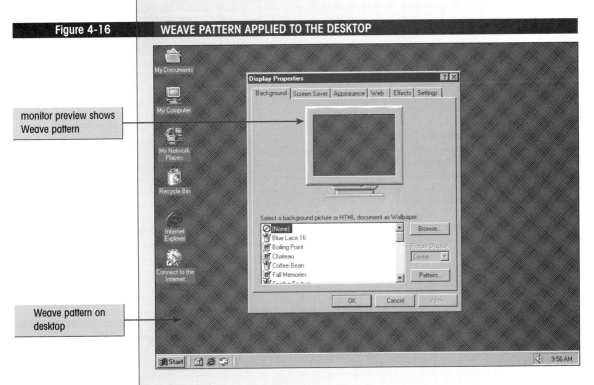

Beth doesn't think this pattern fits her company very well. You decide to experiment with the Windows 2000 wallpapers. Perhaps you can find one that matches the Companions, Inc. corporate look. When you choose a wallpaper, you can display a single image in the middle of the desktop, stretch the image across the width and length of the desktop, or repeat—or **tile**—the image across the desktop.

To select a wallpaper:

1. Click **Prairie Wind** in the Wallpaper list.

TROUBLE? If the Prairie Wind wallpaper isn't available, choose a different one.

2. If necessary, click the **Picture Display** list arrow and then click **Tile** to display multiple copies of the wallpaper image repeated across the entire desktop.

3. Click the **Apply** button. See Figure 4-17. The resulting wallpaper is a little over-whelming. You know Beth wouldn't want this look, so you return to the Background property sheet to make a different selection.

Figure 4-17	PRAIRIE WIND IMAGE APPLIED TO THE DESKTOP

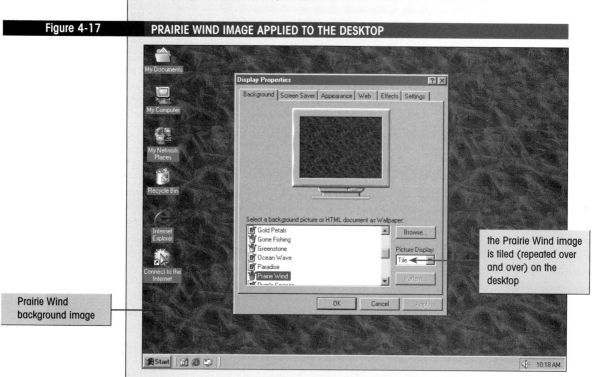

Prairie Wind background image

the Prairie Wind image is tiled (repeated over and over) on the desktop

4. Experiment with the other wallpapers available on your computer by clicking them in the Wallpaper list and previewing them. Click the **Apply** button to see each wallpaper on your desktop rather than just in the preview monitor.

TROUBLE? Some wallpapers will require you to have Active Desktop installed. **Active Desktop** is a feature of Windows 2000 that allows you to place Web components such as Web pages directly on your desktop. If you receive this prompt, click No (so as not to change the configuration of your computer) and try a different wallpaper.

5. Click **(None)** when you have finished examining the wallpaper styles.

6. Click the **Pattern** button, scroll to the top of the Pattern list, click **(None)**, click the **OK** button in the Pattern dialog box, and then click the **Apply** button on the Background property sheet. Your desktop is restored to the default position, and the Display Properties dialog box remains open.

None of the wallpapers that come with Windows 2000 suits Beth's corporate image, so you ask her if she would like to use a graphic of her company logo. She is enthusiastic; it would be great if clients who come to the offices could see the company logo on the office computers.

To use a graphic image as custom wallpaper:

1. If necessary, place your Data Disk in drive A.

2. Click the **Browse** button on the Background property sheet.

3. Click the **Look in** list arrow, and then click **3½ Floppy (A:)**.

4. Click the file **Logo**.

   TROUBLE? If Logo appears as Logo.bmp, click Logo.bmp. Your computer is set to display file extensions.

5. Click the **Open** button.

6. Click the **Display** list arrow, and then click **Center** to center the image on the screen.

7. Click the **OK** button to close the Display Properties dialog box. See Figure 4-18. The logo for Companions, Inc. appears in the middle of the desktop.

Figure 4-18	COMPANIONS LOGO APPLIED AS WALLPAPER

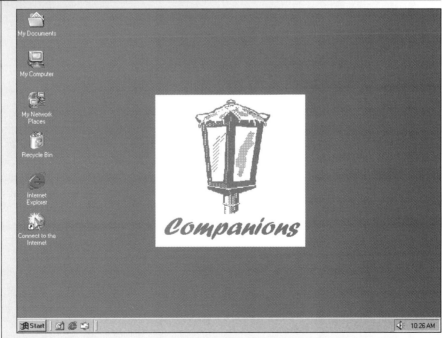

Changing Your Desktop's Appearance

Beth looks over your shoulder and comments that the red of the logo doesn't go very well with the blue of the screen background. She asks if you can try other background colors. The Appearance property sheet gives you control over the color not only of the desktop background but also of all the items on the screen: icons, title bars, borders, menus, scroll bars, and so on.

To view the Appearance property sheet:

1. Right-click an empty area of the desktop, and then click **Properties**.

2. Click the **Appearance** tab. The Appearance property sheet is shown in Figure 4-19.

Figure 4-19	APPEARANCE PROPERTY SHEET

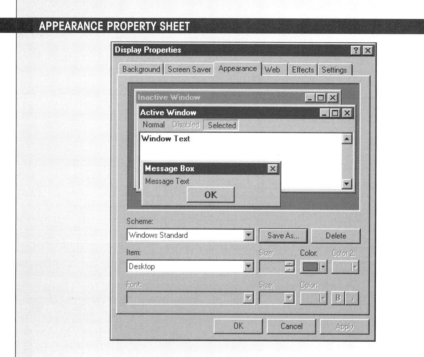

The Appearance property sheet includes several list boxes from which you choose options to change the desktop's appearance. Notice the Scheme list box. A **scheme** is a desktop design. Windows 2000 includes a collection of schemes. You can create your own by working with the Appearance property sheet until you arrive at a look you like, and then using the Save As button to save all the changes as one scheme. The default scheme is Windows Standard. However, if your computer is in a lab, your technical support person might have designed and selected a different scheme. Before you experiment with the appearance of your desktop, you should write down the current scheme so you can restore it later.

The preview in the Appearance property sheet displays many of the elements you are likely to see when working with Windows 2000. You can click an item in the preview to change its color, and sometimes its font or size. You want to change the desktop itself to white. The Item list box currently displays "Desktop," so any changes you make in the Color list affect the desktop.

To change the color of your desktop to white:

1. Write down the name of the current scheme, which is displayed in the Scheme list box.

   TROUBLE? If your Scheme list box is empty, your technical support person might have changed scheme settings without saving the scheme. Each time you change an object's color, write down the original color so you can restore that object's color when you are finished.

2. Make sure the Item list box displays Desktop.

   TROUBLE? If the Item list box does not display Desktop, click the Item list arrow, scroll until you see Desktop, and then click Desktop.

3. Click the **Color** list arrow and then click **white**, the first box in the first row. See Figure 4-20.

Figure 4-20	CHANGING THE COLOR OF THE DESKTOP

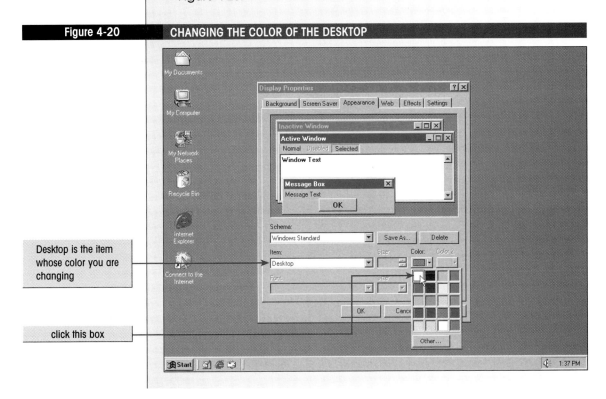

Desktop is the item whose color you are changing

click this box

   The desktop color in the preview changes to white. Notice that the Scheme list box is now empty because you are no longer using the default scheme. You realize that blue title bars might look strange in contrast to the red and white desktop. You decide to change the title bars to red. To change an element, you either click it in the preview or select it from the Item list.

To change the title bars to red:

1. Click the **Active Window** title bar in the preview window. See Figure 4-21 for the location of this title bar. Note that the Item list box now displays "Active Title Bar."

2. Click the **Color** list arrow (in the same row as the Item box) and then click **red**, the first box in the second row. See Figure 4-21.

TROUBLE? If your Color 2 box displays a color, change it to red too. In Figure 4-21 the Color 2 box is gray because in this color scheme, active title bars use only one color.

Figure 4-21	CHANGING THE COLOR OF THE ACTIVE TITLE BARS

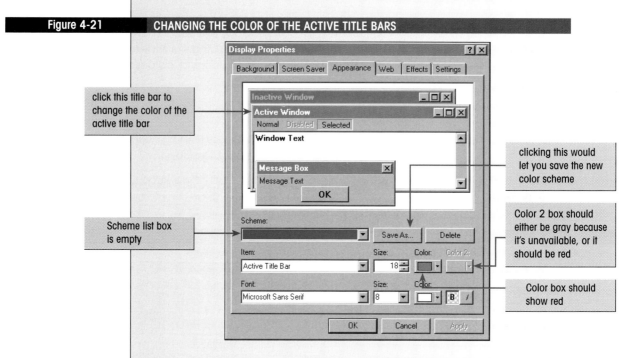

click this title bar to change the color of the active title bar

clicking this would let you save the new color scheme

Color 2 box should either be gray because it's unavailable, or it should be red

Scheme list box is empty

Color box should show red

3. Click the **OK** button to see how the desktop looks. See Figure 4-22.

Figure 4-22	APPEARANCE OF MODIFIED DESKTOP

The next time you open a dialog box, you'll see a red title bar. First you'll open My Computer to view the changed title bar, and then you'll restore the desktop to its original settings. You can do this by simply selecting the scheme you wrote down earlier. You could save the colors that match Beth's logo as a scheme if you wanted to. To do this, you would open the Display Properties dialog box, click the Save As button, type a name for your scheme, and then click the OK button.

To restore the desktop colors and wallpaper to their original settings:

1. Open **My Computer** and observe its red title bar. Then close **My Computer**.

2. Right-click an empty area of the desktop, and then click **Properties**.

3. Click the **Appearance** tab.

4. Click the **Scheme** list arrow, and then locate and click the scheme you wrote down earlier. Most likely this is Windows Standard, which you will find at the bottom of the list.

   TROUBLE? If your Scheme list box was blank when you began working with the Appearance property sheet, skip Step 3 and instead restore each setting you changed to the original color you wrote down in the beginning of this section. Then proceed to Step 5.

5. Click the **Background** tab to open the Background property sheet.

6. Scroll to the top of the **Wallpaper** list and then click **(None)**.

7. Click the **Apply** button. The original desktop is restored, and the Display Properties dialog box remains open.

Activating a Screen Saver

A **screen saver** blanks the screen or displays a moving design whenever you haven't worked with the computer for a specified period of time. In older monitors, a screen saver can help prevent "burn-in," or the permanent etching of an image into the screen, which occurs when the same image is displayed for long periods of time. This is not a concern with newer monitors. Screen savers are still handy for hiding your data from the eyes of passers-by if you step away from your computer. When a screen saver is on, you restore your screen by moving your mouse or pressing a key.

You can select how long you want the computer to sit idle before the screen saver activates. Most users find settings between 3 and 10 minutes to be the most convenient. You can change the setting by clicking the up or down arrow on the Wait box, as you'll see in the next set of steps.

Windows 2000 provides a wide variety of screen savers. Beth would like a screen saver that displays the name of the company. One of the Windows 2000 screen savers accomplishes this. You decide to show her how to set up this screen saver.

To activate a screen saver:

1. Click the **Screen Saver** tab in the Display Properties dialog box.

2. Select **3D Text (OpenGL)** from the Screen Saver list box.

TROUBLE? If 3D Text (Open GL) is not displayed in the Screen Saver list box, do not select a different screen saver, but review the rest of the steps in this example.

3. Click the **Settings** button.

4. Note the text that has been entered into the Text box located in the upper-left corner of the 3D Text Setup dialog box. You'll need to reenter this text later, so write it down now.

5. Select the text in the Text box and then type **Companions, Inc.**. See Figure 4-23.

Figure 4-23   **THE 3D TEXT SETUP DIALOG BOX**

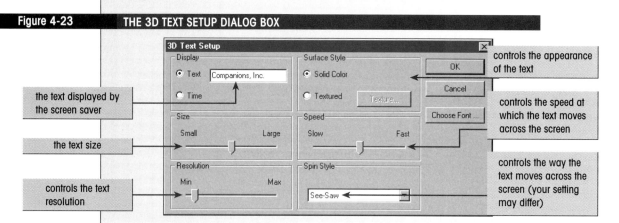

The 3D Text Setup dialog box contains several options you can set to control the screen saver. You can control the speed at which the text appears on the screen, the size of the text, the texture or color of the text, and also the way the text moves across the screen. You'll keep the defaults for all of these options.

6. Click the **OK** button.

The Preview window in the Screen Saver property sheet shows a preview of the screen saver. See Figure 4-24. You can also get a full-screen preview of the screen saver.

7. Click the **Preview** button.

The screen saver fills the screen.

TROUBLE? If you move the mouse after clicking the Preview button, the screen saver will disappear, sometimes so quickly that you can't even see it. Repeat Step 7, but make sure you don't move the mouse after you click the Preview button.

8. When you're done previewing the screen saver, click the **Settings** button again and enter the text that was initially displayed in the Text box. Click the **OK** button to close the 3D Text Setup dialog box.

9. Click the **Cancel** button to cancel your screen saver changes and close the Display Properties dialog box. If you were working on your own computer and wanted to save the changes, you would click the Apply button to save the changes or the OK button to save the changes and close the Display Properties dialog box.

Figure 4-24   **THE SCREEN SAVER PROPERTY SHEET**

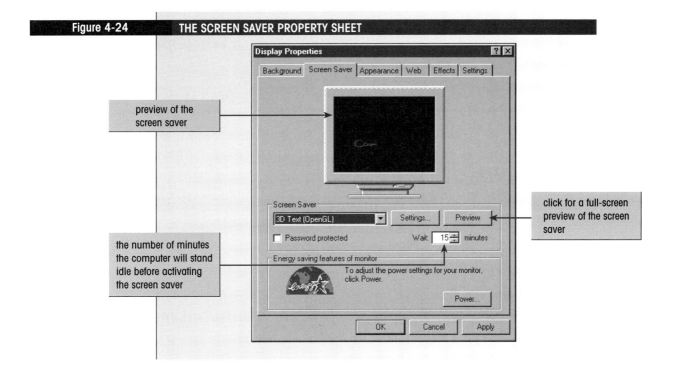

preview of the
screen saver

click for a full-screen
preview of the screen
saver

the number of minutes
the computer will stand
idle before activating
the screen saver

Changing **Display Settings**

The Settings property sheet allows you to control additional settings that you might never need to consider. However, if you want to take full advantage of your monitor type, you should be aware of the options you have on the Settings property sheet. The settings you can change depend on your monitor type and on the **video card** inside your computer that controls visual information you see on the screen. Windows 2000 allows you to use more than one monitor, so you might be able to change settings for multiple monitors.

Changing the Size of the Desktop Area

The Screen area slider bar on the Settings property sheet lets you display less or more of the screen on your monitor. If you display less, objects will look bigger, while if you display more, objects will look smaller. You can drag the slider bar between these two extremes. You are actually increasing or decreasing the **resolution**, or sharpness, of the image. Resolution is measured by the number of individual dots, called **pixels**, short for "picture elements," that run across and down your monitor. The more pixels, the more you see on the screen at one time, and the smaller the objects look.

The 640 x 480 (640 pixels across and 480 pixels down) resolution shows the least information, but uses the largest text and is preferred by most users with 14-inch monitors. The 800 x 600 resolution shows more information, but uses smaller text. Many users with 15-inch monitors prefer the 800 x 600 resolution. This is the setting that Beth's computers use. The 1024 x 768 resolution shows the most information, but uses the smallest text. Most users find the 1024 x 768 resolution too small for comfortable use unless they are using a 17-inch or larger monitor. Users with limited vision might prefer the 640 x 480 setting even on larger monitors, because objects and text are bigger and easier to see. You might also want to change your monitor's resolution, depending on what software you are using.

To change the size of the desktop area:

1. Right-click an empty area of the desktop and then click **Properties**.

2. Click the **Settings** tab to display the Settings properties.

3. Write down the original setting in the Screen area so you can restore it after experimenting with it.

4. To select the 640 by 480 resolution, if it is not already selected, drag the Screen area slider to the left. The preview monitor shows the relative size of the 640 x 480 display. See Figure 4-25.

Figure 4-25	640 BY 480 RESOLUTION

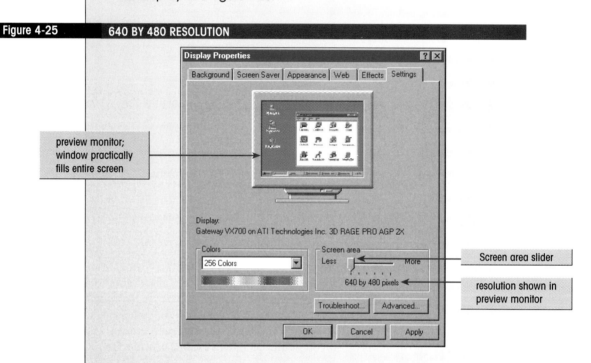

preview monitor; window practically fills entire screen

Screen area slider

resolution shown in preview monitor

5. To select the 800 x 600 resolution, drag the **Screen area** slider to the right. The preview monitor shows the relative size of the 800 by 600 display.

6. Return the slider to the setting you wrote down in Step 3. Leave the Display Properties dialog box open.

Changing the Color Palette

You can also use the Settings property sheet to change the color palette, which specifies the number of colors available to your computer. Beth's computers have a 256-color palette. Figure 4-26 provides additional information on common palettes.

Figure 4-26	COLOR PALETTES
PALETTE	**DESCRIPTION**
16 colors	Very fast, requires the least video memory, sufficient for use with most programs but not adequate for most graphics
256 colors	Relatively fast, requires a moderate amount of video memory, sufficient for most programs and adequate for the graphics in most games and educational programs. This is a good setting for general use.
High color	Requires higher-quality video card and additional video memory. This setting is useful for sophisticated painting, drawing, and graphics manipulation tasks.
True color	Requires the most video memory and runs most slowly. This setting is useful for professional graphics tasks, but might not be available or might be too slow on some computer systems.

Once you change the color palette, you are prompted to reboot Windows 2000. In the next set of steps, you will see how to change the color palette—but to avoid rebooting, you won't actually do so.

To view the color palette options:

1. Click the **Colors** list arrow to display the list of color palettes. See Figure 4-27.

Figure 4-27	COLOR PALETTES

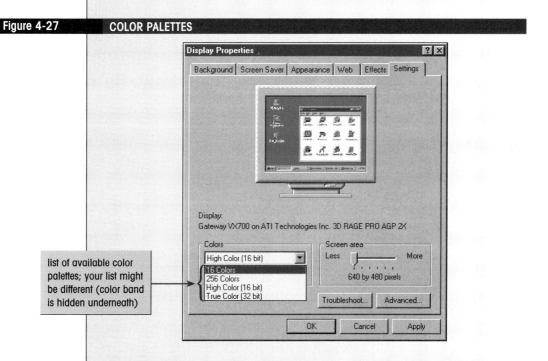

list of available color palettes; your list might be different (color band is hidden underneath)

2. Click **16 Colors** and observe that the color band below the Colors list box displays only 16 colors.

TROUBLE? If 16 Colors doesn't appear in your Colors list, skip Step 2.

3. Click the **Colors** list arrow again, and then click **256 Colors**. Now the color band displays a greater range of colors.

4. Click the **Cancel** button to close the Display Properties dialog box without accepting any changes you might have inadvertently made.

5. If you are working in a school lab, make sure you have changed all settings back to their original state before moving on to Session 4.3.

QUICK CHECK

1. True or False: Although a document is an object, and so is a drive, the desktop is not an object.

2. How do you open an object's property sheet?

3. Name three desktop properties you can change from the Display Properties dialog box.

4. If you have an older monitor and you want to protect it from damage caused by displaying the same image for a long time, what can you do?

5. What does it mean to say that a monitor's resolution is 640 x 480?

6. Users with limited vision might want to use which resolution: 640 x 480, 800 x 600, or 1024 x 768? Why?

7. What is the disadvantage of using a color palette with many colors, such as True Color?

SESSION 4.3

In this session you'll work with your taskbar and Start menu. You'll learn how to modify the appearance and location of the taskbar. You'll see how to add items to the taskbar. You'll work with the properties of the Start menu: how to add items to the menu and how to modify the existing menu items. Finally, you'll learn about the Control Panel, another Windows 2000 tool that makes it easy for you to change the properties of different objects on your computer.

Modifying the Taskbar

So far you've shown Beth how to work with the properties of the Windows 2000 desktop. There are two other parts of the Windows 2000 screen that you haven't worked with yet: the taskbar and the Start menu. You'll start by showing her how to work with the taskbar.

Moving and Resizing the Taskbar

Beth's previous computer was a Macintosh, and she's used to seeing a menu bar at the top of the desktop. She wants to know how to revise the position of the taskbar to create this familiar appearance.

To move the taskbar:

1. Click any blank spot on the taskbar and, with the left mouse button pressed down, drag the pointer to the top of the desktop.

2. Release the left mouse button when the taskbar appears at the top of the desk-top. See Figure 4-28. Notice that the icons moved down slightly to make room for the taskbar.

| Figure 4-28 | MOVING THE WINDOWS 2000 TASKBAR TO THE TOP OF THE SCREEN |

taskbar at top of screen ⟶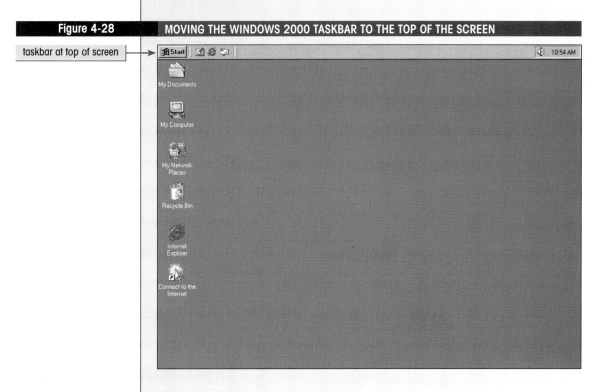

3. Click a blank spot on the taskbar and, with the left mouse button pressed, move the taskbar back down to the bottom of the screen.

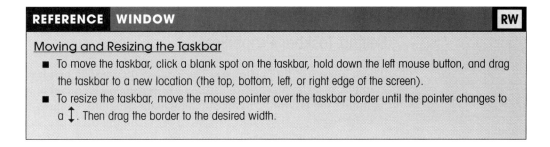

REFERENCE WINDOW **RW**

Moving and Resizing the Taskbar
- To move the taskbar, click a blank spot on the taskbar, hold down the left mouse button, and drag the taskbar to a new location (the top, bottom, left, or right edge of the screen).
- To resize the taskbar, move the mouse pointer over the taskbar border until the pointer changes to a ↕. Then drag the border to the desired width.

Beth has also noticed that when she has several programs running simultaneously, the icons for those programs fill up the taskbar, sometimes to such an extent that the individual icons are compressed beyond recognition. You tell her that one way of dealing with that problem is to increase the size of the taskbar. This is easily accomplished by dragging the taskbar border to a new location. Try this now.

To increase the size of the taskbar:

1. Move the mouse pointer over the upper edge of the taskbar until the pointer changes to ↗.

2. Click and drag the upper border upwards, releasing the left mouse button when the taskbar has increased in height. See Figure 4-29.

Figure 4-29	RESIZING THE TASKBAR

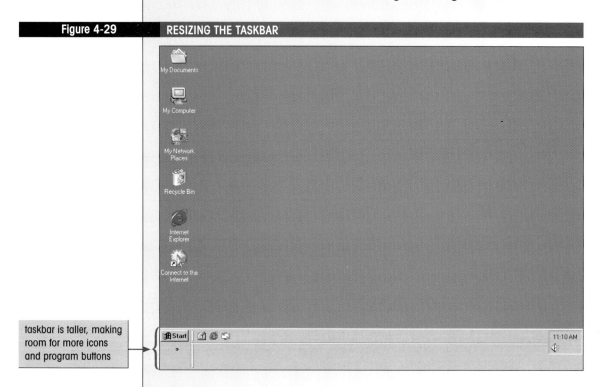

taskbar is taller, making room for more icons and program buttons

3. Click the upper taskbar border again and drag it back to its original height.

Setting Taskbar Properties

There are other properties you can set for the taskbar besides its size and position. For example, you can increase the amount of screen space available for your program windows by hiding the taskbar. Or you can allow your program windows to cover the taskbar rather than letting the taskbar take up space. Try changing these properties now.

To set other taskbar properties:

1. Right-click a blank spot in the taskbar and click **Properties** on the menu.

The Taskbar and Start Menu Properties dialog box appears, as shown in Figure 4-30.

Figure 4-30   THE TASKBAR AND START MENU PROPERTIES DIALOG BOX

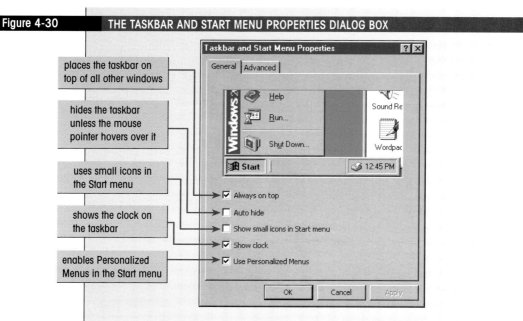

places the taskbar on top of all other windows

hides the taskbar unless the mouse pointer hovers over it

uses small icons in the Start menu

shows the clock on the taskbar

enables Personalized Menus in the Start menu

2. Write down which check boxes are currently selected in this dialog box.

3. Click to select the **Auto hide** check box, and then click the **Apply** button.

TROUBLE? If the Auto hide check box is already selected, skip Step 3.

The taskbar disappears.

4. Move the mouse pointer over the location where the taskbar previously appeared and note that the taskbar is visible as long as the mouse pointer is over it.

5. Deselect the **Auto hide** check box, and then click the **Apply** button.

6. Click to deselect the **Always on top** check box, and then click the **Apply** button.

TROUBLE? If the Always on top check box is already deselected, skip Step 6.

7. Move the Taskbar and Start Menu Properties dialog box over your taskbar. Note that the dialog box now appears over the taskbar.

8. Return the check boxes to their original state, and then click the **OK** button to close the dialog box.

Working with Taskbar Toolbars

One of the features of the taskbar is the ability to display toolbars. By default, the Windows 2000 taskbar will display the Quick Launch toolbar, containing icons for running your Web browser and accessing your mail. You can select other toolbars to display, or you can create your own customized toolbar.

Displaying a Toolbar on the Taskbar

Beth often has several programs running at once, filling up the screen and hiding the desktop. She has seen the benefit of placing icons on the desktop, but she wonders if they're going to be as useful for her. Is there a way that she can access those desktop icons without having to minimize all of her programs? She can do so, if she places a Desktop toolbar on her taskbar. The Desktop toolbar will display all of the icons that appear on her desktop.

To display the Desktop toolbar:

1. Right-click a blank area of the taskbar.

2. On the menu that appears, point to **Toolbars** and then click **Desktop**. See Figure 4-31.

| Figure 4-31 | DISPLAYING THE DESKTOP TOOLBAR |

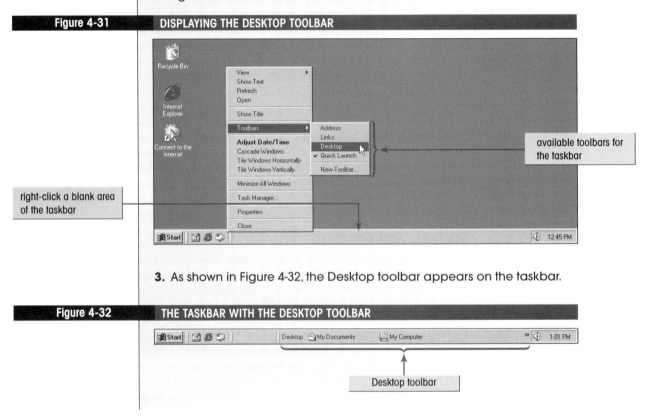

right-click a blank area of the taskbar

available toolbars for the taskbar

3. As shown in Figure 4-32, the Desktop toolbar appears on the taskbar.

| Figure 4-32 | THE TASKBAR WITH THE DESKTOP TOOLBAR |

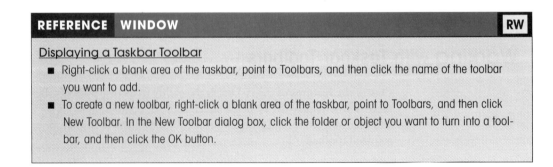

Desktop toolbar

REFERENCE WINDOW | **RW**

Displaying a Taskbar Toolbar

- Right-click a blank area of the taskbar, point to Toolbars, and then click the name of the toolbar you want to add.
- To create a new toolbar, right-click a blank area of the taskbar, point to Toolbars, and then click New Toolbar. In the New Toolbar dialog box, click the folder or object you want to turn into a toolbar, and then click the OK button.

Modifying the Appearance of a Taskbar Toolbar

Beth likes the fact that you can place the desktop icons on a toolbar, but wishes she could see more of them. She would like the toolbar to look more like the Quick Launch toolbar, with no names next to the icon and no title displayed for the toolbar. You explain that you can modify the toolbar's appearance by changing its properties.

To modify the appearance of the Desktop toolbar:

1. Right-click a blank area in the newly created Desktop toolbar.

2. On the menu, deselect **Show Text** so that no check mark appears next to the menu entry.

TROUBLE? If you don't see the Show Text entry on the menu, you may have right-clicked one of the buttons on the Desktop toolbar. Be sure to select a blank area on the toolbar.

3. Right-click a blank area in the Desktop toolbar again and deselect **Show Title** from the menu.

Figure 4-33 displays the final appearance of the toolbar. Note that each item on the desktop is matched by an item in the toolbar and that the icons are small, like those in the Quick Launch toolbar.

Figure 4-33	THE MODIFIED DESKTOP TOOLBAR

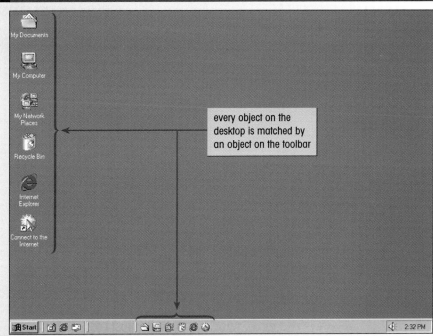

every object on the desktop is matched by an object on the toolbar

Now Beth can access all the items on her desktop without minimizing open windows.

Creating a Custom Toolbar

Beth is happy with the new appearance of the taskbar. She notices that when she clicks the My Computer icon on the Desktop toolbar it opens the My Computer window. Beth finds the My Computer window useful and wonders if you could create a toolbar on the taskbar displaying all of the icons in the My Computer window. This would give her even quicker access to all of the drives on her computer.

To create a toolbar for the My Computer window:

1. Right-click a blank area on the taskbar, point to **Toolbars**, and then click **New Toolbar**.

   A dialog box opens from which you can select a drive, folder, or object whose contents you want to display in a toolbar. You want to display the contents of the My Computer window, which lies at the top of the Windows 2000 hierarchy of objects.

2. Click **My Computer** in the New Toolbar dialog box and then click the **OK** button.

3. The My Computer toolbar appears on the taskbar.

4. Right-click a blank spot on the My Computer toolbar and deselect **Show Text** on the menu.

5. Right-click a blank spot on the My Computer toolbar again and deselect **Show Title** on the menu.

   Figure 4-34 displays the new My Computer toolbar on your taskbar.

| Figure 4-34 | THE MY COMPUTER TOOLBAR |

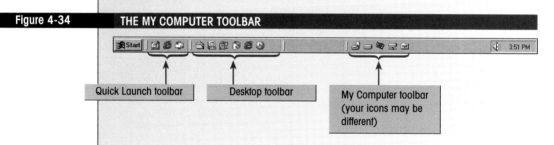

Quick Launch toolbar   Desktop toolbar   My Computer toolbar (your icons may be different)

Removing a Taskbar Toolbar

Having seen how to create and modify toolbars on the taskbar, you should now restore the taskbar to its original state, deleting the Desktop and My Computer toolbars. Note that this will not affect the desktop or the My Computer window. These toolbars contain shortcuts to those objects, not the objects themselves.

To remove a toolbar from the taskbar:

1. Right-click a blank spot on the taskbar and then point to **Toolbars**.

2. Click **Desktop** in the list of toolbars displayed in the submenu to deselect it.

   The menu closes and the Desktop toolbar is removed.

3. Right-click a blank spot on the taskbar again and then point to **Toolbars**.

4. Deselect **My Computer** in the list of toolbars.

Both the Desktop and My Computer toolbars should now be removed from your taskbar.

Editing the Start Menu

The final component on your Windows 2000 screen that you can customize is the Start menu. Most of the items in the Start menu are created for you by Windows 2000 or by the various programs you install. However, you also can determine the content and appearance of your Start menu, removing items you don't use and adding those you do.

Controlling the Appearance of the Start Menu

The first aspect of the Start menu's appearance that you can control is whether the menu uses small or large icons. The default is to use large icons, but you can save screen space by changing this to the smaller icon style.

The second customizable aspect of the Start menu is whether or not personalized menus are used. **Personalized menus** are menus that change depending on your work habits, showing those items in the Start menu you use most often and temporarily hiding items you seldom use. You still have easy access to "hidden" items: you may have noticed a set of double arrows pointing down on some of the menus in the Start menu. If you click those double arrows, you'll display those items that Windows 2000 has chosen to hide. Figure 4-35 shows the Start menu with and without the personalized menu option enabled.

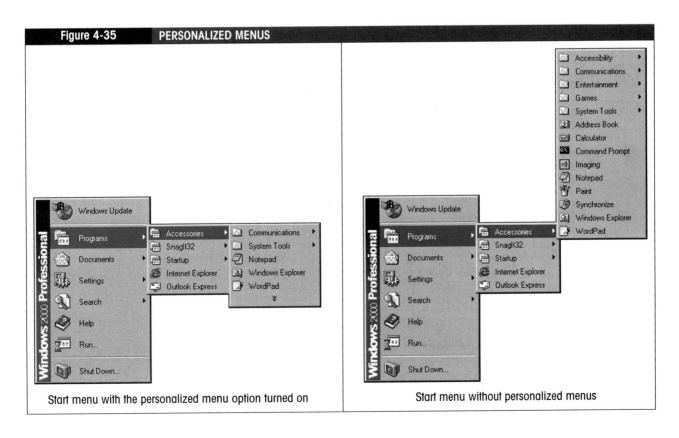

| Figure 4-35 | PERSONALIZED MENUS |

Start menu with the personalized menu option turned on

Start menu without personalized menus

Personalized menus are an effective way to reduce the clutter of the Start menu, a feature you'll appreciate as you add more and more items to the menu. However, at first you may find personalized menus confusing as you try to locate a specific menu item that does not appear right away.

Because the Start button is considered part of the taskbar, you change settings for the Start menu using the same dialog box you used earlier to control the appearance of the taskbar. As shown earlier in Figure 4-30, you can select and deselect the check boxes that turn features on and off.

Adding an Item to the Start Menu

Most of the work you'll do in modifying the Start menu will be to modify its content, adding and deleting items. Like the desktop and the taskbar, the Start menu can contain shortcut icons to give you one-click access to your most important programs, folders, and files.

REFERENCE WINDOW　　　　　　　　　　　　　　　　　　　　　　　**RW**

Adding an Item to the Start Menu
- Right-click a blank area of the taskbar, and then click Properties.
- Click the Advanced tab in the dialog box, and then click the Add button.
- In the Create Shortcut Wizard, locate the file, folder, or object that you want to add to the Start menu, and then specify a name and icon for the item. Finish the Create Shortcut Wizard.

Beth wants to see how she could use the Start menu to get quick access to her floppy drive.

To create a floppy drive icon on the Start menu:

1. Right-click an empty area on the taskbar and then click **Properties** on the menu.

2. Click the **Advanced** tab.

3. Click the **Add** button.

   The Create Shortcut Wizard starts (a **wizard** is a series of dialog boxes that help you complete tasks). From this dialog box you specify the location of the object, folder, or file to which you want to create a shortcut.

4. Click the **Browse** button.

5. Click the ⊞ **3½ Floppy (A:)** icon and then click the **OK** button.

6. Click the **Next** button.

   Now you'll specify where on the Start menu you want to place the shortcut to the floppy drive. In this case, you'll specify the main menu of the Start menu. Note that you could also add an item to any one of the submenus or create a new folder (or submenu) of your own.

7. Click **Start Menu** in the Select Program Folder window, as shown in Figure 4-36, and then click the **Next** button.

| Figure 4-36 | SELECTING THE LOCATION FOR THE NEW START MENU ITEM |

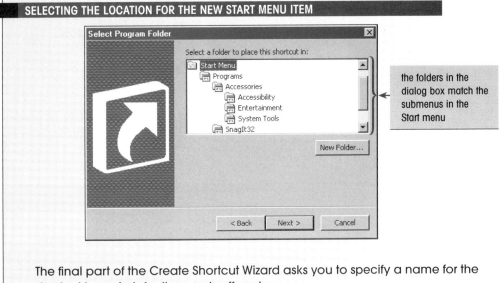

the folders in the dialog box match the submenus in the Start menu

The final part of the Create Shortcut Wizard asks you to specify a name for the shortcut icon. A default name is offered.

8. Keep the default name, "3½ Floppy (A)," offered by the Shortcut Wizard, and then click the **Finish** button.

9. Leave the Taskbar and Start Menu Properties dialog box open.

Now test your new Start menu entry to verify that it will open your floppy drive for you.

To test the new Start menu entry:

1. Click the ⊞Start **Start** button.

2. Click **3½ Floppy (A)** on the Start menu. See Figure 4-37.

| Figure 4-37 | NEW ITEM ON THE START MENU |

new item on the Start menu to access the floppy drive

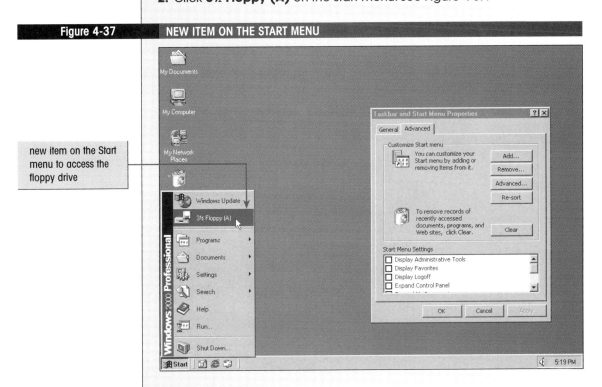

> The contents of the floppy drive are displayed in a window.
>
> 3. Click the **Close** button [X] to close the window.

Removing an Item from the Start Menu

Now that you've seen how to create a Start menu item by yourself, you should remove it so that the Start menu returns to its default position. To remove a Start menu item, you use the same dialog box you opened to create one.

REFERENCE WINDOW   RW

Removing a Start Menu Item
- Right-click a blank area of the taskbar, and then click Properties.
- Click the Advanced tab in the dialog box that appears, and then click the Remove button.
- Select the item in the Remove Shortcuts/Folders dialog box that you want to remove, and then click the OK button.

To remove the floppy drive item from the Start menu:

1. Click the **Remove** button in the Advanced dialog sheet in the Taskbar and Start Menu Properties dialog box.

2. Click **3½ Floppy (A)** in the list of Start menu items and then click the **Remove** button.

   Note that you are only removing the floppy drive shortcut from your Start menu; other methods of opening the floppy drive will remain unchanged.

3. Click the **Yes** button to confirm that you want to remove 3½ Floppy (A) from the Start menu.

4. Click the **Close** button to close the Remove Shortcuts/Folders dialog box.

5. Click the [Start] **Start** button again to confirm that the floppy disk item has been removed from the Start menu, and then click outside the menus to close them.

6. Leave the Taskbar and Start menu Properties dialog box open.

Choosing Start Menu Settings

Windows 2000 also includes a list of options or settings for your Start menu. These settings include the ability to display the contents of your My Documents folder, a list of available printers, or a list of favorite Web pages and files. Figure 4-38 describes the settings that you can turn on or off on your Start menu.

Figure 4-38	START MENU SETTINGS

SETTING	DESCRIPTION
Display Administrative Tools	Display a menu of tools used to administer Windows 2000 and your computer
Display Favorites	Display a list of your favorite Web sites, files, and folders
Display Logoff	Display the Logoff command for use on computers with multiple users
Expand Control Panel	Display individual applets in the Control Panel
Expand My Documents	Display the contents of the My Documents folder
Expand Network and Dial-up Connections	Display individual computers on your network
Expand Printers	Display individual printers attached to your computer
Scroll the Programs Menu	Add scrolling to the Programs Menu (used for very long lists of programs and program groups)

By default, all of these settings are turned off. Beth is interested in adding the printer list to the Start menu so she can have quick access to the printers in her office. You'll show her how this could be done.

To display the printer list in the Start menu:

1. In the Start Menu Settings list box at the bottom of the Advanced tab, scroll to and click the **Expand Printers** check box to select it.

TROUBLE? If the Expand Printers check box is already selected, skip Step 1.

2. Click the **Apply** button.

3. Click the [Start] **Start** button, point to **Settings**, and then point to **Printers** to display the list of printers available on your computer. See Figure 4-39.

Figure 4-39	DISPLAYING THE PRINTER LIST IN THE START MENU

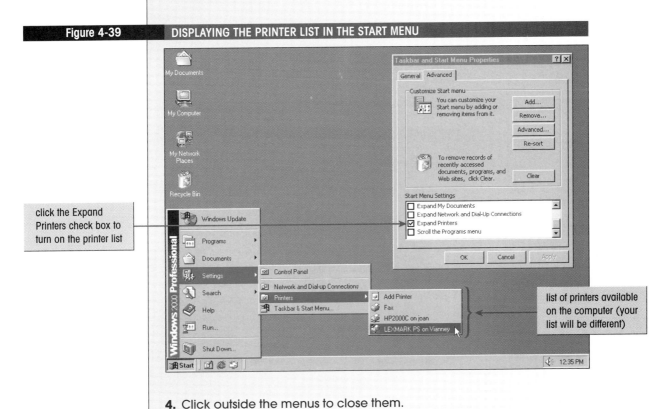

click the Expand Printers check box to turn on the printer list

list of printers available on the computer (your list will be different)

4. Click outside the menus to close them.

As she allows the mouse pointer to hover over each printer icon in the list, a box appears telling Beth the status of the printer (whether it's ready to print or not) and the number of documents queued up (waiting to be printed). This is valuable information for Beth as she works with the variety of printers installed at the company's offices.

To remove the printer list from the Start menu:

1. If the Expand Printers check box was *not* selected before you started this exercise, click the **Expand Printers** check box to deselect it.

2. Click the **OK** button to close the Taskbar and Start Menu Properties dialog box.

Using the Control Panel

You've worked with a variety of objects and properties in this tutorial: the desktop, your display, the Start menu, and the taskbar. There are even more objects and properties on your computer that you haven't examined yet. Windows 2000 organizes some of these objects into the **Control Panel**.

To open the Control Panel:

1. Click the [Start] **Start** button, point to **Settings**, and then click **Control Panel**.

   TROUBLE? If a message appears indicating that the Control Panel is not available, you might be in a computer lab with limited customization access. Ask your instructor or technical support person for options.

2. Click **View** and then click **List** to display the icons in a list, as shown in Figure 4-40.

   TROUBLE? Because some tools are optional, your Control Panel might display different tools than the ones shown in Figure 4-40.

Figure 4-40	CONTROL PANEL

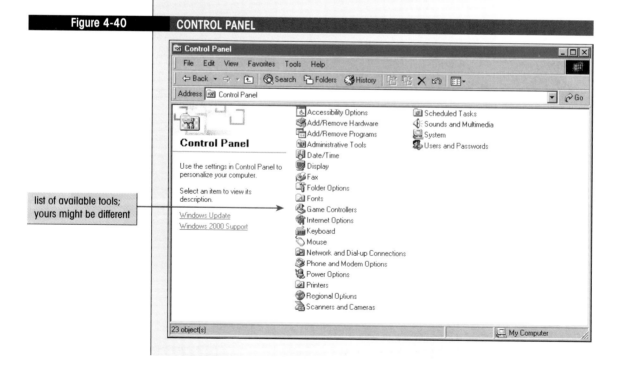

list of available tools;
yours might be different

As you look through the icons in the Control Panel, you'll see some familiar objects. The Display icon opens the Display Properties dialog box, which you've used for controlling the properties of your display (the wallpaper, background, screen saver, etc.). You'll also see many unfamiliar objects. The Folder Options icon allows you to customize how you interact with files on your computer; for example, whether you open files by a single mouse click or a double-click. Other icons allow you to control the workings of your mouse, keyboard, and modem. For more information on working with the Control Panel, see Appendix B.

Beth is impressed with the degree of customization possible with Windows 2000. One of the most exciting features of Windows 2000 is the way it lends itself to the needs of its users. Your ability to customize Windows 2000 in a lab setting is limited, and the settings are likely to be changed by the next user. But if you are running Windows 2000 on your own computer, you will find that designing a desktop that reflects your needs is time well spent. In creating a document-centric desktop you should keep one thing in mind: having too many icons on the desktop defeats the purpose of giving quick access to your documents. If you have icons crowded all over the desktop, it is difficult to locate the one you want quickly.

If you are working in a lab setting, make sure you return all settings to their original state before leaving the lab.

QUICK | CHECK

1. How do you move the taskbar to the left side of your computer screen?

2. To hide the taskbar, select _____ from the Taskbar and Start Menu Properties dialog box.

3. By default, Windows 2000 displays the _____ toolbar on the taskbar.

4. True or False: To create your own customized Start menu, the Use Personalized Menus check box must be selected.

5. To modify the collection of objects and properties on your computer, you can open the _____ _____.

REVIEW ASSIGNMENTS

1. **Creating Shortcuts** Practice placing a document on the desktop and printing it, using a printer shortcut icon.
   a. Create a shortcut on the desktop to the printer you use regularly.
   b. Open Notepad and create a new text document on your desktop, typing your name and the list of classes you are taking. Name this document **Classes**. Close Notepad.
   c. Drag the Classes document icon to the printer shortcut. Your document prints.
   d. Now use the techniques you learned in the previous tutorial to print an image of your desktop. (Use the Print Screen key to save an image of the desktop, open WordPad, type your name and the date at the top of the document, paste the image into WordPad, and then print the image from WordPad.)
   e. When you are finished, delete both icons from your desktop.

2. **Create a Shortcut to a Folder** Beth recently assigned Sally Hanson, an undergraduate at one of the local colleges, to provide housekeeping for three clients. Sally plans to be out of the area over spring break, so Beth needs to write a memo to each client, asking if they need replacement help. Beth would like to be able to get at the correspondence concerning Sally Hanson more easily.

  a. Start Windows Explorer, and then create a new folder called Sally on your Data Disk.

  b. Start Notepad, and then compose the three memos, typing in your own text. Save the memos in the Sally folder on your Data Disk with the names **Smith**, **Arruga**, and **Kosta** (the names of the three clients). Close Notepad when you are finished.

  c. Drag the Sally folder from Windows Explorer to the desktop, using the right mouse button, and then click Create Shortcut(s) Here.

  d. Name the shortcut icon Sally.

  e. Test the shortcut icon by opening the Sally folder, and then open one of the memos. Use two different methods to open these two objects, and write down which methods you used.

  f. Arrange your desktop so you can see the open memo in Notepad, the open folder window, and the shortcut icon. You might need to resize the windows to make them smaller. Then print an image of the desktop (see step 1d, above).

  g. Remove the desktop shortcut to the folder when you are done.

3. **Create a New Bitmap on the Desktop** In this tutorial, you created a new text document directly on the desktop. In this tutorial assignment, you'll create a new bitmap image document on your Data Disk. You'll use the mouse to write your signature. Then you'll use this bitmap image as the wallpaper on your desktop.

  a. Use My Computer to open drive A and display the contents of your Data Disk.

  b. Right-click an empty area of the drive A window, point to New, and then click Bitmap Image.

  c. Name the new file **My Signature**.

  d. Open **My Signature**. What program does Windows 2000 use to open this file?

  e. Drag the mouse over the empty canvas to write your signature (this will be awkward for even experienced mouse users).

  f. Exit the program, and save your changes. Close the drive A window.

  g. Right-click an empty area of the desktop, click Properties, and then make sure the Background property sheet is visible.

  h. Click the Browse button, and then use the Look in list arrow at the top of the dialog box to select the 3½ floppy drive. Select the **My Signature** bitmap image on your Data Disk, and then click the Open button. Your signature appears as the wallpaper in the preview monitor.

  i. Print an image of the screen (see step 1d, above).

  j. Click the Cancel button to preserve the desktop's original appearance.

4. **Explore Your Computer's Desktop Properties** Answer each of the following questions about the desktop properties on your lab computers.

  a. Open the Display Properties dialog box. What resolution is your monitor using? What other resolution settings are available for your monitor? Drag the slider to find out. If it's an older monitor, it might not have higher resolutions available.

b. What color palette are you using?

c. Is Windows 2000 using a screen saver on your machine? Which one? After how many minutes of idle time does it engage?

d. What is your desktop's default color scheme?

e. Does your desktop display a pattern or wallpaper? Which one?

Explore

f. Open the Power Management Properties dialog box from the Screen Saver tab. What power scheme is your computer using, if any? What settings are in effect for that power scheme?

Explore

g. In the Power Management Properties dialog box, click the Advanced tab. Turn on the option to show the power meter on the taskbar. A power icon, like a plug, appears in the tray. Point at the power icon. What ScreenTip appears? Go back to the Power Management Properties dialog box, turn this option off, and then close the Power Management Properties dialog box.

5. **Customizing Your Desktop** The ability to place icons directly on the desktop gives you the opportunity to create a truly document-centric desktop. Figure 4-41 shows Beth's desktop after she's had a chance to create all the shortcuts you recommended and to add additional shortcuts for programs, folders, files, and other resources she uses regularly.

Figure 4-41

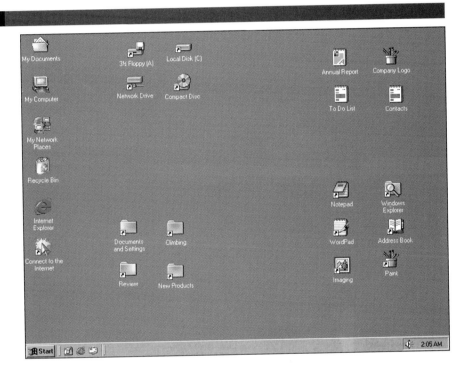

Notice that this desktop has shortcuts not just for drives and documents, but also for programs, utilities, and other Windows 2000 objects. Also notice that the icons are arranged logically and that there aren't so many as to make them hard to find. The amount of time you save by arranging your desktop in this manner cannot be overestimated, if you spend a lot of time at the computer. If you have your own computer, create a desktop that meets your needs.

Use the following strategy:

a. Use Windows Explorer to locate the drives on your computer, and then create a shortcut on the desktop to each of the local or network drives you use regularly.

b. If you haven't done so already, use Windows Explorer to create folders for the work you usually do on your computer. You might want a folder for each class you're taking, letters you write, projects, or hobbies. Then create a shortcut on the desktop to each folder you use regularly.

c. Create shortcuts for each document you use repeatedly. Remember not to overcrowd your desktop.

d. If you know how to locate program and utility files, create shortcuts on the desktop to the programs and utilities you use most often.

e. Group the icons on your desktop so that similar objects are in the same location.

f. Print a copy of your desktop in its final form (see step 1d, above).

6. **Customizing Your Start Menu** A simple way of adding icons to your Start menu is to use drag and drop. For example, you can click a file icon and drag it onto a submenu of the Start menu, and Windows 2000 will automatically create a shortcut to the file for you. Similarly, you can remove any item from the Start menu by clicking the item and dragging it off the Start menu. For example, dragging a Start menu item off the Start menu and onto the desktop moves the shortcut to the desktop. Dragging the same item off the Start menu and onto the Recycle Bin deletes the shortcut.

Figure 4-42 shows a Start menu containing shortcuts to the My Computer and the My Network Places windows. While most Start menu items can be created using either the drag-and-drop technique or the Add method in the Taskbar and Start Menu Properties dialog box, these two new items can be created *only* by dragging and dropping. Try this technique by performing steps a–e below.

Figure 4-42

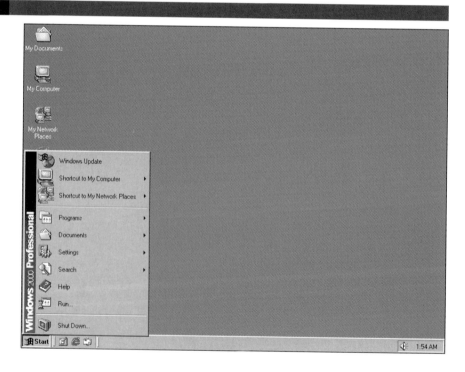

Explore

   a. Drag the My Computer icon to the Start button (you will have to hover over the Start button for a few seconds to allow it to open) and drop the icon at the top of the menu.

   b. Add the My Network Places icon to the top of the Start menu in the same way.

   c. Print a copy of the Start menu you created, showing the two new entries (see step 1d, above).

   d. When you view the contents of the My Computer icon and the My Network Places icon in the Start menu, what you do you see? Discuss how the My Computer icon in the Start menu could replace Windows Explorer as a tool to navigate the contents of your computer's drives and folders. What are the advantages and disadvantages of using the Start menu and My Computer this way? Does this approach work better for floppy drives or for your hard drive—and why?

   e. Remove the My Computer and Network Places icons from the Start menu by dragging them to the Recycle Bin, one at a time.

7. **Customizing a Taskbar Toolbar** You can also use the drag-and-drop technique to customize a taskbar toolbar. By dragging an icon from a folder or the desktop onto one of the toolbars on the taskbar, you can create additional buttons for quick one-click access to your favorite files and programs.

Figure 4-43 shows a modified Quick Launch toolbar with icons for Notepad, WordPad, and Windows Explorer added. Make similar changes to your Quick Launch toolbar by performing steps a–g below.

Figure 4-43

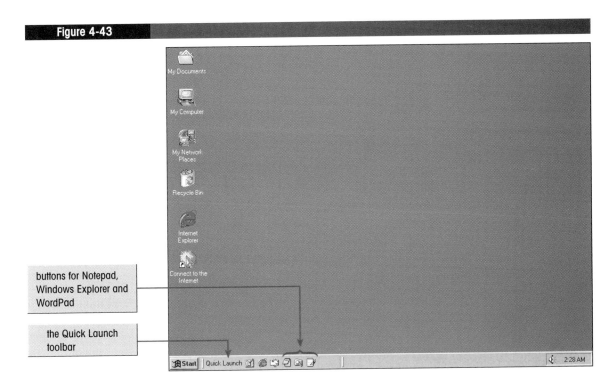

buttons for Notepad, Windows Explorer and WordPad

the Quick Launch toolbar

Explore

   a. Open the Start menu so you can see the Accessories submenu, hold down the Ctrl key, and drag icons for Notepad, WordPad, and Windows Explorer from the Accessories submenu on your Start menu to the Quick Launch toolbar on your taskbar. Be sure to hold down the Ctrl key while dragging and dropping these icons, or you'll move the icons off the Start menu.

b. Modify the properties of the Quick Launch toolbar so that it shows the toolbar's title.

c. Print a copy of your screen showing the revised Quick Launch toolbar (see step 1d, above).

d. Test each new button on the toolbar to verify that it opens the appropriate program.

e. Summarize what you've done and discuss the advantages of using the Quick Launch toolbar to launch your favorite programs. Which is easier, the Quick Launch toolbar or the Start menu, and why? What is the most effective use of the Quick Launch toolbar? Would you place all of your programs on the toolbar? Why or why not?

f. Delete the Notepad, WordPad, and Windows Explorer buttons from the Quick Launch toolbar by dragging and dropping them into your Recycle Bin.

g. Remove the title from the Quick Launch toolbar.

PROJECTS

1. Knowing that you have two years left in your college degree program, your parents decide to splurge and give you a computer, complete with Windows 2000, for your birthday. Your parents spent hours getting everything loaded and configured for you, so when you pick it up this weekend you can get right to work on that major project due on Monday. You have about half an hour before your roommate returns with your car, so take out an 8½ by 11 piece of paper, and draw the desktop that will give you the quickest access to all documents, devices, and/or programs needed to carry out the tasks listed below. Indicate shortcut icons with an arrow. Also draw a window showing your 3½-inch disk contents, using the information provided in the "To Do List."

To Do List

a. Finish typing paper for American History project, using WordPad.

___ currently saved on disk

___ will need to print

b. Finish lab report for Organic Chemistry, using WordPad.

___ currently saved on disk

___ will need to print

c. Insert bitmap image saved on disk into Organic Chemistry lab report.

d. Review outline for Office Procedures class test, created in WordPad.

___ currently saved on disk

___ will need to print

2. You provide computer support at Highland Yearbooks, a company that publishes high school and college yearbooks. Highland has just upgraded to Windows 2000, and you'd like to get right to work customizing the desktops of Highland employees for optimal performance. You start with the computer belonging to John McPhee, one of the sales representatives. Create a desktop for John that takes the following circumstances into account. When you are done, print an image of the desktop (see step 1d, above). Then make sure you remove any shortcuts you created and restore the desktop to its original settings. On the back of your printout, write down which options you changed to meet John's needs.

    a. John keeps a Notepad file with a time-date stamp of long-distance phone calls stored on the desktop with a shortcut to that file on his Start menu.

    b. John wants to be able to print the phone log file quickly, without having to open it first.

    c. The company colors at Highland Yearbooks are blue and gold. John would like a blue desktop with gold title bars.

3. In this tutorial you learned ways to work more efficiently. The shortcut menu is another Windows feature that helps you work efficiently. You've learned that a shortcut menu appears when you right-click an object. The operating system, however, changes the shortcut menu, depending on the object you right-click and what you are doing with that object. Using WordPad, create a chart that summarizes the features available when you right-click:

    a. an object on the desktop

    b. the taskbar

    c. selected text in a WordPad document

    d. nonselected text in a WordPad document

Write a paragraph that explains why these shortcut menus are all different from one another.

4. You recently took a part-time job at the local high school, assisting the computer lab manager. After your first day on the job, you notice how often the lab manager uses property sheets. You decide to spend the evening exploring property sheets so you can be more useful on the job. For future reference, make a chart in WordPad that describes the information you can glean when you look at the property sheets for:

    a. programs

    b. devices

    c. drives

    d. documents (create your own document on the desktop, if there is none available)

After your chart, list which tools you used to locate the property sheets for each of these objects.

5. Your cousin, Joey, has Windows 2000 on his new computer, but has not taken much time to learn about all of the customizable and timesaving features it offers him. In WordPad, type a letter to Joey, explaining three main features covered in this tutorial. Because you know that he is more likely to try to use these features if he has directions in front of him, include basic instructions on how to access them.

6. You just printed your letter to Joey in Project 5, and then remembered the concept of document-centric desktops you learned in this tutorial. You think that if Joey can conceptualize this, it will really expand his Windows 2000 horizons. You decide to add a note explaining the difference between the document- and program-centric desktop. Write a paragraph about this difference.

Explore ▷ 7. You are trying to save money on your electric bill and are wondering if you can take advantage of the Windows 2000 power management features. Open the Power Options Properties dialog box in the Control Panel and print the screen you see, using the techniques you learned earlier in this book. On the printout, write a paragraph describing the power management features available specifically to your computer and how they can help save money.

Explore ▷ 8. You have been asked to give a presentation at a *Computer Users with Special Needs* seminar on campus. You have a half hour to present participants with information on Windows 2000 Accessibility Options in the Control Panel. Using the online Help as a guide, write a handout describing the ways one can configure Windows 2000 for computer users with special needs. Include in your handout instructions for turning these features on and off.

Explore

9. You would like to learn how to create your own pattern to use as a desktop background.
   a. Open the Pattern dialog box, click any pattern, and then click the Edit Pattern button. The Pattern Editor dialog box opens.
   b. Type your name in the Name box and then click anywhere in the Pattern box and observe what happens.
   c. Continue to click until you have the design you want, and then print the screen that shows the pattern you designed. Click the Close button to close the Pattern Editor dialog box, and click No so your changes aren't saved.
   d. Use online Help to learn how you would save your pattern, apply it, and then remove it from the Pattern list.

QUICK CHECK ANSWERS

Session 4.1

1. False
2. False
3. You delete not only the icon but also the document.
4. You delete only the icon but not the document.
5. Dragging and dropping the document icon from one drive to another creates a copy of the document. Dragging and dropping within the same drive moves the document.

Session 4.2

1. False
2. Right-click the object and then click Properties.
3. Here are four: Background, Screen Saver, Appearance, Settings. You could also mention the properties on each of these sheets, such as color palette, resolution, and so on.
4. Activate a screen saver
5. There are 640 pixels across and 480 down.
6. 640 x 480, because it displays the largest objects
7. It requires extra video memory and runs more slowly.

Session 4.3

1. Click a blank area on the taskbar and, with the left mouse button pressed down, drag the taskbar to the left side of the computer screen.
2. Auto Hide
3. Quick Launch
4. False
5. Control Panel
5. Control Panel

OBJECTIVES

In this tutorial you will:

- Explore the structure of the Internet and the World Wide Web

- View, open, navigate, and print Web pages in Internet Explorer

- Download a file

- Enable Active Desktop in order to add, move, resize, close, and remove Active Desktop items

- Schedule the automatic retrieval of data from the Web

- Use an HTML file as a background

- Send and receive e-mail using Outlook Express

LABS

The Internet: World Wide Web

Web Pages & HTML

BRINGING
THE WORLD WIDE WEB TO THE DESKTOP

Using Active Desktop at Highland Travel

CASE

Highland Travel

Highland Travel, a touring company that offers guided tour packages to Scotland, recently hired you as an advertising manager. During your first day at work, you meet with the company's technical support person, Scott Campbell. After describing the training you'll receive, Scott explains that Highland Travel uses the Internet and the World Wide Web to promote the company, to provide services to clients, and to improve communication among employees. The company recently upgraded its computers to Windows 2000, and management wants all employees to be able to use its features to the fullest.

You tell Scott you've heard that one popular feature of Windows 2000 is its integration of the operating system with the Web. Scott nods, and tells you that during your first week on the job, you'll go through a training program to familiarize yourself with Windows 2000, and particularly with its Web features. He explains that Windows 2000 brings the richness of the Web to your desktop with Active Desktop. **Active Desktop** is technology that transforms the Windows desktop into your own personal "communications central"—not only for launching programs and accessing files, but also for obtaining and displaying any type of Web-based information. The Windows 2000 desktop is called "active" because it allows you to access the Internet.

Active Desktop manifests itself in several ways on your computer. For example, you can place updatable Web content, such as weather maps, sports news, and stock tickers, on your desktop so it functions as a personalized newspaper. Scott assures you that the training program will familiarize you with these and more features—and will introduce you to Highland Travel's Web site.

SESSION 5.1

In this session, you will learn how Windows 2000 brings the Internet and the World Wide Web to your desktop. You will learn to use Internet Explorer to view Web sites. You will activate a link, navigate a Web page with frames, print a Web page, and download a file. Finally you'll learn how to quickly access your favorite pages using the History pane and the Favorites folder. For this tutorial you will need a blank 3½-inch disk.

The Internet

Scott begins your training by explaining the basic concepts that make the Internet possible. When two or more computers are connected together so that they can exchange information and resources, they create a structure known as a **network**. Networks facilitate the sharing of data and resources among multiple users. Networks can also be connected to each other to allow computers on different networks to share information; when two or more networks are connected, they create an **internetwork**, or **internet**. "The Internet" (capital "I") has come to refer to the "network of networks" that is made up of millions of computers linked to networks all over the world. Computers and networks on the Internet are connected by fiber-optic cables, satellites, phone lines, and other communications systems, as shown in Figure 5-1. Data travels across these communication systems using whatever route is most efficient.

Figure 5-1	STRUCTURE OF THE INTERNET

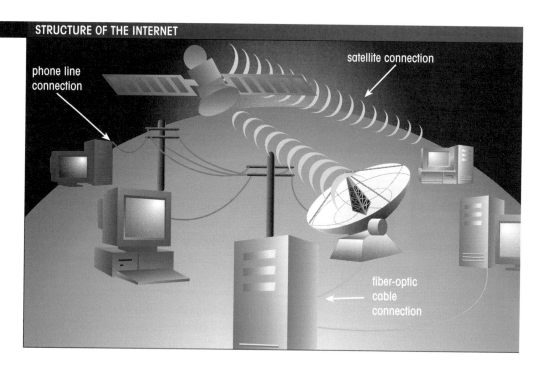

The Internet, by design, is a decentralized structure. There is no Internet "company." Instead, the Internet is a collection of different organizations, such as universities and businesses, each organizing its own information. There are no rules about where information is stored, and no one regulates the quality of information available on the Internet. Even though the lack of central control can make it hard for beginners to find their way through the resources on the Internet, decentralization has some advantages. The Internet is open to innovation and rapid growth, as different organizations and individuals have the freedom to test new products and services and make them quickly available to a global audience. One such service is the World Wide Web.

The World Wide Web makes it easy to share and access data stored on computers around the world with minimal training and support, and for this reason, Microsoft designed Windows 2000 to offer easy Web access. The Web is a system of **hypertext documents**— electronic files that contain elements known as **links**, which target other parts of a document or other documents altogether. A link can be a word or phrase or a graphic image. Figure 5-2 shows a Colorado touring company hypertext document with several links. Each link targets a separate document that offers more information about the company. You can also connect to other file types, including scanned photographs, graphic images, film clips, sounds, online discussion groups, and computer programs.

Figure 5-2	WEB PAGE WITH LINKS TO WEB PAGES CONTAINING ADDITIONAL INFORMATION

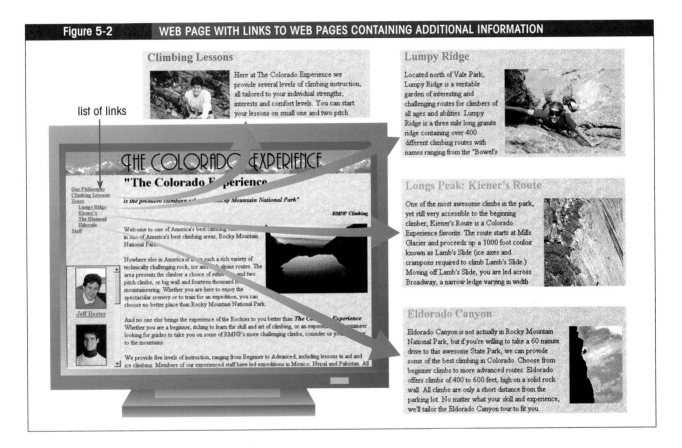

Each hypertext document on the Web is called a **Web page** and is stored on a computer on the Internet called a **Web server**. A Web page can contain links to other Web pages located anywhere on the Internet—on the same computer as the original Web page or on an entirely different computer halfway across the world. The ability to cross-reference other Web pages with links is one of the most important features of the Web.

Navigating Web pages using hypertext is an efficient way to access information. When you read a book you follow a linear progression, reading one page after another. With hypertext, you progress through the pages in whatever order you want. Hypertext allows you to skip from one topic to another, following the information path that interests you, as shown in Figure 5-3.

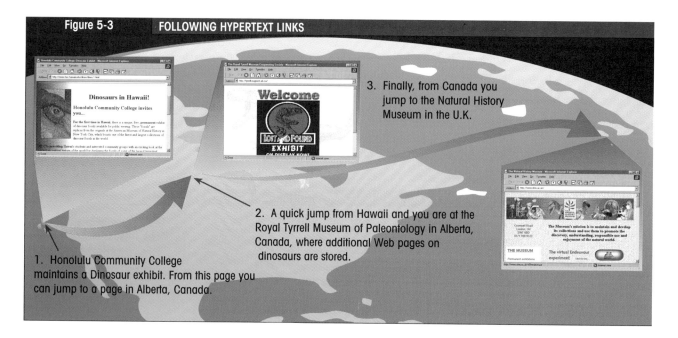

Figure 5-3   FOLLOWING HYPERTEXT LINKS

3. Finally, from Canada you jump to the Natural History Museum in the U.K.

2. A quick jump from Hawaii and you are at the Royal Tyrrell Museum of Paleontology in Alberta, Canada, where additional Web pages on dinosaurs are stored.

1. Honolulu Community College maintains a Dinosaur exhibit. From this page you can jump to a page in Alberta, Canada.

Microsoft has taken advantage of this fact by designing its Windows 2000 operating system to incorporate your experience on the Internet. The techniques you'll learn in this tutorial to navigate Web pages are identical to those you learned in previous tutorials to navigate the objects on your computer. Microsoft's goal with Windows 2000 is to make the user's experience with local files, network files, and files on computers around the world as uniform as possible.

Browsers

To access documents on the Web, you need a **browser**—a program that locates, retrieves, displays, and organizes documents stored on Web servers. Your browser allows you to visit Web sites around the world; view multimedia documents; transfer files, images, and sounds to your computer; conduct searches for specific topics; and run programs on other computers. In Figure 5-3, the dinosaur Web documents that you see appear in a browser window. Windows 2000 includes a set of communications software tools called **Internet Explorer**, which includes the Internet Explorer browser, as well as tools for other Internet functions such as electronic mail, or **e-mail**, electronic messages sent between users over the Internet. Another popular communications software package is **Netscape Communicator**, which includes the Netscape Navigator browser. This tutorial assumes that you'll do your browsing with Internet Explorer. If you're using Netscape Communicator or another browser, talk to your instructor to resolve any difficulties.

Microsoft has integrated the Internet Explorer browser into the Windows 2000 operating system to make its functions available to many Windows 2000 components. For example, the Windows Explorer utility that you used in Tutorial 3 to navigate files on your Data Disk uses Internet Explorer features so that it can function as a browser. The My Computer window works similarly.

There are many advantages to using the same tools to access information regardless of its location. Computer users in the past had to use one tool to access local files, another to access network files, and many additional products to access information on the Internet, such as e-mail, files, and other computers. The Windows 2000 operating system allows you to view information anywhere with a single set of techniques.

When you try to view a Web page, your browser locates and retrieves the document from the Web server and displays its contents on your computer. As shown in Figure 5-4, the server stores the Web page in one location, and browsers anywhere in the world can view it.

 | **USING A BROWSER TO VIEW A WEB DOCUMENT ON A SERVER**

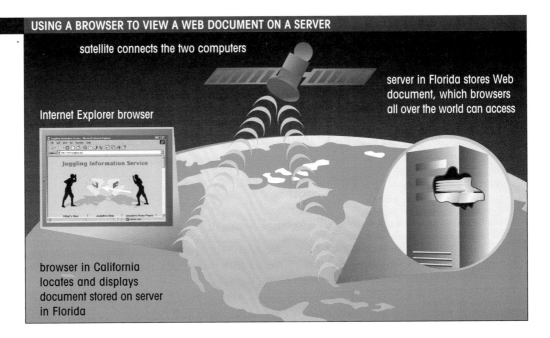

For your browser to connect to the World Wide Web, you must have an Internet connection. In a university setting, your connection might come from the campus network on which you have an account. If you are working on a home computer and gaining Internet access from your modem over a phone line, your connection is called a **dial-up connection** and is maintained via an account with an **Internet service provider (ISP)**, a company that sells Internet access. See Appendix A, "Connecting Computers over a Phone Line," for more information. With a dial-up connection, you are connected to the Internet only as long as your modem "stays on the line," whereas on most institutional networks, you are always connected to the Internet because the network is actually a part of the Internet. If you are using a dial-up connection to connect to your institution's network, you have probably received instructions that help you establish this connection. Use these instructions any time you need to be connected to the Internet during this tutorial. If you are working from home, connect to the Internet using the instructions provided by your ISP.

Starting Internet Explorer

You've already used Windows 2000 to view the files and folders on your disks, and now Scott wants to show you that you can also use it to browse sites on the Web. Scott suggests you start exploring the Web by connecting to the Highland Travel page. When you connect to the Internet without specifying a particular Web page, Windows 2000 automatically loads your **home page**—the Web page designated by the operating system as your starting point. Windows 2000 designates Microsoft Corporation's company page as the default home page, but you can easily designate a different home page. If you are at an institution such as a university, a home page has probably already been designated for you. Note that "home page" can also refer to a personal Web page or to the Web page that an organization or business has created to give information about itself.

Scott suggests that you use Internet Explorer, the browser that comes with Windows 2000, to view a Web page. You'll notice a lot of similarities between Internet Explorer (designed to locate information on the Internet) and Windows Explorer (designed to locate information on your computer or network).

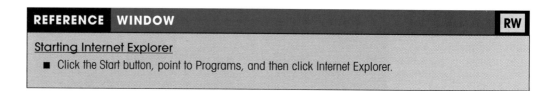

REFERENCE WINDOW   **RW**

<u>Starting Internet Explorer</u>
- Click the Start button, point to Programs, and then click Internet Explorer.

To view your home page in Internet Explorer:

1. Click the **Start** button ⟨Start⟩, point to **Programs**, and then click **Internet Explorer**.

2. If necessary, click the **Maximize** button ⟨□⟩ to maximize the Internet Explorer window.

TROUBLE? If you are in a university setting, you are probably already connected to the Internet, and your home page will appear immediately. If you are working from a computer with a dial-up connection already set up and are not currently connected to the Internet, Windows 2000 will attempt to connect you. Wait and follow the prompts that appear. If you can't establish a connection, check with your technical support person in the lab, or if you are using your own computer, use Dial-Up Networking as instructed by your ISP, or call your ISP's technical support line for assistance. If an error message appears, it's possible that the server on which your home page is stored is temporarily busy or unavailable.

3. Maximize the Internet Explorer window, click **View** on the menu bar, point to **Toolbars**, and then make sure the **Standard Buttons**, **Address Bar**, and **Links** options are checked. The Radio option should *not* be checked.

4. Open the **View** menu again. Make sure **Status Bar** is checked. Your Internet Explorer window should appear similar in form to that shown in Figure 5-5.

TROUBLE? If your Internet Explorer window shows a different Web page and the Address bar shows a different address, don't worry. Your home page is just different.

Figure 5-5	HOME PAGE DISPLAYED IN INTERNET EXPLORER

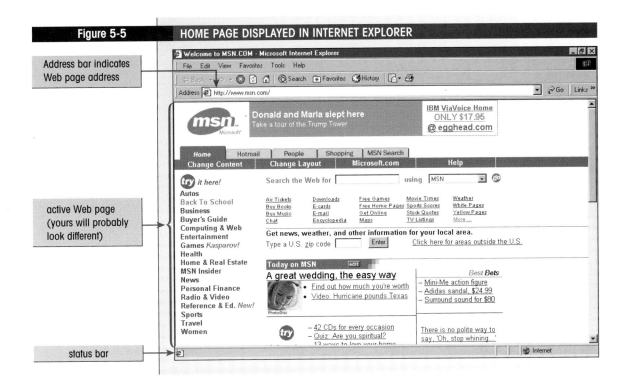

Address bar indicates Web page address

active Web page (yours will probably look different)

status bar

Opening a Page on the Web

Each page on the Web is uniquely identified by an address called a **URL**, or **Uniform Resource Locator**. A company may advertise its Web page by publishing the page's URL, such as "http://www.microsoft.com". A URL consists of three things: a protocol type, a server address, and a file pathname. Let's examine each of these items more closely.

A **protocol** is a standardized procedure used by computers to exchange information. Web documents travel between sites using **HyperText Transfer Protocol**, or **HTTP**. A Web page whose URL begins with the letters "http://" tells the Web browser to use the HTTP protocol when retrieving the page.

The **server address** gives the name of the Web server that is storing the Web page. You can usually learn a great deal about the Web server by examining the server address. For example, in the server address "www.northern.edu" the "www" indicates that the server is on the World Wide Web, "northern" indicates the name of the organization that owns the server (Northern University), and "edu" indicates that it's an educational site. Other common site types include "com" for commercial sites, "gov" for government agencies, and "org" for nonprofit organizations.

Finally, each file stored on a network server must have a unique pathname, just as files on a disk do. The **pathname** includes the folder or folders the file is stored in, plus the filename and its extension. The filename extension for Web pages is usually html, or just htm.

Try deciphering the following URL:

http://www.northern.edu/education/programs.html

The protocol is HTTP, the server address is www.northern.edu, the pathname is education/programs.html, and programs.html is the filename. So the Web browser knows it must retrieve the programs.html file from the /education folder located on the Web server at www.northern.edu, using the HTTP protocol.

Scott has given you the URL for the Highland Travel Web page, which is:

http://www.course.com/newperspectives/windows2000/highland

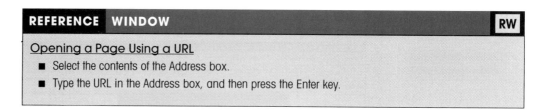

REFERENCE WINDOW   **RW**

Opening a Page Using a URL
- Select the contents of the Address box.
- Type the URL in the Address box, and then press the Enter key.

To open a page on the Web with a URL:

1. Click the **Address** box on the Address bar. The contents of the Address box, which should be the URL for your home page, are selected. Anything you type will replace the selected URL.

   TROUBLE? If the contents of the Address box are not selected, select the address manually by dragging the mouse from the far left to the far right of the URL. Be sure to select the entire URL.

2. Type **http://www.course.com/newperspectives/Windows2000/Highland** in the Address box. Make sure you type the URL exactly as shown.

3. Press the **Enter** key. Highland Travel's Welcome page opens in the Internet Explorer window. See Figure 5-6.

   TROUBLE? If you receive a Not Found error message, the URL might not be typed correctly. Repeat Steps 1 through 3, making sure that the URL in the Address box matches the URL in Step 2. If you still receive an error message, ask your instructor or technical support person for help. If you see a different Web page from the one shown in Figure 5-6, click View on the menu bar and then click Refresh.

| Figure 5-6 | CONNECTING TO THE HIGHLAND TRAVEL SITE |

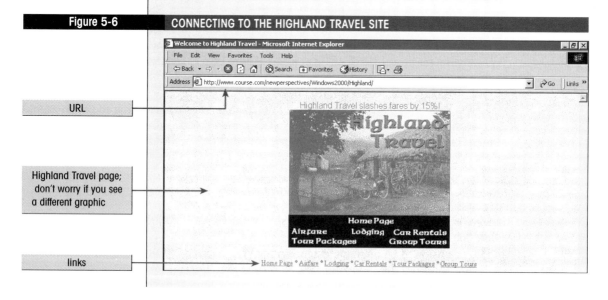

URL

Highland Travel page; don't worry if you see a different graphic

links

You can access information about the Highland Travel company by navigating through its Web pages. Spend some time doing that now.

Navigating **the Web**

The Highland Travel Web page contains links to other Web pages, so you decide to learn more about the company by activating one of the links on the Welcome page.

Activating a Link

A hypertext link on the Web, like a link in a chain, is a connector between two points. Links can appear in two ways: as text that you click or as a graphic that you click. A **text link** is a word or phrase that is usually underlined and often boldfaced or colored differently from the words around it. A **graphic link** is a graphic image that you click to jump to another location (note that graphic images can be or include text). When you aren't sure whether a graphic image is a link, point to it with the mouse pointer. When you move the mouse pointer over a link—text or graphic—the pointer changes shape from ⃕ to ⫛. The ⫛ pointer indicates that when you click, you will activate that link and jump to the new location. The destination of the link appears in the status bar, and, for some graphic links, a small identification box appears next to your pointer.

The Highland Travel page contains both text and graphic links. The text links are at the bottom of the page, underlined, and in color. The graphic links are the words in a fancy font at the bottom of the Highland Travel photo, although graphic links are often images or photos. The links give your browser the information it needs to locate the page. When you activate a link, you jump to a new location. The target of the link can be another location on the current page (for example, you can jump from the bottom of the page to the top), a different page on the current Web server, or a different page located on an entirely different Web server. When you activate a link, there are three possible outcomes:

- You successfully reach the target of the link. The browser contacts the site you want, connects to the site, transfers the data from the site to your computer, and displays the data on your screen.

- The link's target is busy, perhaps because the server storing the link's target is overwhelmed with too many requests. You can click the Stop button ⊗ to prevent your browser from further attempting to make the connection. You'll have to try a different link, or try this link later.

- The link points to a target that doesn't exist. Documents are often removed from Web servers as they become obsolete, or moved to new locations, and links that point to those documents are not always updated. If you click an obsolete link, a message box appears. If an error message box appears, click the OK button and try a different link. Otherwise click the Back button ⇦ to return to the page you were previously viewing.

The amount of time it takes to complete a link, called the **response time**, can vary, depending upon the number of people trying to connect to the same site, the number of people on the Internet at that time, the site design, and the speed of your Internet connection. In fact, one of the differences you might notice between clicking links on your desktop (which target local objects, such as My Computer or a desktop document) and clicking those that target Web pages on the Internet is the difference in response time. Linking to local objects is usually instantaneous, whereas linking to pages on the Web can take many seconds, because of the time required for the data to be transferred over your Internet connection.

As you can see in Figure 5-7, activating a link starts a multistep process. When you point to a link, the status bar displays a message that the browser is connecting to the address of the link's target, its URL. When you click the link, the activity indicator animates. The status bar displays a series of messages indicating that your browser is connecting to the site, is waiting for a reply, is transferring data, and finally, is done.

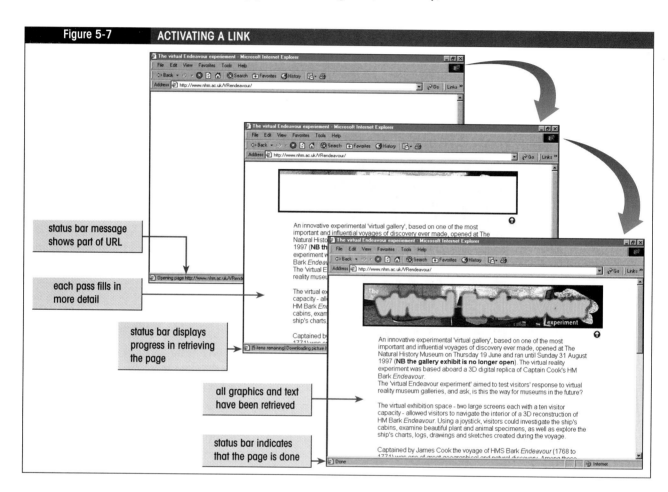

Figure 5-7   ACTIVATING A LINK

status bar message shows part of URL

each pass fills in more detail

status bar displays progress in retrieving the page

all graphics and text have been retrieved

status bar indicates that the page is done

You can see the Web page build as your browser transfers information to the screen in multiple passes. The first wave brings a few pieces to the page, and with each subsequent pass, the browser fills in more detail, until the material is complete. Try activating one of the Highland Travel links to access the company's home page.

To activate a link:

1. Point to the text link **Home Page**—the one at the bottom of the page. (You could also point to the graphic link, the one with the fancy font; both links target the same page.) Notice that the pointer changes shape from ↖ to ↗, indicating that you are pointing to a hypertext link. The status bar shows the URL for that link. See Figure 5-8.

Figure 5-8	CLICKING A TEXT LINK

graphic links

text links

link's target appears
in the status bar

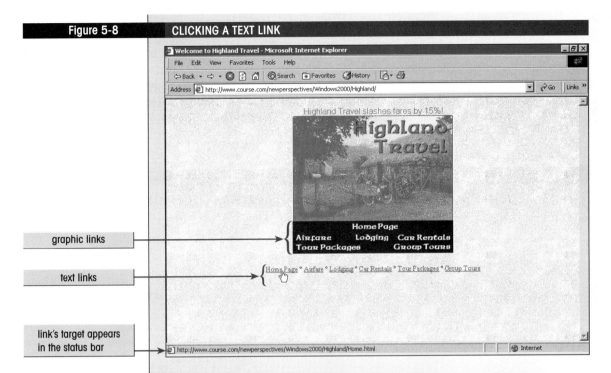

2. Click the **Home Page** text link to activate the link. The status bar notes the progress of the link. When the status bar displays "Done," the link is complete, and the Web page that is the target of the link appears. See Figure 5-9.

Figure 5-9	COMPLETED LINK

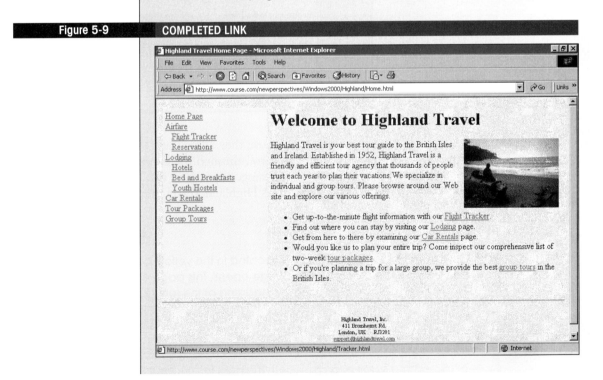

Navigating with Frames

Scott mentions that if you spend time using Windows 2000 to explore the Web, you'll probably encounter Web pages with frames. A **frame** is a section of the browser's display area, capable of displaying the contents of a different Web page. Each frame can have its own set of scroll bars, as shown in Figure 5-10. The NEC Products page is made up of two pages: the one on the left lists graphic links to other pages, and the one on the right displays the list of product categories.

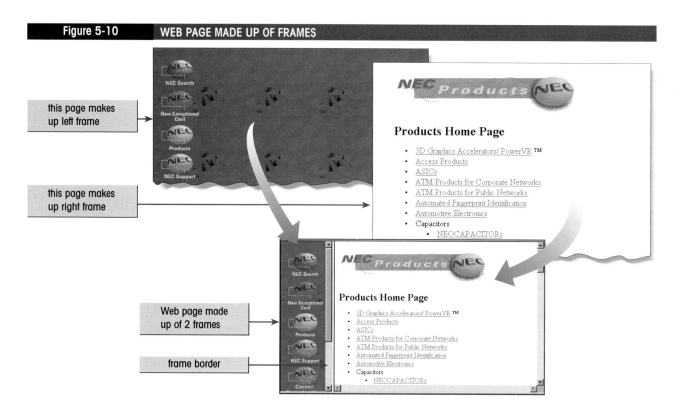

Figure 5-10 — **WEB PAGE MADE UP OF FRAMES**

this page makes up left frame

this page makes up right frame

Web page made up of 2 frames

frame border

Many Web sites today use frames because they allow the user to see different areas of information simultaneously. When you scroll through the contents of one frame, you do not affect the other frame or frames. Scott suggests you view the Tour Packages page, which employs frames, to learn about this season's Highland Travel tours.

To view a page with frames:

1. Click the **Tour Packages** text link, located in the yellow box on the left of the home page. The Tour Packages page opens. This page consists of four frames that contain (1) the Tour Packages heading at the top, (2) information on the left about the specified tour, (3) a scroll box on the right, listing the tour itinerary for each tour, and (4) graphic links to four different tours, on the bottom. See Figure 5-11.

   TROUBLE? If no scroll bars appear in the right frame, your screen resolution is so high that it is capable of displaying the entire itinerary. Skip Step 2, and note that in the rest of the steps you might not find it necessary to scroll.

Figure 5-11	VIEWING A WEB PAGE WITH FRAMES

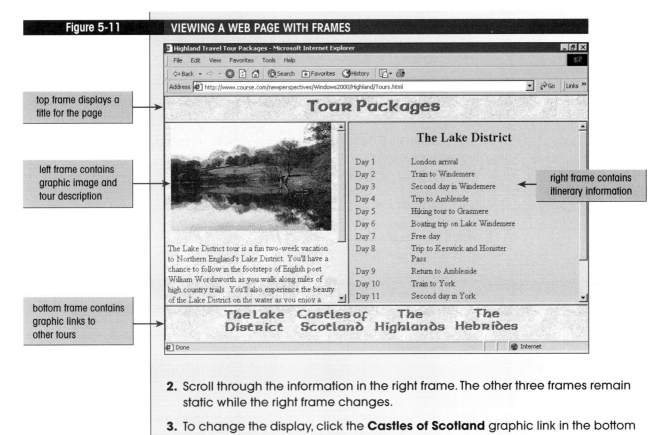

top frame displays a title for the page

left frame contains graphic image and tour description

right frame contains itinerary information

bottom frame contains graphic links to other tours

2. Scroll through the information in the right frame. The other three frames remain static while the right frame changes.

3. To change the display, click the **Castles of Scotland** graphic link in the bottom frame. The information in the left frame changes, and the itinerary in the right frame changes. Scroll through the information in the right frame and again notice that the other frames are static.

4. Click **The Highlands** graphic link to view its itinerary and then click **The Hebrides** graphic link. You have now viewed information on all four tours.

By using frames, the designer of this Web page made it possible for you to view only the information you choose to view.

Returning to a Previously Viewed Page

You've already seen in earlier tutorials how Windows 2000 allows you to navigate the devices and folders on your local and network drives, using the Back ⇦ and Forward ⇨ buttons. These buttons are also found in most browsers. The Back button returns you to the Web page you were most recently viewing, and the Forward button reverses the effect of the Back button. Both the Back and Forward buttons contain lists of visited sites; you can return to those sites by clicking the list arrow to the right of either button and clicking the site.

To return to a previously viewed Web page:

1. Click the **Back** button ⇦ repeatedly, to navigate back through the tour itineraries you viewed. You return to the Highland Travel home page, the page you were visiting before you viewed the Tours framed page.

TROUBLE? If you click the small down arrow (not the Forward button) to the right of the Back button, a list opens. Click the arrow again to close the list and then repeat Step 1. This time make sure you click ⇐.

2. Click ⇐ until the Back button dims, indicating that you have reached your starting point, usually your home page. Now try moving forward again to return to the Tours page.

3. Click the **Forward** button ⇒ repeatedly until the Forward button dims, indicating that you are looking at the last page you visited.

4. Click the **Home** button ⌂ to return to your home page.

5. Now, you'll use the Back list to see how you can return to a page you've visited without having to navigate through all the pages you've seen in a given session. Click the small down arrow to the right of the Back button. The Back list opens. See Figure 5-12.

Figure 5-12	ACCESSING A PAGE VIA THE BACK LIST

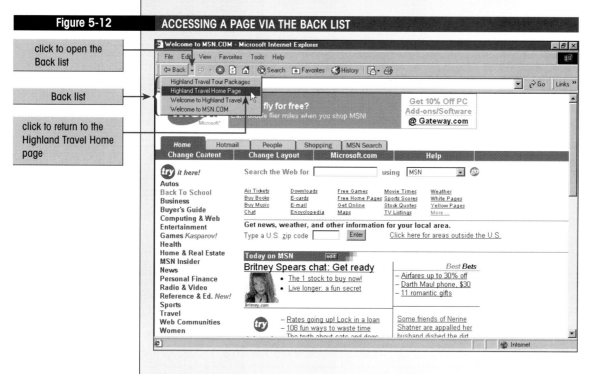

click to open the Back list

Back list

click to return to the Highland Travel Home page

6. Click **Highland Travel Home Page** to return to the Highland Travel home page.

Navigating with the History Pane

Internet Explorer has a lot in common with Windows Explorer. Many of the menu commands and buttons are the same. Internet Explorer also has the same Explorer Bar that Windows Explorer has, and you can always use the Explorer Bar to display a list of the pages you've visited recently (just as you used the History pane to view a list of recently opened files in Windows Explorer).

Scott explains that one limitation of the Back and Forward buttons is that they apply only to your current session on the browser. If you exit Internet Explorer and restart it, the Back list starts afresh. However, you can always use the History pane to quickly access those pages. Scott wants you to try this technique now.

To use the History pane:

1. Click **View**, point to **Explorer Bar**, and then click **History**. Internet Explorer displays the History pane, as shown in Figure 5-13.

Figure 5-13	DISPLAYING THE HISTORY PANE

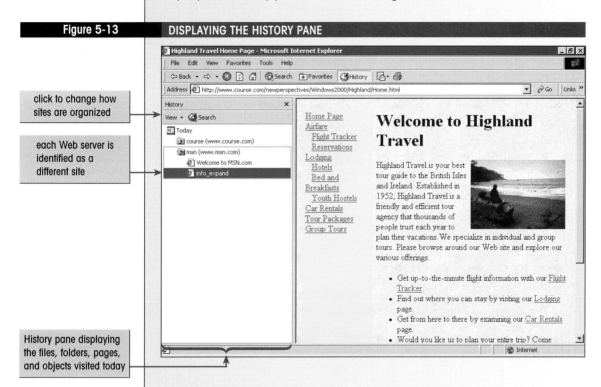

click to change how sites are organized

each Web server is identified as a different site

History pane displaying the files, folders, pages, and objects visited today

2. To make your History pane match the figures, click the **View** button in the History pane (see Figure 5-13) and then click **By Date**.

   In your earlier use of the History pane, you had only one site to examine—the My Computer site for files available on your computer. Now each Web server is identified as a separate site within the History pane.

3. Click the **course (www.course.com)** icon in the History pane. Internet Explorer expands the Course site to display a list of all of the Web pages from the Course Web server that you visited today.

4. Click **Highland Travel Tour Packages** in the list of Web pages. Internet Explorer reopens the tour package page you visited earlier. See Figure 5-14.

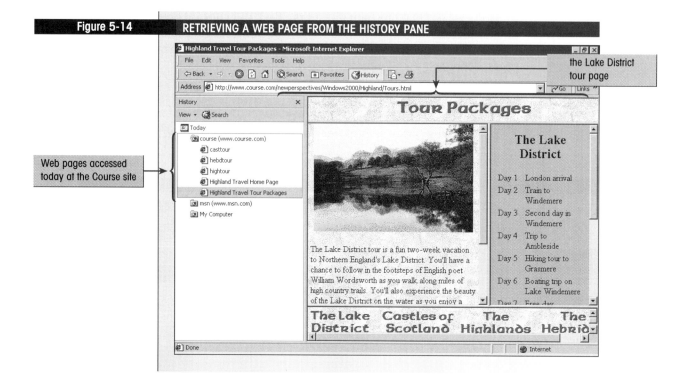

Figure 5-14   RETRIEVING A WEB PAGE FROM THE HISTORY PANE

All of the tools you used in Tutorial 3 with the Windows Explorer History pane apply to the History pane in Internet Explorer. You can change the setup, to view the pages in the History pane by date, by site, by the number of times visited, and in the order visited on the current day. You can also search the pages in the History pane to locate a specific Web site you've recently visited.

Using the Favorites Folder

As you explore the Web you'll find pages that are your favorites. Rather than retyping the URL of a page every time you want to visit it, you can save the location of your favorite pages in a list. In Windows 2000, this is your **Favorites folder**, and it contains shortcuts to the files, folders, objects, and Web pages that you visit most often. With a single click of an icon in the Favorites folder, you can retrieve the Web page and display it on your browser. The Favorites folder is a great tool for organizing your files and Web pages.

Viewing the Favorites Folder

Your Favorites list can be displayed in a variety of ways. You've no doubt seen the Favorites menu available on the Internet Explorer menu bar and the Standard Buttons toolbar. You can also display the contents of your Favorites folder in the Explorer Bar for both Internet Explorer and Windows Explorer. The Favorites folder can even be displayed in your Start menu. The method you use to access your favorites depends on your personal preference. You decide to display the Favorites folder in the Explorer bar.

To display the Favorites folder:

1. Click **View**, point to **Explorer Bar**, and then click **Favorites**. Internet Explorer displays the Favorites pane, as shown in Figure 5-15.

Figure 5-15	DISPLAYING THE FAVORITES FOLDER

you can also click here to add to or organize your Favorites folder

Favorites pane, displaying the contents of the Favorites folder

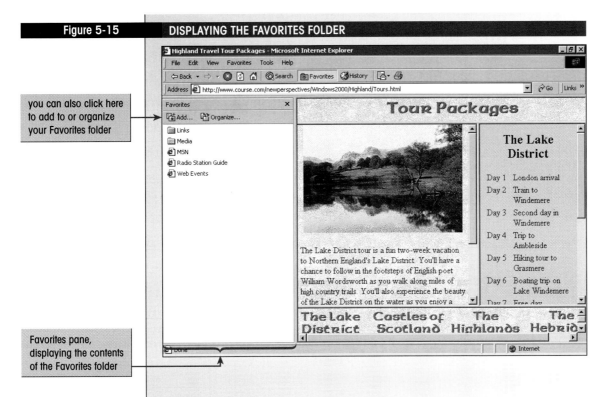

TROUBLE? Your Favorites folder may be different from the one shown in Figure 5-15.

The Favorites folder shown in Figure 5-15 contains shortcuts to a Web page containing a radio station guide, events on the Web, and a page for the Microsoft Network (MSN). It also contains subfolders with additional links. Creating and using subfolders is one way of effectively organizing a long Favorites list.

Adding an Item to the Favorites Folder

Scott suggests that you add the home page for Highland Travel to your Favorites folder. To add a Web page, you must first access the page in Internet Explorer, and then you can use the Add to Favorites command.

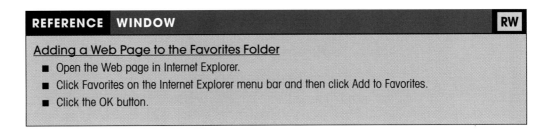

REFERENCE WINDOW **RW**

Adding a Web Page to the Favorites Folder

■ Open the Web page in Internet Explorer.
■ Click Favorites on the Internet Explorer menu bar and then click Add to Favorites.
■ Click the OK button.

To add the Highland Travel home page to the Favorites folder:

1. Click the **Back** button [←] to return to the Highland Travel home page.

2. Click **Favorites** on the menu bar and then click **Add to Favorites**.

   Note that you can also click the Add button in the Favorites pane.

3. Click the **OK** button.

   An icon for the Highland Travel home page is added to the Favorites folder.

   TROUBLE? If you are working on a network, you might not have the ability to change the content of the Favorites folder. If that's the case, you should review this material and the material that follows, but you should not attempt to recreate the steps.

Organizing the Favorites Folder

As you add more and more items to the Favorites folder, you will find that you need to organize its contents: deleting some items and moving others to new folders. Using subfolders is an excellent way to organize your favorite files and pages. You decide to create a subfolder for the Highland Travel Web pages.

To organize your Favorites folder:

1. Click **Favorites** on the Internet Explorer menu bar and then click **Organize Favorites**.

   The Organize Favorites dialog box opens. You can also click the Organize button in the Favorites pane to open this dialog box.

2. Click the **Create Folder** button, type **Highland Travel** for the new folder name, and then press the **Enter** key.

   Now you'll move the Highland Travel home page into the new subfolder you created.

3. Click the **Highland Travel Home Page** icon to select it.

4. Click the **Move to Folder** button. The Browse for Folder dialog box opens.

5. Click the **Highland Travel** folder and then click the **OK** button.

6. Click the **Close** button to close the Organize Folders dialog box.

   A folder for Highland Travel should now appear in the Favorites pane.

7. Click the **Highland Travel** folder.

   The contents of the folder appear as shown in Figure 5-16.

Figure 5-16   **THE HIGHLAND TRAVEL SUBFOLDER OF THE FAVORITES FOLDER**

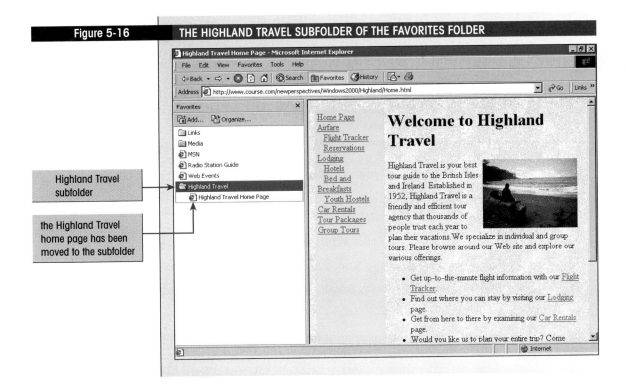

Highland Travel subfolder

the Highland Travel home page has been moved to the subfolder

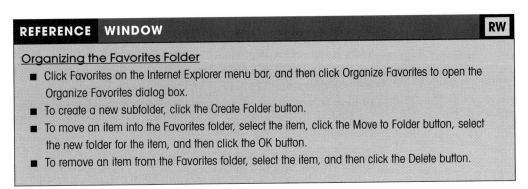

Before completing your work with the Favorites folder, you should remove the folder you created, and you should close the Favorites pane.

To delete an item from the Favorites folder:

1. Click **Favorites** and then click **Organize Favorites**.
2. Click the **Highland Travel** folder in the Organize Favorites dialog box.
3. Click the **Delete** button.
4. Click the **Yes** button to confirm that you want to remove the folder and its contents.
5. Click the **Close** button to close the Organize Favorites dialog box.
6. Click the **Close** button X in the Favorites pane to close the Favorites folder.

Printing a Web Page

Although reducing paper consumption is an advantage of browsing information online, sometimes you'll find it useful to print a Web page. For example, you might want to refer to the information later when you don't have computer access. Although Web pages can be any size, printers tend to use 8½ × 11 sheets of paper. When you print, your browser automatically reformats the text of the Web page to fit the paper dimensions. Because lines might break at different places or text size might be altered, the printed Web page might be longer than you expect. You can specify the number of pages you want to print in the Print dialog box. You decide to print the first page of the Highland Travel Web page.

To print a Web page:

1. Click **File** and then click **Print**.

2. In the Page Range section, click the **Current Page** option button.

3. Click the **Print** button to print the current page of the Highland Travel home page.

Some printers are set up to print headers and footers in addition to the Web page itself, so when you retrieve the page from your printer, you might find the page's title, its URL, the date, and other similar information at the top and bottom of the page.

Downloading a File

Scott explains that Windows 2000 also makes it easy to transfer files stored on the Internet to your computer. **Downloading** is the process of saving a file located on a remote computer (a computer located elsewhere on the Internet) to your own computer. The method you use to download information you find on the Web depends on how the file appears on the Web page. If you want to save the Web page itself, you use the Save As command on the File menu. If you want to save a graphic image located directly on the Web page, you save it by right-clicking the object you want and then using the Save Picture As command that appears in the shortcut menu.

You liked the Lake District graphic on the Tours page, so you decide to download it so you can use it as a background image on your desktop.

To download a file:

1. Click the **Forward** button ⇨ to return to the Lake District tour page.

2. Write "Disk 3—Windows 2000 Tutorial 5 Data Disk" on the label of a blank, formatted 3½-inch disk. Insert your Data Disk into drive A.

3. Return to the Tour Packages page and make sure the Lake District itinerary is visible.

4. Right-click the **Lake District** graphic to open its shortcut menu. See Figure 5-17.

Figure 5-17   SAVING A WEB GRAPHIC

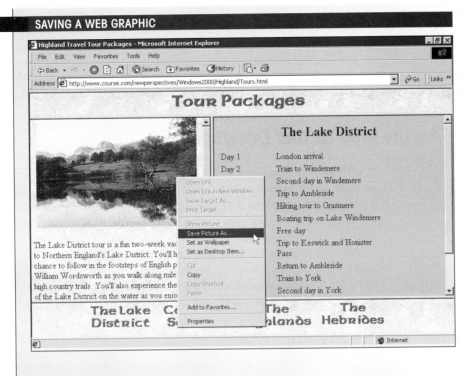

5. Click **Save Picture As**.

6. Click the **Save in** list arrow and then click **3½ Floppy (A:)**. The name "lake" should appear in the File name box and the type should be JPEG, a common graphic image type on the Web.

   TROUBLE? If a name other than "lake" appears in the File name box, replace it with the name "lake."

7. Click the **Save** button. Windows 2000 transfers the file over the Internet from the Tour Packages Web page to your Data Disk.

8. Close Internet Explorer.

The file is now on your Data Disk, and you could open it in a graphics program (such as Paint) and work with it there. Note that content appearing on Web pages is often copyrighted, and you should always make sure you have permission to use it before doing so. Since Highland Travel owns this graphic, Scott tells you that you can use it.

Session 5.1 QUICK CHECK

1. What is a home page?
2. The address of a Web page is called a(n) _____ .
3. If someone gives you the URL of an interesting Web page, how can you view it?
4. What does a URL with "edu" in it tell you about that site's Web server?
5. Each Web server you visit is displayed as a different _____ in the History pane.
6. Describe how you could quickly locate a Web page that you viewed a few days earlier.
7. True or False: Only Web pages and folders can be stored in the Favorites folder.
8. How can you download a graphic image that you find on the Web?

SESSION 5.2

In this session, you will learn how to set up your computer so that it delivers Web page content to your desktop without your having to go look for it. You'll add an Active Desktop item to your Windows 2000 desktop. You'll update the Active Desktop item using the Synchronize command, and you'll set up a schedule for automatic updates. Finally, you'll use a Web page as the new background for your Windows 2000 desktop.

Bringing the Web to Your Desktop

Scott now wants to show you how you can receive content from the Web without having to go look for it. When you connected to the Highland Travel Web page in Session 5.1, you had to go looking for it. You were told where to find the information (that is, you were given a URL), and then you went to that location and "pulled" information from the Web server onto your own computer.

Another way of retrieving data, called **push technology**, brings information to your computer without your having to go get it. True push technology occurs when the author of a Web site modifies the site so that it sends information to users on its own, without requiring the user to manually access the site and retrieve the data. Once the data has been retrieved, the user can view it without being connected to the Internet or any network. This is a technique known as **offline viewing** because the user is not "online" with the Web server.

Scott explains that you're going to begin your exploration of push technology and offline viewing by adding live content to the desktop—Active Desktop items. An **Active Desktop** item is an object that you place on your desktop that receives updates from content providers, who push the updates to users on a schedule. For example, you could place a selection of Active Desktop items on your desktop, as in Figure 5-18.

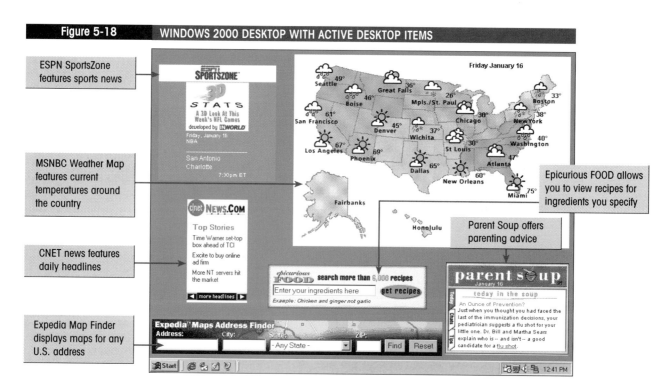

Figure 5-18   WINDOWS 2000 DESKTOP WITH ACTIVE DESKTOP ITEMS

ESPN SportsZone features sports news

MSNBC Weather Map features current temperatures around the country

CNET news features daily headlines

Expedia Map Finder displays maps for any U.S. address

Epicurious FOOD allows you to view recipes for ingredients you specify

Parent Soup offers parenting advice

You can set Active Desktop items to be updated each day, each hour, or on any schedule you choose. Every morning when the user of the computer shown in Figure 5-18 checks her desktop, for example, each component will have been automatically updated. The weather map will show the morning's weather instead of weather from the night before, the news service will display the most recent news, and other Active Desktop items will update in a similar fashion. This user has created her own "mini-newspaper," made up of only the information she's interested in.

Some Active Desktop items are interactive, allowing you to enter information and receive a response. The Epicurious FOOD Active Desktop item, for example, allows you to enter ingredients, such as beans and rice, and when you click the Get Recipes button, Internet Explorer starts (and connects to the Internet if you're not already connected) and displays recipes from the Epicurious site containing those ingredients. Likewise, if you enter a location in the Expedia Maps Address Finder Active Desktop item and then click the Find button, a map will appear showing the location you specified. Microsoft maintains a collection of Active Desktop items at its Active Desktop Gallery Web site, which you'll access in a moment.

Enabling Active Desktop

To add Active Desktop items to your desktop, you must first enable the Active Desktop feature, which allows the desktop to receive pushed information.

To enable Active Desktop:

1. Right-click a blank area of the desktop and then point to **Active Desktop**.

2. Make sure the Show Web Content option is checked; if not, click it to select it.

3. If the My Current Current Home Page option is selected, click it to deselect it.

It might seem that nothing has changed, but your desktop is now poised to receive whatever information you request, on a schedule you set.

Adding an Active Desktop Gallery Item to the Desktop

By enabling Active Desktop, you've added a new list of commands to the menu that appears when you right-click the desktop. You'll use a new command, "New Desktop Item," to add Web content to your desktop.

To add a weather map from the Active Desktop Gallery to your desktop:

1. Right-click a blank area of the desktop.

2. Point to **Active Desktop** and then click **New Desktop Item**.

3. Click the **Visit Gallery** button.

   Windows 2000 opens the Active Desktop Gallery Web page in Internet Explorer.

   TROUBLE? If you are prompted to download a Stock Ticker from Microsoft, talk to your network manager or instructor to decide whether this program can be retrieved and loaded on your computer.

4. Scroll down the icon list if necessary and then click the **Weather** icon, shown in Figure 5-19.

5. Click **MSNBC Weather Map**. After a moment, the weather map appears, along with a button entitled "Add to Active Desktop." See Figure 5-19.

   TROUBLE? If the MSNBC Weather Map doesn't appear, choose a different Active Desktop item.

| Figure 5-19 | ADDING AN ACTIVE DESKTOP ITEM |

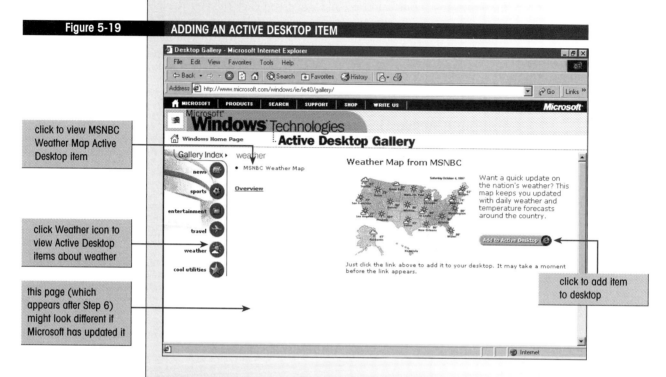

click to view MSNBC Weather Map Active Desktop item

click Weather icon to view Active Desktop items about weather

this page (which appears after Step 6) might look different if Microsoft has updated it

click to add item to desktop

6. Click the **Add to Active Desktop** button. Then click the **Yes** button if a Security Alert dialog box asks if you want to add this item to your active desktop. A dialog box appears that asks you to confirm the procedure. You could click the Customize button to change the default schedule; you'll customize the schedule later.

7. Click the **OK** button to add the item to your desktop.

8. The download process might take one or several minutes, depending on the speed of your Internet connection. Once the download is complete, close your browser. The item you added appears on your desktop. See Figure 5-20.

   TROUBLE? If the Active Desktop item appears but doesn't look like a weather map, the MSNBC site might be busy. A desktop item will still appear, but it won't include the map. Continue with the steps, using the Active Desktop item.

   TROUBLE? If scroll bars appear around your Active Desktop item or the item is off-center, don't worry. You'll learn momentarily how to resize and move it.

Figure 5-20	ADDING AN ACTIVE DESKTOP ITEM

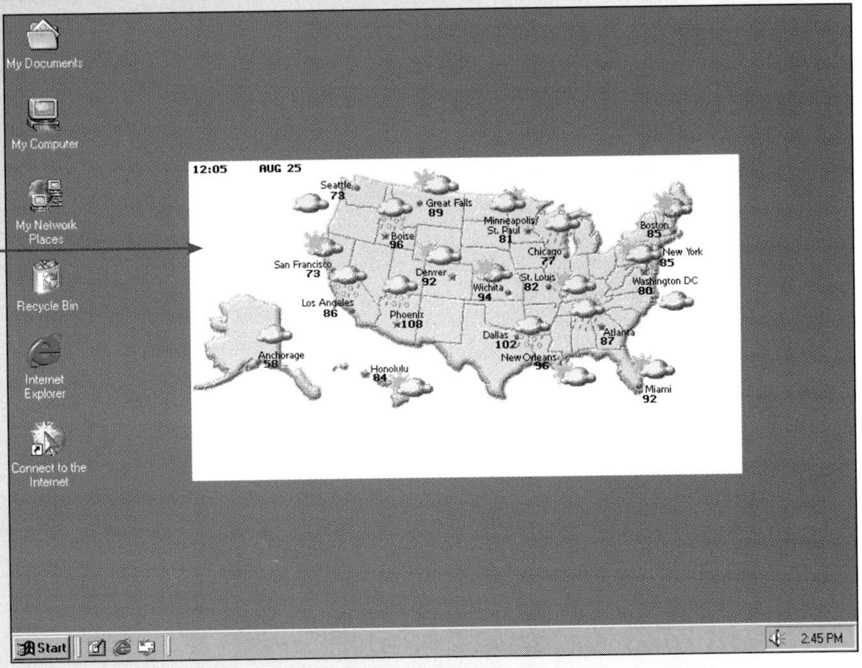

weather map on your desktop (your desktop might appear different)

Resizing and Moving Active Desktop Items

When an Active Desktop item is on your desktop, it occupies a rectangular block that appears as part of the background. To move or resize an Active Desktop item, you must first point to it to select it. When an Active Desktop item is selected, a title bar and border appear, which you can manipulate to move and resize the item as you would any other Windows 2000 window (such as the My Computer window). Practice moving Active Desktop items by moving the weather map.

To move the weather map:

1. Point to the top of the weather map. A gray border appears around the entire Active Desktop item, and a gray bar, similar to a window's title bar, appears at the top. This bar includes a Close button ☒ and a list arrow on the left that opens a menu for that item. See Figure 5-21.

   TROUBLE? If the title bar doesn't appear, move the pointer closer to the top of the Active Desktop item. The title bar should appear just before the pointer reaches the top of the item.

Figure 5-21 ACTIVATING AN ACTIVE DESKTOP ITEM

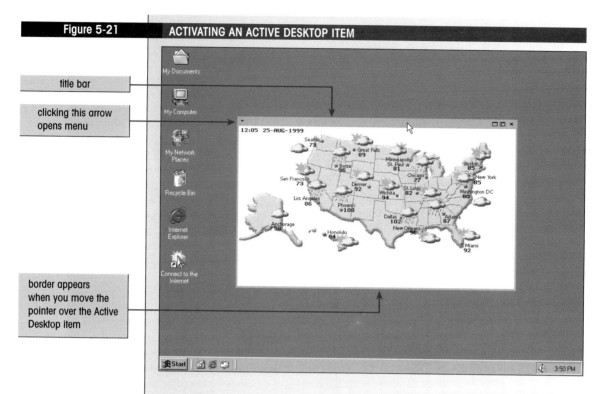

title bar

clicking this arrow opens menu

border appears when you move the pointer over the Active Desktop item

2. Drag the title bar to the center of the screen, if yours was previously off-center. The entire weather map moves.

You can also use the border to resize the item. For example, you drag the left and right borders to widen the item or make it narrower, you drag the top and bottom borders to lengthen or shorten the item, and you drag any corner out to enlarge or reduce both dimensions simultaneously.

To resize the weather map:

1. Point to the lower-right corner of the weather map. The gray border appears, and the mouse pointer changes from ↳ to ↖↘.

2. Drag the corner border to the lower right. The Active Desktop item expands in size. If your map has scroll bars, drag down and to the right until the scroll bars disappear.

You can also change the size of a desktop item by clicking one of the buttons on the upper-right corner of the item border. Figure 5-22 describes the four buttons available on the border and the effect each has on the size of a desktop item.

Figure 5-22 RESIZE BUTTONS FOR THE ACTIVE DESKTOP ITEM

BUTTON	NAME	DESCRIPTION
▭	Cover Desktop	Extend the item across the entire desktop
▯▮	Split Desktop with Icons	Move all desktop icons to the far left and fill the remaining desktop with the item
▫	Reset to Original Size	Reset the item to a window on the desktop
✕	Close	Close the item

To see how these buttons work, you'll try resizing the image: first to fill the whole desktop, then to split the desktop between the icons and the item, and finally to restore the item to its original size and position. Note that you see only three of these buttons at a time. The middle button changes depending on what size the item is currently.

To use the sizing buttons:

1. Move your mouse pointer over the top border of the image to redisplay the title bar (if necessary), and click the **Cover Desktop** button ▣ .

   The weather map fills the entire desktop.

2. Move the mouse pointer to the top of the screen, and then click the **Split Desktop with Icons** button ▣ .

   The weather map is reduced in size, moving to the right of the icons on the desktop.

3. Move the mouse pointer to the top of the screen again and click the **Reset to Original Size** button ▣ .

   The weather map is restored to a window on the desktop.

   Figure 5-23 shows the weather map in each of the three sizes.

Figure 5-23   THE WEATHER MAP IN THREE SIZES

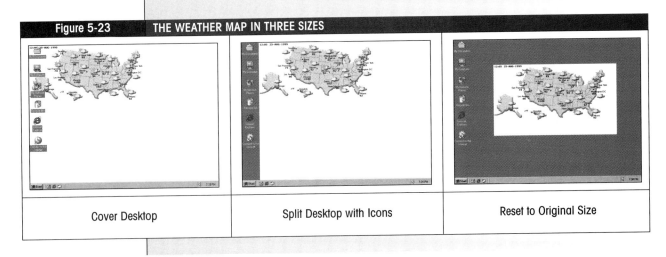

| Cover Desktop | Split Desktop with Icons | Reset to Original Size |

Updating **Web Content**

You may be wondering how you update the weather map to reflect current conditions. The process of retrieving current information is called **synchronization**, and Windows 2000 allows you to synchronize not just Web content, but any information available over your network. For example, if you are working on a corporate network and are leaving on a trip, you can retrieve a file for offline viewing on your laptop. Windows 2000 will make a copy of that file available to you, but it might not be current with the network file when you return. You can change this by synchronizing your copy with the network version. Similarly, you can synchronize the weather map on your desktop with the map available on the Web server.

Updating Content Manually

Files and Web pages can be synchronized on a fixed schedule or manually. To see how synchronization works, you'll manually update the weather map now.

To synchronize the weather map:

1. Move the mouse pointer over the upper border of the weather map to display the title bar.

2. Click the down arrow located on the left edge of the title bar and then click **Synchronize** on the menu. See Figure 5-24.

Figure 5-24	SYNCHRONIZING THE WEATHER MAP

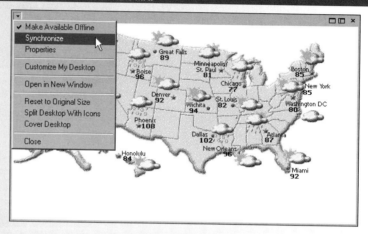

3. Windows 2000 connects to the Web server and updates the weather map with the latest weather information.

REFERENCE WINDOW   RW

Synchronizing an Active Desktop Item
- Move the mouse pointer over the upper border of the Active Desktop item to display the title bar.
- Click the down arrow on the left edge of the title bar to display the menu.
- Click Synchronize.

Viewing an Update Schedule

If you had to manually update the weather map all of the time, having it on your desktop would not be much of an improvement over simply visiting the page on the Web. The advantage of synchronization is the ability of Windows 2000 to access the page for you on a schedule. For example, you could have an Active Desktop item that downloads the latest stock market information every 5 minutes. By glancing at your desktop, you can view data that is no more than 5 minutes old.

Most Active Desktop items retrieved from the Active Desktop gallery have a schedule already set, which you can change. The schedule is one of the properties of the Active Desktop item.

To view the schedule for the weather map:

1. Redisplay the title bar for the weather map, click the down arrow, and then click **Properties** on the menu.

The MSNBC Weather Properties dialog box opens.

2. Click the **Schedule** tab.

As shown in Figure 5-25, the weather map uses the MSNBC Weather Recommended Schedule.

| Figure 5-25 | THE MSNBC WEATHER PROPERTIES DIALOG BOX |

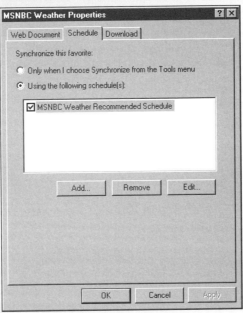

3. To see when the MSNBC Weather schedule downloads updated weather maps, click the **Edit** button.

As shown in Figure 5-26, under the recommended schedule the map is updated every night at 12:00 AM.

| Figure 5-26 | THE MSNBC WEATHER RECOMMENDED SCHEDULE |

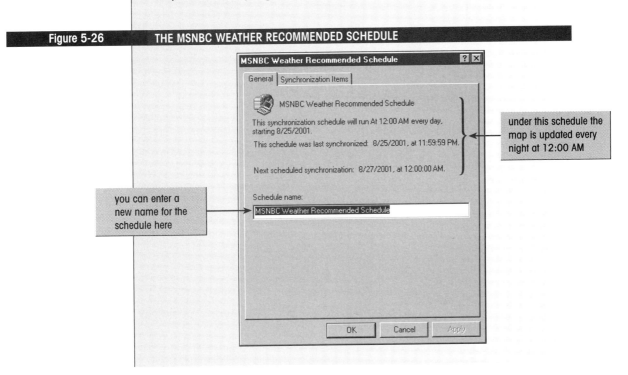

you can enter a new name for the schedule here

under this schedule the map is updated every night at 12:00 AM

4. Click the **OK** button and leave the MSNBC Weather Properties dialog box open.

Editing an Update Schedule

You realize as you examine the current schedule that most of the time your computer will not be turned on at midnight to run the synchronization. A much better time would be 9:00 AM, shortly after you arrive at the office, and 3:00 PM, shortly before you leave. To make this change you have to create two schedules: one for the morning and one for the afternoon.

To create an update schedule:

1. Click the **Add** button.

2. Set the time value to **9:00 AM** (you can set the time value the same way you set the digital clock in Tutorial 4, by selecting each time value and clicking the up and down arrows next to the digital clock).

3. Type **Morning Update** in the Name box.

4. Click the check box to allow Windows 2000 to connect to the Internet automatically to begin synchronization.

Figure 5-27 shows the completed dialog box.

Figure 5-27	SCHEDULING THE MORNING UPDATE

run the update every day ...

click to allow Windows 2000 to automatically connect to the Internet if necessary

New Schedule ? ☒

Please specify settings for your new schedule.

Every ▢ 1 ▢ days at ▢ 9:00 AM ▢ ◄

... at 9:00 AM

Name: ▢ Morning Update ◄

schedule name

☑ If my computer is not connected when this scheduled synchronization begins, automatically connect for me

OK   Cancel

5. Click the **OK** button.

6. Click the **Add** button again and add a new schedule named "Afternoon Update," which will update the map at 3:00 PM every day (automatically connecting to the Internet if needed).

Figure 5-28 shows the new list of scheduled updates. Leave the MSNBC Weather Properties dialog box open.

Figure 5-28	LIST OF UPDATE SCHEDULES

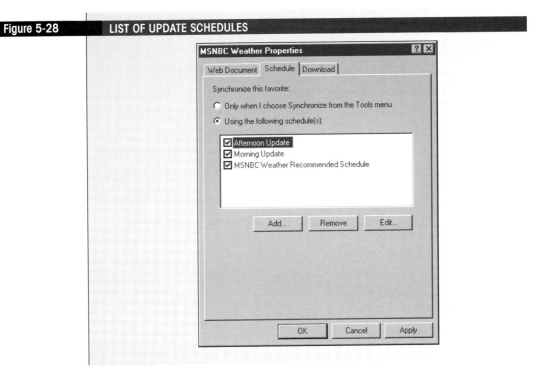

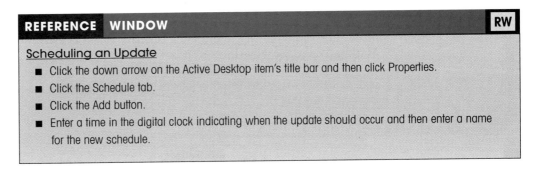

REFERENCE   WINDOW   **RW**

Scheduling an Update
- Click the down arrow on the Active Desktop item's title bar and then click Properties.
- Click the Schedule tab.
- Click the Add button.
- Enter a time in the digital clock indicating when the update should occur and then enter a name for the new schedule.

Removing an Active Desktop Item

Now that you've seen how to work with Active Desktop items and update schedules, you should remove the weather map from your desktop. When you remove an Active Desktop item you can either close the item (by clicking the ✖ button on the title bar) or delete it. Closing the item keeps the information about the item and its update schedule available for future use. You can restore the item later by opening the Display Properties dialog box and selecting the item on the Web property sheet. Deleting the item removes the file and all information about it from your computer. When you delete the item, you have to go back to the Web site and download the item again to reinstall it. Now that you know how to use Active Desktop items, Scott suggests that you delete the item and the update schedules you created.

To delete the update schedules and weather map:

1. Click **Morning Update** and then click the **Remove** button. Click the **Yes** button to confirm the deletion.

2. Remove the Afternoon Update schedule in the same way.

3. Click the **OK** button to close the MSNBC Weather Properties dialog box.

4. Right-click an empty spot on the desktop and then click **Properties** on the menu.

5. Click the **Web** tab in the Display Properties dialog box.

   The Web property sheet shows a list of all of the Active Desktop objects available for your desktop. Those currently displayed on the desktop have their check-boxes selected.

6. Click **MSNBC Weather** and then click the **Delete** button.

7. Click the **Yes** button to confirm that you want to delete the file.

8. Click the **OK** button.

9. If you had to deselect your home page from the desktop earlier, right-click the desktop, point to **Active Desktop**, and then click **My Current Home Page** on the popup menu.

   The map is removed from the desktop.

Using an HTML File as a Background

In Tutorial 4 you worked with the Desktop Properties dialog box to change your desktop's color and pattern, and then to display a graphic image on your desktop. Active Desktop technology extends your control over your desktop's background by allowing you to use Web pages as wallpaper. To create Web pages, you use a language called **HTML**, which stands for **Hypertext Markup Language**. HTML uses special codes to describe how the page should appear on the screen. Figure 5-29 shows a Web page as it appears on your computer screen, and behind it, the underlying HTML code. It is this code that the browser interprets when a Web page is viewed.

Figure 5-29	WEB PAGE AND THE HTML CODE IT EMPLOYS

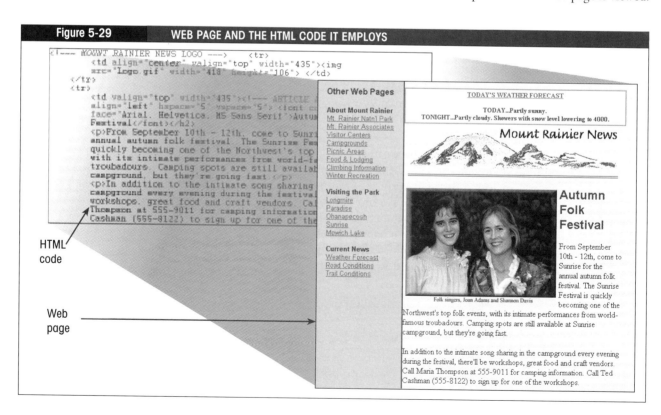

HTML code

Web page

A document created using the HTML language is called an **HTML file** and is saved with the .htm or .html extension. Most Web pages are HTML files.

Because Windows 2000 enables you to use an HTML file as your background wallpaper, your Windows 2000 desktop background can feature text, clip art, photos, animated graphics, links, and multimedia objects such as sound and video. Your desktop can also include **applets**, programs attached to a Web page that extend its capabilities. Some applets add movement and interesting visual effects to your page, whereas others are capable of asking you questions, responding to your questions, checking your computer settings, and calculating data. There are even applets that allow you to play interactive games against the computer or against another person logged on to the Web.

You can use a word-processing program such as Microsoft Word to save a document as an HTML file, or you can create a new one using the Web page editor included with Windows 2000, FrontPage Express. If you learn the HTML language, you can use a simple text editor (such as Notepad) to create a more complex and sophisticated HTML file. Alternately, you can use the Internet Explorer browser to save an existing Web page as an HTML file that you can then use as your wallpaper.

The added control Windows 2000 gives you over background wallpaper makes it possible to make the desktop a launch pad for your most important projects. A corporation, for example, might create an HTML file that contains important company information, an updatable company calendar, links to company documents, a company directory, and so on. Scott wants to show you a Web page he's designing to be used as a background for all Highland Travel computers. He has created an HTML file in his Web page editor and has placed it on a disk for you to examine.

To use a Web page as a background:

1. To view the Highland Travel desktop background Web page, you need to place the files on your Data Disk. Place the Data Disk you worked with in Session 5.1 in drive A. Click the **Start** button ⊞**Start**, point to **Programs**, point to **NP on Microsoft Windows 2000 – Level II**, and then click **Disk 3 (Tutorial 5)**. When you are prompted to insert your disk in the drive, click the **OK** button and then wait as the files you need are copied to your Data Disk.

2. Right-click a blank area of the desktop and then click **Properties**.

3. Click the **Background** tab if necessary, click the **Browse** button, click the **Look in** list arrow, click **3½ Floppy (A:)**, and then click the **highland** file icon.

4. Click the **Open** button. The filename appears in the Wallpaper list and a preview appears in the preview monitor.

5. Click the **OK** button. The HTML file appears on your desktop background. Figure 5-30 points out some of the features an HTML file allows you to employ on a desktop background.

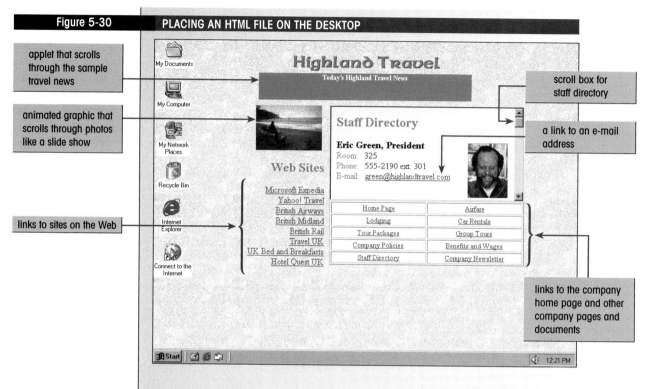

Figure 5-30   **PLACING AN HTML FILE ON THE DESKTOP**

applet that scrolls through the sample travel news

animated graphic that scrolls through photos like a slide show

links to sites on the Web

scroll box for staff directory

a link to an e-mail address

links to the company home page and other company pages and documents

6. Scroll through the Staff Directory to see the various Highland Travel employees. Notice that your experience with these objects is just the same as it would be if you were working with this page in your Web browser.

The difference between using an HTML file as your wallpaper and using a graphic file, as you did in Tutorial 4, is that a graphic is simply a picture that adds interest to your desktop background, whereas an HTML file allows you to interact with the information on your background. If the HTML file contains links, you can click those links to connect to the sites they target. Try clicking one of the links on the page.

To activate a desktop link:

1. Click the **Home Page** link in the first row of the table below the Staff Directory. Your browser starts, and after a moment the link's target appears in the browser window—the familiar Highland Travel page.

2. Close your browser. You return to the desktop.

Scott explains that once he finishes developing his page, the company will place it on all company desktops, so all employees have access to the information it contains. Since it isn't finished, he recommends that you remove it from your desktop.

To restore the desktop to its original appearance:

1. Right-click a blank area of the desktop and then click **Properties**.

> TROUBLE? If you right-click an area of the Web page that has Web content, properties for that object appear, instead of desktop properties. Make sure the dialog box that opens is the Display Properties dialog box. If it isn't, try right-clicking a different area, and make sure it is blank.

2. Click the **Background** tab, if necessary.

3. Scroll up the Wallpaper list and then click **(None)**.

4. Click the **OK** button.

You've completed your work with bringing Web content directly to your desktop. As you've seen, Windows 2000 provides a rich variety of tools to connect your computer with the Internet.

Session 5.2 QUICK CHECK

1. What is offline viewing?
2. What is push technology?
3. An object on the desktop that receives pushed content is called a(n) _____.
4. What is synchronization?
5. How would you schedule an object to be synchronized 24 times a day, once each hour?
6. What is HTML?
7. What are some advantages of using an HTML file for your desktop background?

SESSION 5.3

In this session, you'll learn how to start Outlook Express—the Windows 2000 e-mail program. You'll see how to customize Outlook Express, and you'll examine the properties of your mail account. You'll send and receive e-mail messages and reply to an e-mail message.

Getting Started with Outlook Express

Outlook Express, one of the tools that comes with Windows 2000, allows you to send, receive, and manage **electronic mail** or **e-mail**—electronic messages transferred between users on a network. As more people connect to the Internet, communicating by e-mail is becoming more common. When you need to send information to someone else, an e-mail message saves time and money, because you don't need to wait for postal delivery nor make expensive long-distance phone calls. You can send e-mail to and receive e-mail from anyone in the world who has an e-mail address, regardless of the operating system or type of computer the person is using.

Just as you need an Internet account to browse the World Wide Web, you likewise need an account on a **mail server**, a computer that handles the storage and delivery of e-mail. Most Internet service providers also provide access to mail servers.

Scott informs you that the company's systems administrator has just finished a mail server on the company network to handle all e-mail messages. He hands you a slip of paper with your account information, including your user ID, password, and e-mail address. A **user ID**, also called a **username**, is the name that identifies you on the mail server. A **password** is a personal code that verifies that you have the right to read incoming mail. An **e-mail address** consists of the user ID, the @ symbol, and a host name. For example, Scott's e-mail address is:

SCampbell@HighlandTravel.com

Thus Scott's username is Scampbell, and the address of the company's mail server is HighlandTravel.com. Like URLs, every e-mail address is unique. Many people might use the same host, but user IDs distinguish one e-mail address from another.

Customizing **the Outlook Express Window**

The Outlook Express window offers a number of components that you can choose to display or hide, depending on your needs. These components include:

- **Contacts list**: lists people whose e-mail addresses or other contact information you have saved
- **Folder bar**: identifies the current mail folder
- **Folders list**: displays the hierarchy of mail folders that you can use to store and organize messages
- **Outlook bar**: contains icons for the folders in the Folders list (since this repeats the information in the Folders list, you don't really need to view it unless you find it easier to use than the Folders list)
- **Status bar**: displays messages about the current folder
- **Toolbar**: displays the toolbar buttons used to accomplish most tasks
- **Views bar**: provides you with a quick way to change the message list view so you can switch between showing all messages or hiding read or ignored messages
- **Info pane**: an informational window at the bottom of the Outlook Express window, which may not be an available option, depending on how Outlook Express is installed on your computer

Before you start using Outlook Express, first ensure that your Outlook Express window matches the one shown in the figures. You start Outlook Express by clicking the Outlook Express button 🖳 from the Quick Launch toolbar, clicking the Outlook Express icon on the desktop, or using the Start menu.

To control the Outlook Express display:

1. To open Outlook Express, click the **Start** button 🏁 Start, point to **Programs**, and then click **Outlook Express**.

TROUBLE? If more than one e-mail program is installed on your computer, and Outlook Express is not your current default mail program, a dialog box appears asking if you want Outlook Express to be your default mail program. If you are using your own computer and want to use Outlook Express as your mail program, click the Yes button. If you are using a school or institutional computer, click the No button or ask your technical support person for assistance.

TROUBLE? If the Identity Logon dialog box opens, you are using a version of Outlook Express that is configured for multiple users. If your name appears, click it and then enter the password as requested. Otherwise, ask your technical support person for assistance.

TROUBLE? If a connection dialog box appears, you are probably not connected to the Internet. Click the Connect button and follow the directions that appear on your screen. If you are prompted to enter your username and password and you do not know them, consult your technical support person.

TROUBLE? If the Internet Connection Wizard starts, click the Cancel button and the Yes button twice to exit the wizard. Contact your instructor or technical support person about setting up an Internet account on your computer.

2. If necessary, click the **Maximize** button ▢. Figure 5-31 shows the maximized Outlook Express window.

Figure 5-31 | **OUTLOOK EXPRESS WINDOW**

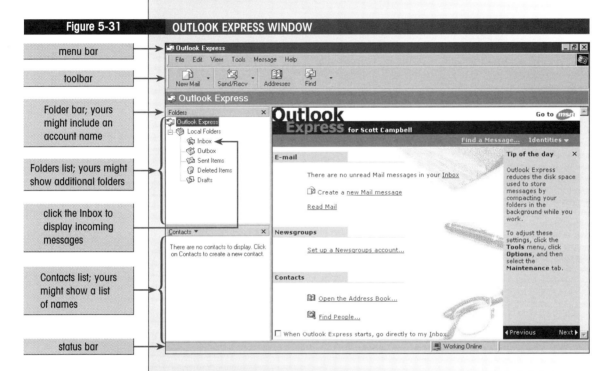

menu bar

toolbar

Folder bar; yours might include an account name

Folders list; yours might show additional folders

click the Inbox to display incoming messages

Contacts list; yours might show a list of names

status bar

3. Click **Inbox** in the Folders list.

TROUBLE? If you see more than one Inbox on the Folders list, you might have more than one mail account. Click Inbox under Local Folders.

4. Click **View** on the menu bar, point to **Current View**, and then click **Show All Messages** so you can view all messages.

5. Click **View**, point to **Sort By**, click **Received**, and then click **View** again, point to **Sort By**, and click **Sort Ascending**. You want to sort your messages in the order they were received, in ascending order (newest first).

TROUBLE? If the Received and Sort Ascending options are already bulleted in the Sort By list, don't worry. Clicking a bulleted menu option does *not* deselect it. Clicking a checked menu option, however, *does* deselect the option.

6. To work with the Outlook Express components layout, click **View** and then click **Layout**.

7. In the Basic area, make sure all check boxes *except* the Outlook Bar, Views Bar, and Info Pane are checked.

TROUBLE? If the Info Pane check box doesn't appear in your Layout dialog box, don't worry. Some installations of Outlook Express do not include this option. Just make sure that the check boxes for Outlook Bar and Views Bar are *not* checked.

8. In the Preview Pane area, make sure the **Show preview pane** and **Show preview pane header** check boxes are both selected and that the **Below messages** option button is selected. See Figure 5-32.

| Figure 5-32 | CHECKING OUTLOOK EXPRESS LAYOUT |

only these two check boxes should not be selected; the Info Pane might be an option as well, depending on your installation. Leave it unselected as well.

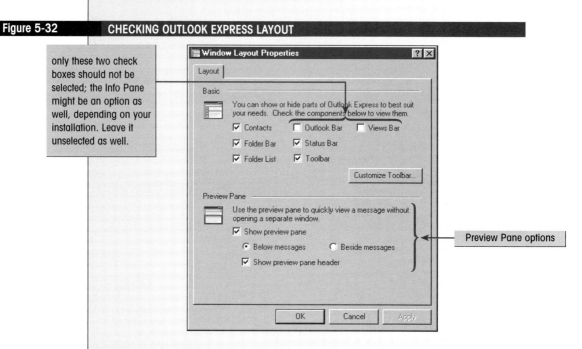

Preview Pane options

9. Click the **OK** button. Your screen should resemble Figure 5-33.

| Figure 5-33 | DEFAULT OUTLOOK EXPRESS WINDOW |

message list appears here; yours might already contain messages

Preview pane displays contents of selected message; it is empty now because the message list contains no message

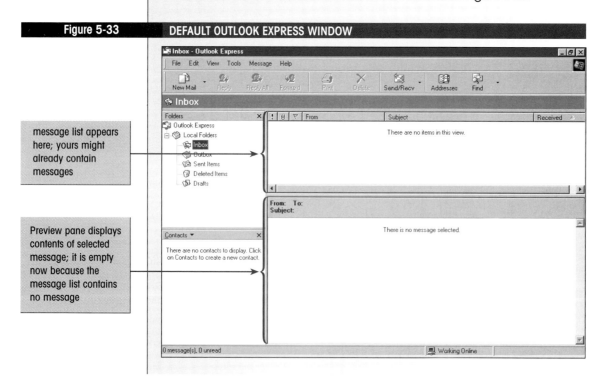

Now that you have ensured that your display will match the one shown in the figures, you are ready to check the status of your Outlook Express account, using the information Scott Campbell gave you.

Setting Up an Outlook Express Account

Once you have an account with a mail service provider (usually this is your ISP), you add your account to Outlook Express. If you are in a university or other institution, this has probably been done for you, but if you are using your own computer, you will probably have to add it yourself.

Most Internet service providers include mail service as part of their Internet services package. What type of mail account you choose depends on how you plan to access your mail. Outlook Express supports POP, IMAP, and HTTP account types.

- With a **POP**, or **Post Office Protocol**, account, your mail server receives incoming mail and delivers it to your computer. Once messages are delivered, they are usually deleted from the mail server. POP accounts work best when you have only a single computer, since POP is designed for offline mail access. To receive POP mail if you are away from your computer, you must be able to set up a POP mail account on a different computer—an impossibility in many places.

- With an **IMAP**, or **Internet Message Access Protocol**, account, mail is stored on a mail server, not on your computer. Thus you can access your mail from any computer on which you have an account, without having to transfer files back and forth between computers.

- With an HTTP account, known as **Web-based e-mail**, you use the same HTTP protocol used on the Web. You set up an account with a Web-based e-mail provider, and your mail is stored on that provider's mail server. You can access your messages from any Web browser. Libraries, hotels, airports, and banks are increasingly making computers with Web access available to the public, so you don't need to own a computer to use Web-based e-mail. Moreover, Web-based e-mail accounts are often free. However, because messages are stored on a server and not on your local computer, mail retrieval is limited by the speed of your Internet connection. Web-based accounts currently don't offer the same breadth of features you find with a traditional e-mail program. The largest provider of free Web-based e-mail is **Hotmail**, a Microsoft service that is made available from Internet Explorer via the Links toolbar or from Outlook Express when you set up a new mail account. Outlook Express allows you to add a Hotmail account to your Folders list, and it treats incoming mail just as it would in a POP account. Hotmail even also allows you to check POP mail.

REFERENCE WINDOW	**RW**

Setting Up an E-Mail Account
- In the Outlook Express window, click Tools and then click Accounts.
- Click the Add button.
- Click Mail. Follow the steps in the Internet Connection Wizard.

The following steps will help you determine whether or not you already have a mail account. If you don't, you will need to set one up before you can continue with this tutorial. Outlook Express can help you with this task. You can set up a Hotmail account almost instantaneously, but to set up a POP or IMAP account, you will need to provide the account information, such as your incoming and outgoing mail server address and type, your user-name and password, and your e-mail address.

To examine your mail account:

1. Click **Tools** and then click **Accounts** to open the Internet Accounts dialog box.

2. Click the **Mail** tab, if necessary. See Figure 5-34, which shows one mail account already set up.

Figure 5-34   **MAIL ACCOUNTS**

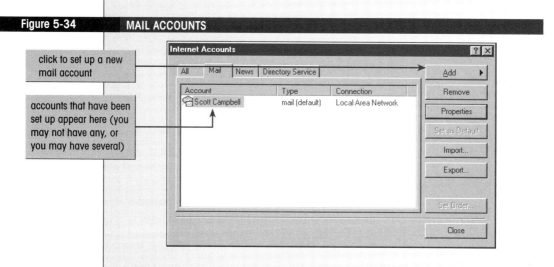

click to set up a new mail account

accounts that have been set up appear here (you may not have any, or you may have several)

---

3. Click the account you want to use.

   TROUBLE? If no account appears with your name, no account has been set up for you. You can set up an account yourself by clicking the Add button and then clicking Mail. The Internet Connection Wizard starts. This Wizard walks you through the steps of setting up a mail account. If you don't know the answers to all the questions the Wizard asks, you will need to get further assistance from your technical support person or your Internet service provider.

4. Click the **Properties** button. Your name and e-mail address should appear in the account Properties dialog box; Outlook Express uses this information when you send and receive e-mail. See Figure 5-35.

   TROUBLE? If your new mail account doesn't appear in the list of accounts, click the Close button in the Internet Accounts dialog box, click No to the question about downloading services and then repeat Steps 1 through 4. Your account should appear. If the name and e-mail address boxes are blank, ask your instructor or technical support person what to enter in them.

| Figure 5-35 | CONFIGURING E-MAIL PROPERTIES |

make sure your e-mail
address appears here

your user information
will differ

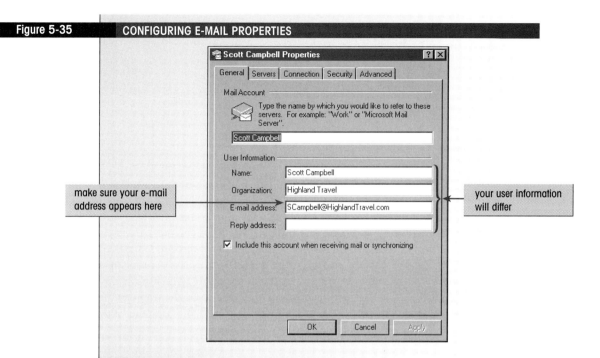

5. Click the **Server** tab to check your mail server information. Your account name (user ID) and password should appear, along with information about your mail server (your password will appear as a series of asterisks so that passers-by cannot see it). For an HTTP account such as Hotmail, you would see the URL of the mail provider's Web page, but Highland Travel uses POP accounts, so each account must identify the incoming and outgoing mail server address, as shown in Figure 5-36.

TROUBLE? If any of these boxes is blank, ask your instructor or technical support person what to enter in them.

| Figure 5-36 | CHECKING MAIL SERVER INFORMATION |

if you have a different
mail server type, such
as HTTP, your server
options will differ

your mail server
addresses will differ

user ID and password;
yours will differ

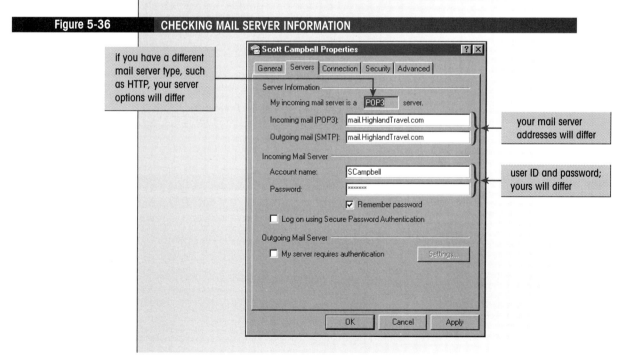

6. Click the **OK** button to close the account Properties dialog box and then click the **Close** button in the Internet Accounts dialog box.

Now that you have ensured that Outlook Express can handle your e-mail, you're ready to send e-mail messages.

Sending E-mail

An e-mail message uses the same format as a standard memo: it typically includes From, Date, To, and Subject lines, followed by the content of the message. The **To line** indicates who will receive the message. Outlook Express automatically supplies your name or e-mail address in the **From line** and the date you send the message in the **Date line** (as set in your computer's clock). The **Subject line**, although optional, alerts the recipient to the topic of the message. Finally, the **message area** contains the content of your message. You can also include additional information, such as a **Cc line**, which indicates who will receive a copy of the message, or a Priority setting, which indicates the importance of the message.

When you prepare an e-mail message, you should remember some commonsense guidelines:

- Think before you type; read before you send. Your name and your institution's name are attached to everything you send.
- Type in both uppercase and lowercase letters. Using all uppercase letters in e-mail messages is considered shouting, and messages in all lowercase letters are difficult to read and decipher.
- Edit your message. Keep your messages concise so the reader can understand your meaning quickly and clearly.
- Send appropriate amounts of useful information. Like junk mail, e-mail messages can pile up quickly. If you must send a longer message, attach it as a file.
- Find out if personal e-mail messages are allowed on a work account. E-mail is not free. (Businesses pay to subscribe to a server.)
- E-mail at your workplace or school is not necessarily confidential. Your employer, for example, might be able to access your e-mail.

Viewing Outlook Express Folders

Outlook Express organizes all the messages it handles, outgoing and incoming, into **folders**, or compartments that allow you to sort your messages, located on the Folders list in the Outlook Express window. Figure 5-37 describes the Outlook Express folders that you can use to store mail.

Figure 5-37	OUTLOOK EXPRESS FOLDERS
FOLDER	**DESCRIPTION**
Inbox	Stores messages that have just been delivered and messages that you've read but haven't discarded or filed
Outbox	Stores messages that you've finished composing and plan to send as soon as you connect to your mail server
Sent Items	Stores a copy of every message you've sent until you discard or file them
Deleted Items	Stores the messages you've discarded. They remain in this folder until you delete them from here, and then they are irretrievable.
Drafts	Stores messages that you have written but not finished

When a folder contains one or more messages that you have not sent or read, the folder name appears in boldface and Outlook Express places the number of new or pending messages in that folder within parentheses.

Any folder that contains subfolders is preceded by a plus box ⊞ or minus box ⊟ in the Folders list. When ⊞ appears in front of a folder, its subfolders are hidden. When ⊟ appears, its subfolders are visible. Outlook Express automatically starts with Local Folders open. To see the contents of a folder, you click it in the Folders list.

To work with Outlook Express folders:

1. Click **Outbox** in the Local Folders list. It will probably be empty, unless you have other outgoing mail. See Figure 5-38.

Figure 5-38	VIEWING THE OUTBOX FOLDER

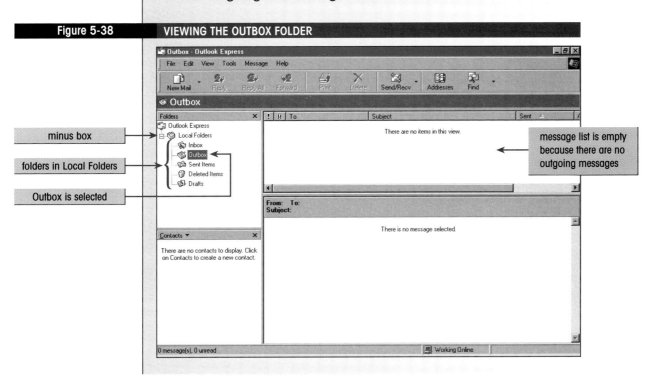

minus box

folders in Local Folders

Outbox is selected

message list is empty because there are no outgoing messages

Now you're ready to compose and send your first message.

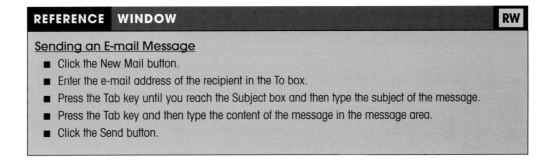

REFERENCE WINDOW   RW

Sending an E-mail Message

- Click the New Mail button.
- Enter the e-mail address of the recipient in the To box.
- Press the Tab key until you reach the Subject box and then type the subject of the message.
- Press the Tab key and then type the content of the message in the message area.
- Click the Send button.

When you click the Send button, Outlook Express places the message in the Outbox and then sends it immediately if you're connected to your mail server and if you haven't changed Outlook's default settings. Because you've opened the Outbox, you'll be able to watch this happen. Remembering that Scott wanted you to contact Katie Herrera about a Highland Travel golf tour as soon as you got settled, you decide to compose your first message to her. Her e-mail address is KHerrera@HighlandTravel.com.

To send an e-mail message:

1. Click the **New Mail** button ▣. The New Message window opens, which allows you to compose a new message.

   TROUBLE? If you receive an error message at any point during these steps, check your mail server properties using the procedure you learned in the previous section. Write down your settings and then ask your instructor or technical support person for help.

   TROUBLE? If you have more than one account, be aware that in the outgoing message, Outlook Express identifies the sender for the currently selected account. If, for example, you want to send a message from your Hotmail account, click Hotmail in the Folders list before you click the New Mail button.

2. Type **KHerrera@HighlandTravel.com**, and then press **Tab**.

3. Type your own e-mail address in the Cc box, and then press **Tab**. Note that normally you would not copy yourself on an e-mail sent to another person. You are sending a copy to yourself only to ensure that you will receive mail later for practice in other sections of this tutorial.

4. Type **Golf Tour** in the Subject box, and then press the **Tab** key.

5. Type the following message in the content area:

   Scott Campbell suggested I contact you regarding the new St. Andrews Golf Tour we're starting next summer.

   Thank you,

   (your name)

6. Before you send the message, make sure you are watching the Outbox. Read all of Step 7 before you perform it, so you know what to watch for.

7. Click the **Send** button. Outlook Express moves your message into the Outbox; the Outbox is briefly boldfaced and followed by a (1) in the Local Folders list, indicating there is one outgoing message. Then, Outlook Express sends the message on its way. The message and the (1) disappear, the Outbox is empty, and the Outbox is no longer boldfaced in the list. See Figure 5-39.

Figure 5-39	SENDING A MESSAGE

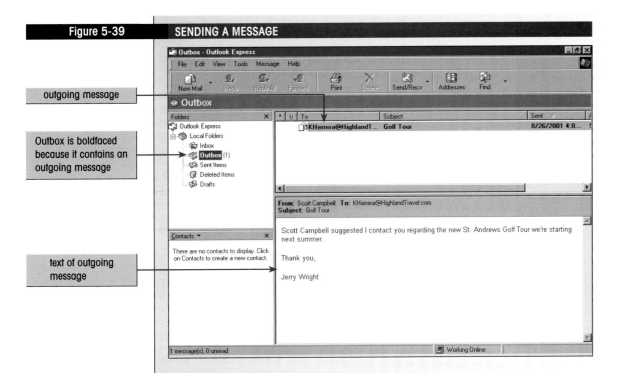

outgoing message

Outbox is boldfaced because it contains an outgoing message

text of outgoing message

TROUBLE? If Outlook Express does not send the message immediately and the (1) does not disappear, Outlook Express might be configured only to send messages when you click the Send/Recv button. Click the Send/Recv button [icon] and watch Outlook Express send the message. Note that you may also receive new messages at this point. You'll deal with reading new messages shortly. If you want to change this setting, click Tools, click Options, click the Send tab, click the Send messages immediately check box, and then click OK to indicate that you want outgoing mail sent immediately.

TROUBLE? If Outlook Express requests a password, you might need to enter a password before you can send and receive your mail messages.

The time it takes to send an e-mail message depends on the size of the message, the speed of your Internet connection, and the quantity of Internet traffic at that time. When you send an e-mail, your outgoing mail server examines the host name in the e-mail address, locates the host, and delivers the message to that host. Because your mail server is not connected to every other host, e-mail is rarely sent along a direct path to the recipient. Instead, the message is handed from one host to another until the e-mail reaches its destination. Figure 5-40 shows how the Internet routes a message from a student at the University of Alaska to a student at the University of the Virgin Islands.

Figure 5-40   **INTERNET E-MAIL ROUTES**

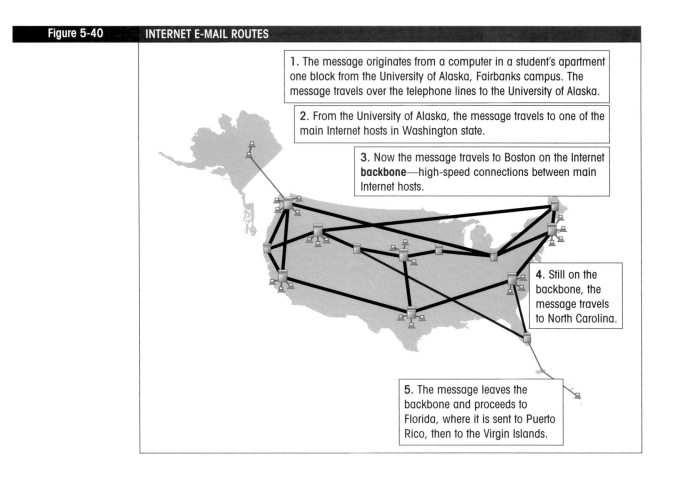

1. The message originates from a computer in a student's apartment one block from the University of Alaska, Fairbanks campus. The message travels over the telephone lines to the University of Alaska.

2. From the University of Alaska, the message travels to one of the main Internet hosts in Washington state.

3. Now the message travels to Boston on the Internet **backbone**—high-speed connections between main Internet hosts.

4. Still on the backbone, the message travels to North Carolina.

5. The message leaves the backbone and proceeds to Florida, where it is sent to Puerto Rico, then to the Virgin Islands.

Receiving E-mail

How you receive e-mail depends on your account. For example, if you are using a Web-based account, you connect to your provider's Web page and view your messages there. If you are using a POP account, your mail server collects your mail and holds it until your mail program contacts the mail server and requests any mail addressed to your user ID. Your mail program then downloads any waiting messages to your computer. (Remember that the Outlook Express mail program allows you to set up a Hotmail account so that it too can receive local mail delivery.)

You can check your e-mail at any time by clicking the Send/Recv button 🖼. Your mail server delivers any e-mail messages that have arrived since you last checked (and sends any messages currently in the Outbox). Some people check for new e-mail messages sporadically during the day, while others check at regular intervals, such as every hour or every morning and evening. If you are always connected to the Internet, Outlook Express automatically checks for messages at a specified interval. You can set this interval on the General tab of the Options dialog box, available on the Tools menu, but you won't do that now.

Remember that you sent a copy of your e-mail to yourself for the purpose of completing this tutorial. You'll now check to see whether the copy arrived.

To check for incoming mail:

1. Click the **Send/Recv** button ⬛. If a dialog box opens requesting your password, enter your password and follow the instructions in the dialog box.

2. Click **Inbox** in the Folders list. New messages appear in the message list, and a number in parentheses appears, indicating the number of new messages you've received. See Figure 5-41. Your Inbox folder might contain additional e-mail messages from other people.

Figure 5-41	RECEIVING MESSAGES

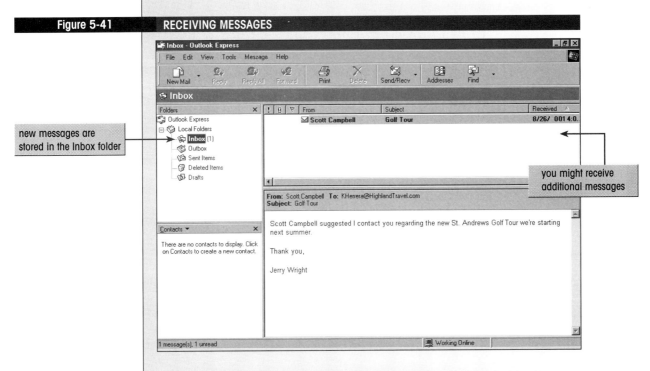

new messages are stored in the Inbox folder

you might receive additional messages

TROUBLE? If you receive a returned mail message in addition to the copy of your message to Katie, don't worry. This happens because the e-mail address you are using for Katie Herrera is fictional. You'll learn more about returned mail shortly.

TROUBLE? If enough time has elapsed since you sent the message, Outlook Express might have checked for incoming mail already. If that's the case, the copy should already appear. If no messages appear, your mail server might not have received or sent the messages yet. Occasionally, some mail servers cause mail to be delayed. Check later to see if your mail has arrived, or consult your technical support person.

Unread messages appear in boldface, preceded by the unread mail icon ✉. The message list displays a **message header** for each message, which identifies the sender, subject (truncated if it's too long), and date received. Your window might list additional columns. You can change the width of the columns in the message list by dragging the column header border in the appropriate direction. You can also click a column button to sort columns by that button. For example, if you click the From button, Outlook Express sorts messages in the current folder alphabetically by name. The default sort order is by date and time received, with newest messages on top.

The message list displays a variety of icons that help you determine the status of the message. For example, ✉ tells you the message has been read; ✉ tells you the message has not been read; ✉ tells you the message is in progress in the Drafts folder.

You can view a message in its own window or in the preview pane. If you click to select an e-mail message from the message list, the contents of that message appear in the preview pane. If you double-click a message from the message list, a separate message window opens. Either way, after a predetermined number of seconds, the message header no longer appears in boldface, indicating that you've displayed the message. You already saw how you can hide the preview pane if you want to view only the message list. You can also resize the preview pane by dragging its upper border up or down. For example, to enlarge the preview so you can see more of a message, drag the top border of the pane up.

Your Inbox should contain the copy of the message you sent yourself. Try reading it now.

To read an e-mail message:

1. If necessary, click the message you sent yourself, which has the subject "Golf Tour" in the message list. The contents of that message appear in the preview pane. After a few seconds (5 is the default), the Unread icon ✉ changes to Read ✉, and the message no longer appears in boldface.

2. Now try adjusting the column widths. Point at the vertical line that forms one of the column borders until your pointer changes to ↔.

3. Drag the pointer slightly to the right to see more of the column, or to the left to see less.

   TROUBLE? If your window shows additional columns, don't worry. You can determine what information to display by clicking View, clicking Columns, and then removing the check from the box of the column display you wish to suppress.

By successfully viewing the copy of the message you sent to yourself, you've verified that Outlook Express is configured properly on your computer.

Handling Undelivered Messages

Sometimes you send an e-mail message to an Internet address that is no longer active, for example when a person switches to a different ISP. When an outgoing mail server cannot locate a recipient's address, it sends an undeliverable mail message to the sender. This is similar to the postal service returning a letter because the street address is incorrect.

Because Katie's e-mail address is fictional, you will probably receive a returned mail message from the mail delivery subsystem of your outgoing mail server, telling you that the host was not found. Check for this message now.

To read a returned mail message:

1. Click the **Send/Recv** button 🖻.

2. Click a message with "Returned mail" or something similar in the Subject column.

   TROUBLE? If no such message appears, don't worry. It might appear later.

3. Read the message. It should inform you that the e-mail address had an unknown host.

If e-mail messages you send are returned undelivered, you should verify the e-mail addresses that you used. Make sure that everything is typed correctly and that the person is still using that e-mail address.

Replying to a Message

Often, you'll want to respond to an e-mail message. Although you could create and send a new message, it's easier to use the Reply feature, which automatically inserts the e-mail address of the sender and the subject into the proper lines in the message window. The Reply feature also "quotes" the sender's text to remind the sender of the message to which you are responding. When you reply to an e-mail message, you can respond to the original sender of the message, or to the sender and everyone else who received the message.

You're first going to view the message you sent yourself, this time in its own window, and then you're going to practice replying to it. To open a message in its own window, double-click the message in the message list. This allows you to display more of the message at once.

Note that this is a *practice* reply. Normally, you would not reply to yourself! Rather, you would reply to someone who sent you a real message.

To open a message in its own window and then reply to it:

1. Double-click the **Golf Tour** message in the message list. The message opens in its own window. Maximize this window if necessary.

2. Click the **Reply** button [icon]. The message window opens, with your name in the To box (because you're replying to your own message) and the original message's subject in the Subject box, preceded by "Re:", which means "regarding." The message quotes your original message.

3. Type the following reply in the message area (the cursor automatically blinks at the beginning of a blank line):

   Thanks for the information.
   (your name)

4. If necessary, scroll down to see how the original text of the message is quoted after the reply you just typed. See Figure 5-42.

Figure 5-42	REPLYING TO A MESSAGE

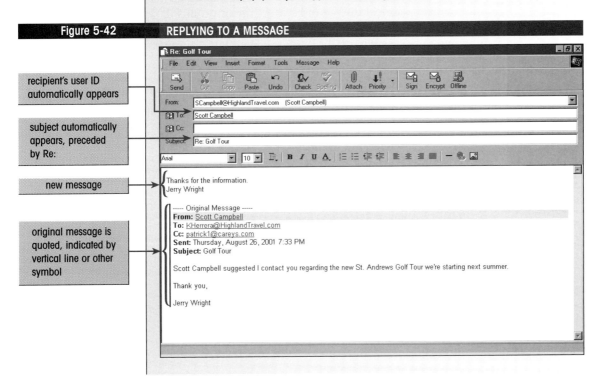

recipient's user ID automatically appears

subject automatically appears, preceded by Re:

new message

original message is quoted, indicated by vertical line or other symbol

> **5.** Click the **Send** button 🖳. Outlook Express sends the message. (You can tell that the message has been sent when there is no longer a number next to the Outbox icon in the Folders list.)

Deciding whether or not to quote the sender's original message when you reply to a message depends on several factors. If the recipient might need to be reminded of the message content, it's appropriate to quote. However, long messages take longer to download, so whenever possible you should delete quoted material from your messages.

Printing a Message

You can print an e-mail message using the File menu's Print command. You decide to print the message you received from yourself.

> *To print an e-mail message:*
>
> **1.** Make sure the message you received is either open in its own window or selected in the message list.
>
> **2.** Click **File** and then click **Print**.
>
> **3.** Check the print settings in the Print dialog box and then click the **Print** button.
>
> **4.** If necessary, click the **Close** button ✖ to close the message.
>
> **5.** Close Outlook Express.

By default, Outlook Express formats messages using HTML. When you print a message formatted in HTML, it includes lines and boldface headings. However, if the message you are printing uses plaintext instead of HTML, the printout will not contain formatting, and some of the lines might be uneven. You can change this setting by clicking Tools, clicking Options, and then specifying HTML on the Send tab. Your messages will then be sent formatted. If you need a high-quality printout of a plaintext message, you can save the message as a text file, open it in a word processor, and edit it there so that it looks professional.

Scott has now finished your training on e-mail. As you continue to work with Outlook Express, you'll see other ways in which e-mail can be integrated with the workings of Windows 2000 and the Web.

Session 5.3 QUICK CHECK

1. What is a mail server?
2. Identify the user ID portion and the host name portion of the following e-mail address: pcsmith@icom.net.
3. How can you view your mail account properties in Outlook Express?
4. Where can you find a copy of a message you sent?
5. Why shouldn't you type your messages in all uppercase letters?
6. Name two advantages the Reply feature has over the New Mail feature when you are responding to an e-mail.

REVIEW ASSIGNMENTS

1. **History of the Internet and the World Wide Web**   Computers have been around for several decades now, but how did the Internet and the World Wide Web get started? Microsoft considered the Internet an important enough development to incorporate many of its features into the Windows 2000 operating system. Go to the library and locate books or articles on the Internet, and write a single-page essay on the history of the Internet. Answer questions such as:

    a. What role did the ARPANET play in the development of the Internet?
    b. What role did CERN play in the development of the World Wide Web?
    c. Over what period of time did the Internet grow? What about the World Wide Web?
    d. When did browsers first become available?

2. **Connecting to the Internet over a Modem**   This tutorial mentioned that home computer users can connect to the Internet using a dial-up connection via an account with an ISP. Assume you have your own computer, and you want to connect to the Internet from home. Contact at least three ISPs in your area, ask for their rates and services, and then write a single-page essay describing your findings. Which ISP would you choose, and why?

3. **Exploring Your Home Page**   In this tutorial the figures showed Microsoft Corporation's home page as the home page. Your home page might be different—take some time to explore.

    a. Start the Internet Explorer browser and print your home page.
    b. Click one of the links on your home page, and continue to click any interesting links that you encounter. Clicking whatever links interest you is often called "surfing." On your printout, circle the link you followed. Write in the margin where it took you.
    c. Use the Home button to return to your home page, and then click another link and go where it leads you. Again, circle the link on your printout, indicate where you ended up, and write what you saw along the way.

4. **Connecting to Specific Web Sites**   You learned in this tutorial that you can enter a URL into the Address box of your browser to connect to a specific Web site. Using the Internet Explorer browser, enter the following URLs, and print the first page of each URL.

    a. http://www.usps.gov
    b. http://www.nps.gov
    c. http://www.cnn.com
    d. Using any one of these pages as a starting point, follow links until you locate a page with frames. Record the URL of the page you found.

5. **Web Page Desktop Background**   Because he will be placing the Highland Web page on your desktop soon, Scott wants you to practice using a Web page as a desktop background.

    a. Apply the Highland Web page (not the folder), located in the root directory of your Data Disk, as your desktop background.
    b. Observe the background carefully and work with the objects that are incorporated into this Web page.
    c. Connect to the Active Desktop Gallery and add a desktop item that would add to the usefulness of this desktop.
    d. Using the Highland desktop you just created as an example, write two paragraphs describing what a Web page background offers that a graphic image file, such as you used in Tutorial 4, does not. Give detailed information about the purpose of each element on the desktop.
    e. Restore your computer's background to its original state.

Explore   6. **E-mailing a Web Page and a Link** Scott wants you to share the Highland Travel Home page with some potential clients. Internet Explorer provides tools to easily e-mail either the entire Web page or a link to the page.

    a. Connect to the Internet and open the Highland Travel home page in Internet Explorer.

    b. Click the Mail button 🖾 on the Standard Buttons toolbar, and click Send a Link to send a link to the home page to your instructor.

    c. Click the Mail button 🖾 again, and send the entire Web page to your instructor.

    d. What problems might there be in sending a Web page to a user? What should you know about the user's e-mail program before attempting to send the page?

Explore   7. **Editing the Links Toolbar** Scott tells you that the Links toolbar is another place, besides the Favorites folder, where you can place shortcuts to your favorite Web sites. The Links toolbar is one of the toolbars displayed by Internet Explorer that displays icons for specific Web sites. Scott wants you to learn how to use it.

    a. Start Internet Explorer and display the Links toolbar in the Web browser (click View on the menu bar, click Toolbars, and then click—if necessary—to place a check mark next to Links).

    b. Click the double arrow on the right side of the Links toolbar, and then click the Customize Links icon (if the Customize Links button is missing, go to the Web page at: http://www.microsoft.com/windows98/usingwindows/internet/tips/advanced/Customize LinksBar.asp).

    c. Print the Web page.

    d. Using the information on this Web page, add a link to the Highland Travel home page to the Links toolbar.

    e. Display the Links toolbar on the Windows 2000 taskbar, making sure that the icon for the Highland Travel home page is visible.

    f. Using the techniques from Tutorial 2, print a copy of your screen with the revised Links toolbar.

    g. Remove the icon for the Highland Travel home page from the Links toolbar.

Explore   8. **Using Rich Text Formatting in E-mail**   Scott tells you that with Outlook Express you can use special fonts and formats to liven up your e-mail messages. You decide to test this by sending an e-mail message to Katie Herrera, telling her of your interest in working on the St. Andrews project.

    a. Start Outlook Express and compose an e-mail message to your instructor with the subject line "St. Andrews Project".

    b. In the message area, enter (in your own words) your interest in the project and willingness to participate.

    c. Turn on formatting for the message by clicking Format on the menu bar of the mail message window and then clicking Rich Text. In the message area, boldface at least one word and italicize at least one word. To boldface a word, you select it and then click the Bold button **B**. To italicize it, you select it and then click the Italic button *I*.

    d. Now color one word red: select the word, click the Font Color button A⏷, and then click the color red.

    e. Send the message to your instructor.

PROJECTS

1. Internet Explorer and Windows Explorer share many of the same menus, commands, and toolbars. In fact, you can modify Windows Explorer to look and operate exactly like Internet Explorer.

   a. Open Windows Explorer.
   b. In the Address bar, enter the URL of your Home page (or use www.msn.com if you don't know the URL of your home page), and then press the Enter key. Connect to the Internet if you are not already connected.
   c. Modify the Explorer Bar so that it displays the Favorites pane.
   d. Using techniques shown in Tutorial 2, print a copy of your screen. Include the taskbar.
   e. Open the same Web page in Internet Explorer and display the Favorites pane in that program. Compare the displays of Internet Explorer and Windows Explorer. Can you see any difference between the two?
   f. Microsoft's goal with Windows 2000 was to create a "single Explorer." Why do you think Microsoft set this goal? What advantages or disadvantages does the single Explorer have?

2. You have a friend who has used Windows Explorer extensively for managing his own files and folders, and you mention to him that he can also use Windows Explorer as a browser. Write him a note, which you'll e-mail to him, that describes how this is possible. Make sure you describe what happens to elements such as the left and right panes, the Address bar, the activity indicator, and the status bar.

3. In this tutorial you learned how to access information on the Web when you either knew the URL or used a link to jump there. Internet Explorer also includes the Search pane (like Windows Explorer), that helps you find the Web pages you need. Use Internet Explorer's online Help to learn about the Search pane and about the general topic of searching the Web.

   a. How would you search for information on a given topic?
   b. Once the Search feature displays a list of search results, what should you do to display the Web page containing the information?
   c. Follow the directions you studied in the Help file to search for information on one of your hobbies, such as snowboarding. While you are using the Search Explorer bar, write down the exact steps you take. Was your search successful? Write down the URL of the page you connected to.

4. You just went to California for a three-week vacation with some friends. On returning, you decide to "capture the moment" by downloading a graphic image that will remind you of your vacation activities.

   a. Use what you learned in Project 3 to locate a graphic image of surfing, rock climbing, wine tasting, or some other vacation activity, and download it to your Data Disk. (If you skipped Project 3, connect to the Highland site or your home page and download a graphic from there.)
   b. Send an e-mail to your instructor containing the image (you can paste the image into the e-mail document by clicking Insert on the New Message window's title bar—then click Picture, click Browse, locate and click the file, and then click OK.

5. Because most labs can't accommodate subscriptions, you probably will need your own computer to complete this project. Your dream is to plan your investments so you can retire by age 55. To keep yourself posted on the stock market:

   a. Locate a Web site that contains stock market information. You could try http://www.nasdaq.com or http://www.djia.com.
   b. Place this Web page on your desktop as an Active Desktop item (you can add in the Web dialog sheet of the Display Properties dialog box).
   c. Set up a synchronization schedule for the Web page so that it is automatically updated every morning at 8 AM.

d. Create a log in Notepad (perhaps using the LOG feature you learned about in Tutorial 4) to record information such as the closing value of an index such as NASDAQ or the Dow on a given day.

e. When you have recorded three days' worth of information in the log, open the log window and your synchronization schedule, and print your screen so your instructor can see which Web page you subscribed to and what information you gained. Make sure you unsubscribe from the Web page once the three days are over.

LAB ASSIGNMENTS

The Internet: World Wide Web

One of the most popular services on the Internet is the World Wide Web. This lab is a Web simulator that teaches you how to use Web browser software to find information. You can use this lab whether or not your school provides you with Internet access. See the Read This Before You Begin page for information on starting the lab.

1. Click the Steps button to learn how to use Web browser software. As you proceed through the steps, answer all of the Quick Check questions that appear. After you complete the steps, you will see a Quick Check Summary Report. Follow the instructions on the screen to print this report.

2. Click the Explore button on the Welcome screen. Use the Web browser to locate a weather map of the Caribbean Virgin Islands. What is its URL?

3. A scuba diver named Wadson Lachouffe has been searching for the fabled treasure of Greybeard the pirate. A link from the Adventure Travel Web site www.atour.com leads to Wadson's Web page called "Hidden Treasure." In Explore, locate the Hidden Treasure page and answer the following questions:

   a. What was the name of Greybeard's ship?
   b. What was Greybeard's favorite food?
   c. What does Wadson think happened to Greybeard's ship?

4. In the steps, you found a graphic of Jupiter from the photo archives of the Jet Propulsion Laboratory. In the Explore section of the lab, you can also find a graphic of Saturn. Suppose one of your friends wanted a picture of Saturn for an astronomy report. Make a list of the blue, underlined links your friend must click, in the correct order, to find the Saturn graphic. Assume that your friend will begin at the Web Trainer home page.

5. Enter the URL http://www.atour.com to jump to the Adventure Travel Web site. Write a one-page description of this site. In your paper include a description of the information at the site, the number of pages the site contains, and a diagram of the links it contains.

6. Chris Thomson is a student at UVI and has his own Web pages. In Explore, look at the information Chris has included on his pages. Suppose you could create your own Web page. What would you include? Use word-processing software to design your own Web page. Make sure you indicate the graphics and links you would use.

Web Pages & HTML

It's easy to create your own Web pages. There are many software tools to help you become a Web author. In this lab you'll experiment with a Web-authoring Wizard that automates the process of creating a Web page. You'll also try your hand at working directly with HTML code. See the Read This Before You Begin page for information on starting the lab.

1. Click the Steps button to activate the Web-authoring Wizard and learn how to create a basic Web page. As you proceed through the steps, answer all of the Quick Check questions. After you complete the steps, you will see a Quick Check Summary Report. Follow the instructions on the screen to print this report.

2. In Explore, click the File menu, then click New to start working on a new Web page. Use the Wizard to create a home page for a veterinarian who offers dog day-care and boarding services. After you create the page, save it on drive A or C, and print the HTML code. Your site must have the following characteristics:

  a. Title: Dr. Dave's Dog Domain
  b. Background color: Gold
  c. Graphic: Dog.jpg
  d. Body text: Your dog will have the best care day and night at Dr. Dave's Dog Domain. Fine accommodations, good food, playtime, and snacks are all provided. You can board your pet by the day or week. Grooming services also available.
  e. Text link: "Reasonable rates" links to www.cciw.com/np3/rates.htm
  f. E-mail link: "For more information:" links to daveassist@drdave.com

3. In Explore, use the File menu to open the HTML document called Politics.htm. After you use the HTML window (not the Wizard) to make the following changes, save the revised page on drive A or C, and print the HTML code. Refer to Figure 5-43 for a list of HTML tags you can use:

Figure 5-43

HTML TAGS	MEANING AND LOCATION
<HTML></HTML>	States that the file is an HTML document; Opening tag begins the page; closing tag ends the page (required)
<HEAD></HEAD>	States that the enclosed text is the header of the page; Appears immediately after the opening HTML tag (required)
<TITLE></TITLE>	States that the enclosed text is the title of the page; Must appear within the opening and closing HEAD tags (required)
<BODY></BODY>	States that the enclosed material (all the text, images, and tags in the rest of the document) is the body of the document (required)
<H1></H1>	States that the enclosed text is a heading
 	Inserts a line break; Can be used to control line spacing and breaks in lines
<UL></UL> <OL></OL>	Indicates an unordered list (list items are preceded by bullets) or an ordered list (list items are preceded by numbers or letters)
<LI>	Indicates a list item; Precedes all items in unordered or ordered lists
<CENTER></CENTER>	Indicates that the enclosed text should be centered on the width of the page
<B></B>	Indicates that the enclosed text should appear in boldface
<I></I>	Indicates that the enclosed text should appear in italics
<A HREF="*URL*"></A>	Indicates that the enclosed text is a hypertext link; The URL of the linked material must appear within the quotation marks after the equal sign
<IMG SRC="*filename*">	Inserts an inline image into the document where *filename* is the name of the image
<HR>	Inserts a horizontal rule

  a. Change the title to Politics 2000.
  b. Center the page heading.
  c. Change the background color to FFE7C6 and the text color to 000000.
  d. Add a line break before the sentence "What's next?"
  e. Add a bold tag to "Additional links on this topic:"
  f. Add one more link to the "Additional links" list. The link should go to the site http://www.elections.ca, and the clickable link should read "Elections Canada".
  g. Change the last graphic to display the image "next.gif".

4. In Explore, use the Web-authoring Wizard and the HTML window to create a home page about yourself. You should include at least a screenful of text, a graphic, an external link, and an e-mail link. Save the page on drive A, then print the HTML code. Turn in your disk and printout.

QUICK CHECK ANSWERS

Session 5.1

1. A home page is the Web page designated by the operating system as your starting point, the Web page that an organization or business has created to give information about itself, or a personal Web page with information about an individual.
2. URL
3. Type the URL in the Address box, then press Enter.
4. It is an educational site.
5. site
6. Open the History pane in Internet Explorer. You can then try to locate the page by viewing the list of pages you accessed on a particular day, or you can search the contents of the History pane to locate it.
7. False
8. Right-click the image, click Save Picture As, enter a filename and destination folder, and then click Save.

Session 5.2

1. With offline viewing, your computer can access a Web page or file off of a network so that you can view it later without being connected to the network.
2. Push technology allows both Web site authors and subscribers to gain more control over content delivery and schedule.
3. Active Desktop item
4. Synchronization is a process by which an offline file is updated with the most recent version of the network file.
5. Right-click the object and open its Properties dialog box. On the Schedule dialog sheet, add 24 new schedules, one for each hour of the day.
6. Hypertext Markup Language, the underlying language of Web documents
7. You can add special items such as animated graphics, links to files and Web pages, and applets to run programs for you from the desktop.

Session 5.3

1. A mail server is a computer on a network that manages the storage and delivery of electronic mail.
2. User ID: pcsmith, host name: icom.net
3. Click Tools, click Accounts, click the Mail tab, click the account with your name, and then click the Properties button.
4. the Sent Items folder
5. The recipient might interpret the uppercase letters as shouting—considered rude in most e-mail exchanges.
6. The recipient's e-mail address is automatically inserted, the subject is automatically inserted, and the original message is automatically quoted.

In this tutorial you will:

- Find files by name, contents, and location using several methods, including wildcards

- Open and work with files from the Search window

- Limit a search to a specific folder

- Locate files by date, type, and size

- Open documents with the Documents menu

- Search for information on the Internet using query and subject searches

- Search for people and maps on the Internet

SEARCHING FOR INFORMATION

Using the Search Feature to Locate Files for a Speechwriter

CASE

Speechwriter's Aide

Like thousands of other college students who are graduating soon, you've been dropping in at the campus job center regularly. Today, you notice that Senator Susannah Bernstein's speechwriter has posted an advertisement for an aide. When you call to inquire, Carolyn King, the Senator's speechwriter, asks you to come by the next morning. Your interview goes very well. You learn that the job would primarily entail locating information that Carolyn could use in writing the Senator's speeches. Carolyn explains that her previous aide collected and organized information in a filing cabinet. In addition to the paper archive, the previous aide started an electronic quotations archive that includes over a hundred files on a 3½-inch disk. These files contain anecdotes, jokes, and commentary on a variety of subjects.

You explain to Carolyn that you could maximize the efficiency of the information retrieval process if you had a computer running Windows 2000 with an Internet connection. Carolyn doesn't think that should be a problem, but she hasn't used Windows 2000 before and asks you to update her on the features that make information retrieval easier.

You explain that Windows 2000 includes a powerful search tool called **Search** that helps you find files on the local or network drives to which you have access and helps you search for information on the Internet. The Internet contains a vast number of computers and networks that store information, much of which can be accessed and retrieved by the search tools that Windows 2000 makes available. With Windows 2000 and an Internet connection, information from around the world is accessible from your office computer. Carolyn is intrigued, and by the end of the interview she offers you the job.

After a week of training and orientation, Carolyn assigns you office space that includes a computer running Windows 2000 and an Internet connection. She promises that your first assignment will come soon, and in the meantime asks that you familiarize yourself with the information available locally.

SESSION 6.1

In this session, you will learn techniques for searching for files by their filenames, by the text they contain, and by file date, type, and size. Finally, you'll examine the Documents menu to explore another way of locating a file.

Preparing Your Data Disk

Before you can begin working, you need to bring a blank 3½-inch disk to the computer lab and use the NP on Microsoft Windows 2000 menu to create a Data Disk containing the files you will work with in this tutorial. If you are using your own computer, the NP on Microsoft Windows 2000 menu may not be available. Once you have made the disk at the computer lab, however, you can use the disk to complete this tutorial on any computer that runs Windows 2000.

To make your Data Disk:

1. Write "Disk 4—Windows 2000 Tutorial 6 Data Disk" on the label of a blank, formatted 3½-inch disk. Insert your Data Disk into drive A.

   TROUBLE? If your 3½-inch disk drive is B, place your formatted disk in that drive instead, and for the rest of this tutorial substitute drive B wherever you see drive A.

2. Point to the **Start** button ⊞Start , point to **Programs**, point to **NP on Microsoft Windows 2000-Level II**, and then click **Disk 4 (Tutorial 6)**. When you are prompted to insert your disk in the drive, click the **OK** button, and wait as the files you need are copied to your Data Disk.

3. Close all the open windows on your screen.

Search Strategies

Windows 2000 offers a useful set of search tools, available on the Search submenu of the Start menu, which help you find several types of information. See Figure 6-1.

Figure 6-1	SEARCH TOOLS
SEARCH OPTION	**DESCRIPTION**
For Files or Folders	Locates files or folders on local or network drives; also gives you access to additional options, including searching for a computer or searching for people and searching on the Internet
On the Internet	Locates information on the Internet
For People	Locates people, using directory services available on your computer and on the Internet

On your own computer, the best way to make sure you can find your files quickly and easily is to start with a well-organized folder structure. But even on your own computer, you might forget the names or locations of certain files. One of the options on the Search menu—For Files or Folders—opens the Search window, which helps you locate files and folders on the devices available to your computer. Search can help you avoid looking manually through the hundreds of files your hard drive contains. It is also useful when you are working on someone else's computer, a network computer, or a computer with multiple users who share documents, or when you have a disk with someone else's data, as is the case with the quotations archive disk that Carolyn gave you.

To search for a file, you provide Search with **search criteria**, one or more conditions you want Search to meet as it searches. For example, you could provide search criteria specifying all or part of a filename and the drive you think the file might be on. Search then locates and displays every file that matches those criteria. You can specify the criteria shown in Figure 6-2.

Figure 6-2	SEARCH CRITERIA AVAILABLE IN THE SEARCH RESULTS DIALOG BOX
OPTION	**DESCRIPTION**
Search for files or folders named	All or part of a filename
Containing text	Any words or phrases contained within the text of the file (not the filename)
Look in	The location (computer, drive, or folder) in which you want Windows 2000 to search
Date	The date or range of dates on which the file was created, last modified, or last accessed
Type	File type
Size	File size
Advanced Options	Allows you to specify search settings, such as whether or not to search subfolders or to perform a case-sensitive search

You start browsing through the quotations archive disk. You discover that the disk is organized into several folders. You open a few files and find quotes from a wide variety of people—historical figures such as Eleanor Roosevelt and Gandhi, as well as more modern personalities such as Jay Leno and Alice Walker. As you are reading through one of the files, Carolyn stops by and asks if you could look for appropriate material for a speech the Senator will deliver next week at Stanton College on successful leadership. You see there are so many files on the disk that opening and reading through every one of them would be time-consuming, so you decide to use the Search feature to locate information on the topic of leadership.

Starting Search

You didn't create the quotations files, and you know very little about them, so Search is just the tool to help you locate quotations for Senator Bernstein's speech. You can start Search from the Start menu, or from within Windows Explorer. When you use Windows Explorer, you click the Search icon 🔍 on the toolbar, or you can right-click the folder or device you want to search, and then click Search. You'll use the Start menu method.

To start Search and specify that you want to search for files or folders:

1. Click the **Start** button 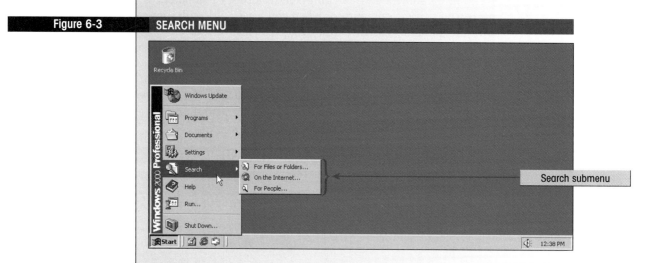 and then point to **Search**. The Search menu opens. Because you are looking for files, choose the first option, **For Files or Folders**, shown in Figure 6-3.

Figure 6-3 | SEARCH MENU

Search submenu

2. Click **For Files or Folders** on the Search menu. A window opens that lets you specify criteria for the file you are looking for. See Figure 6-4.

Figure 6-4 | SEARCH RESULTS WINDOW

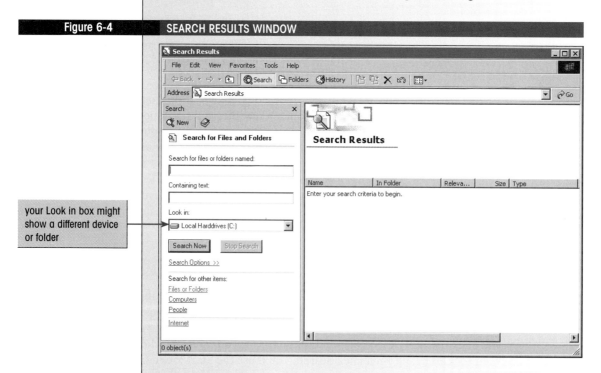

your Look in box might show a different device or folder

The Search Results window is divided into two parts: on the left is the Search Explorer bar, where you enter search criteria, and on the right is the Search Results pane, where Windows 2000 lists any files it found that matched your criteria.

Searching by Name and Location

To find a specific file, enter as much of the filename as you know. The letters you type to define the search are called a **search string**. By default, Search is not case-sensitive when searching for filenames, so you can type the search string in either uppercase or lowercase letters.

REFERENCE **WINDOW** | **RW**

Searching for a File by Name
- Click the Start button, point to Search, and then click For Files or Folders.
- Type a search string in the Search for files or folders named box.
- Click the Look in list arrow, and then click the drive you want to search, or click My Computer to select all the drives on your computer.
- Click the Search Now button.

What search string should you enter when you don't know the filename? You can guess, based on the file contents. You decide to start by looking for files named "leadership." Later you can try other search strings.

To search for files containing "leadership" in the filename:

1. Type **leadership** in the Search for files or folders named box.

You've entered a criterion for the filename. Now you need to specify a file location. When you start Search, a folder or drive name, such as Local Harddrives (C:), appears in the Look in box, which specifies where Search will search. If your computer has multiple drives and you aren't sure which drive contains the file, you can search your entire computer by clicking My Computer on the Look in list. However, if you know which drive contains the file, you can speed up your search by limiting the search to that drive. All the files you are looking for are located on your Data Disk, so specify your floppy drive as your search location.

To specify drive A as the file location and then perform the search:

1. Click the **Look in** list arrow and then click **3½ Floppy (A:)** so that Windows 2000 searches only the files on your Data Disk.

2. Click the **Search Now** button. Search searches for all files on drive A whose names contain the search string you entered. Then it displays any matching files in the Search Results pane.

3. Click **View** and then click **Details** to ensure that you are viewing file details. See Figure 6-5.

   TROUBLE? If nothing appeared, Windows 2000 might not be including subfolders in its search. Click Search Options, click the Advanced Options check box, and then make sure the Search Subfolders check box is selected. This ensures that Search will search all folders on the Data Disk, not just the files contained in the root directory. Click Search Options again to close the menu.

TROUBLE? If your results show "txt" extensions after the filenames, your computer is set to show file extensions. Either way is fine. If you want to hide file extensions, open My Computer, click Tools, click Folder Options, click the View tab, select the Hide file extensions for known file types check box, and then click the OK button and close My Computer.

| Figure 6-5 | SEARCH RESULTS PANE |

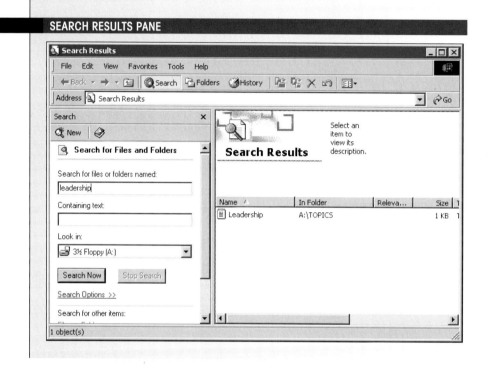

The Search Results list shows one file, Leadership. The In Folder column shows the file location, A:\Topics. The location begins with the drive—in this case, A. If the file is in a folder, a backslash (\) separates the drive from the folder name. Therefore, files in A:\Topics are in the Topics folder on drive A. If there are subfolders, additional backslashes separate the folders from one another. Figure 6-6 shows how this notation works on a drive A that contains two folders, Politics and Speeches, both of which have subfolders.

| Figure 6-6 | FILE LOCATIONS |

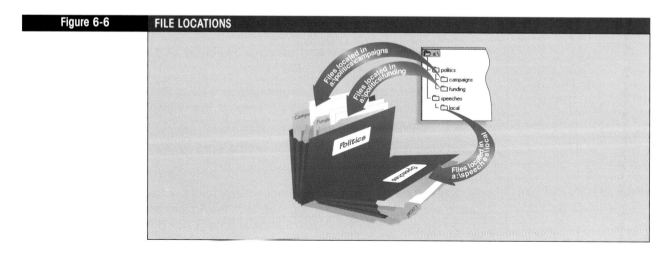

Experimenting with Search Strings

You wonder if you would find more files using a different search string. One rule of thumb is to use the root of your search word as your criterion. For example, if you decide to search for files on political topics for Senator Bernstein's speech, should you enter "politics" as your search string? Probably not, because a file named Politician (for example) will not appear in the Search Results pane. However, the root "politic," without the added "s," would yield files named Politician, Political Quotations, or Politics. Figure 6-7 shows several examples of search strings that use the root of a word (you don't need to try any of these now).

Figure 6-7	CHOOSING EFFECTIVE SEARCH STRINGS	
TOPIC	**USE THIS SEARCH STRING:**	**FINDS THESE FILENAMES:**
politics	politic	Politics, Politicians, Political Quotations
education	educ	Education, Educational Issues, Educators
computers	comput	Computers, Computing, Computerization

Of course, if the root of the word is very general, it might let in unwanted files. Searching for "lead" instead of "leader" would display a file such as "Lead Corrosion." Fortunately, it's easy to adjust your search string until you find only those files you want.

Now that you know there is a file containing quotations specifically about leadership, you look for files on leaders, using "leader" as your search string. To perform a new search, you can change the existing criteria, add a new criterion, or click the New button, which returns all Search settings to their defaults. You change the search string "leadership" to "leader" in the Search for files or folders named box. Drive A is still specified in the Look in box.

To search for files containing the search string "leader" on drive A:

1. Change the entry in the Search for files or folders named box from leadership to **leader**.

   TROUBLE? To change an entry in a text box, often you can simply double-click the text box to select the contents, and whatever you type replaces the existing entry. Or you can click once and then edit the text box contents.

2. Click the **Search Now** button. The Search Results pane now lists three files that might contain information on leadership. See Figure 6-8.

Figure 6-8   EXPANDING A SEARCH

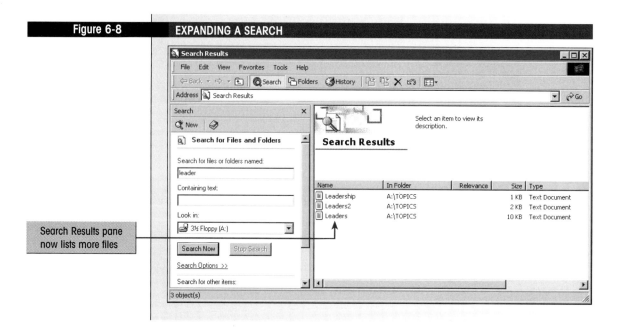

Search Results pane now lists more files

Opening a File from Scratch

Once you locate a file using the Search feature, you can open it directly, as you would from My Computer, Windows Explorer, or any similar window that lists files. You can right-click it and then click Open, click it and then press Enter, or double-click it. Windows 2000 locates and starts the program that created the file, and then it opens the file. If Windows 2000 cannot open your file, it is possible that you don't have the necessary program for that file type installed on your computer. If this is the case, Windows 2000 prompts you to specify the program you want to use to display the file.

You decide to open the Leadership file to see if it contains any quotes the Senator might find useful.

To open a file from the Search Results pane:

1. Right-click the **Leadership** file in the Search Results pane and then click **Open**. The file opens in Notepad.

   TROUBLE? If the text of the quotations extends beyond the right border of the Notepad window, click Format and then click Word Wrap.

2. Browse through the contents of the file and note that it contains several quotations on leadership. When you are finished, click the Notepad **Close** button ☒ to close Notepad. Click **No** if you are prompted to save your changes.

You show Carolyn the files you found for the speech at Stanton College.

Using **Wildcards**

Carolyn is pleased that you found helpful material for her. She mentions that Senator Bernstein will be participating in an atomic energy symposium next month, so anything you can find on that topic would be useful. You decide to check if there are any files on Albert Einstein, but you can't remember how to spell his name. If you make a spelling error, Search won't locate the files you want. You can, however, use wildcards to approximate a filename. **Wildcards** are characters that you can substitute for all or part of a filename in a search string. Search recognizes two wildcards: the asterisk and the question mark. To locate a group of files whose names follow certain specific patterns, such as all files that begin and end with certain characters, or all files with a specified string in a specified location, you can use wildcards.

The * (asterisk) wildcard stands in place of any number of consecutive characters in a filename. With the search string "m*n" for example, Search locates files with names such as Men, Magician, or Modern, but not Male or Women. Here, the files that Search locates have a common characteristic: they all begin with "m" and end with "n." When Search encounters the asterisk wildcard in a search string, it allows additional characters only in those places indicated by the wildcard. Search does not include filenames with characters before the "m" or after the "n." If this is not what you wanted, you can use additional wildcards. If you specify the search string "*m*n*" then Search includes Men, Magician, Modern, Women, and Mention, but not Male. These files have the letter "m" in common, which appears somewhere in the name, followed at a later point by the letter "n."

You can also control the Search Results pane with the ? (question mark) wildcard, which lets you select files when one character in the filename varies. For example, the search string "m?n" locates Men or Man but not Mistaken or Moon.

Files that match the "m?n" criteria must have the letters "m" and "n" in their filenames, separated by a single character. Unlike the asterisk wildcard, however, the question mark wildcard does not cause Search to exclude files with characters before or after the "m" or "n." So although "m*n" excludes Women and Mental, "m?n" does not, because both of these files contain "m" and "n" separated by a single character.

The question mark wildcard is often used to locate files whose names include version numbers or dates, such as Sales1, Sales2, and Sales3, or Tax1997, Tax1998, and Tax1999.

You decide to search for only those files beginning with "e" and ending with "n" because you know those are the first and last letters of Einstein's name, although you aren't sure what's in between. To perform this search, you use "e*n" as your search string. Try this search now.

To locate files using the asterisk wildcard:

1. Select the contents of the **Search for files or folders named** box.

2. Type **e*n** and then click the **Search Now** button. Search locates files on your Data Disk whose names start with "e" followed by any number of characters and then the letter "n." See Figure 6-9.

Figure 6-9   **SEARCHING WITH THE ASTERISK WILDCARD**

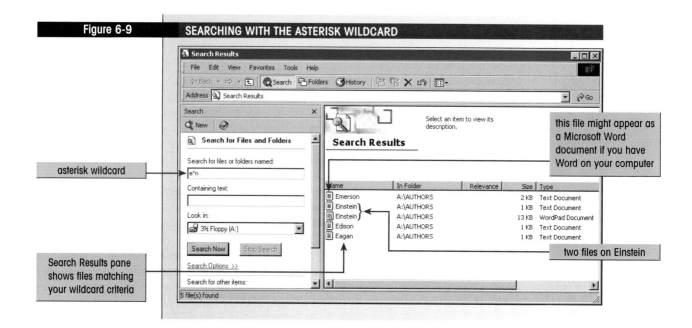

You make a mental note that there are files on Einstein that might be appropriate for the atomic energy symposium.

Finding a Text String in a File

You've found a file on Einstein, and you wonder if there are files specifically on atomic energy. You search for files named "atomic" or "energy" but don't find any. You know, however, that this doesn't necessarily mean there are no quotes on atomic energy within the files. A useful feature of the Windows 2000 Search utility is its ability to search for a word or phrase in the contents of a file, not just in the filename. To use this feature, you enter a text string in the Containing text box. A **text string** is any series of characters, such as a word or a phrase. Search searches through the entire text of every file to find the specified text string.

When you use the text string feature of the Search feature, you can specify whether your search is case-sensitive. For example, if you wanted to find a letter you wrote to Brenda Wolf, you could enter "Wolf" as your text string, and then select a case-sensitive search to locate only files containing Wolf with an initial capital letter. The Case sensitive option affects only the case of letters in the Containing text box—not those in the Search for files or folders named box. The Case sensitive option is available, along with other options, in the Search Options list, which you can view by clicking Search Options and then selecting the appropriate check box.

You decide to search for the text string "atomic energy" in hopes of finding files containing quotations Carolyn could use in writing her speech for the atomic energy symposium.

To look for the text string "atomic energy" within a file:

1. Delete the contents of the Search for files or folders named box.

2. Click the **Containing text** box.

3. Type **atomic energy**, but don't click Search Now yet. Because you aren't sure what case the quote might be in, you want to make sure Search isn't set to perform case-sensitive searches.

4. Click **Search Options** to display a list of options with check boxes, scroll down the Search pane if necessary, and then click **Advanced Options**. Another list of options appears.

   TROUBLE? If search options already appear, you don't have to click Search Options.

5. Make sure the **Case sensitive** check box is not checked. If it is, click it to remove the check mark. Otherwise Search might not locate the file if the case of the search string is not all lowercase. See Figure 6-10.

Figure 6-10	SEARCHING FOR TEXT IN A FILE

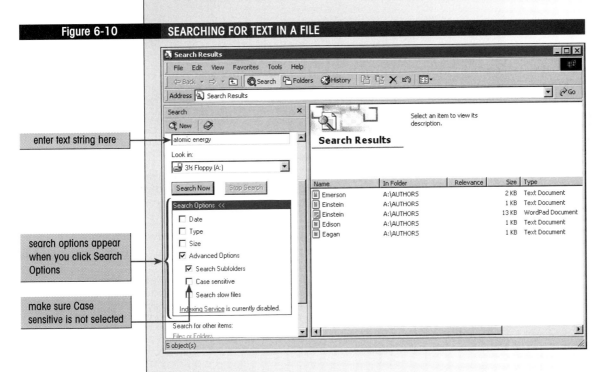

enter text string here

search options appear when you click Search Options

make sure Case sensitive is not selected

6. Click **Search Options** again to hide the search options.

7. Click the **Search Now** button. Search locates one file, Technology, located in the TOPICS folder.

   TROUBLE? Don't worry if Search takes longer than usual. Searching for file contents, even on a 3½-inch disk, is time-consuming.

   TROUBLE? If Search did not locate any file, check to make sure you typed the text string "atomic energy" correctly and that drive A is selected.

8. Delete the entry in the **Containing text** box to clear that search criterion.

If you use the Containing text option on a hard disk, be prepared to wait, because searching file contents one file at a time is time-consuming. If you can narrow the search range using other criteria so that Search searches fewer files—for example, by specifying a folder rather than an entire drive—you will speed things up.

Searching for Files in a Specific Folder

Search can search all drives and folders available to your computer or, as you saw when you selected the drive containing your Data Disk, it can search only a single drive. You can also narrow your search by specifying a specific folder, on your own computer or on a shared network computer.

REFERENCE WINDOW   **RW**

Searching for Files in a Specific Folder

- Start Search and then click the Look in list arrow.
- Click Browse at the bottom of the list.
- Click ⊞ next to the drive containing the folder you want to search.
- If the folder is in the root directory of the drive, click the folder icon 📁 . If the folder is a subfolder, click ⊞ next to the folder icon until you locate the folder, and then click 📁 .
- Click OK, then click the Search Now button.

You report to Carolyn that you've found files containing quotations on atomic energy and on Albert Einstein. She suggests that you spend time looking for material you want, to get a better feel for the disk's contents. You noticed there was a Comedy folder, and you wonder whether it contains any quotes by Woody Allen, one of the Senator's favorite celebrities. You decide to tell Search to look only in the Comedy folder.

To specify the Comedy folder, you navigate a folder tree similar to the one in Windows Explorer.

To search the Comedy folder on drive A for files that contain the string "woody allen":

1. Click the **Look in** list arrow and then click **Browse** at the bottom of the list. The Browse For Folder dialog box opens, displaying a list of devices, drives, and folders.

2. Click ⊞ next to My Computer. Now click ⊞ next to 3½ Floppy (A:). The folders on drive A appear. See Figure 6-11.

   TROUBLE? Your list of devices, drives, and folders might look different, depending on your computer's drives and network.

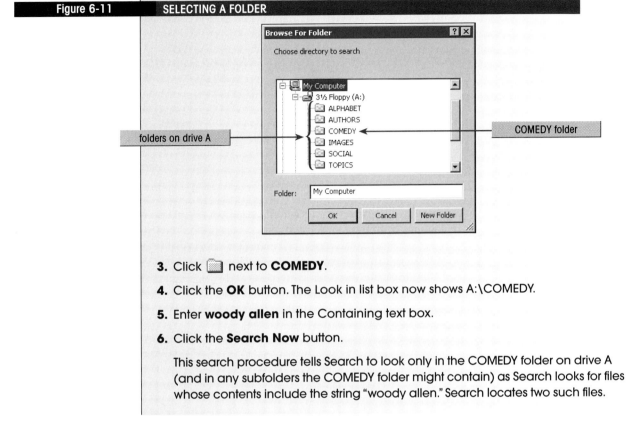

Figure 6-11   **SELECTING A FOLDER**

folders on drive A

COMEDY folder

3. Click 📁 next to **COMEDY**.

4. Click the **OK** button. The Look in list box now shows A:\COMEDY.

5. Enter **woody allen** in the Containing text box.

6. Click the **Search Now** button.

This search procedure tells Search to look only in the COMEDY folder on drive A (and in any subfolders the COMEDY folder might contain) as Search looks for files whose contents include the string "woody allen." Search locates two such files.

So far, you've been deleting your criteria whenever you enter new criteria, but you can also clear all search criteria at once.

Clearing a Search

When you've completed a search, you need to remember to clear the criterion so it won't affect your next search (unless you want to use it as one of several criteria in a subsequent search). You don't want to limit subsequent searches to just the COMEDY folder, so you will use the New button to clear it and any other criteria.

To clear all criteria:

1. Click the **New** button near the top of the left pane.

The Search Results dialog box now displays the default settings. Note, however, that the Look in box still displays A:\COMEDY. Clicking the New button does not change the Search location.

Working with Search Results

Up until now, the Search Results panes that you've examined have been short and manageable. When your search yields a large number of files, you can adjust the Search Results pane to display the information in a more suitable and organized format.

You wonder whether there is a way to find quotations by author. You decide to search the disk for any files or folders whose filenames contain the term "author."

To search for files and folders named "author" on drive A:

1. Click the **Look in** list arrow and then click **3½ Floppy (A:)** to search all folders, not just the COMEDY folder.

2. Type **author** in the Search for files or folders named box.

3. Click the **Search Now** button. The Search Results pane displays all files and folders that have the word "author" located in their filenames. There are 28 such files.

You can view the files in the results list by Large Icons, Small Icons, List, or Details, and you can resize columns by dragging their borders. These options are the same as in My Computer and Windows Explorer. Details view, the default view, is probably the most useful view because it gives you all the information you need (name, location, relevance, size, type, and date modified of each file) to verify that you've found the file you want. Just as in My Computer and Windows Explorer, you can sort the files in the Search Results pane by any of these criteria.

You see files whose names suggest that they contain quotations from authors, labeled by last name. Is there a file for every letter of the alphabet? You can sort the files by name to find out.

To sort the files by name:

1. Click the **Name** button, as shown in Figure 6-12, to arrange the files in ascending alphabetical order by name.

| Figure 6-12 | SORTING THE SEARCH RESULTS LIST |

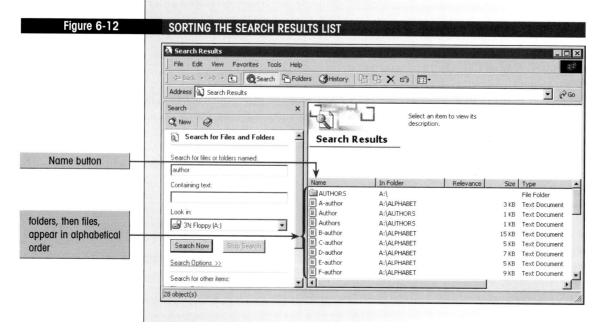

Name button

folders, then files, appear in alphabetical order

2. Scroll down the Search Results list and observe that there are files for most letters of the alphabet.

If you wanted to find quotations by a given author, you could try the file for the author's last name, located in the Alphabet folder. What else can you learn from the Search Results pane? The Type column shows that the first item on the list is a folder and that the rest of the files are text documents. All the files are small (under 16 KB), and you could sort the files by date modified (scroll to the right to see this option), to observe that these files were developed in the years 1996–2001.

Refining a Search

So far you've searched for files with particular filenames or text strings. You can also locate a file using criteria other than the filename or exact contents, including size, date, and type. These options appear when you click Search Options on the Search pane. With these criteria, you can answer questions such as: Are any files more than a few years old? What files were created using a certain program? What files are larger or smaller than a specified size? You enter the characteristic you want to study, and then Search lists all files that share that characteristic, such as all files created after 1998, all Microsoft Word files, or all files larger than 50 KB.

You can use these criteria on their own or in combination with filenames and text strings.

Finding a File by Date

As research assistant, you want to know when the previous aide collected the files. Searching for files by date is also useful when you want a file that you know you were working with on a given date, but you can't remember where you stored it.

You decide to see how many files were created in the years 1994–1996, because you've been told that the aide devoted a lot of time in those years to developing the quotations archive. You'd like to see whether there are any files that haven't changed since then.

To search for files created between 1994 and 1996:

1. Click the **New** button to clear previous search criteria.

2. Click **Search Options** in the Search pane to view additional criteria.

3. Click the **Date** check box. Date options appear; you might need to scroll to see them.

4. Click the **between** option button if necessary.

5. Enter **1/1/1994** as the start date and **12/31/1996** as the end date.

6. Click the **Search Now** button. There are 16 files in that range of dates. Apparently most of the files created in 1994 and 1996 have since been updated. See Figure 6-13.

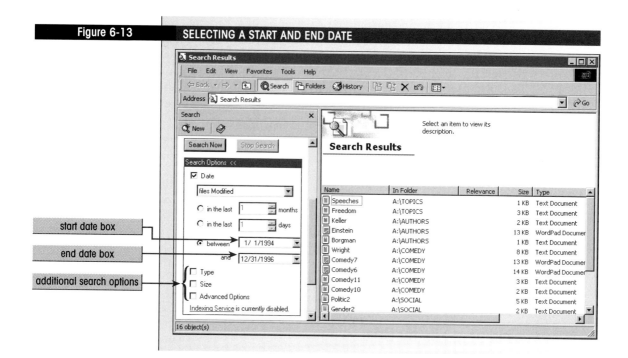

Figure 6-13   **SELECTING A START AND END DATE**

start date box

end date box

additional search options

It might have occurred to you that you could get information about file dates more quickly by opening Explorer or My Computer and sorting the files by date. You'd be right, if the files were all in one folder. However, when the files are scattered among multiple folders, Search can display files from any of those folders that meet your date criteria, whereas Explorer and My Computer can display the contents of only one folder at a time.

Finding a File by Type

You'd like to get an overview of the types of files on the quotations archive disk, to see whether you have the software on your computer to open them. You can look for files by their general file type or by the program that created them. The list of file types from which you can choose includes text files, sound files, bitmaps, Word documents, Web documents, and so on, depending on the resources on your computer.

You already know there are lots of text files, but you'd like to know how many. You also wonder whether there are any sound files that the Senator might be able to use in a multimedia presentation. You decide to use file type criteria to answer these questions.

To view files by type:

1. Click the **New** button to clear previous search criteria.

2. Click the **Type** check box (it's located under Search Options in the Search pane).

3. Click the list arrow below the Type check box and then scroll down the alphabetical list to locate "Text Document."

4. Click **Text Document** and then click the **Search Now** button. The status bar reports that there are 92 text files on your disk.

TROUBLE? If your list is much shorter, you might have forgotten to click the New button to reset the Date setting. Forgetting to reset criteria to their original settings can confuse your search efforts.

5. Next you want to look for sound files. Click the list arrow below the Type check box again. Scroll to and then click **Sound Clip**. Click the **Search Now** button. There are two such files.

Finding a File by Size

In searching for files by type, you found two sound files. You know these files are usually bigger than text files or word-processed documents. If you are short on disk space, you'll want to identify the largest files so you can move them to free up space. You can find this information by looking for a file by its size. You specify either "at least" or "at most" and then pick the number of kilobytes you want. If disk space is a problem, you might want to look for all files that are at least 25 KB in size. Try that search now.

To search for files by size:

1. Click the **New** button to clear previous search criteria.

2. Click the **Size** check box under Search Options, and make sure the **at least** option is selected. If it isn't, click the **Size** list arrow and then click **at least**.

3. Enter **25** in the KB box.

4. Click the **Search Now** button. The Search Results pane shows six such files. You can sort these files to more easily identify the largest.

5. Click the **Size** button twice to sort the files by size, with the largest files first. Not surprisingly, the largest files are the two sound files. See Figure 6-14.

Figure 6-14	SEARCHING FOR FILES BY SIZE

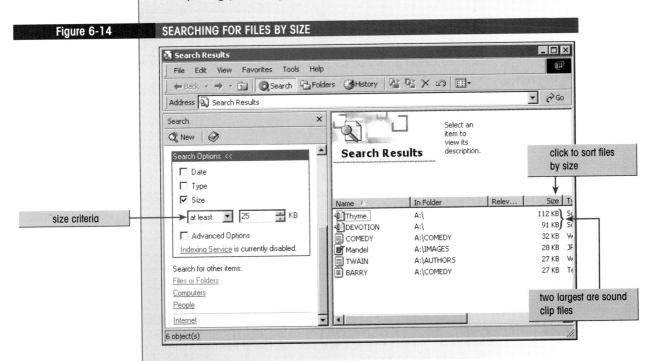

Finding a File Using Multiple Criteria

Carolyn informs you that, because Stanton College is a women's college, Senator Bernstein is interested in having a quote on leadership by a woman. If you specify multiple criteria, such as a likely filename and a likely text string, you might be able to pinpoint such a quote.

You remember that there are files on the archive disk whose filenames contain the search string "women." You guess that the file probably contains the word "leader," so you could specify the root "leader" as your text string. Search uses all the criteria you enter to perform the search.

To find a file with multiple criteria:

1. Click the **New** button to clear previous search criteria.

2. Scroll up to the top of the Search pane, click the **Search for files or folders named** box, and then type **women**.

3. Click the **Containing text** box, type **leader**, and then click the **Search Now** button. One file matches your criteria. See Figure 6-15.

| Figure 6-15 | USING MULTIPLE CRITERIA TO FIND A FILE |

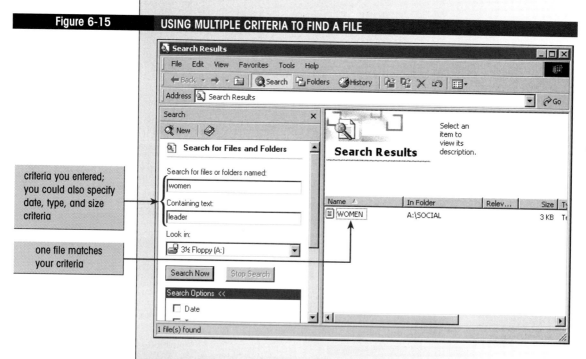

criteria you entered; you could also specify date, type, and size criteria

one file matches your criteria

4. Right-click the **Women** file in the Search Results pane, and then click **Open**. It opens in Notepad. You see a quotation on leaders by Mother Teresa.

5. Close Notepad and the Search Results window.

Opening **Recent Documents**

You have used Search to locate files. There is another way to locate a file you've worked on recently. You can view a list of recently opened documents, using the Documents command on the Start menu. If you click one of the document names on the Documents menu,

Windows 2000 locates and starts the program that created the document, then opens the document. You decide to use the Documents menu to show Carolyn the file you opened that contains a quote on leadership written by a woman.

> ### To view the most recent documents list:
>
> **1.** Click the **Start** button 🅡 Start .
>
> **2.** Point to **Documents**. The Documents menu opens. See Figure 6-16.

Figure 6-16	OPENING A FILE FROM THE DOCUMENTS LIST

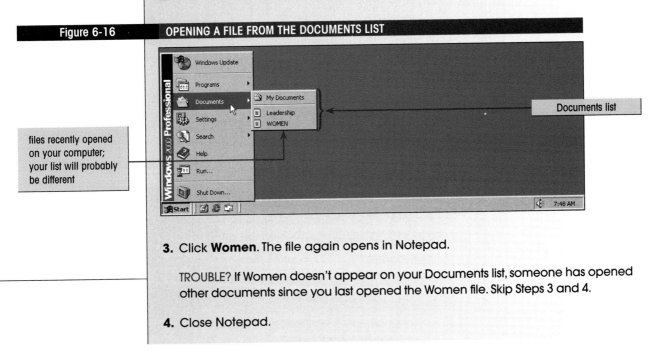

files recently opened on your computer; your list will probably be different

Documents list

> **3.** Click **Women**. The file again opens in Notepad.
>
> TROUBLE? If Women doesn't appear on your Documents list, someone has opened other documents since you last opened the Women file. Skip Steps 3 and 4.
>
> **4.** Close Notepad.

The Documents command is useful only when you have recently worked on a file on your own computer. When this is the case, it can be the quickest way to find and open a file.

The Search utility has helped you locate files on your disks that meet one or more criteria. In the next session, you'll expand your search to locate more quotation files on the Internet.

Session 6.1 QUICK CHECK

1. To search for a file only on drive A, what do you do?

2. True or False: The Search Results pane displays only the files whose names exactly match the search string you entered.

3. What is a wildcard? What is the difference between the asterisk wildcard and the question mark wildcard?

4. How do you display the files in the Search Results pane in alphabetical order?

5. If you want the Search utility to display only the bitmapped images on your floppy disk, what should you do?

6. If the Search Results pane displays the file you were looking for, how do you open the file for editing?

7. Something seems to be wrong with Notepad. You can see only the first 10 words or so of each paragraph. What should you do?

SESSION 6.2

In this session, you will learn about searching on the Internet, including searching by query and by subject. You'll learn to search using Autosearch and the Search Explorer bar. Finally, you'll learn to search for maps and people on the Internet.

Searching on the Internet

The Internet has vast resources, and to locate the information you want, you need to search for it. You can search for information on the Internet with the On the Internet option on the Search menu, which starts the Internet Explorer browser and displays the Search Explorer bar. You can perform a quick search by typing the word *find* in the Internet Explorer Address bar, followed by a search word. When you press Enter, the Microsoft Network **Autosearch** feature displays a list of links you might try.

Searching with Autosearch

You would like to expand the set of quotations on the quotation archives disk, so you decide to search the Internet for sites that make quotation collections available.

To search for a Web page using Autosearch:

1. Make sure you are connected to the Internet.

2. Click the **Start** button [Start], point to **Search**, and then click **On the Internet**. Microsoft starts Internet Explorer and displays the Search Explorer bar.

3. Maximize the Internet Explorer window if necessary.

4. Click the **Address** box on the Address bar, type **find quotations**, and then press the **Enter** key. Internet Explorer connects to the www.quotations.com Web page. See Figure 6-17.

| Figure 6-17 | PERFORMING AN AUTOSEARCH |

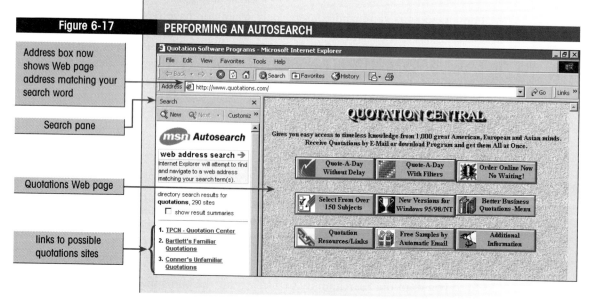

Address box now shows Web page address matching your search word

Search pane

Quotations Web page

links to possible quotations sites

Viewing the Search Explorer Bar

You could look through the links on the quotations.com site, or click any of the links in the Search pane, but for now you'll use the Search Explorer bar to perform a more controlled search.

To view the Search Explorer bar options:

1. Click the **New** button to start a new search.

2. Make sure the **Find a Web page** option button is selected.

3. Click the **More** link below the five option buttons in the Search pane to view all search options. See Figure 6-18.

   TROUBLE? If you are using a different version of Internet Explorer, the search options might look different.

Figure 6-18	SEARCH EXPLORER BAR

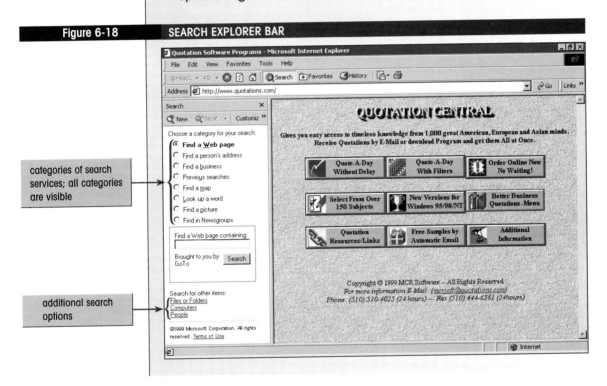

categories of search services; all categories are visible

additional search options

The Search Explorer bar makes available many popular **search services**, software that helps you find information on the Internet. Figure 6-19 describes the categories of search services as they appear on the Search pane shown in Figure 6-18.

Figure 6-19	SEARCH SERVICE CATEGORIES
SEARCH SERVICE CATEGORY	**DESCRIPTION**
Find a Web page	These services help you to search for Web pages, both by subject and by keyword. They include MSN Web Search, InfoSeek, AltaVista, Lycos, GoTo, Excite, Yahoo!, Euroseek, and Northern Light.
Find a person's address	Similar to a telephone book, these services help you locate people's names, e-mail and mailing addresses, phone numbers, and so on. These services include InfoSpace, Bigfoot, and WorldPages.
Find a business	These services provide information about businesses. They include InfoSpace, WorldPages, and Sidewalk YP.
Find a map	These services help you locate maps, addresses, and place names. They include ExpediaMaps and MapQuest.
Look up a word	These services include encyclopedia, dictionary, and thesaurus services, including Encarta, Merriam-Webster, Dictonary.com, and Thesaurus.com.
Find a picture	These services help you locate graphic images. Corbis is the only default service.
Find in Newsgroups	These services help you search newsgroup archives. **Newsgroups**, also called **discussion groups**, bring people with common interests together to exchange e-mail messages on a given topic. Dejanews is the only default service.

Customizing Search Settings

When you use the Search Explorer bar, you first select the category you want to use. The Search Explorer bar displays options appropriate to that category. You then enter a subject and click a button such as Search, Find, Go, or "?". The appearance of the button that starts the search depends on the search service Internet Explorer is using.

You can control the categories and the services that appear on the Search Explorer bar, using the **Search Assistant**. The Search Assistant displays the list of services for each category. When you perform a search, Internet Explorer automatically starts with the first service in that list. If you don't find the information you want with the first search service, you can continue to search, using the next service on the list. You can also control the order in which the services in a category are used, so that Internet Explorer uses your favorite services first.

To customize your search settings:

1. Click the **Customize** button at the top of the Search Explorer pane.

2. Make sure the **Use the Search Assistant** option button is selected at the top of the Customize Search Settings dialog box.

3. Make sure that the **Find a Web page**, **Find a person's address**, and **Find a map** check boxes are all selected. You'll need to scroll through the Customize Search Settings dialog box to see these options. If additional check boxes are selected, leave them selected. Now you'll check the order of services that find Web pages.

4. If necessary, scroll to the top of the Customize Search Settings dialog box. Make sure that at least the **GoTo**, **AltaVista**, and **Yahoo!** check boxes are selected.

5. If GoTo doesn't appear *first* on the list, click **GoTo** in the list of Web page providers on the left, and then click the **Move Up** button ⬆ repeatedly to move it to the top of the list. If AltaVista doesn't appear next, click it and then click ⬆ until Alta Vista is in second place. Finally, move Yahoo! so it is third in the list. See Figure 6-20. If other services appear in addition to these, you can leave them there.

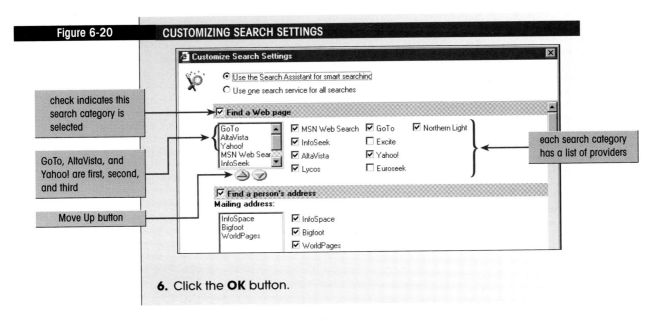

| Figure 6-20 | CUSTOMIZING SEARCH SETTINGS |

check indicates this search category is selected

GoTo, AltaVista, and Yahoo! are first, second, and third

Move Up button

each search category has a list of providers

6. Click the OK button.

Now any searches you perform will use the same settings as those in this tutorial.

Searching for Web Pages

Most Web page search services employ software that regularly searches through Internet documents and compiles a list of Web pages. It organizes and indexes this list by topic. When you use the search service to find Web pages on a specific topic, the service's **search engine** checks the service's index and provides you with links to all the pages it finds on that topic. Because the Internet is changing so quickly, the indexes change regularly too. If you don't find information one day, it might be available the next. Moreover, because different search services use different software to compile their Web page indexes, you might get different results for the same search when using two different search services. If you can't find what you want with one search service, such as Yahoo!, you can try another, such as InfoSeek.

Most search services allow you to perform two types of searches: searches by query and searches by subject. You'll try both kinds of searches.

Searching by Query

A **query** is a request for information. You enter a specific word or phrase, called a **keyword**, into a box, and then click a button, such as Search or Find, that sends your request to the search service. Some search engines allow you to refine your query to get the results you want. For example, if you are looking for information on population statistics, some search engines assume you mean "population" or "statistics" and return pages that contain either word. Other search engines assume you mean "population" and "statistics" and return only pages with both words. These searches take longer and return fewer pages, but the pages are likely to be more useful. Other search engines assume you mean "population" and/or "statistics."

Most search engines allow you to refine your query with symbols called search operators, such as plus (which requires a term or phrase), minus (which excludes a term or phrase), and quotation marks (which identify words that must appear together). Figure 6-21 provides examples of how these operators work in the InfoSeek search engine; other search engines might work differently. You can check a search engine's online Help to learn how to structure your search query using that search engine.

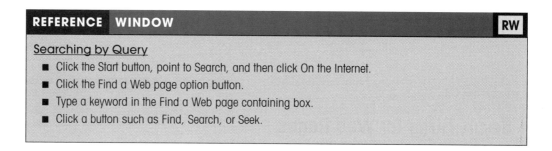

Figure 6-21 **HOW KEYWORD OPERATORS WORK IN INFOSEEK**

KEYWORD WITH OPERATORS	RETURNED PAGES
population statistics	*population* and/or *statistics*
"population statistics"	the word *population* next to the word *statistics*
+population +statistics	*population* and *statistics* but not necessarily next to each other
+population statistics	*population* but not necessarily *statistics*
+statistics –population	*statistics* but not *population*

Using capital letters for proper names can exclude, for example, pages on the color green when you search for information on Greenpeace.

REFERENCE WINDOW   **RW**

Searching by Query
- Click the Start button, point to Search, and then click On the Internet.
- Click the Find a Web page option button.
- Type a keyword in the Find a Web page containing box.
- Click a button such as Find, Search, or Seek.

You want to find information on quotation collections. The Find a Web page option button is already selected, and the "Brought to you by GoTo" line tells you that Internet Explorer will use GoTo as the first search service.

To use the GoTo search service to search for quotation collections:

1. In the Find a Web page containing box, type **quotations**. See Figure 6-22.

Figure 6-22   **USING GOTO TO SEARCH FOR A KEYWORD**

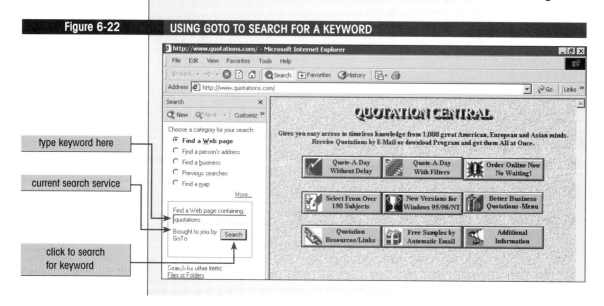

2. Click the **Search** button. After a moment, the Search Explorer bar options are replaced with the GoTo logo and a list of links that GoTo found to match your keyword. See Figure 6-23.

Figure 6-23 | **GOTO'S SEARCH RESULTS**

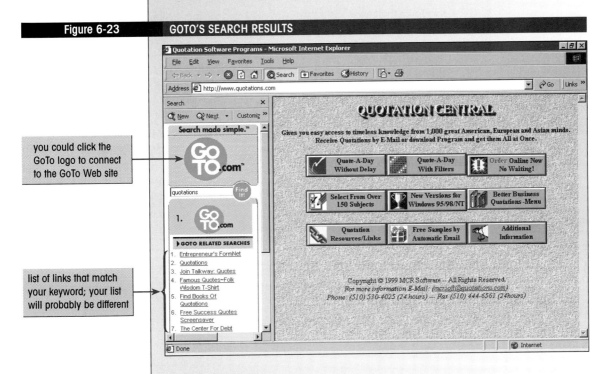

you could click the GoTo logo to connect to the GoTo Web site

list of links that match your keyword; your list will probably be different

Note that since you have not clicked any links in the search results yet, the previous Web page remains in the Internet Explorer window.

3. Scroll down the Search pane to view the list of links.

4. In the Search pane, click the quotation link that looks most promising. In Figure 6-23, there is a link to an entrepreneur's form service, which is probably not what you want, but there are other links that look as if they target quotation collections.

5. Try different links until you locate a collection of quotations.

The search pane usually lists only the first 10 or 20 links; to see the next set of links you need to scroll to locate a link such as More Results, Next, Next 10, or Next 20. Some services rate pages by usefulness according to the keywords you entered, scoring on a 100-point scale and listing the highest scorers first. You can learn about a search service's features by connecting directly to the search service's Web page (for example, www.GoTo.com).

Once you've viewed the links provided by the first search service, you can click the Next button on the Search pane to view results from the next search service. When you customized your search settings, you ensured that AltaVista would be next. Try the same search with AltaVista.

To view the links returned by the next search service:

1. Click the **Next** list arrow at the top of the Search pane. The list of search services appears. You could click any of these services to bypass the predesignated search service order.

2. Press the **Esc** key to close the Next list, and then click the **Next** button. The AltaVista logo now appears in the Search pane, and a list of links returned by the AltaVista service appears in the Search pane.

3. Click the links that look as if they provide promising collections of quotations.

Now you decide to try searching by subject for quotations.

Searching by Subject

Most search services allow you to search by query or subject. When you search by query, you are asking the search engine to locate information on the topic you specify. In a **subject search**, however, you search for information by browsing through a hierarchy of topics, called a **subject guide**. Subject guides are created and maintained by the search service. They are organized first by general and then by successively more specific subjects. Using a subject guide is often more efficient and more effective than searching the entire Web to find pages that contain a few select keywords.

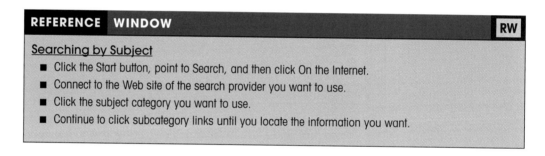

REFERENCE WINDOW | **RW**

Searching by Subject
- Click the Start button, point to Search, and then click On the Internet.
- Connect to the Web site of the search provider you want to use.
- Click the subject category you want to use.
- Continue to click subcategory links until you locate the information you want.

The Yahoo! search engine offers one of the most popular subject guides; you decide to use it to locate additional information on quotations.

To search the Yahoo! subject guide for quotation collections:

1. Click the **Next** list arrow at the top of the Search pane, and then click **Yahoo!**.

2. Click the **Yahoo!** logo at the top of the Search pane. You connect to Yahoo!'s Web site. See Figure 6-24.

Figure 6-24 | SUBJECT GUIDE

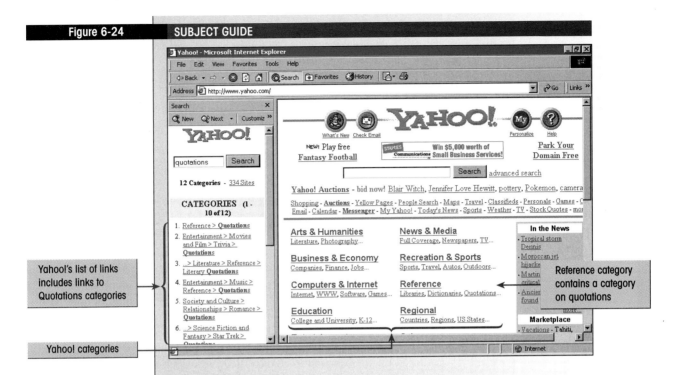

Yahoo!'s list of links includes links to Quotations categories

Yahoo! categories

Reference category contains a category on quotations

3. Click the **Quotations** subcategory on the Yahoo! Web page (it's located below the Reference category). The Quotations category appears, displaying its sub-categories. See Figure 6-25.

Figure 6-25 | YAHOO! QUOTATIONS CATEGORIES

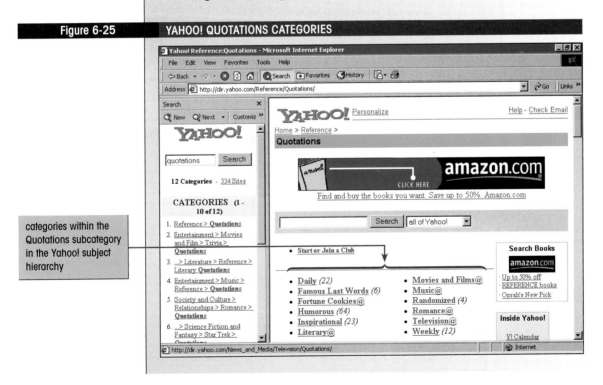

categories within the Quotations subcategory in the Yahoo! subject hierarchy

4. In the category list that appears, click one of the Quotations categories that interests you, and continue clicking relevant links until you locate a quotation collection.

There are many quotation collections on the Web—some have search engines built into them that make it even easier to locate a specific quote. You tell Carolyn that if she isn't satisfied with what you've found on the quotations archive disk, you can easily expand your search to include quotation collections on the Web.

Searching for People

Windows 2000 also includes an option on the Search Explorer bar, Find a person's address, that helps you search for information about specific people. Similar to a telephone book, the Find a person's address option locates information such as a person's mailing address, e-mail address, or phone number from Internet "people search" services such as Bigfoot and SwitchBoard. You enter a name, and the search service returns a list of people with that name. For common names the list is very long; for some names no information is available.

Carolyn has asked you to find contact information for sources she's using to prepare Senator Bernstein's speech. You've managed to do so by searching through journal articles written by the sources, but you wonder if the Internet might give you an alternate method of finding information about people. You decide to test the service by attempting to locate information on yourself.

To find information about a person:

1. Click the **New** button in the Search pane. The Search Explorer bar appears.

2. Click the **Find a person's address** option button. The Search Explorer bar now displays options for a person's address. See Figure 6-26.

Figure 6-26	SEARCHING FOR A PERSON'S ADDRESS

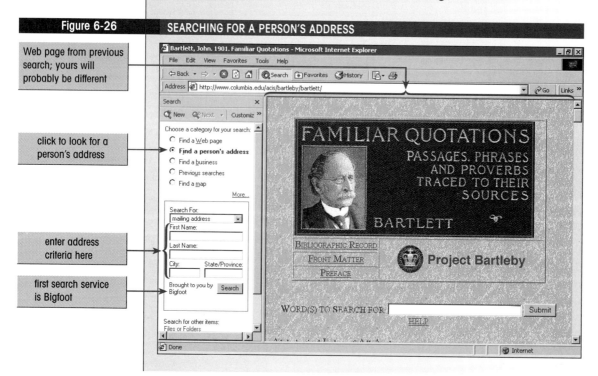

Web page from previous search; yours will probably be different

click to look for a person's address

enter address criteria here

first search service is Bigfoot

3. Type your first name in the First Name box and your last name in the Last Name box. Then enter your city and state.

4. Click the **Search** button. If Bigfoot has any address or phone number information on people with your name, it appears in a list. If Bigfoot wasn't able to find the information you requested, click the New button, then repeat Step 3 using a friend's name, your instructor's name, or a more common name. You could also click **Next** to view results from the next search service.

Searching for a Map

Map services on the Internet provide street maps for addresses you enter. Try searching for your own address. Once the map is located, you can "zoom in" or "zoom out" on the map to view more local detail or more of the surrounding area. Try finding a map of your home or other location.

To locate a map:

1. Click the **New** button on the Search Explorer bar.

2. Click the **Find a map** option button.

3. Enter your address, city, state, and zip code in the appropriate boxes.

4. Click the **Search** button. The map appears in the Internet Explorer window. See Figure 6-27.

   TROUBLE? If the address you tried does not yield a map, try a different address, or try the one shown in Figure 6-27.

Figure 6-27	LOCATING A MAP

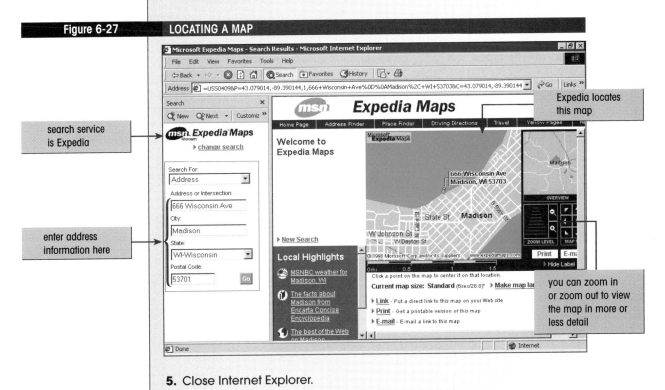

search service is Expedia

enter address information here

Expedia locates this map

you can zoom in or zoom out to view the map in more or less detail

5. Close Internet Explorer.

You're confident that you can use Windows 2000 and the search services it makes available to find just about any information Carolyn needs.

Session 6.2 QUICK CHECK

1. What kind of software searches through Internet documents and compiles a list of Web pages it locates on the Internet?

2. True or False: If you don't find the information you want using Yahoo!, you probably won't find the same information using InfoSeek.

3. What is the difference between a query search and a subject search?

4. If you are using Infoseek and you want information on the dog Toto in *The Wizard of Oz*, but you don't want any pages on the rock band Toto, what search operators can you use?

5. How can you use Windows 2000 to find an e-mail address for your state's governor?

REVIEW ASSIGNMENTS

1. **Using a Search String to Find a File** The governor has asked Senator Bernstein to represent the state in meetings with representatives of Taiwan, to set up a student exchange program. In any international exchange, language is an issue. You remember a funny story about the translation of an ad for Coca-Cola into another language. Might that anecdote be on the quotations archive disk?

   a. To find out, use the For Files or Folders option and enter likely search strings. Make sure you select the drive containing your Data Disk. If you're having trouble locating a file, try using just part of the search string or a different search string.

   b. Once you find a file you think looks promising, open it from the Search Results window.

   c. When you've found what you want, select the text, copy it, and then paste it into a new Notepad document. Type your name in the document you just created. At the end of the document, write a few sentences listing the search string you used and the name of the file(s) you located. Print the document, and then close Notepad and the Search Results window. Don't save the Notepad document.

2. **Learning More About Files** On a sheet of paper, write the answers to the following questions about the files on the Data Disk. You can answer all the questions by examining the filenames.

   a. How many files are there with the search string "comedy" in the filename?
   b. How many files and folders in total are on the disk? What did you do to find the answer? (*Hint*: You can find the answer to this question with a single search.)
   c. Which letters of the alphabet are missing in the filenames of the alphabetically organized Author files?
   d. How many files are there on friendship? What search string did you use to find this answer?

3. **Using Wildcards** What search strings could you use to produce the following results? Write the search strings on a piece of paper. Use a wildcard for each one. For example, a results list of Budget2000.xls, Budget2001.xls, and Budget2002.xls could come from the search string "Budget200?.xls".

   a. Comedy1.doc, Comedy2.doc, Comedy3.doc
   b. Social.txt, Society.txt, Socratic Method.txt
   c. PhotoWorks, Network, Files for Work

4. **Searching for Files by Date** You can answer these questions about the Data Disk by using the Date option. Write the answers on a sheet of paper. Return all settings to their defaults when you are done.

   a. How many files did Carolyn's previous aide modify in 1999?
   b. How many files did the aide modify in August, 1999?
   c. Which file(s) did the aide modify on August 31, 1999?

5. **Locating Files by Size** How many files of 1 KB or less are on the Data Disk? How many files of 15 KB or more? Return this setting to its default when you are done.

6. **Locating Files by Contents** You enjoy Dave Barry's columns. Search the contents of the files on the Data Disk to see how many of them contain the text string "barry", and then record that number. Write down the name of the file that seems to contain the most Dave Barry quotations. Open the file from Search. When you are done, delete the criteria you entered.

7. **Experimenting with Search Criteria** You decide to search for appropriate quotations for Senator Bernstein's upcoming speech topics. For each speech topic, write down the criteria you used to locate a file, and then write down the file location as displayed in the In Folder column of the results list. If you find more than one file, write down the first one in the list.

   a. Senator Bernstein has been invited to give the toast at a football brunch hosted by the president of Riverside College.
   b. The family of a deceased friend has asked Senator Bernstein if she'd like to contribute any thoughts to a written memorial.
   c. Senator Bernstein is cochairing this year's Renaissance Festival downtown. The Festival will feature outdoor performances of three of Shakespeare's plays, including a performance by the Young Shakespearians Guild, a troupe of children under age 18. She's promised to give the opening remarks at the Festival.

8. **Opening Files from Search** You learned how to open a text document from Search in this tutorial. You can open other types of files the same way, as long as your computer contains the program that created the file.

   a. Search for Sound Clip files on your Data Disk. Right-click one of them and then click Play. What did you hear? Click the Close button when the sound file is done playing. If you don't hear anything, your computer might not have speakers, or they might be off.

   b. Search for Video Clip files on your computer's hard drive. If you find any, right-click one of them, and then click the Play button. Describe what you see. Click the Close button when the video clip is done playing.

Explore ▷ 9. **Searching and Viewing File Contents** Find the answers to the questions below. You will probably need to search for a text string in the file's contents. For each answer, write the name of the file you used to find the answer. (*Hint*: Once you've located and opened the file, you can either scroll through it to find the answer, or open it in Notepad, click Edit on the Notepad menu bar, and then click Find. Type the text string in the Find what box, and then click the Find Next button.)

   a. What did Elsa Einstein think about her husband Albert's theory of relativity?
   b. Do you think cartoonist Jim Borgman is an optimist or a pessimist? Why?
   c. What was Helen Keller's opinion of college?
   d. How many children did Erma Bombeck recommend that one have? (Look carefully at the filenames in the results list so you don't open more files than necessary.)
   e. What did Elbert Hubbard have to say about books? (Look carefully at the filenames in the results list so you don't open more files than necessary.)

Explore ▷ 10. **Locating Information on the Internet** Carolyn asks that you help locate information on Taiwan for Senator Bernstein's upcoming participation in establishing a student exchange program.

   a. Use the Yahoo! search service subject guide to locate information on transportation in Taiwan. Write down the subject guide links you navigated to locate information. (*Hint*: Start with Regional.)
   b. Write down the URL of a page on transportation in Taiwan.
   c. Locate a Web page for one of Taiwan's universities. Write down the name of the university and the URL of its Web page.

11. **Locating People** Use three different people search services to locate the e-mail address of the president of your university. Were you able to find it in any of them? Did the search services have e-mail addresses for other people with the same name?

12. **Locating a Map** Locate and then print a map of your home address.

PROJECTS

1. On which drive is your Windows folder? Open the Search window, specify My Computer in the Look in list, and then search for "Windows." Write the answer on a piece of paper. If there are too many files in the results list, sort the files by name so that folders named "Windows" appear near the top.

2. Can you locate the e-mail address of the president of the United States? (*Hint*: The e-mail address will end with ".gov" because the president works for the government.)

3. Specify the following search strings, and, searching your Data Disk, examine the results list for each search string very carefully. What generalizations about wildcards can you make from your observations?

   men

   men.*

   men.

   men*.*

   men?

   men?.*

4. You can use Search to learn about the files on your hard drive. Record how many files of each of the following types exist on your hard drive.
   a. Application. Write down the names of five application files in the Windows folder of your hard drive.
   b. Bitmap Image. Which folders on your hard drive seem to store the most bitmapped images?
   c. Screen Saver. Write down the locations of some of the screen savers on your hard drive.
   d. Text Document. Once the results list shows all the text documents on your hard drive, order them by Name. Are there any files named README? Write down the locations of two of them. Software programs often come with a README text file that lists known software problems and answers to common questions.

5. Write down the names of 10 documents recently accessed on the hard disk.

Explore

6. You can use the Search Explorer bar to locate computers on a network. If you are on a network, open the Search Explorer bar and scroll to the bottom. Click Computers. Your instructor will give you the name of a computer for which to search on your network. Enter this name in the Computer Name box, and then click the Search Now button. Once Search has located the computer, open it from the results list. Make a hard copy of the window that opens and submit it to your instructor (use the PrintScreen key as shown in Tutorial 3 to create the hard copy).

7. Use the Internet search tools to find information on the city where you live, such as a Chamber of Commerce page or a local news service page. Print the first page of the information you located, and write the URL on the page.

QUICK CHECK ANSWERS

Session 6.1

1. Click the Look in list arrow, and then click 3½ Floppy (A:).

2. False

3. A wildcard is a symbol that stands in place of one or more characters. The asterisk wildcard substitutes for any number of characters; the question mark substitutes for only one.

4. Click the Name button in Details view.

5. Click Search Options (if necessary), select the Type check box, click the Type list arrow, click Bitmap Image, and then click Search Now.

6. Right-click it, and then click Open.

7. Click Format, and then click Word Wrap.

Session 6.2

1. search engine

2. False

3. A query search allows you to search by keyword. In a subject search, you search through predefined categories of information.

4. +Toto+Oz

5. Use the Find a person's address option.

CONNECTING COMPUTERS OVER A PHONE LINE

Windows 2000 **Dial-up Accessories**

Windows 2000 makes communicating with computers easier than ever because it provides accessories that allow you to connect your computer to other computers and to the Internet. If you are using a computer on a university or institutional network, you are probably already connected to the Internet, and you can skip this appendix. This appendix is useful for people who are not connected to the Internet but who have their own computer with a modem and access to a phone line.

Computers at universities or large companies are likely to be connected to the Internet via expensive, high-speed wiring that transmits data very quickly. Home computer owners, however, usually can't afford to run similar cables and wires to their homes, and instead rely on phone lines that are already in place, as shown in Figure A-1.

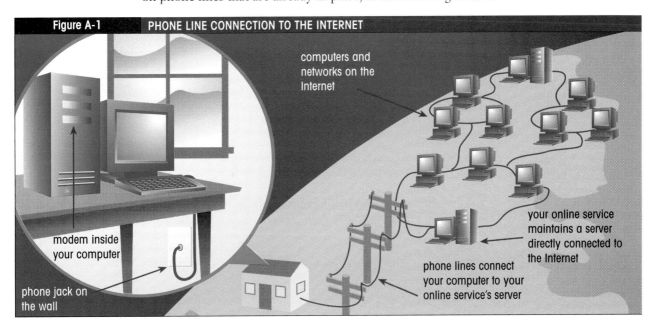

Figure A-1   PHONE LINE CONNECTION TO THE INTERNET

computers and networks on the Internet

modem inside your computer

phone jack on the wall

your online service maintains a server directly connected to the Internet

phone lines connect your computer to your online service's server

When a modem uses an ordinary voice phone line, which uses analog signals, it converts the modem's digital signals to analog, as shown in Figure A-2.

Figure A-2 | **DATA TRAVELING OVER A PHONE LINE**

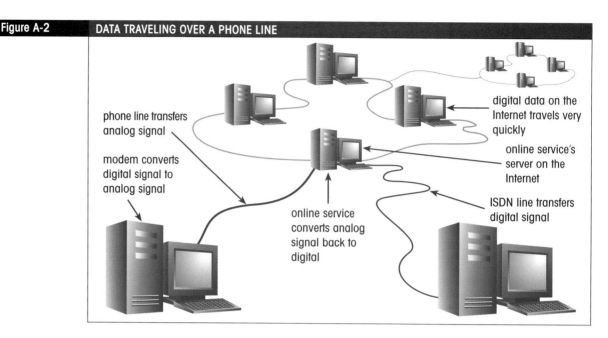

phone line transfers
analog signal

modem converts
digital signal to
analog signal

online service
converts analog
signal back to
digital

digital data on the
Internet travels very
quickly

online service's
server on the
Internet

ISDN line transfers
digital signal

The receiving computer converts the analog signal back to digital. Data usually travels more slowly over phone wires than over the networking infrastructure of the Internet. If there are any problems with the phone connection, data can be lost. But regular phone lines are often the only practical choice for homes and small businesses. In some areas, **ISDN lines**, wires that provide a completely digital path from one computer to another, are dropping in price so that small businesses and homeowners can afford them. Whether you use a regular phone line or a faster ISDN line, Windows 2000 can help you establish a connection to the Internet. You will need to select an Internet service provider (ISP), a company that provides Internet access. ISPs maintain servers that are directly connected to the Internet 24 hours a day. You dial into your ISP's server over your phone line to use its Internet connection. You pay a fee for this service, most often with a flat monthly rate.

Once you've selected an ISP, you can use Windows 2000 to set up your connection. Figure A-3 shows the accessories Windows 2000 includes to help you.

Figure A-3 | **WINDOWS 2000 CONNECTION ACCESSORIES**

ACCESSORY	DESCRIPTION
Dial-up Networking	Some computer users have one Internet account for home use and a different one for business use. The Dial-up Networking accessory helps you manage the accounts that you use to connect to the Internet.
Connection Wizard	The Connection Wizard makes it easy to create an Internet account for the first time by prompting you for information through a series of dialog boxes.

You can also use the Internet Connection Wizard to locate an ISP in your area. There are probably more ISPs in your area than are listed by the Internet Connection Wizard.

Setting Up Dial-up Networking

If you want to connect to the Internet and other networks with your home computer, you can set up a dial-up connection using the Internet Connection Wizard. The Internet Connection Wizard is a series of dialog boxes that prompt you for information your computer needs to connect to the Internet.

Starting the Internet Connection Wizard

If your ISP has provided you with an installation program to set up the connection, install and run that program instead of using the Windows 2000 Internet Connection Wizard. To see how the Internet Connection Wizard works, you'll use it to create a dial-up account. These steps assume you have signed up for an account with an ISP and haven't set up the account yet. Before you perform the steps, you should gather any documentation from your ISP, such as phone numbers, passwords, and special settings.

To begin setting up a dial-up connection:

1. Click the **Start** button, point to **Programs**, point to **Accessories**, point to **Communications**, and then click **Internet Connection Wizard**.

2. Click the **I want to set up my Internet connection manually** option button.

   Choose the first option to connect to a referral service that helps you select an ISP (you use that option only if you haven't already purchased an account). Choose the second option to transfer your account from one of the ISPs listed by the Internet Connection Wizard. Choose the third option when you have an ISP account, but that account is *not* supported by the Internet Connection Wizard referral service, or if you want to set up your account manually.

3. Click the **Next** button and then click the **I connect through a phone line and a modem** option button.

   Choose this option when you are not on a local area network, which you are not if you are connecting your home computer to an ISP.

4. Type the area code and telephone number of your ISP in the appropriate boxes. See Figure A-4. Your numbers will be different.

Figure A-4	ENTERING ISP PHONE INFORMATION

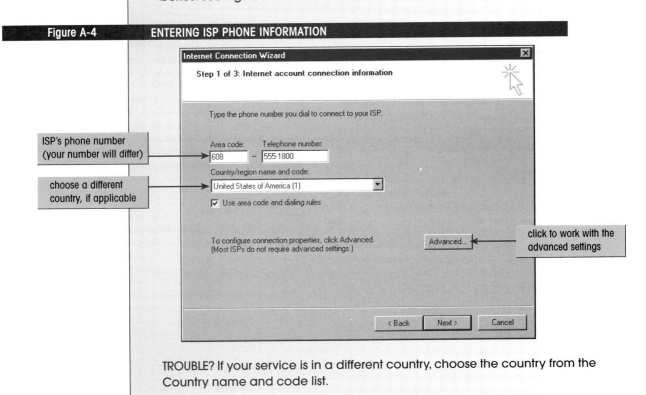

TROUBLE? If your service is in a different country, choose the country from the Country name and code list.

At this point in the Internet Connection Wizard, you have the choice of setting some of the Advanced options in your Internet connection.

Entering Advanced Settings

The advanced settings control the technical aspect of how your computer communicates with your ISP. If you choose not to change advanced settings, you might encounter problems with your connection, if the Windows 2000 default settings don't match those of your ISP.

To enter advanced settings:

1. Click the **Advanced** button to open the Advanced Connection Properties dialog box.

   TROUBLE? If you are sure you can proceed using the default settings, do not click the Advanced button and instead read through the rest of these steps without performing them.

2. Click the **PPP**, **SLIP** or **C-SLIP** option button, depending on what your ISP's documentation specifies.

   A **connection type** is the kind of connection between your computer and your ISP's server. Windows 2000 offers three connection types: PPP, SLIP and C-SLIP. The preferred and more common connection type today is **Point-to-Point Protocol**, or **PPP**, which provides error checking and can cope with noisy phone lines. **Serial Line Internet Protocol**, or **SLIP**, is a basic connection type that runs well on most systems but has no error-checking or security features. **Compressed Serial Line Internet Protocol** or **C-SLIP** is similar to SLIP but compresses some of the data in order to speed up the connection. Most ISPs use a PPP connection, but some require SLIP or C-SLIP; check your ISP documentation to see which one to use.

3. Click the appropriate **Logon Procedure** option button.

   Some ISPs require you to log on before you can use the service. In some cases, you must log on manually, providing the information required by your ISP when you attempt to connect. In other cases, you can use a **logon script**, a program that runs on your computer and logs you on to the service automatically.

4. If you need to use a logon script, click the **Use this logon script** option button, click the **Browse** button, locate and select the logon script specified by your ISP's documentation, and then click the **Open** button. See Figure A-5.

Figure A-5	CHOOSING A CONNECTION TYPE AND LOGON PROCEDURE

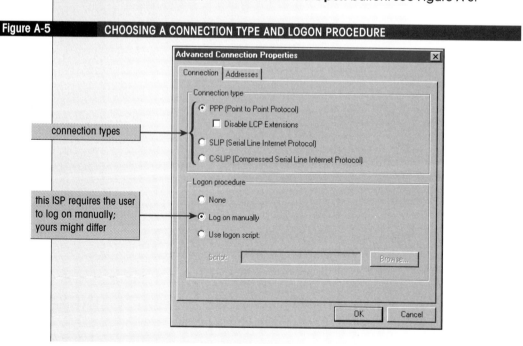

connection types

this ISP requires the user to log on manually; yours might differ

5. Click the **Addresses** tab.

6. Choose the appropriate **IP address** option button, and then, if you selected the second option, enter the IP address. An **Internet Protocol**, or **IP address**, is a unique address that identifies a server on the Internet. Usually your ISP automatically assigns you one when you log on, because you are only a temporary user of the address (only during the period of time that you are logged on).

7. Choose the appropriate **DNS server address** option button, and then, if you selected the second option, enter the DNS numbers. The **Domain Name System**, or **DNS**, is a database service that helps computers look up the names of other computers and locate their corresponding IP addresses. If your ISP documentation provides you with primary and secondary DNS server addresses, enter them here, as shown in Figure A-6.

Figure A-6	CHOOSING AN IP ADDRESS AND DNS SERVER ADDRESS

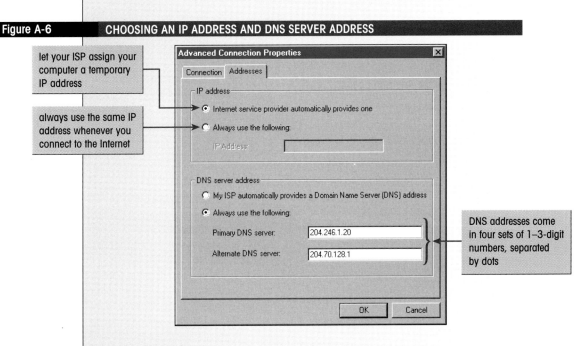

let your ISP assign your computer a temporary IP address

always use the same IP address whenever you connect to the Internet

DNS addresses come in four sets of 1–3-digit numbers, separated by dots

8. Click the **OK** button to close the Advanced Connection Properties dialog box and save your settings.

Entering Account Information

After working with the advanced settings, you are returned to the first step of the Internet Connection Wizard. At this point in the process, you enter information about your account, such as your username and password. You'll also enter a name for your ISP.

To enter your account information:

1. Click the **Next** button to move to Step 2 of the Internet Connection Wizard.

2. Type your username in the User name box, and then press the **Tab** key. Your ISP documentation will provide you with the username and password you should use.

TROUBLE? If you can't find your username in your documentation, it might be called User ID, Member ID, Login Name, or something similar.

3. Type your password in the Password box. As you type the password, asterisks appear instead of the letters you type, as shown in Figure A-7. This protects your password from the eyes of people who might be walking by your computer. You should keep your password secret, so that unauthorized users cannot access your account.

| Figure A-7 | ENTERING A USERNAME AND PASSWORD |

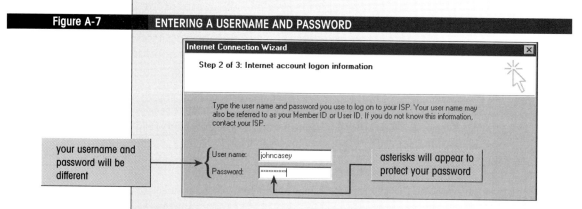

4. Click the **Next** button, type a name for your connection (such as your ISP's name), and then click the **Next** button. Since you are setting up only your dial-up connection, not your mail and news options, proceed by clicking **No** and then clicking **Next**.

TROUBLE? If you want to set up your mail and news options now on your own computer, you can do so by clicking Yes and following the prompts.

5. You've completed the Internet Connection Wizard. You could connect to the Internet right now, but you don't need to yet. Deselect the **Connect to the Internet Immediately** check box, and then click the **Finish** button. The Internet Connection Wizard closes, and you return to the desktop.

Although the steps didn't direct you to set up your mail and news options, you can do that from within Outlook Express, Outlook (if you have Microsoft Office), or whatever mail and news software you are using.

Using the Network and Dial-up Connection Window

Once you have established a dial-up connection, you are ready to use it to connect to the Internet or another network or computer. Windows 2000 will try to connect to the Internet automatically whenever you start a program that requires Internet access, such as your Web browser. If you have more than one ISP, you will be prompted to select which one you want to use to establish the Internet connection.

Another way of establishing your Internet connection is to open the Network and Dial-up Connections window and then to double-click the icon for your ISP. This window also provides tools to change your dial-up settings or any of your network connections (through your modem or local area network).

To view your Network and Dial-up Connections window:

1. Click the **Start** button, point to **Settings**, and then click **Network and Dial-up Connections**.

   The window opens as shown in Figure A-8.

Figure A-8	NETWORK AND DIAL-UP CONNECTIONS WINDOW

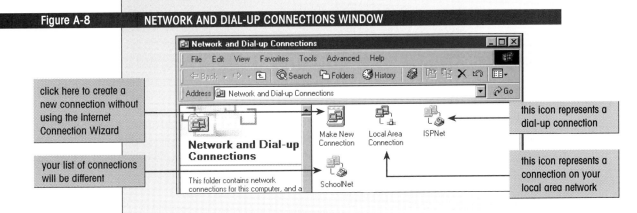

click here to create a new connection without using the Internet Connection Wizard

your list of connections will be different

this icon represents a dial-up connection

this icon represents a connection on your local area network

You can have more than network service, in which case multiple icons appear in the Network and Dial-up Connections window. One connection might provide your business Internet service, another might be for home or family use, and another might access your local area network.

To connect to your dial-up service through the Network and Dial-up Connections window:

1. Connect your phone line to your computer's modem.

2. Double-click the icon for your ISP.

3. The Connect dialog box opens.

4. Click the **Dial** button and then wait as your modem connects.

5. The Connecting dialog box appears and identifies the steps of establishing a connection. First it uses your modem to dial the number, then it verifies your username and password, and finally it establishes a connection. A Connection Complete dialog box (or something similar) may open, indicating that you are connected to your ISP.

6. If necessary, click **OK** to close the Connection Complete dialog box.

7. An icon appears on your taskbar that indicates you are connected. You can now start your Internet browser to view Web pages, check your e-mail, or use any of the other Windows 2000 communications features.

Your dial-up account will remain connected until you leave your computer idle for several minutes, in which case your ISP may automatically disconnect you, or until you disconnect from your account yourself.

To disconnect your dial-up account:

1. Right-click the **Connection** icon 📇 on the taskbar. A pop-up menu appears, shown in Figure A-9.

| Figure A-9 | DISCONNECTING FROM YOUR ISP |

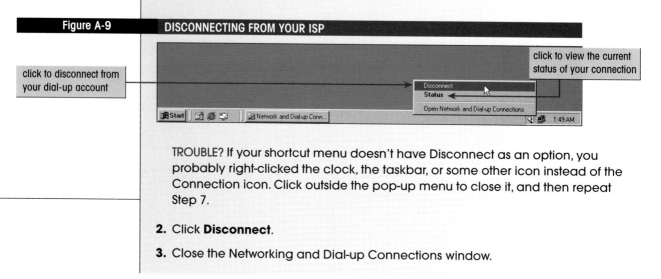

click to disconnect from your dial-up account

click to view the current status of your connection

TROUBLE? If your shortcut menu doesn't have Disconnect as an option, you probably right-clicked the clock, the taskbar, or some other icon instead of the Connection icon. Click outside the pop-up menu to close it, and then repeat Step 7.

2. Click **Disconnect**.

3. Close the Networking and Dial-up Connections window.

The Internet service provider market is changing very rapidly, so make sure you compare prices and features before choosing the ISP you want.

INDEX

TASK	PAGE #	RECOMMENDED METHOD
Active Desktop item, add	WIN 2000 5.23	Right-click a blank area of the desktop, point to Active Desktop, click Customize My Desktop, click Show Web content on my Active desktop, click New, click Yes, click item you want to add, click Add to Active Desktop, click Yes, click OK
Active Desktop item, close	WIN 2000 5.27	Point to item and wait for a title bar to appear, then click ⊠
Active Desktop item, move	WIN 2000 5.25	Point to item and wait for a title bar to appear, then drag title bar
Active Desktop item, remove	WIN 2000 5.27	Right-click a blank area of the desktop, point to Active Desktop, click Customize My Desktop, click item, click Delete, click Yes, click OK
Active Desktop item, remove	WIN 2000 5.31	Open the Display Properties dialog box, click the Web tab and deselect the checkbox for the active desktop item
Active Desktop item, resize	WIN 2000 5.26	Point to item and wait for a border to appear, then drag border or border corner
Active Desktop item, schedule an update for	WIN 2000 5.31	*See* Reference Window: Scheduling an Update
Active Desktop item, synchronize	WIN 2000 5.28	*See* Reference Window: Synchronizing an Active Desktop Item
Active Desktop item, view an update schedule	WIN 2000 5.28	Move over the top of the item to show the title bar, click the down arrow button in upper-left corner of the title bar, click Properties, and then click the Schedule tab
Active Desktop, enable	WIN 2000 5.23	Right-click a blank area of the desktop, point to Active Desktop, click View As Web Page
Character, insert	WIN 2000 2.07	Click where you want to insert the text, type the text
Control Panel, open	WIN 2000 4.40	Click the Start button ⊞ Start, click Settings, click Control Panel
Data Disk, create	WIN 2000 2.15	Click ⊞ Start point to Programs, point to NP on Microsoft Windows 2000 – Level I, click Disk 1, click OK
Desktop background, change	WIN 2000 4.16	Right-click a blank area of the desktop, click Properties, click Background tab, select pattern or wallpaper you want, click OK
Desktop background, use HTML file for	WIN 2000 5.33	Open the Display Properties dialog box, click the Background tab, click the Browse button and select the HTML file
Desktop color palette, change	WIN 2000 4.29	Right-click a blank area of the desktop, click Properties, click Settings tab, click Colors list arrow, click palette you want, click OK
Desktop document, create	WIN 2000 4.02	*See* Reference Window: Creating a New Document Icon on the Desktop
Desktop document, open	WIN 2000 4.04	Click the document icon
Desktop properties, view	WIN 2000 4.15	Right-click a blank area of the desktop and click Properties

TASK	PAGE #	RECOMMENDED METHOD
Desktop resolution, change	WIN 2000 4.25	Right-click a blank area of the desktop, click Properties, click Settings tab, drag Screen area slider, click OK
Desktop, access	WIN 2000 1.14	Click ⬚ on the Quick Launch toolbar
Desktop, change appearance	WIN 2000 4.22	Right-click a blank area of the desktop, click Properties, click Appearance tab, choose a different scheme, or click Item list arrow, change size or color, click OK
Device, select	WIN 2000 3.08	Click the device icon on the Explorer bar of Windows Explorer
Disk, format a	WIN 2000 2.03	Right-click the 3½ Floppy icon and click Format on the shortcut menu. Specify the capacity and file system of the disk and click Start.
Disk, quick format	WIN 2000 3.02	From My Computer, right-click disk icon, click Format, click Quick Format, click Start
Explorer bar, view	WIN 2000 3.04	In the Windows Explorer, or the My Computer window, click View, point to Explorer Bar, click Explorer bar you want
Favorites folder, add a Web page to	WIN 2000 5.17	*See* Reference Window: Adding a Web Page to the Favorites Folder
Favorites folder, organize	WIN 2000 5.19	*See* Reference Window: Organizing the Favorites Folder
Favorites folder, view	WIN 2000 5.16	Click View in Windows Explorer, point to the Explorer Bar, click Favorites
File on the Web, locate by query	WIN 2000 6.24	*See* Reference Window: Searching by Query
File on the Web, locate by subject	WIN 2000 6.26	*See* Reference Window: Searching by Subject
File or folder, delete	WIN 2000 3.27	Click the file or folder icon, then press the Delete key
File, copy	WIN 2000 2.24	*See* Reference Window: Moving and Copying a File
File, copy from one floppy disk to another	WIN 2000 3.26	*See* Reference Window: Copying a File from One Floppy Disk to Another
File, delete	WIN 2000 2.26	*See* Reference Window: Deleting a File
File, download from Web	WIN 2000 5.20	In Internet Explorer, right-click file you want to download, click Save As (or Save Picture As, or something similar), enter a location, click OK
File, locate by contents	WIN 2000 6.10	In Search, click the Containing text box, type the text you want to search for, click Search Now
File, locate by date	WIN 2000 6.15	Click the Search Options link, click the Date checkbox and enter the date criteria

TASK REFERENCE

TASK	PAGE #	RECOMMENDED METHOD
File, locate in a specific folder	WIN 2000 6.12	*See* Reference Window: Searching for File in a Specific Folder
File, locate one you were working with recently using the Documents menu	WIN 2000 6.19	Click **Start**, point to Documents
File, move	WIN 2000 2.24	*See* Reference Window: Moving and Copying a File
File, move or copy from floppy disk to hard disk	WIN 2000 3.24	In Windows Explorer, select files on floppy disk you want to move, right-click selection, click Cut or Copy, right-click folder on hard drive, click Paste
File, move or copy with Cut and Paste	WIN 2000 3.21	*See* Reference Window: Moving or Copying Files with Cut, Copy, and Paste
File, move or copy with the Move To and Copy To Folder commands	WIN 2000 3.22	*See* Reference Window: Moving or Copying Files with the Move To Folder and Copy To Folder commands
File, open from My Computer	WIN 2000 2.11	Open My Computer, open the window containing the file, click the file, press Enter
File, open from Search	WIN 2000 6.08	Locate the file using Search, right-click the file in the Results list, click Open
File, open from within a program	WIN 2000 2.12	Start the application, click Open from the File menu. Select the file in the Open File dialog box and click Open
File, print	WIN 2000 2.13	Within a program, click 🖨
File, rename	WIN 2000 2.25	*See* Reference Window: Renaming a File
File, save	WIN 2000 2.07	Within a program, click 💾
File, select	WIN 2000 3.14	*See* Reference Window: Selecting Files
File, select all but a certain one	WIN 2000 3.15	*See* Reference Window: Selecting All Files Except Certain Ones
File, select in Web style	WIN 2000 3.16	In Windows Explorer or the My Computer window, hover the mouse pointer over the file icon until the icon is selected
Files, locate by type or size	WIN 2000 6.16	Click the Search Options link, click the Type box or the Size box. Enter the search criteria
Files, view as large icons	WIN 2000 2.18	Click View, click Large Icons
Files, view as small icons	WIN 2000 2.18	Click View, click Small Icons
Files, view details	WIN 2000 2.18	Click View, click Details
Files, view in list	WIN 2000 2.18	Click View, click List
Files, view thumbnails	WIN 2000 2.18	Click View, click Thumbnails (Windows Explorer only.)

TASK	PAGE #	RECOMMENDED METHOD
Floppy disk, copy a	WIN 2000 2.28	*See* Reference Window: Copying a Disk
Folder hierarchy, move back in the	WIN 2000 2.23	Click the Back button ⬅
Folder hierarchy, move forward in the	WIN 2000 2.23	Click the Forward button ➡
Folder hierarchy, move up the	WIN 2000 2.23	Click the Up button ⬆
Folder options, restore default settings	WIN 2000 2.21	Click Tools, click Folder Options, click the General tab, click the Restore Defaults button. Click the View tab and click the Restore Defaults button. Click OK
Folder, create	WIN 2000 2.22	*See* Reference Window: Creating a Folder
Folder, create	WIN 2000 3.09	*See* Reference Window: Creating a Folder in Windows Explorer
Folder, rename	WIN 2000 3.10	Right-click the folder icon, click Rename and type the new folder name
Folder, select	WIN 2000 3.09	Click the folder icon on the Explorer Bar of Windows Explorer
Help, display topic from Contents tab	WIN 2000 1.26	From Help, click the Contents tab, click 📖 until you see the topic you want, click ❓ to display topic
Help, display topic from Index tab	WIN 2000 1.27	From Help, click the Index tab, scroll to locate topic, click topic, click Display
Help, return to previous Help topic	WIN 2000 1.28	Click ⬅
Help, start	WIN 2000 1.25	*See* Reference Window: Starting Windows 2000 Help
History pane, display	WIN 2000 3.28	Click View, point to Explorer Bar, click History
History pane, display by most visits	WIN 2000 3.30	Click View in the History pane and click By Most Visited
History pane, display recently opened files in the	WIN 2000 3.31	Click View in the History pane and click By Order Visited Today
History pane, search the	WIN 2000 3.32	Click the Search button in the History pane. Enter the search parameters
Insertion point, move	WIN 2000 2.05	Click the location in the document to which you want to move
Internet Connection wizard, start	WIN 2000 A.03	Click Start, point to Programs, point to Accessories, point to Communications and click Internet Connection Wizard
Internet Connection, set advanced settings for your	WIN 2000 A.04	Start the Internet Connection Wizard and set up the connection manually, click the Advanced button in Step 3 of the wizard
Internet Explorer, start	WIN 2000 5.06	*See* Reference Window: Starting Internet Explorer

TASK	PAGE #	RECOMMENDED METHOD
List box, scroll	WIN 2000 1.23	Click ▼ to scroll down the list box
LOG file, create	WIN 2000 4.05	In Notepad, type .LOG
Menu option, select	WIN 2000 1.08	Click the menu option, or, if it is a submenu, point to it
Menu option, select	WIN 2000 1.21	Click the menu option
My Computer, open	WIN 2000 2.16	Click My Computer on the desktop, press Enter
Objects, display or hide in the Folders pane	WIN 2000 3.06	*See* Reference Window: Displaying or Hiding Objects in the Folders Pane
Outlook Express, receive e-mail from	WIN 2000 5.47	Click the Send/Recv button 📧
Outlook Express, reply to e-mail from	WIN 2000 5.59	Click the Reply button 📧
Outlook Express, send e-mail from	WIN 2000 5.43	*See* Reference Window: Sending an E-mail Message
Outlook Express, set up an e-mail account for	WIN 2000 5.39	*See* Reference Window: Setting up an E-mail Account
Outlook Express, start	WIN 2000 5.36	Click the Start button 🏁 Start, point to Programs, click Outlook Express
Panes, adjust width	WIN 2000 3.10	*See* Reference Window: Adjusting the Width of the Exploring Window Panes
Pattern, apply to desktop	WIN 2000 4.20	Right-click a blank area of the desktop, click Properties, click Background tab, click Pattern, click pattern you want, click OK, click OK
People, locate on the Web	WIN 2000 6.28	Click 🏁 Start point to Search, click For People, choose the service you want, type the name you want to search for, click Find Now
Program, close	WIN 2000 1.12	Click ☒
Program, close inactive	WIN 2000 1.14	Right-click program button, click Close
Program, start	WIN 2000 1.10	*See* Reference Window: Starting a Program
Program, switch to another	WIN 2000 1.13	*See* Reference Window: Switching Between Programs
Properties, view	WIN 2000 4.15	Right-click the object, click Properties
Results list, sort	WIN 2000 6.14	Display the file list in Details view, click the title buttons on the top of the search results list
Screen saver, activate	WIN 2000 4.23	Right-click a blank area of the desktop, click Properties, click Screen Saver tab, click Screen Saver list arrow. Click OK
Screen, print	WIN 2000 3.18	Press PrintScreen, start WordPad, click 📋, click 🖨
ScreenTips, view	WIN 2000 1.07	Position the pointer over the item

TASK	PAGE #	RECOMMENDED METHOD
Search page, view on the Internet	WIN 2000 6.20	Click **Start** point to Search, click On the Internet
Search, clear	WIN 2000 6.13	In Search, click the New button near the top of the left pane
Search, locate by name	WIN 2000 6.05	*See* Reference Window: Searching for a File by Name
Search, start	WIN 2000 6.04	Click **Start** point to Search, click the option you want
Send To command, copy files with the	WIN 2000 3.25	Right-click the file icon, point to Send To and then select the destination of the file
Shortcut icon, delete	WIN 2000 4.14	Select the shortcut icon, press Delete, click Yes
Shortcut, create	WIN 2000 4.07	*See* Reference Window: Creating a Shortcut on the Desktop
Start Menu, add an item to	WIN 2000 4.36	*See* Reference Window: Adding an Item to the Start Menu
Start menu, open	WIN 2000 1.07	Click **Start**
Start Menu, remove an item from	WIN 2000 4.38	*See* Reference Window: Removing a Start Menu Item
Subfolders, view or hide	WIN 2000 3.07	Click **+** or **−**
Taskbar toolbar, create	WIN 2000 4.34	Right-click a blank area on the taskbar, point to Toolbars and click New Toolbar. Select the new toolbar
Taskbar toolbar, display	WIN 2000 4.32	*See* Reference Window: Displaying a Taskbar Toolbar
Taskbar toolbar, modify the appearance of	WIN 2000 4.33	Right-click the taskbar and click Properties. Modify the properties that apply to the taskbar's appearance
Taskbar toolbar, remove	WIN 2000 4.34	Right-click a blank area on the taskbar, point to Toolbars and deselect the toolbar from the list
Taskbar, moving and resize	WIN 2000 4.29	*See* Reference Window: Moving and Resizing the Taskbar
Taskbar, set properties	WIN 2000 4.30	Right-click the taskbar, click Properties
Text, select	WIN 2000 2.06	Click and drag the pointer over the text
Toolbar button, select	WIN 2000 1.22	Click the toolbar button
Toolbars, control display	WIN 2000 2.17	Click View, point to Toolbars, then select the toolbar options you want
Wallpaper, use graphic image	WIN 2000 4.21	Right-click a blank area of the desktop, click Properties, click Background tab, click Browse, locate and select file, click Open, click OK
Web page, activate link	WIN 2000 5.09	In Internet Explorer, click link on Web page
Web page, open with URL	WIN 2000 5.08	*See* Reference Window: Opening a Page with a URL
Web page, print	WIN 2000 5.20	In Internet Explorer, view page, click File, click Print, click OK

TASK	PAGE #	RECOMMENDED METHOD
Web page, return to previous	WIN 2000 5.13	In Internet Explorer, click the Back button
Wildcards, use to find files by name	WIN 2000 6.09	Start Search, type search string in the "Search for files or folders named" box, using ? in place of single characters and * in place of multiple characters
Window, close	WIN 2000 1.18	Click ✕
Window, maximize	WIN 2000 1.18	Click ☐
Window, minimize	WIN 2000 1.18	Click _
Window, move	WIN 2000 1.20	Click and drag the title bar
Window, resize	WIN 2000 1.20	Click and drag ↖
Window, restore	WIN 2000 1.18	Click ⧉
Windows 2000, shut down	WIN 2000 1.15	Click Start, click Shut Down, click the Shut Down option button, click OK
Windows 2000, start	WIN 2000 1.04	Turn on the computer
Windows Explorer, start	WIN 2000 3.03	Click Start, point to Programs, point to Accessories, click Windows Explorer

File Finder

Location in Tutorial	Name and Location of Data File	Student Saves File As...	Student Creates New File
WINDOWS 2000 LEVEL I, DISK 1 & 2			
Tutorial 1	No Data Files needed.		
Tutorial 2 Session 2.1			Practice Text.doc
Session 2.2 *Note:* Students copy the contents of Disk 1 onto Disk 2 in this session.	Agenda.doc Budget2001.xls Budget2001.xls Budget2002.xls Exterior.bmp Interior.bmp Logo.bmp Members.wdb Minutes.wps Newlogo.bmp Opus27.mid Parkcost.wks Proposal.doc Resume.doc Sales.wks Sample Text.doc Tools.wks Travel.wps Practice Text.doc *(Saved from Session 2.1)*		
Review Assigments & Projects	*Note:* Students continue to use the Data Disks they used in the Tutorial. For certain Assignments, they will need a 3rd blank disk.	Woods Resume .doc *(Saved from Resume.doc)*	Letter.doc Song.doc Poem.doc
WINDOWS 2000 LEVEL II, DISK 3			
Tutorial 3 Session 3.1	[16 files] Clients(folder) Advanced (folder) [4 files] Alpine (folder) [3 files] Ice (folder) [2 files] Sport (folder) [2 files] Basic (folder) [4 files] Gear (folder) [3 files] Guides (folder) [3 files]	[16 files] Clients(folder) Advanced (folder) [4 files] Alpine (folder) [3 files] Ice (folder) [2 files] Sport (folder) [2 files] Basic (folder) [4 files] Gear (folder) [3 files] Hardware (folder) Ropes and Harnesses (folder) Guides (folder) [3 files]	Gear (folder) Hardware (folder) Ropes and Harnesses (folder)

File Finder

Location in Tutorial	Name and Location of Data File	Student Saves File As...	Student Creates New File

Session 3.2		[4 files]
		Clients(folder)
		    Advanced (folder)
		        [4 files]
		    Alpine (folder)
		        [5 files]
		    Ice (folder)
		        [2 files]
		    Sport (folder)
		        [2 files]
		    Basic (folder)
		        [13 files]
		Gear (folder)
		    Hardware (folder)
		    Ropes and Harnesses (folder)
		        [5 files]
		Guides (folder)
		    [3 files]	

Session 3.3	No data files needed		
Review Assignments and Projects			C:/Advertise A:/All Clients
Tutorial 4 Session 4.1	Same files used as in Session 3.2		Phone Log.txt
Session 4.2	Logo.bmp		
Session 4.3	No data files needed		

Review Assignments and Projects			Classes.txt
			A:/Sally (folder)
			    Smith.txt
			    Arruga.txt
			    Kosta.txt
			A:/My Signature.bmp

Tutorial 5 Session 5.1	No data files neeeded		lake.jpg
Session 5.2	Highland.htm [15 supporting files]		
Session 5.3			Highland.htm [15 supporting files]

Tutorial 6
Session 6.1
	Alphabet (folder)
	    [25 files]
	Authors (folder)
	    [25 files]
	Comedy (folder)
	    [18 files]
	Images (folder)
	    [2 files]
	Social (folder)
	    [16 files]
	Topics (folder)
	    [19 files]		

Session 6.2	No data files needed		
Review Assignments and Projects	Same as Session 6.1		
Appendix A	No Data Files needed		

BIG BUSINESS,
BIG PROBLEMS

BIG BUSINESS,
BIG PROBLEMS

Timely Reports to Keep
Journalists, Scholars and the Public
Abreast of Developing Issues, Events and Trends

Editorial Research Reports
Published by Congressional Quarterly Inc.
1414 22nd Street N.W., Washington, D.C. 20037

Library of Congress Cataloging-in-Publication Data

Big business, big problem : timely reports to keep
  journalists, scholars, and the public abreast of developing issues, events, and trends / Editorial research reports.
        p.   cm.
     Originally published as individual issues of Editorial research reports.
     ISBN 0-87187-497-0
     1. Industrial management--United States.
  2. Quality of work life--United States. 3. Personnel management--United States.
  I. Congressional Quarterly, inc. II. Editorial research reports.
  HD70.U5B53   1989
  338.6'44'0973--dc20   89-23906
                                                        CIP

CONTENTS

JULY 21, 1989

FUTURE OF EMPLOYEE BENEFITS

FUTURE OF EMPLOYEE BENEFITS

by Robert K. Landers

EDITOR
MARCUS D. ROSENBAUM

MANAGING EDITOR
SANDRA STENCEL

ASSOCIATE EDITOR
RICHARD L. WORSNOP

STAFF WRITERS
MARY H. COOPER
SARAH GLAZER
ROBERT K. LANDERS
PATRICK G. MARSHALL

PRODUCTION EDITOR
LAURIE DE MARIS

EDITORIAL COORDINATOR
DOUGLAS SERY

EDITORIAL ASSISTANT
SHARON C. YOUNG

RICHARD M. BOECKEL (1892-1975)
FOUNDER

PUBLISHED BY
CONGRESSIONAL QUARTERLY INC.

CHAIRMAN AND PRESIDENT
ANDREW BARNES

PUBLISHER
WAYNE P. KELLEY

EXECUTIVE EDITOR
NEIL SKENE

Worried about the rising cost of health insurance and other non-wage benefits, many businesses are abandoning paternalism and seeking to limit their financial commitment to their employees' future welfare. In addition, the shift of the economy from manufacturing to services has resulted in more Americans working without health insurance and other benefits. Taken together, these trends may be spelling the breakdown of the system of employee benefits that Americans have relied on for decades.

Paid maternity leave, unpaid leaves of up to three years, flexible work schedules, help in finding child care and arranging for the care of elderly relatives — these are just some of the benefits enjoyed by the 223,000 employees who work for International Business Machines Corp. in the United States. IBM's generous array of benefits helps the company attract and keep desired employees. About a third of IBM's work force are women and the company was selected by *Working Mother* magazine last year as one of the "five best companies for working mothers." [1]

Most American businesses are not as large or as successful as IBM, however, and the benefits they provide are less liberal than IBM's and less attuned to the changed composition of the work force. A 1987 nationwide survey by the Bureau of Labor Statistics found that although a majority of firms did have work-schedule policies that might help parent-employees, "employers as a group have yet to respond in a significant way to the child-care needs of their workers." [2] (*See story, p. 10.*)

Corporate America's slowness in responding to employees' child-care needs is hardly surprising. Employers now are getting away from traditional corporate paternalism — the belief that companies should "take care" of their workers and their families, should assure their health and security by providing health insurance, pensions and other non-wage benefits.

Under great pressure to be competitive in the world and at home, and faced with ever-increasing health-care costs and an aging work force of future baby-boomer retirees, employers have decided that corporate paternalism, or any pretense of it, is a luxury they can no longer afford. Desperately seeking to contain their rising employee-benefit costs (*see chart, at right*), employers have begun to move away from "defined benefits," in which the employer promises to pay a fixed benefit, determined by a specified formula, and toward "defined contributions," in which the employer promises only to contribute a fixed amount toward the employee's purchase of the benefit. The difference means that the risk of investment and risk of inflation are largely shifted to the employee.

The movement toward defined-contribution benefits began with pensions in the 1970s but has broadened in the 1980s. The emergence of flexible-benefit (or "cafeteria") plans, which allow employees to choose among different types of benefits, gave it a major boost. Flexible-benefit plans, says Meredith Miller, an employee-benefit specialist with the AFL-CIO, were "the beginning of saying, 'Here's $1,000, you buy your own benefits.' "

Although the broader trend toward defined-contribution benefits still remains in "the early stages," it is growing rapidly, according to Dallas L. Salisbury, president of the Employee Benefit Research Institute, a non-profit, nonpartisan research organization based in Washington, D.C.

But this trend is not the only force striking at the nation's system of employer-provided benefits, which developed, mainly as a result of union efforts, in the decades after World War II. There is also the shift of the U.S. economy from manufacturing to services. That has meant that an increasing number of Americans are working for small firms or working part time — often without health insurance or other benefits. About 37 million Americans under the age of 65 were without health insurance in 1985. At least two-thirds of them were working adults and their uninsured dependents, according to an analysis by Congress' General Accounting Office — and their number seems to be increasing. (*See story, p. 5.*)

Under this double assault, the system of employee benefits so familiar to Americans in recent decades may be starting to come apart. "I think we're definitely on a roller coaster down," says Miller of the AFL-CIO. "It's something that's very scary."

Employer Outlays For Employee Benefits

Benefit costs have skyrocketed in recent years, rising from $24 billion in 1960 to $431 billion in 1987. Most of the money is spent on health benefits ($144 billion in 1987) and retirement benefits ($220 billion, which included employers' share of Social Security).

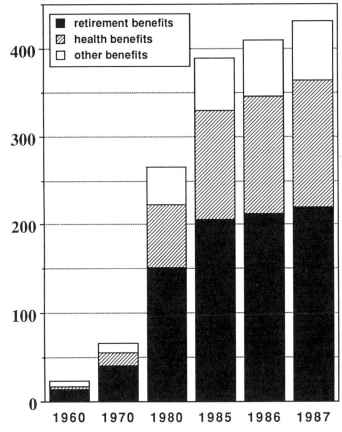

in $ billions

- ■ retirement benefits
- ▨ health benefits
- □ other benefits

Source: Employee Benefit Research Institute.

If the system is indeed breaking down, the fault seems to lie with impersonal forces beyond any private individual's control. Employers, for instance, can hardly be faulted for their concern about the skyrocketing costs of health care — up 8.5 percent in 1986 and 9.8 percent in 1987. With medical expenses estimated at $541 billion in 1988, the United States now spends more than 11.5 percent of its gross national product on health care.[3] In an effort just to limit the growth in their health-care costs, employers increasingly are requiring employees to share the increased costs of medical coverage and hospital stays. In the future, Salisbury says, there is likely to be "a whole lot more" of this sharing.

Employers also worry about the cost of paying for health care for future retirees. Rules proposed by the Financial Accounting Standards Board, a private organization that sets accounting standards for company financial statements, would require companies to recognize the liability on their balance sheets, starting in 1992. In the past, companies have handled retiree health costs on a pay-as-you-go basis out of current revenues. Many companies, particularly those with older workers and many retirees, are worried about how the accounting change will make their balance sheets look to investors and others.

Even without the change in accounting standards, companies have plenty of reason to worry, given the large number of workers from the baby-boom generation who will be retiring early in the next century. The Employee Benefit Research Institute estimates that private employers' liability for retiree health benefits for their current workers amounts to more than $100 billion.[4]

Flexible-benefit plans, which allow employees to choose among different types of benefits, were "the beginning of saying, 'Here's $1,000, you buy your own benefits,'" says Meredith Miller, an employee-benefit specialist with the AFL-CIO.

Many employers are considering reducing retirees' medical coverage, increasing retiree contributions, or both. Over the next decade, Salisbury predicts that many firms will eliminate retiree health coverage altogether, and the result will be that employees will be working longer and not retiring until they become eligible for the federal Medicare program.

Some firms already have moved in this direction. Armstrong World Industries, of Lancaster, Pa., for instance, last month eliminated future retiree coverage for non-unionized employees under age 48; such employees will instead receive annual allocations of shares through a newly established employee stock-ownership plan. (*See At Issue, p. 12.*) The changes don't affect the company's unionized employees, but the subject may come up in Armstrong's negotiations with the unions later this year.

Employees naturally don't like to see fringe benefits eliminated or cut back or even fail to improve. But, under the lash of competition, employers appear to have little choice but to try to control the mounting cost of benefits. Moreover, in leaving paternalism behind, corporations in fact are giving workers what many of them say they want — more of a say in determining which benefits they receive.

Companies more and more, Salisbury points out, have been moving in the direction of saying: "'We should structure programs the way people want them. . . . We should not be telling [employees] what they should do. If they want cash instead of health care, then, gee, maybe we should do that. If they want cash instead of a pension, gee, maybe that's what they should have.'"

Letting workers have what they want may not actually be in the workers' own long-term interest. They themselves may give up benefits they really need, or their employers may more easily shift the costs of certain major benefits to the workers. Nevertheless, it is the workers themselves who are asking for an end to paternalism. "Employees are begging [employers] to abandon it," Salisbury says, "and regrettably for employees, employers are listening."

This does not mean that organizations are evincing a diminished concern for their employees, according to Randall B. Dunham, a professor of management at the University of Wisconsin, Madison. "It's [rather] that their caring behavior is manifested in a different way," he says. By providing flexible-benefit and other plans, organizations are telling their people: "'You understand what you need, you're smart enough to figure out what your preferences are and what you need to have and what you don't have, [and] we're going to let you participate in that.'"

This contrasts sharply with the paternalism of old, which according to John J. Parkington, practice director for organization research and analysis at The Wyatt Co., a benefits and compensation consulting firm, initially grew out of the conviction on the part of the owner that employees were "ignorant slobs" who were incapable of taking care of themselves and their families. Employers later acquired an additional motivation for paternalism: the threat of unionization. But that threat has receded in recent years. Moreover, Parkington notes, workers today are more educated than in the past, and managers are changing, too. "As younger people with different ideas get into more and more senior management roles, it's starting to change the philosophy about [treating] people."

One philosophical change may beget others. Americans have come to rely on employer-provided benefits for their health care and social insurance. Many other Western democracies decided years ago that such social welfare should come from the state, and they instituted national health-care programs, state-funded pensions, and so forth. If American employers no longer can foot the bill — or if a significant proportion of

The Working Uninsured

About 37 million Americans under the age of 65 had no health insurance at all in 1985. This was up 13 percent from 1982, according to an analysis by the General Accounting Office (GAO). At least two-thirds of the uninsured were working adults and their dependents. "Reduced access to health insurance through employment appears to be a major factor in the growth of the uninsured," the GAO stated.†

The report noted that the uninsured are most likely to be young (19-24), non-white, single, poorly educated, and employed in low-income jobs, frequently on a part-time or part-year basis. The businesses least likely to offer health insurance include those that provide low-wage or low-skill jobs, those that have fewer than 100 employees, those that are new, and those in the Southern and Western regions of the country. Construction, retail and service industry jobs are least likely to offer health insurance.

Not having health insurance affects the uninsured, of course: A 1986 study by the Robert Wood Johnson Foundation found that the uninsured are less likely to use health-care services and are more likely to be in poor health than those who have health insurance. But the lack of insurance also affects others. "By billing private insurers at rates exceeding costs . . . ," the GAO reported, "hospitals frequently attempt to shift some of the costs of uninsured patients to insured patients."

Because such cost shifting has been constrained in recent years, as a result of various health-care cost-containment measures, hospitals "increasingly want to treat only insured patients," the GAO report stated. This has led to a practice known as "patient-dumping," in which hospitals "attempt to transfer uninsured patients [to other hospitals or health-care facilities] for economic rather than medical reasons."

† U.S. General Accounting Office, *Health Insurance: An Overview of the Working Uninsured*, February 1989, pp. 10, 12.

workers are employed in jobs that do not provide benefits at all — then Americans will be forced to look outside the work place for help.

Modern system began to take shape in WWII

Before the Social Security Act of 1935 and subsequent legislation provided workers with a measure of security against old age, unemployment or disability, any benefits that workers enjoyed were the result of their employers' largess. "Early in the 20th century, some mass-production employers launched 'employee welfare' programs," historian Robert H. Zieger relates. "Some provided visiting nurses or company-paid

doctors. Others built and maintained housing. Still others established profit-sharing and stock-purchase plans. The electrical products industry, for example, prided itself on its concern for its employees. . . . In the wake of World War I-era strikes, Westinghouse and General Electric began retirement programs, housing projects, group insurance, and stock-ownership plans." [5] Such benefits served to discourage unionization and to bind the worker to the company, but they were far from widespread. Not until World War II did the modern system of employee benefits begin to take shape.

To get around the wartime restrictions on wages, union leaders bargained with employers for non-wage benefits, such as paid vacations and company-financed medical plans. After the war, the industrial unions "mounted major campaigns to establish health care, pension, insurance, and other benefits . . . ,"

Who Gets What Benefits?

Most full-time employees in large and medium-sized firms receive certain benefits including medical insurance, life insurance, paid vacations and holidays, jury duty leave and funeral leave. Other benefits are less widely available and, as the chart below indicates, their availability varies among different types of workers. For example, 90 percent of professional and administrative workers and technical and clerical workers receive paid sick leave, compared with only 69 percent of production and service workers.

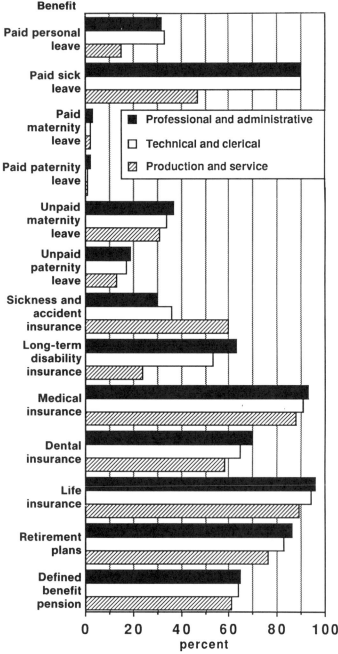

Source: U.S. Bureau of Labor Statistics. Figures are for 1988.

Zieger recounts. "Most large employers ... resisted these initiatives, realizing that 'fringe' benefits would open up vast new areas for bargaining." Employers also argued that federal labor law did not require them to bargain on non-wage issues other than working conditions.

Despite employers' opposition, the unions made swift progress. The United Mine Workers won sweeping medical and insurance benefits in 1947. Two years later, Zieger notes, the Supreme Court "ruled that such non-wage matters were indeed legitimately subjects for collective bargaining, thus undercutting much of corporate America's resistance. The 1949 Steelworkers' contract, hammered out after a lengthy strike, gained pension and insurance funds free from employer control. In 1949 and 1950, the [United Auto Workers] made similar gains, again after long work stoppages."

After these hard-won successes, fringe benefits (as the non-wage forms of compensation came to be known) became an important part of collective bargaining. According to Ziegler, there was "a rapid increase in the percentage of employee compensation taken up by health, insurance, and pension initiatives. Together with the social welfare legislation of the 1930s, as supplemented periodically by postwar improvements, these contract breakthroughs brought a degree of security and thus a kind of freedom to millions of workers and their families." [6]

The gains made by the unions for their members led to similar gains for non-union workers. The union contracts "set a standard for employers everywhere," Zieger writes. "Given the modest levels of social insurance and medical care underwritten by government in the United States, union-negotiated benefits spurred private employers, many of whom sought to prevent the union virus from infecting their employees, to follow suit." [7]

In the 1960s, labor unions pressed for "fully paid health insurance ... , medical coverage for retirees, and pension plans to provide retirement security." [8] The federal government also expanded its role, establishing the Medicare program of health insurance for the elderly in 1965, along with the federal-state Medicaid program, which finances health care for the poor. In addition, the government, by means of tax incentives, encouraged the growth of employee benefits in the private sector.

By the 1970s, although unemployment insurance, health insurance, and other non-wage benefits in the United States still "lagged behind the levels of state-provided services of comparable countries, the main features of the 'mix' of negotiated and state-underwritten benefits were in place," Zieger writes. Indeed, pensions and health insurance "had become so commonplace that millions of Americans took these hard-won benefits for granted."

Shrinking coverage
is trend in pensions

In the 1980s, as the economy has shifted from manufacturing toward service jobs, and as the number of smaller firms has grown, the percentage of the work force covered by pensions has shrunk, falling from 56 percent in 1979 to an estimated 49 percent in 1985. Only 22 percent of service workers were covered by pensions in 1985.[9] The size of the firm often determines whether the workers receive pensions and other benefits. About 90 percent of the full-time employees of large and medium-sized firms are covered by pensions, compared with less than 40 percent of full-time workers at firms with under 100 employees and less than 15 percent at firms with under 20 employees.[10]

Long-term workers at larger firms have enjoyed another advantage: In 1988, about 63 percent of the full-time employees of large and medium-sized firms were covered by defined-benefit pension plans, which specify a formula for determining an employee's annuity.* But this was down from 76 percent in 1986.[11] The trend even at larger firms has been to create defined-contribution retirement plans, which include savings and thrift plans, deferred profit-sharing plans and employee stock-ownership plans.

In savings and thrift plans, employees contribute a predetermined portion of earnings to an account, all or part of which is matched by the employer. Section 401(k) of the tax code allows employers to structure the plans so that the employee's contribution is on a pre-tax basis. In deferred profit-sharing plans, employers make profit-related contributions to employee accounts, and the money is held until retirement or other specified conditions, such as death or disability, are met. Employee stock-ownership plans, usually funded entirely by the employer, provide employees with stock in their company. (*See At Issue, p. 12.*)

The movement away from defined-benefit pension plans was in part a result of the 1974 Employee Retirement Income Security Act (ERISA), which sought to safeguard employees' private pensions. The law didn't oblige firms to provide pensions, but those firms that chose to do so had to adhere to federal standards. ERISA set minimum funding standards for defined-benefit plans and required the plans to obtain benefit insurance through the federally run Pension Benefit Guaranty Corporation, to guarantee the payment of benefits in the event of a bankruptcy. These two requirements raised the cost of defined-benefit plans.

The number of participants in defined-benefit plans has remained relatively stable (about 29 million)

since ERISA took effect, and the number of defined-benefit plans has actually increased. But between 1975 and 1985 the number of defined-contribution plans more than doubled, and the number of participants in such plans nearly tripled (rising from 3.9 million to 11.6 million). According to the Employee Benefit Research Institute (EBRI), the movement toward defined-contribution retirement plans "represents a long-term trend independent of shifts in firm size and industry." Not only did government regulation make defined-benefit plans more costly, but "employers are restructuring their benefits to prepare for the baby boom's retirement." [12]

> *"By providing flexible-benefit and other plans, organizations are telling their people: 'You understand what you need, you're smart enough to figure out what your preferences are and what you need to have and what you don't have, [and] we're going to let you participate in that,'" says Randall B. Dunham, professor of management, University of Wisconsin.*

Companies often justify the move toward defined-contribution retirement plans by saying that this is what workers, particularly younger workers, want. "Younger workers react favorably to defined contribution plans," EBRI reports, "because account balances showing a current cash value appear more meaningful [to them] than the promise of monthly checks for an unknown amount at retirement." Another reason such plans appeal to the baby-boom generation is that

---

*The most common type of defined-benefit pension plan is the terminal earnings plan, which bases pension payments on an employee's earnings in the last few years before retirement. In 1988, according to the Bureau of Labor Statistics, the average benefit formula in such plans was about 1.6 percent of earnings times years of service.

Taxing Highly Paid Workers' Benefits

It originally was just a small and little-noticed part of the 1986 Tax Reform Act, but Section 89 of the tax code eventually prompted a big outcry from business groups and others. As a result, the measure has yet to take effect, and Congress is now in the process of overhauling it.

Section 89 requires employers to run a battery of complicated tests on their health- and life-insurance plans to show that the plans do not favor higher-paid employees at the expense of rank-and-file workers. Employees getting "discriminatory" benefits would have to pay income taxes on them.

Businesses complained about the complexity of the law and the cost of running the discrimination tests. "It will tend to decrease flexibility and increase administrative costs," said Frederick J. Krebs, manager of business and government policy for the U.S. Chamber of Commerce. "The effect will be fewer benefits and fewer businesses offering benefits." †

Labor representatives also objected. They saw Section 89 as a way for the government to begin taxing employee benefits and feared that employers would use the law to override collective-bargaining agreements.

Section 89 originally was set to take effect Jan. 1, 1989, but the date has been twice pushed back and is now Oct. 1. Legislation to revise Section 89 passed the Senate in June, and House Ways and Means Chairman Dan Rostenkowski, D-Ill., was reported ready to modify a revision bill he had introduced in April, to make it more acceptable to employers.††

† Quoted by Roger Thompson in " 'Government Gone Crazy,' " *Nation's Business*, February 1989.

†† Paul Starobin, "Overhaul of Section 89 Rules Making Headway in House," *Congressional Quarterly Weekly Report*, July 1, 1989.

these workers tend to change jobs more often than their parents did, and they prefer defined-contribution plans to pension plans that are based on years of service.

Flexible-benefit plans growing in popularity

Another way companies have responded to workers' changing needs is by providing flexible-benefit plans and reimbursement accounts, which can be used by employees to pay for expenses not covered by the regular package of benefits.* In its 1988 survey of employee benefits in medium and large firms, the

Bureau of Labor Statistics found that 13 percent of the workers — nearly 4 million people — were eligible for one or the other. In 1986, only 5 percent had been. The bureau also found that the arrangements were more common among white-collar workers (19 percent in 1988) than among blue-collar ones (6 percent).

The attraction of flexible-compensation plans is easy to understand: They enable employees to get benefits better suited to their particular situations. Compensation packages that were designed for the traditional family, a working husband with a wife and children at home, do not necessarily meet the needs of two-income families or the increased numbers of single women and divorced mothers in the work force. A working wife, for instance, has no need for health insurance through her job if she is already covered by her husband's policy. An unmarried employee who does not intend to have a family may not be interested in life insurance. The appeal of flexible-compensation plans is not only to workers' needs but also to their preferences. Young workers tend to prefer vacation time and other sorts of paid leave to medical insurance or retirement benefits. As workers grow older, how-

*Reimbursement accounts may be financed by employer contributions, employee contributions or both, but the funds generally come from workers seeking tax advantages through salary-reduction arrangements. The accounts commonly cover such expenses as the employee's share of insurance premiums, dependent care, or health-care deductibles and co-insurance expenses.

ever, medical insurance and pensions move up on their agendas.

How much employees earn also shapes their preferences. "[B]ecause of the non-taxable status of most fringe benefits, high-income workers generally prefer higher overall levels of fringe benefits than do low-income workers," note economists David E. Bloom, of Columbia University, and Jane T. Trahan, of Harvard University. High-income workers "also tend to have stronger preferences for capital accumulation plans, recreation facilities, and child-care assistance." [13] The 1986 Tax Reform Act added a provision to the tax code to penalize benefit plans that "discriminate" in favor of higher-paid employees, but the provision, known as Section 89, is being overhauled by Congress before it goes into effect. (*See story, p. 8.*)

The most common benefits offered in flexible-benefit plans, according to the BLS survey last year, are the traditional ones of health insurance, life insurance and long-term disability insurance — as well as the non-traditional option of receiving cash instead of benefits.

Employees' interest in certain non-traditional benefits is sometimes exaggerated. Take child care, for example. Parkington, who has done work/family studies for various companies, says that frequently "employees who have kids are not interested in on-site day care, because they say, 'Well, I have a babysitter that I know, that I trust. I'm not interested in having my kid go to some place where there are 50 kids running around like crazy people.' ... And so the concern that I've heard a number of parents express in these studies is: 'What I would really like [is] to be able, in emergency circumstances, when my sitter is sick and my backup sitter can't make it, [to have] my employer be flexible enough to understand that my kid comes first and I've got to do something to take care of the kid. And that may require flexible scheduling so that I can be off that day and make up the time some other time.' "

From the employer's point of view, the biggest potential problem with a flexible-benefit plan is "the costliness of its implementation and administration," according to Bloom and Trahan. "Even with the widespread use of high-speed computers, flexible compensation is a tricky program to install and administer, since its acceptability usually requires an extensive communications campaign and its operation requires new computer software and trained personnel who can answer numerous questions from employees about their new benefit options." [14]

That drawback may explain why flexible-benefit plans still are confined to a relatively limited number of firms, mostly larger ones. But the growth of the plans among major firms has been quite dramatic. A recent study of 227 major employers by Hewitt Associates, a benefit and compensation consulting firm, found that 44 percent of them had flexible-benefit plans in 1988,

Employees Are Paying More Out-of-Pocket for Health Care

The number of employer-provided health plans having front-end deductibles rose from 51 percent in 1984 to 70 percent in 1988. During the same period, the percentage of medical plans requiring employee contributions for employee and/or dependent coverage rose from 54 percent to 60 percent.

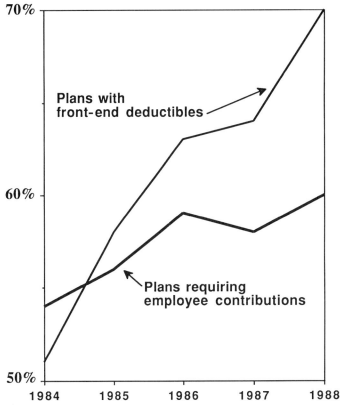

Source: *Hewitt Associates.*

up from just 20 percent in 1985. [15]

Employers may have instituted flexible-benefit plans partly in response to workers' changing needs and preferences, but they soon discovered that such plans could have another benefit: to help the company contain benefit costs. With flexible-benefit plans, Dunham explains, the employer is able to tell his employees: " 'We're going to spend this many dollars for you on benefits, and that's more than we spent for you last year. But here's what these individual benefits cost now, and you can choose where you want to spend that money. ... It's unfortunate the cost of health care went up 20 percent this year and we're only spending 6 percent more. But you can decide. Do you want to contribute cash toward the cost of that health care? Do you want to have us cover the entire cost for you? But it's going to cost you something else, either in life insurance, or maybe in vision care or in vacation time.' "

Flexible-benefit plans don't have to involve shifting the costs of benefits to employees, says Miller of the

Continued on page 11

Employers and Dependent Care

The rise of the working mother has left millions of children in need of some sort of care or supervision while both of the parents or the lone parent are off working. Although employers on the whole continue to play no active role in providing that care, Howard V. Hayghe, a Bureau of Labor Statistics (BLS) economist, observes that "some employers are coming to realize that the difficulties that their employees face in arranging care for their children may result in absenteeism, tardiness, low morale and productivity problems. This may be exacerbated in some areas by worker shortages. Consequently, there is some evidence that employers are looking at steps they can take to help their employees who are parents." †

But a special nationwide survey the BLS conducted in the summer of 1987 of about 10,000 businesses and government agencies indicated that direct aid to working parents was still very limited. Only about 2 percent, or 25,000, of the nation's 1.2 million establishments with 10 or more employees actually sponsored day-care centers for their workers' children, and only 3 percent provided financial assistance toward child-care expenses.

The percentages increased somewhat with the size of the firms. Among large establishments (with 250 employees or more), 5 percent sponsored day-care centers and 9 percent provided financial assistance. Larger proportions offered child-care information and referral and counseling services. (*See table, below.*)

The supply of employer-sponsored day-care centers or other direct aid may be limited, at least in part, because the demand is limited. Many parents prefer to make other, more informal arrangements for care of their children, and what they want from their employers is understanding and flexibility. In that regard, businesses' record appears a good deal better: 60 percent of the firms surveyed by the BLS had work-schedule policies that could help parents meet their child-care needs.

The most common policies — which were at least as much in evidence at small firms as at large ones — involved "flexitime" (in which employees could vary the starting and finishing times of their workday) and flexible leave (such as personal leave, or sick or annual leave that could be taken when needed). More than one-third of the firms surveyed let full-time employees shift temporarily to part-time jobs, with corresponding cuts in pay and benefits.

Children are not the only dependents for whom employees need to provide care. Many workers are also struggling to care for their elderly parents. "[P]roblems associated with this type of dependent care are only beginning to be addressed in the work place," notes a study by the Employee Benefit Research Institute.†† As the work force ages in the 1990s, the institute points out, corporate support for elder care "may become an important employee benefit." Among the forms of assistance that employers might provide: paid and unpaid leave for employees who must care for parents; day care for parents; long-term care insurance; referral services and networks to make it easier to obtain care; and medical coverage.

In the years ahead, with fewer new young workers entering the work force, businesses may become more inclined to accommodate employees' family needs, particularly if, as many expect, the feminization of the work place continues. The Hudson Institute, in *Workforce 2000*, a 1987 study done for the Labor Department, projected that by the year 2000, 61 percent of women will be working and they will constitute more than 47 percent of the work force.

But Randall B. Dunham, a professor of management at the University of Wisconsin, Madison, says employers won't respond directly to general employment trends, but will instead adapt to the situation in their own particular labor markets. "I think the smart organizations aren't going to do it until they see a good reason to do it," he says. ". . . I don't think you'll see organizations changing as quickly as the characteristics of the work force change. But I do think you're going to see those changes happening."

† *Howard V. Hayghe, "Employers and Child Care: What Roles Do They Play?,"* Monthly Labor Review, *September 1988.*

†† *"Dependent Care: Meeting the Needs of a Dynamic Work Force,"* EBRI Issue Brief, *Employee Benefit Research Institute, December 1988.*

While a majority of firms have work-schedule policies that might help working parents, few employers provide day-care services for employees or financial assistance for child-care expenses.

Type of organization	Total organizations (in thousands)	Percent providing: Employer-sponsored day care	Assistance with child-care expenses	Child-care information and referral services	Percent providing: Flextime	Voluntary part time	Job sharing	Work at home	Flexible leave
Total	1,202	2.1	3.1	5.1	43.2	34.8	15.5	8.3	42.9
10 to 49 employees	919	1.9	2.4	4.3	45.1	36.0	16.0	9.2	43.8
50 to 249 employees	236	2.2	4.7	6.3	37.7	32.0	13.7	5.6	39.9
250 employees or more	47	5.2	8.9	14.0	34.9	25.1	15.7	3.8	40.2
Private, total	1,128	1.6	3.1	4.3	43.6	35.3	15.0	8.5	42.9
Goods-producing, total	272	.3	1.9	2.3	31.3	22.4	9.0	8.2	37.3
Service-producing, total	856	2.0	3.5	5.0	47.5	39.4	16.9	8.6	44.6
Government	74	9.4	2.9	15.8	37.5	26.7	23.5	4.0	43.7

Source: U.S. Bureau of Labor Statistics.

Continued from page 9
AFL-CIO. The "good" plans, at a minimum, "preserve the level of benefits that were provided prior to the flexible-benefit plan implementation." However, she says, "the majority of flexible-benefit plans that are created shift health-care costs to workers." In fact, according to Salisbury, the opportunity to have employees share in rising health-care costs has been "the primary motivation" behind the growth of flexible-benefit plans. "[V]ery, very few companies ... have done it because of demographics," he says.

Employers want to share rising health-care costs

Employees generally regard health insurance as being far more essential than other non-wage benefits. It's not "that pensions, group life insurance and vacations are not thought to be important," says Mathew H. Greenwald, of Mathew Greenwald & Associates, a research and consulting company, and former director of social research for the American Council of Life Insurance. "They are. But group health insurance is thought [by employees] to be more than important. It is perceived to be crucial." Faced with the rising costs of health care, employees would prefer "to pay more rather than accept lower benefits." [16] And increasingly, employers are asking employees to pay more.

The recent Hewitt Associates study of major employers' benefit plans found that the percentage of plans providing full reimbursement for hospital room and board charges declined from 53 percent in 1984 to 29 percent in 1988. The use of so-called "front-end" deductibles, applicable to all medical expenses, increased from 51 percent of the plans to 70 percent. There was a "dramatic increase" in annual deductible amounts over the four-year period. The percentage of plans with a per-person deductible of $100 or less dropped from 52 percent to 29 percent. The survey found that "The biggest movement has been to deductibles of $200 or $250 per year and to deductible amounts related to employee pay." [17]

Employees are also paying more direct contributions. The percentage of medical plans requiring employee contributions for employee and/or dependent coverage increased from 54 percent in 1984 to 60 percent in 1988. (*See graph, p. 9.*) "[E]mployers are now forcing people with families to pay more than they ever did before, [so] that getting dependent coverage and keeping dependent coverage has become a very big problem," says Miller of the AFL-CIO. According to the BLS survey of benefits at medium and large firms, the average employee contribution for family coverage was $60 a month in 1988, more than double what it was in 1982. [18]

Some executives contend that it is inequitable for a company to pay larger sums for the medical insurance premiums of an employee with a family than for the premiums of an unmarried employee. Dunham says that in his work with organizations on benefit plans, "that issue has come up over and over again, and in some cases very intensely." Salisbury has also detected growing interest in this issue. "One can argue," he says, "that if you've got two people sitting next to each other, doing the identical job and being paid the identical salary but you're spending twice as much on health insurance for one as the other, that you're discriminating against the individual that doesn't

> *"One can argue," says Dallas L. Salisbury, president of the Employee Benefit Research Institute, "that if you've got two people... doing the identical job and being paid the identical salary but you're spending twice as much on health insurance for one as the other, that you're discriminating against the individual who doesn't have the family health insurance."*

have the family health insurance." One can also argue, of course, that society, including corporations and even single people, has a basic interest in promoting the welfare of families. But that view may not mean much to companies groaning under the weight of rising health-care costs.

Employers' efforts to get employees to pay more of their medical expenses have so far not kept their own share of the costs from ballooning. Public and private employer spending on health insurance reached $115 billion in 1987, almost double what it was in 1980. [19]

For this reason, "one can expect [to] see a whole lot

Continued on page 13

AT ISSUE
Are employee stock ownership plans (ESOPs) a good idea?

YES *writes* **REP. DANA ROHRABACHER**, *R-Calif., in a letter to The Washington Post, June 12, 1989.*

The employee stock ownership plan (ESOP) is not a "hoax," as Robert Samuelson writes, but is a noble endeavor both in theory and in practice. As America searches for more effective ways to promote productivity, we should look to the almost 9,000 privately owned companies that have already transferred stock to employees through ESOPs. Most of these companies — a few brought back from the brink of bankruptcy — are successful money-making entities. At the Brunswick Corp., for example, sales per employee have jumped almost 50 percent since it set up its ESOP.

A study by the National Center for Employee Ownership found that over a 10-year period a company would grow 40 percent faster with employee ownership than without it. Another recent study in the Harvard Business Review asserted: "ESOPs exert a positive influence on corporate performance." Directly contradicting Mr. Samuelson's unsubstantiated gripes, the Harvard study went on to conclude that tax breaks ESOPs provide have no relation to the increase in corporate performance.

As Mr. Samuelson can't or won't understand, nobody is touting the ESOP either as a financial miracle plan or as the exclusive cure to any management-employee conflict. The success of any given ESOP depends greatly on the extent to which it is implemented and how stock values appreciate.... [If] the ESOP concept is integrated creatively and extensively into both the economic and managerial life of a company, employees will begin to feel the power of their own ideas and energy, devising new ways to be more productive together and taking on their own shoulders the traditionally managerial responsibility of providing customer satisfaction.

If some companies, as Mr. Samuelson points out, do in fact implement ESOPs for other reasons (as a defense against hostile takeovers, for example), the superficiality of the maneuver will tell in its level of success; but even implementing an ESOP for the wrong reason results in giving workers something no other financing tool can offer: a stake in the company for which they work.

In the United States today, 1 percent of the population owns 50 percent of all directly held U.S. stock. It is time to expand the blessings of free enterprise to individuals who have lacked access to capital and credit. Expanded use of the ESOP promises millions of new Americans a new and exciting stake in the free enterprise system.

NO *writes* **ROBERT J. SAMUELSON**, *economics writer and columnist, in The Washington Post, May 31, 1989.*

There's something intuitively appealing about ESOPs — employee stock ownership plans. They're sort of workers' capitalism. The idea is that workers become shareholders in their own companies. They're then more committed to its success. Conflicts between workers and managers fade. Cooperation flourishes. The company becomes more productive and profitable. Workers get rich. Society prospers. Who could be against this? No one.

The trouble is that ESOPs don't actually operate this way. They're mostly a hoax. But they're booming anyway. Perhaps 200 major companies have adopted ESOPs in the past year. Procter & Gamble and Anheuser-Busch are among the latest. Don't expect a surge of worker involvement or improved corporate efficiency. The infatuation with ESOPs is strictly expedient. They provide generous corporate tax savings and offer top executives a new defense against hostile takeovers.

Suppose you're one of Procter & Gamble's 77,000 workers. The company will contribute $1 billion in stock to its new ESOP. The stock will be allocated to workers' individual ESOP accounts over 15 years. That's an average of almost $900 per employee a year. Do you suddenly start taking fewer coffee breaks? Do you come to work earlier? Go home later? Suppose you detest your supervisor. Do the two of you now turn into fast friends?...

The ESOPs' rewards are too small and too distant to change how workers work. Most know that individually they can't raise their firm's profits or stock price. Profitability and productivity improve only if the ESOPs are part of a broader program to engage workers and involve them in everyday decisions.

Nor do ESOPs give workers something for nothing. An ESOP is a fringe benefit like health insurance or pensions. Companies can typically spend only so much for salaries and fringes. Spending more on one fringe benefit means spending less on something else.... Sometimes the shift is invisible. But many companies have explicitly cut other fringe benefits when creating ESOPs....

To promote ESOPs, Congress has granted them many tax breaks.... But these tax breaks didn't start corporate America's ESOP stampede. What did was the demonstration — by Polaroid — that ESOPs could be used as a takeover defense. Creating an ESOP places a big block of stock in friendly hands. Employees are less likely to sell their shares, because they fear new owners might fire workers....

Continued from page 11

more [of the cost] shifted," Salisbury says. This is likely to come through "much higher deductibles and much higher co-payments." The result will be a movement "away from programs that are insuring people for discretionary, out-of-pocket [coverage] in many areas and moving much more heavily toward catastrophic-type [coverage]."

Employers have been increasingly trying to "manage" health care so as to keep costs down. One way is through alternative health-care plans, including Health Maintenance Organizations and Preferred Provider Organizations.* Participation in such plans last year was nearly double what it had been in 1986, according to the BLS survey of medium and large firms' benefits. Although most employees still were covered in traditional fee-for-service health plans, 26 percent of medical-plan participants were in the alternative plans, up from 14 percent two years earlier.

Employers also have been seeking to "manage" health care in other ways. They are encouraging use of less expensive alternatives to hospital care, such as home health care and extended-care facilities. Many medical plans now also encourage people to undergo diagnostic testing before hospitalization, so as to shorten hospital stays. Many plans require participants, in order to get full hospital benefits, to obtain the plan's authorization before admission. Requiring second opinions before surgery is another common feature.[20]

Similar approaches are increasingly being used to "manage" outpatient care, particularly mental-health and substance-abuse treatment, which now accounts for one-fourth of health-care expenditures.[21] "Soaring mental-health-care costs in recent years have prompted employers to use the same check/control methods that have typically been applied to medical and surgical benefits," reports Melody A. Carlsen, associate director of research for the International Foundation of Employee Benefit Plans, in Brookfield, Wis. In a recent survey of 245 employee-benefit specialists, three-fourths said they expect mental-health-care benefits to become increasingly "managed."[22]

More health-care "management," more shifting of costs to employees, and drastic curtailment of retiree health benefits — all of this still is not likely to be enough to stop employers' health-care costs from rising. Businesses "can slow the rate of increase, but they can probably not even approach eliminating absolute increases," Salisbury says. That may be why, in a recent survey, 20 percent of 209 chief executive officers of *Fortune* 500 and Service 500 companies said that their interest in some sort of universal national health-insurance plan has grown.[23]

Managing Health Care

Employers in recent years have been trying to "manage" health care to try to keep costs down. The table below shows the percentage of companies that require certain cost-saving procedures, such as second opinions for surgery and diagnostic testing before hospitalization. It also shows that a growing number of companies are providing wellness programs to try to keep employees healthy.

Provision	1984	1986	1988
Preadmission Testing	87%	83%	84%
Precertification of Length of Stay	17	31	61
Second Surgical Opinion †	54	83	81
Home Health Care	68	70	77
Hospice Care	39	52	66
Wellness Programs	15	28	52
Annual Physical	18	41	36
Ambulatory Surgical Facilities	81	89	89

† *Either optional or mandatory.*

Source: Employee Benefit Research Institute.

If businesses are concerned mainly with controlling their costs, their workers have reason to be concerned with what Miller of the AFL-CIO calls the "erosion" of employee benefits. In her view, "the only hope" of overcoming that erosion is in "some kind of national health and pension program. I just don't see that we can provide a comprehensive solution to this problem by only dealing with employer-provided benefits." There is some evidence that many Americans are inclined to agree. A poll conducted last fall by Louis Harris & Associates indicated that 61 percent of Americans would prefer a national health-care system like that in Canada to the one they have.*[24]

Despite such sentiments, however, the erosion of employee benefits in the changed American economy seems likely to continue, for no one appears to be in a position to halt it. The federal government is hamstrung by its massive deficit. The unions are handicapped by the decline in their membership and the tilt of the economy toward the heavily non-unionized service sector. And businesses, under great pressure to do all they can to bring the soaring costs of health insurance and other benefits under control, increasingly see no reason why their employees should not shoulder more of the burden. Employees may not like that, but the fact is unmistakable: The era of corporate paternalism is over.

---

*In a Preferred Provider Organization, subscribers get medical services on a discounted fee-for-service basis from designated hospitals and physicians. Health Maintenance Organizations deliver a wide array of medical services on a prepaid basis.

*In Canada, medical care is free to the entire population, with the costs borne by the federal and provincial governments. The doctors, who practice independently and charge on a fee-for-service basis, are reimbursed according to a fee schedule determined by the provincial governments.

Past Coverage

■ **Fired for No Good Cause: Is it Legal?** This report relates how courts in a majority of states have carved out major exceptions to the "employment-at-will" doctrine that traditionally formed state-court decisions. That doctrine gave employers the right, in the absence of explicit contract provisions to the contrary, to fire employees without notice and for any cause or even no cause. As a result of the court-led change in the law, worried employers throughout the country have over-hauled their procedures for dealing with employees and job applicants, to make it clear that they can be fired at will and to document unsatisfactory employee perfor-mances. By Robert K. Landers, E.R.R., 1988 Vol. II, pp. 597-611.

■ **America's 'Vacation Gap.'** In Europe, workers take extensive vacations, and their time off is often guaran-teed by law. In the United States, vacations are viewed as a privilege and a cost of doing business that should be minimized. American workers typically get only two or three weeks of annual paid vacation, while Western Europeans generally get four to six weeks off. At most U.S. firms, vacations are linked to seniority. To get four weeks of paid vacation, most employees first have to log in 15 or more years of faithful service to the company. By Robert K. Landers, E.R.R. 1988 Vol. I, pp. 313-323.

■ **New Styles in Work-Place Management.** Increased competition has prompted many U.S. corporations to change the way they operate. "As a result, the seemingly stable patterns of worker-management relations that existed in the decades after World War II have unrav-eled," Harrison Donnelly reports. Businesses' most com-mon strategy "has been to try to pare labor costs to the bone. . . . Citing the threat of low-wage producers over-seas, corporate executives have argued that they have no choice but to toughen their stance against unions, make greater use of inexpensive part-time workers and give pay raises to their permanent employees only when they show improved performance." E.R.R. 1988 Vol. I, pp. 97-107.

■ **Part-Time Work.** "As service industries — where part-time work is more prevalent than in manufacturing — take on the role of 'job machine' for the U.S. econ-omy," Richard L. Worsnop writes, "experts are wonder-ing what the future holds for workers, whose careers and lifestyles could be fundamentally altered if part-time work became an integral part of the American work place. . . . In the future, they speculate, jobs will become less secure, benefits less certain, and employees less bound by loyalty to jobs that no longer are likely to last a lifetime." E.R.R. Vol. I 1987, pp. 289-299.

NOTES

[1] IBM, along with Apple Computer; Hill Holliday Connors & Cosmopulos, of Boston; Hoffmann-LaRoche, of Nutley, N.J., and Merck, of Rahway, N.J., were cited by *Working Mother* in the October 1988 issue.

[2] Howard V. Hayghe, "Employers and Child Care: What Roles Do They Play?," *Monthly Labor Review*, September 1988, p. 42.

[3] "Managing Health Care Costs and Quality," *EBRI Issue Brief*, February 1989, Employee Benefit Research Institute, p. 2. Also see "The Failure to Contain Medical Costs," *E.R.R.*, 1988 Vol. II, pp. 509-524.

[4] "Questions and Answers about Employee Benefits," *EBRI Issue Brief*, April 1989, Employee Benefit Research Institute, p. 16.

[5] Robert H. Zieger, *American Workers, American Unions, 1920-1985* (paperback, 1986), pp. 149-150.

[6] *Ibid.*, pp. 150-151.

[7] *Ibid.*, p. 153.

[8] John J. Sweeney and Karen Nussbaum, *Solutions for the New Work Force* (paperback, 1989), p. 76. Sweeney is president of the Service Employees International Union, and Nussbaum is executive director of "9to5," the National Association of Working Women.

[9] *Ibid.*, pp. 86-87.

[10] The figure for large and medium-sized firms is from the Bureau of Labor Statistics, U.S. Department of Labor, *Employee Benefits in Medium and Large Firms, 1986*, June 1987, p. 77; figures for smaller firms are from an interview with Dallas L. Salisbury of the Employee Benefit Research Institute.

[11] About half of the 13 percentage-point decrease stems from the survey's expansion to include smaller establishments and more service industries. Within the industries and sizes of establishments formerly studied, the decline was 6 percentage points — down from 76 percent to 70 percent of workers. See Bureau of Labor Statistics, U.S. Department of Labor, *BLS Reports on Employee Benefits in Medium and Large Firms in 1988*, news release, April 4, 1989.

[12] "Questions and Answers about Employee Benefits," *op. cit.*, pp. 5-6.

[13] David E. Bloom and Jane T. Trahan, *Flexible Benefits and Employee Choice* (1986), p. 3.

[14] *Ibid.*, p. 14.

[15] Hewitt Associates, *Salaried Employee Benefits Provided by Major U.S. Employers in 1984-88*, 1989, p. 4.

[16] Mathew H. Greenwald, "Health Insurance: The 'Crucial' Employee Bene-fit," in *America in Transition: Benefits for the Future* (paperback, 1987), p. 73.

[17] Hewitt Associates, *op. cit.*, p. 3.

[18] Bureau of Labor Statistics, U.S. Labor Department, *BLS Reports on Employee Benefits in Medium and Large Firms in 1988*, *op. cit.*, p. 2; "Questions and Answers about Employee Benefits," *op. cit.*, pp. 12-13.

[19] Bureau of Labor Statistics, *op. cit.*, pp. 3-4.

[20] Bureau of Labor Statistics, U.S. Labor Department, *BLS Reports on Employee Benefits in Medium and Large Firms in 1988*, *op. cit.*, p. 2.

[21] Sharon George-Perry, "Easing the Costs of Mental Health Benefits," *Personnel Administrator*, November 1988, p. 62.

[22] Melody A. Carlsen, "Issues in Managed Health Care," *Census of Certified Employee Benefit Specialists*, May 1989.

[23] "No More Health Care on the House," *Fortune*, Feb. 27, 1989, p. 72. The *Fortune* 500/CNN Moneyline CEO Poll of 209 CEOs was conducted in January.

[24] Dennis Revesi, "Polls Show Discontent With Health Care," *The New York Times*, Feb. 15, 1989.

Graphics: cover, Margaret Scott; pp. 3, 6, 9, S. Dmitri Lipczenko.

RECOMMENDED READING

BOOKS

America in Transition: Benefits for the Future, Employee Benefit Research Institute, paperback, 1987.

This book is a collection of papers presented at a forum sponsored by the Employee Benefit Research Institute in October 1986. Experts in demographics, survey research, public policy and benefits design present their views of what the future holds for employee benefits.

Beam, Burton T. Jr. and McFadden, John J., *Employee Benefits*, 2nd edition, Irwin, 1988.

This 539-page textbook examines medical insurance, life insurance, pensions and various other employee benefits and explains how they work.

Sweeney, John J. and Nussbaum, Karen, *Solutions for the New Work Force: Policies for a New Social Contract*, Seven Locks Press, paperback, 1989.

In a chapter on "The Erosion of Employee Benefits," Sweeney, president of the Service Employees International Union, and Nussbaum, executive director of "9to5," National Association of Working Women, state that "The current benefits system is not working. The implicit social contract that once guaranteed health coverage and retirement security to working Americans is collapsing. And the erosion of employment-based benefits has been accompanied by draconian cutbacks in public programs." However, the authors discern a "growing consensus . . . among business, labor, and government leaders that new public policies are needed both to solve today's health-care crisis and to avert tomorrow's pension crisis."

ARTICLES

Dentzer, Susan, "Benefits Shock," *U.S. News & World Report*, March 28, 1988, pp. 57-61.

"From health insurance to pensions to disability protection, employee benefits have been a staple of corporate life for decades," Dentzer notes. But "now this unique safety net is under assault. A round of staggering health-cost increases has prompted employers to clamp down on health insurance, shifting more of the cost burden to workers. Desperate for revenue to narrow the federal budget deficit, Congress has restricted the tax-free status of many benefits. And U.S. industry is undergoing a structural revolution that has shifted

thousands of jobs from large corporations to upstart firms — many without the wherewithal to offer benefits." Dentzer quotes a benefits specialist as saying that "the next couple of years might be very big years of benefit reduction" for employees.

Farnham, Alan, "No More Health Care on the House," *Fortune*, Feb. 27, 1989, pp. 71-72.

"America's top CEOs view rocketing health care costs as a drain on profits and a threat to the very competitiveness of U.S. industry," Farnham writes, in reporting on a *Fortune* 500/CNN Moneyline poll of chief executives. "While not all executives agree on the cause of this illness, they seem united on treatment: An overwhelming majority have asked present or retired employees to shoulder more of the costs — and nearly as many plan further shifts in the future."

Farrell, Christopher and Hoerr, John, "ESOPs: Are They Good for You?," *Business Week*, May 15, 1989, pp. 116-123.

The employee stock-ownership plan (ESOP) "is fast becoming a way of life at many of the nation's best-known companies, including Anheuser-Busch, Lockheed, Procter & Gamble, and Polaroid," the authors report. Although enthusiasts contend that by giving workers a stake in the company, ESOPs will boost productivity, Farrell and Hoerr write that "it doesn't take a rocket scientist to figure out that the current wave of ESOPs is occurring mainly because it saves money in the short run, even if productivity doesn't go up. It's the latest step in Corporate America's move to replace fixed compensation costs with variable wages and benefits . . . ."

Hayghe, Howard V., "Employers and Child Care: What Roles Do They Play?," *Monthly Labor Review*, September 1988, pp. 38-44.

Hayghe, an economist in the U.S. Bureau of Labor Statistics, reports on a special nationwide survey the bureau did in the summer of 1987 to find out what 10,000 business establishments and government agencies were doing to meet the increasing need of employees for child care. The survey indicated "that direct aid to working parents is still very limited. Only about 2 percent, or 25,000 of the nation's 1.2 million nonagricultural establishments with 10 or more employees actually sponsored day-care centers for their workers' children while an additional 3 percent provided financial assistance towards child-care expenses." However, the survey also found that employers' work-schedule policies often did aid parents in meeting their child-care responsibilities.

REPORTS AND STUDIES

Bureau of Labor Statisics, U.S. Department of Labor, *Employee Benefits in Medium and Large Firms, 1986*, June 1987.

This report presents the results of a 1986 Bureau of Labor Statisics survey of employee benefit plans in medium and large firms. The survey provided representative data for 21.3 million full-time employees. The bureau in 1988 conducted an expanded survey, which included smaller establishments and service industries not previously studied. This recent survey provided representative data for 31 million full-time employees in the private sector. The full report on this survey, similar to the earlier one listed above, is due to be issued this summer.

AMERICA'S 'VACATION GAP'

AMERICA'S 'VACATION GAP'

by Robert K. Landers

In Europe, workers take extensive vacations, and their time off is often guaranteed by law. In the United States vacations are viewed as a privilege, a cost of doing business that should be minimized. America's "vacation gap" with Europe is not new, but circumstances are. As one economist put it, "it used to be we had the living standard, they had the leisure. Now they have both."

Leisure. In the 1950s, it seemed to loom before America like a gigantic sci-fi monster, menacing an unprepared populace. Historian Arthur M. Schlesinger Jr. in 1957 warned that the anticipated increase in leisure was "the most dangerous threat hanging over American society." Novelist and social critic Harvey Swados agreed. "The problem of what 200 million of us will do with our increasing leisure time . . . is so awesome in its magnitude as to be terrifying," he wrote.[1]

In retrospect, the threat seems to have been more than a bit exaggerated. The 40-hour workweek remains the standard for U.S. workers, and annual vacations average little more than two weeks. Americans are scheduled to work more hours than workers in most other industrialized countries and get far less vacation time. (*See chart, p. 25.*) In fact, as a result of the increase in the number of working women in recent years, many American families now enjoy less real leisure than in the past.

"By the latter part of the 1980s, time may well have become the most precious commodity in the land," declared a recent study by Louis Harris and Associates Inc. "Mainly as [a] result of the number of families with both spouses working . . . the press of getting both personal and work tasks done has vastly accelerated."[2]

Including time spent commuting to work and doing housework, the median number of hours of work a week went from 40.6 in 1973 to 47.3 in 1984, the survey firm found. Although the number of work hours declined a bit in 1987, to 46.8, the number of hours available for leisure each week — that is, "to relax, watch TV, take part in sports or hobbies, go swimming or skiing, go to the movies, theater, concerts, or other forms of entertainment, get

Vacations and Seniority

In the United States, vacations are usually linked to seniority. This graph shows the average number of paid vacation days by length of service to the company.

Source: U.S. Department of Labor, Bureau of Labor Statistics, "Employee Benefits in Medium and Large Firms, 1986," June 1987.

together with friends, and so forth" — dropped from 26.2 in 1973 to 16.6 in 1987, a 37 percent decline.

The amount of paid vacation time Americans get has changed little in recent decades. At most firms, vacations still are linked to seniority. "And therefore you have to accumulate a lot of service to get a decent amount of leisure," notes Jerome M. Rosow, president of the Work in America Institute, a research organization in Scarsdale, N.Y. To get four weeks of annual vacation, most employees first have to log 15 years or more of faithful service to the company. (*See graph, above.*) That is far from the situation in Europe, where minimum vacations for all workers are generally guaranteed by law and often improved by collective bargaining. "We [Americans] tend to be much more stingy on vacation time," Rosow observes. And with people apparently changing jobs more frequently these days, and so losing the seniority they had built up, that vacation "stinginess" may be becoming more of a felt reality.

American workers typically get only two or three weeks of annual paid vacation, while Western Europeans generally get four to six weeks off. In Austria, Denmark, Finland, France, Luxembourg and Sweden, the minimum vacation for all workers is set by law at five weeks. The idea of a mere two weeks of vacation strikes many Europe-

ans as incredible. "That's crazy," Sylvie Gueyne, a French translator, told *The Wall Street Journal.* "It would be unthinkable in France. Americans are really exploited." [3]

Europeans have "a very different orientation [toward leisure]," says John D. Owen, a professor of economics at Wayne State University. "As I tell my students in labor economics, the more you read about it, the more you wish you could emigrate. It used to be we had the living standard, they had the leisure. Now they have both."

Despite occasional laments about the decline of the work ethic, most Americans still seem to believe that idleness is the devil's workshop. There has been an enormous growth in consumer expenditures on recreational activities in recent decades,[4] but even that testifies to the persistent notion that leisure is evil unless it can be shown to serve some other purpose, such as self-improvement. "It's a hard concept for most Americans to get . . . that you just do things for pleasure," says Bernard Mergen, a professor of American civilization at The George Washington University in Washington, D.C.

In Europe, many business executives look upon their extensive vacations as "a symbol of how important they are," says Randall B. Dunham, a professor of management at the University of Wisconsin, Madison. But American executives tend instead to give up vacation time to show how indispensable they are.

A 1985 survey of senior executives at America's largest corporations found that four-fifths of them worked between 46 and 60 hours a week, and 10 percent worked more than 60 hours a week. The average executive participating in the survey, which was conducted by Korn/Ferry International, a large executive-recruiting firm, took only 14 days of vacation a year; one-third took 10 or fewer days. A small number took no vacation at all — and undoubtedly boasted loudly about it.[5]

Working long hours may be unnecessary and even unhealthy, not only for the individuals involved but also for their families and, by extension, society. Yet the grim practice is contagious. Senior executives set the example for junior executives, and management determines (in some cases after negotiation with labor unions) work schedules and vacation policies. For management, particularly at smaller firms, vacations are simply a cost that, like other costs, should be kept to a minimum.

U.S. and European attitudes toward leisure and vacations

"Here in Europe, weekends are for lounging with friends and family. During the week, a strict 9-to-5 regimen that includes three-hour lunches is alive and well," reports Susan Carey, a Brussels-based reporter for *The Wall Street Journal.* "Vacations are taken in huge clumps — usually all of July or August — and the weeks around Easter and Christmas also spell a virtual halt of commerce. Visitors from the U.S. often wonder if *anybody* does much work here."[6]

Europeans do work, of course, but, like Americans, somewhat less than they used to do. In recent decades, according to the Organization for Economic Co-operation and Development (OECD), the average number of hours that people in industrialized countries actually work has been falling. Although several factors are responsible for this trend,* "longer paid annual leave has . . . contributed significantly," OECD said. The number of days of paid annual leave guaranteed by law, "is rising very appreciably in some countries and has in fact been increasing in most member countries. In 1960 the statutory minimum . . . was generally two or three weeks, whereas in 1982 it was between three and five weeks."[7]

The "vacation gap" between the United States and European countries is reflected in the number of hours worked annually. A 1986 survey by a West German employer federation found that Americans were scheduled to work more scheduled hours each year than workers in every European country except Switzerland and Portugal. (*See chart, p. 25.*)

Americans can take some solace in the thought that although they work more than their European counterparts, they frequently are paid more. According to calculations based on OECD figures, a manufacturing production worker in the United States earned an average of $20,497 in 1986, whereas a French worker earned only $12,732 and an Italian worker only $12,362. Indeed, the U.S. figure was higher than the amount for every other OECD country except Switzerland, where it was $21,848.[8] The Swiss are scheduled to work about as many hours a year as Americans, but their work week is longer and they get more vacation days — at least four weeks a year. In Norway and Denmark, scheduled work hours are less than in the United States and workers get more vacation time and earn almost as much; Norwegians get more than four weeks of vacation by statute, and Danes get five weeks off.*

In Western Europe, extensive vacations for virtually everyone are accepted as "part of the lifestyle" and "just part of the cost of doing business," says Rosow of the Work in America Institute. "Leisure [there] is placed in a more balanced proportion to the whole mix of life — work, leisure and the family." In the United States, by contrast, "vacations are still treated as very much of a privilege extended by the employer to the employee and not by the society to the workers."

A key reason European workers enjoy more generous vacations than their American counterparts, says economist John Owen, is that in Europe there is "much more influence by collectivities, such as unions and government," than in the United States. American workers, notes Professor Mergen, "aren't as well organized as European workers. And the federal government isn't as strong or as centralized in the U.S. as it is in other countries."

The role of collective bargaining in fixing the length of vacations in Europe varies from country to country. (*See map, p. 23.*) In some countries, the minimum vacation guaranteed by law is substantial and rarely or never lengthened by collective bargaining. That is true in Austria, Denmark, Finland, Luxembourg, Spain and Sweden, where the legal minimum is five weeks, and in Greece and Norway, where it is four.

In other countries, however, collective bargaining has played an important role. In Italy, for example, workers are guaranteed two weeks of vacation, but collective-bargaining agreements provide most workers there with at least four weeks off. West German law requires a minimum three-week vacation for all workers, but collective bargaining has raised the average vacation to six weeks.

Another reason for the U.S.-Europe vacation gap, says Owen, is that living standards — real hourly wages, to use the economists' term — generally have been going up at

---

*"Structural changes . . . in the composition of employment and labor supply have . . . played a by no means negligible part," in reducing working hours, OECD said, "especially because they have combined to favor the development of part-time work." Among the structural changes OECD cited were a decline in the number of agricultural workers, an increase in the number of service workers and a rise in the proportion of women in the labor force.

*The comparison of nominal wages does not take into account the fact that the purchasing power of money varies greatly from country to country. In addition, the European worker receives more assistance from the state than his American counterpart does.

a much faster rate in Europe. There, he says, "they can, so to speak, split the melon — take more time off and also have a much improved living standard, as [they] go from one decade to the next." For Americans, he says, longer vacations "might actually mean some cutbacks in living standards," because real wages have not been going up much.

Europeans, moreover, enjoy the extensive support of the welfare state. They don't have the same economic worries with respect to health, retirement and the education of their children that Americans do. Europeans "are a little bit less pressured economically than Americans," Owen says, and therefore have been more willing to seek additional vacation time as well as higher wages.

Reducing work hours to cut unemployment

This was not possible immediately after World War II, when European nations were recovering from the war's devastation and rebuilding their economies. European workers then mainly sought higher wages. But that started to change in the 1950s, as industrialized countries began to enjoy a long period, lasting through 1973, of rapidly increasing production. Workers decided they wanted to share in the benefits of technological progress by reducing their work hours and enjoying more leisure.

It soon became apparent that work hours could be reduced, or longer paid vacations provided, without a reduction in real earnings. "[T]hese social benefits could be obtained at the cost of no more than a possible slowing down of the rate of growth in real incomes," noted Archibald A. Evans, author of a 1975 International Labor Organization (ILO) study of working hours.[9]

In countries where the work week was longer than 45 hours, reducing work hours became a live issue. Many collective-bargaining agreements were reached that provided not only for a shorter workweek and, in some cases, more extensive paid vacations, but also for an *increase* in weekly earnings. A consensus developed among workers and employers, however, that there should be no reduction in work hours that led to a fall in production or in real earnings. It was generally agreed that the rate at which hours were reduced and other benefits provided should remain below the rate of growth of production.

In recent years, some European workers have experienced a form of leisure they did not choose, the involuntary sort known as unemployment. In France, Great Britain and the Netherlands, unemployment rates reached double-digit levels. During recessions and periods of high unemployment, reducing work hours is frequently talked about as a means of jobs creation, a way of spreading the work around. The idea was extensively debated in OECD countries during the 1970s, particularly after the Organization of Petroleum Exporting Countries dramatically raised oil prices in 1973-74. But a decade later, the debate had resulted in "very little real achievement," according to R. A.

Hart of the International Institute of Management in Berlin.[10] In France, for example, François Mitterrand's Socialist government supported a 35-hour workweek but only managed to reduce the statutory workweek from 40 hours to 39.

The most far-reaching efforts in recent years to increase employment by reducing working hours have been made in the Netherlands. Substantial cuts in working hours were coupled with restraints on wage increases, and in some important industry agreements, employers agreed to recruit additional employees. But even in the Netherlands, the efforts to thus increase employment seem to have had only a modest effect, according to Michael White, a senior fellow and coordinator of the Employment Studies Group at the Policy Studies Institute in London.[11]

Many economists remain skeptical about the effectiveness of using shortened work hours as a way of increasing employment. Various studies have been made. "On the whole, the evidence suggests that jobs are created but not in sufficient numbers to make a *serious* impact on the level of unemployment," the *European Industrial Relations Review* reported last year. In a survey of 17 Western European countries, the London-based magazine found that virtually all workers now have at least four weeks annual paid vacation and that "while there is still pressure from the unions for reductions in working time . . . interest in longer [vacations] has, on the whole, waned." [12]

Vacations in U.S. rare before World War II

"Vacations in 1890? Why, the word wasn't in the dictionary!" That is what a respected citizen of "Middletown" (Muncie, Ind.) told sociologists Robert S. and Helen Merrell Lynd, authors of the classic study, *Middletown* (1929). Certainly vacations weren't common for industrial workers, who labored 10 hours a day, six days a week. But business executives, too, rarely took vacations in the 1890s (although the wives and children of the more well-to-do often went away to a chautauqua or a country resort during the summer). By the early 1920s, however, that had changed. The automobile was mainly responsible.

"Use of the automobile has apparently been influential in spreading the 'vacation' habit," the Lynds wrote. "The custom of having each summer a respite, usually of two weeks, from getting-a-living activities, with pay unabated, is increasingly common among the business class. . . ." The notion of paid vacations for workers was still "very uncommon," they wrote, and it remained so until World War II.*

---

*Foremen in many plants did get a week or two off with pay. In addition, a few Middletown plants closed down for one or two weeks during the summer, allowing their workers an unpaid annual "vacation." And other employers let their workers take up to two weeks off without pay. But of 122 working-class families who provided information on the subject, the Lynds reported, only 24 took a vacation of a week or more in 1923 or 1924.

Japan: Working on Slowing Down

Japan has been trying to stop working so much, but the task isn't easy. The average Japanese worker just doesn't know when to quit.

A revision of Japan's Labor Standards Law — the first major amendment in four decades — went into effect April 1, making the 40-hour workweek and the eight-hour day official. The official *goal*, that is. It's supposed to be achieved during the first half of the 1990s. Meanwhile, the maximum workweek has been pared from 48 hours to 46.

The Japanese worker usually works six days a week and is scheduled to work about 2,100 hours a year. That is less than it used to be, but still about 200 hours — or 25

eight-hour days — more than the American worker.

Vacations are not unknown in Japan, but neither are they the rage. The revision of the Labor Standards Act lifts the statutory minimum from six days to 10, but leaves the maximum at 20. Japanese workers typically do not take all the vacation to which they are entitled. "[Japanese] workers are reluctant to burden their co-workers," *Business Week* reported in 1987. "Often, the company atmosphere discourages time off, especially when the boss doesn't take vacations either."†

When the Japanese do go on vacation, it's not for long. By and large, wrote Bernard Wysocki, Jr., a re-

porter for *The Wall Street Journal*, Japanese "like to take a few days here and there — in May, in August and in early January — at the same time everybody else is off."‡

Tokyo has been trying to get the Japanese to slow down and relax more. The Ministry of Labor's Wages and Welfare Department has been beating the drums for a five-day workweek since 1986. The hope is that, with more leisure, the Japanese will then spend more money — and thus help boost the domestic economy.

† *Larry Armstrong, "Why Tokyo is Tinkering with the Treadmill," Business Week, Sept. 28, 1987, pp. 45-48.*
‡ *Writing in* The Wall Street Journal, *April 21, 1986.*

There were, however, marked reductions in the number of hours Americans worked in the early decades of this century. Average weekly hours for non-agricultural workers dropped from 56 in 1900 to 43 in 1930; for farm workers, they dropped from about 67 to 55. The workweek was further reduced during the Great Depression of the 1930s in an effort to spread the work around. Most of the industry codes promulgated under the National Industrial Recovery Act of 1933 limited the workweek to 40 hours. The Fair Labor Standards Act of 1938 set that as the standard (effective in 1940) for workers in interstate commerce. Longer hours were not prohibited, but overtime pay at the rate of time and a half was required. Longer hours were the rule during World War II, but after the war, the 40-hour workweek became widespread. Insofar as leisure was concerned, attention shifted to paid vacations and holidays.

In 1940, collective-bargaining agreements applying to only about one-fourth of all union members provided for annual vacations with pay. One week off was usually the maximum. But during World War II, relates economist Sar A. Levitan, director of The George Washington University's Center for Social Policy Studies, "the employers couldn't give raises, so they tried to give it in fringe benefits. That's when the vacation time period really started." In 1948, American workers got a total of 55.5 million full vacation weeks, an average of almost one week per employed person. By 1957, when social critics had begun to worry about the threat of too much leisure, 91 percent of the workers covered by major collective-bargaining agreements were eligible for paid vacations, and 84 percent of the agreements provided for a maximum

vacation, usually dependent on time of service, of at least three weeks.[13]

Workers also obtained more leisure in the form of paid holidays, and they got it in a similar way. Before World War II, major holidays often were observed in industry, but hourly employees were seldom paid for the time off. Partly as a result of decisions by the National War Labor Board, the practice of providing paid holidays began to spread during the war, and afterward it became the rule throughout industry. A survey of holiday provisions in major collective-bargaining agreements in 1958 indicated that only 12 percent of the workers covered were not entitled to paid holidays, and nearly three-fifths of the others got seven or more.

But the wartime and postwar expansion in paid vacation and holidays soon decelerated. "By and large," says Levitan, "American workers during the post-World War II [decades] have preferred higher pay [rather] than fringe benefits." An additional week of vacation is equivalent to about a 2 percent increase in pay.

U.S. productivity grew quite rapidly during the 1950s and early '60s, but then the growth slowed down. As a result, so did the expansion of leisure. Workers got additional paid holidays and more annual leave days only "in very, very small doses," says Levitan. By 1986, full-time employees at medium and large firms were receiving an average of 10 paid holidays a year.[14]

Although annual paid vacations have not changed much in recent decades, Americans now enjoy more long weekends than they once did. Congress in 1968 established Columbus Day as a Monday holiday and shifted

Continued on page 24

Eurovacations

Virtually all European workers take extensive vacations. Generally they are guaranteed by law, although in some countries the legal minimums are improved by strong unions through collective bargaining. This map shows the minimum number of vacation weeks workers get in various European countries and describes the role of collective bargaining in obtaining the vacation benefits.

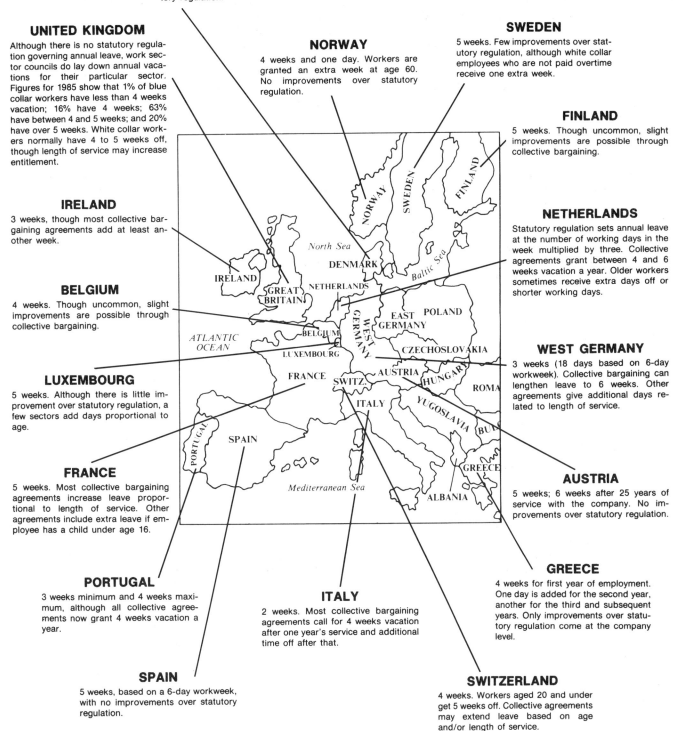

DENMARK
5 weeks. No improvements over statutory regulation.

UNITED KINGDOM
Although there is no statutory regulation governing annual leave, work sector councils do lay down annual vacations for their particular sector. Figures for 1985 show that 1% of blue collar workers have less than 4 weeks vacation; 16% have 4 weeks; 63% have between 4 and 5 weeks; and 20% have over 5 weeks. White collar workers normally have 4 to 5 weeks off, though length of service may increase entitlement.

NORWAY
4 weeks and one day. Workers are granted an extra week at age 60. No improvements over statutory regulation.

SWEDEN
5 weeks. Few improvements over statutory regulation, although white collar employees who are not paid overtime receive one extra week.

FINLAND
5 weeks. Though uncommon, slight improvements are possible through collective bargaining.

IRELAND
3 weeks, though most collective bargaining agreements add at least another week.

NETHERLANDS
Statutory regulation sets annual leave at the number of working days in the week multiplied by three. Collective agreements grant between 4 and 6 weeks vacation a year. Older workers sometimes receive extra days off or shorter working days.

BELGIUM
4 weeks. Though uncommon, slight improvements are possible through collective bargaining.

WEST GERMANY
3 weeks (18 days based on 6-day workweek). Collective bargaining can lengthen leave to 6 weeks. Other agreements give additional days related to length of service.

LUXEMBOURG
5 weeks. Although there is little improvement over statutory regulation, a few sectors add days proportional to age.

FRANCE
5 weeks. Most collective bargaining agreements increase leave proportional to length of service. Other agreements include extra leave if employee has a child under age 16.

AUSTRIA
5 weeks; 6 weeks after 25 years of service with the company. No improvements over statutory regulation.

PORTUGAL
3 weeks minimum and 4 weeks maximum, although all collective agreements now grant 4 weeks vacation a year.

ITALY
2 weeks. Most collective bargaining agreements call for 4 weeks vacation after one year's service and additional time off after that.

GREECE
4 weeks for first year of employment. One day is added for the second year, another for the third and subsequent years. Only improvements over statutory regulation come at the company level.

SPAIN
5 weeks, based on a 6-day workweek, with no improvements over statutory regulation.

SWITZERLAND
4 weeks. Workers aged 20 and under get 5 weeks off. Collective agreements may extend leave based on age and/or length of service.

Sources: European Industrial Relations Review, April 1987; Organization for Economic Co-operation and Development, "Living Conditions in OECD Countries," 1986.

Continued from page 22

observance of three public holidays (Washington's Birthday, Memorial Day and Veterans Day) to Mondays, effective in 1971. Protests from veterans' organizations, however, prompted Congress in 1975 to rescind its Veterans Day move and return the holiday to November 11. But, with Labor Day always falling on a Monday, that still left at least four three-day weekends for many Americans.

The trend toward using holidays to provide long weekends has been evident in other ways in recent years. A 1985 survey of businesses and other organizations by The Bureau of National Affairs Inc. in Washington, D.C., indicated that 63 percent — 9 percentage points more than in 1980 — were giving the day after Thanksgiving off as a paid holiday. "Manufacturers appear far more likely to provide paid days off that create long weekends . . . than they are to give time off for single holidays that occur mid-week," the survey found. The practice of providing employees with one or more "floating" holidays also appeared to be on the increase.[15]

A study released last year by Marriott Hotels and Resorts contended that the two-week vacation "is no longer the norm for American leisure travel." Most Americans now prefer trips of three or fewer days, usually over weekends, the study said. A random survey of 1,513 adults indicated that two-thirds had taken pleasure trips in the preceding 12 months and that 73 percent of those trips were short ones. It was unclear how much of a change from the past that really represented, but the study did indicate that Americans in dual-income households were more likely than those in single-earner ones to take more weekend trips than they had two or three years before. "The increased time pressures in households where two adults are employed most likely requires those Americans to take shorter trips at mutually convenient times," the Marriott report commented. "Weekends are probably the most appropriate time when two working adults can find the time to get away together."[16]

Many Americans now seem to have less free time than they did in the recent past, despite the fact that average weekly hours for non-agricultural employees fell from 40.9 in 1948 to 38.8 in 1987. The decline is deceptive, because, as economist Owen noted a decade ago, it reflects "changes in the composition of the labor force rather than a reduction in the hours of work of the individuals or groups that compose the work force."[17] For one thing, there are proportionally more women and students in the labor force, and they tend to work, on average, fewer hours than men who are not students. Thus, although the overall averages have declined, *full-time* non-agricultural workers in 1987 worked an average of 43.1 hours a week (including overtime).

In fact, the downward movement in average hours worked per adult male apparently stopped at the end of World War II. And with more families with more than one wage-earner now, the hours worked per family has often risen significantly. "Contrary to popular opinion," wrote Owen, "the number of hours supplied to the market by American families — at least by members in the 20 to 55 year age group — appears to have increased, not decreased" in recent decades.*

And when you take into account work outside the work place — after all, housework is work, too — American families are actually working even more than Labor Department statistics indicate. "With two people working, the social costs transfer to both partners," says Rosow of the Work in America Institute. "If your wife is working, who's going to be home to see the repairman . . . do the laundry . . . do the food shopping . . . take the kids to and from school?" The woman may tend to work fewer hours at her outside job than her husband does, but she usually has much more work at home, caring for the household and children. To the extent that the husband becomes more involved in that work, he then has less free time than he otherwise would have. Thus, the net result for both husband and wife is more work and less leisure.

"So we're not a leisure society," Rosow says, "although we've done quite well. . . . But we have not seen much increase in leisure or vacation practices that's significant. And there's very little indication that that's in the [works] right now."

American businessmen insist on long hours

Tom Rath — the man in the gray flannel suit in the popular 1955 novel of that name — was offered a stimulating and very demanding job by his dynamic boss. Rath turned it down. "I don't want to give up the time," he explained. "I'm trying to be honest about this. I want the money. Nobody likes money better than I do. But I'm just not the kind of guy who can work evenings and weekends and all the rest of it forever. I guess there's even more to it than that. I'm not the kind of person who can get all wrapped up in a job — I can't get myself convinced that my work is the most important thing in the world." Rath, having been through one war and refusing to exclude the possibility of another, wanted to spend time with his family.[18]

Social critic William H. Whyte Jr. thought Rath — and his "self-ennobling hedonism" — was representative of young aspiring executives of the day.[19] If so, they must not have risen very far in the corporate world or must have changed their outlook as they did rise. *Fortune* magazine reported last year that "Executives at large companies are working longer hours and taking less vacation than they did just seven or eight years ago."[20] Of the 1,362 senior executives surveyed in 1985 by Korn/Ferry International, only one admitted working 40 hours or less a week.[21] A 1984 survey by Heidrick & Struggles, another large

---

*By Owen's 1978 calculations, non-student males' average weekly hours of work, adjusted for growth in vacations and holidays, amounted to 41.6 hours in 1948 and 41.3 hours in 1977. Owen recently has been examining the data for the years since and, although not ready yet to disclose his calculations, says, "What I said 10 years ago is still true. There's been remarkably little change in that figure over time."

executive-recruiting firm, found that 60 percent of the chief executive officers at *Fortune* 500 industrial and service companies devoted more than 60 hours a week to their jobs.[22]

Management Professor Dunham says that most of this additional executive labor is unnecessary, or would be if the executives delegated less important tasks to other people. "What usually happens is [that] when [executives] work the extra hours, they're doing it because these are critical issues they have to attend to. But had they delegated some less critical things, they could have done those important tasks during the regular work hours."

Executives, however, are often reluctant to delegate tasks. "People want to feel that they have control over what's happening to their organization, and to a lot of executives, delegating means giving up control," Dunham says. Executives also may lack confidence in the people to whom they'd be delegating work. And executives want to make themselves look good, to appear important and indispensable. "There's a culture in many organizations that says: 'Top executives work lots of hours. It sets a good example.' So they do it." It doesn't matter that doing their actual work efficiently may not take lots of hours.

Thus, high-level executives work needless hours to set an example for those below them, and junior executives work needless hours to impress those above them. But when so many people are routinely working so many hours, greater sacrifice is required to stand out. Hence, executives who wish to be considered especially important selflessly give up some or all of their vacation time. And the practice is contagious.

"If you're somebody on your way up in an organization and you hear somebody two or three levels above you bragging about how they gave up their vacation for the good of the organization, and you feel you have to look good in their eyes, what are you going to do?" says Dunham. "Despite a policy that says you get two weeks or three weeks or four weeks of vacation, you're going to think twice before you use it all."

In Europe, it is quite different. A survey of the adult population in 12 European Community countries indicated that senior managers and professionals were most inclined to go away on vacation, to go away often and to go away for long periods (more than 20 days on their main holidays, in 41 percent of the cases).[23] "A lot of executives in Europe will get that extended vacation as a perk, as a symbol of how important they are," Dunham says.

Do longer vacations improve productivity?

According to a survey by the U.S. Chamber of Commerce, American businesses spent an average of $1,357 for each vacationing employee in 1986 and $820 for each employee's holidays. Such expenditures amounted to about

How U.S., European and Japanese Workers Compare

Americans are scheduled to work more hours each year than workers in every European country except Switzerland and Portugal. Japanese workers are scheduled to work about 200 hours more each year than their American counterparts.

	Standard Scheduled Hours *	Annual Leave Days **	Holidays	Annual Hours Worked
West Germany	39	30	12	1708
Netherlands	40	36.5	7	1740
Belgium	38	20	11	1748
France	39	25	9	1771
Italy	40	29	10	1776
Great Britain	39	25	8	1778
Luxembourg	40	25	12	1792
Spain	40	22	14	1800
Denmark	40	25	9	1816
Greece	40	22	6	1864
Ireland	40	20	8	1864
Portugal	45	22	14	2025
Austria	39.3	26.5	11.5	1751
Finland	40	29	8	1792
Sweden	40	25	12	1792
Norway	40	21	9	1848
Switzerland	41.5	22.5	8	1913
USA	40	12	10	1912
Japan ***	44	10.5	13	2116

Figures are from 1986
Sources: Der Arbeitgeber (The Employer). No. 2/39. 1987; U.S. Bureau of Labor Statistics
  * Excludes overtime
 ** Includes personal leave days.
*** U.S. Bureau of Labor Statistics figures.

5 percent and 3 percent, respectively, of the businesses' payrolls.[24]

Many experts say this is a price business should be willing to pay because time off from work increases employees' productivity. "People who take their vacations, who get a break from work, are going to be more productive and more uniformly productive throughout the year," says Dunham. "I'm a believer that vacations are necessary and that they're not just a benefit to employees. . . . It's the same thing you do for a machine when you take it down for a while for routine maintenance." Rosow, a former Exxon Corp. executive, notes that Exxon and some other corporations insist that employees take their vacations, to be sure they get relief from work.

How long vacations should be to provide adequate relief from work "depends a lot on the individual," Dunham observes. "I think what's needed are vacations that are long enough to get the employee's mind away from work. . . . Some people can do that with a long weekend, some people need three or four weeks off to do it."

At some point, however, the costs of longer vacations start to outweigh the benefits of increased productivity. Dunham believes that begins to happen after the fourth week of vacation. And economist John Owen says it is not at all clear that longer vacations lead to greater productivity — "whether [if] you give people five-week vacations instead of three, they're going to be all that more productive during the rest of the year."

Few businesses, however, consider the benefits of vacations when determining their policies. By custom ar d practice, they just treat vacations as an expense — and try to minimize it as they do any other expense.

The common view that vacations benefit only the employees and not the company came out of "a production-manufacturing society, where every hour lost was made up by hiring someone to do that hour's labor," Rosow says. With the shift away from a manufacturing economy, that view, although still prevalent, has become increasingly irrelevant. In many cases now, no one is hired to replace the employee on vacation; he simply makes up the work when he gets back. "Now there's much more elasticity in the performance of work by individuals [but] the policy on vacations hasn't accommodated to that," Rosow says.

Some companies in recent years have adopted flexible-benefit plans, which enable employees to select one benefit, such as additional vacation days, at the expense of some other benefit. Another way people are getting additional time off is through negotiation with prospective employers. With people moving from one company to another more frequently these days, that is becoming more common. At most companies, however, vacation policies remain quite rigid.

And despite the contrast between European and American vacation policies, there seems little pressure on this side of the Atlantic for change. A 1985 survey found that very few workers would trade income for more leisure time. Nearly two-thirds of those responding to the survey were satisfied with the number of hours they currently work; over 27 percent said they would prefer to work more hours and earn more money; less than 8 percent would opt to work fewer hours at the same rate of pay and so earn correspondingly less money.[25] The survey found that women were more willing than men to forgo income for leisure. Even among men earning $750 a week or more, the proportion wanting more hours of work exceeded those wanting fewer hours.

Many people might like more free time if they didn't have to sacrifice income to get it. But most Americans are not in a position to insist on more time off. "I think Americans would love to have four to six weeks [of] vacation," says Professor Mergen. "It's just [that] nobody's going to give it to them, unless they get better organized."

NOTES

[1] Schlesinger is quoted in Swados' 1958 essay, "Less Work — Less Leisure," reprinted in Harvey Swados, *A Radical's America* (1962), p. 104. Swados' comment appears on p. 110.

[2] National Research Center of the Arts, an affiliate of Louis Harris and Associates, Inc., "Americans and the Arts, V," January 1988, p. 20.

[3] Quoted by Roger Ricklefs and Lorie Teeter in *The Wall Street Journal*, Aug. 1, 1986.

[4] Consumer expenditures on recreational activities rose from $42.7 billion in 1970 to $198 billion in 1986. See U.S. Census Bureau, *Statistical Abstract of the United States, 1988*, p. 213.

[5] Korn/Ferry International, "Korn/Ferry International's Executive Profile: A Survey of Corporate Leaders in the Eighties," October 1986, pp. 15, 31-2.

[6] Writing in *The Wall Street Journal*, April 21, 1986.

[7] Organization for Economic Co-operation and Development (OECD), "Living Conditions in OECD Countries: A Compendium of Social Indicators," 1986, p. 65. The OECD was founded in 1961 to promote the economic and social welfare of member countries and to stimulate the economic growth of developing, as well as member, countries. It has 24 members: Australia, Austria, Belgium, Canada, Denmark, Finland, France, West Germany, Greece, Iceland, Ireland, Italy, Japan, Luxembourg, the Netherlands, New Zealand, Norway, Portugal, Spain, Sweden, Switzerland, Turkey, the United Kingdom, and the United States. Yugoslavia is an associate member.

[8] Organization for Economic Co-operation and Development, "The Tax/Benefit Position of Production Workers, 1983-86," 1987, pp. 60-105. The OECD figures are gross annual earnings, given in the national currencies. The U.S. dollar equivalencies were calculated at the exchange rates for Feb. 28, 1986.

[9] Archibald A. Evans, *Hours of Work in Industrialised Countries* (1975), p. 13.

[10] R. A. Hart, *Shorter Working Time: A Dilemma for Collective Bargaining* (1984), p. 12.

[11] Michael White, *Working Hours: Assessing the Potential for Reduction* (1987), p. 15.

[12] "Working Time in 17 Countries: part 2," *European Industrial Relations Review*, April 1987, p. 18.

[13] Peter Henle, "Recent Growth of Paid Leisure for U.S. Workers," in Erwin O. Smigel, ed., *Work and Leisure: A Contemporary Social Problem* (1963), pp. 192, 196. The article by Henle, then with the U.S. Labor Department's Bureau of Labor Statistics, first appeared in *Monthly Labor Review*, March 1962, pp. 249-57.

[14] U.S. Department of Labor, Bureau of Labor Statistics, "Employee Benefits in Medium and Large Firms, 1986," June 1987, p. 7.

[15] The Bureau of National Affairs, Inc., "Paid Holiday and Vacation Policies," November 1986, pp. 1, 3.

[16] Marriott Hotels and Resorts, "The Marriott Report on Leisure Travel: The Demise of the Traditional American Vacation," January 1987, pp. xvii, 9, 16.

[17] John D. Owen, "Hours of Work in the Long Run: Trends, Explanations, Scenarios, and Implications," in National Commission for Manpower Policy, *Work Time and Employment*, October 1978, p. 32.

[18] Sloan Wilson, *The Man in the Gray Flannel Suit* (1955).

[19] William H. Whyte, Jr., *The Organization Man* (1956), pp. 131-132.

[20] Ford S. Worthy, "You're Probably Working Too Hard," *Fortune*, April 27, 1987, p. 136.

[21] Korn/Ferry International, *op. cit.*, p. 31.

[22] The Heidrick & Struggles survey is cited by Worthy, *op. cit.*, p. 136.

[23] Commission of the European Communities, "Europeans and Their Holidays," 1987, pp. 57, 62.

[24] U.S. Chamber of Commerce, "Employee Benefits, 1986," December 1987, pp. 13, 15. The figures include payments in lieu of vacations (or holidays) as well as payments for them. The survey covered 833 businesses.

[25] Susan E. Shank, "Preferred Hours of Work and Corresponding Earnings," *Monthly Labor Review*, November 1986, p. 40.

Graphics: pp. 19, 23, S. Dmitri Lipczenko.

RECOMMENDED READING

BOOKS

Henle, Peter, "Recent Growth of Paid Leisure for U.S. Workers," in Erwin O. Smigel, ed., *Work and Leisure: A Contemporary Social Problem*, College and University Press, 1963.

Henle, at the time with the U.S. Labor Department's Bureau of Labor Statistics, examines the development of paid leisure in the United States. Before World War II, he noted, paid vacations and paid holidays "were quite limited for hourly paid workers, although many salaried workers had been receiving this type of benefit."

Owen, John D., *Working Hours* Lexington Books, 1979.

Owen, an economist at Wayne State University, writes that "It is obvious that a higher material living standard in the United States has not brought with it a concomitant increase in free time. . . . [O]ur high level of consumer goods and services purchases have done little to liberate American men and women from the time required for work (or quasi-work) activities outside the marketplace — what economists call household production — despite the predictions of a number of optimists. The total time spent in commuting, shopping, housework, child care, and the like has not been reduced by very much in some decades."

White, Michael, *Working Hours: Assessing the Potential for Reduction*, International Labor Organization, 1987.

White, a senior fellow and coordinator of the Employment Studies Group at the Policy Studies Institute in London, contends that there are "many ways in which shorter [working] hours may (under appropriate conditions) lead to or form an integral part of productivity improvements, which can be used to offset all or much of the apparent cost of the reductions in working time." Shorter work hours, he writes, "can result in better motivated workers who produce more and give customers higher standards of service, and reduced hours are likely to do so if they form part of a general policy of improving the quality of working life."

ARTICLES

"Working Time in 17 Countries," *European Industrial Relations Review*, March 1987, pp. 18-26 (part one), and April 1987, pp. 18-24 (part two).

According to this survey, "Virtually all workers across Western Europe now have at least four weeks' annual paid holiday [vacation], while those in a third of the countries in our survey have the statutory right to five (excluding public holidays). However, it is not uncommon for this to rise to six under collective agreement. Nowhere are unions concentrating on improving holiday entitlement."

Shank, Susan E., "Preferred Hours of Work and Corresponding Earnings," *Monthly Labor Review*, November 1986, pp. 40-44.

The author, an economist in the U.S. Labor Department's Bureau of Labor Statistics, writes that "If given a choice of working the same, fewer, or more hours at the same rate of pay, most employees would prefer the same number of hours. An additional one-fourth would prefer to work more hours and earn more money, while 8 percent would choose to work fewer hours and earn proportionately less money."

REPORTS AND STUDIES

Korn/Ferry International, "Korn/Ferry International's Executive Profile: A Survey of Corporate Leaders in the Eighties," October 1986.

An executive-recruiting firm's survey of senior executives at America's largest corporations. "As in [a previous survey in] 1979, our data continue to indicate that most senior level executives in large corporations work long hours and spend substantial periods of time away from home. Today, our average respondent works 56 hours a week, up three hours from 1979. . . . In addition to the long work week and many hours spent away from home on business, there also has been a significant decline in the number of vacation days taken by senior level executives." The report is available for $30 from Korn/Ferry International, 237 Park Ave., New York, N.Y. 10017.

Organization for Economic Co-operation and Development, "Living Conditions in OECD Countries: A Compendium of Social Indicators," 1986.

Work and leisure in the OECD countries are among the aspects of life examined in this report. "While the decline [since 1960] in the number of hours actually worked is universal, there may be considerable differences of level between countries." The report is available for $13 from the OECD's Washington Center, 2001 L St. N.W., Suite 700, Washington, D.C. 20036.

U.S. Department of Labor, Bureau of Labor Statistics, "Employee Benefits in Medium and Large Firms, 1986," June 1987.

This survey of large and medium firms finds that virtually all employees get paid holidays (an average of 10 a year) and paid vacations. "Vacation provisions averaged 8.8 days at one year of service, 15.8 days at 10 years, and 20.6 days at 20 years; these averages were virtually unchanged since 1980 — the first year such estimates were developed. . . . Virtually all employees covered by vacation plans had to work for a specified period before being able to take a vacation." The report is available for $5 from the Superintendent of Documents, U.S. Government Printing Office, Washington, D.C. 20402-9325.

THE FAILURE TO CONTAIN MEDICAL COSTS

THE FAILURE TO CONTAIN MEDICAL COSTS

by Sarah Glazer

Nearly everyone agrees that more should be done to hold down increases in health care costs. But can it be done without jeopardizing the quality of health care Americans have come to expect? Are we willing to cap physicians' fees or limit access to expensive procedures and life-saving devices? What are the alternatives?

In some ways, the future of American medical care has never looked better. Doctors routinely perform surgery that was unthinkable just two decades ago. They diagnose illnesses with machines that were unimaginable until the advent of sophisticated computers. New, increasingly effective drugs have greatly increased their ability to treat acute and chronic conditions.

Just this week, the American Council on Science and Health, a consumer health organization in New York, issued an optimistic report about the state of Americans' health: "Life expectancy has reached new highs; infant mortality has plummeted; the overall death rate has declined precipitously. Heart-disease mortality — the leading cause of death — has dropped. Even death rates from most forms of cancer . . . are down except for lung and skin cancer." [1]

But all these advances carry a price tag — and a huge one at that. A computer-assisted tomography (CAT) scanner — a sophisticated X-ray device — costs close to $1 million. Open heart surgery can cost $25,000 to $40,000, a liver transplant, $140,000. Throughout the 1980s, medical bills have consistently risen faster than inflation. As William B. Schwartz, a professor of medicine at Tufts University, puts it, "We're captives of our success as a biomedical research community."

In 1987, the most recent year for which data are available from the Health Care Financing Administration, medical care costs rose 6.6 percent, compared with a general inflation rate of only 3.6 percent. As far back as statistics can be found, medical care prices have tended to grow faster than the prices of other goods and services. *(See chart, p. 32.)* Between 1947 and 1986, the price of a physician visit increased one and a half times as fast as other prices. Over the same period, hospital costs saw an even more phenomenal rise of 9,000 percent.[2]

Technological advances may be the most important cause of the rise in medical costs, but they are not the only one. Economists and insurance companies have come up with a common litany of other factors, too:

■ Labor costs. Hospitals find they must increase nurses' salaries to compete with other industries.[3]

■ The aging population. Medical advances and better general health care are allowing people to live longer, and older people have higher medical costs. As the baby boom generation reaches old age, the problem will get worse.

■ The doctor glut. Some economists believe that, ironically, too many doctors leads to higher medical care costs. With fewer patients, doctors may order more tests or perform more procedures than necessary to keep their incomes up.

■ Health insurance itself. Because the majority of Americans have insurance, economists say, most consumers will remain insulated from the true costs of their health care.

Whatever the causes, the most significant indication of the dangers that lie ahead is the ever-growing share of the nation's income that the medical cost monster has been claiming. Health care now accounts for 11 percent of the gross national product (GNP), almost twice the share it claimed in 1966 and a larger share than in any other Western industrialized nation. *(See charts, pp. 32 and 40.)* By the year 2000, the Health Care Financing Administration predicts, health spending will account for 15 percent of GNP, about two and a half times the portion of GNP now spent on defense. Such phenomenal growth obviously cannot continue forever: This country must produce goods and services other than medical care.

Already there are signs of serious strain. In Washington, D.C., federal workers face a 66 percent increase in the cost of the most comprehensive Blue Cross health insurance premiums next year. In Houston, an unemployed worker forbids his 11-year-old son to play football or soccer because he cannot afford to buy health insurance or to pay the hospital bills if his son is injured.* In Massachusetts, a 91-year-old widow who has had both legs amputated because of gangrene has to exhaust her $60,000 savings account before she can qualify for government medical assistance.[4]

For at least the past 10 years, the problem has received the attention of government and industry, which have tried a variety of ways to hold down medical costs. They have

looked over the doctor's shoulder to make sure hospitalization is needed before authorizing a payment. They have set a fixed reimbursement fee for each procedure. They have instituted or increased co-payments or deductibles, so patients will feel at least some of the cost of the care they are receiving. But nothing seems to have worked.

Some prominent economists in the field say the only solution left is to "ration" health care. Rationing in its harshest form would involve hard decisions about how to distribute expensive health care — decisions like the policy of the British National Health Service to give younger patients preference for such procedures as kidney dialysis. Insurance companies and government officials shy away from rationing and talk instead of inducing doctors to provide health care with a closer eye to the expected costs and benefits. Skeptics worry, however, that such institutionalized cost-consciousness might proceed at the expense of patients' best interests. "The question you have to decide," cautions Judith Feder, co-director of the Center for Health Policy Studies at Georgetown University, "is whether the solution is worse than the problem."

Medical profession favors fee-for-service reimbursement

American doctors traditionally have been paid on a "fee-for-service" basis. Under this system, a doctor charges a separate fee for each service rendered. The more the doctor charges for each service and the more services he provides, the higher his income. Since the 1920s, health care reformers have pushed prepaid group health plans as a cost-effective alternative to the fee-for-service system. The nation's first prepaid group practice was established in 1927 in Elk City, Okla., by Dr. Michael A. Shadid. During the 1930s and 1940s a number of "medical cooperatives" appeared across the country. But according to sociologist Paul Starr, author of *The Social Transformation of American Medicine*, the populist, consumer-oriented cooperatives didn't really catch on, principally because of opposition from organized medicine. "The medical profession was unremittingly hostile [to the cooperatives], and by the end of the [1930s] succeeded in convincing most states to pass restrictive laws that effectively barred consumer-controlled plans from operating." [5]

During this period, in response to growing consumer demand for some form of protection from debilitating health care expenses, both the American Hospital Association and the American Medical Association introduced their own private insurance mechanisms, Blue Cross and Blue Shield, respectively. In 1934, commercial insurance companies began offering health insurance on the same fee-for-service basis, which imposed few, if any, limits on the amount physicians or hospitals could charge. Doctors and hospitals generally boycotted any health insurance plan that sought to make them abide by a fee schedule. "[A]s of 1945," writes Starr, "the structure of private health plans

---

*This is the case Democratic presidential candidate Michael S. Dukakis cited in the first presidential debate on Sept. 25, 1988. Dukakis got the sport wrong; he said Little League.

U.S. Health Bill

Spending on health continued its steep climb during the 1980s. As a percentage of GNP, the '80s have seen increases comparable to the late 1960s.

Expenditures in billions of dollars

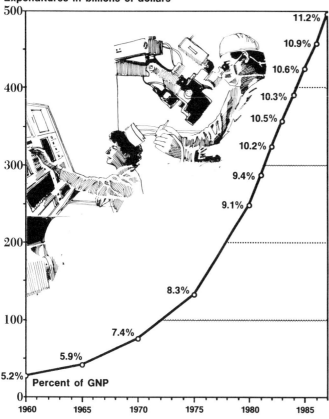

Source: *Health Insurance Association of America*

... and Inflation

Over the last 20 years, the cost of medical care has usually increased at a faster rate than overall inflation, as measured by annual changes in the consumer price index.

Year	All items	Medical care items		Year	All items	Medical care items
1968	4.2%	6.1%		1978	7.6%	8.4%
1969	5.4	6.9		1979	11.3	9.3
1970	5.9	6.3		1980	13.5	10.9
1971	4.3	6.5		1981	10.4	10.8
1972	3.3	3.2		1982	6.2	11.6
1973	6.2	3.9		1983	3.2	8.7
1974	11.0	9.3		1984	4.3	6.2
1975	9.1	12.0		1985	3.6	6.2
1976	5.8	9.5		1986	1.9	7.5
1977	6.5	9.6		1987	3.6	6.6

Source: *Bureau of Labor Statistics*

... was basically an accommodation to provider interests." [6]

In the 1960s, massive amounts of federal money were pumped into the medical system. In 1965, the federal government passed Medicare, which provided federal financial assistance for medical care to all citizens over age 65 regardless of income. That same year Congress approved Medicaid, a joint federal-state program to pay for the medical care of low-income citizens. Under Medicare and Medicaid, the government agreed, as the insurance companies had done earlier, to reimburse hospitals on the basis of their charges rather than to set a schedule of acceptable fees.

Also in the 1960s, unions made health insurance one of their key demands in collective-bargaining negotiations. For large unions like the autoworkers and the steelworkers, employers typically agreed to pay the entire insurance premium and offered "first dollar coverage," covering all medical costs, starting with the first dollar expended by a worker. No limits were placed on how much the insurance plan would pay the hospital or doctor. Richard Cotton, a former aide to Joseph A. Califano Jr., secretary of health, education and welfare in the Carter administration, says management's big mistake was in agreeing to an unquantified benefit. "It was an open checkbook," says Cotton, who now advises employers on how to contain medical costs as president of HCX Inc., a Washington, D.C., firm.

"What happened with Medicare and the development of private insurance is that the government and the employers felt they could not challenge the medical profession and the hospitals," says Starr, now a sociologist at Princeton University. "They had to accept financial arrangements which left all decision-making power with the providers. Employers and government have been trying to change those arrangements in the last decade and they have been finding it exceedingly difficult to turn that around."

HMOs proliferate, but costs escalate

In the 1970s, skyrocketing hospital costs once again grabbed the attention of insurance companies, government policy makers and economists. Conservatives were anxious to apply market notions of competition to the medical care system. So health care policy makers under Republican Presidents Richard M. Nixon and Ronald Reagan enthusiastically embraced the concept of health maintenance organizations (HMOs), prepaid group health plans similar to the medical cooperatives of the 1930s and 1940s. Legislation passed in 1973 under Nixon required businesses with more than 25 employees to offer their employees at least one federally qualified HMO as an alternative to conventional insurance in their health benefit plan. Under President Reagan, Medicare patients for the first time were offered the option of signing up for an HMO in 1982.

Health planners thought that if consumers were offered a choice between the traditional, expensive fee-for-service plan and the cheaper all-inclusive HMO, the majority would opt for the HMO, which in turn would cap medical expenditures through its annual prepayment. The existence of the inherently cost-efficient HMOs, it was hoped, would put pressure on non-participating physicians to keep their prices down as well. But while enrollment in HMOs has grown by leaps and bounds — more than quadrupling since 1976 to an estimated 29 million people* — the ability of HMOs to curb the overall rise in medical costs has been disappointing.

Schwartz of Tufts University says annual costs at HMOs have been rising just as fast as those in the fee-for-service sector. "There's never been a difference historically in the rate at which [their costs] have gone up, going back 20 years." The only thing HMOs have done differently from traditional medical practices, Schwartz says, is to reduce the amount of hospital use and the average length of hospital stays. At the same time, he argues, the HMOs have been just as generous in their use of expensive technology and doctors' consultations as the traditional plans. "If the [HMOs] were going to avoid [higher costs], they couldn't have done [such procedures] as hip replacements . . . or open heart surgery. They couldn't be doing all of the things which are responsible for the rise in costs in the whole health care system."

HMOs today often bear little resemblance to the original models, like Kaiser Permanente in California, which had its own staff of salaried doctors and its own hospitals. Today, the term HMO covers a wide variety of health care arrangements, including loose conglomerations of doctors organized in preferred provider organizations (PPOs). Participating physicians maintain their private practices, but they agree to offer their services at a discount to those who belong to the organization. Faced with growing competition from such groups, the large health insurance companies, including Blue Cross and Blue Shield, began offering HMO and PPO alternatives to their traditional health insurance plans.

One early proponent of HMOs, Alain C. Enthoven of the Stanford University Graduate School of Business, says the new HMOs don't have the same commitment to holding down costs. "When Kaiser found themselves under severe economic pressure, the leader would sit down with the doctors and say, 'You're going to get less of a raise than we thought.' They had loyalty to the cause and what they were trying to do, which was to provide economical health care," he says.

HMOs are still generally cheaper than traditional fee-for-service insurance plans. Although their rates are going up, they are not rising as fast as traditional plans. At Blue Cross and Blue Shield, for example, HMO fees are expected to increase 10-15 percent next year, while premiums for the traditional plans are expected to increase 20-25 percent,

---

*In 1987, more than 27 percent of the nation's employees with group health insurance were enrolled in an HMO or preferred provider organization, up from just 4 percent in 1981, according to the Health Insurance Association of America.

SPEAKING OF HEALTH COSTS

PROSPECTIVE PAYMENT SYSTEM (PPS) The system introduced by the Reagan administration in 1983 to reimburse hospitals for Medicare patients "prospectively" — on the basis of rates established ahead of time — rather than on the basis of the hospital's charges. The system was intended to hold down the federal government's Medicare costs.

DIAGNOSTIC RELATED GROUPS (DRGs) A list of more than 400 medical conditions specified under the PPS system, together with the rates at which the federal government will reimburse hospitals.

UTILIZATION REVIEW Describes several methods used by insurance companies and corporations to reduce the cost of covered employees' medical claims, usually for elective surgery. These include reviewing a doctor's recommended hospital stay for a patient upon admission to a hospital and reviewing the doctor's recommended treatment plan once the patient is in the hospital.

FEE-FOR-SERVICE The traditional system of paying doctors in America, through a separate fee for each medical service, such as a doctor's visit, medical test or operation.

HEALTH MAINTENANCE ORGANIZATION (HMO) An organization of physicians, frequently salaried, that charges each patient a fixed annual fee for all medical care.

PREFFERED PROVIDER ORGANIZATION (PPO) A list of doctors who agree to treat the members of a group health plan. In return for the expected increase in patients, the doctors frequently agree to offer their services at a discount.

---

according to Douglas S. Peters, senior vice president for representation and public affairs.

The proliferation of HMOs in the 1980s created a highly competitive environment. In order to attract and keep members, HMOs were forced to hold down fees at the same time they were facing increasing costs. Some plans went bankrupt. By 1986, the latest year for which figures are available, 75 percent of HMOs faced business losses, according to a study by Jurgovan & Blair, a Potomac, Md., consulting firm. Jurgovan Vice President Robert F. Atlas says the competitive environment also made it harder for HMOs to hold down costs. "There were so many HMOs . . . that doctors and hospitals could pick their deals," he says. "HMOs that were looking to bargain for the best, cheapest prices weren't able to get the best quality providers."

Laws of supply and demand don't apply to health care

Many of the economists who argued in the 1970s that health care costs could be controlled by applying free-market principles have now concluded that health care defies the classical laws of supply and demand. "I'm more pessimistic about it now than I was a couple of years ago," says Victor R. Fuchs, a Stanford University economist who proposed the application of market competition to health care in his 1974 book, *Who Shall Live?* "You really didn't get competition in the sense that we mean competition in other industries, and I don't think you ever really can get it in health care."

Medical care is not like most consumer transactions, where the buyer looks for the product that will give him the most value for his money. "The consumer doesn't demand competition because . . . he pays very little of the bill," says John F. Cogan, a senior fellow at Stanford University's Hoover Institution. Most people don't pay the full cost of the medical care they receive. Usually, a third party, the insurance company or the government, pays the bill, or the bulk of it. "If I don't pay anything," says Cogan, "why would I shop around for the lowest-priced care?"

Another factor that distinguishes medical service from a typical consumer purchase is the information gap between patient and doctor. Frequently, the patient is in a weakened physical or psychological condition and views the doctor as his agent in reaching a decision. "When you buy a videocassette recorder, you can read *Consumer Reports*, you know the prices, you shop around, and the market works. The reason you go to a physician is because you *don't* know . . . what's good for you or what's bad for you," says Jon Gabel, associate director of the department of research statistics at the Health Insurance Association of America in Washington, D.C. "You don't know the prices. You don't even know what you've bought until you've got the bill."

Unlike most commodities, an expanded supply of medical care does not necessarily translate into reduced prices. For one thing, many geographic areas have only enough patients to support one hospital or one specialist, so there is no point in expanding the supply to create competition. In another departure from normal economics, when the supply of physicians in a given area expands, the price of medical care does not seem to fall the way it would if a big truckload of in-season peaches arrived at grocery stores. Some economists have speculated that this is because in an oversupply situation, idle physicians with empty waiting rooms come up with longer, more costly office visits as well as additional tests and procedures per patient to assure a steady income. "When physicians have more time, they do see more things to do," says paul B. Ginsburg, executive director of the Physician Payment Review Commission *(See p. 38.)*

Not everyone agrees that medical spending increases can be traced to the lack of competition. "The cause of the problem is neither physician greed nor an enhanced ability to charge prices that yield monopoly profits," Princeton University economist William J. Baumol argued in a March 1988 report prepared for the American Medical Association. Competition has increased in the medical field far more than most economists believe, he said, noting the increasing number of patients switching from traditional health plans to HMOs. If competitiveness had been declining during the past decade of rising medical costs, Baumol argued, there would have been persistent real rises in physicians' incomes exceeding inflation. Instead, Baumol said, the average physician's income remained level over the 1975-1985 period once adjusted for inflation. (That decade saw the average doctor's income rise in nominal terms from $56,400 to $113,200.)

Baumol blames increases in medical costs on another phenomenon: the inability of the medical profession to increase its labor productivity the way manufacturing does. Historically, the amount of labor devoted to a manufactured good falls as the production process becomes more efficient, permitting savings in labor costs to offset rises in other costs of producing the good. By contrast, the essence of good medical care lies in the amount of attention and labor that the skilled physician devotes to the patient. Since it is almost impossible to reduce the labor component of medical care without harming the quality of the service, the doctor has little opportunity to counterweigh the rising costs of medical technology with a reduction in labor. "The problems of medical care cannot by and large be standardized and rendered routine," Baumol says. "A reduction in the attention that a doctor devotes to a patient results in a concomitant reduction in the quality of medical care." [7]

Cost-containment: Why it hasn't worked

Over the past two decades, the federal government and private companies have been trying to hold down medical costs through a variety of "cost-containment" efforts. Many insurance companies and self-insured employers, for example, now require second opinions before approving an employee's elective surgery. Under a practice known as "utilization review," the insurance company's nurses and medical advisers will review a physician's decision to send a patient to the hospital for elective surgery and decide whether the recommended hospital stay is appropriate before agreeing to pay for it. Once the patient is at the hospital, the insurance company's review team will again review the physician's recommended treatment plan.

Despite the growing popularity of cost-containment programs, many of their original advocates express disappointment over their ability to hold down medical costs. "These programs haven't delivered as much as we'd hoped,"

Continued on page 36

Helping the Uninsured

The growing number of Americans without health insurance has been a prominent theme in the presidential campaign of Massachusetts Gov. Michael S. Dukakis. "I think it's time that when you've got a job in this country, it came with health insurance," Dukakis said in the Sept. 25 presidential debate. Dukakis favors legislation requiring employers to provide health insurance to their employees and to pay a minimum share of the premium. Vice President George Bush has said he favors expanding the Medicaid program to deal with the problem. He claims that the Dukakis plan, by taxing businesses, would "throw some people out of work." †

In 1987, 37 million Americans were without health insurance, 25 percent more than in 1980, according to the Census Bureau's Current Population Survey.†† More than half of the uninsured, 19.6 million people, were in families where at least one member had a full-time job. One reason for this trend is that employers, in an effort to cut their medical insurance costs, are covering fewer dependents of employees than before. The increase also reflects the growth of jobs in the service sector and in smaller firms. These types of jobs are less likely to provide health insurance coverage than jobs in manufacturing or in larger firms.

For those low-income, unemployed persons without health insurance, the lack of Medicaid coverage seems to be the main explanation. Although Medicaid was established to provide health care for the poor, it covers fewer than 40 percent of those who need it, according to Karen Davis, chairman of the Department of Health Policy and Management at the Johns Hopkins School of Hygiene and Public Health.‡ This is because individual states set the income-eligibility levels well below the federal poverty level and because coverage is generally limited to one-parent welfare families — excluding two-parent families, childless couples and single individuals.

On April 21, Dukakis signed a health insurance law for Massachusetts. Beginning in 1992, Massachusetts employers with six or more employees will face a tax of 12 percent on the first $14,000 of each employee's salary. The tax revenues will be placed in a trust fund, which will be used to buy health insurance for those employees not covered through their employer. Employers who already provide health insurance may deduct the cost of their insurance from the surcharge. Beginning in 1990, unemployed persons will be able to buy health coverage from a state trust fund, also subsidized through a separate tax on employers. Dukakis' federal plan is similar to the Massachusetts law in that it would require employers to foot the bill.

The plan has been attacked by the business community as one that will cost jobs, particularly for small businesses that have not previously shouldered the expense of health insurance. Bush's alternative, first proposed at the Sept. 25 debate, is to permit low-income people to purchase health insurance through a "Medicaid buy-in." Rob Quartel, a senior policy adviser in the Bush campaign, at first said the plan would cost the taxpayers only $200 million but later backed down on the number and declined to give a specific figure. Health experts have estimated that the "Medicaid Buy-in" plan could run anywhere from $1 billion to $10 billion, depending on the eligibility levels and the amount that the insurance cost was subsidized.

Although Bush's campaign has attacked universal health insurance as "socialized medicine," the concept is receiving support from a surprising quarter: big business. Last June, for example, several large companies testified in favor of the employer-mandated health insurance bill sponsored by Sen. Edward M. Kennedy, D-Mass. (S 1265). They said they were tired of subsidizing medical care for employees of other firms with no insurance. The cost, they said, is reflected in higher medical bills, higher insurance premiums and larger claims for working spouses whose employers offer no insurance.

"Very simply, we believe that companies like Chrysler . . . should not be allowed to be a dumping ground for other companies' health bills," said Walter B. Maher, director of employee benefits for Chrysler Motors Corp. Robert L. Crandall, president and chairman of American Airlines, complained that if a direct competitor provides no medical insurance, a major cost is eliminated and a competitive advantage can be gained in pricing airline tickets. That, he said, is what happened when Continental Airlines was permitted to eliminate health benefits for retired employees as part of its bankruptcy reorganization.‡‡

---

† *Quotation is from the Sept. 25 debate.*

†† *The majority (67 percent) of those who have health insurance are covered through their employers; 8 percent are covered by Medicare or Medicaid and 7 percent by individual insurance policies.*

‡ *Testimony by Karen Davis before the Senate Finance Committee, July 25, 1988.*

‡‡ *Hearing before the Senate Labor and Human Resources Committee on S 1265, Minimum Benefits for All Workers Act of 1987, June 24, 1987, Part I., pp. 17, 30.*

Continued from page 34
admits Gabel. But, he adds, "I also think we're better off because we have them. If we didn't have them we'd be in worse shape."

Recent studies seem to bear out Gabel's observation. For example, a 1988 study by Blue Cross and Blue Shield says cost-containment efforts saved the plans about $4.8 billion between 1983 and 1986.[8] Yet the savings barely made a dent in the insurance plans' continually rising expenditures. "This money does not appear in the bank account," says Richard M. Sheffler, a health economist at the University of California at Berkeley and author of the Blue Cross/Blue Shield study.

The most impressive savings for Blue Cross/Blue Shield were found in the hospital sector, where most of its cost-review efforts have been directed. Blue Cross and Blue Shield plans reduced the amount they paid for hospital inpatient care by 11 percent in 1986, by cutting back on the number of patients admitted and on the number of days they stayed. But although insurance companies have been successful in holding down hospital costs, their success has not translated into overall cost-saving. For one thing, many procedures that were once performed in hospitals are now performed in physicians' offices or outpatient clinics. The "explosion of outpatient utilization" is just one of the factors that has frustrated efforts to realize net cost reductions, says Peters of the Blue Cross and Blue Shield Association. "We squeeze the balloon in one area only to realize that there are other things that cause the pattern overall."

Henry J. Aaron, a senior fellow at the Brookings Institution, is one of many health care experts who say medical inflation can't be slowed unless something is done to control the use of expensive diagnostic technologies like CAT scans and surgical techniques like coronary bypasses. "That's the engine that's driving everything," he says.

Most of the well-known methods of cost control infringe in some way on the physician's control over patient care. Many of these methods have been bitterly criticized by the medical community as hurting the quality of care patients receive or for tying the doctor up in pointless red tape. Doctors report spending hours trying to reach an insurance company's utilization review nurse before they can send a patient to the hospital.

Representatives of the medical community reiterated these kinds of complaints at a June 6 hearing held by the National Academy of Sciences' Institute of Medicine in Washington, D.C. A representative of the American Hospital Association reported that hospitals must respond to as many as 45 to 50 private review agencies employed by insurers at any one time to review their cases. "Using . . . utilization review . . . to camouflage arbitrary coverage restrictions can lead to clinical standards being established by insurance agents, rather than by qualified clinicians," charged Bruce McPherson, group vice president for the hospital association.*

---

*The Institute of Medicine's Committee on Utilization Management by Third Parties will issue a final report early next year on the effect of utilization management on health care costs and the quality of care.

Doctors say some HMOs penalize doctors financially for referring patients to additional medical services that they need. Under one accounting system, known as "risk" payment, an HMO doctor has a personal account that is debited every time one of his patients receives a service outside the office, like going to the hospital, seeing a specialist or receiving an X-ray. The risk-payment system "introduces a fundamental conflict of interest for the physician and penalizes vigilant patient care," says Dr. Robert A. Berenson of Washington, D.C. Berenson said that when he worked under this system he often resented very sick patients because of the toll they were taking on his income. "To my knowledge no HMO has tried to promote the virtues of this payment system: 'Enroll with us — the less care you receive, the better your doctor does.' "[9]

Most HMOs don't employ the risk-payment system, according to Robert J. Rubin, senior vice president of the consulting firm ICF Inc. and author of a nationwide study of HMOs prepared for the Department of Health and Human Services. Rubin found that the majority of HMOs pool their funds and then distribute them to the physicians on the basis of the group's overall performance, rather than rewarding an individual physician's behavior with incentives.[10]

The cost-quality debate usually comes down to the question, Does the best medical care necessarily mean more medical care? Former HEW Secretary Califano espouses the view that less is more. "Right now, when a physician is uncertain about the value of a medical procedure, his attitude tends to be: Unless it has been proved ineffective, try it," Califano says. "I suggest we adopt a different attitude: Unless the procedure has been proved effective, don't use it."[11]

Prospective reimbursement: How the system resists reform

As the cost-containment efforts of the 1970s and '80s went into effect, medical providers were "very tenacious" in trying to retain or even increase their levels of revenues, says Michael Carter, senior vice president of Hay/Huggins Co., actuarial and benefits consultants in Philadelphia. "When [cost-control] efforts were taken in one area, they just shifted to another."

In the 1970s and early '80s, business and government concentrated their cost-control efforts on the hospitals, which were then responsible for the fastest-growing cost in medical care. In 1983, Congress passed legislation aimed at controlling the hospital costs charged to the federal Medicare program. Instead of reimbursing hospitals on the basis of their historic costs, as had been done in the past, the federal government would decide how much the reimbursement would be ahead of time under a "Prospective Payment System." Under the new system, hospitals were reimbursed based on a fixed schedule of maximum

Continued on page 38

AT ISSUE   *Should Americans adopt some form of national health insurance?*

YES says **HARVEY C. SIGELBAUM,** president and CEO of Amalgamated Life Insurance Co.

"There are 37 million Americans uninsured for health care.... Our inability to forge a universal system for insurance to manage health care for these millions is bad social and economic policy....

The Government and labor leaders who championed this system intended it to be universal, albeit by 'patchwork.' The employment-based, tax incentived, health insurance system . . . ostensibly would cover all American workers. The taxpayer-financed Medicare and Medicaid programs were designed to fill the gaps left at either end for the poor and the elderly....

However well intentioned, this 'patchwork' system simply isn't working. While more families are living below the poverty level, Medicaid enrollment continues to drop. And fewer workers have health insurance . . . as more people work in smaller, service businesses.

Since Americans pay the health care tab for Americans one way or another, why not pay the bill head on, fairly and efficiently, through universal health insurance? Universal access to health insurance is likely to continue the public-private partnership that has been built over the last 50 years. All employees, regardless of health status, should be guaranteed basic health benefits for themselves and their dependents. For those outside the work force, Medicaid coverage should be made universally available, with appropriate subsidies for the poor. The over-65 population should continue on Medicare benefits, which should be further expanded to eliminate all costs to individuals for catastrophic care.

Who will foot the bill? [I] believe that universal access will result primarily in the equitable redistribution of existing costs. Employers who don't provide health insurance will lose their free ride on the coattails of those who do. Small and start-up businesses can be assisted through tax incentives and legislatively mandated insurance pools that extend efficiencies now available only to big groups.... The government will recoup some of its revenue losses by moving a segment of the population out of the publicly financed health care system into the private insurance sector....

[T]he least efficient move is to close the doors of the system to those who can't afford insurance. The smarter move is to put all Americans into insurance systems designed to assure appropriate quality care and contain costs systematically. Without an organized insurance program, we don't know when, where and why care is delivered, and there is no way to manage health care costs...."

From "Universal Health Insurance: Poor Medical Care is Poor Public Policy," The New York Times Sunday Business Section, Sept. 18, 1988, p. 2.

NO says **J. PATRICK ROONEY,** chairman and chief executive officer of Golden Rule Insurance Co. in Indianapolis.

"Sen. Edward M. Kennedy (D-Mass.) is pushing for passage of his 'Minimum Health Benefits for All Workers Act.' It would require all employers — as a condition of staying in business — to provide health insurance for all employees who work 17½ hours or more a week and for their dependents.

If this legislation is enacted, any social benefits would be overshadowed by the permanent increase in unemployment it would cause....

[E]mployers must pay 100 percent of the cost of insurance for employees making less than 125 percent of the minimum wage. So, at the current minimum wage, the cost of insurance would be 17 percent of payroll for full-time minimum wage workers and 34 percent of payroll for half-time minimum-wage workers.

The Kennedy mandate would thus force employers to ask: 'Can't we eliminate some of the lower-paid workers?' This incentive to eliminate lower paid workers threatens minority-group members especially. A disproportionate number of them hold low-wage jobs, jobs that would be the first to be eliminated by the cost of mandated health insurance....

The threat of a permanent high unemployment rate becomes more real when you consider the harm the Kennedy mandate would do to small businesses. Most large corporations already provide health benefits for all employees, and they tend not to employ anyone at the minimum wage.

Most minimum-wage workers are employed by small businesses. These businesses are less likely to provide health benefits and would pay the highest cost, as a percentage of payroll, for mandated health benefits. Small firms not forced out of existence by costs of mandated health care would offset the expense by reducing their work forces and cutting work hours below 17½ hours for remaining employees where possible....

The most important factor influencing the price of medical care is the ability (and willingness) of those receiving that care to pay. The Kennedy mandated-benefits plan would greatly increase the numbers of people able and willing to pay but would do nothing to counter the price escalation, which has historically followed sharp increases in demand for medical services....

We must not, for the sake of extending health benefits to some, establish a regressive employment tax that would coerce employers into eliminating jobs that many Americans need and want."

From "Mandating Health Care Would Eliminate Jobs," Nation's Business, May 1988, p. 4.

Continued from page 36

fees for more than 400 medical conditions, known in the professional jargon as diagnostic-related groups, or DRGs. With this new approach, the Reagan administration hoped to keep a ceiling on federal expenditures and to provide hospitals with incentives to reduce their costs, because the hospitals kept the difference between their actual costs and the reimbursement amount.*

Although the system produced a dramatic drop in the number of people admitted to hospitals and in the length of stay per patient, it is not clear that it has saved the federal government any money. John F. Cogan, who helped set the new rates as associate director for human resources at the Office of Management and Budget (OMB), says the Reagan administration initially set the rates too high and gave yearly inflation increases that were much too generous. "I believe we overpaid hospitals in the first couple of years," he now says. Whatever saving there may have been from reducing hospital admissions, he adds, has "not as yet been passed on to the taxpayer."

One reason is a phenomenon known as "DRG creep." After the new program went into effect, the federal government found that hospitals were claiming they had a sicker group of patients on their hands than ever before. Cogan suspects that hospitals were, to some extent, "gaming" the system by reporting more serious conditions for their patients than actually existed. On the other hand, Paul B. Ginsburg, who examined the phenomenon for OMB when he was at the RAND Corp. in Santa Monica, Calif., says, "We don't know how much was gaming and how much was good management." He points out that the introduction of DRGs coincided with the trend toward outpatient surgery. For example, virtually all cataract surgery, a relatively inexpensive procedure, is now done on an outpatient basis. "As you pulled these easy patients out, the average [expense of the remaining patients] had to go up," Ginsburg says.

As the explosion in outpatient care became increasingly obvious, the government tried to tighten the faucet of funds flowing to doctors under Medicare. The Reagan administration froze physician fees under Medicare in 1984, abandoning its past practice of reimbursing them on the basis of "prevailing" charges. But as that faucet was shut off, doctors responded by opening up another faucet. Because Medicare paid doctors on a piecework basis — so much for each visit, each test, each shot, etc. — doctors "unbundled" all the things that used to be included in an office visit. Each item was submitted as a separate bill. "If you look at the rate of growth in Medicare payments to physicians since 1985," says Cogan, "there's no effect [from the fee freeze]." **

---

*The government also took steps to control Medicaid costs. The Omnibus Reconciliation Act of 1981 removed a requirement that states reimburse hospitals on the basis of actual costs. This freed the states to set caps on hospital reimbursements. This measure has been cited as one of the major reasons that Medicaid spending growth slowed to an average annual rate of 7.5 percent between 1981 and 1984. Between 1978 and 1981, the average annual increase had been 16 percent.

**Over the last six years, Medicare physician payments per beneficiary have been growing at 13 percent per year, according to the Health Care Financing Administra-

Medical practice guidelines to control expensive procedures

After a decade of disappointing experimentation, few analysts see any magic solutions to controlling medical costs. And those who do see solutions wonder whether they would be politically acceptable. Many of the ideas gaining currency in the health policy field involve cutting back on the use of expensive medical care. These proposals range from draconian "rationing" of medical care to routine cost-benefit analyses of medical procedures.

Increasingly, studies show that a surprisingly large number of expensive medical procedures are unnecessary and may actually harm the health of patients. For example, a RAND Corp. study of 2 million Medicare beneficiaries investigated a procedure called carotid end-arterectomy, which removes obstructions from one of the arteries constituting the major blood supply to the brain, and concluded that it had been performed inappropriately in one out of every three cases. In addition, 3.4 percent of the patients died within 30 days of the procedure and 6.4 percent suffered non-fatal strokes during or immediately after surgery. To many experts, that rate of complication — almost 10 percent overall — suggests that the value of the procedure is questionable in the first place.

Mounting evidence of this kind has led some to suggest that doctors may be in need of new standards to specify when such procedures are warranted and when they will be reimbursed for them. Mark R. Chassin, who was the principal investigator for the RAND study, says existing guidelines issued by and for doctors tend to represent the medical profession's bias toward doing procedures when in doubt. "Few current guidelines describe specific circumstances when procedures or tests ought not be used," Chassin noted at a congressional hearing last month on medical practice guidelines.[12]

The cost-saving potential of such an approach has spawned an infant industry that is essentially a sophisticated version of the utilization review system (See p. 34.) On the assumption that expensive medical procedures could be eliminated if there were good information on hand about when to use them, Chassin and others are now developing computerized software packages for use by employers and insurance companies to reduce the extent of inappropriate procedures. Chassin has helped to develop one such package marketed by Value Health Inc., in Avon, Conn. Robert Patricelli, Value Health's president, says his company offers "the first commercially available system to identify inappropriate inpatient and outpatient procedures and to eliminate them before they are delivered." According to Patricelli, the company's computerized system checks out more than 30 high-cost procedures, which account for 20 to 25 percent of employer-paid costs.

The Physician Payment Review Commission (PPRC),

---

tion. Half of the increase is attributed to the increases in volume and in high-reimbursement procedures, the other half to price increases.

a congressionally established commission to reform Medicare costs, sees medical practice guidelines as one route to controlling Medicare costs.* For example, Medicare currently spends more than $300 million per year on physicians' charges for coronary bypass operations. "If just 10 percent of these are inappropriate, $30 million in physicians' charges and millions more for the associated hospital charges could be saved or spent for more beneficial services," PPRC Commissioner Walter J. McNerny said at last month's congressional hearing. Insurance companies like Blue Cross/Blue Shield and private employers like General Electric also have expressed interest in applying medical practice standards to their reimbursement policies. They point to studies indicating that somewhere between 20 percent and 60 percent of the $30 billion annually spent for routine laboratory testing is unnecessary.[13]

Cotton, whose company markets a cost-containment service to employers, sees the sophisticated software packages as a way of holding off the potentially dire consequences of growing medical costs. "The alternatives are economic rationing — making medical care so expensive that only certain parts of society can afford it." The problem with rationing, says Cotton, is that it tends to be arbitrary, penalizing the elderly or the poor. The goal of medical practice standards, he says, would be to cut out unnecessary services in a rational manner, based on the consensus of medical experts. "Whether it can save enough to avoid rationing is not clear," he adds.

Many students of the American health care system have suggested that one reason for the high incidence of costly medical procedures is that physicians are better compensated for doing expensive surgery than for following less costly courses of treatment, such as preventive care. Those who see this bias as a major source of rising medical costs recommend overhauling the current system of paying doctors. In keeping with this line of thought, Congress in 1986 directed the administration to develop a new system of paying physicians under Medicare, known as the "relative value scale."

In response to the congressional mandate, a report issued Sept. 27 by the Harvard School of Public Health recommends increases in payments for office visits and reductions in such high-tech services as inserting pacemakers. The Harvard report develops an entirely new system of compensation that takes into account the time, mental effort, technical skill, cost of training, stress and overhead devoted to each kind of medical service. The administration is required to report to Congress on the advisability of such a system by July 1 of next year.**

---

*The commission held a conference on how such guidelines could be used on Oct. 11 in Washington, D.C.

**William L. Roper, administrator of the Health Care Financing Administration, the government agency that administers Medicare and that commissioned the Harvard study, indicated that he has doubts about this approach. "While the relative value approach may help create fairer relative prices among physicians, it does not address the critical issue of the incentives contained in a fee-for-service system for physicians to increase the volume . . . of services," he said the day the study was released.

Health Benefits Changing

During the 1980s, a major shift has taken place in payment for health benefits, according to a recent survey of 240 large firms. Far fewer companies now pay the entire cost of employee health plans; most now require employees to pay deductibles.

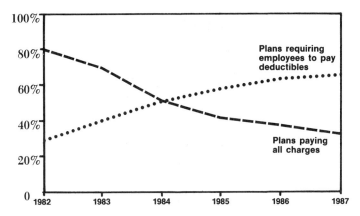

Source: Hewett Associates

Big headaches for big business

Rising medical bills mean big headaches for American businesses. During the first nine months of last year, for example, General Motors Corp. spent more than $2 billion on medical care coverage for its employees; over the same period, the automaker posted profits of $2.7 billion.[14] The cost of employees' health insurance is often passed on to consumers in the form of higher prices for American goods and services — a fact that hurts the competitiveness of American products. "General Motors has to spend considerably more per employee for health benefits for a plant in America than for a plant in Canada," notes Starr. "Similarly, the competitors abroad don't have as big a burden."

Employers' cost-consciousness has grown as more companies have become self-insuring. A majority of employers (51 percent) now act as their own health insurers, according to a survey by the Health Insurance Association of America (HIAA). Employers started to self-insure partly so they could reap the benefits of earning interest on the reserves from insurance premiums and partly because federal law puts fewer limitations on the kinds of insurance that must be provided if the employer is self-insured. The self-insurance trend was also motivated by insurance company rate increases. This year rates will rise an average of 20 percent, according to HIAA. That compares with about a 4 percent average annual increase for the previous three years. Insurers often underprice their product for a few years to attract business, then overprice for another three years or so to recover losses. Another reason for this year's

Health Care Spending in the Industrial World

**Whether measured per capita or as a percentage of gross domestic product (GDP*), the
United States spends more on health care than other industrialized countries. The U.S. has
the smallest government share of the total health bill, however.**

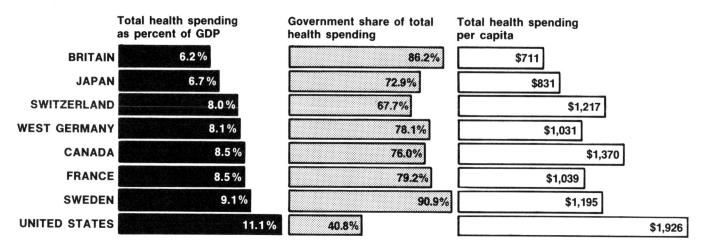

	Total health spending as percent of GDP	Government share of total health spending	Total health spending per capita
BRITAIN	6.2%	86.2%	$711
JAPAN	6.7%	72.9%	$831
SWITZERLAND	8.0%	67.7%	$1,217
WEST GERMANY	8.1%	78.1%	$1,031
CANADA	8.5%	76.0%	$1,370
FRANCE	8.5%	79.2%	$1,039
SWEDEN	9.1%	90.9%	$1,195
UNITED STATES	11.1%	40.8%	$1,926

* *GDP, which is similar to gross national product, does not include income produced abroad.*
Note: Figures are for 1986
Source: Organization for Economic Cooperation and Development and U.S. Health and Human Services Dept.

big rate increase, Gabel says, is that insurance companies
were overly optimistic about the impact of cost-containment
efforts on rising medical costs.

To help pay the rising medical bill, many companies
are requiring employees to pay a larger share through
higher premiums and deductibles. A 1988 survey by the
Hay Group, a management consulting firm in Philadelphia,
found that 43 percent of the surveyed companies now
require some cost participation by covered employees, up
from 29 percent in 1982. According to the study, the
average employee will have $40 removed from his monthly
paycheck for health insurance premiums in 1988, compared with $8 in 1980. In addition to having more taken out
of their paychecks, employees also have to pay deductibles of $150 to $200 before they can qualify for reimbursement. And they often have to pay a specified percentage
— usually 20 percent — of each covered medical bill.

Many believe consumers will become more judicious in
their use of health care services if they are forced to pay
more of the costs. "I think we still have failed in our
society to make people cost-conscious in their choice of
health care plan," says Stanford economist Enthoven.
"What we need is to get a health care economy where
everyone has to make a cost-conscious choice."

Canada's experience with national health insurance

Other countries also have had to grapple with high
health care costs. In Canada, for example, national health

expenditures rose steadily from 2.95 percent of GNP in
1950 to 7.4 percent in 1971 (during that period, medical
spending in the U.S. jumped from 4.4 percent of GNP to
7.8 percent). Then, in 1971, Canada adopted a full-blown
national health insurance scheme. For the next decade,
medical inflation in Canada slowed and health care's share
of GNP remained relatively constant. By 1981, medical
spending accounted for only 7.7 percent of GNP in Canada
while it was a record 9.2 percent in the United States.

Supporters of the Canadian system attribute this mod-
eration in health costs to Canada's adoption of universal
health insurance. Medical care is free to the entire
population, with the costs borne by the federal and provincial governments. Unlike Britain, where all doctors and
nurses in the national health insurance system work for the
government on a salaried basis, Canada retained its
network of independently practicing doctors charging on a
fee-for-service basis. Doctors are reimbursed according to
a fee schedule determined by the provincial governments.

How does Canada avoid the problem of doctors charging for additional services to increase their income? According to Theodore R. Marmor, professor of public policy
and management at the Yale University School of Organization and Management, the key lies in the pre-arranged
grant the federal government makes to the provincial
government for medical reimbursements. If charges by
the province's doctors exceed the provincial government's
medical allocation, the additional funds must come out of
some other area of the provincial government's budget.
"The result," says Marmor, "is that the provincial administrators face 100 percent of the fiscal costs of expansion" in
medical services. In annual negotiating sessions, says

Continued on page 42

The British National Health Service

Americans sometimes refer to it as "socialized medicine" — a cradle-to-grave, tax-funded national health system. The British simply call it the "N.H.S." They take it as much for granted as Americans take Social Security. Most British people take great pride in the National Health Service. They share a strong belief that the national government should be responsible for every citizen's health care because people do not want "health to be related to wealth."

The British system has worked relatively well over most of the last four decades. If any person has an accident, an acute illness or a chronic health problem, he or she is taken care of immediately and without charge for however long is necessary. At least that is how the N.H.S. is designed to work, and usually does.

Problems emerge, however, when non life-threatening illness is involved. The British system "rations" treatment in these cases by lengthy waiting lists. As many as 700,000 people are currently waiting for some kind of treatment. Delays of a year or more are common for such things as hip replacements or elective medical procedures.

The system also requires that priorities be established for treatment. This means that younger people will have a priority for such procedures as kidney dialysis. Overall, of course, the bulk of health care services go to the elderly.

"There cannot be in any system absolute provision for every method of treatment for every single person," says Dr. John Marks, chairman of the British Medical Association (B.M.A.). "We know that's unrealistic. Everyone knows that's unrealistic." But until recently, says Dr. Marks, who supports the N.H.S., Britain has had a reasonable level of care for the vast majority of people.

All that may be in danger, however, because of what the B.M.A. and many other groups say is under funding of the N.H.S. The Conservative-led British government has not cut back money for the N.H.S., but it has also not boosted spending adequately to cover much higher costs from increasingly expensive high technology treatments. The result has been a financial squeeze on the system and a howling political controversy.

The squeeze has meant a record 30,000 nurses are quitting the N.H.S. each year, mostly because of low pay ($11,000-$12,000 a year) and many who stay are staging strikes. In addition, dozens of hospital wards have been closed, including many specialized centers. In cases that have attracted enormous national publicity, children requiring heart surgery have sometimes had their operations repeatedly postponed because of the lack of fully staffed child cardiac units. Some of the children have actually died waiting for treatment.

"The problems are now so acute with underfunding that the health service will simply fall apart within the next few months unless that is recognized," says Toby Harris, director of the British Association of Community Health Councils, an independent consumer watchdog group.

Not surprisingly, the opposition British Labor Party has championed the cause of the health service. Party leader Neil Kinnock has led the attack in Parliament.

Prime Minister Margaret Thatcher's response has been to cite statistics showing that the health service is expanding and funding for it has increased 30 percent over inflation in the nearly 10 years she has been in office.

That's true, more money has been spent, but the British still spend less on health than every other major European country as a percentage of Gross National Product. The United States spends more than 11 percent of their GNP on health; France, 9 percent; West Germany, 8 percent; and Britain less than 6 percent.

As service in the National Health Service has deteriorated because of the funding squeeze, more and more of the British public have opted to use private doctors, at private hospitals, paid for by private insurance. Today, in what is clearly a trend, about one out of every 10 people now has private health insurance.

Although government officials won't admit it, they appear to favor more private spending so eventually a more mixed health care system will develop.

"There is certainly no doubt that the Conservative Party and Mrs. Thatcher think that people should pay extra for health care if they can afford it," says Health Council Director Harris. "The thing that worries us most is that you end up with two classes of medical care — a better class for those who can afford it and a worse class for those who can't." "We do not want a situation in this country where poor people get zero treatment or terrible treatment," says Dr. Marks of BMA.

But what appears to be happening is that the funding crisis in the N.H.S. is moving Britain toward a two-tier system of public and private health spending. That would represent a radical change from the universal health care system started 40 years ago. Its because of fears of such a radical change that politicians and those with a stake in the N.H.S. are fiercely oppposing the government's health funding policies. The only thing government officials will say is that they are conducting a major review of Britain's health service.

— BILL BUZENBERG

Past Coverage

■ **For-Profit Hospitals: Healthy Competition or Unhealthy Medicine?** takes a look at the for-profit hospital chains spawned by Medicare's and Medicaid's initial sky's-the-limit reimbursement policies. The growth of the for-profit hospital chains raised the same question posed by today's cost-cutting efforts: Does cost-consciousness conflict with the quality of care? By John A. Burns Jr., E.R.R., 1986 Vol. II, pp. 533-568.

■ **Health Care: Pressure for Change** was written in 1984, as the Reagan administration's reimbursement ceilings for Medicare were taking hold and as corporations were starting to monitor hospital spending aggressively. The report reflects the early optimism over the cost-saving abilities of health maintenance organizations as well as concerns over the impact of cost-containment on the poor. By Mary H. Cooper, E.R.R., 1984 Vol. II, pp. 569-588.

Continued from p. 40

Marmor, provincial administrators are highly motivated to put pressure on doctors to keep their expenditures down. Canadian citizens are not able to obtain private supplemental insurance to cover medical expenses beyond those covered by government reimbursement. This has discouraged Canadian doctors from charging more than the provincial government's fee schedule allows.

"What the Canadian model shows is that [national health insurance] is doable in a large, decentralized, ethnically varied, equally rich society as ours," says Marmor. But Marmor concedes such a shift for the United States would not be easy: "We have been through 15 years of propaganda about the virtues of market forces, competition and the hidden hand of restraint." At the same time, he says, "We've got cost-containment failure, growing access problems, confusion and distress about market forces and the autonomy of physicians."

There are trade-offs to adopting the Canadian system, and some experts doubt that Americans would find them acceptable. In any system where overall medical spending is capped and every citizen has free access to health care, hard choices must be made about how to distribute the most expensive care. For example, Canadian doctors are much less aggressive than American doctors when it comes to saving underweight premature babies with uncertain prospects. Marmor says that's "a matter of medical judgment" based on a rational weighing of the costs and benefits. But who is to have the authority to make that judgment?

Sociologist Starr argues that in this enormously rich country, Americans could set up an overall health budget without making severe sacrifices. "We have enough doctors and hospital beds in this country to treat everybody," he says. "We have the resources, [but] we can't

seem to find the method of organization and moral rules that will allow us to apportion it in a sensible way."

If Americans cannot agree on a rational method for allocating health care and cannot afford to pay the rising bill, they may be forced into the rationing of health care anyway. In the past two years, individual states have already had to make rationing choices. In Oregon, the state Legislature decided last July to stop funding costly heart, liver, bone marrow or pancreas transplants for Medicaid recipients in order to support regular prenatal care exams for about 1,500 pregnant women. The debate became highly emotional when a 7-year-old boy in need of a bone marrow transplant died of leukemia. Florida's Legislature refused to extend funding to subsidize costly AZT medication for AIDS patients when federal funding ran out this year on the grounds that other life-threatening illnesses were competing for the same funds.

What are the risks to the economy if Americans do not hold down medical costs? Many economists foresee bankrupt industrial firms unable to sustain the rising costs of health insurance, a growing tax burden as Medicare costs continue to skyrocket, and a nation of citizens obliged to spend a growing proportion of personal income on medical care. Yet opinion polls show that a majority of Americans oppose rationing as a solution.[15] Some economists believe this is because the system has anesthetized the average American against the true cost of health care. But it may also reflect the fact that the public is primarily interested in receiving the best health care available — not the most cost-effective.

NOTES

[1] American Council on Science and Health, *America's Health: A Century of Progress*, October 1988.

[2] William J. Baumol, *Price Controls for Medical Services and the Medical Needs of the Nation's Elderly*, March 11, 1988 (Report prepared for the American Medical Association), p. 7.

[3] For background information, see "What is Causing the Nurse Shortage," *E.R.R.*, 1988 Vol. I, pp. 157-168.

[4] The Massachusetts example is cited by Howard H. Hiatt, M.D., in *America's Health in the Balance: Choice or Chance?* (1987), p. 80.

[5] Paul Starr, *The Social Transformation of American Medicine* (1982), p. 302.

[6] *Ibid.*, p. 309.

[7] Baumol, *op. cit.*, pp. 4, 10.

[8] Blue Cross and Blue Shield Association, *The Impact of Medicare's Prospective Payment System and Private Sector Initiatives: Blue Cross and Blue Shield Experience, 1980-1986*, July 1988.

[9] Robert A. Berenson, "In a Doctor's Wallet," *The New Republic*, May 19, 1987, pp. 11-12.

[10] *Study of Incentive Arrangements Offered by HMOs and CMPs to Physicians*, (Report submitted to the Office of the Assistant Secretary for Planning and Evaluation, Department of Health and Human Services), May 18, 1988.

[11] Joseph A. Califano Jr., "The Health-Care Chaos," *The New York Times Magazine*, March 20, 1988, p. 56.

[12] Testimony before the House Energy and Commerce Subcommittee on Health and the Environment, Sept. 23, 1988.

[13] Testimony of Charles R. Buck Jr., General Electric's staff executive for health care programs, before the House Energy and Commerce Subcommittee on Health and Environment, Sept. 23, 1988.

[14] Janice Castro, "Critical Condition," *Time*, Feb. 1, 1988, p. 42.

[15] For example, 71 percent of those responding to a Jan. 25, 1988, Louis Harris poll opposed allowing insurers to set a financial limit on medical treatment that would save lives and 90 percent said everyone is entitled to health care "as good as a millionaire would get." But 75 percent of the respondents recognized that by the 1990s insurers would have to make tough choices about whether to cover new and expensive treatments.

Graphics: cover, S. Dmitri Lipczenko.

RECOMMENDED READING

BOOKS

Hiatt, Howard H., *America's Health in the Balance: Choice or Chance?* Harper & Row, 1987.

"We cannot avoid coming to grips with the reality that we shall never be able to provide everybody with everything that medical care could make possible," writes Hiatt, former dean of the Harvard School of Public Health. First he explains why we cannot afford to dispense the costly fruits of advanced medicine indiscriminately. Then he proposes adopting an American version of the British philosophy: providing "the most for the most, and not everything for a few." Two interesting chapters describe the pros and cons of the British and Canadian universal health insurance plans from an American point of view.

Paul Starr, *The Social Transformation of American Medicine*, Basic Books, 1982.

Starr, professor of sociology at Princeton University, traces the American medical profession's rise from its uncertain stature in the 18th century to the highest-paid professional occupation of modern times. American doctors' incomparable market power in pricing their medical services stems from their historical insistence that they sell their services primarily to individual patients rather than to organizations, Starr argues. "[O]rganizations, had they been more numerous, could have exercised greater discrimination in evaluating clinical performance and might have lobbied against cartel restrictions of physician supply," he writes.

ARTICLES

Faltermayer, Edmund, "Medical Care's Next Revolution," *Fortune*, October 10, 1988, pp. 126-133.

"When we're spending a half trillion a year on health care, we ought to know what works," *Fortune* quotes Dr. Paul M. Ellwood Jr. of Minneapolis as saying. The problem, according to Ellwood and others, is that doctors do not systematically weigh the costs and benefits of medical procedures, leaving insurance companies and patients to foot the bill. The article discusses entrepreneurial efforts to computerize such information for doctors and those who pay for medical care.

"The Managed Care Revolution," Special Issue, *Health Affairs*, summer 1988.

In this special issue on cost-containment efforts of the past five years, distinguished health policy experts, including Victor R. Fuchs and Alain C. Enthoven, take a look at what has been accomplished. Writes William B. Walsh in the opening publisher's letter, "[N]ever again will the medical profession return to the autonomy that once marked its relationship with society, nor will consumers be as insulated from the high cost of care." The issue contains articles on the growth of group health insurance, the uninsured and competition in the health market.

"The Reagan Revolution and Beyond," Special Issue, *Internist*, September 1988.

This magazine issued by the American Society of Internal Medicine asked health policy experts to comment on whether the Reagan administration made health care more competitive. The consensus is that the reality fell short of the rhetoric. Editor C. Burns Roehrig writes, "The competition that had been so touted by administration officials turned out to be a competition among institutions and contractors purely for *price*, and physicians and their patients were left to worry about whether or not the product was any good."

William L. Roper, "Perspectives on Physician Payment Reform," pp. 865-867, and William C. Hsiao, *et. al.*, "Special Article" pp. 835-841, and "Special Report," pp. 881-888, *New England Journal of Medicine*, September 29, 1988.

Hsiao, of the Harvard School of Public Health, presents his exhaustive study of reforming Medicare payments for physicians along a "relative value scale." The proposed reforms would, he says, remove the current "perverse" economic incentives for doctors to operate instead of talking to patients. In a separate commentary, Health Care Financing Administrator Roper says the proposal will not solve Medicare's basic cost problem: the incentives for doctors to provide too many services.

REPORTS AND STUDIES

Frank B. McArdle, ed., *The Changing Health Care Market*, Employee Benefit Research Institute (EBRI), 1987.

A collection of papers examining health insurance and health cost trends presented at a 1986 forum organized by EBRI, a non-profit research organization. A good statistical source on the effects of cost-containment efforts, government policies and the aging work force. Available from EBRI, 2121 K Street N.W., Suite 860, Washington, D.C. 20037-2121.

Physician Payment Review Commission, *Annual Report to Congress*, March 31, 1988.

This congressionally established commission reports on the reasons for rising physicians' bills to Medicare and proposes possible reforms. Available from PPRC, 2120 L Street N.W., Suite 510, Washington, D.C. 20037.

DO ANTITRUST LAWS LIMIT U.S. COMPETITIVENESS?

DO ANTITRUST LAWS LIMIT U.S. COMPETITIVENESS?

by Patrick G. Marshall

For a hundred years Congress has prohibited American businesses from creating monopolies, fixing prices or otherwise restraining trade. Now, critics say that antitrust laws must be amended or even revoked if U.S. businesses are to compete in world markets. Antitrust supporters, however, say such talk is only a ruse to disguise longstanding objections to antitrust restrictions. They say consumers continue to have far more to lose than to gain from any change.

The Sherman Antitrust Act is approaching its 100th birthday,* and America's antitrust laws are under attack. Antitrust laws obstruct rather than encourage competition, critics charge, and with the chronic U.S. trade deficits of the 1980s, the laws are a handicap American companies can ill afford.

"The time has come for us to realistically look at the antitrust laws and try to mold them to our favor and not to the interests of foreigners, [who] have no such restrictions," wrote then-Commerce Secretary C. William Verity Jr. in *The Wall Street Journal* last December.[1] In an unusual double-barreled blast at the statutes, Verity and Attorney General Dick Thornburgh in adjacent articles called for relaxation of antitrust laws to allow U.S. manufacturers to undertake joint production efforts without having to worry about lawsuits from competitors or consumers.

Verity's assessment of our trade competitors' antitrust laws is an exaggeration: Japan and the European

---

*The Sherman Antitrust Act was passed in 1890. See p. 52 for more details.

Community have antitrust legislation.* But it is generally true that the U.S. laws are more restrictive. Where the United States permits private antitrust suits, for example, Great Britain does not. In Japan, antitrust exemptions are routine, and, according to Clyde Prestowitz, a former U.S. trade negotiator, Japan's Ministry of Trade and Industry "has the power to suspend the antitrust laws and to declare cartels, either for the purpose of aiding industries in recession or of developing particular target industries." [2]

America's antitrust laws, say critics, prevent companies from undertaking a wide range of activities that could make them more competitive. Verity and Thornburgh argue, for example, that U.S. companies have refrained from undertaking joint-production ventures out of fear that they will be sued by competitors or consumers for restraining trade. Without being able to share the risk of investing in the development of new technologies by pursuing them jointly, they claim, U.S. companies are at a disadvantage compared with European and Japanese firms.

The industry most often singled out as needing special antitrust treatment is consumer electronics. Mark Rosenker, vice president of the Electronic Industries Association, says the reason is simple: Consumer electronics has been running a major annual trade imbalance to the tune of $20 billion.

Rosenker argues that the antitrust rules make it hard for American companies to compete against foreigners, particularly the Japanese. "We are in a global economy, and the rules have changed," he says. "We're not suggesting that antitrust needs to be shoved down the toilet. What we're suggesting is that there needs to be reform in that area so we can become more competitive in the global economy."

A good example, Rosenker says, is high-definition television (HDTV), a new generation of TV recorders and receivers that deliver twice the resolution of current sets.** "HDTV is the symbolic call sign for bringing competitiveness in the electronics industry, and competitiveness in industry per se, back to America," says Rosenker.

While the Japanese have already initiated HDTV broadcasts, U.S. researchers are still at the experimental stage. And there isn't much of a foundation on which to build an American HDTV industry. Though the United States pioneered television, there is now only one major U.S.-owned TV manufacturer, Zenith.

According to American Electronics Association (AEA) figures, HDTV will be a $20 billion-a-year industry within 10 years. But AEA Vice President Pat

Hubbard says that if the United States is to share in the HDTV bonanza, it will probably need relief from current antitrust laws. "If the goal is to build a U.S. industry, everyone recognizes that individual companies are not going to build that industry alone. They're not going to be able to compete with people who already have the market share unless they come in collectively as an entity."

At least some members of Congress seem to be listening. More than half a dozen bills have been introduced to offer a degree of protection from antitrust laws for joint ventures in U.S. manufacturing. Two of the bills are specifically directed at the development of a high-definition television industry. (*See p. 54.*)

But it's not only companies interested in HDTV that are likely to be lobbying Congress for antitrust relief. On June 21, IBM and six other companies announced the formation of a joint venture, U.S. Memories Inc., that will produce advanced versions of computer memory chips, called dynamic random access memory chips or DRAMs. Though U.S. companies invented DRAM chips, all but three American manufacturers — IBM, Micron Technology and Texas Instruments* — were driven out of the market in the early 1980s as a result of a price war with Japanese chipmakers. To get American manufacturers back in the DRAM market — a market considered vital both commercially and for national defense reasons — the joint venture may need some sort of antitrust waiver. "One of the first things U.S. Memories will look at in drawing up its business plan is the antitrust situation," says IBM spokesman Paul Bergevin.

Some analysts, however, are not so sure that handing out antitrust exemptions is the answer to America's competitiveness problems. "This has become a fad, to blame our competitiveness problems on antitrust policy," says Robert Litan, a senior fellow at the Brookings Institution. "I don't think that the evidence is there yet that exemptions are going to be the elixir that everyone is looking for."

Michigan State University economist Walter Adams adds that the only thing new about the current call for antitrust exemptions is its rationale. "The argument is a phony," he says. "The history of mergers both nationally and internationally has demonstrated that mere size is not the answer to international competitiveness." Rather than a response to foreign competition, Adams says, the current calls for antitrust exemptions are really just another step in the ongoing effort of big business to achieve a "gradual erosion in the thrust of antitrust."

Indeed, long before foreign competition became an issue, critics of antitrust laws were challenging the premise that the laws enhance competition and efficiency. But the worsening of America's balance of trade has given a new twist to the debate, with critics

---

*To be sure, there are differences in the countries' laws. Where U.S. laws aim to prevent monopolies through mergers, for example, the European Community has no effective merger policy and relies on regulating monopolies or near-monopolies when they occur. For more details on European antitrust laws see Tim Frazer, *Monopoly, Competition and the Law: The Regulation of Business in Britain, Europe and America* (1988).

**See "A High-tech, High Stakes HDTV Gamble," *Editorial Research Reports*, 1989 Vol. I, pp. 89-104.

*Of the three, only IBM is currently a participant in U.S. Memories.

Reagan's Antitrust Record

During the Reagan administration, there was a significant increase in the number of criminal cases filed by the Justice Department's Antitrust Division. But the department initiated far fewer investigations into possible violations of Sherman Act prohibitions on restraints of trade or attempts to monopolize.

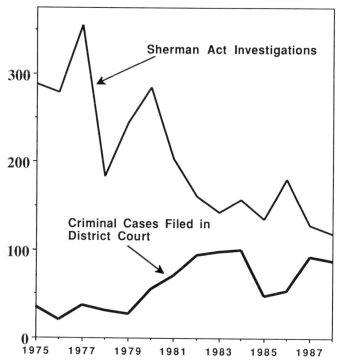

Source: Department of Justice, Antitrust Divison.

painting the laws as woefully out of date. "The world economy has changed, trade patterns have changed, but the antitrust laws have not," then-Commerce Secretary Malcolm Baldrige wrote in a 1985 *Wall Street Journal* article calling for antitrust reform.[3]

In truth, however, antitrust laws *have* changed significantly in recent years, and antitrust *policy* has changed even more. Whether even greater changes are needed for the United States to survive in the global marketplace is the central issue behind the current batch of legislation, and the evidence is far from conclusive.

The Reagan administration's antitrust enforcement record

"Traditional antitrust policy has collapsed like a house of cards," University of Hartford economist Dominick T. Armentano wrote in 1986. "In just 10 years — an extremely short time in matters of such importance — the antitrust regulatory authorities have gone from

an enthusiastic enforcement of traditional antitrust policy in the mid-1970s to a substantial rejection of much of the conventional approach in the mid-1980s."[4]

Generally, both critics and supporters of antitrust policies agree with that assessment. About the only party to claim otherwise is the Justice Department itself. "[The] facts show that the Reagan administration's overall enforcement record has been as vigorous as any in the past," claimed the head of the department's antitrust division, Charles F. Rule, in an October 1988 speech. "And in the area of criminal enforcement — the heart and soul of effective enforcement — no other administration was able to put together a record that even comes close to ours."[5]

Rule's claim of unsurpassed criminal enforcement by the Reagan administration does have some credibility. During the 1970s, the department filed only 20-40 criminal cases per year — mostly for price fixing and bid rigging. Those figures increased dramatically in the early years of the Reagan administration; 94 criminal cases were filed in 1982, 98 cases in 1983, and 100 cases in 1984. The number dropped somewhat in 1985 and 1986, but rose to 92 in 1987. (*See graph at left.*) Last year the department filed 87 criminal cases.

But what this means is another matter. "If you look at antitrust enforcement from January 1981 to June 1989, the only antitrust action has occurred against petty conspirators in the road-paving industry, local bottling companies, conspiracies among small businessmen," says Walter Adams. "I make no brief for these people, but in terms of law enforcement, what the antitrust division has done is to hunt rabbits while lusty elephants have been roaming."

University of Massachusetts economist William G. Shepard agrees: "Antitrust under Reagan, rather than going too far, has disintegrated into a hunting down of a series of petty offenders while coddling the powerful."[6]

The "heart and soul" of antitrust policy, say these economists, is control over mergers and acquisitions, because they create the opportunity for price-fixing and other hard-to-detect antitrust violations. The logic is simple: Mergers and acquisitions tend to reduce the total number of competitors in a specific market. In the extreme case of monopoly, where one company captures the entire market, that company has the power to raise prices at will. When the market is dominated by a handful of competitors, things get more complicated, but there is more temptation for those companies to make an agreement among themselves to raise prices or divide up markets. "Numbers do make a difference," write Walter Adams and James Brock, an economist at Miami University of Ohio. "When numbers are large, conspiracies are difficult to negotiate, difficult to conceal, and difficult to enforce."[7]

In major areas of antitrust enforcement, the Reagan administration made a major shift in policy. Justice Department investigations of violations of Sherman Act prohibitions on restraints of trade and attempts to monopolize, for example, were roughly half the number of similar investigations in the 1970s. Under President Nixon, the Justice Department initiated 434 investigations of Sherman Act violations in 1971; the Reagan administration initiated only slightly more than that during its last *three years*. On the civil side, the Justice Department during the 1970s filed between 27 and 72 cases annually in district courts. Since 1982, the department has filed only between six and 18 cases annually.

Despite sharply rising numbers of mergers over the past 10 years, Justice Department statistics show the number of merger investigations generally holding steady and in some years actually falling. In 1979, the first full year during which merger notifications to Justice were required under the 1976 Hart-Scott-Rodino Antitrust Improvement Act, 859 notifications were made and the department initiated 101 investigations. By 1988, the number of notifications had risen to 2,747, but the number of investigations had dropped to 56. (*See graph, p. 50.*) "They just haven't enforced the law, and they're proud of it," says Walter Adams.

There is another side to the debate, of course. Just as mergers may present the danger of companies getting too much market power, they may also provide economies from which both the companies and consumers may benefit. One large automaker, for example, can realize economies of scale that allow it to produce cars more cheaply than 15 small companies. As long as there are enough competitors left in the market to spur innovation and prevent monopoly pricing, a merger of those 15 automakers into one large company would lead to greater profits for shareholders and cheaper cars for consumers at the same time.

"No one should doubt . . . that whenever analysis indicates that a merger is, in fact, anti-competitive, we will try to stop it," Assistant Attorney General Rule assured the American Bar Association in a 1987 speech. But he also made it clear that the administration was looking at mergers with a different eye — giving new weight to the economic efficiencies to be gained and, by implication, less to the dangers of market concentration. "Today's merger analysis is more sensitive to the economic benefits of mergers and to the various factors that determine whether a merger truly threatens competition," Rule said.[8]

"When we came in, the first step was to define what kinds of mergers we should be concerned about," explains Jeffrey Zuckerman, who joined the Justice Department's antitrust division in 1981 and is now director of the Bureau of Competition at the Federal Trade Commission. "We said the correct question is whether as a result of a certain transaction prices will go up. If they will, then it should be challenged. If that's not likely to happen, then the merger should not be challenged. . . . [E]ven our biggest critics tend not to say that's a bad question to ask."

As for those few recalcitrants who believe the Justice Department *has* been asking the wrong questions, Zuckerman offers a challenge: "Can anyone point to a single merger that we didn't challenge in the last eight years — and we're talking now well over 15,000 transactions — can anybody point to one that we didn't challenge and as a result of the transaction prices went up?"

"I've heard that argument now a dozen times," replies Robert Pitofsky, dean of Georgetown University Law School and an FTC commissioner under President Carter. "I think that's a misleading argument. No single merger is likely to have an effect on price. What will have an effect on price is a process in which more and more mergers lead to more and more concentration. So to say nobody has pointed to a merger where after the merger prices went up is a mischaracterization of the issue."

In fact, according to FTC figures, the market concentration (measured in terms of assets) of the 100 biggest manufacturing companies increased 1.8 percent in the five years before President Reagan took office to 46.8 percent of total manufacturing assets. During Reagan's first five years it rose 2.6 percentage points, to 49.4 percent of total assets.

While the Reagan administration was changing the rules of enforcement, it also was repeatedly proposing antitrust reform legislation. The purpose of the legislation, according to two attorneys on the staff of the Senate Judiciary Committee's Subcommittee on Antitrust, Monopolies and Business Rights, was "to increase the difficulty of proving an antitrust violation or to weaken the remedy available to someone who does."[9]

During both the 99th and 100th Congresses, the administration pushed for a bill that would have changed the Clayton Act's prohibition of mergers whose effect "may be substantially to lessen competition" to a much looser standard: To stop a merger, there would have to be a "significant probability" that it would increase the ability of the new firm to raise prices above competitive levels for "a significant period of time."

Another bill introduced in both the 99th and 100th Congresses — the Antitrust Remedies Improvement Act — would have reduced the current antitrust remedy in private civil suits of automatic triple damages to actual damages, along with interest.

The Reagan administration also called for a bill amending the current Clayton Act ban on directors serving on boards of competing companies. It would also have raised the threshold at which the federal government was interested in a company's activities from $1 million to $10 million. Such a bill passed the Senate in 1987, but died in the House. The Promoting Competition in Distressed Industries Act, introduced in the 99th Congress, would have allowed the president to give antitrust relief to designated "distressed" industries. But according to the two attorneys from the Senate antitrust subcommittee, however,

Merger Investigations

Under legislation passed in 1976, the Justice Department must be notified of proposed mergers and acquisitions that would exceed certain sizes or dollar amounts. As the graph below indicates, the number of premerger notifications grew dramatically from 1978 to 1988, but the number of merger investigations initiated by the department held fairly steady during this period and in some years actually declined.

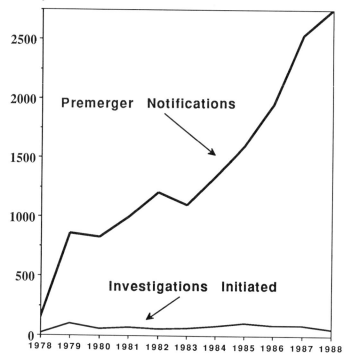

Source: Department of Justice, Antitrust Division.

"A survey of 200 industrial organization economists indicated overwhelming agreement that [the legislation] would not be in the country's best interests." [10] And the FTC found that "Review of the empirical evidence and historical record does not reveal that mergers are efficient in declining industries. . . . But even more importantly, current antitrust policy will not prohibit mergers in declining (or other) industries that are likely to lead to efficiency gains." [11]

Though none of the above legislation made it through Congress, two important pieces of antitrust law did gain approval. The Export Trading Company Act of 1982 amended the Sherman Act to exclude trade or commerce with foreign nations. Applicants, primarily export trading companies, can apply for certification from the Commerce Department. Certification provides protection from criminal antitrust actions. The companies are still exposed to civil actions, but not to treble damages; the most a plaintiff could win would be actual damages and attorneys' fees. According to the Commerce Department, 109 companies have received such certification.

Of even greater importance was the National Cooperative Research Act passed by Congress in 1984. That act allows companies to engage in joint research

and development projects without facing the potential for treble damages from civil antitrust suits. All a company need do is notify the Justice Department and the FTC that it is entering into a joint project, and the potential liability is reduced to actual damages plus attorneys' fees. As of June 15, 1989, 134 such ventures had filed with the government.

All in all, the record of the Reagan administration on antitrust is one of drastic curtailment of enforcement activities. Despite the clear loosening of antitrust restrictions, however, there has been no apparent improvement in the ability of U.S. companies to compete with foreign companies. Indeed, during the Reagan years U.S. trade deficits mushroomed from less than $50 billion in 1981 to $174 billion in 1987.

The 'efficiency paradox' of U.S. antitrust laws

Behind the debate over the antitrust policies of the Reagan administration — as well as behind the more immediate question of whether exemptions should be given to U.S. electronics companies — is a more general disagreement over whether antitrust laws have any redeeming values at all in today's markets.

Ever since the Sherman Antitrust Act was adopted in 1890 (*see story, p. 52*), debate has raged over whether such laws inhibit or encourage competition, whether they benefit or harm the consumer. Much of the disagreement stems from what can be called the "efficiency paradox": antitrust policies may lead to lower prices by prohibiting price fixing and other restraints of trade, but they may simultaneously lead to higher prices by limiting industry's ability to create economies of scale.

The Clayton Act, for example, prohibits mergers or acquisitions where the effect "may be to substantially lessen competition." The "may be" is a crucial phrase in the law. Under the law, the executive branch — and the courts, in the event of legal action — must somehow decide ahead of time what the results of a merger would be, a guessing game that leaves lots of room for argument.

In addition, those words clearly prevent mergers *even if* the mergers provide efficiencies that would benefit consumers. In fact, the mergers that seem to offer the greatest opportunity for increased efficiencies also tend to present the greatest risk of reducing competition by giving the new firms dominance of the market.

Former Appeals Court Judge Robert H. Bork, a Reagan nominee for the Supreme Court, illustrates the problem nicely with the case of Procter & Gamble Co. In 1967, Bork explains in his book, *The Antitrust Paradox*, the Supreme Court declared Procter & Gamble's acquisition of Clorox illegal because Clorox already had 49 percent of the liquid bleach market and Procter & Gamble's ownership could — by giving Clorox access to Procter & Gamble's advertising budget, media discounts and so forth — raise Clorox's market share and prevent new competition. "The real issue is seen to be one of alternatives," Bork wrote. "Should Clorox be allowed to become more efficient, even though that enables it to grow larger? Or is it preferable that the company be denied efficiencies, in order to limit its market share?" [12] Without directly answering the question, Bork characterizes the court's decision to prevent the merger as distinctly "pro-small business," rather than in the interests of efficiency — and, ultimately, perhaps, the consumer.

Weighing the benefits of efficiency against the risks of market dominance is an art, not a science. "Mergers and acquisitions are dangerous, but nobody knows exactly at what point," says Jonathan Cuneo, counsel for the Committee to Support the Antitrust Laws, a Washington-based association of law firms interested in promoting antitrust laws. "The state of economics isn't advanced enough so that you can definitively say in what circumstances what restraints are anti-competitive and what ones aren't." If four firms share 85 percent of a market, will they collude on prices? If one company with 45 percent of the breakfast cereal market merges with a company with 25 percent of the market, is it too much?

Even defining the relevant market for some products can be an exercise in frustration that at times borders on the absurd. According to antitrust attorney Frederick M. Rowe, "Court decisions [have] based illegality on high shares in markets of championship as distinct from other boxing matches, of gospel as distinct from pop music, of collection as distinct from burial of nuclear wastes, and of bubblegum baseball cards as distinct from football cards or other candy premiums. . . . Conversely, antitrust rulings [have] vindicated defendants by refusing to isolate a separate market for chrysanthemums from carnations, for Cadillacs from other cars, and for pipeless from other swimming-pool circulation systems. Always the market [has] seemed prone to manipulation, for how to tell what was *the* relevant market from what was not in any actual case?" [13]

Once the market is defined, the balancing act begins. "If the efficiency gain is trivial, but the change in market concentration is great, then the merger should be stopped," says Swarthmore College economist F. M. Scherer. "If, on the other hand, the market concentration effect is relatively minor but the efficiency gain is great, then the merger should be allowed to go forward." But what should be done when both the effect on the market and the efficiency gain is great? "That's a tough case," Scherer concedes.

To some economists and legal scholars the idea that some types of competition, and even some clear benefits to the consumer, should be forgone in the interest of preventing market concentration is anathema. "The process of attempting to eliminate rivals is inherently competitive," wrote economist Dominick Armentano. He argues that the market itself can be trusted to encourage competition and that antitrust laws are not needed. (*See story, p. 57.*) "Large firms bent on eliminating competitors would presumably seek to reduce final prices, increase their own efficiency and productivity and offer additional services to potential buyers, all in order to secure business from rivals. But such competitive activity is delightful from a consumer perspective and ought not to be discouraged in any way." [14]

Which is to say that the consumer might benefit from a firm's attempt to establish a monopoly. But what happens when the competitors are all gone? Can't the victor then set whatever prices he wishes? "As long as the competitive process is working — regardless of how many firms there are — as long as there are no legal restrictions on entry into the market, then I really don't think we have to worry about consumer welfare," Armentano said in an interview. "Even if there's only one firm in the market, it's still a rivalrous process as long as there's opportunity for entry."

The problem with this reasoning, most economists believe, is that there are always barriers to entry. Time is the most obvious one. If a railroad has a monopoly on freight between Chicago and San Francisco, and doubles or even triples its rates, it might attract competitors. But it would take those new competitors months or even years to build another railroad. And a potential competitor is likely to be deterred by the realization that, after investing millions of dollars in building a new line, all that would be accomplished is that the railroad that had the monopoly would be forced, after months of raking in inflated profits, to cut prices back to a realistic level. The former monopolist might even devote some of the earlier profits to conducting a price war to drive the new competition out of business.

Of course, the antitrust laws cannot, and do not attempt to, prevent companies from gaining dominance in a market solely by outperforming the competition. But the antitrust laws try to ensure that the *only* way for a firm to capture market dominance is through performance, not through purchasing the competition or driving other firms out of business by, say, selling its product at a loss until the competition folds. The consumer might benefit in the short run from such cutthroat competition, but once market dominance is gained, the willingness of the victorious company to maintain low prices is dubious.

There is no doubt that the laws governing mergers and acquisitions can and do — in the name of preserving competition — prohibit some mergers that could greatly increase the efficiency of the companies involved. But according to economist Scherer, all the talk about efficiencies resulting from mergers is overblown. "What the evidence shows is that it's fairly

Continued on page 54

The History of Antitrust Legislation . . .

A hundred years ago, President Grover Cleveland complained in his State of the Union Message about the emergence of "trusts, combinations and monopolies" that rake in immense profits "while the citizen is struggling far in the rear or is trampled to death beneath an iron heel." Corporations, "which should be carefully restrained creatures of the law and the servants of the people, are fast becoming the people's masters," he said.

Cleveland wasn't the only one concerned about the growing power of large corporations. As early as 1872, the Grangers — an activist farmers' association — issued the first real call for anti-monopoly laws, specifically demanding regulation of the railroads.

Ten years later, in 1882, Standard Oil adopted the idea of a trust — a formal combination of companies whose stockholders exchanged their shares, and thus their voting rights, in return for trust certificates. "The effectiveness of this method for making combinations permanently cohesive and easily manageable recommended it to others," writes political scientist William Letwin. The Cotton Oil Trust formed in 1884 and the Linseed Oil Trust in 1885. "Trust-building did not begin in earnest until 1887, but then it took hold quickly," Letwin continues. "That year saw the formation of the Sugar and Whiskey Trusts, which until the end of the century contended for unpopularity only with Standard Oil." †

As companies, trusts and cartels grew, so did the public's distrust of them. Though revisionist historians have challenged some of the charges laid against the early trusts, they were at the time widely despised for a variety of abuses, including setting up dummy companies to drive out competitors by temporarily selling at a loss and then raising the prices to consumers. Trusts also figured in a series of bribery scandals involving state and federal legislators and officials.

"Between 1888 and 1890, there were few who doubted that the public hated the trusts fervently," Letwin writes. "Those who fanned the prejudice and those who hoped to smother it agreed that the fire was already blazing." †† By 1888, both the Republican Party and the Democratic Party had come out in favor of action to break up monopolies and trusts.

In 1890, the pressure finally resulted in legislation: the **Sherman Antitrust Act**. The legislation is, at least on the surface, blunt and to the point: "Every contract, combination in the form of trust or otherwise, or conspiracy in restraint of trade or commerce among the several states or with foreign nations is hereby declared to be illegal," reads the first section.

Under the second section, "Every person who shall monopolize, or attempt to monopolize, or combine or conspire with any other person or persons to monopolize any part of the trade or commerce among the several states or with foreign nations" would be in violation of the law. And the act doesn't just rely on government enforcement: It stipulates that individuals can sue and, if successful, receive treble damages plus attorneys' fees.

The language of the Sherman Act, though bold, was also very vague. Certainly Congress did not mean to outlaw *any* contract that restrained trade, since all contracts, in that they commit parties to specified trade relations, do so. As economists Roger D. Blair and David L. Kasermann note, "Due to the lack of specificity, the Sherman Act was little more than a legislative command that the judiciary develop the law of antitrust. Since the statute did not provide much guidance, the courts would have to be guided by the apparent legislative intent of Congress." ‡

Nailing down the intent of Congress has occupied years of jurists' and academicians' time without producing undisputed answers. In examining the *Congressional Record* of debates leading up to the act, Robert H. Bork, in his influential book, *The Antitrust Paradox*, argues that the legislative intent of the Sherman Act was clearly to promote consumer welfare through "allocative efficiency," a conclusion that would indicate that any monopoly attained through efficiency, rather than an attempt to monopolize, should be allowed.

But Robert Lande, an attorney with the Federal Trade Commission, has argued that Congress had a broader purpose: "The antitrust laws were passed primarily to further what may be called a distributive goal, the goal of preventing unfair acquisitions of consumers' wealth by firms with market power." ‡‡

If Lande is right, Congress meant to prevent a company from obtaining too much market power, whether it was gained through efficiency or not.

In 1914, Congress passed two major pieces of antitrust legislation: the **Clayton Antitrust Act** and the **Federal Trade Commission Act**. The latter act established the FTC as a watchdog agency that would, along with the Justice Department, monitor business conduct and mergers. Where the Justice Department's mandate includes both civil and criminal actions, the FTC is limited to civil remedies.

The Clayton Act was a product of Congress' and President Wilson's dissatisfaction with the vagueness of the Sherman Act. Under the Clayton Act, specific types of business behavior are proscribed. The act's second section makes it unlawful for any person to "discriminate in price between different purchasers of commodities . . . where the effect of such discrimination may be to substantially lessen competition or tend to create a monopoly in any line of commerce."

... *From Cleveland to Reagan*

Section 7 of the Clayton Act prevents corporations from acquiring, "directly or indirectly, the whole or any part of the stock or other share capital of another corporation . . . where the effect of such acquisition may be to substantially lessen competition between the corporation whose stock is so acquired and the corporation making the acquisition . . . or tend to create a monopoly of any line of commerce."

Though the Clayton Act aimed at specificity, it fell short of its goal because of the inclusion of several qualifying words. "The critical words — 'may be,' 'substantially,' 'tend,' and 'monopoly' — [are] about as general as those that set the tone of the Sherman Act. . .," Letwin writes. As a result, "the newly extended body of antitrust law could not do much — indeed, has not done much — to help judges interpret the law uniformly or to help businessmen understand its provisions exactly."‡‡†

The **Robinson-Patman Act**, passed by Congress in 1936, is perhaps the most unpopular of the antitrust laws, finding few supporters even among antitrust proponents. The act amends Section 2 of the Clayton Act to make it illegal for any company to provide "any discount, rebate, allowance, or advertising service charge" to any purchaser unless it is offered to *all* purchasers of goods "of like grade, quality and quantity."

Behind the dry language of the law is a case of hard-sell lobbying. In the early 1930s, chain retail stores were grabbing increasing chunks of various markets, especially in groceries. This upset not only small retailers but also grocery wholesalers, who were being cut out of the market by direct discount deals between producers and chain stores. The wholesalers decided to fight back. Not only did they have enough influence to push the Robinson-Patman Act through Congress, but the legislation itself was drafted by H. B. Teegarden, counsel for the U.S. Wholesale Grocers Association.

While Robinson-Patman may have been in the wholesale grocers' interests, it is not clear that it was in consumers' interests. "[V]irtually everyone in the economics profession who has given thought to the issue would probably put the spotlight on the Robinson-Patman Act as being one part of the overall antitrust arsenal that's been especially pernicious from the consumer standpoint because it has done so much to hinder legitimate price competition," says Ken Elzinga, professor of economics at the University of Virginia.

The next major piece of antitrust legislation came in 1950. The **Celler-Kefauver Act** was aimed at tightening up the laws on mergers. Where the Clayton Act had prohibited mergers that would have anticompetitive effects, as some companies soon discovered, there was nothing to stop them from acquiring the *assets* of companies that the Clayton Act might have prevented them from merging with.

As Frederick Rowe writes, "Closing the 'loophole' that had exempted asset acquisitions, the [Celler-Kefauver Act] implicated all mergers — horizontal, vertical or conglomerate — that threatened to lessen competition 'substantially' within a 'line of commerce' in any 'section of the country.' Aiming at 'large' mergers, the act's framers disclaimed concern with 'local' or 'inconsequential acquisitions' among 'small companies' having 'little economic significance' and unable to affect competition to a 'substantial degree.' " ‡‡††

Mergers were also the focus of the **Hart-Scott-Rodino Antitrust Improvement Act** of 1976. Though the federal government had, since the Clayton Act, the power to stop anti-competitive mergers, it couldn't break up a merger once it had occurred. And with the ever-rising numbers of mergers, undesirable mergers could take place without the government even knowing about it.

The Hart-Scott-Rodino act requires that the Justice Department and the FTC be notified of proposed mergers or acquisitions that would exceed certain size-of-party and/or size-of-sale thresholds. Further, companies involved in a merger must wait 15 days, if a cash offer, or 30 days, if any other kind of offer, in order to give the government time to consider whether to take action against the merger. The act also added sections to the Clayton Act allowing states to file suits on behalf of citizens. The incentive for the state is that the penalties can be distributed to victimized citizens or they can be kept by the state and added to general revenues.

The most recent antitrust legislation — the **Export Trading Company Act** of 1982 and the **National Cooperative Research Act** of 1984 — has been directed at providing exemptions to the antitrust laws, rather than refining the laws themselves. The Export Trading Company Act provides protection for trading companies — after they receive certification from the Commerce Department — from criminal antitrust actions, and reduces their liability in private suits from treble damages to actual damages. The National Cooperative Research Act provides the same protections as the Export Trading Company Act for companies engaged in joint research and development projects.

† *William Letwin,* Law and Economic Policy in America: The Evolution of the Sherman Antitrust Act *(1954), p. 69.*

†† *Ibid, p. 55.*

‡ *Roger D. Blair and David L. Kaserman,* Antitrust Economics *(1985), p. 53.*

‡‡ *Robert H. Lande, "Wealth Transfers as the Original and Primary Concern of Antitrust: The Efficiency Interpretation Challenged,"* Hastings Law Journal, *September 1982, p. 69.*

‡‡ † *Letwin, op. cit., p. 276.*

‡‡ †† *Frederick M. Rowe, "The Decline of Antitrust and the Delusions of Models: The Faustian Pact of Law and Economics,"* Georgetown Law Journal, *Vol. 72, 1984, p. 1523.*

Continued from page 51

unusual that mergers yield substantial efficiencies," he says. "Indeed, the average case seems to be one in which there's either zero efficiency gain or perhaps a small efficiency loss as small, scrappy, fighting-weight-type companies get absorbed into larger corporate bureaucracies and lose their fighting edge." Unless the efficiency gain can be clearly demonstrated, Scherer says "the benefit of the doubt should be on the side of preventing the merger."

It is perhaps worth noting that Japan, for all its reputation of succeeding through huge interlocked companies, increased rather than decreased the number of Japanese automakers as it thrashed America's big-three automakers. "In 1961 MITI [the Ministry of Trade and Industry] announced plans to consolidate Japanese automakers into just three large concerns, to limit each of these firms to a single segment of the market, and to bar newcomers from the field," write Walter Adams and James Brock. "But in the face of intense industry opposition, MITI abandoned its consolidation plan. By 1965, Japan had eight highly competitive car companies, and by 1984, the number had grown to nine. Japanese automakers had prevailed against the world — and against their own government's faith in bigness-by-consolidation." [15]

It is difficult to generalize about whether mergers are "good" or "bad"; it depends on the particulars of each case. But it is clear that there are always enough factors involved, and enough uncertainty in measuring them, that there will almost always be room for argument over each individual merger decision.

Should an exception be made for HDTV?

Despite the demonstrated risks of allowing companies to have too much market power, even strong supporters of the antitrust laws have recognized that under certain circumstances antitrust exemptions are called for — generally, for industries in which economies of scale can be realized only by very large companies operating under essentially monopoly conditions. In the past, for example, exemptions have been given for public utilities, telecommunications, insurance and transportation industries.*

As a rule, such protection from antitrust constraints has been given only in exchange for close regulation by the government, including the regulation of prices or profit margins. That's something the electronics industry is reluctant to accept. "I don't know if [our members] want to get into governing profit margins," says Rosenker of the Electronic Industries

---

*Two exceptions to the "economics-of-scale" rule are the exemptions granted to major-league baseball and labor unions.

Association. "I don't think we want to see that. If people make money, that's good. If they lose money, that's bad."

In offering protection from antitrust laws without imposing a regulatory structure, therefore, the various pieces of proposed legislation now before Congress break an important precedent. But then, as Jonathan Cuneo points out, the suggested legislation is not aimed at protecting consumers or ensuring competition in the marketplace. "These bills are Produce America legislation," he says.

The various bills differ in their particulars. One (HR 2264), sponsored by Rep. Hamilton Fish Jr., R-N.Y., would amend the 1984 National Cooperative Research Act to include production joint ventures along with research and development joint ventures. If passed, a joint venture that files a report with the Justice Department and the Federal Trade Commission listing the companies involved and the purpose of the venture would only be liable for damages and attorneys' fees, instead of the usual treble damages, in the event of a successful antitrust suit. A similar bill, S 1006, was introduced by Sens. Patrick J. Leahy, D-Vt., and Strom Thurmond, R-S.C., last May. Rep. Don Edwards, D-Calif., would extend the Cooperative Research Act to include not only production, but marketing and distribution as well in his bill (HR 1025).

Perhaps the most ambitious of the proposed antitrust bills is HR 1024, introduced by Reps. Rick Boucher, D-Va., and Tom Campbell, R-Calif. Instead of simply allowing companies to file notification of joint ventures, the Boucher-Campbell bill would require them to go through an application process with the Justice Department, the Commerce Department and the Federal Trade Commission. If those agencies judge that the proposed venture "will not possess substantial market power in any relevant market," a certificate would be issued that would, for 17 years or until the certificate is withdrawn, protect companies from all civil and criminal antitrust suits. Unlike the bills amending the Cooperative Research Act, the Boucher-Campbell bill directs the federal agencies to determine that the venture would likely produce "pro-competitive benefits and efficiencies" and that "the innovation sought by the arrangement is of such a character or magnitude that the arrangement will help achieve the economies of scale and scope necessary to mount a successful research and commercialization effort." The government could revoke a certificate if it found the arrangement was harming competition.

In addition to these more general measures, there are two proposed bills that deal specifically with HDTV. Sen. John Kerry, D-Mass., introduced a bill (S 952) that would amend the Cooperative Research Act to allow production joint ventures of HDTV, though not of other products. A bill (HR 1267) introduced by Reps. Don Ritter, R-Pa., and Mel Levine, D-Calif., would, like S 952, extend the Cooperative Research Act to cover HDTV ventures, but would also provide tax breaks and more than $4 million of government funds over the next four years to an HDTV consortium.

The argument for antitrust relief for HDTV is not based on economies of scale, but on the high cost of getting into the business. It is perhaps easier to make a case for such treatment for an HDTV consortium than for other manufacturing ventures, for it would be unique in certain respects. For starters, it is an industry in which the United States has almost no capacity, because Zenith is the only U.S.-owned television-maker remaining. "The cost to set up a manufacturing line is exorbitant," says Pat Hubbard of the American Electronics Association. "No one company is going to have the wherewithal. There's almost no way to become a significant player in HDTV without a collection of energies: money, resources, people."

HDTV is also unique in that there is no existing market, so a joint venture cannot be judged according to how it would affect competition and, therefore, neither the companies nor the government could be certain in advance whether an HDTV consortium might violate antitrust law. "Properly applied, the antitrust laws would not prohibit pro-competitive joint ventures of any kind, whether research, marketing, production, selling, anything," notes Jeffrey Zuckerman of the FTC. On the other hand, he adds, "some people in the business community, being afraid of some applications of the antitrust laws either by the enforcement authorities, or by private enforcement through the courts, say they've been deterred from entering into pro-competitive joint ventures. If that's true, then there's a problem."

The proposed legislation, however, does more than simply clarify what would be considered a legitimate joint venture. The bills amending the Cooperative Research Act would, in addition to clarifying the issue, greatly reduce the damages plaintiffs could collect, which would also make a potential plaintiff less inclined to invest the time and money in a court case in the first place. And the Boucher-Campbell bill goes even further in removing the power to enforce antitrust laws from private citizens. As Campbell notes, private parties could still sue to have a certificate revoked if they felt they were being damaged by anti-competitive actions, but they could only collect for damages incurred after the date of revocation. In short, private parties might have the right to intervene, but the incentive to intervene would be all but removed.

Critics of the legislation also are concerned that there are no explicit guarantees that the exemptions will be lifted if Congress or the president impose import restrictions. Import controls "should be an absolute minimum in this whole thing," says Jonathan Cuneo. "If you're going to do this, then at the same time you've got to legislate that there would be no import controls, so that the joint ventures don't end up with a continental market to themselves and really exploit consumers."

In the case of HR 1024, Campbell says there's nothing to worry about. "If tariff barriers go up, the market then changes" and that would trigger a review of whether the joint venture reduced competition in the market. "If the barriers or quotas, or voluntary restraints go into force, then it is no longer true that the world is the market. Then you do indeed have an argument that America is the market." If the joint venture controlled the American market, its certificate would be revoked and it would be exposed to antitrust remedies, Campbell says.

> *An HDTV consortium "could get [antitrust] exemptions up the kazoo, but if the government doesn't come in as a partner, nobody's going to get it off the ground," says Pat Hubbard of the American Electronics Association.*

Robert Litan of the Brookings Institution doubts whether Campbell's certificate review would work as advertised. "It's going to be very hard to get these things removed even in the event we get protection, and that's precisely the time we should worry about it," Litan says. "The arguments are going to be, 'We've got to do whatever we can to stay alive to help our domestic competitors. To take away our antitrust protection at the time we're trying to kill the Japanese would be ludicrous.' That argument would probably prevail."

Many analysts are concerned about the inclusion of marketing and distribution as protected activities in the Edwards and Boucher-Campbell bills. That's because if companies were allowed to produce a product jointly, but forced to market and distribute it on their own, there would still be room for price competition. But with joint marketing and distribution, there would be no competition at all among consortium members. As Litan puts it, allowing production joint ventures "goes a long way to gutting antitrust law as it is." Including marketing "would gut everything."

Pitofsky agrees. "The joker in the deck is whether you intend it to apply to production joint ventures or whether you intend to include marketing joint ventures," he says. "If it's only the former, most people would say that legislative review is a good idea. The law on production joint ventures is a little obscure, so legislative clarification won't hurt. But if you go beyond research and production to marketing, now you've done something quite radical in terms of antitrust enforcement. And I think there's just no call for that."

Even if HDTV were judged worthy of receiving antitrust exemptions (and government subsidies, as at least one bill proposes), critics charge that the proposed legislation doesn't demand enough in return for such exemption by way of protection for consumers. "I just hope that Congress doesn't get caught up in a maze of blue smoke and mirrors of soft premises and say, 'We've got a problem so let's just throw an antitrust exemption at it,'" says Cuneo. Under the circumstances, he argues "the proponents should have to bear the proof that the antitrust laws are a real impediment and that the legislation is as narrowly tailored as possible to meet the legitimate concerns."

In fact, though the electronics groups are in favor of antitrust exemptions, both the Electronic Industries Association and the American Electronics Association concede that antitrust isn't the biggest problem for HDTV. According to Mark Rosenker, at the top of EIA's list is reducing the cost of capital through lower interest rates. Pat Hubbard of the American Electronics Association says cheap capital and government assistance are what HDTV needs most. An HDTV consortium "could get exemptions up the kazoo, but if government doesn't come in as a partner, nobody's going to get it off the ground," she says. Pointing out that current capital costs are about four times capital costs in Japan, Hubbard says that, if forced to choose, she would rather have capital costs reduced to Japan's level than have antitrust exemptions for U.S. joint-production ventures.

And there are quite a few people who doubt whether HDTV is worth the trouble. "I personally have real qualms as to whether HDTV is the right vehicle for re-emerging into consumer electronics production," says Michael Borrus, deputy director of the Berkeley Roundtable on the International Economy. "It's not obviously the right product. There are a lot of problems with it. Chances are very good that by the time the United States is able to get its act together, the technology will be relatively older."

The uncertainty of betting on a specific technology is the precise reason Rep. Campbell prefers a broad antitrust exemption over a narrowly tailored one. "HDTV may or may not be the flagship industry for the next decade. It could be that superconducting materials are. I don't favor industry-specific exemptions from antitrust. Once in a while you can make a case for them, but in my experience the case is almost always premised in politics rather than economics."

Yet most antitrust proponents, desiring to maintain what they see as the important consumer protections of antitrust law, are loath to grant anything more than narrowly defined exemptions. If a compelling argument for a narrow exemption cannot be made, they believe, no exemption should be granted. "You should do [exemptions] only in exceptional cases," warns Swarthmore economist Scherer. "You can't use a blunderbuss approach."

Clear dangers, uncertain gains

Is the potential efficiency to be gained by allowing companies to cooperate on production, marketing and distribution — of HDTVs or any other product — worth the risk?

The experts are clearly divided. In fact, there is even disagreement about the underlying issue of whether the uncertainties of pursuing such ventures in the United States really puts America at a disadvantage. While Attorney General Thornburgh calls for antitrust exemptions on the grounds that "foreign firms keep pace with ... competitive challenges in part by entering into cooperative production ventures," [16] Michael Borrus of the Berkeley Roundtable says that "as a tool to attack markets, production consortia aren't really used anywhere in the world." In particular, he says, "the Japanese have never had production consortia. One can make the argument that they've broadly coordinated their production in certain industries, and I think that's true. But that can be attacked in different ways than allowing U.S. companies to engage in production consortia."

If the need for joint production is uncertain, the risks of granting antitrust exemptions are clear: By giving protection from antitrust laws the likelihood of anti-competitive behavior, and higher prices for consumers, is increased. "It significantly risks the cartelization of an industry," says Litan of the Brookings Institution.

Supporters of the exemptions claim that foreign competition is enough to keep a U.S. consortium honest. "People who defend this kind of stuff say, 'Well, look, we're in a big new international market now, and even if we only have two or three competitors in the United States, they will be disciplined by the Japanese, the Europeans and everybody else,'" says Litan. "I would feel semi-comfortable with that argument if I had a blanket guarantee that for the next 50 or 100 years there's going to be no significant protection[ist tariffs] in these fields." Of course, nobody can give that guarantee. In fact, a government that made such a promise would be virtually inviting other countries to

Continued on page 58

Does the Free Market Make a Good Watchdog?

Most critics of the antitrust restrictions on mergers and acquisitions would still retain the laws against the "naked violations": price-fixing, bid-rigging, market-sharing, etc. But there is not universal agreement even on that.

Some economists feel that the power of the marketplace is itself enough to prevent most of the abuses antitrust laws are designed to prevent. "Conspiracies in restraint of trade tend to break down eventually without an active antitrust policy," University of Chicago economist Gary Becker has written. "Companies that are part of a conspiracy cheat on their output quotas, and high prices attract new companies into their industry." †

University of Hartford economist Dominick T. Armentano has such faith in the power of free markets that he would repeal all the antitrust laws outright, including those against price-fixing conspiracies. "There's plenty of evidence historically that when firms have attempted either singly or in concert to exercise their so-called monopoly power they've created incentives to entry and there has been competition," Armentano says.

Critics of Armentano's view concede that price conspiracies generally fall apart sooner or later. The problem, they say, is that the process can take considerable time. "The 'sooner or later' is crucial here," says Swarthmore College economist F. M. Scherer. "You can't create capacity in most industries instantaneously. It usually takes years for enough fringe capacity to come into being that the cartel gets undermined. Meanwhile

for years the cartel may be effective."

As for the historical evidence, Armentano's critics say he's reading the evidence incorrectly. The most notable incident of price-fixing — and one cited by Armentano to make his case — took place in the 1950s when more than 30 manufacturers of electrical equipment, including General Electric and Westinghouse, conspired to fix the prices they charged utilities for various types of equipment.

The Justice Department investigation that uncovered the conspiracy began in 1959 after the Tennessee Valley Authority complained about receiving identical sealed bids from different manufacturers. The companies were indicted in 1960 for conspiring to raise and fix the prices of insulators, transformers, circuit breakers and other equipment. The firms pleaded guilty to the charges and, in 1961, seven executives were sent to jail and the firms were fined a total of $2 million. The companies also faced civil suits that resulted in more than $150 million in damages being assessed.

Armentano says that while there was price fixing in this case, the forces of the marketplace prevented it from working very well. He quotes several of the principals involved from court records complaining about how it didn't work. But a July 1982 report by the Federal Trade Commission's Bureau of Economics found clear evidence of increased prices as a result of the conspiracy, with the size of the increase varying from "an average [for all eight types of equipment surveyed] of about 2 percentage points to . . . about 10.5 percentage points for

circuit breakers." ††

Another closely studied case involved bread bakers in Seattle. The FTC found that between 1954 and 1964, when smaller bakers joined the region's largest bread baker, Continental (of Wonder Bread fame), in a price-fixing conspiracy, average prices for bread in Seattle were 15 percent to 20 percent higher than the national average.‡

Likewise, Scherer found that because of a price-fixing conspiracy among cardboard box makers in the 1960s, Pillsbury paid prices 20 percent to 30 percent higher than they should have. "There's a huge amount of information out there if Armentano wanted to dig for it," Scherer says.

Perhaps the strongest argument against depending upon market forces to protect the consumer is that offered by University of Virginia economist Kenneth Elzinga. "Armentano cannot dispute the fact that people keep trying to form cartels," he says. "If there's no money there, are these people fools? Are they crazy? You take a look at the track record of the Justice Department for the past eight years. Dozens and dozens and dozens of price-fixing rings broken up in the paving and contracting industry in the Southeast. We look at the history of American business, and people keep forming cartels, even in the face of jail and fines."

† Gary Becker, "Antitrust's Only Proper Quarry: Collusion," Business Week, Oct. 12, 1987, p. 22.

†† David F. Lean, Jonathan D. Ogur and Robert P. Rogers, Competition and Collusion in Electrical Equipment Markets: An Economic Assessment, Federal Trade Commission, July 1982.

‡ Federal Trade Commission, Economic Papers, 1966-69, p. 136.

Continued from page 56
take advantage of it.

Even Harvard Business School Professor George Lodge, who feels that some sort of antitrust reform is inevitable, cautions that legislation giving broad antitrust exemptions would have far-reaching effects and has to be approached cautiously. "The point is not should we do it — I think there's no alternative if we want to maintain our standard of living," Lodge says. "The danger is that we will do this without understanding the total implications. It's a radical departure from tradition ideology. In the name of competitiveness we are leaving the old idea of how you control the uses of property, namely maximizing open competition in a free marketplace, and going to the idea of community need, or national interest. We are saying that the good corporation, or the good collection of corporations, is that which serves the national interest. You can't do that unless you know what the national interest is. Then the crucial question comes. What is the community interest that this thing is supposed to serve, and who decides what it is?"

One thing Borrus and Lodge agree on is that, if the decision is made that an industry is sufficiently important to the country's interests that antitrust exemptions should be given, it must be done as part of a larger national strategy. "If in fact the judgment is that consumer electronics is sufficiently important to the U.S., and I think that argument can be made, then it would make sense to develop a national strategy to get back in," says Borrus. "One aspect of that strategy might well be that in some market areas it makes sense to permit a production consortium, and to immunize it for a while at least from antitrust. But it has to be as a subset of a large national strategy. As a stand-alone piece of legislation that is going to be pushed through and have broad implications and be applied first to an HDTV consortium, I don't think that's a good idea. I really think that there are more fundamental problems than U.S. companies hesitating about cooperating."

Given the economy-shaping importance of antitrust exemptions, and the potential social impacts, analysts like Litan believe that a better strategy for improving U.S. competitiveness would concentrate on the more obvious problem: the high cost of capital. As Litan notes, the call for antitrust exemptions is being made in terms of getting companies to think long-term and to risk capital on innovation. But, he says, "the economic community has been arguing over the past decade that the reason why American corporations are more short-term in this decade than any other decade is because of high real interest rates. Because of high interest rates, there has to be quicker payback in order to justify investments. The bottom line is, . . . if we were to have a dramatic increase in social savings, translated to mean a dramatic reduction in the federal budget deficit, we'd have much lower interest rates, and our corporations would become long-term again."

NOTES

[1] *The Wall Street Journal,* Dec. 27, 1988.

[2] Clyde Prestowitz, *Trading Places: How We Allowed Japan to Take the Lead* (1988), p. 115.

[3] *The Wall Street Journal,* Oct. 15, 1985.

[4] Dominick T. Armentano, *Antitrust Policy: The Case for Repeal,* Cato Institute, 1986, p. ix.

[5] Rule spoke before the 22nd annual New England Antitrust Conference, Harvard Law School, Cambridge, Mass., Oct. 28, 1988.

[6] William G. Shepard, "The Twilight of Antitrust," *Antitrust Law & Economics Review,* 1986, p. 24.

[7] Walter Adams and James W. Brock, *The Bigness Complex: Industry, Labor and Government in the American Economy* (1986), p. 130.

[8] Rule spoke before the American Bar Association in Washington, D.C., Oct. 9, 1987.

[9] Eddie Correia and Priscilla Budeiri, "Antitrust Legislation in the Reagan Era," *The Antitrust Bulletin,* summer 1988, p. 362.

[10] *Ibid.,* p. 369.

[11] Mark W. Frankena and Paul A. Pautler, *Antitrust Policy for Declining Industries,* Federal Trade Commission, October 1985.

[12] Robert H. Bork, *The Antitrust Paradox* (1978), p. 255.

[13] Frederick M. Rowe, "The Decline of Antitrust and the Delusions of Models: The Faustian Pact of Law and Economics," *The Georgetown Law Journal,* Vol. 72, 1984, p. 1536.

[14] Dominick T. Armentano, *Antitrust and Monopoly: Anatomy of a Policy Failure* (1982), p. 42.

[15] Walter Adams and James W. Brock, "The Bigness Mystique and the Merger Policy Debate: An International Perspective," *Northwestern Journal of International Law and Business,* spring 1988, p. 41.

[16] *The Wall Street Journal,* Dec. 27, 1988.

Graphics: cover, Margaret Scott; pp. 48, 50, S. Dmitri Lipczenko.

RECOMMENDED READING

BOOKS

Adams, Walter and Brock, James W., *The Bigness Complex: Industry, Labor and Government in the American Economy,* **Pantheon, 1986.**

The authors, both economists, present the economic arguments in favor of antitrust laws. They make a convincing case that the increasing concentration of business not only presents social dangers but, in all but a few cases, does not offer economic benefits.

Armentano, Dominick T., *Antitrust Policy: The Case for Repeal,* **Cato Institute, 1986.**

As the title implies, Armentano argues for the complete repeal, not just the reform, of U.S. antitrust laws on the ground that free-market forces will prevent any abuses that truly reduce competition. Readers looking for more detail and historical discussion than is provided in this short work (80 pages) can turn to ...mentano's 1982 book, *Antitrust and Monopoly: Anatomy of a Policy Failure,* published by John Wiley and Sons.

Blair, Roger D. and Kaserman, David L., *Antitrust Economics,* **Irwin, 1985.**

This is a college textbook, complete with questions and problems at the end of each chapter. Though it is sprinkled with some mathematics that is beyond the reach of most non-economists, most of the book is easily accessible and a cogent presentation of the major issues in the antitrust debate.

Bork, Robert H., *The Antitrust Paradox,* **Basic Books, 1978.**

This is the book that established Robert Bork's reputation as an antitrust scholar. Even critics of Bork's view say he has presented a well-written argument for judging antitrust questions on the basis of whether they enhance or inhibit economic efficiency.

Breit, William and Elzinga, Kenneth G., *The Antitrust Casebook,* **Dryden Press, 1982.**

Breit and Elzinga let the courts do most of the talking in their book. The authors provide brief explanations of the historical context of the 56 selected antitrust cases. The majority of the pages are devoted to excerpts from the majority opinions in the cases.

Frazer, Tim, *Monopoly, Competition and the Law: The Regulation of Business Activity in Britain, Europe and America,* **St. Martin's Press, 1988.**

Frazer, a professor at the University of Newcastle in England, writes a bit too densely, but his book provides an invaluable comparison of antitrust laws in the United States, Great Britain and the European Economic Community.

Gellhorn, Ernest, *Antitrust Law and Economics in a Nutshell,* **West Publishing Co., 1981.**

This book provides just what it advertises: a clearly written, no-frills explanation of U.S. antitrust law. It's an excellent primer, though readers interested in a particular topic will likely want to look elsewhere for more details.

Letwin, William, *Law and Economic Policy in America: The Evolution of the Sherman Antitrust Act,* **The University of Chicago Press, 1959.**

Letwin has delivered a delightfully written, cogent political history of the social conditions and legislative events that resulted in the passing of the Sherman Antitrust Act in 1890. Letwin carries the discussion as far as the passage of the Clayton Antitrust Act and the Federal Trade Commission Act in 1914.

ARTICLES

Lande, Robert H., "Wealth Transfers as the Original and Primary Concern of Antitrust: The Efficiency Interpretation Challenged," *Hastings Law Journal,* **September 1982.**

Lande's article is written in response to the idea, championed by Robert Bork, that the sole concern of Congress in passing the early antitrust legislation was with economic efficiency. Lande argues that there is ample evidence that Congress was equally concerned with preventing companies from obtaining too much market power for social and political reasons.

FOREIGN INVESTMENT IN THE U.S.

FOREIGN INVESTMENT IN THE U.S.

by Mary H. Cooper

Foreign investors are buying up U.S. businesses, farm land, real estate, stocks and bonds at a record pace. The Bush administration maintains that the booming foreign investment provides jobs and needed capital for the growth of the American economy. But there are a growing number of critics who worry that the United States may lose control over its own destiny.

Gloomy economic news is so common these days that few people seem to notice when the government releases new data showing the trade deficit is worsening or the federal budget deficit is not shrinking as fast as predicted. But one economic fact makes Americans stand up and listen: Foreigners now own $1.5 trillion worth of assets in the United States.

Foreign investors, who have been purchasing government securities since the early 1980s, are now rapidly buying other kinds of American assets as well, including real estate, banks and other businesses. Known as foreign direct investment, this kind of activity has more than tripled in the 1980s, rising from $83 billion in 1980 to $262 billion in 1987.*

Those $262 billion are still less than the $309 billion in foreign assets held by American citizens. They

---

*This is the last year for which government statistics are available. Foreign direct investment is defined as the ownership of at least 10 percent of the voting shares of an incorporated business enterprise or an equivalent interest in an unincorporated firm, or interest of at least 10 percent in a real-estate transaction. Transactions of lesser value do not appear in the statistics. The figures in the text are cumulative totals.

also represent barely 17 percent of this country's gross national product (GNP). This level of foreign investment hardly suggests a serious erosion of the country's economic resources, supporters of foreign investment say. Among those supporters is President George Bush, who, like his predecessor, Ronald Reagan, sees foreign investment as a beneficial side-effect of the emerging global economy in which goods and money are flowing across borders more easily than ever before. "...[I]t is important if we believe in open markets that people be allowed to invest here, just as I'd like to see more openness for American investors in other countries," the president said at a Feb. 21 news conference.

But, critics point out, foreigners are buying into the United States faster than Americans are investing abroad. Since 1978, U.S. direct investment abroad has grown by about 90 percent, while foreign investment in the United States has increased more than 500 percent. Some observers see this dramatic rise in foreign investment as the latest symptom of this country's waning role as the chief powerhouse of the world economy. "The forces of the international marketplace have begun to overwhelm America's capacity to deal with them," write Martin and Susan Tolchin in their best-selling book, *Buying into America.* "The surge of foreign investment is only one glaring example. The manner in which the nation's leaders respond will determine how we meet the most difficult economic challenge of our times: to retain U.S. sovereignty in the global economy." [1]

The signs of alarm over rising foreign investment are widely apparent. One of the first measures placed before the new session of Congress when it convened in January was a bill that would require stricter monitoring of foreign purchases of U.S. assets. *(See p. 71.)* Like a similar measure defeated last year, the bill has been criticized by the Bush administration, as well as by spokesmen for American multinationals who fear that new restrictions on foreign investment here will meet with retaliation abroad.

Outside the capital, media coverage of foreign investment has focused on cases where foreign firms have bought U.S. companies and then closed inefficient facilities, laying off American workers. Embittered former employees blame the outsiders for usurping their livelihood and the government in Washington for allowing them to do so. Another focus of adverse media coverage is the purchase by foreigners of American real estate, especially large office buildings long identified with American commercial strength.

The main focus of all this negative coverage is Japan. Although Japanese investments in the U.S. are growing faster than those of other nations *(See chart, p. 64),* Japan still ranks third among major holders of U.S. assets, behind Britain and the Netherlands. But Americans seem less concerned about European interests in the United States. In contrast, weekly news magazines illustrate stories on Japanese investments in

From the Editor ...

America has long thought of itself as standing apart from the rest of the world — independent, self-sufficient, proud. But if the world once permitted isolationism (and, arguably, it never did), such certainly is not the case today. The American economy is intricately interwoven with the economies of the rest of the industrialized world, and America's future depends on its relations with them.

How the United States deals with its trading partners — and how they deal with it — are topics for this week's and next week's Reports. This week we analyze foreign investment in the United States; it is helping pay for the deficit, we learn, but there are inherent dangers in letting others control the purse strings. Next week, in "Pacific Rim Challenges," we will examine the Far East. Five Pacific Rim trading partners — Japan, South Korea, Taiwan, Hong Kong and Singapore — are responsible for half the nation's trade deficit. And it is with those countries that the United States will fight what one economist calls "a battle for our standard of living." But as our report will show, American trade policy must be carefully tailored to each country. A false move could have serious economic and geopolitical consequences.

— *Marcus D. Rosenbaum*

the United States with caricatures of samurai swordsmen casting a warlike gaze toward their American readers. [2] Such sentiments are reminiscent of the anti-Japanese sentiment that accompanied the demand for protectionist trade legislation during the early 1980s. Then, workers who were displaced by recession and falling demand for U.S. goods vented their frustrations by taking sledgehammers to Toyotas. Today, Americans seem almost as frustrated by Japan's economic success and its stake in the U.S. economy: 80 percent of the respondents to a recent poll said there should be limits on the number of U.S. companies the Japanese should be allowed to buy; 45 percent said the Japanese should not be permitted to purchase property in the United States at all. [3]

Those who defend foreign purchases of American assets suggest that the public response is largely emotional. Sam Rosenblatt, president of the Association for Foreign Investment in America, a lobbying group that opposes restrictions on foreign direct investment, says much of the opposition reflects an unjustified "perception that [foreign investors] are stealing us blind." "It's a very complex issue," he adds, "and one that doesn't lend itself to easy generalization."

It is also an issue of pragmatism, according to R.

Foreign Direct Investment

(billions of dollars)

This chart shows the cumulative total of foreign direct investment in the United States between 1980 and 1987, the last year for which complete figures are available. Note that although Japan ranks third in such investments, its activity has been growing at a rate much faster than the other four top investors.

	1980	1981	1982	1983	1984	1985	1986	1987
All countries	83.0	108.7	124.7	137.1	164.6	184.6	220.4	261.9
United Kingdom	14.1	18.6	28.4	32.2	38.4	43.6	55.9	74.9
Netherlands	19.1	26.8	26.2	29.2	33.7	37.1	40.7	47.0
Japan	4.7	7.7	9.7	11.3	16.0	19.3	26.8	33.4
Canada	12.2	12.1	11.7	11.4	15.3	17.1	20.3	21.7
Germany	7.6	9.5	9.9	10.8	12.3	14.8	17.3	19.6

Source: U.S. Department of Commerce, Bureau of Economic Analysis.

Taggart Murphy, managing director of Japan Private Placements at Chase Manhattan Asia Ltd. in Tokyo. "The United States has a government deficit to finance, and the money has to come from somewhere," he writes in the current issue of the *Harvard Business Review*. "If we cannot get it by selling Treasury bonds to the Japanese or from our own savings, we must get it by selling our corporations, banks, and real estate. We need the funds, and the Japanese are increasingly in a position to dictate the terms under which they will provide them. We have arranged a Hobson's choice. While we may not want to sell the commanding heights of the U.S. economy, we have little choice if we are to keep the funds flowing." [4]

Finding bargain-basement values in America

Government data help shed some light on the issue. "We feel that the subject of foreign investment in the United States can take two paths," says Greg Fouch, an analyst at the Commerce Department's Bureau of Economic Analysis, one of 16 U.S. government agencies that track foreign investments. "It can take an emotional path, or it can take an economic path, where you study the statistics."

Fouch's data confirm the trend of mounting foreign investment in U.S. businesses and real estate. In 1987, a record $195 billion flowed into the American

economy from abroad. Following a longstanding pattern, most of this money was used to buy financial assets, including Treasury bills and corporate bonds, which fall into the category of so-called portfolio investments. But foreigners also spent an unprecedented $41.5 billion that year, almost a quarter of the total pool of foreign investments, to buy into American industries and real estate. [5]

The United States offers foreign investors a variety of advantages over other potential investment targets. One is the depressed value of the dollar. Since it peaked in February 1985, the greenback has depreciated against the Japanese yen, the West German mark and the world's other major currencies. This makes American real estate and businesses cheaper to buy for holders of other currencies. Another reason foreign investors are interested in the United States is this country's stable political environment — an important lure for real-estate investors, because it lessens the risk that an investment will be lost through political upheaval.

Real-estate purchases by foreigners have drawn a lot of media attention, especially in big cities. In Manhattan, for example, foreigners have bought several billions of dollars' worth of real estate since the city's fiscal crisis of the mid-1970s. Although Canadians were initially the leading foreign holders of New York City's office buildings, Japanese investors have overtaken the Canadians and now own at least 23 office buildings, including such familiar landmarks as the Citicorp Center, the Algonquin Hotel and the Exxon building. Foreigners reportedly own a fifth of Manhattan's office space. [6] Foreign ownership of downtown property is even more concentrated in other American cities, including Washington, D.C., where as much as 30 percent of the commercial real estate is foreign-owned. [7]

According to a recent survey by Kenneth Leventhal & Co., a Los Angeles-based accounting firm, Japanese real-estate purchases in this country increased by 30 percent in 1988, boosting the total value of Japanese-owned property here to $42.9 billion. Because of a shortage of affordable housing in Japan, Japanese investors, aided by the strong yen, are buying up not just office buildings, but houses and apartment buildings in the United States as well. Hawaii and California, because of their proximity to Japan and large Japanese populations, have been the chief targets for this type of investment. Local reaction to such real-estate deals is often hostile: Purchases by one Japanese landlord of $173 million in Hawaiian housing prompted state lawmakers to propose a ban on home ownership by non-resident aliens. [8]

A different pattern is seen in foreign ownership of American agricultural land, including farms and timber. Foreign investors increased their holdings by 202,000 acres in 1987, for a total 12.5 million acres of agricultural land. But such foreign holdings are actually down from 1981, when 12.7 million acres were foreign-owned, and they amount to no more than 1 percent of the country's agricultural land. "At least on the agricultural side, we really haven't seen anything dramatic," says Peter DeBraal of the Agriculture Department's Economic Research Service. Almost a tenth of the foreign-held acreage is accounted for by Maine timberland owned by a few large Canadian lumber companies. The rest of the foreign-held agricultural land is concentrated in the South and West, where British, Canadian, West German and Dutch investors share the holdings. *(See map, p. 70.)*

According to DeBraal, European investors buy American land for a variety of reasons. "Certainly, the cost of farm land in the United States compared to Western Europe is considerably cheaper, because there is so much more of it here," he says. In addition, "there's a certain sense of security of owning real estate in the United States. Despite the fact that we have pooh-poohed the Russian threat, people from Western Europe say they are really concerned about the threat of the Russians on their borders." [9]

Special incentives to buy American

The weak dollar, which has encouraged purchases of U.S. farm land, real estate and businesses, has also encouraged exporters from strong-currency nations to shift production to the United States as a way to maintain their market share in this country. This is because their goods become increasingly expensive to American consumers as their currency strengthens against the dollar. For example, it is more expensive for Nissan to export Japanese-made cars to the United States than it is to produce and sell them here.

Apart from currency considerations, the fear of protectionist trade laws is a special inducement for foreign investors in countries that enjoy sizable trade surpluses with the United States. The merchandise trade deficit has exceeded $100 billion since 1984. By making foreign goods more expensive and American goods less expensive on world markets, the weak dollar was supposed to discourage Americans from buying so many imports and encourage foreigners to buy American products. But while it has boosted U.S. exports, the weak dollar has not reduced American consumers' appetite for Japanese cars, Italian clothing or other imported goods. As a result, last year's trade deficit stood at $126.5 billion.

Businessmen in countries that enjoy the biggest trade surpluses with the United States, such as Japan and West Germany, see investing in the United States as a way to protect themselves should the U.S. government decide to impose restrictions on imports. By setting up U.S. production facilities, the foreign company can sell its American-made products freely in this country even if Congress imposes trade barriers against its country of origin. This is an especially attractive solution for Japanese industries that have been the focus of protectionist measures in the past. Several Japanese automakers — for example, Nissan and Toyota — have entered into joint ventures with American firms or established new factories on U.S. territory as a way to circumvent so-called "voluntary-restraint arrangements," or quotas, that have been erected against their exports to the United States since the early 1980s.

But avoidance of retaliation in trade matters is not the only reason for foreign interest in producing goods in the United States. Britain, for example, is currently one of the few nations with which the United States enjoys a trade surplus, so the threat of retaliatory trade laws should not count as an important lure for British investors. Yet Britain continues to be the main source of foreign direct investment in the United States.

The most compelling reason for foreign investors' growing interest in the United States appears to be their perception that this country offers promising economic conditions in which to maximize profits. Even as U.S. economists and policy makers bewail the persistence of the budget and trade deficits and rising inflation and interest rates, foreign investors continue to regard the American economy as a vigorous "developing economy" that has continued to grow at a healthy rate since 1982. "Twenty years ago, there was a mind-set that the developing economies were limited to the Third World, and that's where investment should move," explains Stephen L. Cooney Jr., director of international investment and finance for the National Association of Manufacturers in Washington, D.C. But those nations are now saddled with debt and have imposed strict austerity measures that prevent growth.

As a result, Cooney says, "the old model that the place for growth is the Third World, because those countries are poorer and less developed, has gone out the window. Most industrialists see their major opportunities for expansion now as being much more significant in the industrial countries than in the Third World countries." Of these, the United States is especially attractive. The 12-member European Economic Community offers great promise of economic growth as it strives to meet its goal of removing all existing barriers to internal trade by 1992.* But, Cooney says, "Europe is still rather hidebound and difficult and has more restrictions. That's why European countries saw a great chance to make headway in the U.S. market and win market share in the United States much more easily than they could increase their sales in Europe."

Continued on page 67

---

*For background, see "Europe 1992: Danger or Opportunity?" *Editorial Research Reports*, 1989 Vol. I, pp. 17-28.

Biggest Foreign Acquisitions of U.S. Firms Since 1984

YEAR	U.S. FIRM principal business	FOREIGN OWNER country	PRICE ($ millions)
1987	Standard Oil Co. (British Petroleum) *(oil and gas)*	British Petroleum Co. PLC *(United Kingdom)*	7,887
1988	Federated Department Stores *(650 stores including Bloomingdales & I. Magnin)*	Campeau Corp. *(Canada)*	7,420
1989	Pillsbury Company *(baking mixes, flour, fast food restaurants, frozen food)*	Grand Metropolitan PLC *(United Kingdom)*	5,757
1988	Farmers Group Inc. *(insurance)*	Batus Inc. (BAT Industries PLC) *(United Kingdom)†*	5,309
1986	Allied Stores Corp. *(Jordan Marsh, Ann Taylor)*	Campeau Corp. *(Canada)*	3,470
1985	Carnation Company *(food and grocery products, including Coffee-Mate)*	Nestle SA *(Switzerland)*	3,000
1988	Triangle Publications Inc. *(TV Guide, Seventeen)*	News Corp. Ltd. *(Australia)*	3,000
1988	Firestone Tire & Rubber Co. *(tires)*	Bridgestone Corp. *(Japan)*	2,652
1988	MacMillan Inc. *(publishing)*	Maxwell Communications PLC *(United Kingdom)*	2,639
1988	Inter-Continental Hotels (Grand) *(international hotel chain)*	Seibu Saison *(Japan)*	2,270
1988	CBS Records Group (CBS Inc.) *(records, tapes, including Columbia label)*	Sony Corp. *(Japan)†*	2,000
1988	First Boston Inc. *(holding company, stock and bond dealers)*	Acquisition Group (Credit Suisse) *(Switzerland)*	2,000
1987	Stauffer Chemical Co. (Chesebrough-Pond's Inc.) *(industrial and agricultural chemicals)*	ICI - ICI Stratos *(United Kingdom)†*	1,923
1988	Koppers Co. *(road construction)*	Acquisition Group (Beazer PLC) *(United Kingdom)*	1,741
1987	Himont Inc. *(plastics)*	Montedison SpA *(Italy)*	1,656
1988	Staley Continental Inc. *(corn sweeteners, starches)*	Tate & Lyle PLC *(United Kingdom)*	1,534
1987	Manpower Inc. *(temporary help service)*	Blue Arrow PLC *(United Kingdom)*	1,328
1987	Heublein Inc. (RJR Nabisco) *(spirits, wine, California grape products)*	Grand Metropolitan PLC *(United Kingdom)*	1,300
1988	G. Heilman Brewing Co. Inc. *(brewing company)*	Bond Corp. Holdings Ltd. *(Australia)*	1,296
pending	Texaco-certain refineries *(oil and gas)*	Saudia Arabia *(Saudi Arabia)*	1,280
1989	Triangle Industries *(metal cans, plastic packaging)*	Pechiney SA *(France)*	1,260
1986	ITT's Telecommunications Business Corp. *(telephone systems)*	Cie Générale d'Electricité *(France)*	1,251
pending	Calmat Co. *(cement, building materials)*	Brierley Investments Ltd. *(New Zealand)*	1,200
1987	Hilton International (Allesis) *(hotel management)*	Ladbroke Group PLC *(United Kingdom)*	1,070
1988	Gould Inc. *(technical instruments, semiconductors)*	Nippon Mining Co. Ltd. *(Japan)*	1,047

† *U.S. subsidiary of foreign company.*
Source: IDD Information Services, Inc.; Mergers & Acquisitions magazine.

Continued from page 65

Mergers and acquisitions of American firms

Foreign investors have long spent more money to buy existing American firms than they have to start up new companies in the United States. Of the $30.5 billion foreigners spent on businesses in the United States in 1987, the Commerce Department reports, $25.6 billion — more than four-fifths — went toward the purchase of 306 existing American firms. Critics say this takeover activity involving foreign buyers is draining the United States of its basic resources. Because they often do not increase employment or otherwise enrich the economy, takeovers by foreign firms merely shift equity out of the country into the hands of people whose interest in the country's well-being may be short-lived. But takeovers by foreign investors account for just a small part — about a tenth in 1987 — of takeover activity in this country, which has mushroomed in recent years with the advent of leveraged buyouts and widespread corporate restructuring.* As American conglomerates shed less productive units or those that are not closely related to the core business, foreign investors have a wide choice of companies to choose from.

As they have in the past, Canadian and Western European investors led the takeover charge in 1987. The biggest deals, in terms of revenue of the acquired companies, were closed by Canadian, Dutch, British and West German concerns. Canada's Seagram Co. Ltd. topped a listing compiled by *Forbes* magazine of the largest foreign investors that year. The Canadian firm bought out Joseph E. Seagram & Sons, producer of alcoholic beverages, and Tropicana Products, maker of orange juice and other beverages. Seagram also purchased a 23 percent share of E. I. du Pont de Nemours Co., the chemical and petrochemical giant. The combined revenues of the Canadian company's purchases in 1987 totaled $33 billion.[10]

Foreigners continued to make megadeals in the United States in 1988. No foreign buyer has come close to the record $24.5 billion offer for RJR Nabisco completed earlier this year by the New York investment firm of Kohlberg Kravis Roberts. But some of the biggest mergers and acquisitions completed in 1988 were made by foreigners: Canada's Campeau Corp.'s $7.4 billion buyout of Federated Department Stores Inc. of Cincinnati, and Britain's BAT Industries PLC's $5.3 billion hostile takeover of Farmers Group Inc., an insurance company based in Los Angeles. And the trend continued into early 1989, when Grand Metropol-

itan PLC, a British food and liquor company, paid $5.8 billion for Phillsbury Co. *(See chart, p. 66.)*

The British are still the main foreign owners of U.S. businesses, and they have shown no sign of retreating from their American commitments. Last year, British investors bought 398 American companies worth $32.5 billion, according to *The British-American Deal Review*, a publication based in New York and London. That continued a two-year streak of record U.S. corporate acquisitions by investors from that country. "The British invest more than three times as much in the United States as they do in their own economy," says Mark Dixon, the *Review*'s editor.

As for Japan, Japanese corporate investors in the United States are beginning to deserve the publicity they have attracted for several years, judging from their activity in 1988. While they still ranked behind the British in terms of the value of deals made in the United States last year, Japanese investors doubled their American corporate acquisitions in 1988 to a record $12.7 billion, according to Ulmer Brothers Inc., an investment bank based in New York City.[11] In terms of the dollar value of 1988 U.S. corporate investments, the Japanese for the first time outranked Canadians, whose 50 mergers and acquisitions in the United States totaled $9.9 billion, according to IDD Information Services, a financial information service based in New York City.

There are some patterns that distinguish foreign investors from different countries. Canadian buyers, for example, tend to be big conglomerates, such as Seagram's and Toronto real-estate developer Robert Campeau's vast enterprise. Canada's relatively small population of 25 million limits Canadian investors' potential for expansion at home, so they are naturally attracted to the giant market next door, with its 247 million consumers. A common language and culture make such transactions all the more attractive. British investors are similarly motivated, as to some degree are citizens of other Western European countries.

As for the Japanese, cultural differences may play a bigger role than economics in Americans' overwhelmingly negative reaction to their investments in U.S. assets. Authors Joel Kotkin and Yoriko Kishimoto say this explains why incidents of "foreign-bashing" in this country have been directed almost exclusively against Japanese interests. "The fact is that in today's supposedly cosmopolitan United States the Europeans can invest at record rates and freely trade in American markets without causing widespread concern. But the success of a nation such as Japan, springing from such alien cultural roots, engenders a very different kind of response."[12]

Thus, for Japanese investors, cultural and linguistic differences increase the risk involved in U.S. deals. Partly for this reason, the Japanese have limited their deals almost exclusively to friendly buyouts of companies they intend to hold over the long term because they further the parent firm's strategic goals.

---

*Official statistics for 1988 will not be made available until May, but privately collected data suggest that the trend is growing. According to IDD Information Services, a financial information service based in New York City, a record 3,637 mergers and acquisitions were completed in 1988, for a total value of $311.4 billion, also a record and an increase of more than 40 percent over 1987.

Dutch Investment in the U.S.

It comes as no surprise that Britain, Japan, West Germany and Canada rank high on the list of foreign direct investors in the United States. But the Netherlands? Only the sixth-biggest economy in the 12-nation European Community, the Netherlands is the second-largest investor in the United States. It even outranks Japan, the world's largest creditor.

The Netherlands' leading position among investors in the U.S. economy is partly a result of the country's favorable accounting and tax policies, which encouraged investors from other countries, chiefly Britain, to set up holding companies there. Through these holding companies, non-Dutch investors have bought interests in the United States.

But even though Dutch accounting and tax policies were tightened several years ago, making the country a less attractive base of operations for foreign businesses, the Netherlands has still retained its strong investment position in the United States. The main reason may be found in the two countries' longstanding commercial ties, according to a joint report by the Netherlands Chamber of Commerce in the United States Inc. and Arthur Young International.†

Poor in resources and heavily reliant on trade for its survival, the Netherlands traces its commercial links with the United States to the activities of the Dutch East India Co. in the early 16th century. Dutch investors bought mainly U.S. farm land until the early 20th century, when they began to invest in light manufacturing and petroleum as well. After World War II, Dutch investors diversified their interests, and since the 1970s they have continued to buy heavily into wholesale and retail businesses, as well as real estate and insurance.

Most Dutch-owned businesses in the United States began as start-up companies rather than acquisitions of existing American firms, and most of those in operation today came under Dutch ownership in the 1980s. Like most European investments, the vast majority of Dutch holdings are headquartered along the East Coast, chiefly in and around New York City and in the Southeast. More Dutch-owned companies are located in Georgia than in New York, a fact that the report attributes to the availability of low-cost and non-union labor as well as to Atlanta's growing role as a business center.

Because Japan is rapidly increasing its direct investments in the United States, the Netherlands probably will soon fall to third place among the biggest foreign investors. But it seems likely to retain its strong investment position in this country and far outrank all the other economic powers, including Canada and West Germany.

† Arthur Young International and The Netherlands Chamber of Commerce in the United States Inc., "Dutch Enterprise in the U.S.A.," 1989.

Whereas European investors have been increasingly aggressive in their use of unfriendly bids for U.S. firms, the only hostile takeover in the United States ever made by a Japanese firm was Dainippon Ink and Chemicals' 1988 buyout of Reichhold Chemicals Inc., a producer of specialty chemicals based in White Plains, N.Y. Another sign of Japanese caution is the size of their U.S. purchases. The $2.6 billion acquisition by Japanese tire maker Bridgestone Corp. of Firestone Tire & Rubber Co. of Akron, Ohio, was unusual. Most Japanese purchases of U.S. firms are relatively small, and a third of the deals made last year were valued at less than $20 million, according to Ulmer Brothers.

One factor that distinguishes foreign corporate buyers from their domestic counterparts is the evident care they take to target acquisitions in the United States that are thought to further the buyer's strategic goals. Since 1985, the bulk of mergers and acquisitions of U.S. firms by foreign investors, especially Western Europeans, have occurred in the manufacturing sector, accounting for $16.3 billion in 1987, as foreign exporters to the U.S. market have increased their presence here to avoid protectionist legislation. Japanese investments, thus far concentrated in the financial and wholesale industries, also are moving increasingly into manufacturing as automakers shift production to this country.

Public attention has focused on foreign entry into the domestic automotive industry. But for at least the past four years, the leading target for outside investors within the manufacturing sector are companies that produce chemicals and related products, including synthetic materials, drugs and soap. They spent $4 billion to buy such companies in 1987, putting fully a third of the industry in foreign hands, more than any other. (See chart, p. 69.) There are a number of reasons for all the foreign interest in U.S. chemical companies. For one thing, American chemical manufacturers are shedding less profitable operations or those that are not closely related to their core businesses, making these available to outside investors. This corporate restructuring is happening at the same time that Western European chemicals producers are preparing for the keener competitive environment taking shape in the European Community. Establishing a foothold in the world's largest market in chemicals is one way to survive.

But the European Community's drive toward 1992 is pushing firms in other industries to invest in the United States as well. Fewer barriers to internal trade within the EC will mean keener competition both at home and abroad for the so-called "national champions," companies that have enjoyed special protection by their governments. One of these is Siemens AG, West Germany's giant electrical and telecommunications manufacturer. Last year, Siemens set out to improve its standing in the electronics field by purchasing specialized companies outside Germany, among them the American firms Bendix, an automobile electronics manufacturer, and Rolm, a division of IBM that makes computerized telephone exchanges.

Many critics of foreign investments in the United States are especially alarmed by signs that foreign investors are beginning to buy heavily into the food products, pharmaceuticals and personal products industries, where brand loyalty plays an especially strong role in corporate profitability. It's one thing to buy an imported Jaguar, Sony television or wedge of Brie cheese on purpose. But often the money American consumers spend on such staples as laundry detergent, fast food or pain relievers ends up in foreign hands without the consumers knowing it. In January, Pillsbury Co., the Minneapolis-based producer of such familiar grocery store items as cake mixes and Green Giant vegetables, and owner of the Burger King fast-food franchise, passed to Britain's Grand Metropolitan. In a deal announced in February, Fabergé Inc. and Elizabeth Arden Inc., makers of toiletries, cosmetics and fragrances, were sold to Unilever Group, a British-Dutch conglomerate, which already owns the Pond's and Vaseline labels. Even the cautious Japanese are buying into the consumer-products industry. Among the 10 biggest Japanese investments in the United States last year, Ulmer Brothers reports, were the purchase of Zotos International Inc., maker of hair products, by the Japanese cosmetics firm of Shiseido Co., and the purchase of Andrew Jergens Co. by Kao Corp. And many consumer electronics products with American names — such as GE and RCA televisions — have been made by foreign companies for years.

Japanese investors have already taken a leading role in the American banking industry. Of the 86 American commercial banks that are owned by foreign banks, 23 are owned by Japanese bank holding companies, according to the Federal Reserve Board. Japanese activity in this field is not surprising, given the country's role as the world's leading creditor. Four of the world's five biggest banks are Japanese, and Dai-Ichi Kangyo Bank Ltd. edged out Citicorp as the world's biggest bank in 1986. The Japanese banks, which have concentrated their presence in the U.S. market on the West Coast, are buying into financial institutions in the Midwest and on the East Coast as

Foreign Share of U.S. Manufacturing

This graph shows the growth of foreign-owned companies as a percentage of all U.S. manufacturing businesses between 1977 and 1986. Although the increase in foreign ownership has been across-the-board in manufacturing, it has been especially high in the chemical industries. Although foreigners owned only a little more than 15 percent of U.S. chemical industries in 1977, by 1986 they owned nearly a third.

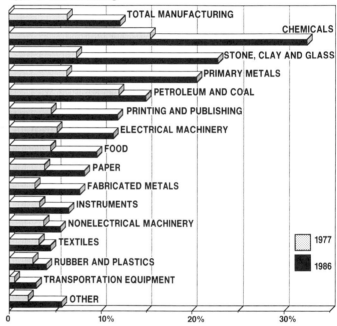

Type of Manufacturing

Source: U.S. Department of Commerce, Bureau of Economic Analysis.

well, competing with British and other European banks for ownership of the increasingly lucrative regional banks that have gained in strength in recent years. The trend is controversial because critics worry that foreign ownership of the institutions where Americans keep their savings poses additional risk to a banking system that has already suffered the shocks emanating from the collapse of so many savings and loans.

Japanese automakers set up shop in U.S.

Although most direct foreign investments in the United States entail mergers and acquisitions of existing American firms, in 1987, foreign investors did spend $4.9 billion to set up 251 new firms in the United States, adding new jobs and tax revenues to the economy. Since the early 1980s, Japanese automakers have been at the forefront of this so-called greenfield

Continued on page 71

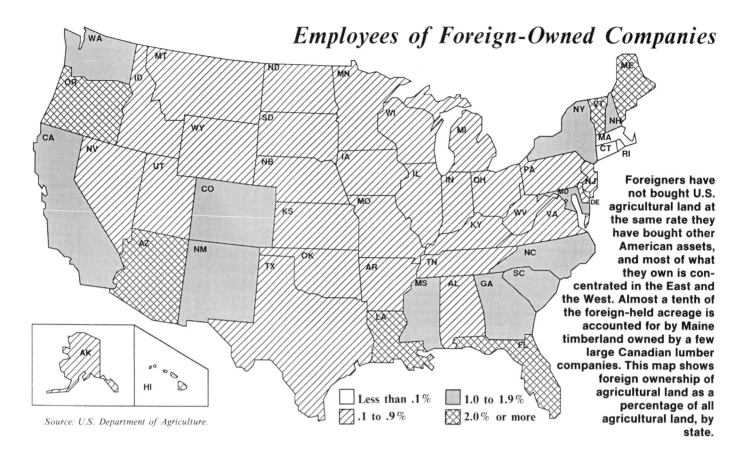

Employees of Foreign-Owned Companies

Foreigners have not bought U.S. agricultural land at the same rate they have bought other American assets, and most of what they own is concentrated in the East and the West. Almost a tenth of the foreign-held acreage is accounted for by Maine timberland owned by a few large Canadian lumber companies. This map shows foreign ownership of agricultural land as a percentage of all agricultural land, by state.

☐ Less than .1%   ▨ 1.0 to 1.9%
▨ .1 to .9%   ▧ 2.0% or more

Source: U.S. Department of Agriculture.

Employees of Foreign-Owned Companies

This chart lists, state by state, the number of employees of U.S. companies owned by foreign investors. The five countries listed here are the five largest foreign employers in the United States.

	United Kingdom	Canada	Germany	Netherlands	Japan		United Kingdom	Canada	Germany	Netherlands	Japan
Alabama	8,435	6,816	2,441	1,281	3,456	Montana	567	1,265	36	†	36
Alaska	†	914	33	†	2,361	Nebraska	1,931	751	710	277	141
Arizona	10,523	10,035	1,029	4,122	689	Nevada	2,701	2,079	656	995	†
Arkansas	2,930	3,808	664	3,934	1,938	New Hampshire	4,604	4,234	1,074	801	†
California	53,029	33,907	20,141	24,793	60,044	New Jersey	32,758	17,826	23,659	12,975	15,369
Colorado	11,523	7,103	1,863	1,042	1,231	New Mexico	2,207	880	†	1,647	61
Connecticut	13,292	6,392	7,615	6,853	1,740	New York	77,987	41,248	20,761	14,984	17,804
Delaware	4,350	†	1,331	202	91	North Carolina	26,490	25,082	20,862	6,018	3,022
District of Columbia	741	2,403	247	77	218	North Dakota	277	960	†	131	6
Florida	24,898	25,864	8,318	7,583	3,247	Ohio	34,620	17,720	10,004	5,705	9,698
Georgia	24,535	21,113	9,317	9,589	7,318	Oklahoma	4,381	8,870	2,068	3,811	610
Hawaii	1,303	700	42	91	11,420	Oregon	2,810	4,163	4,267	707	1,784
Idaho	137	916	56	267	18	Pennsylvania	40,841	32,526	21,160	8,514	3,636
Illinois	38,061	26,890	14,962	10,678	15,060	Rhode Island	3,341	†	1,409	†	144
Indiana	9,566	15,131	8,931	11,482	3,182	South Carolina	8,813	7,507	12,454	10,819	1,726
Iowa	2,194	6,686	2,626	1,639	438	South Dakota	575	641	25	†	15
Kansas	2,922	2,286	1,779	3,104	233	Tennessee	13,904	17,822	5,954	9,057	7,952
Kentucky	6,877	8,444	3,855	3,786	2,137	Texas	39,133	42,471	21,838	30,778	7,175
Louisiana	7,679	9,897	5,473	8,339	235	Utah	2,941	†	592	†	91
Maine	4,925	9,857	565	1,625	106	Vermont	†	2,129	482	14	146
Maryland	8,031	13,573	5,017	7,448	1,755	Virginia	12,569	24,652	10,727	3,212	1,366
Massachusetts	23,260	17,384	8,339	3,098	2,731	Washington	4,526	12,156	2,782	4,098	4,123
Michigan	16,761	19,035	13,311	1,993	10,552	West Virginia	3,947	13,274	4,019	3,282	116
Minnesota	9,825	12,538	2,990	11,442	1,018	Wisconsin	9,361	13,342	7,721	4,503	2,296
Mississippi	4,162	3,547	1,679	543	†	Wyoming	765	759	42	†	†
Missouri	9,019	14,472	4,646	7,285	1,098	ALL COUNTRIES	636,817	602,258	305,337	258,935	216,392

† Suppressed to avoid disclosure of data of individual companies.   *Source: U.S. Department of Commerce, Bureau of Economic Analysis.*

Continued from page 69

investment. By building new plants and hiring workers rather than simply taking over existing facilities, Japanese car and truck manufacturers have hoped to allay protectionist sentiment in their most important consumer market. Honda, which began producing motorcycles in the United States in 1980, expanded its Marysville, Ohio, facilities in 1982 to produce Honda Accords and Civics. The facility created 3,700 new jobs for American workers. In 1983, Nissan set up its light-truck plant in Smyrna, Tenn., hiring 2,500 workers.

Toyota followed suit in 1986 when it entered into a joint venture with General Motors Corp. to co-produce cars at a defunct GM facility in Fremont, Calif. New United Motors Manufacturing Inc. (Nummi) quickly became the object of attention as a model for foreign investment in the United States. Supporters hailed the project's potential boost to American industrial competitiveness. Not only did the venture hire workers who had been laid off from the Fremont facility, but it also brought Japanese management know-how to an American assembly line. The myriad job descriptions and hostile worker-management relations that critics of organized labor say are to blame for this country's industrial decline were jettisoned in favor of the "team concept" prevalent in Japanese manufacturing. Although they continued to be represented by the United Auto Workers, assemblers at Nummi were trained to do several jobs and given greater say in how their work was performed. The results have been dramatic: Even critics of the team concept concede that productivity at Nummi is much higher than at other auto plants in the United States. And, under the company's contract with the United Auto Workers, Nummi assembly-line workers earn $15.46 an hour, making them the highest paid in the American auto industry.[13]

But critics charge that gains in productivity at Nummi exact an unacceptable toll on workers. Mike Parker and Jane Slaughter, former auto workers, call the team concept "management-by-stress" and warn that it is being adopted by managers throughout the industrial world and that its effects on workers are far from benign. "Management-by-stress," they write, "uses stress of all kinds — physical, social, and psychological — to regulate and boost production. It combines a systematic speedup, 'just-in-time' parts delivery, and strict control over how jobs are to be done, to create a production system which has no leeway for errors — and very little breathing room." [14]

Assembly-line workers are not the only critics of management techniques in Japanese-owned factories in the United States. Higher-level employees have complained that some management positions in these firms are reserved for Japanese nationals and Japanese-Americans. This was the basis of a discrimination suit filed by two mid-level managers in February 1988 in federal court in New York against Sumitomo Corp. of America, an affiliate of a Tokyo-based trading company.[15] The suit is still pending.

Efforts to control foreign investments

One of the advantages of foreign corporate investment was supposed to be an improvement in the trade deficit. Foreign affiliates such as Honda's Ohio plant produce for export from the United States as well as for the local market. Even when considering sales to American consumers alone, each Honda Civic car produced in the United States for domestic sale means one less Japanese import and should whittle about $10,000 off the $100 billion deficit.

But the overall relationship is not so neat. In fact, the Commerce Department reported that in 1987 the value of imports by U.S. affiliates, $124 billion, far exceeded the value of their exports, which amounted to only $51 billion. While foreign-owned assembly plants include some domestic content in the products they turn out in this country, they also import parts for final assembly. Often, these imported parts are such high value-added components as automobile engines. Furthermore, foreign investors often bring with them the capital equipment — machines used on the assembly line, for example — used in the U.S. plant. This practice actually worsens the U.S. trade deficit, at least in the plant's early operating phase.

One of the main threats posed by the wave of foreign investments in U.S. industry, critics have said, is to the country's national security. Without limits on foreign purchases of defense contractors, a hostile power could obtain sensitive military information and technological expertise by simply buying into the right American firm. This fear is the only aspect of foreign direct investment on which Congress has taken action. The Exon-Florio amendment to the 1988 Omnibus Trade Bill, sponsored by Sen. Jim Exon, D-Neb., and Rep. James J. Florio, D-N.J., grants the president explicit authority to void a merger, acquisition or takeover by a foreign investor of an American company on national security grounds.

This new authority has not been exercised by the Bush administration, which like its predecessor is on record as favoring foreign investments in the American economy. The Committee on Foreign Investment in the United States, an agency led by the Treasury Department that screens controversial investments, has never barred a foreign investment since it was created in 1975, according to the committee's staff chairman, Steve Canner. In February, the committee decided not to intervene in a case involving the planned purchase by Huels AG of West Germany of Monsanto Electronic Materials Co., the last major U.S. producer of silicon wafers used in semiconductor

State and Local Governments Seek Foreign Investors

Fear of protectionist laws that would cut into their share of the world's largest consumer market is only one reason foreign investors are setting up new plants in the United States. They also are responding to aggressive campaigns launched by states and cities eager to lure foreign investment to their jurisdictions. "In the 1980s, states have emerged as the most direct and primary public sponsors of business development in the United States," according to a report prepared for the National Governors' Association. "Most states now administer comprehensive economic development programs to retain existing businesses, promote new firm starts, and attract industry from other jurisdictions." † The report notes that at least 27 states have offices in Japan and 25 states have representatives in Europe for this purpose.

State and local interest in attracting foreign direct investment stems from two forces. First, the decline of traditional U.S. industries such as steel and heavy manufactured goods that began in the mid-1970s led to factory closings and has forced state and city governments to compete with one another to attract corporate investment, both domestic and foreign. The Reagan administration's cut-

backs in federal support for these governments, beginning in 1981, compounded the problem.

State representatives often provide tax breaks and other incentives to attract foreign investors. Susan Tolchin, a professor of public administration at The George Washington University in Washington, D.C., is among those who question the advisability of such efforts to attract foreign capital. Among the issues she says that need to be examined more closely is "the wisdom of having states compete for foreign capital, providing millions of dollars in tax abatements and other incentives, thus letting United States taxpayers subsidize foreign acquisitions and investments." ††

Another frequently stated concern is that by bringing in foreign plants, state and local governments may be hurting their domestic competitors. But Stephen L. Cooney Jr., director of international investment and finance of the National Association of Manufacturers, disputes this notion. "[Our members] have never been worried about more competition as long as the competitors have to pay the same taxes and obey the same labor standards American companies do," he says. But like Tolchin, Cooney criticizes state governments that offer special tax

incentives to foreign investors. This, he says, amounts to "government subsidization" that places domestic industry at an unfair disadvantage to their foreign-owned competitors.

Whatever their merits, the state and local governments' campaigns have paid off. The Commerce Department estimated than in 1987 about 3 million American workers were employed by about 5,100 U.S. affiliates of foreign companies. While this is only about 3.5 percent of the American work force, it is double the number of workers employed by foreign affiliates a decade earlier. The greatest number of affiliate employees were found in California, New York and Texas, each with more than 200,000 people working for foreign-owned firms. But other states depend more heavily on foreign investment for overall employment. In Delaware, for example, one worker in eight was employed by a foreign affiliate.‡ Given the rapid growth in foreign investment last year, those numbers are surely greater today.

† *Blaine Liner and Larry Ledebur,* Foreign Direct Investment in the United States: A Governor's Guide, *National Governor's Association and the Urban Institute, July 1987, p. 5.*

†† *Writing in* The New York Times, *June 22, 1988.*

‡ *Commerce Department figures cited by Liner and Ledebur, op. cit.*

chips. The committee had been urged by other U.S. manufacturers of silicon wafers to recommend a presidential rejection of the deal on national security grounds.*

---

*The Committee on Foreign Investment in the United States, set up by executive order in 1975, fell under the International Economic Emergency Powers Act until the Exon-Florio amendment extended its authority to consider the national security implications of foreign corporate investments. Upon receipt of a complaint regarding a foreign purchase, the committee has 30 days to decide whether to launch an investigation, not to exceed 45 days, at the end of which the president has 15 days to decide whether to void the deal.

Some critics say foreign acquisitions will continue to have a negative impact on America's defense industry and the country's national security because the public lacks timely and adequate information about the extent of foreign purchases of key businesses.[16] Although the Commerce Department's Bureau of Economic Affairs provides aggregate statistics on foreign direct investments, it is slow to publish the data — the most recent available figures are preliminary numbers for 1987. Furthermore, the bureau withholds statistics that would reveal the identity of partners in specific deals. That information must be obtained piecemeal from private sources. "We have 16 federal agencies that collect some kind of information, all of which is inaccurate, incomplete or basically worthless in terms of assessing the phenomenon and its impact on our economy," said Carlton Carl, press secretary for Rep. John Bryant, D-Texas. Bryant sponsored an amendment to last year's trade legislation to require foreign investors to register their U.S. purchases. Defeated last year, the measure was reintroduced by Bryant as one of the first legislative proposals offered before the 101st Congress in January.*

The Bryant measure would apply to foreign investors buying more than 5 percent of an American property or business worth $5 million or more or that had annual sales of more than $10 million. They would have to reveal their identity, nationality, the American firm or property they acquired and the amount of the transaction to the Commerce Department, congressional committees, the General Accounting Office, a special office in each state and a researcher authorized by the Secretary of Commerce. The measure's intent, Carl explained, is not to limit foreign direct investment, but to allow government agencies to assess its impact. "Basically, it's clear that foreign investment has a great impact on our economy, but we don't know the extent, the concentration or the impact, or who's doing it in what sectors of the economy." Opponents of the measure, including the Bush administration, say that forcing foreigners to register their purchases would discourage them from investing here.

Carl rejects that position, and says the Bryant legislation would merely bring the U.S. practices closer in line with foreign-investment regulations already imposed by America's trading partners. But critics of the measure say registration of foreign investments would undermine American industry's efforts to eliminate such requirements for U.S. companies that invest overseas. As Stephen Cooney of the National Association of Manufacturers puts it: "People will turn around and say, 'Well, if it's such a great idea and investments should flow according to economic opportunity, why are you guys thinking about restrictions, now that the shoe's on the other foot?'"

Portfolio investments pose greater risk

Critics of measures such as the Bryant legislation say the emphasis on foreign investment in U.S. industries and property is overblown. For all the alarm

*House Speaker Jim Wright, D-Texas, originally scheduled the Bryant measure (HR 5) for floor action on Feb. 23, but postponed action after several administration officials opposed to the measure complained that it had not been subjected to hearings. For background, see *Congressional Quarterly Weekly Report*, March 4, 1989, pp. 428-429.

over direct investments in American industry and real estate from abroad, they say, this is only a small part of the issue of foreign investment in the United States. "If you really want to scare people, it's portfolio investment that has the greater portent because you can move it in a matter of milliseconds," said Sam Rosenblatt of the Association for Foreign Investment in America. "You can't move a factory out of the United States."

Flush with export earnings from sales to the United States and attracted by relatively high interest rates in this country, investors in Japan and Western Europe have poured funds into Treasury bills and other securities in the 1980s. About 80 percent — $153 billion — of the foreign investments in 1987 were in such portfolios. This influx of foreign money has allowed the United States to finance a federal budget deficit that has exceeded the $100 billion mark since 1982. As foreign holdings of U.S. government securities have increased, so, too, have interest payments by the government. Almost 20 percent of net U.S. government interest payments currently go to foreigners.[16]

Experts across the political spectrum agree that the country's dependence on foreign money will continue until the deficit is greatly reduced. Although the deficit peaked in 1986 at $221 billion, it still stood at $155 billion last year. According to projections by the Congressional Budget Office, current budgetary policies will derail efforts to balance the budget by 1993, as mandated by the Balanced Budget and Emergency Deficit Control Reaffirmation Act of 1987. The budget office predicts the deficit will grow to $159 billion in 1989 and fall to $135 billion in 1993.[18]

The danger of depending so heavily on capital from abroad to finance the budget deficit lies in the ease with which foreigners could withdraw their money if they no longer perceived the U.S. economy to be a safe place for their investments. Indeed, the power of this kind of foreign investment has already been demonstrated — most notably, according to R. Taggart Murphy's article in the *Harvard Business Review*, in the October 1987 stock market crash. "Japanese fund managers triggered the crash when the dumped U.S. Treasuries on October 14, five days before Black Monday, in a panicked reaction to the announcement of America's poor August trade performance," he writes. "The collapse in bond prices and concomitant sharp rise in interest rates led, in turn, to the worldwide sell-off in equities." [19]

But according to C. Fred Bergsten, director of the Institute for International Economics in Washington, D.C., foreign direct investment, by contrast, actually protects the U.S. economy. In his view, foreign companies, and by extension their governments, that buy a stake in American companies have every interest in avoiding moves that will harm the U.S. economy.

Instead of discouraging foreign acquisitions of American business enterprises, Bergsten says, the United States should press for a new international

Past Coverage

■ **A High-Tech, High-Stakes HDTV Gamble** explains why billions of dollars are at stake in the development high-definition television. "The problem is a familiar one," writes author Patrick G. Marshall. "Japan has a clear lead in the race to provide high-definition television to the world. . . . Just as the videocassette recorder was invented in the United States only to be developed and manufactured in Japan, so, too, did HDTV find its origins in U.S. research labs." E.R.R., 1989 Vol. I, pp. 89-104.

■ **Soviet Trade: In America's Best Interest?** examines U.S. trade with the communist world. Author Mary H. Cooper writes that the Bush administration "must decide whether [Soviet leader Mikhail] Gorbachev's reforms bode well or ill for the United States. The debate will reflect fundamental perceptions of the world." E.R.R., 1989 Vol. I, pp. 73-88.

■ **Europe 1992: Danger or Opportunity?** looks at U.S. trade with Europe as the European Community moves toward removing all internal trade barriers by 1992. The report explains what U.S. businesses can and should do to prepare for the economic competition posed by a united Europe. By Mary H. Cooper. E.R.R., 1989 Vol. I, pp. 17-28.

regime to govern the flow of investments among countries. In much the same way that the multilateral trade agreement GATT (the General Agreement on Tariffs and Trade) seeks to expand trade as a means of raising world living standards, the "GATT for Investment" Bergsten proposes would aim to facilitate investment flows and provide rules governments and firms would have to follow, as well as an institution to enforce them. By taking the lead in such a plan, Bergsten says, the Bush administration could "begin the process of resolving the interminable debate on [foreign direct investment]." [20]

There is no sign, however, that the Bush administration is ready to take on the task of initiating a new multilateral initiative to regulate the flow of global investments. Judging from its immediate opposition to the Bryant measure, the administration appears likely to maintain the laissez-faire approach embraced by its predecessor. As long as the U.S. economy offers foreigners the best deal for their money, the debate over foreign investment seems destined to continue.

NOTES

[1] Martin and Susan Tolchin, *Buying into America: How Foreign Money Is Changing the Face of Our Nation* (1988), p. 274.

[2] See, for example, the cover of *Business Week*, Sept. 7, 1987.

[3] *The Washington Post*-ABC News Poll was conducted in late January. See *The Washington Post*, Feb. 21, 1989.

[4] R. Taggart Murphy, "Power without Purpose: The Crisis of Japan's Global Financial Dominance," *Harvard Business Review*, March-April 1989, p. 79.

[5] "Foreign Direct Investment in the United States: Detail for Position and Balance of Payments Flows, 1987," *Survey of Current Business*, August 1988, p. 69.

[6] See Thomas J. Lueck, "New York City Is Challenged as Giant of Global Economy," *The New York Times*, June 27, 1988.

[7] See Paul Farhi, "How Foreign Money Is Changing Washington," *The Washington Post*, June 20, 1988.

[8] See Stewart Toy and Ted Holden, "Japan Buys into the American Dream," *Business Week*, Nov. 7, 1988, p. 42.

[9] For more information, see J. Peter DeBraal, *Foreign Ownership of U.S. Agricultural Land through December 31, 1987*, U.S. Department of Agriculture, April 1988.

[10] See "The 100 Largest Foreign Investments in the U.S.," *Forbes*, July 25, 1988, pp. 240-46.

[11] Figures reported in *Japan M & A Reporter*, January-February 1989. The newsletter is published by Ulmer Brothers Inc.

[12] Joel Kotkin and Yoriko Kishimoto, *The Third Century: America's Resurgence in the Asian Era* (1988), p. 14.

[13] See George Ruben, "Collective Bargaining and Labor-Management Relations, 1988," *Monthly Labor Review*, January 1989, p. 29.

[14] Mike Parker and Jane Slaughter, *Choosing Sides: Unions and the Team Concept* (1988), p. 14.

[15] See *The Wall Street Journal*, Nov. 7, 1988.

[16] See, for example, "Tracking a Foreign Presence in U.S. Military Contracting," *The New York Times*, Jan. 1, 1989.

[17] See *Economic Report of the President*, January 1989, p. 133.

[18] Congressional Budget Office, *An Analysis of President Reagan's Budgetary Proposals for Fiscal Year 1990*, February 1989. The 1987 law, popularly known as Gramm-Rudman II, amended the original Balanced Budget and Emergency Deficit Control Act of 1985, sponsored by Sens. Phil Gramm, R-Texas, Warren B. Rudman, R-N.H.

[19] Murphy, *op. cit.*, p. 73.

[20] C. Fred Bergsten, *America in the World Economy: A Strategy for the 1990s* (1988). p. 156.

Graphics: S. Dmitri Lipczenko.

RECOMMENDED READING

BOOKS

Bergsten, C. Fred, *America in the World Economy: A Strategy for the 1990s*, **Institute for International Economics, November 1988.**

Bergsten, director of the Institute for International Economics in Washington, D.C., disagrees with the notion that foreign direct investment (FDI) is getting out of control. "No one has demonstrated that inward FDI hurts the American economy, or even has the potential to do so," he writes. "The imposition of major restrictions on FDI by the United States, like the adoption of any far-reaching restrictions on trade, could cause a run on the dollar and thus undermine the entire international economic policy of the new administration."

Tolchin, Martin & Susan, *Buying into America: How Foreign Money Is Changing the Face of Our Nation*, **Times Books, 1988.**

The authors examine the increase in foreign investments in the United States during the 1980s and conclude that the phenomenon is fast outstripping policy makers' ability to understand its implications and formulate policies to deal with it. "The forces of the international marketplace have begun to overwhelm America's capacity to deal with them. The surge of foreign investment is only one glaring example. The manner in which the nation's leaders respond will determine how we meet the most difficult economic challenge of our times: to retain U.S. sovereignty in the global economy."

ARTICLES

Curran, John, "What Foreigners Will Buy Next," *Fortune*, **Feb. 13, 1989.**

Foreign investors will continue their buyout of U.S. companies, the author predicts, and they will expand beyond the chemicals, metals and publishing industries that have attracted most foreign capital to date. Firms that produce semiconductors, small industries such as paints and adhesives, and biotechnology firms are likely targets for foreign investors in the future. According to the author, foreign investors will continue to avoid large, diversified companies and concentrate on purchasing healthy companies that produce goods that fit in with their overall production strategies.

"Japan's Clout in the U.S.," *Business Week*, **July 11, 1988.**

This cover story includes several articles describing the growing political power of Japanese interests that has accompanied the influx of direct investments from Japan in the U.S. economy. Lobbyists, the authors say, are pushing Japanese corporate and government interests on Capitol Hill, while Japanese endowments to U.S. educational institutions are subtly changing the way Americans think about Japan.

Rohatyn, Felix, "America's Economic Dependence," *Foreign Affairs*, **America and the World 1988/89.**

Rohatyn, a senior partner in the investment firm of Lazard Freres & Co., says U.S. policy makers are more permissive toward foreign investors than are other governments. "Selling permanent assets is an easy solution at this time and it relieves the U.S. government from having to sell equivalent amounts of government bonds, possibly at higher rates of interest to finance its deficits. But it creates a permanent claim on our economy, as opposed to the temporary claim represented by borrowing." Rohatyn says this policy relieves the pressure on Congress to take more painful steps to lower the deficits by further devaluing the dollar or raising interest rates.

Tsurumi, Yoshi, "The U.S. Trade Deficit with Japan," *World Policy Journal*, **spring 1987.**

The author, a professor of international business at Baruch College, City University of New York, blames poor U.S. planning and management practices for America's trade deficit with Japan. To illustrate his point, Tsurumi describes the success of Japanese corporate investors in turning around abandoned enterprises in the United States. "Illustrations of the Japanese paradox can be found increasingly across America's industrial landscape. A common thread runs throughout: management, in cooperation with labor, restoring the vigor of firms abandoned by American executives as uneconomical. The Japanese are successful because they understand that sustained improvements in competitiveness and productivity can only be achieved by a long-term investment in automation and people, and not by quick-fix remedies like migration to low-wage countries."

REPORTS AND STUDIES

Jackson, James K., "Foreign Direct Investment in the United States," **Congressional Research Service, Jan. 19, 1989.**

This report from the research branch of the Library of Congress reviews the rise in foreign investment in the United States and U.S. policy toward it. The report details recent proposals to limit or more closely monitor foreign purchases of American assets and includes a bibliography of congressional studies on the subject.

Parker, Mike, and Jane Slaughter, "Choosing Sides: Unions and the Team Concept," **Labor Education and Research Project, May 1988.**

Former auto workers review the track record of "team management" introduced by Japanese managers in their U.S. plants and joint ventures with American firms. The authors conclude that the team concept is less beneficial to working conditions than is popularly believed. The traditional role of labor unions is eroded, only to be replaced by what they call "management by stress," as workers are pressed to work faster. They point to the spread of the team concept beyond Japanese-owned auto plants to other U.S. enterprises as well.

IS AFFIRMATIVE ACTION STILL THE ANSWER?

IS AFFIRMATIVE ACTION STILL THE ANSWER?

by Robert K. Landers

Affirmative action survived the Reagan administration's assault and is now an established fact, both in government and in big business. But with the success of the black middle class and the troubles of the largely black underclass, is affirmative action still relevant to the needs of today's black Americans?

The Supreme Court is taking a "giant step backward," Justice Thurgood Marshall bitterly asserted. But his protest last January was to no avail. By a 6-3 vote, the court ruled unconstitutional a Richmond, Va., ordinance setting aside 30 percent of the city's public works contracts for minority-owned firms. *(See story, p. 83.)* Only where a state or local government was trying to rectify the effects of "identified discrimination" might "some form of narrowly tailored racial preference" be necessary, Justice Sandra Day O'Connor wrote for the court's majority. Thirty-six states and 190 cities and counties had minority set-aside programs similar to Richmond's, and many of the governments have begun to re-examine them in the light of the court's decision.

Less than a week before its ruling in *City of Richmond v. J. A. Croson Co.*, the Supreme Court heard arguments in *Wards Cove Packing Co. v. Frank Atonio et al.*, an employment discrimination case that could be "very significant," according to William L. Robinson, dean of the District of Columbia School of Law and former director of the Lawyers' Committee for Civil Rights Under Law. A crucial issue that could be resolved by the court's ruling in this case is whether an employer whose practices have had a statistically "disparate impact" on minorities must prove (as he has in the past) the "business necessity" of his practices, or whether he must merely produce some evidence that the practices serve a legitimate business interest. *(See story, p. 80.)* If, as many anticipate the court lifts the heavier burden of proof from the employer, the result, in Robinson's view, will be "to insulate the informal discriminatory practices which occur so frequently."

Despite the Richmond ruling and the prospect of another major setback in the *Atonio* case, affirmative action in employment is not likely to disappear any time soon from American life. The Supreme Court has clearly upheld affirmative action in principle, even if the court now seems to be moving to limit its use somewhat. Affirmative action survived the vigorous assault on it by the Justice Department during the Reagan administration, and it is an established fact in both government and big business.

Although it was not the main factor in the enormous progress that black Americans have made in the past half-century, affirmative action has had an effect. The principal beneficiaries have been young black college graduates. But the benefit to them may have proved somewhat mixed. Many blacks in business and academia have come to resent being perceived as "affirmative action hires," that is, as somehow unqualified for, or incompetent at, their jobs. Wrong and even racist as that perception often is, some blacks have ruefully come to regard it as a predictable result of affirmative action.

But whatever its disadvantages, some middle-class blacks did at least benefit from affirmative action. To unskilled blacks trapped in the underclass, however, affirmative action has meant virtually nothing. "It seems to me that affirmative action would be all right if it were designed to help the economically disadvantaged," says Shelby Steele, a professor of English at San Jose State University who has written about race for *Harper's* and *Commentary* and is at work on a collection of essays on the subject. "But any time it's based solely on color or ethnicity or gender, I think it's absolutely wrong and it's going to create backlash and . . . other difficulties."

Steele's view is still apparently a minority one among blacks. Nevertheless, it is evident that affirmative action is a much smaller part of "the solution" for black America than was once imagined, and, indeed, it may even have become a part of "the problem" — a distraction from the real difficulties facing unskilled blacks and irrelevant to the troubling question of why more blacks have not taken advantage of the opportunities that opened up for them as a result of the hard-fought struggle for racial justice.

Affirmative action is, of course, a fruit of that struggle, a symbol of blacks' successful assertion of their rightful claim on the American conscience. "[E]ven though [affirmative action] is not what we really need right now," Steele says, "we cling to it as a symbol of our power, and we feel that to lose it would be to indicate that we've lost power in American life."

Others believe that affirmative action is more than a symbol and more even than just an established fact, that it remains a vital tool in the quest for a just and ultimately color-blind society. Whatever the truth of the matter, it is clear that the impassioned debate about affirmative action is not quite over.

Federal rules, courts changed the meaning

The meaning of affirmative action has changed greatly over the years. As originally used by Presidents Kennedy and Johnson, the term meant that federal contractors would act affirmatively to recruit workers, without discrimination. " 'Affirmative action' originally meant that one should not only not discriminate, but inform people one did not discriminate; not only treat those who applied for jobs without discrimination, but seek out those who might not apply," notes sociologist Nathan Glazer.[1] In the Civil Rights Act of 1964, the term "affirmative action" was used to refer to the sort of action — such as hiring or reinstatement of employees, with or without back pay — that a court might order an employer found guilty of discrimination to take. But employers otherwise were explicitly *not* to be required "to grant preferential treatment to any individual or group" on the basis of race (or sex) "on account of an imbalance which may exist with respect to the total number or percentage of persons" of any race (or sex) employed.

In subsequent years, however, affirmative action came to mean something quite different. As a result of interpretations made in federal regulations and court rulings, federal contractors and private employers who had *not* been found guilty of discrimination began to be required to take race (and gender) into account in their hiring and promotions. If their work forces were found to be racially imbalanced, the employers had to establish numerical "goals" to correct the imbalance, along with "timetables" for reaching the goals — and then to make "good faith" efforts to do so. Critics said all this amounted to illegal racial quotas, but advocates of affirmative action (in its new meaning) denied this and insisted that, as Justice Harry A. Blackmun once put it, "In order to get beyond racism we must first take account of race."[2]

With the shift in its meaning, affirmative action became controversial. Critics maintained that the way to get beyond racism in employment was to see to it that employers did *not* take race into account. Employment decisions should be based, as much as possible, on the individual applicant's or employee's ability to perform the job. If the result was less than proportional equality for blacks and whites, then so be it. Equality of opportunity for individuals, no matter what their race, was the object to be achieved, after all,

'Disparate Impact' and Alaska Canneries

There are indications that the Supreme Court's forthcoming ruling in *Wards Cove Packing Co. v. Frank Atonio et al.* may mark a significant change in the interpretation of Title VII of the 1964 Civil Rights Act, making it easier for employers to defend their challenged employment practices. The court heard arguments in January in the employment-discrimination case involving Alaskan salmon canneries.

Wards Cove Packing Co. and Castle & Cooke operate canneries in remote areas of Alaska during the summer salmon runs. Skilled workers, most of them white, are brought in before the fishing season begins to assemble canning equipment, repair any damaged facilities and prepare the cannery for the salmon run. Those workers stay after the season is over to disassemble the equipment and shut down the facilities for the winter. Unskilled cannery workers, most of them non-white (predominantly Filipino or Alaska Native), make up the bulk of the summer work force. They arrive shortly before the fishing season begins and leave when it is over, three weeks to two months later.

The plaintiffs, unskilled cannery workers, contend that they were discriminated against in the hiring for and promotion to the skilled jobs, as well as in the companies' housing and "messing" (providing of meals) practices. The plaintiffs also contend that even if there was no intent to discriminate, the companies' employment practices (including English-language skill requirements and alleged nepotism) had an adverse impact on non-whites and were not necessary to the employer's business.

Ever since the Supreme Court's 1971 ruling in *Griggs v. Duke Power Co.*, employers whose hiring or promotional practices have been shown to have a "disparate impact" statistically on blacks or other protected groups, have

had to prove the "business necessity" of those practices. But the ruling in the *Atonio* case could change that.

In the landmark *Griggs* case, black workers charged that the North Carolina power company had discriminated against them when it required a high-school diploma or the passing of a standardized general intelligence test as a condition for employment or promotion. There was no evidence the company intended to discriminate. But the requirements disqualified blacks at a substantially higher rate than whites and were irrelevant to successful job performance, the workers contended. The Supreme Court agreed, and ruled that in the circumstances, the requirements were discriminatory. Rulings in subsequent cases reaffirmed the "disparate impact" reasoning.

Last year, however, a plurality of Supreme Court justices signaled that the court may be ready to ease the employer's burden. In *Watson v. Fort Worth Bank*, the court actually extended (by an 8-0 vote) the applicability of "disparate impact" analysis to include subjective employment practices, not just "objective" practices such as written tests. However, Justice Sandra Day O'Connor, joined by Chief Justice William H. Rehnquist and Justices Byron R. White and Antonin Scalia, expressed concern that the extension "could increase the risk that employers will be given incentives to adopt quotas or to engage in preferential treatment," and said that the *Griggs* ruling should not be taken to mean "that the ultimate burden of proof can be shifted to the defendant [employer]. On the contrary, the ultimate burden of proving that discrimination against a protected group has been caused by a specific employment practice remains with the plaintiff at all times." The employer, in the plurality's apparent view, has merely to "produc[e]

evidence that [his] employment practices are based on legitimate business reasons." It's up to the plaintiff to show that alternative practices would serve "the employer's legitimate business goals" equally well.

Justices Harry A. Blackmun, Thurgood Marshall and William J. Brennan Jr. dissented from the plurality's opinion. Justice John Paul Stevens expressed no view on the matter. Justice Anthony M. Kennedy was not on the court when the case was heard and took no part in the decision.

In a memorandum last July to members of the Equal Employment Advisory Council, an association of about 190 large employers and trade and industry groups, Jeffrey A. Norris, the association's president, noted that if in future cases either Stevens or Kennedy should join the O'Connor plurality, "plaintiffs will find it much more difficult to prevail in adverse impact cases involving *both* objective and subjective practices."

The *Atonio* case, which the court selected for review the day after its *Watson* decision, may provide the opportunity for such a ruling. However, William L. Robinson, dean of the District of Columbia School of Law, points out that the court, "in all of its major decisions that involve questions of affirmative action or questions of description of the burden of proof, [has] been horribly divided. Indeed, in many of the cases, you've been forced to piece together the central holding of the case by looking at majority opinions, concurring opinions, and even dissenting opinions in some instances." As a result, he says, "I think it's very difficult nowadays for a lawyer in advance of the decision to predict either the outcome or the likely significance of a case." Still, he adds, the *Atonio* case "has the potential for being a very significant case."

not necessarily equality of result. According to this view, black Americans had made substantial progress and would continue to do so, without the aid of preferential treatment or discriminatory quotas.

Proponents of affirmative action (in its new and current meaning) took a different position. The historical fact of racial discrimination, they contended, had consequences that simply could not be ignored. "There

was rigid racial segregation and individual definition of opportunity on the basis of race for hundreds of years," Robinson says. "[If] you proclaim no more discrimination and you inculcate in society broadly the feeling that it is wrong to be motivated by the race of the person with whom you are dealing, that just simply doesn't undo racial discrimination. And if that's all you did, then for the foreseeable future you would essentially have changed the legal status but would have left people where they were. And that's just not a proper response to the fact of racial discrimination as it has occurred in our society. That does not create for us the society of genuine equal opportunity, the non-race-based society that I think even the pro- and anti-affirmative action debaters would agree is the ultimate goal."

There may be agreement about the ultimate goal, but there is sharp disagreement about existing social reality, and that disagreement has underlain much of the debate about the use of affirmative action as a "temporary" means to achieve the ultimate goal. Justice Marshall, in his dissent in the Richmond case, complained that the court majority was signaling "that it regards racial discrimination as largely a phenomenon of the past, and that government bodies need no longer preoccupy themselves with rectifying racial injustice. I, however, do not believe this nation is anywhere close to eradicating racial discrimination or its vestiges."

Other proponents of affirmative action do not believe that, either. To Josh Henkin, assistant editor of the liberal Jewish magazine *Tikkun*, for instance, "[T]he American ideal of meritocracy is a sham. . . . [I]t is absurd to argue . . . that people who achieve academic and career success do so by winning the meritocratic race. The starting line is radically different for different people, and these divergent starting lines all too often reflect racial and sexual divisions." Racism, he thinks, "[goes] a long way toward explaining . . . why a black man with more than an elementary-school education earns 30 percent less than a white man with the same education, and why the black poverty rate is nearly three times as high as the overall poverty rate." [3]

Critics of affirmative action, however, believe that racial discrimination is a far less significant force than it used to be. Glazer points out that the "barriers to economic activity and education [which] had been overwhelming for blacks . . . [were] lifted through the success of the civil rights struggle." Although discrimination, to be sure, did not completely cease to exist, the laws against it "were powerful and powerfully enforced. Blacks . . . made great progress in the 1960s without affirmative action." In his 1975 book, *Affirmative Discrimination*, Glazer cited econometric studies that had found, as one of them put it, that "traditional discriminatory differences in the labor market [were] abating rapidly." [4]

But statistical disparities in the racial composition of work forces continued to exist, and from such disparities, apparent discrimination has been inferred. As the Equal Employment Opportunity Commission (EEOC), one of the main government agencies charged with enforcing affirmative action, asserted in one case, in reference to entry-level jobs: "A substantial underrepresentation of women or minorities in certain job categories manifestly cannot be attributed to their lack of skill. Absent discrimination, one would expect a nearly random distribution of women and minorities in all jobs."

Glazer strongly disagrees with that argument: "Absent discrimination, . . . one would expect nothing of the sort. . . . [The] various elements that contribute to the distribution of jobs of minority groups [include]: level of education, quality of education, type of education, location by region, by city, by part of metropolitan area, character of labor market at time of entry into the region or city, and many others. These are factors one can in part quantify. Others — such as taste or, if you will, culture — are much more difficult to quantify. Discrimination is equally difficult to quantify. To reduce all differences in labor force distribution (even for entry-level jobs) to *discrimination* is an incredible simplification." [5]

Still, some of the other factors that affect job distribution undoubtedly reflect, to some extent, *past* discrimination. "Thus," stated a Wharton Center for Applied Research study group on affirmative action, set up at the request of the U.S. House Committee on Education and Labor, "although current acts of discrimination might be widely condemned as incompatible with contemporary American values, and punished because they are unlawful, the mere enforcement of laws against discriminatory behavior will not assure equal opportunity. Something more is required to secure and protect the right of all persons to participate fully in the economy." [6] The study group went on to cite a statement made by President Johnson in a 1965 speech at Howard University: "You do not take a person who, for years, has been hobbled by chains and liberate him, bring him up to the starting line of a race and then say, 'you are free to compete with all the others,' and still justly believe that you have been completely fair."

Yet to critics of affirmative action, complete fairness also would not include "reverse discrimination," which is what they believed affirmative action had been reinterpreted to be. In their view, special efforts at education or encouragement or recruitment — affirmative action's original meaning — were warranted to increase minority representation in the work place — but not numerical goals, quotas or racial preference. "Until Jackie Robinson broke the color bar in organized sport in the United States, the most virulent kinds of prejudice prevailed against members of minorities," philosopher Sidney Hook observed. "Today who would argue that in compensation for the gross injustices of the past the composition of our basketball, football, baseball, and track teams be determined by any kind of ethnic quota system or numerical ratios reflecting either the relative distribution of ethnic groups in the general population or in the pool of those available? It would be absurd to propose any other criterion except color-blind merit in filling the available posts regardless of what the numerical distribution turns out to be." [7]

Court has followed
a tortuous course

The division of opinion about affirmative action, as that term had come to be understood and applied, was reflected in the decisions of the Supreme Court. After sidestepping the "reverse discrimination" question in 1974,* the court four years later seemed to come down on both sides of the issue, in a case that captured the public's attention. *University of California Regents v. Bakke* involved Allan Bakke, a 38-year-old white engineer who had been twice denied admission to the medical school at the University of California at Davis. To ensure minority representation in the student body, the university had set aside 16 seats in each 100-member medical school class for minority applicants. Each year that Bakke's application had been rejected, minority applicants with qualifications inferior to his had been accepted.

The Supreme Court, by a 5-4 vote, ruled that state universities may not set aside a fixed quota of seats in each class for minority-group members, denying white applicants the opportunity to compete for those places. Bakke was ordered admitted to the medical school. At the same time, by a different five-justice majority, the court held that the equal protection clause of the 14th Amendment did not bar colleges from considering race as a factor in their decisions on applicants. Only one of the nine justices — Justice Lewis F. Powell Jr. — agreed with both halves of the decision.

Although the *Bakke* case concerned admission to an educational institution,** the court's ruling was widely taken as having some application to employment practices. And in Glazer's view, the "schizophrenia" that the court manifested in the *Bakke* decision has "shaped the many decisions over employment that have come down year after year." [8]

In 1979, the court took up its first affirmative-action employment case, *United Steelworkers of America v. Weber.* Kaiser Aluminum and the United Steelworkers of America had agreed on an affirmative-action plan that reserved half of all in-plant craft training slots for minorities. Brian Weber, a white employee at the Kaiser plant in Gramercy, La., applied and was rejected. He had more seniority than the most junior black who had been accepted. Weber sued, charging that he had been a victim of "reverse

discrimination." He won in the lower courts but lost in the Supreme Court.

In its 5-2 decision, the high court held that the prohibition against racial discrimination in Title VII of the 1964 Civil Rights Act did not bar "all private, voluntary, race-conscious affirmative-action plans." The court refused to "define in detail the line of demarcation between permissible and impermissible affirmative-action plans. It suffices to hold that the challenged Kaiser-USWA affirmative-action plan falls on the permissible side of the line."

The pattern evident in the *Weber* case has persisted in the decade since. As Glazer noted, "Those affected by affirmative action — employers and employees, enforcement agencies and lawyers, applicants to selective programs and good jobs, jobholders threatened with termination — have waited for that final, clear decision that tells us just how to separate the constitutional and the legal in preference for minorities from the unconstitutional and illegal. But the court has shown a remarkable skillfulness in chopping up the issue into finer and finer pieces — still without drawing that clear line that settles the controversy over affirmative action." [9]

Although no such clear line has been drawn, the court has clearly upheld the legitimacy of affirmative action, even when it came under vigorous attack by the Justice Department during the Reagan administration. William Bradford Reynolds, then assistant attorney general for civil rights, expressed the administration's position in September 1981, when he told the House Education and Labor Subcommittee on Employment Opportunities that the Justice Department "no longer will insist upon or in any respect support the use of quotas or any other numerical or statistical formulae designed to provide to non-victims of discrimination preferential treatment based on race, sex, national origin or religion." [10] In the administration's view, remedies for discrimination should go only to specific individual victims of past discrimination.

The Reagan administration tried to bring the principal affirmative-action enforcement agencies into line with the view that affirmative action amounted to reverse discrimination. Clarence Thomas, who became EEOC chairman in 1982, criticized his own agency's reliance on statistical disparities as evidence of employment discrimination, and said he didn't think use of numerical goals and timetables for affirmative action worked.

Critics said the EEOC's enforcement work was being undermined, that it was shifting away from systemic discrimination cases against large companies or entire industries and toward cases involving discrimination against specific individuals.[11] But according to Jonathan Leonard, an economist at the University of California, Berkeley, the EEOC has not typically gone after large firms that allegedly discriminate systematically. Instead, he says, the commission "has

Continued on page 84

---

*In *DeFunis v. Odegaard* (1974), a five-justice majority ducked the opportunity to rule on the constitutionality of minority set-asides by finding the case moot because the white plaintiff, who had charged that he was denied admission to a state law school so that a less-qualified minority applicant could be accepted, had been admitted to the school as the result of a court order and was about to graduate.

**The term affirmative action has been widely applied to the voluntary efforts by colleges, universities and professional schools to increase minority enrollment. However, there is no legal requirement for affirmative action in admission to institutions of higher learning, except for public institutions, mainly in the South, that formerly were restricted to whites or to blacks.

Minority Set-Asides: The Richmond Case

Six years ago, the city of Richmond, Va., adopted a plan requiring that at least 30 percent of city construction contracts be subcontracted to minority-owned businesses. The City Council declared that the "remedial" plan had "the purpose of promoting wider participation by minority business enterprises in the construction of public projects." Half of Richmond's population is black, but, according to one study, less than 1 percent of Richmond's prime construction contracts had gone to minority businesses in the period 1978-83.

Later in 1983, the J. A. Croson Co. went after a contract to install plumbing fixtures in the city jail. The company contacted several minority-owned businesses about supplying the fixtures, but, according to Croson, they were uninterested, unresponsive or unable to submit a bid for the subcontract.

The Croson firm, which was the only bidder on the city contract, then sought a waiver of the 30 percent set-aside requirement. The city denied the request and decided to rebid the contract. Croson sued, and the case eventually reached the Supreme Court.

By a 6-3 vote last January, the court ruled that Richmond's minority set-aside ordinance violated the 14th Amendment's equal protection guarantee. The city had failed to provide any evidence of any "identified discrimination" in the Richmond construction industry, and so had failed to demonstrate a "compelling interest" that would justify such a race-based remedy, Justice Sandra Day O'Connor said on behalf of the court's majority.

Moreover, she said, the 30 percent quota "cannot be said to be narrowly tailored to any goal, except perhaps outright racial balancing. It rests upon the 'completely unrealistic' assumption that minorities will choose a particular trade in lockstep proportion to their representation in the local population." The city had not ascertained how many minority businesses there were in the local construction market, or what percentage of city construction dollars they received

as subcontractors.

"While there is no doubt that the sorry history of both private and public discrimination in this country has contributed to a lack of opportunities for black entrepreneurs," the court majority said, "this observation, standing alone, cannot justify a rigid racial quota in the awarding of public contracts in Richmond, Va."

A majority of the justices made it clear that the same "strict scrutiny" by which the constitutionality of laws favoring whites over blacks is tested must also be applied to laws favoring blacks over whites. Dissenting Justice Thurgood Marshall called this "an unwelcome development. A profound difference separates governmental actions that themselves are racist, and governmental actions that seek to remedy the effects of prior racism or to prevent neutral governmental activity from perpetuating the effects of such racism." He cited "the tragic and indelible fact that discrimination against blacks and other racial minorities in this nation has pervaded our nation's history and continues to scar our society."

Responding to Marshall's dissent in her opinion, O'Connor contended that the "relaxed standard of review" he favored would mean "that race will always be relevant in American life, and that the 'ultimate goal' of 'eliminat[ing] entirely from governmental decisionmaking such irrelevant factors as a human being's race' . . . will never be achieved."

In a 1980 case, *Fullilove v. Klutznick*, the Supreme Court had held that Congress had not violated the 14th Amendment's guarantee of equal protection when it set aside 10 percent of federal funds for local public works projects to be awarded, if possible, to minority businesses. But Congress, O'Connor said in the Richmond case, has "a specific constitutional mandate to enforce the dictates of the 14th Amendment. . . . That Congress may identify and redress the effects of society-wide discrimination does not mean that, *a fortiori*, the states and their political subdivisions

are free to decide that such remedies are appropriate."

The court's decision in the *Richmond* case, O'Connor said, did not preclude a state or local government from acting "to rectify the effects of identified discrimination within its jurisdiction. If the city of Richmond had evidence before it that non-minority contractors were systematically excluding minority businesses from subcontracting opportunities, it could take action to end the discriminatory exclusion. Where there is a significant statistical disparity between the number of qualified minority contractors willing and able to perform a particular service and the number of such contractors actually engaged by the locality or the locality's prime contractors, an inference of discriminatory exclusion could arise. . . . In the extreme case, some form of narrowly tailored racial preference might be necessary to break down patterns of deliberate exclusion."

Even where there was no evidence of identified discrimination, O'Connor noted, the city could use various "race-neutral devices to increase the accessibility of city contracting opportunities to small entrepreneurs of all races. Simplification of bidding procedures, relaxation of bonding requirements, and training and financial aid for disadvantaged entrepreneurs of all races would open the public contracting market to all those who have suffered the effects of past societal discrimination or neglect."

The Supreme Court's Richmond ruling has prompted the many state and local governments with similar programs to take another look at them. "These programs were important because they were very helpful in . . . building an entrepreneurial class in the black and minority community and among women," says Eleanor Holmes Norton, a professor of law at Georgetown University Law Center and former head of the Equal Employment Opportunity Commission. "Most of [the programs] will have to be modified substantially."

Losing Ground

Despite affirmative action and overall black economic progress, a smaller proportion of black men aged 20-24 were employed in 1987 than in 1972; a larger proportion were unemployed; and a higher percentage were out of the labor force altogether — that is, not looking for work. The same trends hold true for older black men.

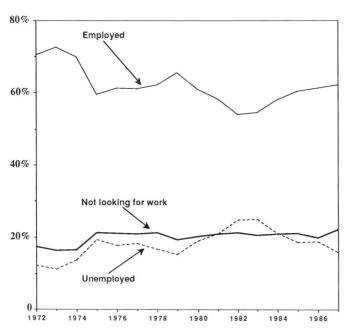

Source: Bureau of Labor Statistics.

Continued from page 82

normally been a reactive body slowly working its way through a mountain of individual complaints, many of which it discards as lacking substance." The agency's "major contribution ... has probably been in helping to establish far-reaching principles of Title VII law in the courts which can then be used by private litigants, rather than in directly providing relief from systematic discrimination through its own enforcement activity." [12]

The other main affirmative-action enforcement agency was the Labor Department's Office of Federal Contract Compliance Programs (OFCCP), which President Johnson had established in a 1965 executive order to combat discrimination by federal contractors.[13] Beginning in 1968, such contractors (which include most large American corporations) had been required to submit affirmative-action plans, complete with "specific goals and timetables." Violators ran the risk of becoming ineligible for federal contracts or of suffering lesser (and more common) penalties such as fines or back-pay awards.

A 1987 investigation by the staff for the majority Democrats on the House Education and Labor Committee found that "enforcement at the OFCCP has come to a virtual standstill since 1980." According to the

staff's report, the number of persons receiving back pay as a remedy for past discrimination decreased from 4,336 in fiscal year 1980 to 499 in fiscal 1986. The report also said that the office's "use of goals and timetables" as a requirement for contractors "has been severely limited." [14]

Nevertheless, when Reynolds and Attorney General Edwin Meese III in 1985 began pushing a proposal that President Reagan rewrite the 1965 executive order so as to relax the affirmative-action requirements, they ran into opposition from Secretary of Labor William E. Brock III, who told a NAACP national convention that he believed "the country would have to have some form of affirmative action for the foreseeable future." [15] The Justice Department officials encountered other opposition, too — from civil rights groups, from Congress, and, perhaps to their surprise, from big business. Although many small businesses objected to what they consider the burdensome regulations and paperwork, large corporations such as IBM, Merck & Co., and the Monsanto Corp. actually supported affirmative action.

"Some corporate managements, no doubt, push affirmative action only because government pushes them," *Fortune* magazine noted. "But persuasive evidence indicates that most large American corporations want to retain their affirmative-action programs, numerical goals and all." [16] The National Association of Manufacturers opposed "quotas," but favored affirmative action, with numerical goals and timetables. "Business sets goals and timetables for every aspect of its operations — profits, capital investment, productivity increases," an association representative said. "Setting goals and timetables for minority and female participation is simply a way of measuring progress." [17] It is also, of course, a way of avoiding expensive litigation.

Business people "want to know what the rules are," law school Dean William Robinson notes. "They know what the rules are with affirmative action being the law. They can comply with it, and they can operate their businesses consistent with their basic business purpose. ... [In addition,] many of them have found that affirmative-action techniques and principles assist them in identifying quality workers and maintaining a sound employer-employee relationship with their work force. Business people don't talk about it widely, but the fact is they don't have any magic way to identify who's going to turn out to be a good worker and who's not. ... And the way that business people have done it in the past as a matter of fact excluded from their work force a significant number of minority and women employees, who, now that they've got them in the work force, turn out to be good employees. So it gives [the businesses] an additional benefit."

Faced with strong opposition from business and others to changing the affirmative-action requirements, the Justice Department officials ultimately lost the battle over the executive order. Reagan never had it rewritten. He may have been influenced in his decision by the outcomes of the most important battles in the administration's war on affirmative action, which took place in the courts.

The administration hailed as a great victory a 1984 Supreme Court ruling that a federal judge had erred in 1981 when he directed the Memphis Fire Department to ignore its seniority system in order to save the jobs of black officers in the face of budget-dictated layoffs. The blacks had been hired as a result of a court-approved 1980 affirmative-action consent decree. Meese's predecessor, Attorney General William French Smith, claimed the Supreme Court decision in *Firefighters Local Union #1784 v. Stotts* meant that "federal courts cannot impose quotas based upon racial considerations in employment relationships." [18] The administration advised 51 cities, counties and states to scrap their affirmative-action plans. (Most rejected or ignored the advice.)

In the ensuing years, however, the Reagan administration's sweeping interpretation of *Stotts* proved to be just wishful thinking. Although in May 1986 the Supreme Court did declare that a Michigan school board had violated white teachers' constitutional right to equal protection when it laid them off in order to preserve the jobs of blacks with less seniority, a majority of the justices also made it clear that affirmative-action plans are not inherently unconstitutional. "We have recognized ... that in order to remedy the effects of prior discrimination, it may be necessary to take race into account," Justice Powell stated. "As part of this nation's dedication to eradicating racial discrimination, innocent persons may be called upon to bear some of the burden of the remedy." * Justice O'Connor said she and her fellow justices agreed that an affirmative-action plan "need not be limited to the remedying of specific instances of identified discrimination for it to be deemed sufficiently 'narrowly tailored' or 'substantially related,' to the correction of prior discrimination by the state."

Although the Justice Department publicly praised the court's 5-4 decision in that case, the handwriting on the wall was quite legible. That July, the court not only upheld a federal court order requiring a union that had persistently refused to admit blacks to increase its non-white membership to 29 percent, but also, in a different case, ruled that Title VII of the 1964 Civil Rights Act did not prohibit the city of Cleveland from resolving a discrimination complaint by a consent decree that committed it for a limited period to promote one black firefighter for every white promoted. Less than eight months later, the court ruled that, despite the administration's argument to the contrary, the 14th Amendment's equal protection guarantee had not been violated by a one-black-for-one-white promo-

tion quota that a federal judge had imposed on Alabama's state troopers.

In March 1987, by a 6-3 vote, the court gave its broadest endorsement yet to affirmative-action programs. The case involved the voluntary affirmative-action plan of the Transportation Agency of Santa Clara, Calif., and the agency's promotion of a woman to road dispatcher instead of a man who had scored slightly higher in an interview. There was no proof of any past discrimination, although the agency had never employed a woman as a dispatcher. The court, in an opinion by Justice William J. Brennan Jr., said that a voluntary affirmative-action plan that was moderate, flexible, and aimed at gradually eliminating manifest racial or sexual imbalances in traditionally segregated job categories did not conflict with Title VII's purpose. "Such a plan is fully consistent with Title VII, for it embodies the contribution that voluntary employer action can make in eliminating the vestiges of discrimination in the work place," he said.

"In determining whether an imbalance exists that would justify taking sex or race into account," Brennan said, "a comparison of the percentage of minorities or women in the employer's work force with the percentage in the area labor market or general population is appropriate in analyzing jobs that require no special expertise, or training programs designed to provide expertise." But "[w]here a job requires special training, ... the comparison should be with those in the labor force who possess the relevant qualifications."

Justice Antonin Scalia was scathing in his dissent. The purpose of the Santa Clara agency's affirmative-action plan, he said, "was assuredly not to remedy prior sex discrimination by the agency. It should not have been, because there was no sex discrimination to remedy. ... It is absurd to think that [the absence of many women on road-maintenance crews was due to] systematic exclusion of women eager to shoulder pick and shovel. ... [B]ecause of long-standing social attitudes, it has not been regarded by women themselves as desirable work."

By its decision, Scalia said, the court was completing "the process of converting [Title VII] from a guarantee that race or sex will not be the basis for employment determinations, to a guarantee that it often will. Ever so subtly, without even alluding to the last obstacles preserved by earlier opinions that we now push out of our path, we effectively replace the goal of a discrimination-free society with the quite incompatible goal of proportionate representation by race and by sex in the work place."

This crushing defeat ended the Reagan administration's long war against affirmative action. Not only is there no indication that the Bush administration has any notion of waging the war anew, but the Supreme Court, despite its recent ruling in the Richmond case, is hardly likely any time soon to change its collective mind about affirmative action.

Justice Marshall's comment that the Richmond

---

*However, Powell said that layoffs were "too intrusive" a burden. "Denial of a future employment opportunity is not as intrusive as loss of an existing job," he observed.

decision indicates the court majority regards racial discrimination as largely a thing of the past "may be too harsh an evaluation," says Eleanor Holmes Norton, a professor of law at Georgetown University Law Center and a former EEOC chairman. "I think that the Richmond plan, with its large quota [and] without the detail of justification that the court has indicated in the past would clearly be necessary . . . was a sitting duck."

The Richmond decision, although "a setback," in Norton's view, should not be read to mean that the court is belatedly adopting as its own the views of Meese and Reynolds. The court "has been telegraphing substantially what's in this [majority] opinion all along," she says. "What Meese and Reynolds wanted really was a theory that would return us to the way discrimination was proved in the '40s and '50s — that is to say, that only identifiable victims of discrimination could get the advantages of so-called affirmative action. Well, the Supreme Court [has] roundly refuted that doctrine and held that you can use goals and timetables and they do not have to apply only to identifiable victims."

"The problem with the identifiable-victims theory," Norton says, "is that there'd be no way to find them, and the effect of discrimination is [also] to ward off people, not simply to victimize people. Women won't apply to be construction workers in the first place if they know they won't be hired, and blacks didn't go 'downtown' in the first place because they didn't think they would be hired — until affirmative action."

Black middle class is a real success story

The economic progress made by black Americans in the last half-century has been dramatic. The "real story" of the years since 1940, economists James P. Smith and Finis R. Welch have written, has been "the emergence of the black middle class, whose income gains have been real and substantial." In 1940, more than 75 percent of black men were "destitute, with little hope that their lot or even that of their children would soon improve." Only 22 percent of black men were in the middle class. And the black "economic elite resembled an exclusive white club" — only 2 percent of black men belonged. By 1980, all that had changed: By then, 80 percent of black men were *not* destitute. More than two out of three black men were in the middle class, and membership in the economic elite had swelled to 12 percent. "For the first time in American history, a sizable number of black men [were] economically better off than white middle-class America," Smith and Welch pointed out.[19]

Norton contends that this immense progress would

have been "absolutely impossible without affirmative action. There were two things that did it: Businesses [began] to employ people they had routinely turned away before, and schools — some of the best schools and schools of all kinds — opened up to minorities. . . . Blacks did not prepare themselves in the same fields before affirmative action as they do today. . . . [The] most popular college major for blacks [today is] business, because affirmative action has had the effect of opening jobs, [and] young black people think it matters that you get a job if you major in business. The proverbial story all my life was that black men who had college degrees worked in the post office, where white men who had eighth-grade educations worked, because they couldn't get hired [in business or professional jobs] downtown. . . . [Now,] affirmative action [has] had such a high profile that young black people [have] understood that you should go to law school, you can now be hired by a firm; you can go to business school and you [can] get a job in the corporation, [even though] your father could not."

There is no doubt that affirmative action has been effective, Welch says. Skilled and qualified blacks "[have] gotten into larger firms [and] they're being taken much more seriously." He and Smith found that affirmative action "significantly shifted black male employment toward EEOC-covered firms and industries, and particularly into firms with federal contracts.* Affirmative action also increased the representation of black male workers in managerial and professional jobs in covered firms." The big shift took place mainly in the late 1960s and was largely over by 1974. During those years, "there was a remarkable surge in incomes of young black males," as firms covered by the EEOC "rapidly increased their demand for black workers, bidding up their wages. However, once the stock of black workers had reached its new equilibrium, this short-run demand increase was completed and wages returned to their long-run levels."[20]

For black men as a whole, affirmative action had no significant long-term impact on their narrowing wage gap with white men, according to Smith and Welch's analysis. The relative improvement after affirmative action was instituted took place (until about 1980) at about the same rate as it had before.** The massive

Continued on page 88

*All private firms with 100 or more employees, and all federal contractors with more than $50,000 in contracts and 50 or more employees, must report annually to the EEOC on how their employees break down by ethnic and racial group and occupation. Because not *all* firms must report to the EEOC, Smith and Welch noted, "affirmative-action coverage varies widely across industries. Coverage is almost universal in the large-scale, durable goods manufacturing sector, but less than 10 percent of the workforce is covered in the retail trade, personnel services, and construction industries, where small establishments are common. . . . [O]nly about half of the non-government, non-education work force is directly covered by affirmative action."

**The rate of progress has not been maintained in the 1980s. "What one sees, in general," Welch says, "is that if you take average earnings of working black men and express that as a percentage of average earnings of working white men, the data trace a fairly smooth trend up through about 1980; [it] level[s] off then, there's actually a dip [during] the '82-'83 recession, and then it returns to about the 1980 level." (*See graph, p. 209.*)

Landmark Supreme Court Rulings

Griggs v. Duke Power Co. (1971): Black workers charged that the North Carolina power company had discriminated against them in violation of Title VII of the 1964 Civil Rights Act when the company required a high-school diploma or the passing of a standardized general intelligence test as a condition for employment or promotion. There was no evidence the company intended to discriminate. But the requirements disqualified blacks at a substantially higher rate than whites and were irrelevant to successful job performance, the workers contended. The Supreme Court agreed, and ruled that in the circumstances, the requirements were discriminatory. *Vote*: 8-0.

Washington v. Davis (1976): Two black men challenged as unconstitutionally discriminatory the District of Columbia Police Department's requirement that recruits pass a verbal ability test. They argued that the number of black police officers was not proportionate to the racial mix of the city, that more blacks than whites failed the test, and that the test was not significantly related to job performance. The challenge, however, was based not on the 1964 Civil Rights Act but on the Constitution's equal protection guarantee. A federal district court rejected the challenge, ruling that there was no evidence that the Police Department intended to discriminate against black applicants. The Supreme Court agreed. In order to prove an employer guilty of violating the 14th Amendment's equal protection guarantee, the court ruled, it was necessary to prove discriminatory intent as well as effect. *Vote*: 7-2.

Regents of University of California v. Bakke (1978): The court ruled that Title VI of the 1964 Civil Rights Act prohibited state universities from setting aside a fixed quota of seats in each class for minority group members. *Vote*: 5-4. By a different five-justice majority (with only Justice Lewis F. Powell Jr. voting in the majority both times), the court also held that the equal protection clause of the 14th Amendment did not bar college admissions officers from considering race as a factor in their decisions on applicants. *Vote*: 5-4.

United Steelworkers of America v. Weber (1979): The court held that Title VII did not bar an employer from establishing an affirmative-action training program that gave preference to blacks. *Vote*: 5-2.

Fullilove v. Klutznick (1980): Congress, the court ruled, had not violated the constitutional guarantee of equal protection when it set aside 10 percent of federal funds for local public works projects to be awarded, if possible, to minority businesses. *Vote*: 6-3.

Firefighters Local Union #1784 v. Stotts (1984): The court held that a federal judge erred in 1981 when he directed the Memphis Fire Department to ignore its seniority system in order to save the jobs of black officers in the face of budget-dictated layoffs. The blacks had been hired as a result of a court-approved 1980 affirmative-action consent decree. *Vote*: 6-3.

Wygant v. Jackson Board of Education (1986): The court declared it unconstitutional for the Jackson, Mich., school board to lay off white teachers in order to preserve the jobs of blacks with less seniority. The school board's plan, the court found, denied white teachers their right to equal protection of the laws. However, the court made it clear that affirmative action plans are not inherently unconstitutional. *Vote*: 5-4.

Local 28 of the Sheet Metal Workers International Association v. Equal Employment Opportunity Commission (1986): The court upheld a federal court order requiring a union that had persistently refused to admit blacks to increase its non-white membership to 29 percent by August 1987. *Vote*: 5-4.

Local 93 of the International Association of Firefighters v. City of Cleveland and Cleveland Vanguards (1986): The court ruled that Title VII did not prevent the city of Cleveland from resolving a discrimination complaint by a consent decree that committed it for a limited period to promote one black firefighter for every white promoted. *Vote*: 6-3.

United States v. Paradise (1987): A one-black-for-one-white promotions quota imposed on Alabama's state troopers by a federal judge in 1983 was upheld by the court. *Vote*: 5-4.

Johnson v. Transportation Agency, Santa Clara County, Calif. (1987): The court upheld a voluntary affirmative-action plan that led to the promotion of a woman over a man who had scored slightly higher on a qualifying interview. There was no proof of any past discrimination. The court said that a voluntary affirmative-action plan that was moderate, flexible and aimed at gradually eliminating manifest racial or sexual imbalances in traditionally segregated job categories did not conflict with Title VII's purpose. *Vote*: 6-3.

Watson v. Fort Worth Bank (1988): The court extended the applicability of "disparate impact" analysis to include subjective employment practices, not just "objective" practices such as written tests. *Vote*: 8-0. However, four justices expressed concern that the extension "could increase the risk that employers will be given incentives to adopt quotas or to engage in preferential treatment," and said that the *Griggs* ruling should not be taken to mean "that the ultimate burden of proof can be shifted to the defendant [employer]." The employer, in their apparent view, has merely to "produc[e] evidence that [his] employment practices are based on legitimate business reasons." Three justices disagreed with them.

City of Richmond v. J. A. Croson Co. (1989): The court struck down a Richmond, Va., affirmative action plan that set aside 30 percent of the dollar amount of city construction contracts for minority-owned firms. In dissent, Justice Thurgood Marshall called the court's decision a "giant step backward." *Vote*: 6-3.

Continued from page 86
migration of Southern blacks to the cities of the North in the decades from 1940 to 1970 was one reason for blacks' economic progress. Education was another. Blacks were not only becoming better educated, but their education was counting for more economically. However, Smith and Welch noted, "the increase in the economic benefits of the black schooling began long before the affirmative-action pressures of [the 1960s and '70s]." Thus, the economists argue, it was "the slowly evolving historical forces" of education and migration that "were the primary determinants of the long-term black economic improvement. At best affirmative action has marginally altered black wage gains about this long-term trend." [21]

Some black Americans did achieve significant economic benefits from affirmative action, however. As might perhaps have been expected, they were mainly young college graduates. In 1967-68, the wages of young black male college graduates had been only about 75 percent of their white peers' wages; four years later, the blacks' wages reached and slightly exceeded the whites'. Once the EEOC-covered firms obtained their targeted numbers of blacks, however, the wage gap began to widen again, so that in 1979, young, black college graduates' wages were 91 percent of the whites' wages. Even so, the wage gap was substantially smaller than it had been just a decade or so earlier — and affirmative action had helped to reduce it.[22]

But affirmative action's beneficiaries have found that its benefits are not inexhaustible. It enabled many blacks and women "to enter occupations and industries from from which they had long been excluded," the Wharton study group said. "But ... [m]any minority and female employees are now in middle-level positions [in private firms] where they feel frustrated about their prospects for promotion. Breaking ... into higher management and executive positions is especially difficult because of the greater importance of subjective performance measures at that level. ... Under such circumstances, the failure of minority and women workers to advance in numbers commensurate with their overall participation in the work force sparks cries of discrimination, even when other legitimate factors are involved." [23]

"Most black managers are convinced that their best is never seen as good enough, even when their best is better than the best of white colleagues," notes Edward W. Jones Jr., who is president of his own consulting firm in South Orange, N.J., and a former manager at New York Telephone Co. and at AT&T. "The barrier facing black managers is no less real than a closed door. But in the minds of many of their superiors, if people can't make it on their own, it must be their own fault." Because of people's tendency "to act favorably toward those with skin color like theirs and unfavorably toward those with different skin color," Jones maintains, "many of [the] best qualified managers are seen as unqualified 'affirmative ac-

tion hires.'" In his view, this is hardly the fault of affirmative action, whose objective is simply "to ensure that all qualified persons compete on a level playing field." [24]

"We ought to get rid of people's attitudes," Norton says, not get rid of affirmative action. Not only does "affirmative action in fact ... not mean hiring less-qualified people, [but] if you hire less-qualified people, there's a [legal] cause of action. And there are reverse-discrimination suits brought every day that are won. They are very small in number compared to discrimination suits, however."

The perception that a particular black person in business or the professions is an unqualified "affirmative-action hire," may well be inaccurate, unfair and even, in some instances, racist. "But, in any case, certainly that perception does exist and does affect those blacks who, whether through affirmative action or otherwise, have moved ahead," Steele, the San Jose State English professor, says. However, in his view, the perception is a predictable consequence of affirmative action. "[A]ny time you grant affirmative action to people on the basis of color alone, then I think inevitably you're going to diminish the importance of those people who have been let in. I don't think there's any easy way around that. People are going to say, logic following logic, that 'You're here because you're black.' ... And this is going to be difficult for you, in whatever professional setting it may be."

Steele used to believe affirmative action was fine, but over the years he has gradually changed his mind. "Certainly, as a college professor, it irks me deeply when people perceive or feel that I'm here because of affirmative action. I find that a very demeaning sort of view and resent it deeply. And I think certainly most other blacks also resent it, because the suggestion is, well, you wouldn't be here otherwise or you're incompetent in some way. There's a lot of racial stereotyping that blacks have always endured, [and it] now can pass under this 'affirmative action' label."

Racial discrimination is the real issue, Steele contends. "The goal, obviously, is to get race out of the picture as much as possible, if not to end discrimination. And I think affirmative action, as it's now practiced, probably contributes more to racism than it eradicates it."

Some blacks still are losing ground

Despite all the progress black Americans have made, too many still remain mired in poverty. The growth of the black middle class is only part of the story. The other part is the emergence of the underclass, which, in political scientist Lawrence M. Mead's description, "comprises those Americans who *combine* relatively low income with functioning problems such as difficulties in getting through school, obeying the law, working, and keeping their families together." The underclass is about 70 percent non-white.[25]

The two trends appear to contradict one another. "Among those [men] who work, there is clear evidence that earnings of blacks are rising relative to whites, but increasing fractions of black men do not work," Welch observes. In 1960, nearly 78 percent of black men in their early 20s were employed or in school. Two decades later, after the great advances in civil rights and the enforcement of affirmative action, only 70 percent were employed or in school. Not only were 12 percent unemployed (about 3 points higher than in 1960), but nearly 13 percent of black men in their early 20s — more than 4 percentage points higher than in 1960 — were not in the labor force (that is, not even actively looking for employment). Nearly 5 percent of black men in their early 20s were in jail.[26] As author Charles Murray famously put it, young black males, when compared with young white males, "lost ground."[27]

Ground was lost not only in employment but in education. A report last year by the Commission on Minority Participation in Education and American Life, sponsored by the American Council on Education, said that in higher education "the picture of stalled progress is dramatically clear. During the same period when the pool of minority high-school graduates was becoming bigger and better than ever, minority college attendance rates initially fell, and have remained disproportionately low." The percentage of black high-school graduates in their early 20s who had completed one or more years of college had jumped from 39 percent in 1970 to 48 percent five years later, while the corresponding rate for whites remained steady at 53 percent. But between 1975 and 1985, while the college participation rate for white youths increased to 55 percent, the rate for blacks dropped to 44 percent (before going back up to 47 percent in 1986, which was still less than in 1975).[28] The college participation rate for black males fell even more precipitously.

Not only were not enough blacks going to college, but too many who did were dropping out before graduation. In 1984-85, although blacks made up 9 percent of all undergraduates, they received only 8 percent of the associates' degrees and only 6 percent of the bachelor's degrees conferred that year.* At the graduate level, the commission noted, the falloff was dramatic. Between 1976 and 1985, the number of blacks earning master's degrees declined by 32 percent, and the number earning doctorates dropped by 5 percent. "In certain critical fields of study, the minority presence is nearly non-existent," the commission said. In computer science, for instance, only one black received a doctorate out of 355 awarded in 1986. In mathematics

*By contrast, whites made up 80 percent of the undergraduates in 1984-85, but received 85 percent of the bachelor's degrees conferred.

Closing the Gap

In 1940 the typical black male worker earned only 43 percent as much as his white counterpart. By 1960 the average black male was earning 58 percent as much. The wage gap continued to narrow in the late 1960s and early 1970s as a result of the migration of Southern blacks to the North, increased education and affirmative action. However, the rate of progress has not been maintained in the 1980s.

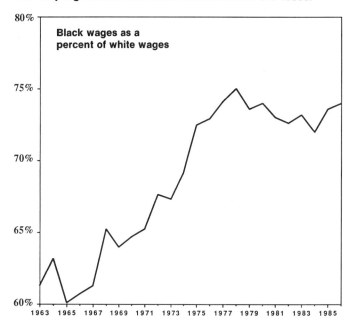

Black wages as a percent of white wages

Source: Kevin Murphy, associate professor of business economics and industrial relations, University of Chicago Graduate School of Business.

that year, blacks received only six of the 730 doctorates awarded.[29]

Opportunity increasingly beckoned, but not as many black Americans seized it as should have. "By most [socioeconomic] measures — infant-mortality rate, teen pregnancy, and so forth — the gap [between blacks and whites] is wider today than it was in the '50s," Steele says. "The startling thing . . . is that just as we have declined, our opportunities have increased. We have certainly a great deal more opportunity today than we did in the 1950s. And yet at the same time, we've had this decline. Well, obviously that points the finger back at us. What kinds of things are going on in black life that account for that kind of decline? We should have at least held even, if not progressed a great deal."

Many factors, including the deterioration of the traditional black family structure, clearly are involved. But Steele says that "in a general sort of way, I think that . . . we have not really looked at our own anxieties about inferiority, our own fear of moving into the mainstream, of taking opportunities, of making efforts to get ahead, and so we've held back and hesitated, and certainly in a competitive society like America, you can't hesitate and hold your ground, you're going to decline, and we have declined."

Steele contends that the "victim-focused black identity" is holding blacks back. "We think of ourselves too much as victims. It makes you more passive, it makes you more demoralized, it robs you of individual initiative. ... We're so busy seeing ourselves as victims, seeing racists everywhere, that we're unable to see opportunity and simply unable to take advantage of it in the way that we should be taking advantage of it. Because we have an enormous amount of opportunity. Anybody can go to college. Or if [the opportunity is denied], there's an entire body of laws there that you can rely on to seek redress. And we're not doing it, we're not taking advantage."

The employment opportunities for blacks and other minorities are expected to increase in the coming years, thanks to demographic change. "With fewer new young workers entering the work force, employers will be hungry for qualified people and more willing to offer jobs and training to those they have traditionally ignored," the Hudson Institute pointed out in a 1987 study done for the U.S. Labor Department. "At the same time, however, the types of jobs being created by the economy will demand much higher levels of skill than the jobs that exist today." To take advantage of the increased opportunities, then, blacks and other minorities will have to acquire the higher levels of skill. If they don't, affirmative action will be of little help.

"If the policies and employment patterns of the present continue," the institute warned, "it is likely that the demographic opportunity of the 1990s will be missed and that, by the year 2000, the problems of minority unemployment, crime, and dependency will be worse than they are today. ... Now is the time to renew the emphasis on education, training, and employment assistance for minorities that has been pursued with limited success over the past several decades. These investments will be needed, not only to insure that employers have a qualified work force in the years after 2000, but finally to guarantee the equality of opportunity that has been America's great unfulfilled promise." [30]

For the next 20 years, Robinson says, "the spotlight that emphasizes education, job training, must burn more brightly than it has before, it must burn more brightly than the spotlight of affirmative action. But that is not to say that the spotlight of affirmative action can be immediately turned off. Instead, I think that as it expires, it will do so gradually. It will dim, dim, dim, dim and fade out of the picture, at some point in the future. I don't know exactly when."

For the foreseeable future, affirmative action is here to stay. But it no longer seems to have as much practical significance for black Americans as it once appeared to have. Education and job training clearly are the greater need now. And they, as it happens, were part of what affirmative action originally was all about.

NOTES

[1] Nathan Glazer, *Affirmative Discrimination* (1975), p. 58

[2] Quoted in U.S. House Committee on Education and Labor, *A Report of the Study Group on Affirmative Action to the House Committee on Education and Labor*, August 1987, p. 33. The report was prepared by the Wharton Center for Applied Research, The Wharton School, University of Pennsylvania. As the result of a typographical error in the committee's published print of the report, the date of the print is mistakenly given as August 1986.

[3] Josh Henkin, "The Meretriciousness of Merit: Or, Why Jewish Males Oughtn't Be So Smug," *Tikkun*, January-February 1989, p. 54. Henkin's article is a rejoinder to Michael Levin, "Affirmative Action vs. Jewish Men," in the same issue.

[4] Nathan Glazer, "The Affirmative Action Stalemate," *The Public Interest*, winter 1988, p. 104; Glazer, *Affirmative Discrimination, op. cit.*, pp. 42-43. The quoted econometric study was by Richard B. Freeman.

[5] *Ibid.*, pp. 62-63.

[6] U.S. House Committee on Education and Labor, *op. cit.*, p. 32.

[7] Sidney Hook, "Foreward," in Barry R. Gross, *Discrimination in Reverse: Is Turnabout Fair Play?* (1978), p. xi.

[8] Glazer, "The Affirmative Action Stalemate," *op. cit.*, p. 99.

[9] *Idem.*

[10] Reynolds testified on Sept. 23, 1981.

[11] See "Equal Employment Opportunity Commission," in *Federal Regulatory Directory* (1986), fifth edition, pp. 147-158.

[12] Jonathan Leonard, "The Impact of Affirmative Action Regulation and Equal Employment Law," in U.S. House Committee on Education and Labor, *op. cit.*, pp. 289-290.

[13] The office was originally called the Office of Federal Contract Compliance.

[14] Majority staff of the U.S. House Committee on Education and Labor, *A Report on the Investigation of the Civil Rights Enforcement Activities of the Office of Federal Contract Compliance Programs, U.S. Department of Labor*, October 1987, pp. 3, 7.

[15] Quoted by Nadine Cohodas in "Administration Ignites New Conflict Over Affirmative Action Enforcement," *Congressional Quarterly Weekly Report*, Oct. 19, 1985, p. 2106.

[16] Anne B. Fisher in "Businessmen Like to Hire by the Numbers," *Fortune*, Sept. 16, 1985, p. 26.

[17] Quoted in *ibid.*, p. 28.

[18] Quoted by Elder Witt in "Administration Hails Ruling on Affirmative Action Case: Seniority Prevails in Layoffs," *Congressional Quarterly Weekly Report*, June 16, 1984, p. 1451.

[19] James P. Smith and Finis R. Welch, *Closing the Gap: Forty Years of Economic Progress for Blacks*, February 1986, pp. 12-13.

[20] *Ibid.*, pp. 92-93, 99.

[21] *Ibid.*, pp. xi, xiii, 91, 95.

[22] *Ibid.*, pp. 94-95, 100.

[23] U.S. House Committee on Education and Labor, *op. cit.*, p. 16.

[24] Edward W. Jones, Jr., "Black Managers: The Dream Deferred," *Harvard Business Review*, May-June 1986, pp. 88, 92.

[25] Lawrence M. Mead, *Beyond Entitlement: The Social Obligations of Citizenship* (1985), p. 22.

[26] Finis Welch, *The Employment of Black Men*, unpublished report, Feb. 3, 1988, pp. 12, 26.

[27] See Charles Murray, *Losing Ground: American Social Policy, 1950-1980* (1984), pp. 69-82. For a discussion of Murray's book and the debate over welfare reform, see "Working on Welfare," *E.R.R.* 1986 Vol. II, pp. 729-752.

[28] Commission on Minority Participation in Education and American Life, *One-Third of a Nation*, May 1988, p. 11. The minority population studied by the commission included Hispanics and American Indians. The Education Commission of the States was a cosponsor of the study commission.

[29] *Ibid.*, pp. 12-13.

[30] Hudson Institute, *Workforce 2000: Work and Workers for the 21st Century*, June 1987, p. 114.

Graphics: S. Dmitri Lipczenko.

RECOMMENDED READING

BOOKS

Glazer, Nathan, *Affirmative Discrimination: Ethnic Inequality and Public Policy*, Basic Books, 1975.

Harvard sociologist Glazer writes that affirmative action "has developed a wonderful Catch-22 type of existence. The employer is required . . . to state numerical goals and dates when he will reach them. There is no presumption of discrimination. However, if he does not reach these goals, the question will come up as to whether he has made a 'good faith' effort to reach them. The test of a good faith effort has not been spelled out. From the employer's point of view, the simplest way of behaving to avoid the severe penalties of loss of contracts or heavy costs in back pay (to persons selected at random who have not been discriminated against, to boot) . . . is simply to meet the goals."

Landry, Bart, *The New Black Middle Class*, University of California Press, 1987.

Landry, a University of Maryland sociologist, says the emergence of the "new" black middle class in the 1960s "marked a major turning point in the life of black people in the United States. New opportunities at this level of the class structure gave renewed hope to the aspirations of working-class black parents. No longer were the doors of many colleges and universities closed to them. And a college degree need not automatically mean preparation for a career teaching black children or as a social worker in the black community. Now there was the chance that their sons and daughters could also aspire to become accountants, lawyers, engineers, scientists, and architects."

ARTICLES

Glazer, Nathan, "The Affirmative Action Stalemate," *The Public Interest*, winter 1988, pp. 99-114.

The author, a critic of affirmative action, writes that it "has been institutionalized and has become an accepted part of the American economic scene. It will be very hard to uproot. There is now a serious question whether one should try. . . . [A]fter about 15 years of affirmative action, we have created expectations among blacks and practices in business and government that sustain it. Whatever black doubts about affirmative action there may be (and they do exist), moving against it would appear to black leaders, and to other blacks, as an attack on their interests and their well-being. . . . Today affirmative action looks back on a long history, and the memory of what was intended in 1964 recedes further and further into the distance."

Jones, Edward W., Jr., "Black Managers: The Dream Deferred," *Harvard Business Review*, May-June 1986, pp. 84-93.

Jones, president of his own consulting firm, writes that

black managers "have not gained acceptance on a par with their white peers. They find their careers stymied and they are increasingly disillusioned about their chances for ultimate success. They feel at best tolerated; they often feel ignored. . . . To get ahead, a person depends on informal networks of cooperative relationships. Friendships, help from colleagues, customers, and superiors, and developmental assignments are the keys to success. . . . Black managers feel they are treated as outsiders, and because of the distance that race produces they don't receive the benefit of these networks and relationships."

Steele, Shelby, "On Being Black and Middle Class," *Commentary*, January 1988, pp. 42-47.

The author, a professor of English at San Jose State University, says that middle-class blacks are caught in "a very specific double bind that keeps two equally powerful elements of our identity at odds with each other. The middle-class values by which we were raised — the work ethic, the importance of education, the value of property ownership, of respectability, of 'getting ahead,' of stable family life, of initiative, of self-reliance, etc. — . . . urge us toward participation in the American mainstream. . . . But the particular pattern of racial identification that emerged in the '60s and that still prevails today urges middle-class blacks (and all blacks) in the opposite direction. This pattern asks us to see ourselves as an embattled minority, and it urges an adversarial stance toward the mainstream. . . ."

REPORTS AND STUDIES

***Workforce 2000: Work and Workers for the 21st Century*, Hudson Institute, June 1987.**

"Though it appears very likely that the labor market will be increasingly comprised of disadvantaged minorities over the [coming] years, it is much less clear whether the disadvantages these groups suffer will be getting better or worse during this period of tighter labor markets," says this study done for the U.S. Labor Department.

Smith, James P., and Welch, Finis R., *Closing the Gap: Forty Years of Economic Progress for Blacks*, Rand Corp., February 1986.

The economist authors write that "the real story" about black Americans in the years 1940-80 "has been the emergence of the black middle class, whose income gains have been real and substantial. The growth in the size of the black middle class was so spectacular that as a group it outnumbers the black poor. Finally, for the first time in American history, a sizable number of black men are economically better off than white middle-class America."

U.S. House Committee on Education and Labor, *A Report of the Study Group on Affirmative Action*, August 1987. (As a result of a typographical error, the date on the print is mistakenly given as August 1986.)

According to this Wharton Center for Applied Research study, affirmative action has had "an uneven impact. . . . The better educated, experienced, and highly motivated minority group members and women have taken advantage of wider opportunities made possible through affirmative action programs. This has contributed to a widening gap within minority communities between those whose income and social status have improved, and others within the community whose status has worsened."

FIRED FOR NO GOOD CAUSE: IS IT LEGAL?

FIRED FOR NO GOOD CAUSE: IS IT LEGAL?

by Robert K. Landers

For a century, the legal doctrine of employment-at-will permitted American businesses to fire most employees without notice, for any cause or for no cause at all. But courts in California, Michigan and other states have changed the law in recent years, and employers have discovered that dismissing employees is not quite as easy as it used to be.

A legal revolution has been taking place in this country, and a case now before the California Supreme Court may signal whether it is at an end — or at least at a stopping point. The revolution involves attacks on the traditional right of American employers to fire employees whenever they see fit, and the case involves a man named Daniel Foley, who, in March 1983, was fired from his job at Interactive Data Corp.

Foley had worked for Interactive Data for nearly seven years, first in Waltham, Mass., later in Los Angeles. His performance as a middle manager had been considered superior; he'd been given regular promotions and pay increases. He earned $55,164 a year and had just received a merit bonus of nearly $7,000.

But a few months earlier Foley had heard some disturbing information about his new supervisor, Robert Kuhne — that Kuhne had been suspected of embezzlement and fired from his previous job with Bank of America. The information was accurate; Kuhne later pleaded guilty to the crime. But when, two weeks after Kuhne became his boss, Foley told his former supervisor what he had heard, he was told to stop spreading rumors. And on March 17, Foley was fired. The claimed reason: inadequate performance of his job.[1]

Contending that Interactive Data Corp. had fired him without just cause, Foley sued. A lower court threw his case out, and an appeals court upheld the decision. When the California Supreme Court first heard arguments in *Foley v. Interactive Data Corp.*, liberal Rose Elizabeth Bird was chief justice. But she and two associate justices were ousted from the bench by California's voters two years ago, and now the court is headed by conservative Chief Justice Malcolm Lucas. Employers are hopeful that the Lucas court will see the *Foley* matter their way.

In California, the court's decision should clarify the murky common law* on wrongful discharge. More importantly, even though the *Foley* decision will be legally binding only in California, its impact is likely to be felt well beyond the state's borders. That's because California has been among the revolutionary leaders in recent years as courts in a majority of states have carved out major exceptions to the "employment-at-will" doctrine that traditionally informed state-court decisions.** That doctrine gives employers the right, in the absence of explicit contract provisions to the contrary, to fire employees without notice and for any cause or even no cause. "Absolute employment-at-will is a relic of early industrial times, conjuring up visions of the sweatshops described by Charles Dickens, . . ." Texas Supreme Court Justice William W. Kilgarlin declared in a 1985 case. "The doctrine belongs in a museum, not in our law." [2]

The mainly court-led change in the law has been swift and significant. Wrongful-termination litigation has mushroomed in California and other states. More than 20,000 unjust-discharge cases are now pending in state courts, according to Columbia University political scientist Alan F. Westin and employment-law attorney Alfred G. Feliu. In the late 1970s, fewer than 200 unjust-discharge cases a year were filed by private-sector employees in the state courts. [3]

Seeking to reduce their potential liability, worried employers throughout the country have overhauled their procedures for dealing with employees and job applicants, to make it clear that they can be fired at will and (in case that argument fails to impress a court) to document unsatisfactory employee performances. Employers have become more cautious about dismissing employees without cause. "The fact that management must now think twice before acting whimsically is surely a step in the right direction," contends Professor William B. Gould IV of Stanford Law School. "All employees deserve, at a minimum, some notice of their deficiencies before dismissal and, where practicable, an examination of alleged improprieties or inadequacies by a disinterested third party." [4] Many employers disagree, of course.

*The common law is the unwritten law, based on custom and precedents, expressed in judicial decisions.
**In California, the court-led change in the common law regarding the employment-at-will doctrine has taken place even though the California Legislature in 1937 put the doctrine in the form of a state statute. Section 2922 of the California Labor Code provides that "An employment, having no specified term, may be terminated at the will of either party on notice to the other."

Growing Number of Cases

The number of wrongful-discharge cases has exploded in recent years. This chart shows the number of cases at the appellate level for the years indicated.

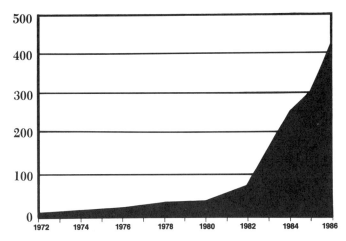

Source: *Andrew D. Hill, 'Wrongful Discharge' and the Derogation of the At-Will Employment Doctrine.*

Those who favor the traditional employment-at-will doctrine argue that it conferred benefits equally on employee and employer alike: The former is free to quit his job whenever he wants, and the latter is free to fire the employee whenever *he* wants. But critics say this superficial neutrality masked a fundamental inequality between the two parties. An employer whose employee quits usually is little affected; he simply hires another employee. But an employee who is fired may well be devastated, psychologically as well as economically, and, stigmatized by being fired, he may find it very hard to get another job quickly. In recognition of that basic inequality, some limitations were in fact placed on the employment-at-will rule well before the court decisions of recent years — most significantly by labor legislation in the 1930s and civil rights legislation in the 1960s.

Recent change in the common law has left both employers and employees less than fully satisfied thus far. Employers now "are subject to volatile and unpredictable juries that frequently act without regard to legal instructions," Gould notes. And the employees who directly benefit from jury verdicts in wrongful-discharge cases "are few and far between, first, because of the difficulties involved in staying the course of a lengthy and expensive judicial process, and second, because of limitations inherent in the legal doctrines adopted by the courts." [5]

The change in employers' treatment of all their employees in response to the change in the common law is part of a larger trend. Now under great pressure to be competitive, businesses are increasingly making it clear to their employees that they feel no long-term commitment to them. [6] "And the response of employees [to the organization]," says Randall B. Dunham, a professor of management at the University of Wisconsin, Madison, "has been: 'Well, then, I suppose there's no need for me to develop a commitment to you.' "

In the long run, this new absence of organizational commitment on the part of managers and professionals may well make the organization itself (as well as, perhaps, society) the loser. Employees' psychological attachment to the organization "has all kinds of potential benefits for the organization, including good attendance and reduced turnover and increased motivation," Dunham says. "I think we're going to see those things suffer very deeply, and [they're] going to suffer the most in organizations [that] make the biggest deal about how clearly they are not committed to the employee."

Still, there is probably no going back to the older ethos. "Given the ferocity of competition today, international and domestic, [and] the volatility of technological change . . . which changes the way work is done and the way people relate to work, we now have a Darwinian survival model for the worker in the work place, as opposed to the paternal, the company-is-your-home kind of ethos," Westin says. "If we were to try to shift back to the paternal model of the '50s and '60s, given those other forces, it would take a lot of cohesive policy making by unions and management and government. And I don't see the signs that they're interested or that the capacity to rebuild that kind of system is out there."

How employment-at-will became accepted doctrine

The United States is the only major industrial country that has embraced the employment-at-will doctrine. *(See story, p. 97.)* It first did so in the late 19th century, when it was becoming a full-fledged industrialized nation. The ancient relationship of master and servant, bound together in a domestic setting by familiarity and mutual concern, had been succeeded by one of worker and owner, bound together in a commercial and more impersonal way. It was the era of financial titans, industrial barons and big business. With the economic principle of laissez faire and the legal principle of freedom of contract holding sway, American law began to depart from the English law on duration-of-service contracts.

The employment-at-will rule "developed in America in response to cases presented by a particular group of workers — middle-level managers," Jay M. Feinman wrote in his study of the subject. "Educated, responsible, and increasingly numerous, the middle-level managers and agents of enterprises might have been expected to seek a greater share in the profits and direction of enterprises as the owners had to rely more heavily on them with the increasing size of business organizations. But the employment-at-will rule assured that as long as the employer desired it (and as long as the employee was not irreplaceable, which was seldom the case) the employee's relation to

the enterprise would be precarious." [7]

The legal doctrine was first formulated in 1877 by an Albany, N.Y., lawyer named Horace Gray Wood, in a treatise on master-servant relations. Wood announced: "With us the rule is inflexible, that a general or indefinite hiring is *prima facie* a hiring at will. . . . [I]t is an indefinite hiring and is determinable at the will of either party, and in this respect there is no distinction between domestic and other servants." [8] Wood cited four American court decisions in support of his rule, although commentators have pointed out that, in fact, none of the four upheld a discharge of an employee without notice or cause. [9]

Despite the deficiencies of Wood's explanation, his rule spread across the country until it was generally adopted as a principle of common law. A Tennessee court gave the doctrine vivid expression in an 1884 decision: "All may dismiss their employee[s] at will, be they many or few, for good cause, for no cause, or even for cause morally wrong without being guilty of legal wrong." In that doctrinal light, the Alabama Supreme Court, for instance, had no choice in 1932 but to reject the suit of a man who contended he had been fired because his wife had rebuffed his boss's sexual advances. [10]

Wood's rule was elevated to a constitutional principle by the U.S. Supreme Court in 1908, when it struck down a section of federal law banning discrimination by railroads against their operating employees because of union membership. Relying on that decision seven years later, the high court, as Andrew D. Hill, author of 'Wrongful Discharge' and the Derogation of the At-Will Employment Doctrine, recounts, held "that a Kansas statute prohibiting 'yellow-dog' contracts (in which employers demand as a condition of employment that their workers not become union members) was unconstitutional since it infringed on an employer's right to determine whom to hire, a violation of the due process clause of the 14th amendment. These opinions have been seen as the 'high water mark' of the court's insistence on laissez-faire principles in the labor area." [11]

In the 1930s, the first major legislative and judicial limitations on the employment-at-will doctrine were imposed. The Norris-LaGuardia Act of 1932 — enacted despite the contention of Pennsylvania Republican Rep. James Beck that it represented "a long march toward Moscow" [12] — made yellow-dog contracts unenforceable in the federal courts, although still not illegal. The National Labor Relations Act of 1935 outlawed such contracts and prohibited dismissals of workers for engaging in union activity. Those provisions of the act were upheld by the U.S. Supreme Court in 1937. The court, however, made it clear that only a limited exception to the employment-at-will doctrine had been created. The National Labor Relations Board "is not entitled to make its authority a pretext for interference with the right of discharge when that right is exercised for other reasons than the antiunion intimidation and coercion," the court declared. [13]

The next major restrictions on the employment-at-will doctrine were imposed during the 1960s and '70s, in the form of federal laws against discrimination. Title VII of

U.S. Marches to a Different Drummer

In not having legislation that requires employers to justify their dismissal of employees, the United States is out of step with much of the rest of the world. Several countries enacted such legislation in the 1940s and 1950s, and many more have done so since 1960, according to the International Labor Organization (ILO).†

Every major Western European nation, except Switzerland and Greece, has legislation explicitly requiring justification for dismissal of an employee. (Switzerland, however, insists on due notice and Greece, on compensation). Closer to home, Canada (in the federal jurisdiction, Nova Scotia and Quebec) provides such legislative protection to workers not covered by collective-bargaining agreements.

In most countries that provide protection against wrongful discharge, the worker can appeal his dismissal to a judicial body that, if it finds the dismissal unjustified, can provide remedies in the form of reinstatement or compensation.

At the ILO's annual conference in 1982 in Geneva, a "convention" (similar to an international treaty and subject to member-state ratification) was adopted establishing a standard regarding "Termination of Employment at the Initiative of the Employer." It provides that workers will not be dismissed without valid reason and that workers who consider they have been will be able to appeal "to an impartial body, such as a court, labor tribunal, arbitration committee or arbitrator." The final vote to accept the convention was 356-9, with 54 abstentions.

The United States is a member of the ILO. The U.S. delegation — consisting of two government representatives, one employers' representative and one workers' representative — cast three votes against the convention and one vote (the workers' delegate's) in favor of it.

In discussion of the measure the preceding year, Paul Weinberg, an American Express vice president who advised the U.S. employers' delegate, contended it would severely curtail the flexibility employers needed to run their businesses. The burden of proof that there was a valid reason for dismissal was shifted to the employer, he complained. David A. Peterson, a Commerce Department official who advised the U.S. government delegates, said the best way to accomplish the measure's ultimate objectives was through reduced government intervention in the free marketplace.††

Eight countries‡ so far have ratified the ILO convention (meaning they pledge to bring their national legislation into conformity with it). The United States is not among them.‡

† International Labor Office, Termination of Employment at the Initiative of the Employer, 1980, Report VIII (1) for the International Labor Conference, 67th Session, 1981.

†† Weinberg and Peterson are quoted indirectly in International Labor Office, Termination of Employment at the Initiative of the Employer, 1981, Report V (1) for the International Labor Conference, 68th Session, 1982.

‡ The eight nations are Cyprus, Malawi, Niger, Spain, Sweden, Venezuela, Yugoslavia, and Zaire. Sometimes only minor differences between a nation's law and an ILO convention cause the nation not to ratify it.

---

the Civil Rights Act of 1964 barred discrimination in hiring or firing on the basis of race, sex, religion or national origin. The Age Discrimination in Employment Act of 1967 prohibited discrimination against employees over 40 years of age. The Rehabilitation Act of 1973 prohibited discrimination against handicapped employees. Many states enacted similar laws.

The labor laws and the civil rights acts were only the most far-reaching exceptions Congress made to the employment-at-will doctrine. There have been many others. The Selective Service Act of 1940, for instance, forbade employers to fire employees who were drafted for military service; draftees were assured of getting their old jobs back when they returned. Other exceptions included the Fair Labor Standards Act of 1938, which prohibited discharge of an employee for exercising rights guaranteed by minimum-wage and overtime provisions of the act; the Consumer Credit Protection Act of 1968, which prohibited discharge of an employee because of garnishment of wages for any one indebtedness; the Occupational Safety and Health Act of 1970, which prohibited discharge of an employee in reprisal for exercising rights under the act;

and the Employment Retirement Income Security Act of 1974, which prohibited discharge of employees in order to prevent them from attaining vested pension rights.

But despite the "long list of federal and state statutory limitations on employment-at-will, the doctrine continued to be the dominant force in the workplace until the early 1980s," the authors of a recent RAND Corp. study observe.[14] Workers whose employment was governed by collective-bargaining agreements usually were protected from unjust dismissal by "just cause" provisions in their union contracts, and virtually all collective-bargaining agreements included grievance and arbitration procedures. Civil servants and college teachers with tenure also enjoyed job security. But union membership was declining, and most American employees — 70 million to 75 million workers, by one estimate [15] — were not protected from unjust dismissal.

Even employees who fell into groups defended by law against discrimination could still be fired for any reason or for no reason at all — as long as the reason was not membership in the protected group. However, workers who thought they had been wrongfully fired sometimes tried to stretch the statutory exceptions to the employment-at-will doctrine to cover their cases. "Employees who believe that their discharges are unjust attempt to characterize them as a form of discrimination," Clyde W. Summers, a professor of law at the University of Pennsylvania, noted in 1980. "Thus charges of discrimination have been filed by long-haired and/or bearded male workers and by females who allegedly were fired for rejecting their male supervisors' sexual advances, gaining weight, getting married, getting pregnant, or refusing to shave their legs." Discharged workers who could do so often claimed age discrimination.[16]

The Civil Rights Act of 1964 and related measures against discrimination encouraged, as the National Labor Relations Act three decades earlier had encouraged, rising expectations and demands on the part of employees. But many corporations, under the lash of technological change and intensified competition, or as a result of mergers and increased corporate debt, sought to cut their labor costs. More and more middle managers and professionals, often after many years of service to their companies, suddenly found themselves out of work. Some of them turned to the courts. And in the changed environment, the courts changed the common law.

Public-policy exception to the at-will doctrine

The major court decisions that have reshaped the employment-at-will doctrine were foreshadowed by a California appeals court ruling in 1959 in a case called *Petermann v. International Brotherhood of Teamsters.* The union's business agent had been called before a legislative committee investigating the union. His boss, he said, directed him to give false testimony. He didn't, and was fired. Although there was no statute then that explicitly protected an employee who refused to commit perjury, the court found the union's action violated "public policy." "It would be obnoxious to the interests of the state and contrary to public policy and sound morality to allow an employer to discharge an employee on the ground that the employee declined to commit perjury," the court declared.[17]

Although the court admitted the concept was imprecise, it said "public policy" meant "that principle of law which holds that no citizen can lawfully do that which has a tendency to be injurious to the public or against the public good," and it rested on "the principles under which freedom of contract or private dealing is restricted by law for the good of the community. Another statement sometimes referred to as a definition, is that whatever contravenes good morals or any established interests of society is against public policy."[18]

Courts in California and many other states in recent years have followed that reasoning in carving out a public-policy exception to the employment-at-will doctrine. Courts have held that employees may not be fired for

refusing to commit such unlawful acts as engaging in illegal price-fixing, illegally performing a medical operation or illegally manipulating pollution-sampling results. In an Arizona case, a nurse was fired after she refused her supervisor's request, on a company rafting and camping trip, to "moon" her fellow employees while singing *Moon River*. Noting the state's law against indecent exposure, the Arizona Supreme Court ruled: "We hold than an employer may fire for a good cause or for no cause. He may not fire for bad cause — that which violates public policy."[19]

Perhaps the most important "public policy" case, according to the RAND Corp. analysts, was *Tameny v. Atlantic Richfield Co.*, which involved an employee who claimed he had been fired for refusing to fix gas prices in violation of antitrust laws. In its 1980 decision in the case, the California Supreme Court "held that discharging an employee contrary to public policy was a tort,* and the employee was entitled to tort damages." Tort damages, as the RAND authors note, "can include punitive damages and recovery for emotional distress, both of which are difficult to quantify and can amount to millions of dollars, depending upon the jury's impression of the employee's distress and the employer's motive." The result was an enormous increase in an employer's potential liability — and a corresponding increase in the incentive of fired employees and their attorneys to bring suit.[20]

Some courts have extended the public-policy exception to cover so-called "whistleblowers." The Illinois Supreme Court in 1981, in *Palmateer v. International Harvester*, for instance, held that an employer's dismissal of an employee who had informed police about suspected crimes by a fellow employee was contrary to public policy, even though no specific statute required citizens to take an active role in ferreting out crime. The court, as a matter of public policy, wanted to encourage citizen crime-fighting. "Courts in other states have since also found discharges contrary to public policy even when the discharge was not for exercising a statutorily guaranteed right or refusing to violate a statute," the RAND analysts note.

On the other hand, a minority of states have not recognized a public-policy exception to the employment-at-will doctrine at all. New York is one of them. In *Murphy v. American Home Products Corp.*, the New York Court of Appeals, the state's highest court, emphatically stated in 1983 that "this court has not and does not now recognize a cause of action in tort for abusive or wrongful discharge of an employee; such recognition must await action of the legislature." In the particular case, the employee, Joseph Murphy, had alleged he was fired, at age 59 and after 23 years with the company, because of his disclosure to top management of alleged accounting improprieties on the part of corporate personnel and because of his age. Although sympathetic to the plaintiff's plea to go along with the trend toward a public-policy exception, the court

Continued on page 100

---

*A tort is a private or civil wrong, other than breach of contract, for which the wronged person may collect damages.

Landmark Cases

Petermann v. International Brotherhood of Teamsters (California, 1959). In this early "public policy" case, the union's business agent said he refused his boss' request to give false testimony to a legislative committee investigating the union and was fired. Although there was no statute then that explicitly protected an employee who refused to commit perjury, the California Court of Appeal found the union's action violated "public policy."

Monge v. Beebe Rubber Co. (New Hampshire, 1974). Olga Monge, a machine operator, said she was told by her foreman that if she wanted a promotion she had sought she would have to go out with him. She refused and was fired. The New Hampshire Supreme Court upheld a jury's verdict in her favor and said "a termination by the employer of a contract of employment at will which is motivated by bad faith or malice . . . is not [in] the best interest of the economic system or the public good and constitutes a breach of the employment contract."

Fortune v. National Cash Register Co. (Massachusetts, 1977). This was one of the first cases involving an "implied covenant of good faith." A 61-year-old salesman who had worked for the National Cash Register Co. for 40 years had a written contract that included an explicit employment-at-will provision. But he contended he had been demoted and later fired because the company wanted to avoid having to pay him the full commission on a particularly large sale. The Massachusetts Supreme Judicial Court declared there was an implied covenant of good faith and fair dealing in any written contract and upheld a jury's verdict awarding $45,649 to the salesman.

Tameny v. Atlantic Richfield Co. (California, 1980). An employee of the Atlantic Richfield Co. claimed he had been fired for refusing to fix gas prices in violation of antitrust laws. The California Supreme Court held that discharging an employee in violation of "public policy" was a tort and the employee was entitled to tort damages.

Toussaint v. Blue Cross & Blue Shield of Michigan (Michigan, 1980). In this major "implied contract" case, Charles Toussaint said that when he had been interviewed for a middle-management job at Blue Cross & Blue Shield, he had been told he could stay with the company "as long as I did my job." He also had been given a handbook that stated it was company policy to discipline or dismiss employees "only for cause." Yet, after five years with the company, he was fired — he claimed, without cause. He sued for breach of contract. The Michigan Supreme Court upheld a jury's verdict, awarding him nearly $73,000. The oral assurance and the handbook statement had created an implied contract, the court said.

Cleary v. American Airlines (California, 1980). An American Airlines employee with 18 years of apparently satisfactory service had been accused of theft and fired; the employee claimed the dismissal had been a result of his union activities. The California Court of Appeal held that a covenant of good faith and fair dealing was implicit in every employment contract, even when the employment was at-will. The employee could not be fired without good cause, the court said.

Palmateer v. International Harvester (Illinois, 1981). The Illinois Supreme Court held that an employer's dismissal of an employee who had informed police about suspected crimes by a fellow employee was contrary to public policy, even though no specific statute required citizens to take an active role in ferreting out crime.

Pugh v. See's Candies (California, 1981). Wayne Pugh was fired by See's Candies after 32 years of service and given no specific reason for the sudden dismissal. The California Court of Appeal found "the duration of [Pugh's] employment, the commendations and promotions he received, the apparent lack of any direct criticism of his work, the assurances he was given, and the employer's acknowledged policies" were sufficient evidence to allow a jury to conclude that See's had made an "implied-in-fact" promise not to dismiss him arbitrarily.

Weiner v. McGraw Hill Inc. (New York, 1982). Walton Lewis Weiner said he had been told by McGraw Hill supervisors before he was hired that the firm's policy was to discharge for cause only. That policy was clearly expressed in the company's employee handbook. After eight years of apparently satisfactory performance at his job, Weiner was fired for "lack of application." Weiner claimed the dismissal was the result of a dispute with his supervisor. The New York Court of Appeals sided with Weiner, saying that "a limitation on the employer's right to terminate an employment of indefinite duration might be implied from an express provision in the employer's handbook or personnel policies and procedures."

Gates v. Life of Montana Insurance Co. (Montana, 1983). The Montana Supreme Court upheld the award of $50,000 in punitive damages to a woman who had worked as a cashier for the Life of Montana Insurance Co. for more than three years and been fired without warning. The court held that an employer's breach of an implied covenant of good faith and fair dealing was not only a breach of contract, but a separate, independent tort.

Woolley v. Hoffmann-LaRoche Inc. (New Jersey, 1985). Engineer Richard M. Woolley, after nine years with Hoffmann-LaRoche, a pharmaceutical company, was fired. The New Jersey Supreme Court ruled that job-security assurances in the company's employee handbook meant the company could discharge only for cause. The old employment-at-will rule, the court said, "must be tested by its legitimacy today, and not by its acceptance yesterday."

Exceptions to the At-Will Doctrine

Because this law is being made by courts and not by legislatures, the exact status of the law in each state is imprecise. The fact that a state currently does not recognize an exception to the employment-at-will doctrine does not necessarily mean that it has been explicitly rejected; it is possible that the doctrine simply has never been challenged properly. On the other hand, the extent to which one state recognizes an exception may differ from the extent to which another state recognizes it, and in some cases rulings have not been made by the state's highest court. For these reasons, the interpretations in this chart should not be taken as the absolute truth of the matter.

	Alabama	Alaska	Arizona	Arkansas	California	Colorado	Connecticut	Delaware	District of Columbia	Florida	Georgia	Hawaii	Idaho	Illinois	Indiana	Iowa	Kan...
Public Policy	✔	✔	✔	✔		✔					✔	✔	✔	✔			✔
Implied Contract	✔	✔		✔	✔	✔		✔				✔	✔				
Good Faith Covenant	✔				✔												

* Montana is the only state to have passed a law defining exceptions to the employment-at-will doctrine. Parts of that law are now being challenged in the state's Supreme Court. (See story, p. 606).

Continued from page 98
maintained that the Legislature was better suited to deal with the matter. As yet, however, the Legislature hasn't done so, perhaps because of strong opposition from both business and organized labor.[21]

Courts have found an implied contract

The public-policy exception to the employment-at-will doctrine is widely accepted — recognized in some form in about 30 states. But it is not the only exception the courts have fashioned. Recognized in about as many states and much more pertinent to most employers and employees is the implied-contract exception. Even though no explicit contract between employer and employee may exist, courts have found there may be an *implicit* contract not to fire an employee except for just cause — because of promises or statements made by the employer in job interviews or in employee handbooks, or because of the employer's conduct over the course of the employee's time with the company.

In *Toussaint v. Blue Cross & Blue Shield of Michigan,* Charles Toussaint said that when he had been interviewed for a middle-management job at Blue Cross & Blue Shield, he had been told he could stay with the company "as long as I did my job." He also had been given a handbook that stated it was company policy to discipline or dismiss employees "only for cause." Yet, after five years with the company, he was fired — he claimed, without cause. He sued for breach of contract. A Michigan jury awarded him nearly $73,000, but the judgment was reversed on appeal. The Michigan Supreme Court, however, in a 4-3 decision in 1980, sided with Toussaint. The oral assurance and the handbook statement had created an implied contract, the court ruled.

When an employer establishes personnel policies or practices and makes them known to the employees, "the employment relationship is presumably enhanced," the Michigan court said. "The employer secures an orderly, cooperative and loyal work force, and the employee the peace of mind associated with job security and the conviction that he will be treated fairly." Therefore, the court ruled, the employer has created a situation in which he has an obligation to the employee.[22] Courts in other states, including the New York Court of Appeals in a case in 1982 and the New Jersey Supreme Court in a case in 1985, reached similar conclusions.

Length of an employee's service and other indications of an employer's conduct during the employment relationship also have been held to imply a contract giving the employee the right to continued employment in the absence of just cause for dismissal. Wayne Pugh was fired by See's Candies after 32 years of service, during which he had worked his way up from dishwasher to vice president in charge of production and a member of the board of directors. The company's president gave Pugh no specific reason for the sudden dismissal, but, according to Pugh, only told him to "look deep within [him]self." In 1981, the California Court of Appeal, in *Pugh v. See's Candies,* found in "the duration of [Pugh's] employment, the commendations and promotions he received, the apparent lack of any direct criticism of his work, the assurances he was given, and the employer's acknowledged policies," sufficient evidence to allow a jury to conclude that See's had made an "implied-in-fact" promise not to dismiss him arbitrarily.[23]

In addition to the implied-contract and the public-policy exceptions to the employment-at-will doctrine, there is a third one: the "implied covenant of good faith and fair dealing." Although only a handful of states have embraced this exception, it is the most far-reaching of all. It holds, as Michigan State University economist Jack Stieber has explained, "that no matter what an employer says or

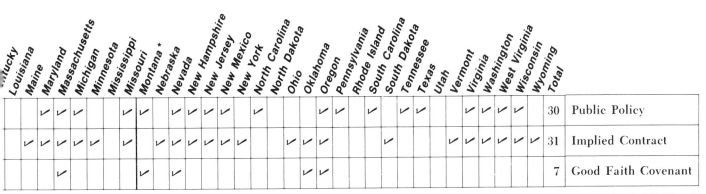

Kentucky	Louisiana	Maine	Maryland	Massachusetts	Michigan	Minnesota	Mississippi	Missouri	Montana*	Nebraska	Nevada	New Hampshire	New Jersey	New Mexico	New York	North Carolina	North Dakota	Ohio	Oklahoma	Oregon	Pennsylvania	Rhode Island	South Carolina	South Dakota	Tennessee	Texas	Utah	Vermont	Virginia	Washington	West Virginia	Wisconsin	Wyoming	Total	
			✔	✔	✔			✔	✔			✔	✔	✔	✔		✔			✔	✔		✔		✔	✔			✔	✔	✔	✔		30	Public Policy
✔	✔	✔	✔	✔		✔		✔	✔	✔	✔	✔	✔			✔	✔	✔				✔				✔	✔	✔	✔	✔	✔			31	Implied Contract
			✔					✔		✔								✔	✔															7	Good Faith Covenant

Sources: David A. Cathcart and Mark S. Dichter, eds., *Employment-At-Will: A 1986 State-By-State Survey* (1987); Andrew D. Hill, *'Wrongful Discharge' and the Derogation of the At-Will Employment Doctrine* (1987); William B. Gould IV, "The Idea of the Job as Property in Contemporary America: The Legal and Collective Bargaining Framework." *Brigham Young University Law Review,* 1986, No. 4; James N. Dertouzos, Elaine Holland and Patricia Ebener, *The Legal and Economic Consequences of Wrongful Termination,* 1988.

does to make it clear that employment is at-will and that an employee may be dismissed without cause, he must deal with the employee fairly and in good faith." [24]

Thus, despite a written contract with an explicit employment-at-will provision, the Massachusetts Supreme Judicial Court in 1977 upheld a jury's verdict awarding $45,649 to a salesman who had been dismissed by the National Cash Register Co. The 61-year-old man, who had worked for the company for 40 years, contended it had demoted and later fired him to avoid having to pay him the full commission on a particularly large sale he had made. The court declared there was an implied covenant of good faith and fair dealing in any written contract. [25]

A California decision three years later "suggested that *any* termination of a long-term employee without just cause would violate the implied covenant of good faith," Charles G. Bakaly Jr. and Joel M. Grossman, two attorneys who specialize in labor and employment law, have written. In that case, an American Airlines employee with 18 years of apparently satisfactory service had been accused of theft and fired; the employee claimed the dismissal had been a result of union activities. The California Court of Appeal could have resorted to the public-policy exception, but instead it held that a covenant of good faith and fair dealing was implicit in every employment contract, even when the employment was at-will. The court cited two factors as paramount in its decision: the longevity of the employee's service and the expressed policy of the employer for adjudicating employee disputes. These meant that such an employee could not be fired without good cause, the court said. [26]

The California court's decision in *Cleary v. American Airlines* "created a potential lawsuit in every employment discharge, entitling the discharged employee to tort damages, including punitive damages and damages for emotional distress," the RAND analysts observe. [27] Other states followed California's example. In 1983, the Montana Supreme Court upheld the award of $50,000 in punitive

damages to a woman who had worked as a cashier for the Life of Montana Insurance Co. for more than three years and was fired without warning. The court held that an employer's breach of an implied covenant of good faith and fair dealing was not only a breach of contract, but a separate, independent tort. [28]

The common law on wrongful discharge "is still in a state of flux in many states," the RAND analysts note. "Many are considering which theories to accept; others are still considering whether to adopt any form of the doctrine. Even in California, where the theory is most fully accepted, many questions remain unanswered in part because many of the major decisions have come from intermediate appellate courts, rather than the highest state court." [29] One of the key unanswered questions has to do with whether a fired employee must show longevity of service in order to claim a breach of a covenant of good faith. In the *Cleary* decision, which opened the floodgates for wrongful-discharge suits, the individual had worked for the company for 18 years. "Subsequently, having apparently appreciated the chaos created by [the] ruling in *Cleary,* a different division of the same Court of Appeal in [*Foley v. Interactive Data Corp.*] placed some constraints on claims for breach of a covenant of good faith and fair dealing by holding that employees had to show longevity of employment," write attorneys Michael J. Lotito and Michael E. Caples. "However, in *Foley* seven years of employment was not long enough." [30] The anticipated decision in *Foley* by the California Supreme Court should clear up some of the confusion.

Worried employers look to their policies

Employers throughout the country have been alarmed by the explosion in wrongful-discharge litigation that has

Montana Law Challenged

Montana last year became the first — and so far the only — state to enact a law to protect employees from being fired without good cause. The statute, which was backed by Montana employers, also limits employer liability. A state trial judge ruled in March, however, that the restriction on liability violates Montana's Constitution. The Montana Supreme Court is expected to decide the issue next year.

According to Montana's Wrongful Discharge from Employment Act, "A discharge is wrongful only if: (1) it was in retaliation for the employee's refusal to violate public policy or for reporting a violation of public policy; (2) the discharge was not for good cause and the employee had completed the employer's probationary period of employment; or (3) the employer violated the express provisions of its own written personnel policy."

The act defines "public policy" as "a policy in effect at the time of the discharge concerning the public health, safety, or welfare established by constitutional provision, statute, or administrative rule." It defines "good cause" as meaning "reasonable job-related grounds for dismissal based on a failure to satisfactorily perform job duties, disruption of the employer's operation, or other legitimate business reason."

The law restricts employer liability by limiting a wrongfully discharged employee's recovery to lost wages and fringe benefits (with interest) for no more than four years. The employee could recover punitive damages only if it were "established by clear and convincing evidence that the employer engaged in actual fraud or actual malice" in firing the person. Otherwise, the statute says, "There is no right under any legal theory to damages . . . for pain and suffering, emotional distress, compensatory damages, punitive damages, or any other form of damages."

On July 2, 1987, the day after the law went into effect, Judith Johnson was fired from her $46,000-a-year job in the state's office of public instruction. She brought suit and challenged the constitutionality of the new law's four-year cap on back wages that could be recovered and its restriction on punitive and other damages. In March, Judge Bart Erickson struck down those provisions, saying that they "clearly limit, restrict and modify the right to full legal redress [for injury]" guaranteed by the state's constitution, and also discriminate between employees who had suffered loss of wages for less than four years and those whose loss was for a longer period.

The Montana Supreme Court, in considering the constitutional issue, is taking up the Johnson case along with a separate case involving a man who was fired from his $26,000-a-year job as assistant administrator at a Great Falls nursing home.

Setting aside its constitutional problems, Montana's first-in-the-nation statute still leaves a good deal to be desired, in the view of some specialists in labor and employment law. "It's a very limited law; it doesn't really do very much," says Stanford Law School Professor William B. Gould IV, a prominent advocate of legislation that would establish a just-cause standard for dismissal and require arbitration of wrongful discharge disputes, with back pay and reinstatement at stake, but without any punitive or compensatory damages. The Montana law permits binding arbitration if both sides agree but does not require it. Unless his ex-employer agrees to arbitration, then, a dismissed employee must wage his battle in the courts.

Wrongful-discharge legislation should "provide fairness for both sides," Gould says, "and that means you give the employee the opportunity to get an inexpensive, expeditious forum [to resolve the dispute], and you give the employer limited liability. The Montana statute gives the employer limited liability but it still requires the employee to go to court." ∎

occurred in California and other states as a result of the court-led change in the common law. In Los Angeles Superior Court alone, the number of wrongful-discharge suits filed increased from about 90 in 1980 to about 600 in 1986. Most suits are settled out of court or thrown out, but those that go to trial in California and elsewhere tend to be won by employees (and that fact, of course, influences the out-of-court settlements). Employees emerged victorious in 81 — more than two-thirds — of 120 jury trials decided in California between 1980 and 1986. Although ages and salaries varied widely, the average plaintiff in those trials was a 45-year-old white male executive or middle manager with eight years service who had been making $36,254 a year. The defendants often were large corporations. In four out of five cases, poor performance or misconduct was given as the reason for dismissal of the employee; in the fifth case, economic factors unrelated to the performance or behavior of the person were cited.[31]

The plaintiffs at wrongful-discharge trials are disproportionately corporate managers or professionals. They are educated, have money, often have documentation to support their cases, and "they're in the kind of positions where if they get fired, it's not that easy to walk into another job," Westin points out. That is not so, for instance, in much of the low-wage service sector of the economy. "If you're fired at Burger King, you can walk down the street to McDonald's and get a job usually at 20 or 50 cents more an hour, just for the asking, because the labor market is so acutely underserved in that kind of service business," he notes. Those fired workers have no need to fight their dismissals.

Moreover, lawyers who represent wrongful-discharge plaintiffs prefer higher-salaried clients, because the attorneys operate on contingency fees (of 30-40 percent) and wrongful-discharge awards are usually related to the fired employee's salary. "Lawyers for the plaintiffs will not take cases of lower-compensated employees unless they have a very strong case, just because you don't seem to have as good a chance of coming out with a large recovery; whereas if you have somebody with a very high compensation, $200,000 or $300,000 a year, then even if you don't do all that well, just the notion that the recovery could be in the millions will tend to spur some kind of settlement discussions," says Los Angeles attorney Joel Grossman, who generally represents employers in wrongful-discharge suits.

Jurors in wrongful-discharge cases often tend to be more sympathetic to dismissed employees than to large corporations, particularly if they are perceived to have "deep pockets." And juries "often impose liability and large damage awards according to their own standards of fairness rather than the legal instructions provided by the judge," Gould observes.[32] The average award in those 81 California verdicts was $646,855; in one case, an award of $8 million was made.*

Such outcomes appalled many employers. Even though the common law varied from state to state, employers throughout the country anxiously consulted their lawyers. And then they started doing what they could to avoid potential liability and to preserve what they had regarded as their traditional right to fire employees at will. The main hurdle that could be surmounted seemed to be the implied-contract exception. Hence, employers sought to avoid making any promises or statements in job interviews or in employee handbooks that could be construed as implying that employees who performed satisfactorily could feel secure in their jobs.

Employers instructed company interviewers to avoid any talk of job security or even of "promotions from within," and they scoured their employee handbooks and other company documents of dangerous language. Terms such as "permanent" or "career" or "probationary" were excised. Indications that dismissal would be only for just cause were eliminated. Promises of fairness or equitable treatment were taken out. Even pleasantries such as "Best wishes for a long and happy relationship" were scrapped. In some cases, employers went beyond sanitizing the handbooks and inserted disclaimers in them explicitly stating that the employment was at-will. Some employers insisted that job applicants sign such disclaimers (a practice critics have likened to the yellow-dog contracts outlawed in the 1930s).

At-will disclaimers have been upheld by courts as effective counters to dismissed employees' claims that they could be fired only for just cause. But use of such

---

*On average, such awards are reduced by more than 50 percent in appeals or post-trial settlements. The largest awards generally are reduced the most.

Costs and Benefits

Plaintiffs win most of the wrongful-discharge suits that make it through the court system. The cost to the losing businesses is high, but much of the money they pay goes to lawyers. The information is based on 120 California cases.

	All Cases	Plaintiff Verdicts
Average award	$436,627	$646,855
Average final payment	208,212	307,628
Average net payment (minus fees)	127,590	188,520
Median net payment	30,000	74,500
Average plaintiff contingency fee	80,622	119,108
Average defense legal fees	83,862	90,483

Source: RAND Corporation

Plaintiff Profile

As this chart shows, plaintiffs in wrongful-discharge trials — at least in the 120 California cases these data represent — generally are white males who had held middle-management jobs.

Average age	45.3	Average salary	$36,254
Median age	45.0	Median salary	$30,000
Age range	24-65	Salary range	$8,000-250,000

Tenure:	(percent)
Under one year	18.2
1-5 years	34.2
6-10 years	15.7
11-15 years	8.3
Over 15 years	23.1
White	89.3
Male	68.6
Executive	13.6
Middle management	39.8
Defendant reason for termination:	
Inadequate performance	80.8
Exogenous economic factors	19.2

Source: RAND Corporation

---

disclaimers represents "a very difficult call" for employers, says attorney Grossman. "It's not a real big boost for employee morale to put in the handbook, 'We can fire you at any time, for any reason, and there's nothing you can do about it,'" he points out. "People just do not want to see that in their handbook. So you have to make a judgment call as to whether you prefer to have more security from a lawsuit vs. higher employee morale."

An employer's decision on use of at-will disclaimers often depends on the likely effect on recruiting. Montgomery Ward and Sears, Roebuck & Co. have used at-will disclaimers for years without apparent harm to their ability to recruit people. But the situation changes "as you get into different industries that are more competitive for employees — like the high-tech or aerospace industries — where a disclaimer like that could just mean that you'd have a harder time finding people," Grossman says. In such cases, employers do without disclaimers.

As an alternative to at-will disclaimers, some management consultants have urged employers to consider using written contracts for a specified term, usually one year. If the employer wants to get rid of the employee, he simply waits until the year is up and then does not renew the contract. A disadvantage, from the employer's point of view, is that he has to have good cause to dismiss the employee before the contractual year is up. Grossman says such written contracts have been used in some instances for high-level employees, but otherwise "I haven't seen that particular piece of advice being followed very much."

Given the larger forces that have pushed companies to trim their labor costs and their commitments to their employees, Westin contends, most employees are not especially distressed now by the inclusion of at-will disclaimers in employee handbooks. "Ten or 15 years ago — when the ethos in the United States was that if you went to work for a well-known company, if you were any good and you performed well, it was kind of a lifetime job — putting these kinds of disclaimers in would have been a cultural shock and probably would have led to significant employee discontent," he says. Today, however, "the average employee knows that there [is] no job security in the overwhelming majority of companies. . . . Employees know that that's the reality, so what's the difference if it's in the handbook. . . ? The company has no loyalty to them and . . . the employee feels no loyalty to the company, either."

Besides avoiding making explicit or implicit promises of job security they do not intend to keep, many employers altered their conduct toward their employees in other ways, in order to be able to show, if need should one day arise, that not only was there no implied promise of job security but there was indeed "good cause" for firing a particular employee. "One of the most difficult arguments company attorneys have had to make to judges and juries in wrongful discharge cases," Westin and Feliu write, "has been that the employee who had received consistently excellent performance evaluations through his long years of employment with the company was legitimately terminated because of suddenly poor performance, particularly when this arose in connection with management actions the employee alleges to have been improper or negligent." [33]

The employer's past evaluations of the employee's performance became the fired employee's attorney's "most important tool" in demonstrating that the reason given for the dismissal was only a pretext, Westin and Feliu note. Consequently, many employers have taken to regular written evaluations of employees' performances, evaluations that avoid excessive praise and document perceived failings. Some corporate attorneys have advised employers to forswear use of the word "excellent" in their evaluations, to forbid employee responses to the appraisals and to destroy evaluations more than three years old. When an

employee is fired, some attorneys have advised, he or she should not be told the reason, lest the company's defense in court be hindered.

Documenting employees' unsatisfactory performances is now "very, very widespread," Grossman says. "That's what we management lawyers pound on when we lecture groups of employers or when we counsel with our clients: that someday you may be before a jury trying to defend what you've done, and you'll make my life as your lawyer a lot easier if I have solid documentation that there were good reasons for doing what you did."

Thus, although employers persist in maintaining that they can fire at will, they nevertheless, as a result of the change in the common law, have actually moved toward dismissal only for cause — at least what the employer considers to be cause. "Just as all of the discrimination laws when they first came out in the '60s probably made employers tend to stop discriminating, I think that a lot of the wrongful-termination cases have tended to make employers a lot less arbitrary in termination," Grossman says. Whereas an employer once might have fired someone just because he didn't like him, now he "is more likely to pick up the phone and call his labor lawyer and say, 'Here's the facts of the case. Do you think I have grounds to fire so-and-so?' I get calls like that several times a week."

And now, when an employer wants to dismiss an employee who he fears might bring a lawsuit for wrongful discharge, he often tries to arrange a "voluntary" resignation with severance pay, in return for an agreement not to sue. "That's very widespread," Grossman says, more so than in the past, when an employer usually could just fire an individual, without feeling any need to bargain with him about it.

Even when a dismissed employee's case appears legally deficient, if it is likely to arouse the sympathy of a jury, many companies in states that have moved sharply away from the employment-at-will rule prefer to settle the dispute out of court. "A lot of companies that I know," Westin says, "just settle and settle and settle, and buy [the fired employees] out for what they think is acceptable, given the exposure if the case goes to trial in places like California, Michigan, and so forth."

But Westin and Feliu think that employers' most significant response to the explosion in wrongful-discharge litigation has been "the decision by a growing number of companies to either create new dispute-resolution systems inside their organizations, or to improve existing systems they have had for some time." Such internal-complaint systems allow management "to learn about and have the opportunity to deal equitably with almost all the employee complaints that are truly meritorious." [34] In addition, Westin says, such systems enable employers, in general, to take to trial "only those cases where they feel that they have such a solid case that they're going to fight it 'on the beaches and in the cities,' because in those kinds of cases they know everything that the employee is saying, because they've heard it inside. . . ." Also, "the fact that a good company with a good internal program has provided a

Continued on page 106

AT ISSUE

Have the changes in the law on employment-at-will tied employers' hands too much?

YES says **RICHARD A. EPSTEIN**, James Parker Hall Distinguished Service Professor of Law, University of Chicago.

"The modern law of unjust dismissal has created a work-place nightmare. Advertised as a means to place the employee on equal footing with the employer, it has no such effect. Instead it operates as a wasteful tax that harms workers and employers alike.

To see why, shift your focus from the time of dismissal to the time of hiring. As a general rule, contracting leaves both the employer and employee better off than before. Workers and employers, therefore, must have reasons to stick to the at-will contract. And they do. An at-will contract lets the employee signal his or her willingness to work hard in the long haul and thus command a higher wage.

Similarly, the at-will contract pressures the employer to maintain salary and working conditions at competitive levels, for workers can (and do) quit to work elsewhere. The rule is cheap to administer, because the deal is adjusted informally day by day, without squads of lawyers. At-will contracts avoid expensive and error-prone inquiries as to whether this dismissal or that demotion was made 'for cause.'

Of course, a worker will regret an at-will contract when his deal goes sour. Belatedly, the claim will be that the original contract was unfair. If successful, one disgruntled worker can impose upon both employers and other workers a legal rule that none of them wants. At the very least, employer handbooks must be redrafted to restate what everyone understood in the first place, that at will means at will. At worst, the at-will contract may be illegal, cutting off all voluntary escape.

And for what gain? Long-term relationships were common before the at-will contract was subjected to the present judicial assault. Employers who fire on a whim have to interview and train new workers, and they earn a bad reputation to boot. Informal checks on employer abuse are stronger than believed.

Getting jobs will also be harder with unjust dismissal rules. Employers will become more circumspect, less willing to hire inexperienced or unknown workers. The unjust dismissal rule erects large obstacles for new workers or those who want to change jobs. Tying the employers' hands ties workers' hands as well. But every cloud has a silver lining: Litigating an unjust dismissal case makes the lawyers on both sides rich."

NO says **PETER LINZER**, Professor of Law, University of Houston Law Center.

"The restraints that have been placed on employer discretion in the past 10 or 15 years are pretty small beer. Most of them are based either on public policy or promises made in employee handbooks. The public-policy rule means only that employers may not threaten to fire workers to coerce conduct that no one should be able to force on another person. Thus, in *some* states (not all), employers may no longer fire a worker for refusing to break the law, for refusing sexual favors, for whistle-blowing, for filing a workers' compensation claim, for serving on jury duty.

Some say that when employees are told 'do it or get fired,' they can always go out and find another job, but that is an answer that works only for the talented few. For the great majority of people, employer discretion to fire them for any reason, including a bad one, means that their self-respect and their economic and political rights have to be balanced against the ability to feed their families and pay their rent.

The handbook exceptions hold employers to glowing promises of job security or procedures they say they will follow before a worker will be fired. The important point to remember is that no one forced the company to make the promises; presumably the management made the promises to get something in return — employee loyalty, a better atmosphere on the line or even a work force that would take a little less money because its jobs were protected. Some courts have held that the company can go back on its word, but the better decisions have held it to its promise — no more, but no less. Any employer who is unhappy with these cases need only make no promises that it doesn't want to keep. That is how the rest of us run our lives.

All that the changes in the employment-at-will rule have done so far is to remove gross unfairness, but they could start us thinking in the right direction.

Our companies are really joint ventures among capital providers, management, workers and often the locality that has helped and become dependent on the company. Most workers have more company loyalty and have made more of a permanent investment than the shareholders who buy and sell stock at the rate of hundreds of millions a day. They can't give themselves the sweetheart contracts and golden parachutes that management gives itself. But if they are guaranteed some amount of job security and compensation based on productivity and profits, we just might see American business able to compete again with Asia and Europe."

Continued from page 104
complete internal hearing system affects either the judge or the jury in deciding whether there's any liability or not."

Companies' internal-complaint systems have their limitations, however. Of 90 companies surveyed by Westin and Feliu in 1984 that had systems with "a formal adjudicative mechanism," only one in five provided "that a fellow employee can be selected to assist the complaining employee or represent him/her at hearings, or have the employees as members of hearing and appeal committees," and only one in 20 provided "voluntary, outside mediation or arbitration of the final internal appeal." [35]

Even with outside arbitration, Professor Gould says, "there's not a guarantee that the hearing would be a fair one, because all of these procedures are devised without employee input, without employee selection of the arbitrator, and without employee sharing of the costs of the system." Fairness would be assured only if employees, as well as the employer, were thus involved, he contends. But employers "don't want to turn to a group [of employees] because that might be a foot in the door for a union, and they don't want to turn to the [individual] employees [making the complaints] because that might encourage them to bring outsiders into the process."

Gould, who co-chaired a committee on termination-at-will and wrongful discharge appointed by the Labor and Employment Law Section of the State Bar of California in 1983, favors (as did most members of the committee) legislation that would establish a just-cause standard for dismissal and require arbitration by an impartial third-party of wrongful-discharge disputes. The remedies would include back pay and reinstatement (or up to two years' pay if reinstatement were deemed inappropriate), but no punitive or compensatory damages.

"The benefits of arbitration for employee and employer are obvious," Gould has written. "The employer would be rid of the unpredictability of the jury system and the accompanying possibility of unlimited punitive and compensatory damages and would also have a forum in which the peculiarities of managerial performance could be handled more expertly. The employee would have relatively unencumbered access to a process that would promise prompt relief." [36] However, the prospects for such legislation are "not so good," Gould acknowledges, given the strong opposition of two groups: "The trial lawyers, who are doing very well, thank you, under the existing system, where they go into court and get big contingency fees, and the employers, who would rather live under the existing system, where fewer employees are able to get at them, even though [some of the fewer employees are] able to get these enormous judgments."

"Business in America doesn't like to have its hands tied, and they clearly view [legislation establishing a just-cause standard for dismissal] as something that would tie their hands," management Professor Dunham points out. Businesses would like to decide on their own what is just cause for firing an employee. "And they'd like to think that they're responsible enough to make that decision well, and I think a lot of organizations in this country are responsible enough to do that. But unfortunately there's a lot of others that aren't. And there is where we have problems." The California Supreme Court's decision in the *Foley* case may indicate whether employers in the near future will need to rethink their position.

NOTES

[1] See Michael J. Lotito and Michael E. Caples, "Life After *Foley*: What Will It Be?," *Personnel*, June 1988, pp. 82-84, and *The Los Angeles Times*, July 28, 1987, and Sept. 16, 1988.

[2] Quoted by David A. Bradshaw and Linda Van Winkle Deacon in "Wrongful discharge: The tip of the iceberg?," *Personnel Administrator*, November 1985, p. 76.

[3] Alan F. Westin and Alfred G. Feliu, *Resolving Employment Disputes Without Litigation* (1988), p. 2.

[4] William B. Gould IV, "Stemming the Wrongful Discharge Tide: A Case for Arbitration," *Employee Relations Law Journal*, winter 1987-88, p. 412.

[5] *Ibid.*, p. 413.

[6] For background on this trend, see "New Styles in Work-Place Management," *E.R.R.*, Vol. I, No. 8, Feb. 26, 1988.

[7] Jay M. Feinman, "The Development of the Employment at Will Rule," *American Journal of Legal History*, Vol. 20, 1976, pp. 118, 133.

[8] Quoted by Feinman in *ibid.*, p. 126.

[9] See Clyde W. Summers, "Protecting *All* Employees against Unjust Dismissal," *Harvard Business Review*, January-February 1980, p. 134.

[10] See Brian Heshizer in "The New Common Law of Employment: Changes in the Concept of Employment at Will," *Labor Law Journal*, February 1985, p. 96.

[11] Andrew D. Hill, '*Wrongful Discharge*' and the Derogation of the At-Will Employment Doctrine (1987), p. 7.

[12] Quoted by Norman L. Zucker in *George W. Norris: Gentle Knight of American Democracy* (1966), p. 106.

[13] Quoted by Hill, *op. cit.*, pp. 7-8.

[14] James N. Dertouzos, Elaine Holland, and Patricia Ebener, *The Legal and Economic Consequences of Wrongful Termination*, 1988, p. 5. Dertouzos is an economist, Holland is an attorney, and Ebener is a behavioral scientist.

[15] The estimate, by Professor Theodore St. Antoine of the University of Michigan Law School, is cited by Hill, *op. cit.*, p. 9.

[16] Summers, *op. cit.*, pp. 135-136.

[17] Quoted by John Hoerr *et al.* in "Beyond Unions: A Revolution in Employee Rights is in the Making," *Business Week*, July 8, 1985, p. 75.

[18] Quoted by Hill, *op. cit.*, p. 28.

[19] Quoted by David A. Cathcart and Mark S. Dichter, eds., *Employment-At-Will: A 1986 State-By-State Survey*, 1987, p. 15. See also Daniel Murnane Mackey, *Employment at Will and Employer Liability*, 1986, p. 41.

[20] Dertouzos *et al.*, *op. cit.*, pp. 8-9.

[21] Cathcart and Dichter, *op. cit.*, p. 287; Hill, *op. cit.*, pp. 121, 126-128.

[22] Quoted by Peter Linzer, "The Decline of Assent: At-Will Employment as a Case Study of the Breakdown of Private Law Theory," *Georgia Law Review*, winter 1986, pp. 346-351. See also Hill, *op. cit.*, pp. 19-20.

[23] Quoted by Linzer, *op. cit.*, p. 354. See also Hill, *op. cit.*, p. 61, and Hoerr *et al.*, *op. cit.*, p. 75.

[24] Jack Stieber, "Most U.S. Workers Still May Be Fired under the Employment-at-Will Doctrine," *Monthly Labor Review*, May 1984, p. 35.

[25] Cathcart and Dichter, *op. cit.*, p. 212.

[26] Charles G. Bakaly, Jr. and Joel M. Grossman, "How To Avoid Wrongful Discharge Suits," *Management Review*, August 1984, pp. 43-44; Cathcart and Dichter, *op. cit.*, p. 39; Hill, *op. cit.*, pp. 35-36.

[27] Dertouzos *et al.*, *op. cit.*, p. 10.

[28] Cathcart and Dichter, *op. cit.*, pp. 254-255.

[29] Dertouzos *et al.*, *op. cit.*, p. 11.

[30] Lotito and Caples, *op. cit.*, p. 84.

[31] Dertouzos *et al.*, *op. cit.*, p. 15-16, 20-22, 25. The figures on suits filed are derived from a survey of documents filed in Los Angeles Superior Court during March and April of selected years.

[32] Gould, *op. cit.*, p. 406.

[33] Westin and Feliu, *op. cit.*, p. 252.

[34] *Ibid.* pp. 4, 16.

[35] *Ibid.*, p. 15.

[36] Gould, *op. cit.*, p. 415.

Graphics: cover, S. Dmitri Lipczenko.

RECOMMENDED READING

BOOKS

Hill, Andrew D., *'Wrongful Discharge' and the Derogation of the At-Will Employment Doctrine*, Industrial Research Unit, Wharton School, University of Pennsylvania, 1987.

The court-led change in the common law on employment-at-will has left the traditional doctrine "riddled with exceptions and exemptions depending on the jurisdiction and focus of each individual case," the author says. Hill examines the legal doctrines that have evolved, legal defenses, and preventive measures employers can take. He devotes separate chapters to the situations in California, Michigan, Pennsylvania and New York. An appendix provides a state-by-state survey.

Westin, Alan F. and Feliu, Alfred G., *Resolving Employment Disputes Without Litigation*, Bureau of National Affairs Inc., 1988.

Westin, professor of public law and government at Columbia University, and Feliu, an employment-law attorney, focus on what they consider the "most important response" that U.S. corporations have made to the rise in wrongful-discharge litigation, namely, the decision by a growing number of companies to establish or improve "dispute resolution systems inside their organizations."

ARTICLES

Bakaly, Charles G., Jr., and Grossman, Joel M., "How to avoid wrongful discharge suits," *Management Review*, August 1984, pp. 41-46.

"In a wrongful discharge lawsuit, the employer has essentially two defenses," note the authors, both attorneys specializing in labor and employment law. "The first is that the employee was an employee at-will and could be discharged at any time. . . . [T]his defense is not nearly as potent as it once was. The second defense is that the discharge was for good cause. In many cases this will be the only defense for the discharge, and the employer should be prepared to document its reasoning."

Gould, William B., IV, "Stemming the Wrongful Discharge Tide: A Case for Arbitration," *Employee Relations Law Journal*, winter 1987-88, pp. 404-425.

The author, a Stanford Law School professor, writes, "It is unlikely that there will be substantial change providing for comprehensive wrongful discharge legislation in the foreseeable future. The time for that idea has not yet come. Nevertheless, the idea that a job is property and that the employee deserves and needs protection has arrived on these shores, even if there is no clear consensus about how to cope with this idea in resolving disputes. Arbitration in the organized sector is a useful model. . . ."

———, "The Idea of the Job as Property in Contemporary America: The Legal and Collective Bargaining Framework," *Brigham Young University Law Review*, 1986, No. 4, pp. 885-918.

Gould examines the changed common law regarding the relationship between employer and employee. He writes that "the starting point for evaluation of these issues is the realization that in a modern industrialized economy employment is central to one's existence and dignity. One's job provides not only income essential to the acquisition of the necessities of life, but also the opportunity to shape the aspirations of one's family, aspirations which are both moral and educational. Along with marital relations and religion, it is hard to think of what might be viewed as more vital in our society than the opportunity to work and retain one's employment status."

REPORTS AND STUDIES

Cathcart, David A. and Dichter, Mark S., eds., *Employment-At-Will: A 1986 State-By-State Survey*, National Employment Law Institute, 1987.

This detailed, 493-page survey reflects "the current status of a revolution in American employment law which is transforming employer policies and practices toward the 80 percent of the nation's work force which is not covered by collective bargaining agreements," the editors write. The report, covering the 50 states and the District of Columbia, is the main annual project of the Employment and Labor Relations Law Committee of the Litigation Section of the American Bar Association.

Dertouzos, James N.; Holland, Elaine; and Ebener, Patricia, *The Legal and Economic Consequences of Wrongful Termination*, RAND Corp., Institute for Civil Justice, 1988.

These RAND analysts examined 120 wrongful-discharge jury trials in California between 1980 and 1986, and found that defense and plaintiff lawyer fees represented more than half of the money changing hands. "Despite the rather large average jury award of $650,000, the typical plaintiff receives much less. In fact, the median employee bringing suit can expect to pocket only $30,000 after we account for the losing cases, post-trial reductions, and deducting contingency fees." Not only the discharged employees but also the employers "would probably have benefited from an early resolution of the dispute. Considering legal fees, most defendants would be better off paying the initial demands rather than going to trial. . . . Of course, this ignores the effect on other employees who may be contemplating wrongful discharge actions."

RACKETEERING LAW COMES UNDER ATTACK

RACKETEERING LAW COMES UNDER ATTACK

by Kenneth Jost

The Wall Street Journal called it a "monster."[1] A high Justice Department official, on the other hand, called it a "thermonuclear weapon" in the war on organized crime.[2] "It" is RICO, the Racketeer Influenced and Corrupt Organizations Act. Passed in 1970, the federal racketeering law was scarcely used during its first decade of existence, but prosecutors and private lawyers alike have made up for that during the last 10 years. Gangsters and drug dealers, politicians and pornographers, securities firms and labor unions — all have been caught in its web. And as the law has expanded its reach, calls to rein it in have grown louder. Here's what is behind all the noise.

Almost two decades after its enactment, RICO has come of age. Federal prosecutors have used the anti-racketeering law to cut a wide swath through organized-crime families and put crooked politicians behind bars from coast to coast. Terrorists, white supremacists, pornographers, even Ferdinand and Imelda Marcos have felt RICO's sting. Private lawyers have discovered the statute as well. Lured by lucrative treble-

Kenneth Jost, a lawyer, is a free-lance journalist who lives in Washington.

damage and attorney-fee provisions, lawyers representing big corporations, forlorn investors and a variety of other plaintiffs have filed racketeering suits against established businesses ranging from big accounting firms and white-shoe law firms to securities dealers, banks and *Fortune* 500 corporations.

But the growing use of the 1970 law — formally called the Racketeer Influenced and Corrupt Organizations Act — has brought with it growing criticism. RICO's looming presence in the government's successful plea negotiations with junk-bond dealer Drexel Burnham Lambert Inc. raised doubts on Wall Street and beyond about the leverage the law gives to prosecutors. Expansion of the law to obscenity cases was challenged on First Amendment grounds. And injection of racketeering allegations into private litigation of all sorts — sexual harassment, wrongful discharge and an array of what critics call "garden variety" fraud — has produced broad-based calls to restrict the law's civil remedies.

Congress passed RICO as a way to remove the influence of organized crime from legitimate businesses and labor unions. Critics charge that because RICO was meant to attack gangsters, it should not be used as just another tool in business disputes. Today, they say, RICO is being used to label as racketeers the legitimate businesses it was designed to protect.

Indeed, RICO suits against established businesses are multiplying. A major accounting firm, for example, paid out $15 million after a jury in Sacramento, Calif., found it liable for aiding and abetting a fraudulent investment scheme. Two brokerage houses paid multimillion-dollar settlements in an insider-trading suit. A big Chicago law firm paid $7.3 million to settle a class action brought by investors in a failed real-estate investment concern. Ashland Oil Inc. was ordered to pay $70 million after a jury said it fired two executives to cover up illegal foreign bribes. And late last year, a jury in New York ordered the Long Island Lighting Co. to pay almost $23 million after finding the utility had lied in rate-making proceedings before the state Public Service Commission (the award later was thrown out by the judge in case).

With headline-grabbing suits like those in mind, a coalition of business groups, backed by the AFL-CIO and the American Civil Liberties Union, is urging revisions in the law that they say will reduce its abuse in civil suits. Opposing them in trying to preserve RICO's potent civil provisions are consumer organizations and state law-enforcement groups, who say RICO is the most effective federal remedy against the estimated $200 billion-a-year problem of business fraud.[3]

RICO, passed by Congress in 1970, was technically only one part of an omnibus bill crafted by the Senate's veteran crime fighter, Democrat John L. McClellan of Arkansas, to provide stronger tools to federal prosecutors to attack organized crime. The law gave prosecutors new authority to convene special grand

RICO in a Nutshell

RICO is a powerful legal tool in the hands of the federal government or private citizens to prosecute or seek compensation from perpetrators of a broad range of criminal activities. Many states have enacted laws similar to the federal statute, which has these provisions:

Criminal: Anyone who engages in a "pattern of racketeering activity" consisting of at least two violations within the past 10 years from a list of more than 40 state or federal offenses — so-called "predicate offenses" — and uses the proceeds to acquire, control or operate an "enterprise" can be convicted under RICO. The person can also be convicted of the predicate offenses themselves.

Each RICO count carries a prison term up to 20 years and a fine of up to $25,000. In addition, any assets or property found by the jury to be proceeds from the racketeering activity are subject to mandatory forfeiture to the government.

Civil: Anyone "injured in his business or property" as a result of a RICO violation — including private citizens, corporations and state or local governments — may bring suit in federal court and recover triple damages plus costs, including "a reasonable attorney's fee."

The government may also bring civil suits and seek any of a number of court remedies to prevent racketeering violations.

In a civil RICO suit, the plaintiff needs to prove the RICO violation only by a preponderance of the evidence. As the law stands today, the defendant need not have been convicted first of any of the predicate offenses, which would require proof beyond a reasonable doubt.

juries in metropolitan areas to hear organized-crime cases and a powerful new weapon — "use immunity" — to force testimony from witnesses without foreclosing later prosecution. It established the witness protection program, permitted use of depositions in organized-crime cases if a witness was in danger or likely to flee, and provided for special sentences of up to 25 years for anyone convicted as a "habitual" offender, "professional" criminal or "organized crime figure."[4]

The RICO section, which addressed the problem of infiltration of organized crime into legitimate businesses, made it illegal to use "dirty" money to set up or operate "clean" businesses. Specifically, RICO defined a laundry-list of 32 offenses as "racketeering activity" * and made it a crime to use profits from those

---

*The so-called "predicate offenses" included eight felonies covered by state law — murder, kidnapping, gambling, arson, robbery, bribery, extortion and drug-dealing; and such federal offenses as bribery, counterfeiting, embezzlement from pension or welfare funds, mail fraud, wire fraud, obstruction of justice, gambling violations, transportation of stolen property, "white-slave traffic," illegal loans or payments to unions, embezzlement from union funds, bankruptcy fraud, securities fraud and felony drug violations. Offenses added since 1970 include trafficking in contraband cigarettes (1978), state or federal obscenity violations (1984), money-laundering (1984) and child pornography (1988). The total number of offenses now covered is 41.

activities to establish, acquire or operate any "enterprise" in interstate or foreign commerce. Violations could be punished by fines of up to $20,000 and up to 20 years' imprisonment and were also to result in forfeiture to the federal government of any assets or profits derived from the pattern of racketeering activity. In addition, the law allowed the government — before trial — to seize or freeze assets that might later be forfeited if the defendant were found guilty.

That was the essence of the criminal side of RICO, but, borrowing from antitrust law, RICO included a *civil* section, too. It allowed anyone "injured in his business or property" as a result of the racketeering activity to sue the persons responsible and recover triple damages plus the cost of the suit, "including a reasonable attorney's fee."

Despite these tough criminal and civil provisions, in the law's early years, "What happened is nothing," says McClellan's chief aide on the bill, G. Robert Blakey, now a professor at Notre Dame Law School. "The government didn't use it criminally, and the private civil bar was oblivious to it." The Justice Department approved only 217 prosecutions under the law through 1980. The private bar was even less active. An American Bar Association (ABA) task force found only 14 written court decisions in civil RICO suits during the entire decade.[5]

Paul Coffey, deputy chief of the Justice Department's Organized Crime and Racketeering Section, says government lawyers were reluctant to use the statute because of its complexity and the lack of court rulings to guide them. Private lawyers give similar reasons for their slowness to take up the statute and cite one other factor: federal judges' overt hostility to the use of RICO in what they saw as ordinary commercial disputes.

Then, beginning in the mid-1970s, Blakey says, FBI agents persuaded assistant U.S. attorneys around the country to see the potential of RICO prosecutions. According to Coffey, the key developments in expanding use of the law were two decisions by the U.S. Supreme Court that endorsed prosecutions against strictly "illegitimate" enterprises like an organized-crime family[6] and upheld broad application of RICO's forfeiture provisions.[7] And with those two decisions the stage was set for RICO to become, in Blakey's phrase, "the prosecutor's tool of choice in sophisticated crime." (Civil lawyers had to wait two more years for the key ruling on private RICO suite. *See p. 117.*)

'Unprecedented successes' in taking on the mob

Prosecutors loved RICO, and they had good reason. The 20-year prison term set for a RICO violation was longer than the sentence for most of the predicate offenses. RICO's forfeiture provision opened up a whole new area of punishment and, in combination with the longer prison term, gave prosecutors a powerful hand in plea bargaining. At trial, the broad definition of "enterprise" allowed the government to present a more complete picture of a defendant's criminal activities and also helped persuade judges to allow larger and larger joint trials.

Many of the early cases, and the most common single category of cases over the past four years, involved government corruption. By labeling state or local government as an "enterprise," prosecutors could charge officials from county commissioners and police officers up through legislators and governors with "a pattern of racketeering activity" carried out through their public offices. The theory snared, among others, Maryland's Gov. Marvin Mandel in a race-track favoritism scandal, judges in Chicago's Operation Greylord, Bronx Democratic leader Stanley Friedman in the so-called parking meter case, and New York Rep. Mario Biaggi for his role in the Wedtech scandal.

Beginning in the early 1980s, the Justice Department turned RICO's force against the mob. Testifying before a Senate panel on RICO in October 1987, Assistant Attorney General William Weld said the government had achieved "unprecedented successes" in securing convictions of the heads and principal lieutenants of La Cosa Nostra families in Boston, Buffalo, Kansas City, Cleveland, Los Angeles, New Orleans and four of the five principal families in New York City.[8]

Blakey exults in the government's successes: "It's blowing them out of the water . . . ," he says. "They're actually destroying the Mafia families." Gerard E. Lynch, a professor at Columbia Law School and a critic of some expansive uses of criminal RICO provisions, concurs. He calls the drive against the Mafia "one of the great success stories of RICO."

David C. Williams, director of the General Accounting Office's office of special investigations, told a Senate panel in 1988 that the results of the RICO assault on the mob would be lasting.[9] Crime families are being forced to replace seasoned leaders with "inexperienced, violent wiseguys" who lack the skills needed to direct sophisticated financial enterprises, Williams said. Recruitment of entry-level replacements is difficult because convictions are making the line of work less attractive, and even some current members are being encouraged to defect, he said.

The government's drive against the Mafia was marked by larger and longer trials. Nine defendants were convicted in May 1988 after a 13-month trial in the so-called "Commission" case — an unprecedented prosecution of the ruling body of New York City's five organized-crime families. Thirty defendants were convicted in the Pizza Connection heroin smuggling case after a 14-month trial. The trend toward "RICO

Continued on page 114

Grabbing the Loot

"No conviction or judgment shall work corruption of blood or forfeiture of estate," the First Congress provided in 1790.† That prohibition, however, didn't stop the authors of RICO in 1970 from giving federal prosecutors unique powers to go after racketeers' money, business interests and other property.

After strengthening amendments passed in 1984, RICO †† now provides that anyone convicted under the law "shall forfeit to the United States" any proceeds "obtained, directly or indirectly, from racketeering activity" and any interest in "any enterprise" used to conduct the racketeering. While the statute appears to be mandatory, in fact prosecutors have great discretion in deciding what assets — including money, personal property, business assets, real estate and so forth — to include in an indictment.

To prevent a defendant from hiding or destroying assets that would be forfeited upon conviction, the law allows the government to apply for a court order to tie up the property before a final conviction. The court may enter a restraining order or injunction, require a performance bond "or take any other action to preserve the availability of property" that may eventually be forfeitable to the government.

The pretrial seizure provisions may be invoked after indictment or, with some additional proof, before indictment. The statute doesn't specify a right to a hearing after indictment, but many courts have given defendants the chance to contest restrictions imposed before trial.

In pre-indictment situations, the law does state that a defendant is entitled to prior notice and a hearing. But if there's a risk the assets will be removed or destroyed, the government can ask the court to delay the hearing until after the property is physically seized.

RICO's original forfeiture provisions were upheld by the Supreme Court in 1983. ††† In the next few years, they were invoked with increasing frequency and relatively little controversy against drug dealers and grafters, labor racketeers and white-collar criminals. But when the U.S. attorney's office in New York tried to tie up the assets of the Princeton/Newport investment firm after five of its partners were indicted in August for RICO and securities fraud, much of Wall Street arose in indignant defense of due process and the presumption of innocence.

In the end, the government lost its bid to oversee Princeton/Newport's affairs while the indictment was pending, and the firm was required only to post a $14 million bond. That did not stop the criticism of the prosecutors' tactics, though, especially after the firm liquidated in December.

But a ranking official in the U.S. attorney's office in New York, which prosecuted the case, insists that the action against Princeton/Newport was nothing more or less than evenhanded enforcement of the law. "All that's going on in those cases is that the law is being applied in the exact same manner as in other cases," said Louis Freeh, deputy U.S. attorney.

Legally, the Oct. 17 ruling by the 2nd U.S. Circuit Court of Appeals in New York ‡ was a significant precedent, because it allows the application of RICO's pretrial provisions to companies that are themselves not criminally charged. And the U.S. attorney's office followed in December with an even more innovative use of prosecutorial power. As part of a plea bargain, the prosecutors got the investment house of Drexel Burnham Lambert Inc. to agree to withhold 1988 salary and bonuses from Michael Milken, the head of Drexel's lucrative Beverly Hills operations and a major target of the 2½-year probe.

Drexel itself was never charged under RICO, and the plea agreement doesn't give any legal justification for the move. Milken, claiming he was due more than $100 million, asked a federal judge in New York to invalidate the provision as an unconstitutional interference with his property rights. The U.S. attorney's office countered that Milken should bring a contract suit against Drexel directly for whatever he was entitled to. A hearing is scheduled for March 22.

Meanwhile, the U.S. Supreme Court is to hear arguments March 21 on an issue of broad significance to the RICO defense bar — whether the pretrial seizure and forfeiture provisions can be applied so stringently as to deny a defendant funds needed to pay for a lawyer. Defense lawyers contend the practice violates the defendant's right to counsel under the Sixth Amendment and, not coincidentally, might deter many attorneys from taking on RICO cases.

Most federal appeals courts have upheld the government's efforts to go after the funds paid to defense lawyers, but in a complex and divided ruling the full 2nd U.S. Circuit Court of Appeals last July held that legitimate attorneys' fees are not subject to forfeiture under RICO either before trial or after conviction. ‡‡ To resolve the conflict, the Supreme Court agreed to hear the case along with a ruling by the 4th U.S. Circuit Court of Appeals in Richmond, Va., that defense lawyers can be ordered to turn over money already paid to them once a defendant is convicted. ‡‡‡ The betting among experts is that the justices will opt for an expansive interpretation of the law and find nothing unconstitutional in the practice.

† *Quoted in* H Rept 91-1549 (1970).

†† *See* 18 U.S.C. Section 1963.

††† Russello v. United States, *464 U.S. 16 (1983).*

‡ United States v. Regan, *858 F.2d 115 (2nd Circuit, 1988).*

‡‡ United States v. Monsanto, *836 F.2d 74 (2nd Circuit, 1988).*

‡‡‡ *In re Forfeiture Hearing as to Caplin & Drysdale, 837 F.2d 637 (4th Circuit, 1988).*

State RICO Statutes

Twenty-six states have adopted civil and criminal RICO statutes. They are Arizona, Colorado, Delaware, Florida, Georgia, Hawaii, Idaho, Illinois, Indiana, Louisiana, Mississippi, Nevada, New Jersey, New Mexico, North Carolina, North Dakota, New York, Ohio, Oklahoma, Oregon, Pennsylvania, Rhode Island, Tennessee, Utah, Washington and Wisconsin. Two other states, California and Connecticut, have only criminal RICO statutes.

Continued from page 112
megatrials," however, drew sharp criticism from a defense lawyers' group, the National Association of Criminal Defense Lawyers, which said the length and complexity of the prosecutions prejudiced individual defendants, taxed the mental and physical energies of judges and juries, and led to huge, unnecessary costs for court-appointed counsel.* [10]

A jury in Newark, N.J., appeared to validate the criticisms in the record-breaking, 21-month-long trial of 20 defendants depicted as members of the Lucchese crime family. After just 14 hours' deliberation, the panel acquitted all defendants on all charges. "The jury said never, never again should the government waste the public's money this way," Maria Noto, one of the defense lawyers, said after the verdict.[11]

And in the next few months, the government suffered two more setbacks in labor-racketeering cases brought under RICO's civil provisions. In New Jersey, the corruption-ridden Teamsters Local 560, which had been under a court-supervised trusteeship for four years, elected as its new president the brother of the man ousted as president at the beginning of the racketeering case. Columbia's Lynch called it "a rather dispiriting result" — all the more so since it came as the government prepared for an even higher-stakes RICO suit to oust the leaders of the national Teamsters organization.

Then in January 1989, a federal judge rebuffed a bid by U.S. Attorney Rudolph W. Giuliani in New York to gain control of the United Seafood Workers local at New York's famous Fulton Fish Market. Judge Thomas P. Griesa said prosecutors had failed to show

the local and its officers were controlled by the Genovese crime family. And this week the Justice Department agreed to settle its longstanding suit against the Teamsters union hours before the civil trial was to begin. The settlement provided for some reforms in the union, including the Teamsters' first direct election for its leadership, but the reforms were considerably less than the suit had demanded.

Meanwhile, a Supreme Court decision last month may blunt a Reagan administration initiative of using RICO in obscenity cases. Attorney General Edwin Meese III's Commission on Pornography had advocated use of state and federal racketeering laws against pornographers, and some 20 states and the federal government now include obscenity as a predicate offense in RICO-type laws.

To booksellers, publishers, and civil-liberties groups, however, the laws encroach on the First Amendment by permitting authorities to seize — either before trial or after conviction — books, magazines, and the like, even those not obscene, as the assets of a racketeering enterprise. "It means," explains Michael A. Bamberger, a New York lawyer for the American Booksellers Association, "that if you make a mistake and sell a book that is held to be obscene or that is not obscene but is held to be harmful to minors, you may lose your stock in goods, you may lose your chain of bookstores, you may lose your publishing house if you go after the publisher. That's inappropriate when you're dealing with First Amendment materials."

A case involving a state RICO law in Indiana, *Fort Wayne Books v. Indiana*, was the first to reach the U.S. Supreme Court, and in its Feb. 21 ruling the court gave something to both sides. The justices voted 5-3 to permit application of RICO-type provisions and penalties in obscenity cases, but held unanimously that pretrial seizure of books and the like violated First Amendment principles. As for post-conviction forfeitures, the justices left the issue for a future case.

"It was a very good decision for the government," said Lawrence J. Leiser, an assistant U.S. attorney in Alexandria, Va., who was the prosecutor in the only federal RICO/obscenity trial so far. The major defendant, Dennis Pryba, was given a three-year prison term and a $75,000 fine, but most significantly his entire chain of three adult bookstores and eight video clubs — valued at $1 million — were forfeited to the government.[12] Leiser notes that Justice Department policy is not to seek pretrial seizure of materials in obscenity cases, as was done in the Indiana case. But the Pryba case, which will be argued before the 4th U.S. Circuit Court of Appeals in Richmond, Va., later this year, apparently will be the first test of the constitutionality of ordering the forfeiture of an entire bookstore under the federal RICO law.

Despite setbacks, though, prosecutors from Attorney General Dick Thornburgh down still praise RICO as an important crime-fighting tool. And they were voicing no second thoughts about its value even while

*In a rebuttal presented to the American Bar Association's criminal justice section meeting in March, Prof. Blakey statistically challenged the defense lawyers' critique. Analyzing some 100 RICO decisions containing information about the length of trial, Blakey found only six lasted more than six months and 19 others lasted three to six months, while the rest — 76.4 percent — were less than three months long. Similarly, he found that one or more of the defendants were acquitted on one or more charges in 12.6 percent of the cases — undermining the warnings of indiscriminate mass verdicts.

they prepared to push the racketeering law into a new area: sophisticated financial crime. "It's designed to attack the business of crime," Thornburgh said of RICO in a January television interview. "And when people are in the business of crime, we have aggressively sought not only to prosecute them, but to seize the ill-gotten gains that they've derived from that activity. And I think most American citizens will think that's only fair." [13]

Crime in the pits; fear in the board room

Few people raised questions as prosecutors began pushing RICO beyond traditional organized-crime and public-corruption cases in the early 1980s into such areas as domestic terrorism. Federal prosecutors in New York secured convictions of members of a Croatian terrorist group under RICO, citing evidence of extortion in raising funds to finance the organization. On the other side of the country, prosecutors in Washington state won RICO convictions of 10 members of the neo-Nazi group Order of the Silent Brotherhood for a series of bank robberies used to finance the organization and two murders, including the killing of a Jewish radio talk show host, Alan Berg, in Denver.

If the moves to target pornographers and political terrorists with RICO went largely undebated, so, too, did its extension into the world of high finance. RICO has applied to business fraud since its inception. Mail fraud, wire fraud, bankruptcy fraud and securities fraud were all included as predicate offenses when RICO was passed in 1970. The Supreme Court's 1983 decision upholding RICO's forfeiture provisions arose from an arson-insurance fraud ring operating in Florida in the mid-1970s. For the past four years, cases involving business fraud have accounted for 11 percent of the RICO prosecutions approved by the Justice Department — the third-largest category, after public corruption and narcotics charges.

Supporters and critics of RICO agree that Congress' principal target was organized crime. But Blakey, the primary draftsman, and more detached law professors like Lynch at Columbia and Michael Goldsmith of Brigham Young University Law School say the legislative history also shows there's nothing contrary to congressional intent in prosecutors' use of the law to fight white-collar crime, too. *(See story, p. 119.)* "You can have a white collar or a blue collar — or indeed no collar at all — and violate this statute," says Blakey.

Nevertheless, it was September 1983 before RICO was used in a big way against financial fraud. Giuliani, then in his first year as federal prosecutor in New York, invoked the statute in charging wealthy oil trader Marc Rich with evading $40 million in federal taxes by shifting income from a domestic company to a foreign subsidiary and by concealing the transactions with phony documents. But Rich never came to trial, remaining a fugitive in Switzerland and Spain and not subject to extradition on tax charges.

The Rich case was one small episode in a decade when high-rolling financial deals drew close scrutiny from regulators and prosecutors. In the fall of 1986, the Securities and Exchange Commission's crackdown on insider trading landed its biggest catch — financier Ivan F. Boesky, a man who had made millions of dollars by buying and selling stocks in companies that were "in play" in the dizzying world of mergers, acquisitions and takeovers. The SEC investigation disclosed that Boesky's good fortune depended on use of inside information gathered from a network of informants in brokerages and investment houses. Boesky agreed to plead guilty to a single felony count — making false disclosures to the SEC — and cooperate with authorities in further investigations.

Boesky had been implicated by Dennis Levine, who had been a junior trader at the investment house of Drexel Burnham Lambert. As the SEC pursued its leads from the Levine-Boesky case, so, too, did Giuliani's office in New York, targeting Drexel and its star trader, junk-bond wizard Michael Milken.

Nearly two years after the Drexel investigation was opened, Giuliani fired a warning shot over Drexel's bow. His office obtained indictments for conspiracy, mail and wire fraud, and RICO violations against a former Drexel official and five partners of the investment firm Princeton/Newport Partners — the first RICO charges ever against officials of a securities firm. Most significantly, prosecutors cited RICO's forfeiture and pretrial restraint provisions in seeking an order to freeze the defendants' assets and prevent them from withdrawing any funds from the investment firm itself. A federal appeals court ruled the pretrial restraint was permissible under RICO, but ordered the lower court to hold a hearing on whether a pretrial bond would suffice to protect the government's interest in securing the assets while the charges were pending.[14]

Judge Robert L. Carter's ruling that set a $14 million bond was viewed as a setback for the government, which had asked for $24 million. Two months later, however, Princeton/Newport liquidated, with the defendants still awaiting trial. Defense lawyers said the government had succeeded in shutting the firm down without a trial, and their complaints were echoed by critical observers. "In the context of a securities firm, this reversal of the presumption of innocence meant that Princeton/Newport did not survive long enough to have a chance to defend itself in court," wrote L. Gordon Crovitz, assistant editor of The Wall Street Journal's editorial page, in a signed article, one of his many sharp attacks on use of RICO.[15] The trial still has not begun.

Other observers more sympathetic to RICO, however, see nothing untoward in the outcome. "The reason they went bust was because of the bad publicity from the indictment," says Brigham Young's Goldsmith. "It had nothing to do with RICO."

Regardless, the appeals court ruling fueled speculation at Drexel that Giuliani's office could get a restraining order on its business if RICO charges were brought. Drexel's attorneys met with Justice Department lawyers in late October in an unsuccessful effort to block RICO charges. For two months, Drexel officials mulled their legal options and then, on Dec. 21, agreed to plead guilty to six still-unspecified felonies and pay $650 million for fines and compensation of investors.

What had Drexel done? In its 24-page formal charge against Drexel filed Jan. 24, the government alleged securities fraud and mail fraud in five stock deals involving Drexel and Boesky, and a scheme with Princeton/Newport to generate bogus tax deductions. The deals with Boesky included stock price manipulation involving MCA Inc., Phillips Petroleum Co. and Stone Container Inc., and rigged takeovers of Fischbach Corp. and Harris Graphics Corp. The charges said Boesky got stock profits and phony tax losses from the deals, while Milken earned about $6.5 million in profits from stock he held personally in Harris Graphics.

Drexel issued a statement saying it was "not in a position to dispute" the charges, but its guilty plea was held up pending settlement of the parallel suit by the Securities and Exchange Commission (SEC). Milken issued a statement saying his lawyers were "continuing to prepare to defend him against any charges that may be brought."

Drexel said it spent $75 million in legal fees on the combined SEC-criminal investigations, but RICO critics said the firm had been bludgeoned into a guilty plea. "It has really eliminated much of the constitutional right to a jury trial," says securities law expert Alan R. Bromberg of Southern Methodist University Law School.

Ivan Fisher, a defense lawyer who represented one of the defendants in the Pizza Connection heroin-smuggling trial, agrees. But he also doubts that Drexel's viability as an ongoing business was really jeopardized. "I have a feeling that Drexel might very well have persuaded a district court here to leave them unrestrained," he says. Significantly, Drexel's chief executive, Frederick H. Joseph, said precisely as much to firm employees before the decision was made to plead guilty. "We expect that the firm will have the opportunity to post a bond to forestall any pretrial restraint on the firm's assets," his written statement read.

With the debate over the Drexel case still raging, RICO surfaced in another investigation: a probe of suspected fraud in the heart of the nation's commodities market, the Chicago Board of Trade and the Chicago Mercantile Exchange. While the Justice Department and U.S. Attorney Anton Vukas have been tight-lipped about the investigation, defense lawyers representing some of the futures traders questioned in the probe have been quoted as saying their clients were threatened with RICO charges and possible pretrial seizure of assets like their cars or homes.[16]

The accusations of abusive tactics in both the commodities and securities investigations focused unaccustomed attention on the Justice Department's review process in RICO cases. Department guidelines adopted in 1980 call for the statute to be "selectively and uniformly used."[17] They require prior approval of any RICO case, criminal or civil, by the department's Organized Crime and Racketeering Section in Washington. U.S. attorneys must submit a detailed "pros memo" along with a copy of the draft indictment in the case at least 15 days in advance of presenting any RICO charges to a grand jury. The guidelines caution against use of RICO for plea-bargaining purposes or for gathering evidence and disapprove of " 'imaginative' prosecutions . . . which are far afield from the Congressional purpose of the RICO statute."

When questioned about the tactics, U.S. Attorney General Thornburgh vouched for his prosecutors' actions. "The United States attorneys have, I think, without exception . . . followed the guidelines that are laid down in some detail for the use of the RICO statute," Thornburgh told a Jan. 31 news conference called to announce a new prosecutorial task force on financial fraud.

The department's review process also gives defense attorneys the chance to argue against institution of the RICO charges before they are brought. "We like to give them a conference," says Coffey, the section's deputy chief. He says the defense lawyers' presentations are often helpful and sometimes result in modification of charges. Despite his complimentary remarks, however, the widespread view among the RICO defense bar is that Coffey's review is a rubber-stamp process. And statistics lend credence to that view.

Since the department began keeping annual statistics in 1981, the number of RICO prosecutors approved by the section has averaged about 100 a year. Coffey won't give out the number of requests, but another Justice Department official — Stephen S. Trott, assistant attorney general for the criminal division at the time and now a judge on the 9th U.S. Circuit Court of Appeals — did give Congress the figures on prosecution requests in testimony for RICO oversight hearings in 1985.[18] Combining the two sets of figures shows that from 1981 to 1984, the section approved 94 percent of the requested RICO prosecutions — rejecting just 22 charges out of 371 requests over the four-year period.

Procedural disputes aside, however, at the heart of the debate over RICO's use in financial-fraud cases is whether the law should apply to securities fraud at all. Critics like Bromberg and Fisher say probably not. "These insider-trading notions, these parking violation notions, where do we see their precedents?" Fisher asks. "How much real notice was there in the commu-

Criminal Prosecutions

During RICO's first 10 years of existence, the law was scarcely used at all. There were only 217 criminal prosecutions brought between 1970 and 1980. Now, there are a hundred cases a year. The majority of those cases involve drugs or corruption of government officials.

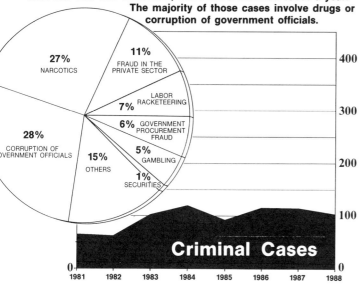

Source: U.S. Department of Justice

Civil Suits

Separate information on RICO suits was not officially maintained until 1985. Unofficial statistics compiled by Andrew Weissman, the former executive director of the American Bar Association's task force on civil RICO, measure the number of written decisions, not the number of suits filed. Weissman found only 14 such decisions between 1970 and 1980. The number remained low until 1985, when the Supreme Court approved a broad interpretation of the law. Now, so many suits are filed that there are hundreds of written RICO decisions in federal courts each year. The majority of cases involve commercial fraud (breach of contract, franchise disputes, etc.) or securities and commodities fraud. Only about 5 percent involve activities commonly associated with professional criminals, such as gambling, arson, murder, drugs, and extortion, and so on.

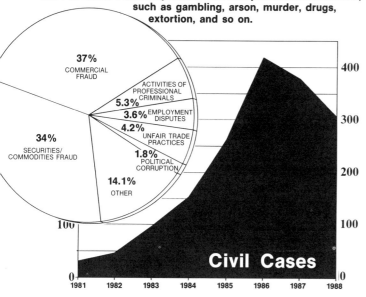

Source: Andrew Weissman

nity that this was conduct that violates the criminal law? To what extent were these genuine violations of RICO? I don't know."

On the other hand, Louis Freeh, deputy U.S. attorney in New York, contends the office's use of RICO in securities cases has been "well within the statutory authority and statutory history." And Columbia's Lynch concurs. "If one agrees that the firms involved have committed securities violations, the use of RICO is absolutely standard...," he says. "The main thrust of their unprecedentedness is that these guys think they are or ought to be exempt from these statutes. They're not."

How common is RICO in 'garden variety' fraud?

RICO may be only a looming presence in the Chicago commodities probe and the Drexel-Milken case, but use of the law in civil litigation over the past five years has been very real indeed. Multimillion-dollar verdicts and settlements in RICO suits against established businesses galvanized corporate lawyers into taking steps to weaken the law long before Wall Street or LaSalle Street came under the scrutiny of federal prosecutors.

It was a 1985 Supreme Court ruling that paved the way for a quantum leap in the number of RICO suits. A Belgian corporation, Sedima, S.P.R.L., became convinced that a U.S. firm, Imrex Co., had been padding its bills for electronic components to the tune of about $175,000. Sedima brought a suit in U.S. District Court in New York. It alleged conventional legal theories — unjust enrichment, conversion and breach of contract — but it buttressed them by three RICO counts based on charges of mail fraud, wire fraud and conspiracy.

Sedima's suit was thrown out at the trial level and thrown out again, in a split decision, by a federal appeals court.[19] Both courts held that a civil RICO suit required "a racketeering injury" on top of the injury resulting from the underlying offense, although they left vague precisely what they meant by such an injury. In addition, the appeals panel said the plaintiff couldn't bring a RICO suit unless the defendant had first been convicted of the underlying offense or a RICO count; in other words, Imrex would have to be convicted of a RICO-related charge in a *criminal* court, where the burden of proof is much greater, before Sedima could bring a RICO suit in *civil* court and collect triple damages.

In 1985, however, the Supreme Court, in a 5-4 decision, rejected both requirements.[20] The court said that nothing in RICO's language or legislative history imposed such preconditions for civil recovery. But the ruling was no ringing endorsement of RICO. The justices produced three opinions — a majority opinion by Justice Byron R. White and dissents by Justices Lewis F. Powell Jr. and Thurgood Marshall — and all voiced doubts that Congress had intended the statute to be used against what White called "respected businesses" rather than "the archetypal, intimidating mobster." For the majority, however, White said the defect — "if defect it is" — was for Congress, not the judiciary, to correct.

The plaintiff's bar needed no further invitation and began including RICO in suits great and small. Within two years the number of RICO suits topped 1,000.* RICO seminars and RICO newsletters started to appear.

The opponents of the law claimed that RICO was being abused, and they found ample evidence in the growing number of suits.[21] A free-lance journalist charged ABC News with racketeering because he didn't receive on-air credit for his contribution to a story on irregularities in President Carter's personal finances. One rabbi cited RICO against another in a dispute over the succession to leadership of a Chassidic congregation. RICO counts showed up in a divorce action, a landlord-tenant dispute and uncounted numbers of cases that critics said involved "garden variety" fraud and properly belonged in state rather than federal courts. Citing the ABA task force's report, they said only 9 percent of RICO suits involved activities traditionally associated with organized crime.[22]

Interest groups facing RICO suits kept the debate going. The AFL-CIO spoke out after word leaked in late 1987 that the Justice Department was readying a suit to oust the entire leadership of the Teamsters union and place it under trusteeship. Labor had more to fear. A ruling by a federal appeals court in Washington, D.C., upheld an employer's civil RICO suit against its union for alleged violence and intimidation during a strike.[23]

The American Civil Liberties Union (ACLU), which had opposed RICO in 1970 because of its criminal provisions, discovered another threat to civil liberties in use of the law by abortion clinics against anti-abortion protesters. Half a dozen civil suits were filed around the country, and one — in Philadelphia — resulted in a $93,000 jury award against the protesters in June 1987. Four months later, ACLU legislative counsel Antonio Clifa told Congress that the abortion clinic suits showed RICO had "enormous" potential for chilling free speech rights and said the ACLU joined in urging general RICO reform.**[24]

The AFL-CIO and ACLU were junior partners, though, to three business groups that provided the real

muscle for the RICO reform coalition: the National Association of Manufacturers (NAM), the American Institute of Certified Public Accountants and the Securities Industry Association. For NAM's members, the Sedima case illustrated the kind of commercial litigation that under RICO could be converted into a treble-damage federal court suit. Accountants, already facing more litigation for involvement with phony investment schemes and failed businesses, said charges amounting to nothing more than negligence now carried the racketeering label and the threat of triple damages. And securities dealers argued that existing law provided all that was needed to deal with any abuses in the securities market. The beefed-up RICO suits gave plaintiffs' lawyers too powerful a club, they argued, and upset a carefully constructed 50-year body of court rulings for handling securities suits. In the late days of the 100th Congress, commodities dealers chimed in, too, seeking an exemption from RICO suits like the one securities dealers were proposing for themselves.

For their part, supporters argue the critics are exaggerating the abuses and ignoring RICO's benefits to plaintiffs, including businesses as well as individuals. The journalist's suit against ABC, they point out, was thrown out before trial.[25] So, too, the suit between the two rabbis.[26] In fact, according to a study by Robert Blakey, motions to dismiss were granted in 50 percent of reported RICO decisions in 1985 and 1986.[27] A later count — by Andrew B. Weissman, the former executive director of the ABA task force on civil RICO — found that two-thirds of RICO decisions from 1970 to 1988 ended up either as dismissals or as summary judgments in the defendants' favor.

A study by Brigham Young's Goldsmith documented the exaggerations by RICO opponents. In testimony before the House Criminal Justice Subcommittee in 1986, the professor analyzed some 34 "abuse" cases cited by previous witnesses and found that the majority — 19 — had been dismissed for failure to satisfy RICO requirements and another six disposed of on other grounds. Of the remaining nine, Goldsmith's account suggested most involved allegations of serious fraud — like a $1.8 million commercial kickback case or a scheme to defraud elderly rich people out of their estates.[28]

Michael Waldman, legislative director of Public Citizen's Congress Watch, argues that RICO's treble-damage provisions are exactly what's needed to go after such large-scale financial crime. "Law enforcement against such economic crimes succeeds only when the potential penalty exceeds the gain from the illicit conduct," Waldman wrote in an editorial in *RICO Law Reporter* in July 1988.[29]

In fact, however, damages actually paid in many of the big cases have not even equaled the amounts plaintiffs claimed to have lost, much less exceeded the loss. Anheuser-Busch settled a RICO/insider-trading suit against the brokerage houses Bear Stearns &

---

*Despite the increase, RICO cases amounted to less than 1 percent of the federal judiciary's entire caseload of about 240,000 cases in 1988, according to the Administrative Office of the Courts.

**Paradoxically, RICO damages in the case amounted to only $887 (which were tripled, so totaled $2,671). The remainder of the $93,000 award included $42,000 on trespass counts for security costs and $48,000 in punitive damages, an award that was later set aside.

What Did Congress Intend?

Abner J. Mikva didn't intend to turn the federal anti-racketeering law loose on American business. But he helped.

As a Democratic congressman from Chicago, Mikva was one of a handful of House liberals in 1970 who opposed enactment of RICO, warning in particular that its civil damage suit provisions could allow "disgruntled and malicious competitors to harass innocent businessmen." †

Today, as a judge on the U.S. Circuit Court of Appeals for the District of Columbia, Mikva wishes he hadn't spoken out. "The plaintiffs' bar loves me," Mikva explains, because his comments can be used to show that Congress knew all along that RICO applied far beyond organized-crime cases.

What Congress intended in 1970 is a focal point of today's debate over RICO, and the record provides ammunition for both sides. No doubt, the law derived from increasing concern in Congress and among the public about organized crime. For the Senate sponsor of the measure, Democrat John L. McClellan of Arkansas, the bill was the culmination of more than a decade of work on organized crime, including hearings on underworld connections with labor unions in the late 1950s and the electrifying hearings featuring ex-Mafia member Joseph M. Valachi in 1963.††

Working with recommendations of a presidential commission, McClellan introduced the Organized Crime Control Act on Jan. 15, 1969, and followed three months later with the Corrupted Organizations Act, an innovative anti-racketeering package that would be rechristened later as RICO.‡ The Nixon administration had its own law-and-order measure — a crime bill for the District of Columbia containing such provisions as pretrial detention and no-knock search warrants — but it enthusiastically embraced McClellan's bill, too. Civil libertarians fought both measures, but few in Congress opposed the law-and-order tide.

The civil provision for treble damages found its way into the bill in a less-than-straightforward way. McClellan's original racketeering proposal included it, but it was removed before the bill passed the Senate. McClellan's chief aide, G. Robert Blakey, says the provision was dropped because the bill "was getting too complex." Critics today say civil remedies were slipped back into the bill in the House without hearings. Blakey, however, notes that the American Bar Association testified in favor of restoring the private damage suits provisions — and President Nixon backed the idea, too — while the measure was before the House Judiciary Committee.

The Judiciary Committee's liberal leadership kept the bill bottled up for months, but supporters mounted a discharge petition as midterm elections neared to force the bill out of committee. The panel's chairman, Rep. Emanuel Celler of New York, yielded and, in return for some minor amendments, agreed to report the bill to the House floor.

Mikva tried but failed to blunt the law's civil provisions by giving defendants the right to recover triple damages for injury caused by a frivolous or harassing racketeering suit. Today, the judge wishes he had been craftier and worked out a dialogue with Celler on the floor to show that the law didn't apply to white-collar crime and business fraud. "Manny would have said whatever I told him to say . . . ," Mikva says. "But I didn't realize that was the way to do it until I got here."

Blakey, now a professor at Notre Dame Law School, says Mikva's rueful recollection may make for a good story, but it's not right. McClellan and House sponsor Richard Poff of Virginia had both stated the law extended beyond organized crime, he recalls. If Celler had said anything different, Blakey insists, the bill's managers would have pounced.

The House vote on final passage Oct. 7 was 341-26. In the Senate, McClellan opted to accept the House bill without a conference. A voice vote Oct. 12 completed congressional action, and Nixon signed the bill into law Oct. 15. Despite the rush to enactment, years would pass before many of the law's most significant provisions would see wide use.

† H Rept 91-1549 (1970).

†† *For background, see "Organized Crime: The American Shakedown,"* Editorial Research Reports, *1981 Vol. I, pp. 451-467.*

‡ *See* 1970 Congressional Quarterly Almanac, *pp. 126, 545-553.*

Co. and A. G. Edwards and Sons for less than one-third of the extra $60 million its expert witness said the company paid as a result of the inflated price of its acquisition target's stock. The $15 million Laventhol & Horwarth, the nation's ninth-largest accounting firm, paid to settle a RICO suit in California was less than the $20 million-plus that investors in the failed business lost, according to testimony introduced at trial.

Even some of the critics of RICO concede that plaintiffs are not routinely collecting windfalls beyond the amount of their actual losses. "You tend to get closer to the untrebled amount because of the trebling," says Edward F. Mannino, a Philadelphia attorney and a member of the American Bar Association's Special RICO Coordinating Committee. Susan Getzendanner, who handled many RICO cases as a federal judge in Chicago and is now with a private law firm, says in her tenure on the bench she never saw a settlement she considered unjust or a settlement by an innocent party.

On closer examination, the recent extensions of RICO suits also appear less novel. The sexual-harassment case, for example, cited as RICO offenses allegations by an apprentice carpenter in Cambridge,

Mass., that she was forced by union leaders to withdraw an assault-and-battery complaint against a fellow worker and that she was coerced into buying raffle tickets to support the union's political fund. U.S. District Judge William Young said the allegations amounted to obstruction of justice and extortion, both specifically included as RICO offenses.[30] In the whistleblower case against Ashland Oil, Judge William O. Bertelsman said the RICO counts were permitted not because the two executives were fired but because the firings were alleged to be part of "a conspiracy to operate the petroleum company through a pattern of racketeering activity" — that is, illegal foreign bribes.[31]

"We just haven't seen the evidence that there are so many abusive civil RICO lawsuits and, more importantly, haven't seen the evidence that they ever succeed in court," says Pamela Gilbert of the U.S. Public Interest Research Group, an organization connected with consumer activist Ralph Nader.

Prospects for revision are not clear

This year, for the third time in five years, RICO critics returned to Capitol Hill with proposals to amend RICO to cut back its civil remedies. Before they had completed work on a new bill, the reformers picked up an important ally: Chief Justice William H. Rehnquist. Addressing the ABA midwinter meeting in Denver on Feb. 6, Rehnquist said: "A sharp curtailment of the basis for civil RICO actions ... would ... help to cut down on the work of the federal courts."

An effort to reduce RICO's scope is now before the Supreme Court in a case called *H. J. Inc. v. Northwestern Bell Telephone Co.* Lawyers representing telephone customers in Minnesota filed a class action against Northwestern Bell, claiming that a pattern of bribes and other favors to members of the state's Public Utilities Commission had resulted in unjustified rate hikes. Northwestern Bell denied the allegations, but also argued in a motion for dismissal that the accusations involved only one scheme rather than a "pattern of racketeering activity," as RICO required.

RICO itself said "pattern" required at least two offenses, and the Senate Judiciary Committee report said it required "continuity plus relationship." [32] Federal appeals courts had grappled with defining the term, and the appeals court for Minnesota — the 8th Circuit — had arrived at the strictest standard: multiple, separate illegal schemes. By that test, the court held, Northwestern Bell was accused only of one scheme — to raise rates — and, whether true or not, the allegations didn't suffice for a RICO suit.[33]

The high court, which had upheld expansive interpretations of RICO in its four previous rulings on the

law, agreed to review the case to resolve the conflict. Minneapolis attorney John French, representing Northwestern Bell, reminded the justices of the concern they had voiced in *Sedima* about RICO's effect on established businesses.

But plaintiffs' attorney Mark A. Reinhardt, with the St. Paul firm of Reinhardt & Anderson, countered that "legitimate businesses" had nothing to fear from the law. "Only those who commit not one but a pattern of racketeering activity are within RICO," Reinhardt said. "Such businesses forfeit the right to call themselves legitimate."

Two major partners in the RICO reform coalition — the manufacturers and accountants — filed briefs urging the justices to tighten the definitions for RICO suits. A decision is expected before the court's summer recess in July.

While the justices ponder the fate of RICO in the Minnesota case, Congress has taken up the issue formally. The RICO Reform Act of 1989 was introduced on Feb. 22, with bipartisan sponsorship: Rep. Rick Boucher, D-Va., in the House, and Sens. Dennis DeConcini, D-Ariz., and Orrin G. Hatch, R-Utah, in the Senate. Like the bill that failed in the last days of the 100th Congress, its key provisions would impose a prior-criminal-conviction requirement for treble-damage suits, exempt commodities and securities violations other than insider trading from civil RICO, and allow actual damages plus up to double punitive damages for three types of suits — insider trading, certain consumer-fraud cases and suits brought by special-purpose local governmental bodies such as transit authorities or utility districts. Suits by federal, state or local governments would be unaffected.

The sponsors slightly modified the prior-conviction requirement to get around the argument of critics who had dubbed it "the Boesky Bailout" because Boesky's plea to a non-RICO charge wouldn't have been included. So the 1989 bill permits a RICO suit as long as there's been a conviction on any charge relating to the subject matter of the suit. Nonetheless, opponents say the requirement would still bar RICO suits by many victims of offenses covered by RICO because prosecutors do not — and cannot — prosecute every crime.

"You don't need a criminal conviction to bring an antitrust action," adds Arizona Attorney General Robert Corbin, who has represented the National Association of Attorneys General in lobbying against the changes. "You don't need a criminal conviction to bring a civil rights suit. What's the difference? It's an added tool to bring action against something that the courts think is illegal."

The reform coalition began the year with guarded optimism about prospects for their proposal, partly because of their near success in 1988 and partly because of changes on the House Judiciary Committee. The committee's former chairman, Peter W. Rodino

Continued on page 122

AT ISSUE

Should securities fraud be exempt from RICO's civil provisions?

YES writes **M. DAVID HYMAN**, *senior managing director of Bear, Stearns & Co. Inc. and chairman of the Securities Industry Association's Ad Hoc Committee to Reform Civil RICO.*

The real issue in any discussion of RICO and securities fraud must be the automatic trebling of any damage award. The provision totally distorts civil litigation because it stacks the deck in favor of the plaintiff.

Federal securities laws already provide numerous remedies for defrauded investors. In fact, proof of wrongdoing is relatively easy, and the Securities and Exchange Commission has earned high marks for its vigorous enforcement of these laws. Brokers, issuers, accountants and others involved in the distribution of securities have learned to conduct "due diligence" before offering stock to the public or pay the price.

Securities fraud, of course, does exist. But such misconduct represents only a tiny fraction of the billions of dollars in securities traded daily. And the fact that fraud occurs does not mean that every plaintiff who alleges fraud should be presumed to be acting in the role of public prosecutor.

Private litigation should not favor either party. RICO does. Its automatic treble-damage provision gives the plaintiff an enormous advantage simply by raising the stakes by a factor of three. Any case with merely enough evidence to get to a jury has a good chance of being settled with some payoff to the plaintiff.

That's legalized extortion, and Justice Thurgood Marshall recognized as much in his dissenting opinion in *Sedima, S.P.R.L. v. Imrex Co.*, the case that opened the floodgates for civil RICO suits. "Many a prudent defendant facing ruinous exposure," he wrote, "will decide to settle even a case with no merit."

The dangers of doing otherwise are clear. In the past year there have been several staggering treble-damage awards against large publicly held corporations. These awards, which run into the hundreds of millions of dollars, are higher than any fine a judge would have imposed on a corporation convicted of a crime. And if they are not reversed on appeal, they will be paid by the public shareholders, who had nothing to do with the alleged wrongdoing. In one reported case, the award threatened to bankrupt a large public utility. Such windfall awards are a clear threat to our economy. At a minimum they will result in higher costs to business which will ultimately be borne by consumers.

The many private recovery provisions of federal securities laws, coupled with the very real threat of punitive damages that can be awarded at common law, provide adequate means to compensate defrauded investors and punish unreasonable conduct. But RICO's treble damages go far beyond these remedies and distorts private litigation in securities claims. It should be repealed.

NO write **PAMELA GILBERT**, *consumer program director of the U.S. Public Interest Research Group, and* **MICHAEL WALDMAN**, *legislative director of Public Citizen's Congress Watch.*

Wall Street is experiencing a crime wave unparalleled since the scandals of the 1930s. From E.F. Hutton to Kidder Peabody to Goldman Sachs to Ivan Boesky, the securities industry and takeover "game" are permeated with illegality.

Drexel Burnham Lambert recently pleaded guilty to six criminal counts to settle federal racketeering charges resulting from the largest securities fraud case in history. In the words of Drexel chronicler Connie Bruck, in her book, *The Predators' Ball*, Drexel has been accused of being "the brass knuckles, threatening, market-manipulating Cosa Nostra of the securities world."

Not surprisingly, prosecutors and victims have turned to the Racketeer Influenced and Corrupt Organizations Act (RICO) to prosecute massive, ongoing securities crimes. RICO, passed by Congress in 1970, provides enhanced penalties and prosecutorial tools to combat patterns of organized criminal behavior conducted through an "enterprise." Although the law was primarily intended for organized crime, Congress purposefully included the offenses of mail, wire and securities fraud so that RICO would reach so-called "legitimate" businesses that had perpetrated large-scale criminal schemes.

Remarkably, in the wake of this supernova scandal on Wall Street, some representatives of the securities industry are asking for an *exemption* from RICO's civil provisions. They claim that the "carefully crafted" securities laws are sufficient to address stock fraud.

But the securities laws simply are not adequate to punish and deter the type of criminal activity currently being perpetrated on the stock market. First, remedies under the securities laws are limited to actual damages, while civil RICO provides triple damages to successful claimants. Multiple damages are necessary to deter difficult-to-detect economic crimes such as securities fraud — just telling the criminals to "give the money" back is not enough.

Second, regulators and prosecutors lack the resources to pursue the continuous flow of stock market fraud. It is wise to recall that the SEC had allocated *half* its enforcement budget to fight Drexel — until the firm admitted guilt. Hence, lawsuits by victims must augment public prosecutors.

RICO is one of the few federal laws designed, in the words of Attorney General Dick Thornburgh, "to attack the business of crime." For Wall Street, of all industries, to ask for special exemptions is more than laughable. It is outrageous. Congress must spurn these pleas and *toughen* the laws against crime in the suites, not weaken them.

Continued from page 120

Jr. of New Jersey, retired, yielding his post to Rep. Jack Brooks of Texas, who is viewed as more favorable to business interests. Perhaps more significantly, jurisdiction over RICO was transferred from a subcommittee headed last year by Rep. John Conyers Jr. of Michigan, an opponent of the legislation, to one headed this year by Rep. William J. Hughes of New Jersey, who supported RICO reform legislation in the 99th Congress.

Kim Pearson, a Washington lawyer representing the manufacturers' group, says he expects retroactivity to be the most contentious issue this year. Under the bill, the new restrictions on RICO suits would apply to pending cases unless a judge ruled including them would be "clearly unjust." Opponents argue that's unfair to plaintiffs with suits pending.

For their part, however, opponents say widening investigations of fraud in securities and commodities markets and probes linking the accounting industry to the $100 billion savings and loan crisis actually create a worse climate for the groups pushing reform. "The big red flags are still there: retroactivity, the special exemptions," says Gilbert. "And criminal activity — at least the disclosure of criminal activity — is more than it has been since I've been involved in this."

Supporters of the law say they are willing to consider some compromises, such as changing the term "racketeering" to a less ominous phrase like "business misconduct." Brigham Young Professor Goldsmith has a nine-point compromise plan that he thinks would correct some abuses under civil RICO without "eviscerating" the statute.[34] Some outside observers, however — Judge Abner J. Mikva and former Judge Getzendanner, for example — believe the movement to revise or repeal RICO has peaked. "The people who follow the issue are becoming hopeless it's going to be reformed," says Getzendanner.

As for the Supreme Court, Professors Goldsmith and Blakey both expect the justices to reject the strictest standard for RICO suits and at most describe general, somewhat tighter guidelines for lower courts to follow in determining what constitutes "a pattern of racketeering activity." A ruling along those lines might slow the growth of RICO litigation a bit, but it wouldn't be much help to the major business groups leading the reform drive.

To its supporters, RICO is a great success story: a tool against organized crime, government corruption and — in the hands of prosecutors or private plaintiffs — white-collar crime. Its successes in attacking Mafia bosses and politicians on the take brought virtually unanimous cheers, but when the law was turned on the country's corporate-financial-legal establishment the howls of protests were loud and long. For Congress, the issue is whether RICO's new face shows the law is being abused or that it is being used effectively for the first time.

NOTES

[1] "Lights Out for RICO?," an editorial in *The Wall Street Journal*, Feb. 17, 1989.

[2] Stephen S. Trott, former assistant attorney general for the criminal division and now a judge on the 9th U.S. Circuit Court of Appeals, quoted in *Governing* magazine, April 1988, p. 42.

[3] U.S. Department of Justice, *Annual Report of the Attorney General*, 1984, quoted in Michael Goldsmith, "Civil RICO Reform: The Basis for Compromise," *Minnesota Law Review*, Vol. 71, 1987, p. 833. Goldsmith notes other estimates ranging from $27 billion up to $200 billion.

[4] *1970 Congressional Quarterly Almanac*, pp. 546-47.

[5] *Report of the Ad Hoc Civil RICO Task Force of the ABA Section of Corporation, Banking and Business Law*, 1985.

[6] *United States v. Turkette*, 452 U.S. 576 (1981).

[7] *Russello v. United States*, 464 U.S. 16 (1983).

[8] *Proposed RICO Reform Legislation: Hearings Before the Committee on the Judiciary*, 1987, pp. 29-53.

[9] "Effectiveness of the Government's Attack on La Cosa Nostra," Statement of David Williams, before Permanent Subcommittee on Investigations, Senate Committee on Governmental Affairs, 1988.

[10] See *NACDL Report on RICO Megatrials* (1988).

[11] Quoted in *The New York Times*, Aug. 27, 1988.

[12] See "A Jury Wrestles With Pornography," *The American Lawyer*, March 1988.

[13] *Moneyline*, Cable News Network, Jan. 31, 1989.

[14] *United States v. Regan*, 858 F.2d 115 (2nd Circuit, 1988).

[15] "RICO's Broken Commandments," *The Wall Street Journal*, Jan. 26, 1989.

[16] See "Lawyers See Hurdles for Futures Inquiry," *The New York Times*, Feb. 20, 1989; "Traders in Chicago Reassured by Talk Focusing on RICO," *The Wall Street Journal*, Feb. 15, 1989.

[17] *U.S. Attorneys' Manual*, Title 9, Chapter 110, reprinted in *RICO Reform: Hearings Before Subcommittee on Criminal Justice, Committee of the Judiciary*, 1985, pp. 336-362.

[18] *Oversight on Civil RICO Suits: Hearings Before the Committee on the Judiciary*, 1985, p. 95.

[19] *Sedima, S.P.R.L. v. Imrex Co.*, 741 F.2d 482 (2nd Circuit, 1984).

[20] *Sedima, S.P.R.L. v. Imrex Co.*, 473 U.S. 479 (1985).

[21] See, for example, "Statement of Bernard Z. Lee, on behalf of American Institute of Certified Public Accountants," in *Proposed RICO Reform Legislation: Hearings Before the Committee on the Judiciary*, 1987, op. cit., pp. 160-279; "Statement of Ray J. Groves, chairman, AICPA," in *Oversight on Civil RICO Suits: Hearings Before the Committee on the Judiciary*, 1985, op. cit., pp. 240-327.

[22] *ABA Task Force*, op. cit., pp. 55-56.

[23] *Yellow Bus Lines, Inc. v. Local Union*, 639, 839 F.2d 782 (D.C. Circuit, 1988). Ironically, the opinion was authored by Judge Abner J. Mikva, a RICO critic both as congressman and judge.

[24] *Proposed RICO Reform Legislation: Hearings Before Committee on Judiciary*, 1987, op. cit., pp. 306-320.

[25] *Peckarsky v. American Broadcasting Co.*, 603 F.Supp. 688 (District of Columbia, 1984).

[26] *Congregation Beth Yitzhok v. Briskman*, 566 F.Supp. 555 (Eastern District of New York, 1983).

[27] G. Robert Blakey and Scott D. Cessar, "Equitable Relief Under Civil RICO: Reflections on *Religious Technology Center v. Wollersheim*: Will Civil RICO Be Effective Only Against White-Collar Crime?," in *Notre Dame Law Review*, Vol. 62, 1987, pp. 526, 619-622.

[28] *RICO Reform: Hearings Before the Subcommittee on Criminal Justice of the Committee on the Judiciary*, 1985-1986, pp. 1279-1285. See also Michael Goldsmith and Penrod W. Keith, "Civil RICO Abuse: The Allegations in Context," *Brigham Young University Law Review*, 1986, p. 55.

[29] Michael Waldman, "Opinion," *Rico Law Reporter*, July 1988.

[30] *Hunt v. Weatherbee*, 626 F.Supp. 1097 (Massachusetts, 1986).

[31] *Williams v. Hall*, 683 F.Supp. 639 (Eastern District of Kentucky, 1988).

[32] *Senate Report*, 91-617, 1969, p. 158.

[33] *H. J., Inc. v. Northwestern Bell Telephone Co.*, 829 F.2d 648 (8th Circuit, 1987).

[34] Goldsmith, *op. cit.*, pp. 858-882.

Graphics: S. Dmitri Lipczenko.

RECOMMENDED READING

ARTICLES

Cohodas, Nadine, "Advocates of RICO Revision Gird for Third Try," *Congressional Quarterly Weekly Report*, Vol. 47, No. 7, Feb. 18, 1989.

The author, who regularly covered the House and Senate Judiciary committees, provides an assessment of the prospects for RICO reform legislation as it was introduced in the 101st Congress.

Goldsmith, Michael, and Keith, Penrod W., "Civil RICO Abuse: The Allegations in Context," *Brigham Young University Law Review*, 1986, pp. 55-107.

Professor Goldsmith, who has written extensively on RICO, concludes in this article that allegations of abuse of the law's civil provisions are seriously overstated. He believes that courts can — and should — use existing sanctions for frivolous suits to deal with those abuses that do occur without undermining a needed vehicle to remedy fraud in the society.

Mikva, Abner J., and Blakey, G. Robert, "RICO and Its Progeny: Good or Bad Law?," *Notre Dame Journal of Law, Ethics & Public Policy*, Vol. 2, Issue No. 2, 1986.

In this transcript of a debate at Notre Dame Law School in November 1985, Judge Mikva and Professor Blakey vigorously argue what Congress intended to do when it passed RICO in 1970. Blakey, who wrote the law as an aide to Sen. John L. McClellan, D-Ark., finds no violation of congressional intent in the expanding use of RICO in civil litigation. Mikva, who led a small group of congressmen in opposing the measure, says Congress was sold a bill of goods and ought now to wipe the law off the books.

Queenan, Joe, "RICO Strikes Again! A Growing List of Businesses Are Hit by Racketeering Charges," *Barron's*, Dec. 12, 1988.

A skillful writer examines the business community's beef with RICO with great insight into the legal and political complexities of the issue. The story notes the use of RICO *by* businesses as well as against them and also discusses such tactical considerations as insurance coverage in bringing about some RICO settlements. The perspective is critical but balanced.

Strasser, Fred, "State Racketeering Laws Are Giving Prosecutors a New Weapon Against Crime," *Governing*, April 1988.

Some 27 states have enacted racketeering laws patterned after the federal RICO statute. The author, Washington bureau chief of the *National Law Journal*, reports on their use — and concerns about their abuse.

REPORTS AND STUDIES

Report of the Ad Hoc Civil RICO Task Force of the ABA Section of Corporation, Banking and Business Law, **March 28, 1985.**

A special task force of the American Bar Association's business law section documented use of RICO in civil suits, surveyed legal and constitutional issues, and concluded with 10 "practical" recommendations for legislative changes to make the law fairer without eliminating the civil remedy altogether.

CONGRESSIONAL HEARINGS

Oversight on Civil RICO Suits: Hearings Before the Committee on the Judiciary, United States Senate, **1987.**

This three-day set of hearings includes testimony from more than 30 witnesses. Particularly valuable are two items printed as exhibits: excerpts from House and Senate floor debate at the time RICO was enacted and the Department of Justice's manual for U.S. attorneys on use of RICO.

RICO Reform: Hearings Before the Subcommittee on Criminal Justice, Committee on the Judiciary, House of Representatives, **1985-1986.**

Nearly 70 witnesses testified before the House Judiciary's Subcommittee on Criminal Justice in the most extensive hearings to date on RICO reform legislation. The information and range of views are invaluable in exploring issues on use of the law's criminal and civil provisions alike and in examining proposed revisions in the law.

Proposed RICO Reform Legislation: Hearings Before the Committee on the Judiciary, United States Senate, **1987.**

This two-day airing of RICO issues includes testimony of a dozen witnesses with more recent listings, in particular, on use of the law in prosecution of Mafia figures and in suits against such established businesses such as investment bankers, accounting firms, law firms, banks, insurers and manufacturers.

NEW STYLES IN WORK-PLACE MANAGEMENT

NEW STYLES IN WORK-PLACE MANAGEMENT

by Harrison Donnelly

As American businesses have faced greater competition from abroad and at home, they have turned to two radically different, and perhaps incompatible, styles of managing their employees. Both approaches have shown promise during relatively good economic times, but no one knows which one will better withstand the strain of a recession.

If, as many economists predict, a recession does begin this year, there is likely to be a new wave of on-the-job turmoil for many of America's 113 million workers. The working lives of millions of people — from the lowest minimum-wage earners to the upper reaches of corporate executives — will continue to be shaped by the developments that have already transformed employee-management relations in the past decade.

An economic downturn, if it occurs, will come at the end of a period of extraordinary stress and change for American businesses. Faced with an array of economic challenges posed by increased competition — from abroad, from deregulation, from ever-changing technology — many U.S. corporations have had to undergo a radical rethinking of the ways in which they operate.

As a result, the seemingly stable patterns of worker-management relations that existed in the decades after World War II have unraveled. For most white-collar workers, the world of work in that bygone era was one of stability and security, in which loyal service to a company was rewarded with steady advancement in pay and power. Blue-collar workers usually found themselves in a more adversarial relationship with their employers. But the labor unions that represented them were mostly accepted by management as a permanent aspect of industrial relations, and all workers could expect to share in the growing wealth produced by the nation's dominance in the world economy.

Out of the breakup of the postwar system, two approaches to employee-management relations have emerged. Both approaches share the goal of making businesses economically stronger by making their workers more pro-

The Changing Work Place, 1981-1987

Total civilian employment has increased substantially (Graph A), but the number of people employed by the nation's largest corporations is down (Graph B). Although many of the jobs lost by these large corporations have been mid-level management positions, the number of employed managers in the country is actually up (Graph C), and management salaries continue to grow faster than blue-collar ones (Graph D).

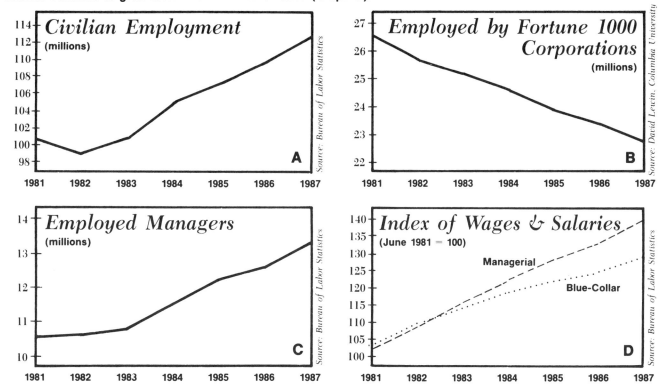

ductive. But the two trends are based on sharply different ideas about how to do so, and, ultimately, on contrasting views of the nature of the relationship to which most people devote half or more of their waking hours. Which will hold up better under the strain of a recession remains to be seen.

The first, and more common, employee-relations strategy followed by companies faced with this increased competition has been to try to pare labor costs to the bone. As hundreds of thousands of white-collar workers can testify, this "lean-and-mean" approach has led to mass layoffs, particularly among people at the middle-management level of major corporations. Citing the threat of low-wage producers overseas, corporate executives have argued that they have no choice but to toughen their stance against unions, make greater use of inexpensive part-time workers and give pay raises to their permanent employees only when they show improved performance.

This strategy embodies a marked shift in the conception of the duties and responsibilities of workers and employers to each other. Notions of "company loyalty" and job security are outmoded, in this view, as is the tradition of the employee who spends his whole career working up through the hierarchy of a single corporation. The employee-management relationship has become a much more strictly economic one, in which workers are loyal only to their own careers, and employers do not hesitate to dispose of workers when their usefulness is over. In economic terms, employees have come to resemble commod-

ities, such as steel or coal, which may be bought (hired) or sold (fired) as economic conditions warrant.

Many business analysts argue that the "lean-and-mean" approach is vital for hard-pressed companies. Companies will be able to respond to changing economic conditions, they say, only by becoming more flexible and efficient in the way they handle employees; and workers will be better off, too, once they recognize that their company is not their family or their friend, but simply another temporary stop on their lifelong career path. Critics, on the other hand, warn that the spread of this hard-nosed philosophy is undermining the spirit of cooperation and commitment in the work place, which they say is crucial to improving productivity.

As that criticism suggests, the opposing strategy aims to improve competitiveness through fuller use of the talent and commitment of employees. Inspired by the success of management techniques used in Japan, where company loyalty and worker involvement in improving the quality of products is widespread, this approach seeks to make employees more productive by giving them a greater opportunity to manage themselves. Although it has been adopted by a relatively small number of firms, this approach can be seen in a variety of forms. They range from informal "quality circles" in small firms to the massive cooperative programs that have sprung up between U.S. automakers and the United Auto Workers (UAW) union.

Advocates of "participative management" argue that companies need to strengthen, rather than weaken, their ties to their workers in order to become more competitive. Through tactics such as job guarantees, profit-sharing and employee stock ownership, they say, firms can build a sense of commitment and trust among their employees. That will encourage workers to help develop and participate in new and more effective ways of operating. Some economists wonder, though, whether these programs are luxuries that will wither in the face of economic stress. And many union members continue to suspect that these innovative work programs are merely a cover for management efforts to take away worker rights.

To be sure, these two strategies are not always mutually exclusive. Some firms attempt to do both at once — as General Motors Corp. (GM) has done in recent years, by laying off large numbers of white-collar workers while participating in cooperative programs with the UAW. Others, influenced by Japanese successes and the popularity of management "gurus" such as Tom Peters, * have followed the first strategy while paying lip service to the second, says Arizona State University management Professor Mark Pastin. "We're going through a period in which managers are still mouthing the management theories of the early 1980s. But they're actually operating differently," Pastin says. "Competition has imposed a strain on corporations that makes these new theories seem like luxuries. There's a kind of schizophrenia."

And the two approaches seem to be fundamentally at odds. "Many companies face short-run pressure to cut labor and other costs. But they also face strong pressure to restructure to become more competitive, by bringing employees into the decision-making process, and by using teamwork and involvement," says labor-relations scholar Thomas A. Kochan of the Massachusetts Institute of Technology (MIT). "Some companies are trying to go both ways at once. But the two strategies are almost diametrically opposed." Although the value of these employee-management philosophies will be tested in the next recession, the issue of which is better for the U.S. economy in the long run is not likely to be settled any time soon, Kochan predicts. "The tension between the two strategies will be with us for a long time."

'Lean-and-mean' approach allows quick response to change

Competition from low-wage foreign producers is not the only reason that many U.S. corporations have pursued "lean-and-mean" campaigns. The strategy also reflects some basic changes in the ways that businesses develop, produce and market products. In previous decades, the pace of business innovation was often relatively slow and

stable. A company that developed a successful product could generally count on having the market to itself for enough time to become profitable through long, steady production runs designed to make maximum use of economies of scale. Early this century, for example, the Ford Motor Co. designed the Model T automobile and then produced it, essentially unchanged, for nearly 20 years.

Today, however, businesses must react far more quickly to technological and marketing developments. The creator of a new product, notes business psychologist Srully Blotnick, frequently has only a short time to exploit its advantage before competitors seek to capture its market with similar products. As a result, to maximize their profits, companies must make an all-out effort to saturate their market quickly. "Somebody designs a better mouse-trap and starts selling it locally," Blotnick writes. "If our mousetrap man doesn't quickly blanket the country, indeed the world, he will soon find local and Taiwanese knock-offs have beaten him to most of the juiciest markets." [1]

The consequence of this stepped-up business schedule is that many companies feel they cannot afford the large, stable work forces that were appropriate in past years. Instead, employers have sought the flexibility to respond rapidly to changing market conditions. Like a farmer who needs extra help only when his crops are ripe, they want to be able to expand or contract their work force according to their current needs. "When the hot market a firm has been exploiting becomes saturated," Blotnick writes, "the 'season' is over and many workers are shown the door."

For many corporate executives, old-fashioned ideas about stable employment and job security are clearly unsuited to the new business environment. To underscore their need for labor flexibility, they are making clear to their employees that the relationship begins and ends with a paycheck, and that it will last only so long as the company profits from it. "Many companies are trying to put their relationship with their workers on a market basis," says Audrey Freedman, executive director of the human-resources program of The Conference Board Inc. * "They are depersonalizing the relationship and taking out its unbusinesslike aspects."

The massive layoffs of experienced white-collar workers in major corporations are an obvious sign of this new relationship. While the exact size of this corporate "downsizing" phenomenon is hard to measure — estimates range up to half a million people already affected — it is clear that a wide swath has been cut through exactly the sort of employees who, in previous years, might have counted on virtually ironclad job security. One measure of the decline, according to Columbia University business Professor David Lewin, is that total employment among the nation's 1,000 largest corporations is 11 percent below its level of a decade before. [2] Half of the companies surveyed by the American Management Association in 1987 reported employment declines in the previous 18 months, with

---

* Peters, co-author (with Robert H. Waterman Jr.) of *In Search of Excellence* (1982) and author of *Thriving on Chaos* (1987), has attracted a wide following with his theories on innovative business management, including efforts to increase involvement of all workers in the success of the firm.

* The Conference Board is a New York-based economics research organization funded by business, labor and other institutions.

large companies reporting an average job loss of 2,770.[3]

Perhaps the most telling instances of the strength of the downsizing movement have been the cutbacks in corporations that for generations had prided themselves on providing secure employment. International Business Machines Corp. (IBM) — the paradigm of paternalistic corporate security, where most employees traditionally have spent their whole careers — has reduced its employment rolls substantially in recent years, cutting 13,000 workers through early retirement alone. American Telephone & Telegraph Co., another haven for lifetime employment, has laid off more than 30,000 workers since 1984. GM is in the process of eliminating some 40,000 white-collar jobs.[4]

While these layoffs have hit people at all levels of the corporate structure, the heaviest blows often have fallen on middle-level managers — the people who take the decisions of top corporate executives and translate them into specific actions to be carried out by employees. "Staff" employees, who fill such ancillary corporate functions as public relations and economic research, have been affected more than "line" workers, who participate directly in the process of production.

Freedman of The Conference Board argues that the corporate downsizing campaign has cut out a lot of fat that had grown under the protection of white-collar job security. "Executives had more security in the past, but it was not the security of a truly caring environment. It was the security of those who didn't have to hustle. The rest of the economy was supporting them," she observes. "That was not sustainable under conditions of intense competition."

For many of these employees, cut down in the prime of their careers, the layoffs have been a devastating personal experience, made worse by the fact that their chances of finding work at some other downsizing corporation are slim. But most seem to have found new jobs, frequently with smaller companies. In fact, the number of managerial positions in manufacturing has actually increased considerably faster than other manufacturing jobs since 1983, according to Sar A. Levitan, who directs the Center for Social Policy at The George Washington University. "If there has been a pervasive 'lean-and-mean' approach, it doesn't show up in the numbers," Levitan says. Moreover, notes AFL-CIO economist John Zalusky, the income gap between white-collar and blue-collar workers has continued to grow despite the layoffs. Bureau of Labor Statistics figures show that salaries for managerial personnel increased an average of 38.6 percent between 1981 and 1987, compared with a 27.7 percent increase for blue-collar workers. *(See charts, p. 127.)*

Part-time, temporary workers give companies greater flexibility

Another aspect of the "lean-and-mean" strategy involves greater use of "contingent" workers. These include part-time and temporary workers and contract employees, who provide services to a company but are not part of its full-time, permanent work force. Many corporations are moving toward a policy in which a relatively small core of permanent workers is surrounded by a large group of contingent employees, who are called on only when they are needed. Contingent workers usually cost less, because they do not receive expensive health-care and other benefits given to the permanent work force. Even more importantly, they can be let go with a minimum of expense and trouble. Because of those advantages, the number of contingent workers has grown rapidly. There were 34.3 million contingent workers in 1986, according to Conference Board analyst Richard S. Belous, compared with 28.5 million in 1980 — a 20 percent increase, which was twice the growth rate of the labor force as a whole.

Companies are also trying out a variety of strategies for holding down the costs of their permanent work forces. An increasingly popular method calls for basing employee pay levels on individual performance. Under these "performance-based" systems, a significant portion of employee compensation is paid only to those who are found to have contributed substantially to the firm's profitability. One of the biggest experiments with performance-based pay is taking place at GM. Beginning this year, 112,000 white-collar employees of the automaker will in effect compete against each other for the largest raises. Many firms are also relying more often on cash bonuses for annual pay increases. The advantage of a lump-sum payment is that, unlike an increase in an employee's base pay, it does not add to compensation costs in subsequent years. Moreover, employees usually find the loss of an annual bonus easier to accept than an outright cut in salary.

By contrast, another cost-cutting strategy, the two-tier wage system, seems to be losing favor among business leaders. These plans, which were frequently included in union collective-bargaining agreements in the early 1980s, allow workers doing the same jobs to receive widely different rates of pay. Thus, a union member with seniority at a grocery store, for example, might continue to receive relatively high pay while newly hired workers earned little more than the minimum wage. As might be expected, two-tier wage systems stirred considerable resentment on the job — especially when, as often occurred, the plans were designed so that a worker hired after a certain point could never catch up with other workers, no matter how long he or she stayed on the job. Because the costs in low morale outweighed the wage savings, many employers have begun to abandon the plans. The number of workers covered by union contracts containing two-tier systems fell from 700,000 in 1985 to 200,000 in 1986.

The corporate cost-cutting drive is also evident in an increasingly combative approach toward unions, after decades in which the management of most corporations seemed to have become accommodated to the existence of unions. Non-unionized firms have mounted sophisticated campaigns to block organizing efforts among their workers. Partially unionized companies have transferred much of their production from union to non-union facilities. Management's anti-union drive has been aided by a substantial decline in support for unions, both among workers and in the public at large. "Certainly not since the days of . . . company unionism that followed World War I has it been as socially or politically acceptable for U.S. management to embrace publicly a 'union-free' preference as it is today," writes Kochan.[5]

Even firms that have remained unionized have moved aggressively to remove obstacles to their economic flexibility. One target of their efforts are union-negotiated work rules, which often spell out in great detail the rights and duties of each type of job. Managers typically view these work rules as highly inefficient, because they can block efforts to shift workers between jobs as market conditions warrant. Management has made the removal or loosening of work rules a key demand in many collective-bargaining negotiations in recent years. Another trend has been to curtail the formerly widespread use of "pattern bargaining." Under that method, union wages were often set according to wages at other companies or in comparable industries. But many corporations now insist that wages of each group of workers be based specifically on the business conditions affecting the product they are making. This allows companies that face strong low-wage competition from abroad to hold down pay increases. In the rubber industry, for example, wages were set industrywide in the 1970s. Since then, however, the industry has negotiated separate wage levels for each product — tires, industrial belting, rubber shoes, and so on.

Critics of such corporate tactics argue that companies will pay a heavy price for the efficiency and flexibility they are trying to obtain. A corporate downsizing campaign usually generates considerable turmoil within the organization, as employees spend much of their time gossiping and maneuvering over who will be the ones to lose their jobs. Even among those who survive the cuts, there is often a lingering atmosphere of resentment and mistrust, which can harm productivity. In short, a company that demonstrates its lack of commitment to employees often receives a reduced degree of commitment in return.

Moreover, the transformation of most people's expected career patterns — from relatively stable employment with a small number of companies to a succession of jobs with different employers — has occurred before other social institutions have been able to respond. Most pension and health-insurance programs, for example, are based on the model of a permanent, full-time work force. Part-time workers and those who change jobs frequently often are not covered by these vital protections.

The changes also have left many individual workers unprepared to deal with a world in which job security has disappeared and hunting for a new job has become a regular and unavoidable process. "It's something of a new ball game, and career-development structures haven't kept pace," says Anthony Carnavale, labor economist for the American Society for Training and Development. "If we're going to expect people to take responsibility for their own careers, we need new tools, in counseling and training. But we don't have those yet."

'Participative management' seeks closer ties to the company

The alternative employee-relations strategy — known as "participative management" and "work innovation," among other things — is also an attempt to help companies become better able to respond to changing economic conditions. Instead of depersonalizing the relationship between company and employee, this approach seeks to strengthen the connection into one of mutual assistance and benefit — "collective entrepreneurialism," in the words of Harvard University economist Robert B. Reich.[6] Proponents of this approach argue, as does management theorist Peters, that "The chief reason for our failure in world-class competition is our failure to tap our work force's potential." The wide array of participative work programs undertaken by U.S. companies in recent years in effect represents an attempt to implement the solution offered by Peters to that problem: "Truly involved people can do anything!"[7]

Efforts to increase workers' involvement in their employer's economic health are not new. In 1867, the Bay State Shoe and Leather Co. started one of the first employee profit-sharing programs. In the 1930s, the Lincoln Electric Co. of Cleveland began a no-layoff policy that, with one exception after World War II, it has maintained ever since. In the 1960s, the Donnelly Corp., of Holland, Mich., established a system under which workers were given considerable authority over production and a share in company profits. Even so major a corporation as the Polaroid Corp. experimented with a participative management program at about that time.

However, such innovative programs did not begin to receive widespread attention until 1973, when GM and the UAW established the first of their "quality of work life" programs. The eventual spread of such programs to other U.S. automakers, and the obvious success of Japanese corporations in using similar ideas, led many other companies to experiment with their use. By 1982, the Work In America Institute Inc., a leading advocate of work innovations, proclaimed, "Work innovations are no longer unknown quantities; they have been tested in the cauldron of experience and they work."[8] These programs have continued to spread since then, according to University of Southern California management Professor James O'Toole. "One has to give credit to American industry, particularly among medium-sized firms, where there has been a tremendous amount of innovation," O'Toole says. "American managers have gotten a lot smarter. They know that a key to productivity is to get workers more involved. The ideas about changing jobs that seemed radical a few years ago are much more popular now."

There are four general categories of programs among the many work innovations being tried by American businesses. They are:

Consultation With Workers. The most common type of work innovation, these programs seek to create a forum through which worker ideas about their jobs and the

Scarcity of Entry-level Workers Predicted

While U.S. employers have been busy revamping their employee-relations policies in recent years, major changes in the nation's supply of workers have also been taking place. Changes in the composition of the work force, projected to occur between now and the end of the century, will have an important impact on the success or failure of those policies.

The most important change will be a marked slowdown in the influx of young people into the pool of available workers during the next 22 years. For much of the last two decades, employers have enjoyed a steady flow of new workers created by the maturing of the "baby-boom" generation born between 1946 and 1964. Along with the arrival of millions of married women in the work force, this has allowed employers to pick and choose from an abundant supply of potential employees. The long-term "buyers' market" in employment has made it possible for many corporations to adopt a tougher stance in relation to their employees.

But U.S. Bureau of Labor Statistics (BLS) projections show that the number of new entrants into the work force will fall substantially in the next decade, as the relatively few babies born in the low-birthrate years after 1964 begin looking for work. The effects of the "birth dearth" will be combined with a leveling off in the number of new women workers, because most of the adult females who need or want to take jobs have already done so. The 1986 federal law imposing sanctions on employers who hire illegal aliens will help dry up another source of new workers.

The BLS expects that the number of workers will grow by only 21 million, or 18 percent, between 1986 and 2000. In the preceding 14 years, by contrast, the labor force added 31 million people, for an increase of 35 percent.*

Although the rate at which the economy creates new jobs is also expected to slow during the 1986-2000 period, the slowdown in the growth of the labor force clearly will create major new problems for employers, particularly among service industries that usually rely on low-wage young workers. The shortage of available young people is already forcing fast-food chains and similar employers to go to great lengths to recruit the help they need.

Some labor experts predict a major shift in the balance of power between employers and employees. Columbia University business Professor David Lewin, for example, foresees "perhaps the most severe and sustained period of labor shortages that has been experienced in this century." As a result, Lewin believes, "Power in the employment relationship, which has largely resided with the employer in the 1982-1987 period, will increasingly rest with the employee in the 1988-1990 period."**

Changes in the composition of the work force will also pose challenges to employers. While the number of workers aged 20-34 will decline about 14 percent by 2000, the ranks of those aged 45 to 54 will grow by 63 percent. The median age of workers will increase significantly, from 35.3 years in 1986 to 38.9 years in 2000.

Older workers frequently bring a greater degree of experience and skill to their jobs, which will help improve productivity. But they also tend to be less willing or able to learn new skills and accept new jobs. Consequently, employers will have to devote more effort to training and retraining in order to have a work force flexible enough to respond to changing economic conditions. ■

*Statistics are from "Projections 2000," a special BLS report contained in the September 1987 issue of the Monthly Labor Review.
**Quoted in "Human Resources Outlook 1988," The Conference Board, 1988, p. 11.

Labor Force Growth Rate

Figures show average annual rate.

1965-72	1972-79	1979-86	1986-2000
2.3%	2.7%	1.7%	1.2%

Source: Bureau of Labor Statistics

---

products they make can be incorporated in the company's decision-making process. Ranging from informal "work circle" discussion groups to large union-management bureaucracies, they are based on the idea that "the person on the job knows more about that job and how to improve it than anyone in the organization," as Corning Glass Works Chairman James Houghton puts it.[9]

At Xerox Corp., for example, employees participate in the "Leadership Through Quality" program, under which organized teams provide a channel for worker suggestions on improving efficiency and product quality. The program has led to improvements in everything from loading-dock procedures to the design of a national telecommunications network. At GM's Delco-Remy Division plant in Fitzgerald, Ga., workers belong to teams with authority to make decisions on a wide range of operations, including quality control, safety and recruiting. GM's Pontiac Fiero factory in Pontiac, Mich., not only has worker participation in problem-solving teams, but also includes a UAW official on the plant's top administrative committee, with access to all its business information.

Job Redesign. A related concept — often linked with consultative programs under the general rubric of "quality of work life" — calls for a restructuring of the way jobs are organized within a facility. Many of these programs seek to reduce or eliminate job classifications on the factory floor, and to encourage workers to receive training on how to do different jobs. One goal is to make production-line jobs more satisfying to workers, by replacing the mind-numbing repetition of a single operation with a variety of more challenging tasks. Moreover, these programs seek to improve efficiency by allowing managers to transfer workers to different duties as conditions warrant.

One far-reaching version of this concept calls for doing away with assembly-line production. Instead of having each worker perform a single task, the company organizes workers into teams that are responsible for producing an entire product or unit. So each worker must do a variety of operations in coordination with his colleagues. A prime example of work-redesign is the New United Motor Manufacturing Inc. (NUMMI) plant in Fremont, Calif., operated jointly by GM and the Toyota Motor Corp. Under the team concept of production, the plant has substantially increased its efficiency and now produces cars with some of the highest quality ratings of any made in the United States.

Job Security. Many advocates of work innovations argue that they will work in the long run only if accompanied by some sort of promise to workers that they will not end up the victims of the process. Few workers have an interest in making suggestions for improved efficiency or job redesign if they suspect that they will lose their jobs as a result. So a number of companies are experimenting with job guarantees as a way of fostering employee commitment both to the company and to other work-innovation programs.

Because of the vagaries of the business cycle, job-guarantee programs are not easy to maintain. Many companies, such as Motorola Inc., minimize the possibility of layoffs in slow times by keeping staffing levels somewhat under full strength during times of normal operations. Workers must be willing to accept temporary transfers to other, perhaps less desirable jobs — as sometimes happens at Hallmark Cards Inc. in Kansas City, Mo., where production workers may find themselves assigned at times to the company cafeteria. Moreover, most job-guarantee programs do not necessarily ensure that workers will continue to receive their full pay during periods of reduced production.

The most elaborate job-security program is the one negotiated between the UAW and the U.S. automakers during the past decade. Management-labor agreements in that industry have established complex protections for workers facing layoffs. In 1982, for example, the union obtained the establishment of a "guaranteed income stream" program, under which workers with 10 years of seniority whose plants were closed would be given 55 percent to 75 percent of their pay until retirement. A "job bank" program allows workers whose jobs were lost due to technological changes to continue receiving full pay, while remaining available for reassignment to temporary jobs within the company. Such security programs, observes UAW spokesman Reg McGhee, were crucial to union participation in other work innovations. "Job security was the underpinning of the whole notion that we can work cooperatively. I doubt that we would have agreed to changes without job security."

Gain-Sharing. Another method of increasing worker involvement in productivity improvements is to give them a share of the benefits. Advocates of work innovations argue that such strategies are truly effective only when workers have the financial incentives to participate fully. One way to do this is through programs that reward workers for cost-saving efforts. Some companies use the Scanlon plan, named for the union official who designed it in the 1930s, under which workers receive a share of the money saved by the company through their suggestions.

Workers who own a share of their companies have an even greater incentive to assist in increasing profitability. The major form of worker ownership is the Employee Stock Ownership Plan (ESOP), under which employers receive federal tax breaks for establishing stock programs for their employees. There are about 8,100 companies with ESOPs, involving more than 8 million employees, according to a 1987 report.[10] In some cases, employees have assumed complete ownership of their firm. A prime example is the Weirton Steel Corp., a failing West Virginia firm that was bought by its employees in 1984 and since returned to financial health.

The 1987 study, conducted by the National Center for Employee Ownership, maintains that ESOP companies show strong economic performance. A group of ESOP firms grew an average of 1.9 percent faster a year than a comparison group of non-ESOP companies, the study found. Moreover, 73 percent of the firms studied improved their performance after ESOP programs were begun. "Ownership and participation together have a considerable impact," wrote study authors Corey Rosen and Michael Quarrey. "There is no escaping the conclusion that American workers sense a difference between working for their own benefit and merely being employed for the company's benefit."

An even more common way of involving employees in the financial health of a company is through profit-sharing plans. Such plans set aside a portion of company profits each year for the benefit of employees. According to the Profit Sharing Research Foundation of Evanston, Ill., there are about 375,000 firms with profit-sharing plans. Many profit-sharing plans do not distribute funds directly to workers on an annual basis. Instead, such plans operate through contributions to deferred-compensation accounts, which are given to workers only when they retire or leave the firm. Others, such as Ford, distribute substantial cash payments to workers during good years. Ford announced Feb. 19 that its hourly and salaried employees would receive an average of $3,700 each as a result of 1987 profits. A small number of firms take a step further by basing actual wages and salaries on profitability. Worthing Industries Inc., for example, a Columbus, Ohio, steel-processing firm, determines as much as 50 percent of employee pay according to profits.[11]

Despite its spread, the work-innovation movement continues to be viewed skeptically by much of both management and labor. Economists frequently describe such programs as more the products of the idiosyncratic visions of a few corporate chief executives than as a coherent strategy for coping with competition over the long term

They note that many of the companies that first experimented with work changes in the 1960s and 1970s have since dropped them. "Many companies undertake these programs because of the strong views of their chief executives. But business conditions change. Competition is so intense that even a strong philosophical drive will have to fail," says Freedman of The Conference Board. "A lot of companies that used to be praised as 'caring' don't follow that strategy anymore."

Many workers and labor unions, however, view work innovations not merely as well-meaning but ineffective experiments — that is the way business economists often see them, too — but as dangerous and devious attacks on protections won through decades of struggle. Given the history of labor-management antagonism, it is not surprising that many in the labor movement continue to resist cooperation with management as a sellout of worker rights. The UAW's cooperative efforts with the automakers, for example, have drawn vocal criticism from a sizable segment of auto workers and dissident union officials. To many such workers, ideas about "quality circles" and work-redesign are just a cover for schemes in which workers give up a lot in return for minimal concessions by management. "The biggest problem in cooperation is management's unwillingness to share information and power," says the AFL-CIO's Zalusky. "A lot of stuff travels under the rubric of work innovations. But it's often just management's way of getting workers to sign on to their agenda."

The legacy of labor-management discord is not the only reason unions are frequently reluctant to participate in work-innovation programs. The whole idea of redesigning jobs in order to achieve more flexibility and involvement by workers represents a fundamental challenge to unionism, argues Marvin H. Kosters, director of economic studies at the American Enterprise Institute in Washington, D.C. For more than a century, Kosters notes, one of the chief goals of unions has been to force management to define the exact responsibilities and rights of each worker. Such detailed job descriptions help protect workers from management abuses, but they also limit the ability of firms to respond quickly to changing conditions. "There's something deep in our culture that requires that jobs be sharply delineated. A major function of unions, historically, has been to press for exact definitions of jobs," Kosters says. "But many companies have been trying to move toward more flexibility in jobs. That is difficult for unions, because it cuts against their very core. What is the role of the union, if not to carefully delineate jobs?"

No definitive answer
to which system is better

So far, the experience of businesses using the alternative strategies has not yet produced any definitive answers to the question of which is the more effective way to improve productivity and competitiveness. A recent study by the Industrial Relations Research Association

(IRRA) [12] found no clear distinctions between industries — whether, for example, the "lean-and-mean" approach is usually better in heavy industry, or participatory management is the superior strategy for computer firms, or vice versa. The IRRA report, which described itself as the first comprehensive examination of the relationship between employee relations and employer success, did note, however, the choice of an employee-relations strategy is of varying degrees of importance to different types of firms. In the airline industry, where labor costs are a crucial factor determining profitability, employee policies are a central strategic issue facing management. In the capital-intensive steel industry, by contrast, employee-relations policies are less important in determining the success of a firm than other aspects of company strategy, such as marketing or investment.

The IRRA study also found no strong relationship between the economic health of a firm and the way it handled its employee relations. "It's not that clear which is the best model," observes study co-editor Richard N. Block, director of the School of Labor and Industrial Relations at Michigan State University. "IBM, which traditionally has prided itself on maintaining full employment, has been successful for many years. But General Electric, which has stressed a hard-nosed, performance-based approach, also has done well in recent years. Who's to say what's better, or how much each company's employment policies contributed to its success? Firms move back and forth on the continuum of employment policies. Ford, which is doing very well, has worked hard to be nice to its employees. But a few years before, it sharply reduced employment. We can't say whether they are doing better because of the new relationship, or because of what they did before."

Nor is it clear which approach will better help a company to survive a recession. But for most jobholders, whether their employers will do well in a recession is beside the point; they worry whether they themselves will be able to keep their jobs when times get hard. Labor experts hold some sharply different views on how the two main employee-management strategies will affect workers in the midst of a recession.

Perhaps the most vulnerable group are employees of major corporations that have resisted major changes in the way they deal with their employees even in the face of the threat of increased competition. The added weight of overall economic troubles may leave them no choice but to respond, probably by conducting large-scale layoffs. "Those firms that have not experienced a major shake-out and that operate in highly competitive, mature environments will probably be forced to downsize or restructure," predicted Alan R. Ewalt, senior vice president of the California-based National Medical Enterprises. [13]

Economists are more divided, however, about the recessionary prospects of workers at firms that have already gone through extensive downsizing. Many firms have already cut so deeply into employee ranks that those who remain on the payroll would seem to have a good chance of keeping their jobs through all but the most catastrophic

Past Coverage

■ **Part-Time Work** provides an in-depth analysis of the way many employers have sought to reduce labor costs by making greater use of part-time and other "contingent" workers. "Experts are wondering what the future holds for workers, whose careers and lifestyles could be fundamentally altered if part-time work became an integral part of the American work place," writes author Richard L. Worsnop. E.R.R., 1987 Vol. I, pp. 290-299.

■ **Industrial Competitiveness** looks at the ways American businesses are trying to improve their performance to match the economic threat from abroad. New approaches to the competitiveness problem include not only greater labor-management cooperation, writes author Sarah Glazer, but a fundamental reexamination of the emphasis on short-term profits that prevails among American corporate executives and financiers. E.R.R., 1987 Vol. I, pp. 126-135.

economic problems. A staff that has been reduced to the "bare bones" cannot be cut any further without eliminating major aspects of the company's operations.

Those employees may not be as secure as they think, however. "Many business people say that there has been so much downsizing that they are much more able to withstand a recession without having to cut severely," says Freedman. "But these companies have also learned to do things so much faster. They have made themselves more flexible and adaptive. The first sign that demand is diminishing will be responded to faster. Because of the changes that have occurred in recent years, there will be far less employment security in a recession. When companies have to, they will move very swiftly, because they know how to."

Employees of companies that have adopted work-innovation policies, such as job-security programs, may also expect to ride out a recession in relative safety. But they, too, may face problems if the economic situation deteriorates too far. Some of the auto industry's job-security programs, for example, protect the jobs of only those workers whose positions have been eliminated by technological changes — not those who are thrown out of work by a drop in the market demand for autos. No matter how strong a company's commitment to participatory policies, its management may someday be forced to cut costs and lay off workers in order to survive.

In a crunch, many participatory-management companies will try to reduce costs by reducing employees' working hours and pay, rather than by laying off workers completely. Examples of this have already occurred in Japan, where companies have struggled with falling export demand caused by the rising value of the yen. Japanese

industry, where employees typically work longer hours than in other advanced countries, is moving toward a shorter workweek. A similar, but more drastic, approach is evident at a GM plant in Van Nuys, Calif. In response to falling demand for the autos made at the plant, union and management officials recently approved a job-sharing plan in order to head off massive layoffs. Under the plan, workers will work half their previous number of hours each month, for between 76 percent and 95 percent of their previous pay.

Looking even further down the road, some employee-relations experts see a new type of worker-management relationship evolving in the coming decades. In this vision, which in some ways combines elements of both of today's competing approaches, workers will grow increasingly mobile and independent in their relations with their employers. But, once they have joined a firm, these workers will bring the greater degree of commitment that comes when equals participate on the basis of a common vision.

"In the past, people saw loyalty as the measure of commitment. If the company said 'do this,' they went and did it," said John E. Ellsworth, vice president for human resources of the Canadian firm of Northern Telecom Ltd. "But that didn't carry companies forward in competitiveness. There need to be thinking people who can engage the vision of the company, rather than merely putting in long years of service. Work relationships of the future will be fragile in terms of tenure. Instead, passionate engagement in a common vision will be the measure of commitment."

NOTES

[1] Srully Blotnick, "Just-in-Time People," *Forbes*, July 13, 1987, pp. 110 and 112.

[2] Lewin's remarks were included in *Human Resources Outlook 1988*, a publication of The Conference Board. Lewin was one of a number of academic, union and corporate labor-relations experts brought together by The Conference Board for a round-table discussion of employment trends in 1988.

[3] See *Responsible Reduction in Force: American Management Association Research Report on Downsizing and Outplacement*, 1987.

[4] Amal Kumar Naj, "GM Now Is Plagued with Drop in Morale as Payrolls Are Cut," *The Wall Street Journal*, May 26, 1987, p. 1.

[5] *The Transformation of American Industrial Relations*, Thomas A. Kochan, Harry C. Katz and Robert B. McKersie, Basic Books Inc., 1986, p. 9.

[6] Reich outlines his views in *Tales of a New America*, Times Books, 1987.

[7] *Thriving on Chaos*, Alfred A. Knopf, 1987, p. 286.

[8] *Productivity Through Work Innovations*, Pergamon Press, 1982, p. 9. The Work in America Institute Inc., is located in Scarsdale, N.Y.

[9] "For Better Quality, Listen to the Workers," *The New York Times*, Oct. 18, 1987, p. F3.

[10] Corey Rosen and Michael Quarrey, "How Well is Employee Ownership Working?" *Harvard Business Review*, September-October 1987, pp. 126-129.

[11] See Jeffrey A. Leib, "The Promise of Profit-Sharing," *The New York Times*, Feb. 9, 1986, p. F10.

[12] *Industrial Relations and the Performance of the Firm*, Richard Block, Morris Kleiner, Myron Rommkin and Sidney Salsburg, eds., Industrial Relations Research Association, 1988.

[13] *Human Resources Outlook 1988*, op. cit., p. 8.

RECOMMENDED READING

BOOKS

Kochan, Thomas A., Harry C. Katz and Robert B. McKersie, *The Transformation of American Industrial Relations*, Basic Books, 1986.

The authors of this volume survey the broad range of worker-management relations in the 1980s and come to the conclusion that some fundamental changes are taking place. The system that had grown up as a result of the New Deal of the 1930s, in which formal collective bargaining between unions and employers was the dominant element of worker-management relations, has broken up, the authors argue. The decline of unions and the growth of corporate "human resources" programs has given management the upper hand in its relations with employees.

Peters, Thomas J. and Robert H. Waterman Jr., *In Search of Excellence*, Harper and Row, 1982; and Peters, *Thriving on Chaos*, Alfred A. Knopf, 1987.

Peters is one of the best-known of the management experts who have sought to exhort American business to change radically the way it operates in order to survive. A hallmark of "excellent" companies, and those that can thrive in the midst of a "revolution," as Peters sees it, is that they "involve all personnel at all levels in all functions in virtually everything."

Work in America Institute Inc., *Productivity Through Work Innovations*, Pergamon Press, 1982.

This study provides a step-by-step guide for corporate executives interested in introducing innovative work practices into their firms. While acknowledging the frequent reluctance of workers, union officials and managers to accept such new ideas, the report argues that companies have no alternative but to get workers more involved. "Companies that compete in today's and tomorrow's markets have no choice but to raise sharply the quality standards of their products and services without raising costs," it argues. "And there is no known way to accomplish these goals except to engage every member of the enterprise, from top to bottom, in this pursuit."

ARTICLES

Levitan, Sar A., "Beyond 'Trendy' Forecasts: The Next 10 Years for Work," *The Futurist*, November-December 1987.

Levitan, an economist who studies employment and other social issues, examines what he views as four popular myths about changing work relations in the next decade: "the declining middle"; "the future belongs to robots"; "eliminating government regulations will boost productivity"; and "labor-management cooperation." In fact, Levitan argues, the pace of change in the work place is likely to be considerably more glacial than many analysts acknowledge.

Massing, Michael, "Detroit's Strange Bedfellows," *The New York Times Magazine*, Feb. 7, 1988.

The United Auto Workers (UAW) and the U.S. automakers have moved from the confrontational stance of a few decades ago to one of cooperation in the face of a growing threat from international competition. Union and management officials are eating and traveling together, building an array of "joint" programs and, in effect, staking their futures on the possibility of industrial peace. But, "The move toward jointness is not unanimously popular," Massing writes. "In Dearborn, Pontiac, Flint and other U.A.W. strongholds, the union's conciliatory stance has sparked a vigorous debate."

Saporito, Bill, "Cutting Costs Without Cutting People," *Fortune*, May 25, 1987.

Many corporations have responded to economic troubles, Saporito writes, with a policy of "throw the crew overboard." But, Saporito discovers, a significant number of other companies are finding economic health even while retaining full employment. "What sets these companies apart from others is that their managers direct the cost containment effort first at how work gets done — and how work will change in the future — and not just at how many people are doing it."

Rosen, Corey and Michael Quarrey, "How Well is Employee Ownership Working?" *Harvard Business Review*, September-October 1987.

The authors, associated with the National Center for Employee Ownership, report the results of a study of the economic health of companies that have instituted employee stock-ownership programs. Employee-ownership companies "grow fastest when ownership is combined with a program for worker participation," they write.

REPORTS AND STUDIES

The Conference Board, "Human Resources Outlook 1988," Research Bulletin No. 217, 1987.

This publication contains the results of a round-table discussion of corporate, union and academic labor-relations experts, held on Nov. 5, 1987. It provides valuable insights into the way that corporate executives view the current state and future course of their relationship with their employees. Available from The Conference Board, 845 Third Avenue, New York, N.Y. 10022.

HELP WANTED: WHY JOBS ARE HARD TO FILL

HELP WANTED: WHY JOBS ARE HARD TO FILL

by Mary H. Cooper

Employers now face a double dilemma: There are fewer young people entering the labor force each year, and many of them lack the skills needed for even entry-level jobs. So businesses must find new ways to recruit and keep qualified workers.

The baby bust has hit the labor market. Children born after the postwar baby boom are beginning to look for jobs, and they are finding a sellers' market. They are coming of age at a fortuitous time. The economy is expanding and generating entry-level jobs. And because there are fewer young people to fill these positions, the "busters" are able to pick and choose in ways their older brothers and sisters could not only a few years ago.

Employers are actively competing for the shrinking pool of young job-seekers. Newspaper advertisements for entry-level jobs highlight benefits once reserved for higher-level positions: more pay, extensive training, flexible working hours, health insurance, paid vacations, etc. "Young folks can name their price," says Doug Wesley, principal consultant of the Hall-Wesley Group, a management consulting firm in Lakeland, Fla.

Nearly 17 million new jobs have been created since the current economic recovery began in November 1982. The civilian unemployment rate has fallen to 5.6 percent from 9.7 percent at the depth of the 1981-82 recession. The labor crunch is most evident in places like Boston, Mass., where a booming high-tech economy pushed unemployment down to 3 percent in June. But the employment picture is not so rosy for all job seekers. In the Rust Belt city of Flint, Mich., for example, the jobless figure stood at 14.6 percent. Jobs in depressed rural areas also are hard to come by. Employment prospects are mixed even for the declining number of young workers. In fact, since the busters began entering the job market in 1979, the jobless rate among 16-to-19-year-olds has actually risen, from 16.1 to 16.9 percent.

The labor mismatch in urban areas all over the country is especially worrisome. Employers in the booming suburbs are begging for entry-level workers, while downtown, young people are idle. Distance is one factor. Potential applicants for such low-paying jobs as fast-food restaurant workers or janitors can ill afford the transportation costs to the suburban work place. In many cities, these unskilled youths, many of whom did not finish high school, have simply dropped out of the job market altogether.

But another aspect of today's job market worries the experts even more. At a time when the nation's economic progress depends increasingly on workers' ability to use high technology, new entrants into the work force are bringing fewer basic skills to their jobs. Recent surveys have shown an appalling lack of basic knowledge — much less technological know-how — among high-school graduates. As a result, employers are forced to offer their new recruits extensive job-training programs, often including remedial academic courses.

Because of aggressive recruiting and intensified training, employers are spending more today to hire qualified workers. They're also offering higher wages to lure entry-level job-seekers away from their competitors. These higher labor costs frequently are passed along to consumers in the form of higher prices. Economists are worried that the stage may be set for a period of "wage-push" inflation. Inflation climbed to 4.7 percent in the second quarter of 1988, its highest level since 1982, prompting the Federal Reserve Board to raise interest rates to slow the price spiral.[1]

The shrinking pool of skilled young workers that distinguishes today's labor market is good news for those women, members of minority groups and older workers who possess adequate education and skills. For them, the minimum wage — $3.35 an hour since January 1981 — is a thing of the past. But there is little cause for optimism among the unskilled and the poorly educated, whose prospects for productive participation in a technology-based economy appear dim indeed. If the experts are right, these people will become increasingly unemployable and mired in poverty.

Such a scenario also bodes ill for the society as a whole. "There is no way we can ever attain a high-wage economy if 20 percent of our high-school graduates are functionally illiterate," says Robert B. Reich, an economist at Harvard University's Kennedy School of Government.

Tomorrow's jobs are in the service industries

The jobs available to those entering the work force today are different from those their parents held. Blue-collar employment was once the key to financial success for middle-income workers. Bolstered by union contracts that virtually guaranteed substantial annual raises, factory workers with only a high-school diploma or less earned good wages. In 1979, for example, construction workers earned an average $21,660, while operators of metal and plastic processing machines made an average $19,500.[2] But blue-collar work no longer holds such promise for most new job seekers. Manufacturing jobs, which peaked at 21 million in 1979, fell by nearly 3 million during the 1981-82 recession and have never recovered. The dollar's value in relation to other currencies soared in the first half of the 1980s, making U.S. goods more expensive than foreign-made goods both here and abroad. Factories closed, and those that continued operations cut their work forces and demanded wage concessions from employees.

The trend has slowed but will continue for the foreseeable future. "There is a demand for cost-effectiveness which we are seeing in the restructuring and downsizing of a lot of companies," says Alexander B. Trowbridge, president of the National Association of Manufacturers. "There are going to be more efficient methods of manufacturing, and that means more automation and computerized activity, more tight controls on inventory and just-in-time delivery. It's painful, it's no fun for the company, and it's particularly no fun for the people involved. But in the competitive world marketplace, it's one of those developments that had to come." * The Labor Department predicts that employment in the goods-producing sector will fall slightly, from 27.9 million jobs in 1986 to 27.6 million in the year 2000; within that sector, increases in construction jobs are expected to be outweighed by decreases in manufacturing and mining jobs.

By contrast, the service-producing industries are expected to provide almost the entire net increase in new jobs — some 20 million — by the turn of the century. Broadly speaking, these include transportation, communications and public utilities; wholesale and retail trade; financial services, including insurance and real estate; government; and a catchall "services" division. (See Chart Nos. 1 and 2, p. 142.) This last category of industries, which is expected to generate most new jobs in coming years, includes a wide range of activities from legal services to building maintenance, from teaching to car repairs. More than half the growth of service jobs will come in the areas of business services and health care. Employment is expected to more than double at computer and data-processing firms, outpatient care facilities, doctors' and dentists' offices and personnel supply agencies providing temporary help to businesses. But by far the biggest increase in demand for workers will come from eating and drinking establishments. Bars and restaurants, be they fast-food or gourmet, will hire an additional 2.5 million employees by the year 2000. These trends appear to support the notion that the new service economy is generating more low-wage than high-wage jobs.

The quality of newly created jobs has become a pivotal issue in the presidential campaign. Vice President George Bush, defending the Reagan administration's economic policies, emphasizes the 17 million jobs that have been created since the end of the 1981-82 recession and points

---

*For a thorough discussion of the "lean and mean" approach to business, see "New Styles in Work-place Management," p. 125.

to data showing that these new jobs are challenging, well-paid positions. Massachusetts Gov. Michael S. Dukakis, the Democratic nominee, presents different statistics to shore up his argument that the biggest growth in employment is occurring in low-paid, menial jobs.

The campaign debate reflects an equally heated dispute among academics that was sparked by a 1986 study for the Congressional Joint Economic Committee. The study reported that three out of five jobs created in the early 1980s were low-wage jobs, compared with only one out of five new jobs from 1973 to 1979.[3] These findings have been alternately challenged and defended ever since, with no resolution in sight. There is no reliable information about precisely which jobs are created each year and which ones are eliminated. So the same data are often given widely different interpretations — generally depending on the political leanings of the interpreter.

Growing mismatch between skills and requirements

Of course, not everyone entering the job market is destined to flip hamburgers for a living. When the new job market is examined in terms of the *rate* of growth rather than the simple *numerical* increase in jobs, the picture changes dramatically. The fastest job growth will occur in higher-paying occupations, including paralegal personnel, medical assistants, physical therapists and data-processing equipment repairers. And those fast-growing, better-paying jobs will go to the workers who possess the requisite education and skills.

The Labor department predicts that more than half the new jobs created by the end of the century will require education beyond high school. *(See Chart No. 4, p. 143.)* Today, fewer than a quarter of all occupations require a college degree; by 2000, almost a third of the jobs will be held by college graduates.

Another way to judge the requirements for employment ignores formal education and examines instead the skills needed to enter different occupations. In a 1987 report entitled, *Workforce 2000*, the Hudson Institute, a non-profit policy research organization in Indianapolis, Ind., compared skill levels needed for current jobs with skills needed for jobs in the year 2000. The group predicted that the number of jobs available in the broad category of occupations requiring moderate-skill levels — precision production workers, service occupations, administrative jobs, construction and marketing and sales — will remain fairly steady. But jobs with low-skill requirements — including laborers, machine setters, farmers and transport workers — are becoming scarcer, while those requiring higher skills — technicians, teachers, managers, engineers, lawyers and scientists—are growing the fastest.[4] *(See Chart No. 3, p. 143.)*

Unfortunately, recent test results and surveys suggest that large numbers of young people are grossly unqualified

for tomorrow's jobs. The International Association for the Evaluation of Educational Achievement provided alarming evidence of this fact with its 1981-82 mathematics survey of eighth and 12th graders in 24 industrialized and developing countries. American students scored below average in all subjects, ranging from mathematics to statistics, and fell far behind their Japanese peers. But the problem goes beyond mathematics. According to the National Assessment of Educational Progress, a 1985 literacy test given by the Educational Testing Service, three out of five 21- to 25-year-olds were unable to trace the path between two points on a map, describe what they had read in a newspaper article or figure how much tip to leave based on 10 percent of the price of a restaurant meal.

The academic achievement level required for graduation from high school has fallen so low that most colleges and universities now offer remedial reading, writing and math courses to incoming freshmen who otherwise would be unable to master the curriculum. But these young people at least have a chance to acquire the skills necessary for employment. The job prospects for the million or so youths who drop out of high school each year are bleak indeed. In 1985, about 25 percent of 18- to 19-year-olds left high school before graduation; that figure was 40 percent for blacks and about 50 percent for Hispanics. High-school dropouts have always been less likely to find jobs than graduates, and they are finding it increasingly difficult to enter today's work force. Among dropouts who were seeking jobs in 1985, fewer than half were working.

This fact supports the view that the economy is producing a "two-tiered" labor market. While demand for the relatively small number of highly qualified young workers is growing, job opportunities for the growing pool of underqualified job seekers, many of them black or Hispanic, are shrinking. Because these minorities account for a growing share of the work force, the gap between the demand for adequately trained workers and the supply seems destined to widen.

The metropolitan area of New York City provides a stark example. "The quality of the labor force may become *the* limiting factor on the New York City economy," said Samuel Ehrenhalt, regional commissioner of the Bureau of Labor Statistics in New York.[5] Employers there are clamoring for qualified workers to fill jobs in such expanding service industries as finance, telecommunications and computer software design. But the New York Telephone Co., for example, says that only a fifth of the applicants for telephone operator positions pass the required test. And there is evidence that the skills level of entry-level workers is slipping: The share of applicants who pass Chemical Bank's basic math test for prospective bank tellers sank from 70 percent in 1983 to 55 percent in 1987. Meanwhile, an estimated 45 percent of the city's residents are outside the labor force. While this figure includes full-time mothers, students and other people who are voluntarily unemployed, many are unskilled youths who have simply given up finding a job and have stopped looking. According to one account, only 23 percent of the city's 16- to 19-year-olds hold part-time or full-time jobs or are actively seeking employment. In the nation as a whole, more than half the people in this age bracket are in the labor force.[6]

Company training programs to bridge the skills gap

Employers are trying to bridge the skills gap by spending more time and money on training for both longtime employees and new hires. And because computer technology is finding its way into even the most mundane tasks, they are forced to provide training for jobs that in the past required few skills. Federal Express Corp., an overnight parcel-delivery service, only requires a high-school education of its typical entry-level worker. But even couriers must receive special training to do their jobs. "Most of our couriers carry microcomputers that have wand scanners on them, basically a personal computer they carry in their pockets," explained Steve Rutherford, manager of human resource planning for the Memphis-based company. "When they get back to their trucks, they have to be able to use a video display terminal that transmits information from the truck back to the station."

Federal Express devotes one to five weeks to "basic training" for the company's 1,200 to 1,500 new hires each year who deal directly with customers. In addition, the company provides "recurrence training" for older employees as new services or job requirements are introduced. Federal Express has 40,000 employees scattered among 1,000 facilities in the United States alone. Training so many employees in so many different locations would be prohibitively expensive in a classroom setting. So the company computerized the training process to save time and money.

Federal Express is one of several large firms that have adopted "interactive laser-videodisc" training (IVD). New employees sit down in front of a television screen hooked up to a laser disc video player and a computer. The laser disc allows realistic scenes to be presented to the trainee. He responds to questions (usually by touching the screen), and the computer selects the next question based on his response. "Not only is it an economical way to have consistent training throughout the organization," Rutherford said, "but people can proceed at their own pace and go only as far in the training course as is appropriate for their jobs."

Adequate training is even more essential for companies that manufacture high-technology goods like electronic equipment and components. Motorola Inc., based in Schaumburg, Ill., faces stiff competition from Japanese electronics firms and companies based in the newly industrialized countries of the Pacific Rim. Motorola fell from the No. 2 position in worldwide sales of semiconductors in 1982 to fourth place in 1987. In an effort to reverse its fortunes, the company has poured more than

$150 million over the past four years into training programs for its 94,400 employees.

In its effort to compete on the international market, Motorola also has adopted management techniques that are reminiscent of its Japanese competitors: more flexible jobs, requiring employees to be able to perform several tasks and to work in teams. But the company has found that more than 40 percent of its current workers lack sufficient communication and other basic skills to participate in its flexible work environment. As a result, Motorola requires these employees, as well as those who fail tests in basic math and communications skills, to take remedial courses that the company provides on site.

Managing diversity in the work place

As the baby bust progresses, employers are discovering new ways to attract young workers. In a shrinking labor market, employers seeking entry-level workers can no longer stop at the promise of training with the potential for advancement. Even such traditional lures as health insurance and profit sharing often are not enough. "You've got to be more direct and give them toys because they're kids," says Anthony Carnevale, chief economist of the American Society for Training and Development in Alexandria, Va. "You've got to raffle off a car or a winter vacation. For the college kids, you might have a spring break package." Some fast-food restaurants and other companies that rely heavily on young workers are offering what Carnevale calls "more socially responsible" benefits to lure new employees. Miami-based Burger King Corp., for example, provides scholarships and other education benefits to their new hires.

The shortage of young males, the traditional source of entry-level workers, is beginning to change recruiting techniques in ways that are likely to persist as the supply of younger workers continues to shrink. According to the Hudson Institute, white males became a minority of the labor force in 1980. It predicts that 85 percent of new workers at the turn of the century will be women and minority men. *(See Chart No. 5, p. 143.)*

But managers have been slow to adapt to the changes in the labor market. "There are no managers today who know how to manage in this sellers' market because there hasn't been one since World War II," consultant Wesley says. "Before, managers could fire people. If they were polite to workers, that was nice but not necessary. We now have management by begging because we can't replace them."

Employers are beginning to offer benefits, geared especially toward female employees, that they resisted before the baby bust made them scurry for entry-level workers. "I have a feeling that a great deal of the corporate discussion of what is called women's issues is really generated not out of a sense of charity or equality, but is

Continued on page 144

The Changing Job Market

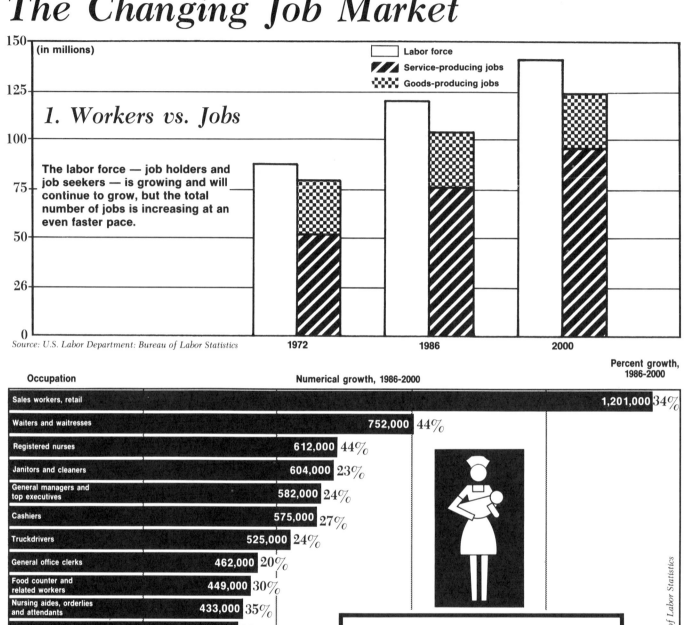

1. Workers vs. Jobs

(in millions)

Labor force
Service-producing jobs
Goods-producing jobs

The labor force — job holders and job seekers — is growing and will continue to grow, but the total number of jobs is increasing at an even faster pace.

Source: U.S. Labor Department: Bureau of Labor Statistics

1972 1986 2000

Occupation	Numerical growth, 1986-2000	Percent growth, 1986-2000
Sales workers, retail	1,201,000	34%
Waiters and waitresses	752,000	44%
Registered nurses	612,000	44%
Janitors and cleaners	604,000	23%
General managers and top executives	582,000	24%
Cashiers	575,000	27%
Truckdrivers	525,000	24%
General office clerks	462,000	20%
Food counter and related workers	449,000	30%
Nursing aides, orderlies and attendants	433,000	35%
Secretaries	424,000	13%
Guards	383,000	48%
Accountants and auditors	376,000	40%
Computer programmers	335,000	70%
Food preparation workers	324,000	34%
Teachers, kindergarten and elementary	299,000	20%
Receptionists and information clerks	282,000	41%
Computer systems analysts	251,000	76%
Cooks, restaurant	240,000	46%

0 250,000 500,000 750,000 1,000,000 1,250,000

2. What the Jobs Are

As Graph No. 1 indicates, the growth in jobs is in the service sector of the economy. Most of the occupations listed here are growing faster than the average for all occupations. Those growing less rapidly are very large, so that the numerical increase is still great.

Source: U.S. Labor Department: Bureau of Labor Statistics

3. Skills Needed

Although many new jobs will continue to require only moderate skills, a much greater proportion of new jobs will need high-level skills than is currently the case. Workers with the skill level of engineers or teachers will be more in demand than workers with the skill level of laborers or farmers. (A representative sample of the skill levels required for various occupations is provided.) This need for highly skilled workers will exacerbate the growing gap between the number of jobs and the number of workers, because it is always more difficult to find skilled workers than unskilled ones.

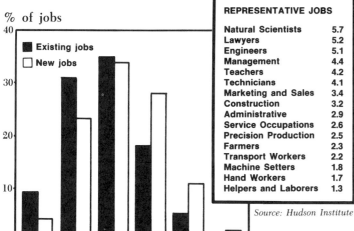

% of jobs

- ■ Existing jobs
- □ New jobs

SKILL-LEVEL OF WORKERS

REPRESENTATIVE JOBS	
Natural Scientists	5.7
Lawyers	5.2
Engineers	5.1
Management	4.4
Teachers	4.2
Technicians	4.1
Marketing and Sales	3.4
Construction	3.2
Administrative	2.9
Service Occupations	2.6
Precision Production	2.5
Farmers	2.3
Transport Workers	2.2
Machine Setters	1.8
Hand Workers	1.7
Helpers and Laborers	1.3

Source: Hudson Institute

4. Education Needed

The new jobs will also require more education than the old ones, and that, too, will make them harder to fill.

Education	Current Jobs	New Jobs
8 Years or Less	6%	4%
1-3 Years of High School	12%	10%
4 Years of High School	40%	35%
1-3 Years of College	20%	22%
4 Years of College or More	22%	30%
TOTAL	100%	100%
Median Years of School	12.8	13.5

Source: U.S. Labor Department: Bureau of Labor Statistics and Hudson Institute

5. The New Work Force

Workers are becoming more homogeneous in terms of age, but less so in terms of race and sex. Workers between the ages of 25 and 54 will account for an increasing share of the labor force, as will women and minorities.

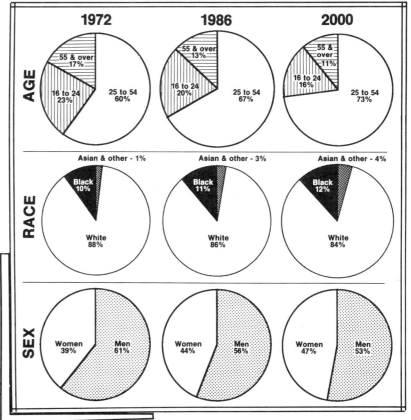

Source: U.S. Labor Department: Bureau of Labor Statistics

Continued from page 141
coming from the labor shortage," says Audrey Freedman, a labor expert at the Conference Board, a business research institute in New York City. "In other words, employers

realize that in order to avoid reaching very far down into the barrel for men, they can get higher quality women."

In their attempts to attract women workers, some employers are opening day-care centers on the premises,

Work Place Demographics

Until recently, the labor market — the number of people at work or seeking employment — was inflated by the large generation of "baby boomers" born after World War II.

The labor force will continue to increase, according to Labor Department forecasts, rising by 21 million workers and job seekers by the year 2000. But the rate of increase — 18 percent over the next 14 years — will be only about half that of the 1972-86 period when the baby boomers went to work. Young workers, those between the ages of 16 and 24, can expect to benefit from the demographic trend well into the future, as employers step up their efforts to lure entry-level workers.

With fewer young workers entering the job market each year, the work force is taking on a new appearance. Not only are there fewer young workers, there are fewer older workers, those 55 and older. Although they are growing in number, older Americans are being lured out of active employment by Social Security and private pension benefits. In many cases, they are also being offered special incentives to retire early by employers eager to trim their labor costs as a way to enhance competitiveness in today's global marketplace. These early retirees are part of a growing pool of part-time and temporary workers, which numbers some 20 million people.

The dwindling number of jobholders at both extremes of the age spectrum has already made the labor force more homogeneous from the generational standpoint. Since 1972, the 25- to 54-year-old group has increased from 60 to 67 percent of the labor force. The trend is expected to

continue, with these younger members of the baby boom generation representing almost three-quarters of all workers by 2000.

Factors other than age are also helping to reshape the work force. One is the erosion of living standards over the past 15 years. Frank Levy, an economist at the University of Maryland, estimates that average wages grew between 2.5 and 3 percent a year from the end of World War II until 1973. Since then, he writes in *Dollars and Dreams*, a study based on Census data, "inflation-adjusted wages have stagnated and, in many cases, declined." † Both falling productivity and the rise in inflation that followed the oil-price increases of the 1970s are linked to the fall in earnings over the past 15 years. A man who turned 40 in 1973, Levy estimates, now earns 14 percent less than he did that year, while a young man who went to work in 1973 now earns 25 percent less than his father earned in the early 1970s.

Families have fared somewhat better than individuals since 1973 for the simple reason that fewer families now depend for their livelihood on a single wage earner. Women, including those with small children, have flocked to the job market in an effort to slow the fall in living standards. After declining by 7 percent from 1973-80, the average family's inflation-adjusted income rose by 5 percent from 1980-84, Levy found. But not all families have fared as well. According to Jim Weill, program director of the Children's Defense Fund in Washington, D.C., young workers, those in the prime child-rearing years, have suffered the most. "Between 1973 and 1986, the

median income for families headed by a person under age 30 fell 13.5 percent," he says. "The median income for families headed by a person under 25 fell 26 percent." As living standards continue to decline, there is every reason to believe that more currently non-working women will seek employment. Women's share in the work force, only 39 percent in 1972, rose to 44 percent by 1986, and is expected to reach 47 percent by the turn of the century.

If tomorrow's work place will be more balanced by gender, it will also be more culturally diverse. The Labor Department predicts that the proportion of whites on the job will fall slightly, from 88 percent in 1972 to 84 percent by 2000. Blacks, Asians, Hispanics and people of other ethnic backgrounds will account for a greater portion of workers. There will be more black workers because blacks continue to have a higher birth rate than whites. Asians, too, tend to have more children, but their 71 percent increase in the labor market from 1986 to 2000 — the fastest of all groups — is also explained by the high numbers of Asian immigrants into the United States. The biggest ethnic change in tomorrow's work force will come from Hispanic workers, whose numbers are expected to rise from 8 million in 1986 to 14 million in 2000. Because of increased immigration and high birth rates, Hispanics will account for one-tenth of the work force by the turn of the century.

(For further details on the makeup of tomorrow's work place, see Chart No. 5 on p. 143.)

† *Frank Levy,* Dollars and Dreams: The Changing American Income Distribution *(1987), p. 4.*

while others offer subsidies for outside child care. Still others provide referral services for mothers who are having trouble finding adequate care for their children during working hours. Employers also are introducing innovative work schedules to employees whose family responsibilities prevent them from taking on full-time, year-round work. "Flextime" benefits allow employees to work at odd hours, while "job-sharing" allows two part-time workers to perform a task ordinarily assigned to one full-time employee.

It remains to be seen whether the competition for female workers will mean higher wages for them. It is true that the male-female earnings gap has narrowed slightly in recent years: Full-time female workers earned on average 70 cents for every dollar earned by men in 1986, up from 62 cents in 1979, according to the Census Bureau. The Hudson Institute predicts that the wage gap will continue to narrow as women increase their share of the work force and enter higher-paying occupations traditionally dominated by men. But day care is expensive, and some analysts say employers may deduct at least part of the cost of such "women's benefits" from their female workers' wage earnings.[7]

The growing diversity of the work force has led Avon Products Inc. to develop specific management techniques for each type of worker. "Most people, no matter what their background, don't want to be 'blended' into anything," said Jim Preston, president and chief operating officer of the New York cosmetics manufacturer, which employs 38,700 workers.[8] "They want to be themselves — preserve their own culture, heritage and customs. They don't think 'being themselves' should deny them equal opportunity. And they're right." But corporate America, he said, has been slow to understand. "Minority men were expected to be the most blue-suited, white-shirted, wing-tipped people in the office. And all the women who were managers, or hoped to be, felt they had to wear semi-masculine pin-stripe outfits with floppy ties."

Avon reasons that women perform better if they are treated differently from men. The company has also adopted special management techniques designed to enhance the productivity of black, Hispanic and Asian workers. "It has to do with understanding, valuing and managing diversity in the work place," Preston said. "If a company doesn't recognize that talent is color-blind and gender-blind, and doesn't provide an environment where minorities and women are comfortable and have the opportunity to advance, they'll go elsewhere — and that company will be at a competitive disadvantage," he said.

Jim Cox, Avon's senior vice president in charge of communications, explained that falling sales led the company to change its approach. "We had a head start both in seeing the problem and adapting to it over other companies because our products are sold to, for and by women. We also serve a whole lot of different ethnic groups." Avon created a "minority and women's participation council" to find ways to make use of its workers' talents, and has promoted women and minorities to top management positions.

As the work force is becoming more diverse, calls to protect these new workers are mounting in Congress. According to Jim Weill of the Children's Defense Fund, temporary and part-time workers are not only a growing share of the work force but are especially vulnerable because they do not receive the benefits granted full-time, year-round workers. He estimates that 35 million Americans lack health insurance, largely because of the rise in part-time work. "We need a substantial federal investment in child care and some form of guaranteed health insurance, be it public or private, for these workers," he said. Rep. Patricia Schroeder, D-Colo., this year proposed a measure that would require employers to offer health insurance and pensions on a prorated basis to part-time and temporary workers.

At a time of growing concern over the federal budget deficit, both Congress and the next administration will be hard put to solve these problems in the near future, no matter which candidate wins the White House this November. But both presidential candidates have acknowledged the difficulties faced by parents who are trying to juggle work requirements and child care. Meanwhile, Congress is now considering a bill Weill's group supports, called the Act for Better Child Care Services, known as the ABC bill (HR 3660). The measure would authorize $2.5 billion for child-care subsidies to low- and moderate-income families. Under current law, families may take a federal income tax credit for child-care expenses of up to $2,400 a year for a child under 15 and up to $4,800 for two or more children. Critics say the credit benefits mainly upper-income families. Another measure (S 2488) would require employers to grant workers limited unpaid leave to care for a seriously ill child or to care for a newborn or newly adopted baby.

Businesses are getting involved in public education programs

Some of the loudest cries for government intervention are coming from business leaders who say that public education must be improved to prepare young people better for employment. Criticism of the school system is not new: it has been five years since a government report documented the declining quality of education at the elementary- and high-school levels.[9] But businessmen say the reforms introduced in response to that report have not made young job seekers better qualified for the kinds of jobs that are now available. Employers complain that the schools have failed to teach such basic skills as reading, writing, mathematics and communication.

Business leaders are lobbying for better schooling as a necessary step in America's efforts to gain a competitive edge over its trading partners. Not surprisingly, education reform has become a prominent issue in the presidential campaign. Both candidates promise to introduce reform measures if elected. Vice President Bush would give higher merit bonuses to outstanding teachers, grant awards to schools where test scores improve and fund the creation of magnet schools. He also has proposed giving each state $1 million to come up with innovative teaching methods. Gov. Dukakis would set up a $250 million special fund to provide college scholarships, encourage college graduates to become teachers and lure other professionals into public education.

But employers also are demanding that the schools enlarge their standard course offerings to teach students how to solve problems, adapt to new surroundings, work in teams and take initiative. Workers must have these skills, businessmen say, if they are to function in the changing work place. Many employers are including such new work skills in their training programs for new employees. But, says Carnevale, "it's a slow process, and employers don't do these things readily. Their first instinct is to go to the schools and say, 'Give us better people now.'"

In some areas, employers are taking the message directly to the educators by becoming actively involved in local school systems. Many look to Boston for guidance. In the late 1970s, as the high-tech boom took off and created a strong demand for entry-level workers in the Boston area, employers were forced to recruit outside the city. The local public schools, plagued by high dropout rates, were not producing enough qualified graduates to satisfy the demand. As a result, employers, union representatives, government officials and educators formed the Boston Private Industry Council in an effort to improve the schools. In 1982, local employers and educators signed a formal agreement that has served as a model for other initiatives across the country.

Under the "Boston Compact," employers promised to create summer jobs and give hiring preference to an increasing number of qualified graduates of Boston high schools each year. In return, the schools promised to reduce truancy and raise scholastic achievement scores, and they guaranteed that graduates would possess basic skills. The compact later included local colleges and universities, which granted additional placements and scholarships for local students. Unions also signed on, promising to provide vocational training for Boston youth.

In just a few years, the Boston Compact produced significant results: 94 percent of the 1985 and 1986 high-school graduates in Boston went on to college, got a job or enlisted in the armed forces. According to the National Alliance of Business, a non-profit organization of business representatives that supports job training programs, this is the highest placement rate in the country. The organization is setting up business-education partnerships based on the Boston Compact model in seven other cities — Albuquerque, Cincinnati, Indianapolis, Louisville, Memphis, San Diego and Seattle.[10]

But even as support for business involvement in the education system builds, there are critics who say the creation of a qualified work force requires a different approach. "Bashing the public school system is really unfair," says Sar Levitan, a labor economist at George Washington University's Center for Social Policy Studies.

Levitan attributes the high dropout rates, high youth unemployment and poor academic achievement among those who do graduate from high school to profound social problems that are beyond the schools' control. "It goes back to the deterioration of the family and a general permissiveness in our society," he says. "What we have to pay attention to is the American family." When almost one out of every four children is born out of wedlock, and fewer than half the fathers of these children give even limited support for the children, Levitan concludes, it is not surprising that young people lack the encouragement and drive to excel. "Until we stabilize the family and create responsibility of parents for socializing their kids, then this problem is going to persist and exacerbate."

In Levitan's view, the keen interest shown by corporate leaders in the school system is a temporary phenomenon driven by the current shortage of qualified workers. "In the next recession employers are going to lose interest, and rightly so," he predicts. "Business is ill-equipped to provide basic education."

If Levitan is right, the burgeoning employer-school partnerships may be short-lived. A recession would dampen demand for entry-level workers, and even well-trained baby busters might face unemployment. But the birth dearth is a long-term demographic reality that will affect business practices for the rest of the century. Even with a moderately growing economy, employers will have to make adjustments to the decline of younger workers. Audrey Freedman predicts the baby bust will have a beneficial effect on American business in the 1990s. The labor shortage, she says, will force businesses to practice "labor conservation" to get more output from a limited number of workers. That would mean better productivity, a necessary ingredient in any formula to improve the country's competitiveness on the global market.

NOTES

[1] In August the Federal Reserve Board raised the prime rate, the interest it charges member banks, from 9.5 to 10 percent.

[2] Frank Levy, *Dollars and Dreams: The Changing American Income Distribution* (1987), p. 88.

[3] Barry Bluestone and Bennett Harrison, "The Great American Job Machine: The Proliferation of Low Wage Employment in the U.S. Economy," Joint Economic Committee, December 1986. For an opposing view, see Marvin H. Kosters and Murray N. Ross, "The Quality of Jobs: Evidence from Distributions of Annual Earnings and Hourly Wages," American Enterprise Institute, July 1988.

[4] William B. Johnston and Arnold H. Packer, *Workforce 2000: Work and Workers for the 21st Century* (June 1987), pp. 97-101.

[5] Quoted in *American Demographics*, September 1988, p. 13.

[6] See stories by Thomas J. Lueck in *The New York Times*, June 26 and Aug. 3, 1988.

[7] See Gary Becker, *Business Week*, Aug. 22, 1988.

[8] Preston spoke Aug. 2, 1988, at a conference sponsored by the American Productivity Center in Boston.

[9] National Commission on Excellence in Education, *A Nation at Risk* (1983).

[10] For further information on business-education partnerships, see National Alliance of Business, *The Fourth R: Workforce Readiness* (1987), and *Building a Quality Workforce* (1988), a joint study by the Departments of Labor, Education and Commerce.

Graphics: cover, pp. 142-143, S. Dmitri Lipczenko.

RECOMMENDED READING

BOOKS

Lampe, David, *The Massachusetts Miracle: High Technology and Economic Revitalization*, MIT Press, 1988.

This series of articles by academics, public officials and business representatives describes the development of Massachusetts' booming high-tech economy. Concentrated along Boston's Route 128 corridor, the manufacturers of computers and related materials, and the businesses that support them, have created enough jobs to eliminate the unemployment and economic stagnation faced by other areas dependent on traditional manufacturing.

Levy, Frank, *Dollars and Dreams: The Changing American Income Distribution*, Russell Save Foundation, 1987.

Family incomes doubled from the end of World War II until 1973. Since then, Levy writes, inflation-adjusted incomes have stopped growing and, in some cases, have actually declined. The author, a professor of public affairs at the University of Maryland, bases his conclusion on Census data. "Put simply," he writes, "there is a rapidly increasing *inequality of prospects*, an inequality in the chance that a family will enjoy the 'middle-class dream.'"

ARTICLES

Bloom, David E., and Todd P. Steen, "Why Child Care Is Good for Business," *American Demographics*, August 1988.

Because more and more women, including those with small children, are entering the labor market, the need for adequate child care is growing. Employers can attract skilled female labor, reduce absence from work and raise productivity, the authors write, by adding child care to their list of employee benefits.

Nelton, Sharon, "Meet Your New Work Force," *Nation's Business*, July 1988.

Businesses are beginning to change their ways of managing workers because their employees are no longer predominantly white males. Some companies, including Avon Products Inc., are developing distinctive management techniques aimed at helping women and minorities do their jobs better and advance to managerial positions.

REPORTS AND STUDIES

Berlin, Gordon, and Andrew Sum, *Toward A More Perfect Union: Basic Skills, Poor Families, and Our Economic Future*, Ford Foundation, February 1988.

The authors show how poor academic achievement leads to high dropout rates, youth unemployment, teen pregnancies, welfare dependency and falling productivity. Demographic trends mean that there will be fewer young workers in coming years and that more of these will come from disadvantaged backgrounds. For this reason, schools need to focus on helping these people improve their skills.

Johnston, William B., and Arnold H. Packer, *Workforce 2000: Work and Workers for the 21st Century*, Hudson Institute, June 1987.

This study analyzes the economic changes that await us over the next 12 years. It predicts that the economy will grow "at a relatively healthy pace," that manufacturing will account for a smaller share of jobs, that the workforce will grow slowly and become more diverse and that new jobs will require greater skills. To cope with these changes, the authors recommend that employers make special efforts to integrate women and minorities into the workforce and improve the quality of education to job preparedness for all workers.

National Alliance of Business, *The Fourth R: Workforce Readiness*, November 1987.

The Boston Compact, a business-education partnership initiated by the community's business leaders to improve the quality of high-school education, is the focus of this study. Frustrated by the lack of adequately trained high-school graduates to fill entry-level positions in the area's booming high-technology industry, employers agreed to help graduates find work if the schools improved the quality of education. The study also describes similar community efforts modeled on the Boston experience.

U.S. Department of Labor, Bureau of Labor Statistics, *Projections 2000*, March 1988 (Bulletin 2302).

The bureau predicts employment trends using three alternative scenarios for economic growth over the next 12 years. A detailed breakdown of expected changes in employment opportunities for all occupations shows a fall in most blue-collar jobs and significant growth in service-producing jobs, especially those requiring specialized training.

U.S. Departments of Labor, Education and Commerce, *Building a Quality Workforce*, July 1988.

This joint study addresses the growing gap between requirements for entry-level workers and the skills most job seekers possess. The "skills gap" is forcing employers to spend more and more money on job training. The study describes several community partnerships between local businesses and schools, which are designed to improve young people's preparedness for work.

MANAGEMENT'S HIGH-TECH CHALLENGE

MANAGEMENT'S HIGH-TECH CHALLENGE

by Roy Furchgott

Computer-based technologies are changing the way America works. New technologies aren't just making workers' tasks easier or more efficient — they're altering the very ways offices operate. But many companies aren't getting the most out of their information systems because managers are reluctant to give up their traditional role as the "guardians of all useful knowledge."

For America's white-collar workers, the 1980s are a period of transition. The office of the 1990s may look — and operate — as differently from the office of today as the office of the 1980s does from the office of the 1950s. Perhaps the biggest change will come from the maturing role of computers. "When computers were in the back room, they were just a tactical tool," says John Donovan, chairman of the Cambridge Technology Group. "Now computers are in the corner office. They are a strategic tool." [1]

Computer-based technologies are not just making office workers' tasks easier or more efficient. They are altering the very ways offices operate. "Office automation changes the way that information flows between and within organizations, the way that work is distributed in an office, the way that people do their work, and the skills they need," the congressional Office of Technology Assessment (OTA) has pointed out. [2]

But while the changes have been profound, old management habits often hinder the effective use of computers. "[M]ost top managers are applying complex and fertile new technologies as though they simply are new versions of Henry Ford's assembly line," notes Shoshana Zuboff, an associate professor at the Harvard Business School and the

Roy Furchgott is a business reporter living in Baltimore.

author of *In the Age of the Smart Machine: The Future of Work and Power*. "They have failed to recognize that their organizations need to be fundamentally changed to fully exploit the potential of information technologies. In fact, the kinds of innovations needed to foster better use of technology are being hindered — sometimes intentionally — by managers who resist re-examining their roles and who hew to notions of managerial status inherited from an earlier age." [3]

This is certainly not the first time management has been slow to take advantage of new office technologies. Take the case of Chester Carlson. Fifty years ago next month, on Oct. 22, 1938, this little-known patent attorney perfected a process that would make copies of a document without carbon paper or wet chemicals. Carlson was convinced that his invention would make office work easier and more efficient. But even though he demonstrated his process to more than 20 companies, all of them unceremoniously showed him the door. It took him more than 10 years — until 1949 — to get his idea off the drawing board and into the marketplace. And it was another 10 years before his electrostatic copying machine, dubbed the Xerox 14, caught on. *(See article, p. 155.)*

As is often the case with new technologies, the ramifications of the xerography process took years to unfold. No one realized in 1959 that Carlson's unheralded idea would create a $27 billion industry, do away with carbon paper and the office mimeograph room and permanently alter office operations. By giving managers a way to send messages quickly and directly, the photocopier made it possible for information to move faster through the company to a greater number of employees. Now, of course, the offspring of Carlson's invention are standard office fixtures in even the smallest businesses.

As for the spread of the latest office technology, one analyst estimates that in 1980, approximately 10 million Americans interacted daily with a video display terminal and that this number will increase to 25 million by 1990. Another study predicts that in 1990, 65 percent of all professional, managerial, technical and administrative workers will depend upon computer-based work stations. [4] According to OTA, there will be one computer terminal for every two or three office workers by 1990. By the year 2000, OTA predicts, computer terminals will be as common as telephones are now. [5]

It's not as if no one saw these changes coming. Back in 1962, two University of Chicago professors predicted that the introduction of computers into the work place would alter the way corporations are organized and transform the role of managers. "Information technology built around the computer and focusing upon vital flows of information through an organization will rechannel these flows and, in the process, alter basic organization structure and change managerial jobs," they wrote. [6] Now, people whose jobs didn't even exist a few years ago are in senior management positions — the new "computer elite," for example, who control the information systems on which companies depend. New information systems also mean other unpredictable changes for the work place.

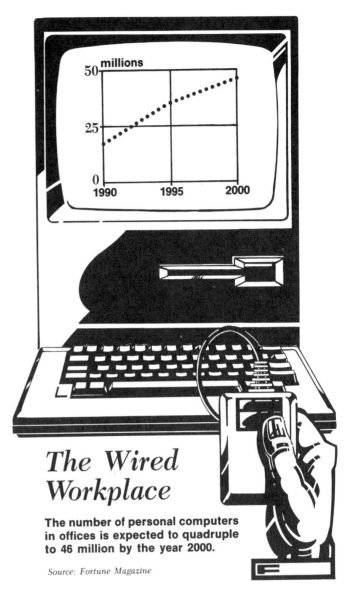

The Wired Workplace

The number of personal computers in offices is expected to quadruple to 46 million by the year 2000.

Source: Fortune Magazine

"We discover that [phenomenon] with all technology, with all infrastructure," says Professor Donald A. Norman, Director of the Institute for Cognitive Science at the University of California, San Diego (UCSD). "We invent the automobile to get us between two points faster, and suddenly we find we have to build new roads. And that means we have to invent traffic regulations and put in stop lights. And then we have to create a whole new organization called the Highway Patrol — and all we thought we were doing was inventing cars."

The proliferation of office technology can be partially attributed to the changing nature of the American economy. The production and dissemination of information has replaced manufacturing as the principal activity of the U.S. economy. According to a January 1988 report prepared at the request of the Office of Management and Budget and the President's Council on Management Improvement, "the number of workers employed in producing information (*i.e.*, in the fields of education, research and development, the media, design, and engineering) and in using information (*i.e.*, finance, government, insurance and real estate) [grew] from 30.8 percent in 1950 to 46.6 percent in 1980." [7]

The economy's appetite for information — and for systems and machines to manage that information — has been a boon to the companies that produce computer hardware, software and printers and telecommunications systems. Sometimes it seems that they are making new products faster than companies can assimilate them.

Facsimile, or FAX, machines, are a good example. They take a handwritten or typed message, or even simple graphics, and in a half-minute or less, transmit a likeness across phone lines anywhere in the world. About 475,000 FAX machines were installed last year, up from 190,000 in 1986. But while most companies are still deciding whether to purchase their first FAX machines, a new generation is already on the horizon. The new systems will take a step out of — and therefore speed up — the FAX process. Instead of feeding in hard copy at one end to be reproduced at the far end, a computer equipped with the new technology can send data directly to the distant FAX machine, avoiding modem and compatibility problems that can arise going computer to computer.

And FAX machines are just one example of the speed with which new technology is being created. In fact, new systems are evolving so rapidly that the experts can't assess their impact. "We all see the marriage of high-band communications that will allow access to better images, better audio and huge amounts of information from libraries and data bases," says Norman of UCSD. "The combination of telephone, telefax, audio and video bases is imminent — we predict that. But can we predict the impact? My reading of the history of technology says no."

One problem is that managers are sometimes so anxious to acquire the latest technologies that they install the equipment before they've determined how best to use it. "When people were inventing the typewriter, they just thought of the typewriter — they thought of the keys and how they work with the levers and so on," says Dr. Harlan Mills, a 24-year IBM veteran and director of the Information Systems Institute in Vero Beach, Fla. "The inventors never imagined the idea of touch typing. So [when] touch typing comes along, . . . it turns out to have a much larger impact on the typing industry than good typewriters. Good use of systems is a tougher problem than good systems."

Early readings of the effects of technology indicate that the future could go either way: New office technology could mean improved office conditions, greater efficiency and more job satisfaction. But it could just as easily lead to worse office conditions, no increase in efficiency and low job satisfaction. The key difference seems to lie not so much in the nature of the new technology as in developing the ability to use it. And to use it properly requires new management techniques — techniques that are often hard to sell to managers.

Electronic utopias, or electronic sweatshops?

From the earliest days of civilization, man has devised machines to lighten his physical and mental labors. But it was not until the development of power machinery during the 18th-century Industrial Revolution that the average worker was able to enjoy the benefits of automation. With advances in computer science in the mid-20th century, automated technology moved from the factory floor to the office.

At first, businesses used computers simply to "automate" the office. They saw computers only as super-clerks, capable of handling repetitive operations millions or trillions of times without ever becoming bored or tired and therefore error-prone. Computers also were able to perform these tasks in a fraction of the time required by human beings. So as increasing numbers of computers were put to work in information storage and retrieval, the experts confidently predicted that automation would cut costs, increase productivity and make workers more efficient.

However, it didn't take long for the experts to realize that computers could be used to enhance jobs as well as automate them. Computers didn't have to be just a better mousetrap; they could be a whole different kind of exterminator. "Computer-based technologies differ from earlier technologies in that they generate new information about the very processes of production and administration that they are designed to automate," says Zuboff. She has coined the term "informating" to describe the capacity of computer technologies to produce information about their own activities. "Because of this informating capacity," she writes, "computer-based technologies can increase rather than decrease the intellectual content of work. When people have their work reorganized by these technologies, they find that they spend less time doing things. . . . They spend proportionally more time dealing with abstract information presented to them by their computer systems." [8]

The Office of Technology Assessment uses the term "bundling" to describe the "electronic reintegration of tasks" to expand the boundaries of jobs and enhance their interest for the worker. This approach, OTA said, allows the worker to "concentrate on a coherent objective from the beginning to the end of a series of tasks, such as providing a service to the satisfaction of a specific customer, rather than being forced to endlessly repeat one suboperation."

"Informating," or "bundling," represents the promise of the computerized work place. In practice, however, many businesses are still using computers only for automation. Barbara Garson, author of *The Electronic Sweatshop: How Computers Are Transforming the Office of the Future into the Factory of the Past*, says that most companies are "bringing 19th century Taylorism to the office in the guise of 20th century technology. . . .* Managers are . . .

---

*"Taylorism" refers to Frederick Winslow Taylor, the American industrial engineer who was the father of scientific management. *(See article, p. 153.)*

Frederick Taylor: The Father of Scientific Management

Who is Frederick Taylor, and why are people saying such terrible things about him?

Taylor is the father of scientific management whose time and motion studies systematized management and manufacturing, and created the discipline of efficiency experts. He was then, and is now, equally revered and reviled for his contributions to the work place.

Born in 1856 in Philadelphia, to a lawyer-father and abolitionist-mother, Taylor himself intended to become a lawyer. Forced from his studies by a temporary vision problem, Taylor went to work for the Midvale Steel Company as a common laborer. He worked his way up the ranks over 12 years to become chief engineer while he was also getting a masters degree in education from Stevens Institute of Technology in Hoboken, N.J.

His years on the shop floor convinced him that with careful observation, every step in a manufacturing plant could be quantified. Such a process would cut out wasted time and effort by employees and could be used to set reasonable work quotas he believed would end labor-management antagonism. He began his first study in 1881, at the age of 25 (the same year he, with partner Clarence M. Clark, won the United States tennis doubles championship).

Taylor summarized the basic precepts of industrial automation in his books *Shop Management* (1904) and *The Principles of Scientific Management* (1911). "The managers assume . . . the burden of gathering together all of the traditional knowledge which in the past has been possessed by the workman and then of classifying, tabulating and reducing the knowledge to rules, laws and formulae . . . ," he wrote. "All possible brain work should be removed from the shop and concentrated in the planning or laying out department."

In one way his methods were successful; for example, he developed a treatment for tool steel at Bethlehem Steel that increased tool cutting capability 200 to 300 percent. But Stuart Leslie, associate professor of history at John Hopkins University says managers "felt his methods took control out of the hands of management and put it in the hands of an outside efficiency expert." And laborers, fearing they would be turned into robots, performing mindless tasks repititiously, weren't any more accepting than management. "From labor, there was incredible resistance. At the Watertown [Mass.] Arsenal they tried to implement Taylor's methods. There was a bitter labor strike, and the result was Taylor's methods were kept out of government facilities for a long time," says Leslie.

Before his death in 1915, Taylor saw his methods adopted by industrialized nations all over the world. "It did give tremendous productivity gains, and that sort of wore down the skepticism," says Leslie. "When companies realized they could bring an efficiency expert into their management instead of hiring him as an outside consultant, the skepticism wore off."

However, Taylor's name has lived on colloquially to connote the worst side of his work, his methods carried to an extreme, turning laborers into unskilled, unthinking automatons.

doing what Taylor did, breaking down jobs and handing them out to people who become replaceable units." They are, in OTA's terminology, using computers to "de-skill" work — "to reduce it to simple, precise, repetitive actions that require no thought or judgment." This approach, OTA said, "tends to produce job dissatisfaction, poor motivation, and high employee turnover because it is tedious and boring. At the extreme, this can result in an 'office factory' that recreates some of the worst problems of the early manufacturing-plant production lines." [9]

Garson, in her book, offers an example of how even jobs that would seem to need flexibility and a personal touch can be standardized. She quotes an American Airlines reservations agent who explains how conversations are broken into carefully pre-scripted "modules," including the sales pitch, probe questions and close. "They provide me with the scenario, the basic script and props, and I have to keep that alive," the agent told her.

"American Airlines," Garson wrote, "had divided the two-minute conversation into segments . . . and provided a set of interchangeable conversation modules for each segment. . . . On one level it's obvious why this is considered efficient. In industry, production is routinely arranged so that the bulk of the work can be done with a minimum of skill. The more an airline can standardize the reservation conversation, the less they need to depend on the agents' experience and judgment. This should make the agents cheaper and more interchangeable. . . . [T]his process [also] produces . . . a more uniform product."

Garson, however, doesn't hide her own objections to such a system. "As a customer," she writes, "I'd like to reach an agent . . . who feels free to use his discretion and common sense." [10]

UCSD's Norman says managers who use computer technology to standardize white-collar jobs overlook the fact that the social and business processes of an office are more complex than those of a factory. "If you go into an office," he says, "and try to analyze what is going on, and you get everyone to tell you what job they do, and you write it up and you show it back to them and they agree that is exactly what they do, then you watch them, you see that is not what they do at all. So you say, 'How come this item doesn't follow your procedure?' They'll say, 'Oh, well, this is a special case.' So you look at the next piece. 'This isn't what you said you do either.' 'Oh, well, this is a special case.' It turns out that almost everything is a special case. The normal case turns out to be the rare one. Even the people who do the work think they are doing something different than they really are. So when you go to automate, you can really destroy the social interaction that allows people to deal skillfully with the special case."

Managers also rely on information generated by computers to judge employees' efficiency and productivity. Norman says he doesn't approve of such methods. "I've never liked efficiency measures, because what you have to talk about is worker output per unit of time," he says. "But how do you measure output? You can only measure it in things you can count — you can measure how many letters are produced a week, but you can't measure quality. . . . The other thing is unseen cost. If workers feel they are being monitored in that way, the stress level is high, the job satisfaction is low, turnover is high, and turnover . . . almost always leads to high costs."

Managers sometimes equate knowledge with power

Experts like Norman and Zuboff say there are better ways to use computers in the work place — making them tools for creativity and development rather than tools for standardization and measuring efficiency. Zuboff suggests managers give their employees the skills they need to take advantage of the information produced by technology. "With new skills," she writes, "those who work at the front lines of an organization and who monitor its pulse can use the data to improve products and services."

Despite the potential benefits of this strategy for the company's bottom line, however, many managers are reluctant to do it. "[G]iving the 'front lines' the skills, information and opportunity to act on what they are learning would require new roles and relationships [within the company], particularly for management. And too often managers have viewed sharing information and skills as if it were a zero-sum game in which more knowledge for others means less status for themselves." [11]

"The terrain of information in the work place has been a battleground on which the conflicts over managerial authority have typically been waged," Zuboff says. "Over the centuries, managerial authority has evolved in a way that says, 'Managers are the guardians of the organization's knowledge base, and no one else is allowed to have access to this knowledge.' This has been an important part of the legitimization process for managers."

But the spread of office automation already has blurred conventional notions of the division of labor between managers and workers. "In many offices," OTA noted, "clerical workers become expert at using computers to access data, monitor production activities, and formulate reports ('the professionalization of clerical work'), while professionals and managers begin to do their own word processing in drafting letters and documents ('the clericalization of professional work')." [12] The result is often a flattening of the corporate hierarchy.

Sharon Gentry, office automation development manager for Texas Instruments, says clerical work has been professionalized through automation at her company. "I know that initially what one expected when you have automation is that you'd start getting rid of people, that you could start replacing them with machines," she says. "What we saw instead was a job stayed there, but it was enhanced due to automation. What used to be a secretarial position became more an administrative assistant position." Gentry says she found that thanks to automation, secretaries have, on their own, gone from simply typing reports and presentations to producing charts and graphic information and support materials as well.

According to Norman, it's middle managers who are most threatened by such changes. "Why do we have middle management?" he asks. "They are the sort of people who serve the top level by gathering information at the low level and putting it up in digestible form, or take the intentions and goals of the high levels and try to restructure it in a way that makes sense on the shop floor. As you automate the shop floor and make it more powerful, the middle disappears. Middle management does its funny paper-shuffling work — it's sort of a communications interface between the top and bottom, and it either won't be necessary or it will be required in some completely different form."

For her part, Zuboff doesn't think middle managers should be so concerned. "[Flattening] may be true [for the] short-term in some places, but I don't think that is a fair characterization of what is happening in any broad way," she says. "Just because there is more technology, it doesn't mean you are going to wipe out a whole class of people, and that has never been true of any type of office automation, going back to the typewriter. The more office automation there has been, the more people in the office there have been."

But although middle managers may not disappear, their jobs are being redefined, Zuboff says. Middle managers no longer "have to fulfill the function of passing around information like they used to," she says, "but they are still needed in a number of very important functions. They are the people who educate, who help develop skills. They are the vital people who do what I call creating the learning environment."

Creating this kind of environment will become increasingly important as American companies struggle to stay competitive in the global economy. "The old-style corporation, with a fixed hierarchy of authority and information flow, is becoming a dinosaur," says H. J. Maxmin, chairman and chief executive officer of the home electron-

Chester Carlson: The Xerox Man

If ever there was a legitimate subject for a Frank Capra movie, Chester F. Carlson was it. Rising from an impoverished childhood, he went on to discover a process of copying documents that would make him a multimillionaire and form the basis of a $27 billion industry.

Carlson was born Feb. 8, 1906, to an immigrant father and a mother who died while Carlson was in his teens. His father, a barber, had arthritis, so Carlson supported his parents from an early age. While Carlson was busy at odd jobs, he managed to graduate with a B.S. in physics from the prestigious California Institute of Technology. While working as a research assistant at Bell Telephone Laboratories and then as a patent lawyer — a degree he picked up at night while working for Bell — he grew frustrated at how hard it was to obtain copies of documents. In the late 1920s and early 1930s, the only two viable methods for reproduction of text and graphs were photography and the Photostat process, which were slow and relatively expensive.

So Carlson took it upon himself to create an easier, more efficient way to make copies. With the aid of his degree from the California Institute of Technology, he began to investigate the possibility of using electric

charges to produce a copied image.

This process, called electrostatics, uses the forces inherent in electric charges to produce an image on a plate, which is then covered with a powder. A sheet of paper is passed between the plate and a charged object, and as the powder is drawn to the paper, heat is applied to fuse the powder to the paper. In 1937, Carlson applied for and received a patent for the process. The following year, with the help of a German physicist named Otto Kornei, Carlson produced the world's first dry-copy machine.

This cornerstone in office technology didn't immediately catch the interest of big business, or small business for that matter, and Carlson had difficulty finding financial backing for his innovative process. In 1944, after rejections from I.B.M., General Electric and Remington Rand, a small photographic paper manufacturer, Haloid Company, bought the rights to Carlson's process. The company later changed it's name to Xerox Corporation and called the process xerography — after the Greek words for dry writing.

It took 15 years for the kinks to be ironed out, but with the introduction of Xerox model 914 in 1959, sales began to pour in and Xerox's profits

began to skyrocket. Thanks to a generous consulting position with Xerox — and even more generous royalties — Carlson's fortunes increased at the same rate as that of the company. By the time of his death in 1968, he had donated millions to charities and to his alma mater.

In recognition of Carlson's achievements and the 50th anniversary of his invention, Xerox recently introduced the Xerox 50 Series copier. The United States Postal Service will release a 21-cent stamp honoring Carlson on Oct. 21.

— DOUGLAS SERY

---

ics division of the British firm Thorn EMI. "In the last decade, excellence in business meant doing one thing well. In the decade to come, though, you'll have to do everything well, and do it everywhere. The image of the corporation as a pyramid is dead; the new corporation will be more like a hologram, with shared information making each person, each part, contain the whole."

Only 10 to 15 percent of senior managers regularly use computers today, but experts say more than half will be doing so in 10 years. According to David De Long of the Harvard Business School, "Chief executives going on-line today say they want help with three tasks — communications, analysis and the monitoring of business perfor-

mance and the external environment. The most common use is monitoring." [13]

One factor speeding the move of computers into the executive suite has been the development of "user-friendly" software that can be customized to fit their specific needs. Experts expect the trend to continue as more computer-literate managers make their way to the top. "Companies that are reluctant to move electronic information into the executive suite are naive," says Robert Wallace, president of Phillips 66 Co. "Their reluctance is going to be a significant limitation on their managerial and competitive ability in the 1990s." [14]

Overcoming resistance to new technologies

Managers aren't the only ones who resist new office technologies. "Many employees initially fear new technology and have doubts about their ability to use it," OTA points out.[15] That means that high-powered information systems often get used on a very low-power scale. Mills, the former IBM official, says most firms don't get all the benefits they could from their computer technology. "They use maybe 20 percent of it," he says.

The reasons for the underutilization are multifold. First, there is the cost of educating and training employees. "It's just a simple fact of life, that when a company has laid out a big chunk of money for a system, it is hard to get them to shell out another big chunk to get good use of it," says Mills. "In any business, as fortunes prosper and wane . . . the capital-funding is probably affected less than the people-funding. In a bad year, the education programs are the first to go." And even if companies are willing to spend the money, Mills contends, good education programs are hard to find. "It's harder to think up good education for people than it is to think up good systems."

The way management introduces new technologies also can affect its acceptance by employees. Even when a system is properly designed and the employees properly trained, it will fail, Norman says, "if the people it is being thrust upon don't believe that it serves their needs, and don't believe they had some say in selecting it." The key, he says, is employee involvement. "If through the participation of the people who are going to use it, you bought a less efficient system, the results will still be superior. It is their system and they feel happy with it."

Management must also be sensitive to employees' concerns about the health risks of new technologies. While there is no hard evidence, studies have linked concentrated work at computer visual display terminals (VDTs) to eye disorders, miscarriages and muscular, skeletal and neural disorders, including carpal tunnel syndrome, a crippling nerve disorder.

A study conducted by the Kaiser Permanente health maintenance organization revealed that women in administrative or clerical positions who worked at VDTs 20 or more hours a week had twice as many miscarriages in the first trimester of pregnancy as all other women. But the study could not explain the correlation. "There was insufficient data to tell us why it was," says Bob Hughes, a spokesman for Kaiser Permanente. "The suspicion is it has something to do with the working conditions because it only affected women in certain job categories rather than all women using VDTs 20 hours or more. If it was radiation, you would expect it to affect all women working at VDTs 20 hours or more."

Many companies, including Kaiser Permanente, are experimenting to see if discomforts can be reduced through such things as better work-station designs, the types of chairs employees use and the amount of time allowed for breaks. "We have put together a task force to determine

what guidelines should be as to ergonomics . . . but there are still a lot of unknowns," says Hughes.

Not everyone is waiting for a conclusive answer to make changes in the office environment. Suffolk County, N.Y., has enacted legislation regulating work-place standards for VDT operators. The law requires eye exams for VDT operators, limits the time a worker can sit at a terminal without a break and requires employers to provide machines with adjustable screens, detachable keyboards, adjustable copy holders and adjustable lighting. They must also provide employees with both written and oral training.

Communicating in the 'wired workplace'

When they introduce new technologies into the work place, managers must recognize that they are changing more than the ways individual employees do their jobs. They are changing the entire social structure of the office. "[Previously] when something unusual happened, you knew somebody to call in another office and work it out," says Norman. "Now'days, you can't do that. All you know is information that comes on the computer screen."

But at the same time technology is breaking down some forms of office socialization, it is creating new ones. One increasingly popular medium is electronic mail, a system through which messages are sent over computer lines. Because messages can be sent without identifying the status of the sender, company hierarchy and corporate norms break down.

Electronic mail also tends to strip away superficialities. A study by social psychologist Sara Kiesler and her colleague Lee Sproull, both of Carnegie-Mellon University, found that "when managers in mixed-sex groups were talking face to face, four out of five times the first person to make an explicit suggestion for a decision was male. When we put those same groups in an electronic mail network where the same kinds of problems were discussed, women made the first move to get to a decision as frequently as men did." [17]

The flip side to "E-mail," as electronic mail has come to be known, is a phenomenon called "flaming." Because of the immediate nature of E-mail, some strongly worded messages are sent out before there is time for reflection, so office quarrels can escalate quickly. The messages also can seem worse than intended because they are not delivered personally, where nonverbal cues such as body language may modify meaning. But a new phenomenon of E-mail hieroglyphics has evolved to give a better clue to a message's actual intent. "Symbols have developed to indicate the mood of the sender," says Norman, an admitted flamer. "For instance, you type a colon, hyphen and right paren[thesis] as a happy face. [:-)] There are a lot more. . . . What this is proving is that the written word, and

Continued on page 158

AT ISSUE   *Do monitoring technologies threaten employee privacy rights?*

YES say **GARY T. MARX**, a Massachusetts Institute of Technology sociology professor, and **SANFORD SHERIZEN**, a security information consultant.

"In a less technological age, our expectations about privacy were defined partly by what the unaided senses — sight, sound, smell, taste, and touch — were capable of detecting. The traditional physical boundaries of the workplace offered other limits to the gathering of information. Today's monitoring technologies easily transcend traditional barriers to data collection. Since monitoring is increasingly done automatically by machines, supervisors are no longer limited to what they can immediatly observe. Nor are workers always able to know when they are being monitored. . . .

Workers increasingly participate in their own monitoring — even though such participation may be unwilling or unconscious. Technical devices automatically record data that workers generate: they capture information from the workers' voices or movements such as keystrokes or assembly-line actions, and they measure workers' effectiveness by monitoring security and quality-control systems. In data-processing jobs, for instance, the devices monitor the number of errors and corrections made, the speed of work, and the time away from the desk. . . .

The new technologies, of course, may bring greater equity. After all, 'pre-technological' monitoring by a human supervisor sometimes meant high-handed or discriminatory treatment. Technological monitors have no favorites; all workers are treated alike. Because so many parameters of job performance can now be monitored, the total result might be a fairer system. . . .

However, intrusive monitoring may conflict with workers' traditional expectations of what is fair on the job. . . .

Monitoring may also create more adversarial relationships in the workplace. Workers may feel violated and powerless in the face of the new monitoring technologies. The result could be low morale, reduced productivity, and destructive countermeasures. Monitoring may even increase the violations or abuses it is intended to stop. Workers may feel challenged to beat the system or react out of anger and estrangement. . . .

American companies today are at a crossroads. They can use new electronic technologies to increase their control over worker behavior and reinforce traditional patterns of nonparticipatory management. But such efforts will erode individual rights to privacy and may cause psychological stress and reduce productivity."

From "Monitoring on the Job," Technology Review, November/December 1986, pp. 44-72.

NO says **ALAN F. WESTIN**, a Columbia University professor of public law and government.

"The move into office automation has made video display terminals (VDT) a staple in most American offices. . . . At the same time . . . VDTs have generated some very important social policy issues. . . . One of the most well-publicized issues in the past few years is employee monitoring. . . .

[S]hould we be changing laws and regulating this area of employer conduct? Should this be an area in which arbitrators reach out to find improper and impermissible standards of conduct or unacceptable invasions of privacy? I do not believe that regulation by law or an arbitrator importation of public-law standards is called for on privacy grounds. . . . [T]his is a basic labor-management issue, or, in non-union settings, a basic employee relations issue. There are important questions involving fairness of the work measurement process and how it is conducted and the fairness of the evaluation and recognition criteria used in the observation. . . .

Where employees told us that they were angered and stressed by monitoring, our interviews invariably found that it was really the fairness of work standards, measurement techniques, and evaluative criteria that were the cause. The mere banning of monitoring in such workplaces without the provision of overall fairness and equity in employee relations would not represent progress. In fact, it could cause a return to favoritism, subjectivity, and discrimination in supervisory evaluations, since it would withdraw the one essentially objective and factual component of employee evaluation.

But some . . . say, why not use the invasion-of-privacy issue and the good emotional and political-ally sentiment this attack on the computer and Big Brother can generate to champion better treatment of employees? . . . .

My answer has to be that the end does not justify the means in this instance any more than others. There is oppressive, dignity-destroying, and unfair monitoring of employees and there is monitoring that is fair, dignity-respecting, and a proper tool of personnel administration. I am an advocate of the fair and proper use of monitoring, and I write and speak constantly to advance its use by all employers. I am also too devoted an advocate of privacy rights in American society to join those who want to stretch that basic right and concept beyond its proper limits. To do that . . . risks creating confusion and backlash that could retard the expansion of genuine privacy protections for employees in all the dimensions."

Based on a presentation at the 41st annual meeting of the National Academy of Arbitrators, June 1988. To be published in Arbitration 1988: Emerging Issues for the 1990s (BNA Books, Washington, D.C., March 1989).

Continued from page 156
sometimes even the spoken word, isn't enough. We convey a lot through facial expressions, and the new technologies will allow that."

In fact, the Xerox Corp. in Palo Alto, Calif., conducted an experiment with its facility in Portland, Ore., leaving a two-way TV hookup in a room at each office. A worker in one office had only to go to the room and call out for someone at the distant operation, and that person would come in the room for a face to face video meeting. "It was actually quite effective," says Norman. "People there told me it was actually easier to talk to people in Portland and work with them on joint projects than with someone on the far end of their own building. To do effective group work you need immediate access, and what this experiment demonstrated was that immediate access didn't mean you were physically close. It meant the amount of physical and mental effort you had to do to talk to them was small."

Managing in the age of the smart machine

As the pace of office automation accelerates, many corporate executives are struggling to keep up. Some say the companies that manufacture and sell the new technologies should do more to ensure that their clients get the most out of their products.

"We've got technology growing very fast," says Mills, "and right behind it we've got a lot of hucksters and systems sellers and so on. They sell the systems, and once they're sold, they are sort of demotivated — they don't show you how to use them well. They are making their money on the sales of the systems, not particularly on the follow-through of making them work."

One of the main selling points for the new technology is that it increases productivity — for both individual employees and the company as a whole. The Office of Technology Assessment says that while "it is not yet possible to quantify the gains in productivity that can be achieved through widespread office automation . . . they are significant." OTA estimates that "office automation shortens that time required for many basic tasks from 15 to 85 percent." But, OTA goes on to say, "The consequences of office automation in terms of overall productivity for an organization are far more difficult to measure and document, and to compare with those in other organizations." [17]

Increases in productivity aren't the only benefits of automation, says Norman. For example, an efficiency study of word processors found that they did not reduce the amount of time it took to produce letters or reduce the number of employees in the typing pool. But because word processing made revisions easier, the quality and appearance of the letters improved. There was another benefit as well, Norman says. "Because the employees got to use their heads, they thought they were contributing

more of their own effort, so turnover was less."

Not everyone thinks these labor-saving devices are a blessing. In fact, some believe they may actually be making it easier to work harder, not smarter. "So-called 'time-saving' inventions and innovations make it possible to try to squeeze more tasks into less time," says management consultant Marilyn M. Machlowitz. "Technological advances have much to recommend them. But portable computers, FAX machines, Federal Express, the Filofax and Daytimer calendars, as well as phones in cars, on trains and on planes as well as in hotel bathrooms, also make it far more possible to work anytime, anywhere. And . . . what formerly was impossible may now be temptingly possible. Instead of responding, 'No, I can't get this to you tomorrow,' with overnight couriers we now may knock ourselves out trying to." [18]

For good or ill, however, office automation is here to stay. How effectively the new technologies are used will depend largely on those who run America's corporations. "The new computer-based technologies will not do the job by themselves," says Zuboff. "At best, they provide only short-term advantages. At worst, they can turn managers into police officers and companies into police states. It rests with the visionary chief executive to create an organization that celebrates learning, risk-taking and creative thinking. Without these innovations, more top managers will join the ranks of the CEOs who lament the false promises and broken dreams so often associated with new information technologies." [19]

NOTES

[1] Quoted by Joel Dreyfuss in "Catching the Computer Wave," *Fortune*, Sept. 26, 1988, p. 78.

[2] Office of Technology Assessment, *Automation of America's Offices: Summary* (December 1985), p. 16.

[3] Shoshana Zuboff, "Short-Circuiting New Technology," *Los Angeles Times*, June 5, 1988.

[4] The studies were quoted by Shoshana Zuboff, *In the Age of the Smart Machine* (1988), p. 416.

[5] Office of Technology Assessment, *op. cit.*, p. 8.

[6] George P. Schultz and Thomas L. Whisler, "Automation and the Management Process," *Annals of the American Academy of Political and Social Science*, March 1962, p. 82.

[7] *Meeting Public Demands: Federal Services in the Year 2000* (January 1988), p. 15.

[8] Zuboff, the *Los Angeles Times*, *op. cit.*

[9] Office of Technology Assessment, *op. cit.*, p. 22.

[10] Barbara Garson, *Electronic Sweatshops: How Computers Are Transforming the Office of the Future into the Factory of the Past* (1988), pp. 40-70.

[11] Zuboff, *op. cit.*

[12] Office of Technology Assessment, *op. cit.*, p. 16.

[13] Writing in *The New York Times*, Feb. 7, 1988.

[14] Maxmin and Wallace were quoted by De Long, *op. cit.*

[15] Office of Technology Assessment, *op. cit.*, p. 22.

[16] Quoted in the *Los Angeles Times*, May 5, 1988.

[17] Office of Technology Assessment, *op. cit.*, p. 12.

[18] Speech to the American Psychological Association, Aug. 31, 1987.

[19] Zuboff, *op. cit.*

Graphics: cover, p. 151, S. Dmitri Lipczenko.

RECOMMENDED READING

BOOKS

Betz, Frederick, *Mananging Technology: Competing Through New Ventures, Innovation and Corporate Research*, Prentice-Hall, Inc. 1987.

Dr. Betz, a professor of physics at the University of California at Berkeley, focuses on technological innovation in creating new products and services and, in turn, new business opportunities. "Managing technology means to use new technology to create competitive advantages. . . ," he writes. "Technology played a vital role in the original industrial revolution of the 18th and 19th centuries. Technological innovation continues to play an important role in industrial competitiveness and in the globalization of markets and industry that is occurring in the 20th century and into the 21st."

Davis, Donald D., et al., *Managing Technological Innovation*, Jossey-Bass Publishers, 1986.

Davis, an assistant professor of psychology and research scientist at the Center for Applied Psychological Studies at Old Dominion University, has brought together a number of scholars and experts in manufacturing to help explain why America is not using modern technology to its fullest advantage and what to do to correct the problem. "New technologies force organizations to reconsider their purpose and methods of operation," Davis writes. "Organizational strategies receptive to new technologies contribute to successful adaptation. Organizations that do not modify themselves to absorb newly adopted technologies never achieve their technological promise. Many American firms have disregarded these basic facts."

Garson, Barbara, *The Electronic Sweatshop: How Computers are Transforming the Office of the Future into the Factory of the Past*, Simon and Schuster, 1988.

Playwright Garson, through anecdotal sketches and interviews, shows the insidious side of office automation. Garson shows how human functions and intellect in industry are being replaced by machines, and says that everyone from cooks at McDonald's to Proctor and Gamble executives are in the process of becoming little more than clerical machines. "Right now a combination of 20th century technology and 19th century scientific management is turning the Office of the Future into the factory of the past," she writes.

Norman, Donald A., *The Psychology of Everyday Things*, Basic Books, 1988.

Norman, a professor of cognitive psychology at University of California, San Diego, shows why devices from light switches to computers work — and why they don't. Norman discusses the design process, the all too common design errors that make products and systems hard for humans to use and how those errors can be corrected.

Zuboff, Shoshana, *In the Age of the Smart Machine: The Future of Work and Power*, Basic Books, 1988.

Zuboff, an associate professor at the Harvard Business School, argues that we are at a watershed in technology history, where office automation can be used to rob workers of skills and job gratification, or where it can be used to give workers more information and autonomy than ever before. The theory is illustrated with case histories drawn from interviews of workers and managers. "Choices that appear to be merely technical will redefine our lives together at work," she writes. "This means more than simply contemplating the implications of consequences of a new technology. It means that a powerful new technology, such as that represented by the computer, fundamentally reorganizes the infrastructure of our material world. It eliminates former alternatives. It creates new possibilities. It necessitates fresh choices.

ARTICLES

Dreyfuss, Joel, "Catching the Computer Wave," *Fortune*, Sept. 26, 1988, pp. 78-82.

For executives who master the emerging office technologies, the payoff will be more power and greater control, the author states. The challenge is to stay on top of the technology as it evolves.

Kirkpatrick, David, "How Sage Are Video Terminals?" *Fortune*, August 29, 1988, pp. 66 +.
Just how much do we know about the effects of video terminal on the people who use them? Very little is the conclusion drawn by Kirkpatrick, who outlines the conflicting information now being uncovered and the questions that remain unresolved.

REPORTS

Office of Technolgy Assessment, *Automation of America's Offices*, December 1985.
This study analyzes trends in office automation through the year 2000, examining social and economic issues and the effects of federal policy on the development and use of office technology. "Office automation is more than the replacement of typewriters by word processors and of bookkeeping machines by computers; it is a basic far-reaching change in the technology that supports fundamental economic and social activities," the report summary states.

FREE MARKET ENVIRONMENTAL PROTECTION

FREE MARKET ENVIRONMENTAL PROTECTION

by Tom Arrandale

With pressure mounting to cut the budget deficit and make U.S. industry more competitive, some Bush administration officials say they have a way to make environmental protection more cost-effective: Offer industries financial incentives to clean up their own acts by charging them for polluting and rewarding them if they don't. It is a free-market approach to the environment that has gained support even among some environmental groups, but critics worry that it simply will give businesses a license to pollute.

In the nearly 20 years since environmentalists galvanized public opinion with the celebration of Earth Day, the federal government has passed dozens of laws and spent billions of dollars to clean up the environment. With a few notable exceptions, however, the environment still seems to be a mess. Summer smog alerts have become almost commonplace. Toxic wastes continue to leach into groundwater. Acid rain continues to fall. Medical wastes wash up on once pristine beaches. Scientists warn of the threat of global warming — the so-called "greenhouse effect" — caused by burning fossil fuels.

Now Congress and the Bush administration are weighing new campaigns to protect the environment. But even as they do so, the federal budget remains

Tom Arrandale is a free-lance writer in Albuquerque, N.M. He last wrote for E.R.R. in October 1988 on "The Battle for Natural Resources."

mired in deficit and U.S. industry is under siege from Japanese and European competition. Under current circumstances, says economist Robert N. Stavins of Harvard University's John F. Kennedy School of Government, "if we're going to have environmental protection, we've got to do it at the least cost possible."

The Reagan administration, when it was faced with that problem, opted for slashing EPA's budget, imposing "cost-benefit" tests for environmental protection rules, and promoting private development of resources from federally owned lands. The Reagan approach provoked the wrath of environmentalists, who said the policies only allowed environmental problems to get worse.

For its part, the Bush administration, joined by some economists, environmentalists and industry leaders, say they have a better idea — one that Stavins says is "180 degrees different" from Reagan's brand of environmental deregulation. Arguing that the old "command-and-control" approach embodied in the environmental laws of the 1970s* has bogged down in red tape and courtroom battles, they say it's time to let market forces rather than government edict be the driving force behind cleaning up the environment. Congress would still set national environmental standards, they say. But instead of regulating the way factories operate, the government would give businessmen and communities incentives to meet pollution control goals as cheaply and efficiently as possible.

Current laws give federal and state officials authority to fine polluters, and in recent years the threat of legal liability judgments costing millions of dollars has given industry an incentive to do better. On Aug. 15, for example, Alaska sued Exxon Corp. and six other oil companies for unspecified damages, charging negligence in the *Exxon Valdez* grounding that spilled nearly 11 million gallons of crude oil into Prince William Sound. But some businesses have used the current law to their advantage, finding it more profitable to stall action through time-consuming regulatory and legal challenges than to comply promptly with regulations. Economists suggest that market-based policies could provide more powerful financial incentives than the threat of legal action for limiting or preventing pollution.

Not only would such an approach be much less expensive for the federal government, the proponents say, but it might actually work. Current regulatory efforts often pose choices between preserving the environment and promoting economic activity, says Stavins, but "economic-incentive approaches ... make the market a partner, rather than an adversary, in the search for environmental protection."[1]

Last year, Stavins was commissioned by two U.S.

*Under the "command and control" approach, the government sets the amount of pollutants industry or individuals can discharge into the environment, with the Environmental Protection Agency and other government agencies monitoring and enforcing the limits.

Environmental Expenditures

Strong public support for environmental improvement resulted in the adoption during the 1970s of a host of environmental protection laws. These laws, in turn, stimulated significant increases in environmental expenditures by both government and the private sector. During the early 1980s, however, business and government spending on pollution control declined. The decline in government spending was due primarily to changes in spending for sewer system construction, which is the largest single component of government spending on pollution control. Business spending dropped primarily because of declines in new plant and equipment expenditures for pollution control. Total spending increased substantially in the mid 1980s. The slight drop in 1987 was largely the result of declines in personal and business purchases of emission abatement devices on motor vehicles.

billions of constant 1982 dollars

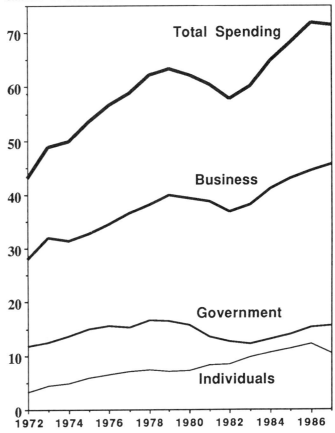

Source: Bureau of Economic Analysis, U.S. Department of Commerce

senators — Timothy E. Wirth, D-Colo., and John Heinz, R.-Pa. — to review market-based alternatives to current environmental programs. That effort, known as Project 88, presented the incoming Bush administration with 36 broad-brush recommendations to curb pollution and protect natural resources by taking advantage of economic incentives.[2] Proposed market incentives take several forms, but here are some of the more compelling ones:

■ **Imposing taxes or fees on pollution.** The government would charge businesses for each ton or other unit of pollution discharged, setting the fees high enough to encourage businesses to curtail emissions and to develop efficient pollution-control systems.

■ **Issuing pollution permits that corporations could buy and sell.** Under this program, EPA would set limits on the amount of pollution a company could legally discharge. Companies that reduced emissions below their allocation could sell their unused emission rights to companies having difficulty meeting their allocation levels. Some companies might find it cheaper to buy emission credits from other companies than to invest in expensive pollution control equipment for aging factories; others might find investing in anti-pollution equipment and selling surplus emission credits to be more profitable.

■ **Requiring deposits on hazardous materials.** The government would charge a tax on hazardous materials, then grant refunds for each unit of waste that was recycled or disposed of in proper fashion. The difference between the deposit and refund would amount to a net tax on wastes that companies failed to reclaim. By raising the net tax to higher levels, the government could strengthen incentives for recycling and waste disposal.

■ **Ending archaic government subsidies.** The government would repeal existing subsidies that promote destructive harvesting of national forest timber, inefficient irrigation systems, overgrazing on federal rangelands, and other practices that waste public resources and degrade the environment.

In concept, such mechanisms would force businesses and consumers to take costs to the environment into account in day-to-day economic decisions. The devices, in effect, would be a cost for businesses and communities that damage the environment — while offering financial rewards for those that take the strongest cleanup measures. Once in place, economists argue, market incentives would prod polluters to devise innovative ways to control emissions more effectively — and at lower cost — than less flexible federal and state regulations can order.

The U.S. Environmental Protection Agency (EPA), the agency charged with enforcing federal pollution-control laws, has been experimenting with the so-called market approach to environmental protection for more than a decade. Since 1976, the agency has approved the trading of emission rights among factories in industrial zones with heavily polluted air. (*See story, p. 172.*) "Emission trading sounds weird," *Newsweek* contributing editor Gregg Easterbrook wrote recently, ". . . but nearly everyone who studies pollution regulation concludes that what's missing is a positive inducement that works from the bottom up, supplanting the conventional structure of costs imposed from the top down. Emission trading will allow engineers rather than regulators to judge which factories can meet standards most

efficiently while adding a profit motive for inventing improved controls." [3]

Current EPA Administrator William K. Reilly, a former Conservation Foundation president, has frequently called for fresh approaches to environmental protection, such as "debt-for-nature" swaps that forgive Third World nations' international debt in return for protecting imperiled rain forests. At EPA, Reilly has met with Project 88 participants and named an agency task force to study market-based approaches.

So far, the Project 88 approach has met a mixed reception in Congress. Rep. Henry A. Waxman, D-Calif., a leading proponent of tougher air-quality regulations as chairman of the House Energy and Commerce Subcommittee on Health and Environment, has given guarded support to using economic incentives in some cases. But Waxman also warns that he supports market-based controls "only when we can be certain that the measure will not be used by industry to delay or derail pollution reductions."

Many environmentalists and government pollution-control officials are even more skeptical. They worry that market incentives amount to granting industries "licenses to pollute" without producing real improvements in environmental quality. The basic question, they say, is whether the federal government could better protect the environment by devising economic incentives or by strengthening pollution-control laws and enforcing them more vigorously.

Michael McCloskey, the Sierra Club's national chairman, contends that the case for market incentives "really is built around how to save costs to the economy. It's not an argument for how you get more cleanup." Even industry, which has spent 20 years adjusting to the command-and-control system, may be reluctant to junk it in favor of untested market mechanisms. "Project 88 is so vague — 14 pages on air pollution," notes William D. Fay, administrator of a business lobby coalition called the Clean Air Working Group. "I'm not sure we're ready to jettison volumes and volumes of air-quality regulations and proceedings . . . for a 14-page summary."

Nevertheless, market-based incentives seem to have caught President Bush's eye and have every indication of holding a prominent place in environmental protection in the future. Take acid rain, for example. The clean-air proposals Bush sent Congress in July featured market incentives as part of its strategy for curbing sulfur dioxide and nitrogen oxide emissions from utility plants in Midwestern states. The emissions from those plants are believed to be responsible for acid rain that has devastated lakes, streams and forests in the East, Northeast and Canada. The president's plan, instead of taking the usual command-and-control tactic of forcing the utilities to install costly smokestack "scrubbers," would permit plant managers to choose any emissions-reduction technology they wanted.

Market Forces and Water Conservation

In Western states, market forces already are at work encouraging water conservation. In a predominantly arid region, access to water supplies has always been critical for economic activity. After Congress passed the Reclamation Act of 1903, the federal government built huge dams across the West's scattered rivers and streams to generate electric power and supply low-cost water for irrigated farms and municipal water systems. Federally subsidized projects supplied farmers with cut-rate water that encouraged wasteful irrigation practices. But federal budget deficits have helped bring the dam-building era to an end, and Western states no longer can count on new projects to augment their supplies. As fast-growing cities seeking more water now have started buying farmers' rights, prices have risen and lively water markets evolved across the region. Water's increasing value is creating new economic incentives to conserve scarce supplies and protect them from pollution.

But federal water policies and Western state water laws still present obstacles to using water more efficiently. U.S. Bureau of Reclamation rules have cast doubt on whether many water rights could be bought and sold, and the "use it or lose it" doctrine embedded in most Western state water laws means that farmers risk forfeiting rights if they cut water consumption.

In one pioneering step, proposed by the Environmental Defense Fund, the Metropolitan Water District (MWD) serving Los Angeles last year struck a deal to obtain additional supplies by financing water conservation by Southern California farmers. Under that agreement, MWD will pay $155 million for water-saving investments by the Imperial Irrigation District. In return, Los Angeles will obtain rights to at least 100,000 acre-feet of Colorado River water. Environmental Defense Fund attorneys and economists say the deal sets a precedent for similar water-conserving agreements across the West. In addition to ending wasteful use, more efficient irrigation practices will reduce "non-point" runoff from fields bearing pesticides and concentrated salts that eventually reach groundwater or rivers.

An acre-foot of water is the quantity needed to flood one acre to a depth of one foot. Equal to 325,851 gallons, an acre-foot of water is enough for one family of five for a year.

With Congress no longer willing to fully fund construction of new dams and aqueducts, the U.S. Bureau of Reclamation and the Army Corps of Engineers are shifting their missions away from building new projects to managing existing water delivery and flood control systems.

But continuing subsidies still allow California farmers to pay as little as $10 for water to irrigate an acre of cotton, while Los Angeles pays $600 for the same quantity. Some Denver suburbs now pay more than $2,500 for the right to use an acre-foot of water.

The Project 88 report called on the U.S. Interior Department to clear away regulations that present obstacles to marketing rights to water that federal projects supply to farmers. Environmental Defense Fund officials Tom Graff and Zach Willey have called for a thorough overhaul of federal water policies that encourage wasteful uses that contribute to water pollution.

As one step, Graff and Willey recommend that EPA scrap existing technology-based water-pollution regulations and replace them with tradable discharge permits. Under their plan, EPA would set a total discharge limit for each river basin, then issue marketable permits to communities, firms, farms and other facilities that release sewage, discharge industrial wastes or serve as the source of "non-point" runoff to its waters. To improve water quality in the basin, EPA could periodically purchase and retire discharge permits.†

† *Zach Willey and Tom Graff, "Federal Water Policy in the United States — An Agenda for Economic and Environmental Reform,"* Columbia Journal of Environmental Law, *1988 Vol. 13, No. 2, p. 346.*

For example, they might substitute low-sulfur coal for the high-sulfur coal now used. Plants that exceeded their required reductions would be allowed to trade or sell unused emissions permits to other plants. The Project 88 report concluded that "a market-based approach to acid-rain reduction could save us $3 billion per year, compared with the cost of a dictated technological solution."

Command and control: Regulations and red tape

Public concern for the environment has been growing steadily since 1962, when Rachel Carson published *Silent Spring*, a plea to curb the use of the pesticide DDT. Many Americans came to believe that industry would not control air and water pollutants or conserve natural resources unless the federal government forced it to. On Earth Day, April 22, 1970, millions attended environmental teach-ins and anti-pollution rallies around the country, a dramatic testimonial to public sensitivity to environmental degradation — and to the potential political power of the environmental movement.

President Nixon responded with an executive order creating the Environmental Protection Agency on Dec. 2, 1970, which immediately assumed the existing environmental responsibilities of other departments and agencies. Congress quickly gave EPA responsibility for several new laws, including the landmark Clean Air Amendments of 1970, which set limits on auto pollutants and strengthened air-quality standards, and the Water Pollution Control Act Amendments of

> *"Economic-incentive approaches . . . make the market a partner, rather than an adversary, in the search for environmental protection," says economist Robert N. Stavins of Harvard University's John F. Kennedy School of Government.*

1972, which expanded the government's powers to clean up the nation's waters. In later years EPA was also given authority to control noise, pesticides and other toxic substances, provide clean drinking water and clean up toxic contaminants.*

In writing the environmental-protection laws, Congress opted for a strategy that required polluting facilities to obtain federal permits that set limits on the amount of pollutants they could release into the environment. In granting a permit, EPA and state environmental agencies usually directed plant managers to install smokestack "scrubbers," filters or "the best

available technology" to reduce or eliminate harmful emissions.

But drafting and enforcing federal environmental standards proved to be exceedingly difficult. If often took EPA years to come up with pollutant standards, and it was often many more years before state governments drew up implementation plans that EPA found acceptable.

From the beginning, EPA has been pulled by competing political pressures: Environmentalists pressure the agency to punish polluters, while businesses want to reduce red tape. Business interests complain that EPA often imposes tougher requirements on new facilities than on older ones, a practice critics say encourages firms to keep operating outmoded plants while discouraging investments that would make U.S. companies more competitive in world markets. Critics also argue that the current system favors existing pollution-control methods but gives companies little incentive to develop superior emission-control equipment with greater long-term pollution reductions.

EPA's enforcement efforts have often bogged down in detailed regulation drafting, lengthy administrative proceedings, courtroom hearings and negotiations. Take the case of Kennecott Copper Corp. Kennecott closed a Nevada copper smelter in the 1970s after a court upheld EPA regulations requiring the facility to install equipment to control sulfur dioxide (SO_2) emissions. Kennecott subsequently persuaded the state of Nevada to revise its air-quality implementation plan to allow firms to control SO_2 emissions through tall smokestacks or production cutbacks, then went to court to force EPA to accept the state's decision. The suit was successful, and the court annulled the EPA regulations.

EPA's regulatory efforts have also been subject to congressional meddling. For instance, in the 1977 amendments to the Clean Air Act, Congress ordered EPA to require electric utilities to install costly emission scrubbers on all new coal-burning power plants.* Congress was responding in part to pressure from Eastern coal companies and the United Mine Workers, who wanted to preserve jobs in Appalachia's high-sulfur coal mines by preventing firms from complying with sulfur dioxide emission limits by burning low-sulfur Western coal.

In an unlikely political alliance, environmental groups joined with Eastern coal interests in lobbying for the scrubber requirements. Environmentalists said the scrubbers would ensure the maximum possible reductions in emissions from each new power plant, including those built near low-sulfur coal deposits in Rocky Mountain states with nearly pristine air, and would reduce demand for Western coal extracted by destructive strip-mining techniques. But what really

---

*For background, see "Closing the Environmental Decade," E.R.R., 1979 Vol. II, pp. 821-840.

*The resulting EPA regulations were upheld by a 1981 District of Columbia Circuit Court ruling, *Sierra Club v. Costle.*

happened, according to Yale University Law School scholars Bruce A. Ackerman and William T. Hassler, was "an extraordinary decision that will cost the public tens of billions of dollars to achieve environmental goals that could be reached more cheaply, more quickly, and more surely by other means." [4]

The scrubber decision was not unusual. When Congress passed the major environmental laws during the 1970s, cost was not often a consideration. But by the 1980s cost had become a major concern. Between 1983 and 1987, the United States spent $336 billion on pollution control, according to the Bureau of Economic Analysis in the U.S. Department of Commerce. In 1987 alone, total expenditures for pollution control amounted to over $71 billion (in constant 1982 dollars). Private industry paid more than 60 percent of the bill, government more than 20 percent and consumers paid the rest. (*See graph, p. 163.*)

Such expenditures might have been acceptable if they worked, but critics contend that what the government bought for all that money was not much at all. What happened, the critics say, is that early on EPA officials, instead of making tough political judgments, defended proposed regulations against industry challenges by trying to marshal scientific data on pollution effects.

But that task required EPA to make complex scientific and engineering judgments that overloaded agency administrators and invited legal challenges from companies that found it cheaper to go to court than to comply. The resulting heavy workload prevented EPA from dealing with other emerging environmental problems.

It also seemed to prevent the government from keeping track of how well its environmental regulations were working. While committing enormous resources to devise and defend regulations, EPA delegated most enforcement power to state agencies; between 1979 and 1985 the agency spent only 8 to 10.5 percent of its own budget on enforcement actions. The Conservation Foundation reports that by 1984, "approximately 70 percent of EPA's day-to-day responsibilities for environmental enforcement had been delegated to the states." [5]

"Our current environmental regulatory system was an understandable response to a perceived need for immediate controls to prevent a pollution crisis," Harvard Law School professor Richard B. Stewart wrote in 1988. "But the system has grown to the point where it amounts to nothing less than a massive effort at Soviet-style central planning of the economy to achieve environmental goals. It strangles investment and innovation. It encourages costly and divisive litigation and delay. It unduly limits private initiative and choice. The centralized command system is simply unacceptable as a long-term environmental protection strategy for a large and diverse nation committed to the market and decentralized ordering." [6]

Pollution Control: How the Money Was Spent

The great bulk of the expenditures for pollution control have gone for activities that directly reduce pollutant emissions. Critics of the current "command-and-control" system say environmental quality would be better if more money had been spent on monitoring how well environmental regulations and equipment were working.

billions of constant 1982 dollars

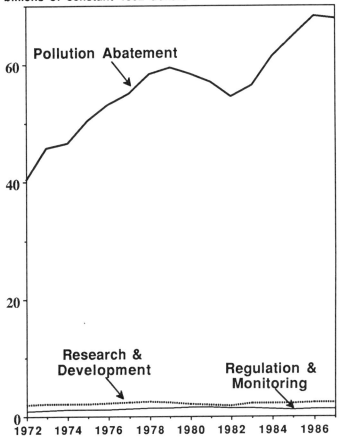

Source: Bureau of Economic Analysis, U.S. Department of Commerce

Tradable emission permits: Will financial incentives work?

Stewart and other advocates of controlling environmental risks through economic incentives would rely on the "invisible hand" of market forces to guide decisions on how the nation should meet its pollution-reduction goals. Through various means, they would set a price on conduct that creates pollution or environmental risk, then let each company or other entity decide for itself how much to pay and how much to reduce emissions.

One way this could be done is with "tradable emission permits." Under this approach, the government would set a national cap on certain pollutants

Discouraging Destructive Development...

Current environmental policy debates focus primarily on using market incentives to encourage steps to control pollution. But some economists also call on the federal government to review current laws and practices that invite environmental destruction by promoting destructive use of the nation's land and natural resources. Those policies grant subsidies or provide government support that artificially encourages wasteful resource development projects that by themselves cannot stand the test of economic efficiency.

Those policies are often holdovers from the era when the federal government was encouraging settlers to convert swamplands to fields, harvest timber and grasslands, and turn other untapped resources into commodities for economic expansion. Those incentives reflect a philosophy that environmentalists say is no longer appropriate to a nation that now values wildlife, wilderness and outdoor recreation.

Previous generations, for instance, regarded wetlands simply as swamps that stood in the way of progress. From colonial times, landowners have drained wetlands, cleared their trees, filled them with soil, and converted them to farm fields and residential areas. Federal flood control and soil conservation programs have provided financial assistance to those efforts. As a result, less than half of the nation's original wetlands are left, and development continues to destroy them at the rate of 458,000 acres a year.

Biologists now see natural wetlands as vital wildlife breeding grounds that purify water supplies and regulate water flows to retard flooding. But landowners cannot profit from those benefits, so they instead alter wetlands to earn economic returns from development. And federal efforts to regulate wetland conversion and to buy them for wildlife refuges meet stiff resistance from development interests.

Bush has endorsed a "no net loss" policy calling for steps to discourage wetland conversion and artificially replace those that are developed. Congress in recent years has repealed tax benefits for wetland conversion and denied federal farm subsidies for "Swampbusters" who drain wetlands for cultivation. The impact of those changes has yet to be felt, and the Project 88 report called for more comprehensive strategies, including "self-enforcing inducements for people to take account of the full social value of wetlands."

Near major cities, the spread of suburban development also is threatening open spaces provided by farmland. As housing tracts and shopping malls move outward from city lines, farmers can earn more by selling lands to developers than by keeping them in production. Near Brentwood in California's Contra Costa County, a farming region that lies in the path of suburban expansion eastward from San Francisco Bay, farmlands that sold for $6,000 an acre five years ago could be worth $85,000 an acre once they are an-

nexed and zoned for subdivisions. Some Contra Costa County farmers, environmentalists and planners have come up with a plan for the county to buy development rights to about 17,000 acres of prime crop lands, in effect paying landowners to keep the land in farming by making up the difference from what they could earn by selling to developers.

Over the last two decades, several states and some county governments have created tax breaks and bought development rights to provide financial incentives to preserve open space around metropolitan regions. Wisconsin, for instance, grants state income tax credits to farmers who agree to restrict development of their lands for 10 years. The Nature Conservancy and other private groups have protected millions of acres by purchasing them outright or buying conservation easements from owners who agree to keep lands in natural condition. In a 1987 report that the Reagan administration disavowed the President's Commission on Americans Outdoors recommended a national "greenway" program to preserve streamside habitat in fast-growing areas through financial incentives for donations, easements, leases and restrictive land-use covenants.

In managing its own public lands, conservation groups for decades have charged that the federal government encourages destructive resource use without adequately protecting natural values. Producers pay the government fees for access to federally owned resources.

and allocate pollution rights among polluters. A firm could either invest in new technology to reduce its emissions or buy permits or credits from another firm whose emissions fall below the standard. To assure further progress in cleaning up the environment, the

government could "ratchet down" overall emissions of pollutants by cutting the total number of permits.

Some economists favor a system in which emission permits would be auctioned off instead of granted free of charge. They say this approach would enable the

...of Land and Natural Resources

But in many areas, the government spends far more to manage public lands than it takes in from leasing or selling resources. Commodity production on federal lands in recent years has brought the government between $2.5 billion and $3 billion a year in revenues. But the government has been spending $5.5 billion to $6 billion to manage those lands and share mineral leasing and timber sale revenues with state and local governments.

Except for national parks and wilderness areas, the government manages most of its 700 million acres of federal lands for multiple uses. While Congress directs the U.S. Interior Department and U.S. Forest Service to give equal weight to wildlife and recreation, environmentalists complain that the agencies favor commodity production from mining, logging and livestock grazing. Land managers typically give less weight to hard-to-quantify benefits from wildlife and recreation that show no immediate returns in federal receipts and in revenue-sharing payments to local governments where public lands are located.

Both the Interior Department and the Forest Service lease public range lands for grazing at fees far below what private range lands command; bankers and real-estate agents recognize that access to low-cost federal grazing confers a "permit value" that raises a ranch's worth. Stockmen maintain that the below-market fees are justified by the expense of feeding and controlling livestock on public lands, but envi-

ronmentalists argue that they provide a subsidy that encourages overstocking of federally owned range.

In recent years, The Wilderness Society and other conservation groups have begun challenging Forest Service timber sales in the Appalachians, the Rocky Mountains and Alaska on economic grounds. After subtracting the costs of preparing sales and sharing 25 percent of receipts with county governments, two out of three national forests actually lost money selling timber in 1985, according to Randall O'Toole, an Oregon forestry consultant. Critics contend that Forest Service accounting practices encourage logging on steep slopes and other sensitive lands while ignoring the growing value of national forests for wildlife and recreation. O'Toole contends that the Forest Service loses $22 million a year selling timber for logging on six national forests surrounding Yellowstone National Park that produce $20 in recreation benefits for every dollar of timber benefits. "These losses are irrational from a conservation as well as an economic viewpoint," he says.†

Critics say the Forest Service prices its timber through an archaic system that virtually ignores the government's cost of growing trees and offering them for harvest. O'Toole recommends that national forest management be "marketized" by requiring the Forest Service to earn market prices for its timber, halting current practices that in effect subsidize timber sales with federal funds for road-building and

planting new trees, and forcing the agency to pay its own way without congressional appropriations.

However, the ranchers and loggers who benefit from those policies are small but well-organized groups that lobby Western congressional delegations vigorously against changes. Congress for years has refused to raise federal grazing fees to market levels, instead imposing a formula that keeps fees low by tying them to ranching costs and livestock prices. And low-cost timber sales provide logs for sawmills that often provide most of the jobs in small towns near national forests. State and local governments dependent on revenue sharing from federal lands also resist proposals that would curtail timber harvests and other economic development.

Wilderness Society economists are studying a proposal that would reduce political resistance to reforms by severing the link between revenue sharing and commodity production, no longer basing local government shares on the amount of timber harvested or minerals extracted. Environmental groups generally remain suspicious that economists' approaches would lead to recreation fees for backpackers, hunters, and others who now enjoy free use of public lands. "Most of these ideas are fairly controversial politically," Hahn observes, "so it will take time [to implement them]."

† Randall O'Toole, "Reforming the Forest Service," Columbia Journal of Environmental Law, *1988 Vol. 13, No. 2, p. 299.*

government to raise substantial revenue for environmental research or for reducing the federal deficit. One study cited in a 1988 article by Stewart and Bruce Ackerman estimates that the sale of emission permits could raise between $6 billion and $10 billion annually.[7]

Robert W. Hahn, a senior staff economist for the President's Council of Economic Advisers, and a colleague have estimated that the EPA's current program allowing limited marketing of air-quality permits has saved industry more than $4 billion in costs without making air quality worse.[8] (*See story, p. 172.*)

President's Bush's recommendations for reducing acid rain follow a similar line. Past congressional proposals to combat acid rain would have required Midwestern utilities to install smokestack scrubbers to control sulfur dioxide and nitrogen oxide emissions. In his clean-air bill, Bush proposed steps to force more than 300 electric power plants to cut SO_2 emissions by 10 million tons and nitrogen oxide emissions by 2 million tons. But the White House plan would let

> *"Our current environmental regulatory system . . . has grown to the point where it amounts to nothing less than a massive effort at Soviet-style central planning of the economy to achieve environmental goals. It strangles investment and innovation. It encourages costly and divisive litigation and delay," says Harvard Law Professor Richard B. Stewart.*

utilities decide for themselves how to achieve those reductions. Incentives for meeting the reductions would come from marketable emission permits. Companies that reduced pollutants below their allocation could sell their unused emission credits to firms that were unable to meet their limits.

EPA has released studies concluding that meeting similar emissions goals by installing smokestack controls would cost $2.3 billion, while a measure allowing emission permit trading would meet the same goal at a cost of $1.5 billion. A report by ICF Inc., a Virginia-based environmental consultant, suggests that scrubbers would still be the cheapest way for some power

plants to comply, and that tighter limits would force even more utilities to adopt smokestack controls.[9] But Bush's plan would let others select less costly alternatives. These might include switching to low-sulfur coal, trying new coal-cleaning technologies, shutting down heavily polluting plants except during peak demand periods, replacing older units with natural gas-fired generators, or offering customers incentives to cut electricity use by buying high-efficiency appliances and lighting fixtures.

The administration program also would grant marketable emission credits to automobile manufacturers that produce vehicles outperforming federal emissions standards and to refiners that surpass clean-fuel standards. "We've provided the goals but we won't try to micro-manage them," the president said in announcing the plan. "We will allow flexibility in how industry achieves these goals, but we stand firm on what must be achieved." [10]

Business and environmental lobbyists still are sorting out the president's proposals. While businessmen want more flexible air-quality controls, they are waiting to see how marketable emission permits would fit in the existing command-and-control structure. Among other unanswered questions is whether the government would issue the marketable permits free of charge or auction them off to the highest bidders.

Industry also fears that regulators would defeat the purpose of market-incentive mechanisms by imposing complicated monitoring and reporting requirements. "We're a little skeptical of the agency that's going to be issuing the permits," says William Fay of the Clean Air Working Group. "Just like the Treasury always interprets the tax laws to raise more government revenue, EPA when it interprets a law always interprets it for more control."

The Edison Electric Institute, a utility industry trade group, and several utilities have criticized Bush's acid-rain plan as harsh, inflexible and too costly. W. S. White Jr., chairman of American Electric Power Company, the nation's largest coal user, predicts that utilities seeking to buy marketable emission-offset credits in order to build new power plants or run older facilities at full power will find that demand outstrips supply. Eventually, White says, "it may become impossible to find additional offsets at any price."

Some influential environmentalists also have serious questions about Bush's acid-rain plan, but they've indicated a willingness to keep an open mind about it. Says the Sierra Club's McCloskey, "I come out as a guarded skeptic, not as a hard-core opponent." And Edward J. Barks, a spokesman for the National Clean Air Coalition, which represents most of the major conservation groups on clean-air issues, says his organization is willing to consider a marketable-permit system, but adds that the coalition insists that pollution standards still be set by the federal government to prevent threats to human health.

William Becker, executive director of the State and

Territorial Air Pollution Administrators Association, says an emissions-credit system must be closely monitored to make sure that utility transactions produce overall acid-rain reductions. "There can be good trades and there can be sloppy trades, and the latter will exacerbate the problem we're trying to solve in the first place," Becker says. "It would be ludicrous to allow a Midwestern utility to pollute more and a Florida utility to pollute less. The result would be more acid rain [in the Northeast]." Even if emissions trading is allowed between existing plants, Becker adds, new plants still should be fitted with state-of-the-art emission equipment to assure maximum control of pollutants.

The Project 88 report: An alternative approach

The debate over Bush's clean-air proposals will test how much Congress is willing to trust market forces to protect the environment. "Whether the clean-air bill is the first of a series [of market-based proposals], it's just too early to tell," says Robert Hahn of the Council of Economic Advisers. But market-approach advocates like Hahn now hold several White House and EPA posts, and the administration now is studying wider use of economic incentives. The Project 88 report suggests that Congress encourage wider use of EPA's emissions-trading program by writing authority into the Clean Air Act itself, thus giving businesses greater confidence that credits they accumulate will remain available for future use.

The Project 88 report also advocates extending the marketable-permit system to the federal clean-water program. Instead of just requiring industry to install effluent-control equipment, the report suggests that EPA set overall limits on polluted discharges to watersheds and then issue tradable permits to control pollution levels. While conceding that regulatory approaches may play a larger role, the report also urges combining them with marketable permits as incentives for reducing hard-to-control water pollution from "non-point" sources, such as runoff from farmers' fields and urban streets.

Hahn says the administration also is considering market incentives for removing asbestos from buildings and is looking at recommendations in the Project 88 report for using economic incentives as part of international efforts to control global warming and phase out chemicals that destroy the atmosphere's protective ozone layer.

EPA in 1987 outlined a plan to issue marketable permits as part of its strategy to implement an international agreement to freeze and subsequently reduce use of chlorofluorocarbons (CFCs) and other chemical compounds that scientists have found deplete the

Spending on Major Pollution Control Programs

During the 15 years from 1972 to 1987, the bulk of the expenditures for pollution control were for water and air, with the remainder going primarily to solid waste. The fall in total pollution control spending in the early 1980s (see graph, p. 163) was caused primarily by the large decline in spending on water pollution control.

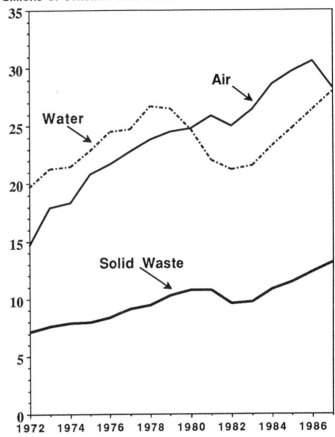

billions of constant 1982 dollars

Source: Bureau of Economic Analysis, U.S. Department of Commerce

ozone layer protecting the earth's surface from ultraviolet radiation. The agency envisions granting tradable permits allowing manufacturers to produce or import specified annual quantities of potential ozone depleters. As annual quotas are cut, permits are expected to rise in value, giving users incentives to replace or recycle the gases where possible and to commit limited supplies for the most essential purposes.

Project 88 suggests applying similar market approaches to reverse global warming, which is occurring, many scientists say, because of a "greenhouse effect" caused by the release of carbon dioxide into the atmosphere when fossil fuels are burned. The report calls for a comprehensive national energy policy to promote alternative fuels; debt-for-nature swaps that would

Trading Air Quality Permits

By the mid-1970s, it was obvious that many major metropolitan areas in the country would be unable to comply with the air quality standards that Congress had set in the 1970 Clean Air Act. EPA officials realized there would be unacceptable economic consequences if the agency barred construction of any new factories or other polluting facilities in these "non-attainment" regions.

As a way out of this dilemma, EPA in 1976 devised an "offset" policy enabling businesses that reduced emissions from one facility to earn emission credits they could use to increase emissions from a new facility nearby. Firms could also bank credits for future use, or sell them to other companies wishing to expand their facilities.

Then, in 1979, EPA gave firms more flexibility in reducing pollution from existing plants. It approved a "bubble" policy that allowed existing plants to make major changes in their facilities without complying with all of the standards governing new sources of pollution. Under the bubble approach, as long as pollution from a new source in one part of a plant is offset by reductions in emissions from another part, the plant as a whole would be treated as though it were a single unit enclosed in a bubble.

The goal is not just to allow flexibility for economic reasons. These policies also have been designed to help assure overall improvements in air quality by requiring that offsetting reductions exceed new pollutant emissions. In Los Angeles, for instance, every pound of pollutant produced by a new company must be counterbalanced by reducing emissions somewhere else by 1.67 pounds.

Those who say emissions trading works often cite a 1987 study by G. L. Hester and Robert W. Hahn, a senior staff economist for the President's Council of Economic Advisers. They estimated that EPA's emission trading policies had saved more than $4 billion in pollution control costs with no adverse impact on overall air quality.[†]

But many environmentalists remain skeptical. They contend that the policy prevents the country from achieving the best possible air quality by letting heavy polluters buy credits instead of forcing them to reduce emissions. Critics also complain that EPA has tolerated "paper trades," in which companies claim credits for previously achieved emission cutbacks, for closing outmoded facilities, or for steps they probably would have taken without market incentives.

Not all environmentalists are categorically opposed to emissions trading, however. Daniel Dudek, a senior economist with the Environmental Defense Fund, and John Palmisano, president of an emissions trading consulting firm, contend that EPA's program has demonstrated that "market incentives which enlist the expertise of on-site managers can achieve more pollution control results for less money, now instead of later." But they complain that widespread trading in emissions credits remains "handicapped by bureaucratic inertia and infighting, dogmatic opposition by environmentalists, hostility in Congress, as well as indifference by polluters." [††]

EPA does not require states to permit emissions trades. Even where trading is allowed, advocates acknowledge that companies have been reluctant to participate unless they are forced to buy credits to open new facilities. For one thing, companies fear that the government will tighten air quality standards in the future, denying use of credits companies have saved for future expansion. "Before industry can widely use emissions trading concepts, Congress, EPA, and states must make the rules more certain," Dudek and Palmisano argue.

[†] *Robert W. Hahn and G.L. Hester, "The Market for Bads: EPA's Experience with Emissions Trading,"* Regulation, 1987, pp. 48-53.

[††] *Daniel J. Dudek and John Palmisano, "Emissions Trading: Why Is This Thoroughbred Hobbled?"* Columbia Journal of Environmental Law, 1988 Vol. 13, No. 2, p. 218.

forgive Third World nations' international debt in return for preserving tropical rain forests; and an international system for trading permits to continue emitting carbon dioxide, CFCs and other gases that contribute to the greenhouse effect.

Economists contend that market incentives also can play major roles in forcing safe handling of hazardous substances. As federal regulation of such substances has tightened, the cost of placing hazardous wastes in a dump has risen from about $10 a ton in 1980 to as much as $500 a ton, giving firms an incentive to reduce how much waste they produce and to recycle hazardous materials. And the threat of financial liability may be emerging as a forceful spur for firms to handle toxic materials more carefully. Near Rochester, N.Y., for instance, a Xerox factory paid a $95,000 fine for failing to report that trichloroethylene from the plant was seeping toward nearby residential wells. But more significantly, the company also paid $4.75 million to two families whose wells were contaminated.

Several states have adopted "bottle" laws to reduce solid waste by imposing refundable deposits on glass beverage containers. Seattle is trying to encourage recycling by collecting cans, bottles, newspapers and junk mail for free, but charging $13.55 a month to pick up one garbage can of refuse weekly. West Germany has encouraged motor oil recycling by charging a levy on new lubricants and using revenues to subsidize development of an oil recycling industry. Norway and Sweden tax new cars and refund the levy to owners when they deliver unusable vehicles to authorized scrap dealers.

Project 88 suggested a similar deposit-refund system for small quantities of hazardous materials that can be transported in containers and dumped just about anywhere. A front-end tax would be imposed on newly manufactured solvents and other products. It would be refunded on toxic wastes that were turned in to designated facilities for disposal or recycling. The tax would encourage producers to substitute less dangerous substances, while the refund would provide an incentive for recycling and disposal. The system would discourage illegal dumping that is nearly impossible to control. Wirth and Heinz have proposed legislation setting up incentives modeled on Project 88 proposals for recycling used motor oil.

Doubts about market approaches

Proponents make clear that economic approaches are not a cure-all for every form of ecological damage. Pollution taxes, permit trading, deposit systems and other proposals can work only for pollution or health risks that can be measured and monitored. Stewart suggests that such devices may be unworkable for managing risks from pesticides, for instance, or from pollutants that become dangerous only if they exceed "threshold" concentrations at a single location. Even the Project 88 report acknowledged that setting more stringent motor vehicle emission standards may be the most effective way to reduce air pollution by automobiles.

Proponents also acknowledge that their ideas face resistance from Congress, environmentalists and regulatory officials steeped in a regulatory system designed to punish, not reward, private-sector actions that affect the environment. A marketable-permit system would require EPA and state environmental officials to monitor permit transactions and emission levels instead of evaluating how industry controls emissions. "Regulators may at first feel that they have less control over the system, because actual pollution-control decisions will be made by polluters, not by the government," the Project 88 report points out. "This, of course, is the whole point of the marketable-permit approach."

So far, state officials and leaders of environmental organizations say they are willing to look closely at proposed market incentives, but skeptics argue that although market incentives may be attractive in theory, they might turn out to be just as difficult to administer as existing regulations. As Rutgers University law Professor Howard Latin put it in a 1985 law review

> *"We're a little skeptical of the agency that's going to be issuing the [pollution] permits," says William Fay of the Clean Air Working Group. "Just like the Treasury always interprets the tax laws to raise more government revenue, EPA when it interrupts a law always interprets it for more control."*

article, market approach theories "represent wishful thinking rather than a realistic appraisal of present environmental knowledge and regulatory capabilities." [11]

Some environmentalists also offer a more fundamental objection to substituting market influences for direct controls on contaminants that threaten human health or the quality of life. Removal of direct regulatory controls would let some industries continue to pollute without taking steps to control emissions as much as possible, they contend, making it more difficult to bring about overall pollution reductions.

Despite its imperfections, environmentalists contend, the existing command-and-control system has improved the environment at a cost that most Americans find acceptable. "Most of us would grant that EPA seems to be badly bogged down right now, but it's an open question whether with good leadership it will be able to generate some progress," says the Sierra Club's McCloskey. Nevertheless, even McCloskey agrees that market approaches offer an appealing vision of "what seems to be an automatic system sending the right signals to all of the actors."

Past Coverage

■ **Setting Environmental Priorities** compares the multitude of environmental problems facing the nation and the world in order to determine which problems are the most serious and which should be tackled first. Mary Cooper reports that this is not an easy task, but that many scientists believe the dangers of global warming present the most pressing challenge, if not the most difficult one to resolve. E.R.R., 1988 Vol. II, pp. 613-628.

■ **The Battle for Natural Resources** reviews the government's management of federal lands. President Reagan reversed his predecessor's stringent regulation of public lands and opened them to mining, logging and grazing. Critics say excessive development is destroying the environment. By Tom Arrandale, E.R.R., 1988 Vol. II, pp. 537-548.

■ **Living with Hazardous Wastes** examines EPA's effectiveness in cleaning up toxic waste dumps. Despite the creation in 1980 of a "superfund" to remove abandoned hazardous substances, 1,177 highly toxic waste dumps are still awaiting action, and their number is likely to grow. By Robert K. Landers, E.R.R., 1988 Vol. II, pp. 377-388.

■ **America's Biological Diversity** is declining. The number of endangered species of animals and plants native to this country has risen by 25 percent since 1981, victims of development and pollution. By Tom Arrandale, E.R.R., 1988 Vol. I, pp. 70-80.

■ **Air Pollution Countdown** describes the state of urban air pollution 10 years after Congress tightened the 1970 Clean Air Act. More than 60 American cities failed to meet federal air-quality standards at the end of 1987. By Tom Arrandale, E.R.R., 1987 Vol. II, pp. 617-628.

■ **Garbage Crisis** examines alternatives to landfills for disposing of this country's mounting trash. Incineration and recycling offer help, but not enough to solve the problem. By Sarah Glazer, E.R.R., 1987 Vol. II, pp. 473-488.

■ **Ozone Mystery** analyzes the depletion of stratospheric ozone, which protects us from the sun's cancer-causing ultraviolet rays. Discovered in 1985, the ozone "hole" is caused by the industrial production of chlorofluorocarbons (CFCs). Since the report was published, 34 nations have agreed to phase out CFC production. By Sarah Glazer, E.R.R., 1987 Vol. I, pp. 165-180.

NOTES

[1] Robert N. Stavins, "Clean Profits, Using Economic Incentives to Protect the Environment," *Policy Review*, spring 1989, p. 59.

[2] *Project 88, Harnessing Market Forces to Protect Our Environment: Initiatives for the New President*, Washington, D.C., December 1988.

[3] Gregg Easterbrook, "Cleaning Up," *Newsweek*, July 24, 1989, p. 33.

[4] Bruce A. Ackerman and William T. Hassler, *Clean Coal/Dirty Air* (1981), p. 2.

[5] *State of the Environment: A View Toward the Nineties*, The Conservation Foundation, 1987, p. 32.

[6] Richard B. Stewart, "Controlling Environmental Risks Through Economic Incentives," *Columbia Journal of Environmental Law*, 1988, p. 154.

[7] Bruce A. Ackerman and Richard B. Stewart, "Reforming Environmental Law: The Democratic Case for Market Incentives," *Columbia Journal of Environmental Law*, 1988 Vol. 13, No. 2, p. 172.

[8] Robert W. Hahn and G. L. Hester, "The Market for Bads: EPA's Experience with Emissions Trading," *Regulation*, 1987, p. 48.

[9] See Peter Passell, "Selling Rights to Pollute: Bush Backs Idea in Acid-Rain Fight," *The New York Times*, May 17, 1989.

[10] Quoted by Larry Liebert in "Washington Perspective: Bush and the Environment," *California Journal*, August 1989, p. 318.

[11] Howard Latin, "Ideal Versus Real Regulatory Efficiency: Implementation of Uniform Standards and 'Fine-Tuning' Regulatory Reforms," *Stanford Law Review*, May 1985, p. 1267.

Graphics: Cover, Margaret Scott; pp. 491, 495, 499, S. Dmitri Lipczenko.

RECOMMENDED READING

BOOKS

Ackerman, Bruce A., and Hassler, William T., *Clean Coal, Dirty Air,* **Yale University Press, 1981.**

Yale University legal scholars Ackerman and Hassler trace congressional and EPA decisions leading to regulations requiring new electric utility power plants to install smokestack scrubbers. The authors take a critical view of a political process they contend subverted efficient environmental protection to assure markets for high-sulfur Eastern coal mines. "Instead of a solution responsive to the evolving will of a national majority, congressional intervention mixed clean-air symbols and dirty-coal self-interest in a way that invites cynicism about democratic self-government," they write.

Magat, Wesley A., editor, *Reform of Environmental Regulation,* **Ballinger Publishing Co., 1982.**

The author draws together seven chapters commissioned by Duke University for a 1982 conference assessing different approaches to revising environmental regulations that were commonly discussed in the early years of the Reagan administration. In an introductory chapter, Magat suggests that using economic incentives for environmental protection faces "two substantial hurdles. First, more extensive use of incentive-based approaches would require statutory change before EPA could adopt them," opening up a wide range of conflicting political interests during congressional debate. "Second, the reason for probable congressional inaction is precisely that major wealth transfers would be involved."

ARTICLES

Easterbrook, Gregg, "Cleaning Up," *Newsweek,* **July 24, 1989, p. 27.**

Easterbrook discusses President Bush's proposal for an emission-trading system to combat acid rain. "Emission trading sounds weird," he writes. ". . . But nearly everyone who studies pollution regulation concludes that what's missing is a positive inducement that works from the bottom up, supplanting the conventional structure of costs imposed from the top down. Emission trading will allow engineers rather than regulators to judge which factories can meet standards most efficiently while adding a profit motive for inventing improved controls."

Faludi, Susan, "Selling Smog," *California Business,* **June 1987, p. 68.**

Contributing editor Faludi takes a critical look at emission trading in California under the federal Clean Air Act. Faludi reports environmentalists' complaints that emission trading prevents improvements in air quality: "Cleaner companies make money off their good records, and dirtier companies save money because it is always cheaper to buy emissions-reduction credits than to actually invest hundreds of thousands of dollars in pollution-control equipment. So everyone in the deal walks away happy, unless one happens to be a member of the general public worried that all this swapping of smog is not making our lungs any cleaner."

Latin, Howard, "Ideal Versus Real Regulatory Efficiency: Implementation of Uniform Standards and 'Fine-Tuning' Regulatory Reforms," *Stanford Law Review,* **May 1985, p. 1267.**

Latin, a Rutgers Law School professor, dismisses proposed market-based incentives for environmental protection as unrealistic and unproven. "Despite its imperfections, command-and-control regulation has fostered significant improvements in environmental quality at a societal cost that has not proved prohibitive," he writes. ". . . In many environmental contexts, society's real choice may be to rely either on crude regulation or on no regulation."

Main, Jeremy, "Here Comes the Big New Cleanup," *Fortune,* **Nov. 21, 1988, p. 102.**

Main looks at potential responses to environmentalists' calls for a "third wave" of government programs addressing newly emerging environmental problems. He focuses more than Easterbrook does on economic-incentive approaches. "The third-wave attack demands a fresh, third-wave approach that learns from the errors of the past," Main writes. ". . . With a more common-sense, market-oriented strategy, the U.S. could get on with the cleanup without drowning the economy in unnecessary regulation and expense."

Stavins, Robert N., "Clean Profits, Using Economic Incentives to Protect the Environment," *Policy Review,* **spring 1989, p. 58.**

Stavins, a professor at Harvard University's John F. Kennedy School of Government, outlines the conclusions of the Project 88 study he directed for U.S. Sens. Timothy Wirth, D-Colo., and John Heinz, R-Pa. (*See below.*) Stavins argues that economic incentives will be essential if the nation wants to address environmental problems while reducing the federal budget deficit and keeping its industries competitive in international markets. "Incentive-based approaches have an added benefit: They can make the environmental debate more understandable to the general public," he adds. "Because they do not dictate a particular technology, these approaches can focus attention directly on the selection of environmental goals, rather than on complex questions concerning technological alternatives for reaching those goals."

REPORTS AND STUDIES

"Law and Economics Symposium: New Directions in Environmental Policy," *Columbia Journal of Environmental Law,* **1988 Vol. 13, No. 2, pp. 153-401.**

The journal, published by the Columbia University Law School, prints papers that leading advocates of economic incentives presented at an Oct. 1, 1987, symposium.

Project 88, Harnessing Market Forces to Protect Our Environment: Initiatives for the New President, **sponsored by Sen. Timothy E. Wirth, D-Colo., and Sen. John Heinz, R-Pa., Washington, D.C., December 1988.**

Prepared under the auspices of Wirth and Heinz, the report summarizes arguments for using economic incentives to solve environmental problems. It makes 36 recommendations to President Bush for steps to address acid rain, the greenhouse effect and other emerging problems.

Index